D1094442

E
159
U53

(Front end paper)

An imaginative artist's version of San Mateo (Fort Caroline), a Spanish fort on the St. Johns River, Florida, in the last half of the 17th century. In 1564, French Huguenots had constructed Fort Caroline. The following year, the Spanish, after founding St. Augustine, captured and renamed it. From the 1671 engraving "Arx Carolina," by an unknown artist. Courtesy, Chicago Historical Society.

EXPLORERS AND SETTLERS

Courtesy, Office of the Architect of the Capitol; color separations, United States Capitol Historical Society and the Eastern National Park and Monument Association.

De Soto's discovery of the Mississippi, in 1541, is romantically portrayed in this 19th-century painting by William H. Powell, which hangs in the rotunda of the U.S. Capitol. Though historically inaccurate, it symbolizes the courage and daring of the European explorers, who probed a new continent.

THE NATIONAL SURVEY OF HISTORIC SITES AND BUILDINGS VOLUME V

EXPLORERS AND SETTLERS

Historic Places Commemorating the Early Exploration

and Settlement of the United States

ROBERT G. FERRIS

Series Editor

CONTRA COSTA COLLEGE LIBRARY SAN PABLO, CALIFORNIA DISCARD

UNITED STATES DEPARTMENT OF THE INTERIOR

NATIONAL PARK SERVICE WASHINGTON, D.C. 1968

MAY 4 1970

E
159
U53

This volume was prepared by the Division of History Studies, National Park Service, under the general supervision of the Chief, Robert M. Utley. One of a series designed to make available to the public the studies of the National Survey of Historic Sites and Buildings, directed by John O. Littleton, it incorporates survey and evaluation reports prepared by the following National Park Service historians: John Porter Bloom, S. Sydney Bradford, William E. Brown, William C. Everhart, Ray H. Mattison, Frank B. Sarles, Jr., Charles E. Shedd, Jr., Horace J. Sheely, Jr., Charles W. Snell, and Robert M. Utley. These reports were reviewed by the Advisory Board on National Parks, Historic Sites, Buildings, and Monuments and the Consulting Committee for the National Survey of Historic Sites and Buildings. Members of these groups are listed in the Acknowledgments.

The background narrative for this volume is based on a study prepared under contract by Dr. Seymour V. Connor, Texas Technological College. Special contributions to the entire volume were made by Richard E. Morris and John W. Walker, Editorial Assistant and Staff Archeologist respectively, National Survey of Historic Sites and Buildings.

LIBRARY OF CONGRESS CATALOG CARD NUMBER: 66–60013

For sale by the Superintendent of Documents, U.S. Government Printing Office, Washington, D.C. 20402 - Price $3.50

Contents

Photographs are by the National Park Service except where specified

MAPS

Foreword

The United States today is a mixture of diverse nationalities, cultures, and races. The mixing process began when Europeans first probed the land and has continued into modern times. This volume, which emphasizes significant historic sites and structures, tells the fascinating story of early exploration and settlement and contributes to understanding our past. It commemorates the daring men who conquered a strange, forbidding wilderness and in so doing fostered a heritage of overcoming the unknown—a heritage carried on today in our exploration of space.

We need physical reminders of our past. Otherwise we tend to lose the sense of being part of a continuous process. Visits to historic places provide a refreshing awareness of immediacy and historical reality. They provide an association with our past that is impossible to achieve with the written or spoken word.

This volume has two parts. The first offers a brief, narrative background for the period of early exploration and settlement. The second consists of evaluations and descriptions of historic sites and structures associated with the period.

Historians and archeologists of the National Park Service, United States Department of the Interior, after comprehensive fieldwork, prepared the basic studies from which this publication has been drawn. The studies were reviewed by the Consulting Committee for the National Survey of Historic Sites and Buildings, composed of eminent historians, architects, and archeologists not otherwise connected with the National Park Service; and by the Secretary of the Interior's Advisory Board on

National Parks, Historic Sites, Buildings, and Monuments, which has a similar membership. The findings of the National Survey of Historic Sites and Buildings, achieved through this process, are made available to the public by means of this series of volumes.

The purpose of the Survey is the evaluation of places important in our history and prehistory. Those sites judged to possess exceptional value in illustrating or commemorating the history of the United States are declared eligible for designation as Registered National Historic Landmarks. Upon request, the Secretary of the Interior will provide the owner of a Landmark property with an engraved certificate and a bronze plaque attesting to its value and encouraging its continued preservation. A very few Landmarks may, in addition to possessing national historical significance, meet the standards of suitability and feasibility for park purposes and be considered for addition to the National Park System.

Credit for the preparation of this volume is shared widely by persons both in and out of the National Park Service. In particular, the work of the Service in the general field of historic preservation has benefited inestimably from the assistance provided by the National Trust for Historic Preservation in the United States, cosponsor of the Survey.

We believe that this book will assist students, teachers, travelers, historians, archeologists, preservation groups, and other Americans in understanding and appreciating a period of our history that is both complex and difficult, yet basic to a proper comprehension of American democracy and culture. We earnestly hope that this volume will also focus attention on, and stimulate further activities in, the field of historic preservation. Important as progress is, it should not result in the thoughtless destruction of sites and buildings that commemorate our national heritage.

GEORGE B. HARTZOG, Jr.
Director
National Park Service

EXPLORERS AND SETTLERS

PART I

Explorers and Settlers:

Historical Background

THE LAND THAT BECAME the United States was in colonial times an extension of the Old World into the New. Through the centuries, the descendants of the original colonists blended their European heritage into the new Nation that evolved. But for the courage and resourcefulness of the Europeans who first explored and settled the unknown wilderness, that evolution would not have been possible.

Our European Heritage

The United States is an amalgam of nationalities, cultures, and races whose basic heritage is European. The amalgam began to take shape long before the Declaration of Independence and is still being formed today. European nations discovered the area of the present United States, explored it, and settled it. For decades after the Nation came into being, they continued to possess or claim substantial territories within its ultimate limits. They also affected the growth and course of the Republic by their alinement in international affairs.

During the first half of the 19th century, the United States trebled in size by acquiring Florida from Spain and the lands west of the Mississippi

River and their historical heritage from France, Mexico, and England. She also benefited during the century from the reinfusion of European influences during the great immigrations, which have carried into the 20th century.

From the beginning, the emergent Nation molded its diverse European heritage with other cultural influences into a new way of life. It modified the English language into a uniquely American form and reshaped the legal and governmental systems of England. It utilized the architectural styles not only of England, but also of France, Spain, Holland, and Sweden. In the trans-Mississippi West, it incorporated Spanish land, mining, and water laws into the legal fabric; and it adapted the ranching terms and methods of Spain to cowboy life. Across the face of the land are registered numerous other European contributions—in language, religion, place names, literature, the arts, music, and social mores.

Thus our Nation has been profoundly enriched by its European heritage. A source of strength, this heritage still lives today—centuries after the initial European exploration and settlement—even though, in the meantime, during prolonged contact with a fresh environment, a distinctive American civilization has been created.

The Old World in the New

In the summer of 1492, a daring Genoese navigator set his sails westward from Palos, Spain, his three tiny ships flying the banners of his royal benefactors, Ferdinand of Aragon and Isabella of Castile. Christopher Columbus was sailing west into the unknown to reach the fabled Cathay of the East. Behind him lay the familiar shores of Europe; ahead stretched two mighty continents whose virgin lands, dense forests, untapped mineral resources, and aborigines were almost completely unknown to him and the civilizations of Europe and Asia. The Old World had earlier made some contacts with the New. Venturesome Norsemen, under Leif Ericson and other leaders, founded Vinland and explored elsewhere along the North Atlantic coast. And fishermen from France may have periodically visited the banks and shoals of Newfoundland. But none of these contacts yielded any permanent fruits.

Such, also, might have been the result of Columbus' heroic voyage but for a variety of factors. In the 15th and 16th centuries, for the first time since the fall of the Roman Empire, Europe was ripe for

"Christopher Columbus at the Court of Isabella." From a mid-19th-century lithograph by V. de Turgin. Courtesy, Chicago Historical Society.

exploitative expansion. It was undergoing cataclysmic changes. The Crusades to save the Holy Lands, in the 11th and 12th centuries, had strengthened and unified the European principalities; the plunder that footmen and knights had hauled back from the opulent East introduced Europeans to new luxuries and stimulated the reopening of trade.

The revival of trade between Western Europe and the East was inevitable, and the commercial revolution that revitalized the stagnate society of the Western World—sparked by the voyages of discovery in the 15th century—was almost as certain. A merchant class arose to serve the demands of commerce, and cities grew up to protect and serve the merchants. An ascendant Western Europe resented the exorbitant prices charged by merchants in the Italian city-states, who dominated trade with the East, and sought to break their monopoly by finding other trade routes.

The intellectual awakening of the Renaissance, which came to full flower in the 15th and 16th centuries, opened new horizons of interest in the sciences and arts. It stimulated learning and the recapture of classical knowledge, and fostered a fresh curiosity and a more pragmatic way of thinking. In the wake of the Renaissance emerged a movement to reform the "universal" church. The Reformation, beginning early in the 16th century, introduced wide-scale religious conflict, ruptured the medieval unity of Christendom, and produced a sectarian fragmentation of the Christian religion. These interrelated changes in European society spelled the doom of the feudal system of the Middle Ages. Feudalism yielded to a stronger political force, the rise of national states.

The four movements—economic, intellectual, religious, and sociopolitical—might have exhausted their strength in Europe had it not been for Spain's accidental discovery of a New World while seeking a better route to the East. This discovery resulted in a major shift in the world trade pattern and gave Europe mastery of the globe for centuries to come.

Who would have believed a few centuries earlier that the "barbarian" heirs of the great Roman Empire in Western Europe would some day dominate the earth, or that their culture would influence all peoples from the Volga to the Yalu and from Lapland to Tasmania, or that London and Paris rather than Mecca and Istanbul would be the cultural and financial centers of civilization? Even more preposterous would have been any idea that some yet unfounded English-speaking nation born on a strange continent would be a world power—that a nation then undreamed of would rise from those distant shores to join the vanguard of civilization.

The New World provided Europe with a vast frontier of expansion and, perhaps even more important as a stimulus, an incredible source of wealth. Within two decades after Columbus' discovery, Spain was importing more than a million dollars a year from the "Indies"; by the end of the first half-century, gold and silver treasures poured into Madrid from the Aztec and Inca fields and increased the expendable wealth of Europe some fifteenfold. Had the rewards not been so immense, the Spaniards might not have been so daring and persistent in their exploration.

From his initial voyage (1492–93), Columbus returned with gold bracelets and ornaments, as well as tales of greater wealth farther west. On this first voyage and three subsequent ones (1493–96, 1498–1500, and 1502–4), he explored extensively throughout the West Indies. Yet he died in 1506, only 2 years after his last voyage, not realizing that he had discovered a continent. But the promise of abundant gold, silver, and other treasure that could be wrenched from the arms of natives enticed adventurous Spanish conquistadors (conquerors), strengthened by long conflict in their homeland with the intrusive Moors, to the New World in search of gold and glory. Missionary padres sought to serve God by converting the native masses.

Conjectural portrait of Ferdinand Magellan, the Portuguese navigator. He died in 1521, during his attempt to circumnavigate the globe. One of his five vessels succeeded. From a late 18th- or early 19th-century painting by an unknown artist. Courtesy, Chicago Historical Society.

Within a few decades, Spanish navigators became familiar with the northern coast of South America, the Isthmus of Panama, the Pacific Ocean, the Gulf of Mexico, the Atlantic shore of North America, and ultimately the general outlines of most of the New World—though for some time enough hiatuses existed in their knowledge so that the dream of a Northwest Passage persisted. The Spanish benefited from the earlier pioneering efforts of the nautical-minded Portuguese, especially those of Prince Henry, "The Navigator," to find a water route to the East. Though King John II of Portugal turned a deaf ear to the pleas of Columbus for sponsorship, between 1429 and 1460 Portuguese seamen had explored 2,000 miles of Africa's northwest coast. In 1498, Vasco da Gama pioneered a route to India around Africa's southern tip. While Portugal directed her energies to the south and east, Spain pursued opportunities to the west, a division of interest formally recognized in 1494 by the Papal Line of Demarcation.

Spain, of all European nations, was particularly qualified to exploit the opportunities. The marriage of Ferdinand and Isabella, in 1469, had united the Houses of Aragon and Castile, and started the country on a spectacular rise to power. The two monarchs finished driving the Moors from the country, consolidated royal power, diminished the pretensions of the lesser nobility, conquered new lands, and advanced homogeneity of religion. Spain became Europe's strongest power. Treasure poured into her coffers as Cortés conquered the Aztec Empire and Pizarro overran the Peruvian Incas. Little wonder, then, that Spain was spurred to ever-quickening exploration or that the other nations of Europe dared to send their own expeditions into the unknown hemisphere—or to plant their flags on soil that Ferdinand and his haughty Hapsburg successors claimed for Spain.

The acquisition of colonies was an integral part of the economic policy of mercantilism, to which many European powers in the course of time adhered. According to mercantilistic theory, gold, silver, and precious gems were the prime measurement of national wealth and power. To obtain these, a nation should export to the maximum extent and restrict imports. The theory further held that colonies, important as sources of raw materials and as captive markets for the mother country's products, should be rigidly controlled.

Because of national pride, too, monarchs vied with one another in subsidizing exploration and colonization. Monarchs and individuals alike sought wealth in precious metals, furs, and other natural resources. Other individual motives were escape from religious, political, and economic oppression and the devastation of the seemingly endless wars in Europe; the desire to convert the pagan Indians to Christianity; land hunger; and the lure of adventure.

During the 16th century, navigators of all nations sought a water passage around or through the American continental block to the fabulous

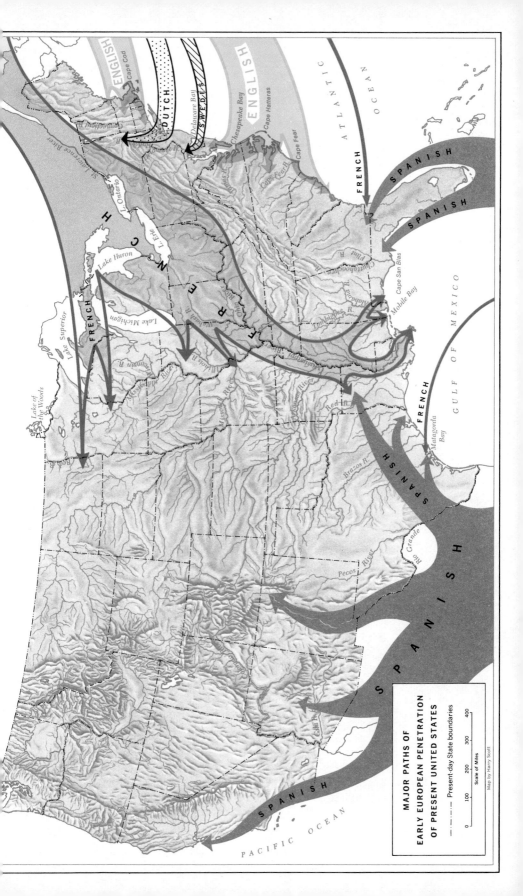

MAJOR PATHS OF
EARLY EUROPEAN PENETRATION
OF PRESENT UNITED STATES

--- Present-day State boundaries

0   100   200   300   400
Scale of Miles

Map by Harry Scott

East while overland expeditions searched North America for the fabled Seven Cities of Gold or other easily conquered and wealthy empires like those of the Aztecs and Incas. Spain, from well established bases in the New World, explored extensively along both coasts of North and South America; and, in addition to exploring much of the Southeastern and Southwestern parts of the present United States, founded at St. Augustine, in 1565, the first permanent settlement by Europeans in what is now the United States.

French explorers claimed the land between the Carolinas and the St. Lawrence, and Huguenots attempted to settle in South Carolina, Florida, and Nova Scotia. Though late in the preceding century John and Sebastian Cabot had provided Henry VII of England with a New World claim, English "sea dogs" preferred to raid Spanish treasure galleons making their cumbersome voyages to Seville's treasury rather than colonize the empty coasts of North America.

Notable exceptions were Sir Humphrey Gilbert and Sir Walter Raleigh, who late in the 16th century threw their fortunes—mostly Spanish gold—into settlement attempts in Newfoundland and "Virginia." Ironically, England's decisive sea victory in 1588 over Philip II's "invincible" armada indirectly caused the doom of Raleigh's colony at Roanoke in "Virginia" by seriously delaying John White's return trip with supplies. But, over the years following the defeat of the armada, the "Spanish Sea" was opened to all comers.

In the next century, imperial rivalry for control of the New World increased in intensity, as other European powers sought to catch up with Spain. The British founded a permanent settlement at Jamestown in 1607; the French at Quebec in 1608; and the Dutch at Nieuw Amsterdam in 1626. During the century, the British spread staunch colonies on the Atlantic coast from South Carolina to Maine. In 1638, the Swedes settled the Delaware Bay region and in 1654 lost possession to Peter Stuyvesant, Director General of New Netherland. Stuyvesant, a decade later, watched in frustrated anger as the English raised their flag over Nieuw Amsterdam and renamed the surrounding area for its new owner, the English Duke of York. Meanwhile, the French pushed up the St. Lawrence and the Great Lakes waterways into the heart of the continent, following such intrepid leaders as Samuel de Champlain to the Great Lakes and La Salle to the mouth of the Mississippi.

The frontiers of three mighty colonial empires now stood in dangerous proximity, and in the 18th century imperial rivalries flared into a vital struggle for control of North America. In a series of four wars, beginning with King William's War (War of the English Succession) in 1689 and ending in the Treaty of Paris of 1763, which ended the French and Indian War (or Seven Years' War), France was forced off the continent. The wars were fought largely in Europe and all except the fourth stemmed from European power struggles, but they resulted in a reshaping of the North American map. England and Spain divided the spoils, the English claiming the eastern third of the present United States and the Spanish the area west of the Mississippi.

Little did the rulers of England and Spain dream that their vast New World empires were to be shattered in paroxysms of revolution or that new nations would arise from the feeble colonial beginnings. But this was to be—and in the course of time the young United States of America grew strong and mature by molding into the vibrant mainstream of her British legacy the diverse heritages of Spain, France, Holland, Sweden, and other European nations.

The Spanish: Conquistadors and Padres

Between 1513, when Ponce de León first set foot in Florida, and 1821, when Mexico gained her independence as well as the Spanish possessions in the present United States, Spain left an indelible influence—especially in the trans-Mississippi West, which the United States began to acquire in 1803. Spain was the leading European power in the early imperial rivalry for control of North America and for centuries dominated the Southeastern and Southwestern parts of what was later the United States—particularly the States of Florida, Texas, New Mexico, Arizona, and California.

Spain held Louisiana territory between 1762 and 1803, and was for the most part content to foster the settlements founded there by France rather than to initiate new ones. She lost Florida temporarily in 1763, but regained it in 1783. Her possessions reached their maximum extent between 1783 and 1803, when they ranged in a crescent from Florida to California.

Except in California, Spain happened to colonize less fruitful regions than did England and France. Yet she tenaciously clung to them long after she had lost her dominance in Europe, some years after the English defeated her armada in 1588. Frustrated in their search for gold and precious metals, the Spaniards were usually forced to try to wrest a living from the barren soil of an inhospitable land by farming and ranching. Finding native labor much scarcer in the present United States than in her possessions to the south, Spain was forced to spread her colonial empire dangerously thin. A small number of soldiers, settlers, and friars controlled the native masses and through their labors obtained what wealth was to be had.

Spain's motives for colonization were threefold: to locate mineral wealth, to convert the Indians to Christianity, and to counter French and English efforts. The Spanish colonization system was highly successful. First, an armed force subdued the natives and established forts, or presidios, for future protection. Then, zealous missionaries moved in to convert the Indians to the religion of Spain and teach them the arts of civilization. Finally, representatives of the King founded civil settlements in conjunction with the presidios and missions. The Crown controlled the highly centralized process through a bureaucracy that burgeoned as the empire expanded. But the story begins in the first years of the 16th century, when Spain first realized that Columbus had discovered, not island outposts of Cathay, but a New World!

SUCCESSES TO THE SOUTH

In the two decades after the first voyage of Columbus, Spanish navigators only began to realize the nature and extent of his remarkable find. The presence of a continental landmass was surmised but not known. Columbus himself had sailed around Puerto Rico; charted most of the remainder of the West Indies; touched on the shores of South America, but without realizing that it was a continent; and mapped the Central American coast from Panama nearly to southern Yucatan. On his first voyage, late in 1492, he had established the colony of Navidad on Hispaniola, but, finding it destroyed on his second voyage, he founded Isabella, in January 1494. Isabella also failed within 2 years, and the colonists established Santo Domingo, the first permanent European settlement in the New World. In 1508–9, while Ponce de León was occupying Puerto Rico and subduing its natives, Vicente Pinzón explored the southern Yucatan coast and Sebastián de Ocampo circumnavigated the island of Cuba. In 1510, the Spaniards occupied Jamaica, and, the following year, Cuba. In 1513, Vasco Núñez de Balboa, who dominated a struggling colony in present Colombia, hacked a trail across the Isthmus of

Panama and discovered the Pacific Ocean. In 1522, one of the five vessels of the Ferdinand Magellan expedition completed the first circumnavigation of the globe. The lure of adventure and the thrill of discovery whetted the Spanish desire to explore.

FLORIDA AND THE FOUNTAIN OF YOUTH

Juan Ponce de León was the first Spaniard to touch the shores of the present United States. As Columbus had not remotely realized the extent of his momentous discovery, so De León never dreamed that his "island" of Florida was a peninsular extension of the vast North American Continent. After coming to the New World with Columbus in 1493, he had led the occupation of Puerto Rico in 1508 and governed it from 1509 to 1512. In 1509, he started a colony at Caparra, later abandoned in favor of San Juan. He was one of the first of the *adelantados*—men who "advanced" the Spanish Empire by conquest, subjugation of the Indians, and establishment of quasi-military government.

In 1513, the aging King Ferdinand awarded De León a patent to conquer and govern the Bimini Islands, in the Bahamas, of which the Spaniards had heard but not yet seen. According to a persistent legend, there De León would find the marvelous spring whose waters would restore lost youth and vigor. So many wonders had the Spaniards already

The first Spaniard to touch the shores of the present United States, Juan Ponce de León. He discovered, named, and explored Florida. From an 18th-century engraving, probably conjectural.

encountered in the Western Hemisphere that only a cynic would have doubted the existence of such a spring.

In March 1513, De León sailed off confidently from Puerto Rico for the Bahamas. Landing briefly at San Salvador, Bahamas, he wound through uncharted islands until he sighted an extensive coastline. He had no reason to suspect that it was anything more than an island, but he followed the coast for a day without rounding its end or finding a suitable landing place. He named the "island" *La Florida,* probably because of the season—*Pascua Florida,* or the Easter festival of flowers. The name came to be applied by the Spanish to the entire present Southeastern United States and beyond.

Then near the 30th parallel, not far from the site of St. Augustine, De León landed at the mouth of the St. Johns River. Determined to be the first to circumnavigate the "island," he turned south, traced the coast around the tip of the peninsula, passed through the treacherous waters of the Florida Keys, and moved up the western coast, perhaps reaching Tampa Bay. After 7 weeks, he gave up hopes of circling the northern tip of his "island"; it was incredibly large—bigger even than Cuba—and he may have suspected that he had discovered the long-sought mainland. If so, it all belonged to his King, for he had earlier planted the Spanish flag and claimed Florida and all lands contiguous to it for Ferdinand.

Of gold and restorative waters, De León had seen nothing; of hostile Indians, predecessors of the Seminoles, he had seen too much. Returning to Puerto Rico in September 1513, he reprovisioned and then spent the next 6 weeks back in the Bahamas fruitlessly searching for the fountain of youth. Before the year was out, he sailed for Spain emptyhanded. Ferdinand rewarded him, however, with new patents to the "islands" of Bimini and Florida, but he was to bear the expense of conquest.

Not until 1521 was De León able to return to take possession of his grant. By that time, his search for the fountain of youth took on a more immediate importance—for he was 61 years of age. At large cost he equipped 2 ships, enlisted 200 men, and set out to found a permanent base from which an exhaustive search could be conducted for the fabled fountain. Not only did he fail to find the fountain, but he also lost his life. Almost as soon as he landed on the western shore of Florida, probably near Tampa Bay, Indians attacked, killed scores of men, and mortally wounded De León himself. The expedition hastily retreated to Cuba, where the "valiant Lion," as his epitaph was to read, died.

Exploring the Atlantic and Gulf Coasts

By the time of De León's hapless attempt to exercise his patent rights to the "island" of Florida in 1521, many geographers and navigators realized that Florida was likely the giant arm of a continent. Two expeditions had indicated that this was true, one in 1519 by Alonso de Pineda and another in 1521 by Francisco Gordillo.

The Pineda expedition was the inspiration of Francisco de Garay, Governor of Jamaica. He placed four vessels under the command of Pineda and ordered him to find a water passage around or through the landmass whose existence had been indicated by a series of Spanish explorations during the period 1515–18. Pineda circled west and south around the coast from Florida to Vera Cruz. He named the land off his starboard bow "Amichel"; he called what was probably the Mississippi River "Rio del Espíritu Santo"; and he recommended a settlement at the mouth of the "Rio de las Palmas"—possibly the Rio Grande. Most important of all, he gained a substantial knowledge of the unbroken coastline and revealed that to the west of Spain's island headquarters in the Caribbean lay a huge continental landmass.

Lucas Vásquez de Ayllón, a prominent magistrate in Hispaniola, in 1521 sent out Capt. Francisco Gordillo to sail northward through the Bahamas, strike the shore of the continent, follow part of De León's route, and try to round the "island" of Florida from the east. Up the coast he tacked, extending De León's exploration at least 3° northward, and landing on the shores of present South Carolina. Ignoring orders, he loaded his ship with innocent and friendly natives and put about for Hispaniola. He planned to sell his cargo into slavery to replace the large losses of natives during the first years of the Spanish conquest.

De Ayllón reprimanded him and released the unfortunate captives, but listened greedily to the report of the fair land to the north. Rushing to Spain, he obtained a patent to colonize the region. A reconnaissance expedition in 1525, led by Pedro de Quexos, extended De Ayllón's knowledge of the coast as far as present Virginia. The following year, after extensive preparation, De Ayllón himself set out with 3 vessels, more than 500 colonists, 3 padres, and ample supplies and livestock to establish a lasting settlement on the Atlantic shore. He failed. Attempting to settle first at an unknown site, possibly in present North Carolina, he shifted about 100 miles to the south and founded a crude settlement named San Miguel de Gualdape (Guandape), in South Carolina. He died of a fever before the year was out, and internal dissension rent the settlement into anarchy. Less than a third of the colonists survived to return to Hispaniola.

The previous year, 1525, a Portuguese navigator named Stephen Gómez, also flying the flag of Spain, had completed the exploration of the Atlantic coast by sailing from Newfoundland south to the Florida peninsula in search of the Northwest Passage. Clearly the continental block extended from Newfoundland to Tierra del Fuego. Intrepid Spanish explorers were to be forced off their ships and onto the land if they wished to make additional discoveries, as had Balboa and Cortés before them.

THE FIRST INLAND PENETRATION

Cortés' one-time rival for command, Pánfilo de Narváez, made the first inland exploration in the area of the present United States. In 1526, he obtained title to all lands between the Rio de las Palmas and the Cape of Florida, and the next year left Spain. After stopping at Spanish bases at Santo Domingo and Cuba, in 1528 his expedition of 5 ships and more than 600 colonists, including friars and Negro slaves, landed on the west coast of Florida, probably in the region of Tampa Bay. Narváez split his command and sent his vessels along the shoreline while he led the main body of the expedition by land toward an intended rendezvous point up the coast. The two parties never met. The sea party missed the rendezvous and, after a futile search, returned to its home base.

Harassed by hostile Indians and scourged by privation and disease, the overland group struggled along the coast. Reaching the vicinity of Apalachicola Bay, the men, greatly reduced in numbers as well as strength, built crude rafts on which they courageously launched themselves westward toward Spanish settlements in Old Mexico. They sailed along the coast to Texas, where storms sank some of the rafts and drove others onto a low-lying, sandy island, probably Galveston Island. Thus began one of the most amazing adventures that has ever befallen any group of men.

The 80 or so survivors were so weak from starvation they could scarcely pull themselves out of the water. They scattered in small groups. Some wandered off and others joined the Indians; many died of hunger and disease. Winter hardships took more lives. The natives, at first friendly, turned belligerent and enslaved the remaining Europeans. Months of miserable captivity stretched out to 5 unbearable years.

Álvar Núñez Cabeza de Vaca, the treasurer and second officer of the Narváez party, obtained a reputation as a medicine man—his knowledge of medicine being a little more advanced than that of the Indians. In 1534, he and three others, including a Negro slave, Estévan, escaped and began an arduous 3-year trek across Texas and into Old Mexico that represented the first exploration by Europeans of any part of the present Southwestern United States. Their reports of great riches were to excite the imagination of men in the Viceroyalty of New Spain and stimulate exploration of the unknown area of New Mexico, to the north.

To the Mississippi and beyond

On her fourth expedition to "Florida," Spain scored a major success. Hernando de Soto and Luís de Moscoso, during the years 1539–43, explored extensively throughout the present Southeastern United States and obtained a wealth of information about the lands and peoples of the interior—beyond the Mississippi and as far west as Oklahoma and Texas. De Soto was perhaps the most determined and successful of all Spanish explorers. He had made a fortune as one of Pizarro's lieutenants in the

Hernando de Soto led the fourth Spanish expedition to Florida. He explored much of the present Southeastern United States, and his survivors penetrated Texas. From an 18th-century engraving, probably conjectural.

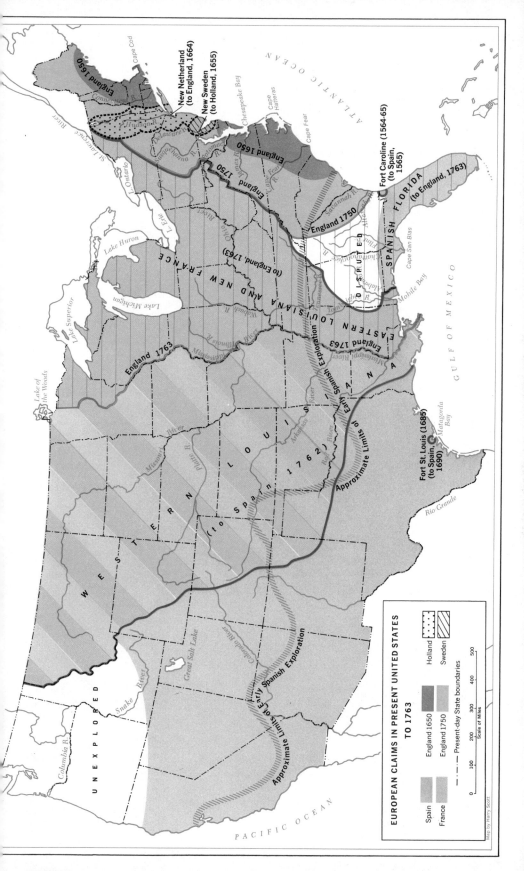

EUROPEAN CLAIMS IN PRESENT UNITED STATES
TO 1763

Map by Harry Scott

Spain
France
England 1650
England 1750

Holland
Sweden

Present-day State boundaries

Scale of Miles
0 100 200 300 400 500

New Netherland
(to England, 1664)

New Sweden
(to Holland, 1655)

England 1650

England 1750

England 1650

England 1750 (to England, 1763)

England 1750

Fort Caroline (1564-65)
(to Spain, 1565)

SPANISH FLORIDA
(to England, 1763)

EASTERN LOUISIANA AND NEW FRANCE
(to England, 1763)

England 1763

England 1763

DISPUTED

Early Spanish Exploration

WESTERN LOUISIANA
(to Spain, 1762)

Approximate Limits of

Fort St. Louis (1685)
(to Spain, 1690)

Approximate Limits of Early Spanish Exploration

UNEXPLORED

ATLANTIC OCEAN

GULF OF MEXICO

PACIFIC OCEAN

Cape Cod
Connecticut R.
Hudson R.
Delaware R.
St. Lawrence River
Susquehanna R.
Chesapeake Bay
Cape Hatteras
Cape Fear
Cape Fear R.
Savannah R.
Cape San Blas
Mobile Bay
Matagorda Bay
Rio Grande
L. Ontario
Lake Erie
Lake Huron
Lake Michigan
Lake Superior
Lake of the Woods
Ohio River
Wabash R.
Illinois River
Mississippi River
Missouri River
Platte R.
Arkansas River
Red River
Great Salt Lake
Colorado River
Snake River
Columbia R.

conquest of Peru. As a further reward, Charles V granted him the right to conquer—at his own expense—the land of "Florida," which had not yielded to De León, De Ayllón, and Narváez before him.

Artist's rendition of De Soto at Tampa Bay, Florida, in 1539. From an engraving by James Smillie, after a drawing by Capt. S. Eastman. Courtesy, Library of Congress.

In May 1539, De Soto and more than 600 men landed on the west coast of Florida. Marching north, they spent the winter of 1539–40 in the region of Apalachee, in the Florida Panhandle. In the spring, De Soto led his men northeast through present Georgia to the Savannah River. He then turned northwest, traversed part of South Carolina, fought his way through the mountains, circled back across northern Georgia and central Alabama, and in October reached the head of Mobile Bay.

There a severe battle with the Indians occurred, but the indefatigable De Soto would let nothing deter him. In a remarkable tribute to his leadership, after 18 months of fruitless wandering and the loss of more than 100 men to disease and Indians, De Soto's men continued to follow him when he turned his back on the sea and the outside world and plunged once more into the unknown continent. Moving northwest into present Mississippi, the explorer set up winter quarters.

In March 1541, Indians launched a sudden and catastrophic attack. Although they killed only 11 men, they burned the expedition's clothing and destroyed 50 horses and a large drove of swine. Though many of his followers were clad only in skins, De Soto resumed the march in a northwest direction and on May 8, 1541, discovered the Mississippi River. A month later, he crossed the swollen river on specially constructed barges and set out across present Arkansas. After several months of hard marching, the expedition may have penetrated as far as Oklahoma—at the same time as Coronado, who from a base in New Mexico had reached the same general region and was probably only 300 or 400 miles to the west. De Soto then turned back east and set up his third winter quarters, in southwestern Arkansas.

That spring the expedition started down the Mississippi—not to return home, but for the purpose of sending to Cuba for badly needed supplies. De Soto, however, sickened and died on May 21, 1542, and the men sank his body in the middle of the great river he had discovered so that the Indians would not find it and realize that he was mortal. Command devolved upon Luís de Moscoso, who promptly agreed with the men that it was time to abandon the wild venture.

The party decided to strike overland toward Spanish bases to the southwest rather than follow the Mississippi to the coast. Moscoso penetrated Texas, perhaps as far as the Trinity River, before becoming discouraged and returning to the Mississippi. Then, during the fourth winter, 1542–43, the men built small brigantines and prepared for a precarious voyage down the river and out into the gulf. They butchered and dried all the pigs and most of the remaining horses and filled barrels with fresh water. Liberating some 500 Indians whom they had enslaved, they embarked on July 2, 1543. Sixteen days later they floated out into the gulf, and on September 10 landed near Tampico. At the end of the amazing 4-year expedition, only half of the original members were still alive.

THE SETTLEMENT OF FLORIDA

Four times had the Spanish Crown given patents to its bravest *adelantados* to conquer and settle Florida—De León, De Ayllón, Narváez, and De Soto. Each had lost his life in the attempt. But the importance of the Florida peninsula in controlling the Gulf of Mexico could not long be overlooked. Three more Spaniards were to make futile attempts to tame the region before a permanent settlement was at last accomplished.

A Florida Indian village. From a 1591 engraving by Theodore de Bry, after an on-the-scene drawing by Jacques le Moyne de Morgues. Courtesy, Library of Congress.

In 1549, Friar Luís Cancer de Barbastro led a group of missionaries, supported by a few friendly Indians, from Vera Cruz to the vicinity of Tampa Bay, where hostile Indians massacred them. Only little more successful was the expedition of Tristán de Luna y Arellano a decade later from Vera Cruz to the Pensacola Bay area. It consisted of 1,500 colonists, soldiers, and friars, and 1 year's provisions. A hurricane nearly destroyed the fleet shortly after it landed; more than half the supplies were ruined; fever decimated the group; and the Indians, if not openly hostile, were zealous thieves. But some of the colonists survived. In 1561 Angel de

Villafañe replaced De Luna, who proceeded to Havana. That same year Villafañe, at the direction of the Spanish authorities, set out to found a colony on the Carolina coast. After landing temporarily, probably at Port Royal Sound, in present South Carolina, and later at the mouth of the Santee River, the group sailed for Old Mexico by way of Pensacola Bay.

The prospect of a permanent settlement in "Florida" must then have seemed remote to Spanish officials. But the establishment of French settlements there caused Spain to react with urgency. In 1562, Jean Ribaut and a small party of French Huguenots put ashore at Port Royal Sound to found the religious refuge that the farsighted Adm. Gaspard de Coligny was planning. Before the year ended, Ribaut abandoned the settlement, Charlesfort, but neither he nor Coligny was discouraged. In 1564, a second Huguenot expedition, under René de Laudonnière, landed at the mouth of the St. Johns River and erected a small stockade, Fort Caroline. Discipline soon broke down. Thirteen men stole the only vessel and set out to raid Spanish shipping in the Caribbean. Laudonnière immediately put the remainder of the men to constructing another vessel; when finished, it, too, was stolen by would-be buccaneers.

The French settlement aroused Spanish fury. Philip II, ruler of Spain and Europe's strongest monarch, allotted 600 troops and 3 ships to Pedro Menéndez de Avilés and ordered him to drive the Frenchmen out of his domain. Menéndez furnished a party of colonists and obtained De León's old patent to "Florida." Menéndez and his King were convinced that the Huguenot colony was intended as a base for French piracy. Ten years earlier, French pirates had sacked and burned Havana. Such a New World base as Laudonnière's could not be tolerated—and to add insult to the defenders of the Catholic faith, the Frenchmen were Protestant heretics. Late in August, Ribaut arrived from France with reinforcements.

On September 8, 1565, the Spaniards put ashore and began constructing a fort, around which grew the city of St. Augustine—the oldest permanent European settlement in the United States. Then, Menéndez marched northward and wiped out the settlers at Fort Caroline, which he renamed San Mateo. He next moved southward below St. Augustine, attacked a French party under Ribaut that had set out to fight the Spanish but had been shipwrecked, and put the few survivors to work constructing St. Augustine.

Despite the tireless energy of Menéndez, the Spanish colony in Florida

This fanciful artist's rendition of St. Augustine, pioneer Spanish settlement, is of interest despite its historical inaccuracies. The Castillo de San Marcos at no time resembled the fort as portrayed. The artist probably included the high hills because he mistook the Spanish word for thick forests to mean hills. From the 1671 engraving "Pagus Hispanorum," by an unknown artist, probably prepared in Amsterdam. Courtesy, Chicago Historical Society.

grew slowly. From 1566 to 1571, determined Jesuit missionaries strove to bring Christianity to the reluctant natives in the region. They founded a number of small and temporary missions, but were not too successful in their overall effort. In 1566, they established San Felipe Orista on the Carolina coast, and a few years later may have reached as far north as Chesapeake Bay with other evanescent missions. After 1571, brown-robed Franciscan friars carried the word of God into the marshes and forests of the Florida region. At the height of their success, about 1635, they were ministering to thousands of neophytes at a number of tiny missions, mainly in the provinces of Guale, Timucua, and Apalachee, in northern Florida and coastal Georgia.

None of these missions proved to be permanent, and few of the "converted" Indians could actually be counted as Christians. When, in

1763, Spain surrendered Florida to England, little more than a feeble colony at St. Augustine evidenced two centuries of occupation. Besides the missions, two small outposts in the region called Apalachee, on the northwestern fringe of the peninsula, had been established to help supply St. Augustine: San Marcos de Apalache on the gulf coast, which originated in 1660 but was abandoned and reestablished several times thereafter; and San Luís de Apalache, a few miles north, the center of a temporarily flourishing mission field that was later relinquished during Queen Anne's War.

Over the years, Spanish Florida had suffered countless vicissitudes. In 1586, only 2 years before England ravaged Spain's mighty armada, Sir Francis Drake almost destroyed St. Augustine. Less than a century later, in 1668, another English force again nearly decimated it. Before many more years passed, British settlers from the Carolinas began a series of raids on the Spanish settlements in Florida. During Queen Anne's War, in 1702 the English captured and burned St. Augustine, although they failed to conquer the redoubtable Castillo de San Marcos, constructed in 1672. In 1704, Col. James Moore, attacking from the Carolinas, destroyed five mission-settlements in Apalachee and later that year drove the Spanish out of the province. From then on, Spanish Florida was almost constantly in a state of war with the Carolinas and, after 1733, with Georgia. Attacks on St. Augustine by Gen. James Oglethorpe, the founder of Georgia, resulted in the construction of Fort Matanzas in 1743 as a part of Spain's last desperate effort to hold the region.

Even as British intrusion began to threaten Spanish Florida in the east, the French again encroached on the empire—this time in the west. To meet the threat of France's advance to the mouth of the Mississippi, the Spanish founded an impotent post—Fort San Carlos de Austria—at Pensacola in 1698 and undertook to settle Texas.

New Mexico and Arizona: outposts of empire

The second major penetration by the Spanish of the present United States was in the Southwest. There, in an arid and inhospitable land, Spanish dreams of gold and precious metals were to become nightmares. But before the reality were the myths. After Cortés' conquest of the rich Aztec Empire and Pizarro's looting of Inca wealth in Peru, should not great or greater riches be found to the north of Old Mexico? Mythmakers and dreamers began to spin wild fabrications. Soon their fantasies were given a touch of reality by the reports of a strange party of three men led by Cabeza de Vaca—survivors of the Narváez expedition to Florida— which arrived in present Mexico after an amazing cross-country trek from the gulf coast of Texas. Thus, interestingly enough, a tenuous thread from Florida stimulated the northward march of New Spain into the unknown lands of New Mexico.

When De Vaca, the other two Spaniards, and the Negro slave Estévan—after 5 years of captivity among the Indians—sought to escape in 1534, they were somewhere inland in Texas, possibly near the site of San Antonio. Traveling sometimes alone, but more often with roving bands of Indians, they wandered south and west. Probably crossing the Rio Grande into present Mexico, they moved westward for several hundred miles, crossed the Rio Grande again in the vicinity of the Big Bend, and then turned to the southwest. In June 1536, they stumbled across a party of Spaniards, who could hardly believe that the starving, nearly naked "savages" who rushed sobbing up to them were really aristocratic hidalgos and their slave.

What a story the men had to tell! The credulous Spaniards, who after the discovery of the riches of the Aztec and Inca Empires might be expected to believe anything of the new continent, were beside themselves with joy. The men's report of the fabled Seven Cities of Gold spread like wildfire, although the narrators made it plain that they had not seen these fabulous cities—only heard of them from the Indians. The Viceroy, Antonio de Mendoza, cautiously decided upon further reconnaissance of the region to the north before sending out the army of conquest for which his eager subordinates clamored.

When De Vaca and his two Spanish companions, not surprisingly, refused to return, Mendoza dispatched Estévan with Fray Marcos de Niza to gain further information. In 1539, the Franciscan friar, accompanied by Estévan and several Indian guides, crossed into the present United States, possibly near the Arizona border community of Lochiel. Nearing the Zuñi pueblos at the Arizona-New Mexico border, he sent Estévan ahead with some of the Indian guides. When the Zuñis killed the Negro, the friar took to his heels. After a hasty trip back, he reported to Mendoza that he had seen a city, one of the Seven Cities of Cíbola, that was more impressive than Montezuma's capital itself. He probably had seen one of the Zuñi pueblos. From a distance, the sun-baked walls may indeed have glittered like gold.

Coronado marches through the Southwestern United States, in 1540–42. Disappointed at not having found the Seven Cities of Gold, he returned to Mexico. From a painting by Frederic Remington. Courtesy, Library of Congress.

Immediately Mendoza began organizing one of the grandest expeditions that Spain ever assembled in the New World. He appointed as commander his young friend Francisco Vásquez de Coronado, Governor of Nueva Galicia, and sent along Fray Marcos. In February 1540, about 250 mounted Spanish troops, nearly 100 footmen, several hundred friendly Indians, 4 priests, remudas of extra horses, and herds of cattle, sheep, and swine left Compostela. At Culiacan the impatient Coronado rushed ahead with 100 mounted men, leaving the slow-moving main body, with the livestock and baggage train, to follow. Crossing into the area of the present United States southwest of Bisbee, Ariz., he struck out toward the northeast until he came upon the Zuñi pueblo of Hawikuh—a jolting disappointment. It was not a magnificent city surrounded by gold-crusted walls ornamented with jewels, but a motley rock-and-clay pueblo. Furthermore, its Indian defenders were hostile. Though tired from the rapid march and debilitated by a rationed diet, the Spaniards took the pueblo by storm.

The mounted men with superior arms won the fray. Coronado ensconced himself in the pueblo and sent back one of his lieutenants, Melchior Díaz, to order the main army forward. After doing so, Díaz took a detachment and cut west to the Colorado River, roughly along the southern boundary of Arizona. He failed in his attempt to rendezvous with the expedition's ships—two supply vessels under Hernando de Alarcón—that had sailed the length of the Gulf of California and up the mighty Colorado for a distance of perhaps 50 miles.

The pueblo of Hawikuh was undoubtedly one of the fabled Seven Cities of Cíbola; Fray Marcos shamefacedly returned home, but Coronado determined to pursue the search. During the summer of 1540, another lieutenant, Pedro de Tovar, led a side expedition to Awatovi and the other Hopi villages in northeastern Arizona. López de Cárdenas explored as far west as the awesome walls of the Grand Canyon of the Colorado. He was the first European to view the canyon. Another small expedition under Hernando de Alvarado followed Indian guides northeast to Taos and Pecos Pueblos. Meanwhile, Coronado shifted his headquarters eastward to the pueblo of Tiguex on the Rio Grande, a few miles north of the site of Albuquerque. Heavy fighting ensued with the Indians, who finally surrendered.

From an Indian the Spaniards called the Turk, "because he looked like one," Coronado heard marvelous tales of the rich land of Quivira farther to the east. In the spring of 1541, the entire army, with renewed hope, marched eastward under the Turk's guidance. In truth, the Indian was a native of the Plains country, seeking to escape from captivity among the Pueblo Indians. But he easily duped the Spaniards, who so avidly sought gold and conquest—even though Ysopete, another Plains Indian who accompanied the expedition, denied the Turk's stories. Somewhere along the eastern edge of the Texas high plains, Coronado sent the main army back to Tiguex. With 30 cavalrymen, 6 infantrymen, some servants, and the 2 Plains Indians, he trekked toward the northeast into present Oklahoma and Kansas, which did not yield the riches the Spanish sought. The Turk confessed his duplicity and the Spanish garroted him. At the very time that Coronado was in Kansas, the De Soto expedition—which had originated in Florida—was probably only a few hundred miles to the southeast.

Coronado, frustrated at finding no wealth in Kansas, turned back to Tiguex, where the Spaniards spent a dreary winter before dragging themselves back to their homeland in the south. Not only had their high hopes of riches been dashed, but the inhospitable lands they had traversed were unsuitable for colonization. The discovery by Díaz and Alarcón that Baja (Lower) California was a peninsula and not an island was the only concrete result of the expedition. For about 40 years, New Spain's interest in the north country waned.

New Mexico—which then included present Arizona and the rest of the Southwest—was colonized in 1598 by Juan de Oñate because of the lingering suspicion that the fabled land of Quivira might, in truth, be real, and because of persistent rumors of mineral wealth in the mountains. The Rodríguez and Espejo expeditions of 1581–82 stimulated these rumors. In 1581, Friar Agustín Rodríguez, with two other Franciscans and a small band of soldiers, entered the upper Rio Grande region to convert the Pueblo Indians. The priests remained there without military escort. Fearing that they were lost, the following year Antonio de Espejo went to their rescue. The three friars had been killed; Espejo had little to report, but his return quickened Spanish interest again in the lands to the north. An unlicensed expedition under Castaño de Sosa in 1590 was thwarted when soldiers from Chihuahua overtook it and arrested the leader. About 1590, Indians slaughtered another group, led by Francisco Leyva de Bonilla and Antonio Gutíerrez de Humaña, somewhere in the Plains country.

It was Oñate, sanctioned by the Crown and leading a powerful force, who made the first permanent settlement. Crossing the Rio Grande at present El Paso, he and some 400 followers proceeded up the river to the juncture of the Chama. In that vicinity, in the summer of 1598, they founded the colony of San Juan de los Caballeros in one of two Indian pueblos. Late in the year or early in 1599, they established San Gabriel de Yungue-ouinge at the other pueblo as the capital of New Mexico. From these bases, Franciscan friars scattered to the pueblos and in 1601 Oñate himself rode grandly off with an expedition to find Quivira. He traveled down the Canadian River, across the Texas Panhandle, and probably into the same general region of southern Kansas that Coronado had reached in 1541. On another trip, in 1604–5, he passed though the Gila country of Arizona to the Colorado River, but again found no gold or silver.

The little colony on the Rio Grande grew discontented under Oñate's leadership; he resigned about 1608 and Pedro de Peralta replaced him the following year. Probably in 1610 Peralta moved the capital southward and reestablished it at Santa Fe, which he founded in the foothills of the Sangre de Cristo Mountains. The priests continued to expand their evangelical work among the neighboring pueblos, but otherwise the province grew slowly. In the second decade of the 17th century, perhaps 20 priests were serving some 30,000 converts in more than 40 small churches in the upper Rio Grande area. Military and civilian personnel numbered

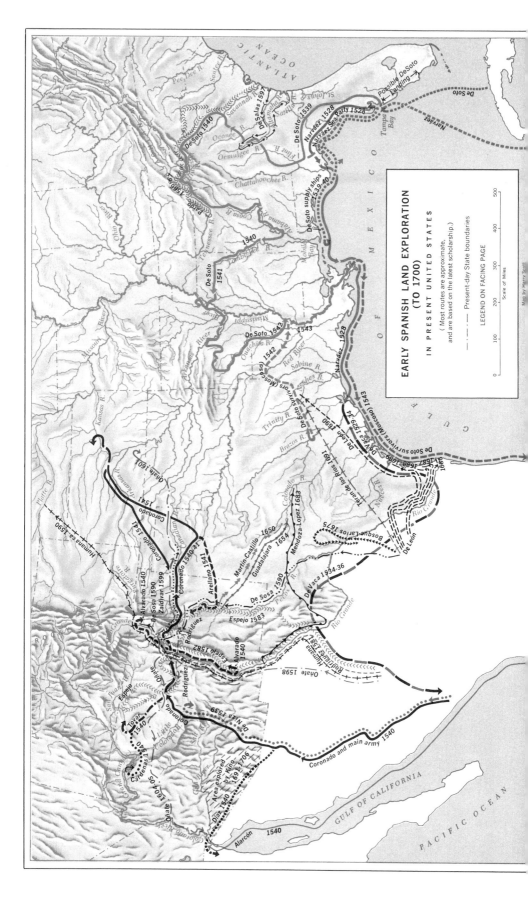

EARLY SPANISH LAND EXPLORATION
(TO 1700)

IN PRESENT UNITED STATES

(Most routes are approximate,
and are based on the latest scholarship.)

- - - - - Present-day State boundaries

LEGEND ON FACING PAGE

Scale of Miles

0   100   200   300   400   500

Map by Harry Scott

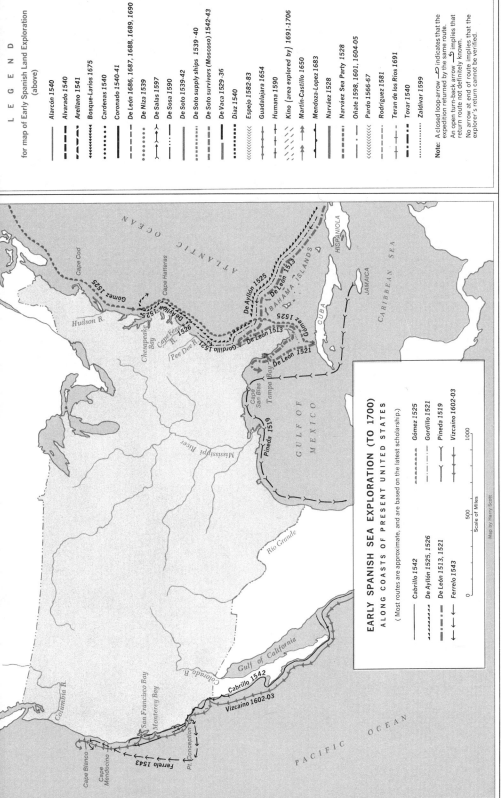

L E G E N D

for map of Early Spanish Land Exploration
(above)

Alarcón 1540
Alvarado 1540
Arellano 1541
Bosque-Larios 1675
Cardenas 1540
Coronado 1540-41
De León 1686, 1687, 1688, 1689, 1690
De Niza 1539
De Salas 1597
De Sosa 1590
De Soto 1539-42
De Soto supply ships 1539-40
De Soto survivors (Moscoso) 1542-43
De Vaca 1529-36
Diaz 1540
Espejo 1582-83
Guadalajara 1654
Humana 1590
Kino (area explored by) 1691-1706
Martin-Castillo 1650
Mendoza-Lopez 1683
Narváez 1528
Narváez Sea Party 1528
Oñate 1598, 1601, 1604-05
Pardo 1566-67
Rodriguez 1581
Teran de los Rios 1691
Tovar 1540
Zaldivar 1599

Note: A closed loop-arrow ⟲ indicates that the
expedition returned by the same route.
An open turn-back arrow ⤳ implies that
return route not definitely known.
No arrow at end of route implies that the
explorer's return cannot be verified.

EARLY SPANISH SEA EXPLORATION (TO 1700)
ALONG COASTS OF PRESENT UNITED STATES

(Most routes are approximate, and are based on the latest scholarship.)

Cabrillo 1542
De Ayllón 1525, 1526
De León 1513, 1521
Ferrelo 1543

Gómez 1525
Gordillo 1521
Pineda 1519
Vizcaino 1602-03

Scale of Miles

0   500   1000

Map by Harry Scott

PACIFIC OCEAN

ATLANTIC OCEAN

CARIBBEAN SEA

GULF OF MEXICO

Gulf of California

BAHAMA ISLANDS

CUBA

HISPANIOLA

JAMAICA

Cape Cod
Cape Hatteras
Hudson R.
Chesapeake Bay
Pee Dee R.
Tampa Bay
Cape San Blas
Mississippi River
Rio Grande
Colorado R.
San Francisco Bay
Monterey Bay
Pt. Conception
Cape Mendocino
Cape Blanco
Columbia R.

Gómez 1525
De León 1513
De Ayllón 1525
De León 1521
Gordillo 1521
De León 1513
Pineda 1519
Cabrillo 1542
Vizcaino 1602-03
Ferrelo 1543

only a few hundred. Several minor expeditions searched the surrounding mountains and made other tours—as far as west Texas—in the vain pursuit of treasure.

Only the apparent success of the mission effort among the sedentary Pueblo Indians kept the tiny colony in New Mexico alive, for the venture proved unrewarding otherwise. New Mexico settled quickly into an isolation and pastoral lethargy that was to be its chief characteristic for the next two centuries. The small number of Spanish settlers and soldiers—competing with the clergy—exacted burdensome tributes and forced labor from the Indians in an attempt to derive a livelihood. The clergy and civil leaders clashed on many other issues, and civil-military discord seriously weakened the small colony.

Disaster struck in 1680. The padres' success had been more apparent than real, and the Indians proved to be more recalcitrant than they had seemed. Resenting the tributes and the new religion that was forced on them, they rebelled under an unusual leader, Popé. They killed more than 400 Spaniards and drove the rest off their scattered estates and out of Santa Fe. The survivors fled panic-stricken southward into the province of Chihuahua, where the following year they founded El Paso del Norte, now Juarez, Mexico. One small group of friars and loyal Indians continued on and stopped on the north bank of the Rio Grande a few miles southeast of present El Paso. There, also in 1681, they established the mission community of Corpus Christi de Isleta.

That same year, Gov. Antonio de Otermín made an attempt to reconquer New Mexico but failed. A decade elapsed before Diego de Vargas received a commission to reestablish dominion over the province. In 1692, he led a strong force up the Rio Grande. The pueblos submitted with little resistance, and the Spaniards reoccupied Santa Fe. In their absence, the Tano Indians had moved into the town. Friction between them and the newcomers erupted soon into a bloody fight, the Tanos being driven into the mountains. For the next 6 years, like brush fires on the prairie, sporadic rebellions burst out in the pueblos; De Vargas was kept busy chasing from one to another before, finally, he reinstituted complete and lasting Spanish authority.

The history of the province from the time of the reconquest until the newly independent Mexico took it over in 1821 is a record of the ebb and flow of missionary activity in the Indian pueblos; civil-military-religious clashes; the slow spread of ranchos and haciendas into the plateaus away

774-955 O-68—4

from the rivers; the coming and going of a long line of royal Governors; the building of little villages along the rivers and in the valleys; frequent warfare with the Apaches, Navajos, and Comanches; occasional explorations into the vast, unknown regions surrounding the upper Rio Grande; and, finally, visits by French fur traders from the northeast.

New Mexico was hopelessly separated from the pulse of the Spanish Viceroyalty. It was a distant outpost from which twice a year long caravans made the wearisome trek to Mexico City and back, bringing news, gossip, and supplies. For the most part, the widely scattered towns and ranches were self-sustaining, and even the smallest had some fortifications against Indian attack. The largest town during this period was not the capital of Santa Fe but the village of Santa Cruz, about 20 miles north on the Rio Grande. Twice destroyed by Indian raids late in the 17th century, in 1706 it was reestablished by Gov. Francisco Cuervo y Valdez, who also founded that same year a small post southwest of Santa Fe that he named San Felipe de Alburquerque (later Albuquerque) in honor of the Viceroy. The latter remained a sleepy, pastoral village until after the coming of the Anglo-Americans in the middle of the 19th century.

In the Taos Valley, in northern New Mexico, were three distinct villages: the Indian pueblo; a Spanish villa, Fernando de Taos, a short distance away; and tiny Ranchos de Taos, about 3 miles farther south. The Indians of the Taos Pueblo had been the first to rebel in 1680 and were the last to submit, in 1696, to the reestablishment of Spanish authority. San Gerónimo de Taos, the mission church of the pueblo and one of the earliest in New Mexico, constructed in 1620, was rebuilt in 1706 after being razed during the Pueblo Revolt. In 1723, the Spanish officially established the Taos Fair, whose origins reached far back into prehistoric times. Conducted annually almost every year thereafter for more than a century, it became an important source of contact and commerce with the Plains Indians and French trappers.

From some Plains Indians (Cuartelejo Apaches) the Spaniards learned of a French expedition that had left the Illinois country for the purpose of trading in New Mexico. The Spanish response, as always to French intrusion, was reflexive. In 1720, an expedition under Pedro de Villasur rushed north from Santa Fe. In a fight along the North Platte River with Pawnee Indians, Villasur and his interpreter, Jean l'Archeveque, lost their lives. Months later, 12 survivors of the expedition struggled back to Santa Fe.

In 1727, New Mexicans heard alarming rumors of a French settlement

160 leagues north of Santa Fe, which proved, indeed, to be a French
trading post at a Cuartelejo Apache village. Then, in 1739, the Mallet
brothers and a party of fur traders appeared in Santa Fe. Spain and
France were at peace in Europe, but the Spanish Crown directed the
capture of any other Frenchmen who appeared in New Mexico. After
1746, despite the royal injunction, French trappers apparently began to
visit the Taos Fair. In the years following 1762, when Spain acquired
western Louisiana from France, royal Governors in both New Mexico and
Texas made good use of the French traders in dealing with the Indians
of the "northern tribes."

In Pimería Alta—the northern region of the province of Sonora,
which included present Arizona south of the Gila River—the Spanish
were far less active than in neighboring New Mexico. This was especially
true in southern Arizona (northern Pimería Alta), where the Spaniards
made only a nominal penetration of an area not more than 60 miles
square south of Tucson in the Santa Cruz Valley; they had little or
no effect on the rest of modern Arizona. Ultimately, in Arizona the
Spaniards established three missions, only two of which were active at
any one time, and founded a few *visitas* and a small presidio. In southern
Pimería Alta, in contrast, Spanish activities were more intensive. There
at one time three presidios protected a series of missions and *visitas,*
and miners were quite active.

The entradas of De Niza, Coronado, and Oñate, in 1539, 1540, and
1604–5, merely passed through Pimería Alta, but the Jesuit Father
Eusebio Francisco Kino thoroughly explored it, beginning in 1687. After
founding a group of missions in southern Pimería Alta, in 1691 he
entered present Arizona. For the rest of the decade he visited the Indians;
stopped at the future sites of the Tumacacori, San Xavier, and Guevavi
missions; established Indian rancherías to support envisioned missions;
and wandered north to the ruins of Casa Grande on the Gila. In 1700,
under his direction, Indians laid the foundations of San Xavier del Bac
Mission, ultimately one of the most magnificent in North America, and
Kino soon founded San Gabriel de Guevavi Mission. Unable to obtain
funds or missionaries from the Spanish Government to operate the missions, however, he returned to his headquarters in southern Pimería Alta,
from where he directed activities until his death, in 1711. His successors
carried on his efforts there.

In 1732, a new group of Jesuits—mainly Germans—renewed the

apostolic effort in northern Pimería Alta. From Guevavi and San Xavier, despite occasional Apache raids, they continued Kino's work by founding six *visitas* at the rancherías in the Santa Cruz Valley. An uprising of the

This scene illustrates life at San José de Tumacacori Mission, Arizona. The mission Indians engaged in religious, educational, farming, and handicraft activities. From an exhibit at Tumacacori National Monument.

Pima Indians in 1751 jolted the Spanish authorities into a greater awareness of the area, and the following year they founded a presidio at Tubac to protect the small group of settlers in the region; and padres built a mission 3 miles away at the village of San José de Tumacacori. It was from Tubac that Juan Bautista de Anza set out in 1774 to open an overland route to California.

To better cope with Apache depredations, in 1776 the Spanish authorities replaced the presidio at Tubac with one at the site of Tucson. In 1767, the Crown had expelled the Jesuits from all the Spanish colonies, and the Franciscans had moved in. In 1773 they abandoned Guevavi and centered their activities at Tumacacori, and in 1785 began construction of present San Xavier del Bac Mission, which they completed in 1795.

In the 1790's, in addition to the few hundred missionaries and settlers in present Arizona, about 20,000 Hispanic people were living in New Mexico in scores of isolated estates and hamlets scattered along the upper Rio Grande. Their quiet, near-indolent retirement was rudely shattered by the appearance of the Americans on the northern frontier just after the turn of the century. But Spain lacked the power or the energy to push back the tide. After Mexico gained her independence in 1821, together with the Spanish possessions in the present United States, she opened the province to the Yankees, who gained a major inroad into the Southwest via the Santa Fe Trail.

TEXAS—REACTION TO THE FRENCH

Texas was the third major area to be penetrated by the Spanish. Despite sporadic interest by Spanish officials, it received little attention until the founding of San Antonio, in 1718. During the next century, only a few sparse settlements were made, and a handful of missionaries, soldiers, and settlers sought to link the vast province with the rest of New Spain.

As in Florida, Spanish settlement in Texas was in response to a French threat. In 1682, the remarkable French explorer René Robert Cavelier, Sieur de la Salle, floated down to the mouth of the Mississippi, planted the gold and white banner of his country on the riverbank, claimed the entire river system for France, and named it Louisiana in honor of his sovereign, Louis XIV.

La Salle's next venture was an even more serious menace to Spain. Sailing from France and planning to establish a permanent post at the mouth of the Mississippi, in 1685 he landed instead on the Texas coast at the mouth of the Lavaca River. How could such an experienced explorer have missed his destination so far? Was his actual purpose, perhaps with the secret support of his inscrutable King, to move even nearer the Spanish mines of Nueva Viscaya, to the West?

In any event, La Salle erected Fort St. Louis and set out in a *westerly* direction, allegedly to locate the Mississippi's estuary, before turning northeast and headed back to the Illinois country for provisions. Some of his discouraged followers, however, assassinated him somewhere in east Texas. A few survivors made their way back up the Mississippi to Canada; the remainder of the complement at Fort St. Louis succumbed to disease, starvation, and the Indians.

Spanish authorities, learning from coastal Indians of the threat to their northern outposts, began a frantic search by land and water. On his fourth overland expedition, in 1689, Capt. Alonso de León located the French post. Finding it deserted, he burned it to the ground to obliterate any trace of French occupancy on Spanish soil.

In the heat of the alarm over the French, Father Damian Massanet, who had accompanied De León, had little difficulty in obtaining official support for the establishment of a mission among the friendly Tejas Indians, a branch of the Caddo Confederation, in east Texas. Emissaries of the Tejas tribe, whose very name was translatable as friendly, had witlessly invited the Spanish into their midst. In 1690, De León and Massanet founded the San Francisco de los Tejas Mission. The following year they began an offshoot, Santísimo Nombre de María, a few miles away. Domingo Teran de los Rios, appointed "Governor" of the province, crossed Texas bringing additional priests and supplies.

Two years later the disillusioned Indians—among the most civilized in North America—drove the padres out. But a combination of a zealous priest and a forward Frenchman was to bring Spain rushing back into Texas shortly after the turn of the century. Father Francisco Hidalgo, one of the Franciscans who had been at the Tejas mission, feared for the souls of his Indian converts in east Texas. When Spanish authorities failed to support his return, he sent a message to the French, then ensconced at the mouth of the Mississippi, praying that a priest be sent to the Tejas to minister the sacraments to the handful of faithful. Nothing could have delighted the French commander more than this invitation. In 1713, he dispatched a young French woodsman—the clever and charming Louis Juchereau de St. Denis—to the Spanish outpost on the Rio Grande.

Carmel Mission, California, in 1839. Mission activities included farming and stockraising. From a multivolume series, published during the years 1841–54. Courtesy, Bancroft Library, University of California.

St. Denis did not intend to save Indian souls; he sought trade with the northern Spanish settlements. In the next 4 years, he pursued one of the most romantic adventures in the history of the North American frontier. Arriving in July 1714 at San Juan Bautista on the Rio Grande—opposite modern Eagle Pass—he was promptly arrested for trespassing. But his silken tongue and gracious manners won the friendship of the post commandant and he began ardently to court his daughter, or niece. A jealous rival for the girl's hand, however, quickly caused his detention and he was sent to Mexico City.

With facile grace, St. Denis convinced the Viceroy that, although born a Frenchman, he was at heart a Spaniard. The Viceroy not only released him but appointed him cocommander of a Spanish expedition returning to east Texas to set up a presidio and mission field. The sizable expedition of friars, soldiers, and friendly Indians, under the joint command of Domingo Ramón and St. Denis, moved across Texas. During the autumn of 1716, it founded six missions, scattered from the Neches River eastward to present Louisiana, as well as the presidio of Dolores near the midpoint of the chain. No sooner were the Spaniards well established than St. Denis became a Frenchman once again. He hastened to a cache of trade goods that he had left on the Red River, erected a trading post at Natchitoches, and entered into an entirely illegal commerce with his Spanish friends.

In 1718, Martín de Alarcón stopped along the San Antonio River on his way to supply the east Texas outposts. Establishing there a halfway post between the Rio Grande and east Texas, he founded the presidio of Bexar and the mission of San Antonio de Valero, which came to be known much later as the Alamo.

In 1719, the sudden appearance at Los Adaes—the easternmost mission—of a French soldier from Natchitoches caused a wildfire panic. Padres and soldiers alike fled to Bexar seeking safety from what they imagined to be a French attack. Chagrined and embarrassed, Spanish officials appointed the capable Marqués de San Miguel de Aguayo as Governor and captain-general of Texas and sent him into the region with a formidable force of soldiers to reoccupy and strengthen it. In 1720, the beautiful San José y San Miguel de Aguayo Mission was founded in his honor at San Antonio. The Marqués went to east Texas in the summer of 1721. To prevent any further French incursions, he reestablished the six missions and the Dolores presidio and established a presidio at Los Adaes a few miles away from the French settlement of Natchitoches. Then, to extinguish forever any claim France might have to Texas, he marched down the coast and erected a mission and a presidio on the very site of Fort St. Louis, which 30 years earlier De León had burned to the ground.

When Aguayo left Texas in 1722, there were four presidios, nine missions, and small clusters of settlers at San Antonio and at Los Adaes. For the next half-century, Spain's hold on the region was stubborn—if shaky and unsure. In 1731, the Spanish relocated three of the east Texas missions at San Antonio. That same year, a shipload of Canary Islanders, consisting of about 15 families—the first civil colonists in Texas—arrived after a tortuous overland trek from Vera Cruz and settled at San Antonio. For about the next two decades, no major developments occurred. In 1749, the Spanish moved the mission and presidio known as La Bahía del Espíritu Santo back from the mouth of the Lavaca River to the site of Goliad. Six years later, they founded the mission Rosario nearby.

Spanish Franciscans endeavored, without success, to establish missions at the mouth of the Trinity (1756); on the San Gabriel River, in central Texas (1751); on the San Sabá River, 100 miles farther west (1757); and near the headwaters of the Nueces (1762). None of these missions lasted more than a few years, but the one at San Sabá had the most tragic history. Its purpose was to attempt to convert and teach agricultural methods to the terrifying Apaches, who were struggling with the even more frightening Comanches—intruding into west Texas from the north.

In 1758, the year after the founding of the mission, a horde of Comanches swooped down, destroyed it, and massacred the missionaries and their pitiable Tlascalan Indian charges—most of whom had been imported from northern Mexico. Frightened troops in the San Luís presidio across the river were unable—or unwilling—to come to the mission's aid. The next year the Comanches decisively defeated on the Red River a punitive Spanish expedition, consisting of 500 soldiers and Indian allies, which had moved into Comanche country. The reconstructed stone walls of San Sabá stand today as a memorial to the fierce might of the "Lords of the South Plains"—the Comanches. Spain was never able to defeat or contain these Indians, whose raiding range soon extended even farther south and separated San Antonio from the settlements in New Mexico.

By the middle of the 18th century, Spain's occupation of Texas reached its acme. Soon thereafter interest and strength began to wane. In 1762, the year before Florida passed to the English by the Treaty of

Paris, Spain acquired western Louisiana from France. The eastern frontier of New Spain thus moved to the Mississippi and the fear of French encroachment in Texas ended. For this reason, and in the interest of economy, the Spanish authorities completely abandoned the east Texas mission field in 1773. They even ordered the settlers at Los Adaes to move to San Antonio. Before long, some of these settlers insisted on returning to east Texas, even though they had no military protection. In 1779, some of them founded Nacogdoches. By the end of the century, Spanish Texas had shrunk to this feeble village in east Texas, the presidio-settlements in the Goliad vicinity and at San Antonio, and a handful of scattered missions.

During the next two decades, these isolated settlements figured in the movement for independence from Spain. Filibustering expeditions, organized by Mexican patriots, adventurers professing the Mexican cause, or pirates, several times ranged into Texas, captured settlements, and clashed with Spanish forces. When, at last, in 1821, Mexico achieved independence, Texas passed with hardly a tremor from Spanish control; the royal Governor, Antonio Martínez, simply turned his coat about and raised the Mexican tricolor over the 100-year-old plaza of San Antonio. Even before then, however, the preliminary American penetration of Texas that augured independence from Mexico in 1836 had already begun.

CALIFORNIA: THE LAST COLONY

The California coast, endowed with a wonderful climate and peopled by docile Indians, was ideally suited for the pastoral mission system by which New Spain had been slowly extending her northern frontiers. Elsewhere in the present United States the system had either failed or met with only moderate success; in California it thrived and reached perfection. Nevertheless, California was the last area in the United States to be penetrated by Spain—and not until the frontier lay virtually dormant elsewhere. Located as it was so far out on the lifelines of the Spanish Empire in the New World, California was sparsely populated and neglected.

Though the Spanish explored the Pacific coast extensively only a few decades after they began to explore the Atlantic and gulf coasts, they had but meager information about California. At the same time that Moscoso was leading the weary survivors of the De Soto expedition across

Carmel Mission, California, in 1835. From a lithograph by Day & Haghe, published in 1839. Courtesy, Bancroft Library, University of California.

east Texas and Coronado was returning dejectedly homeward from New Mexico, in 1542–43, the Juan Rodríguez Cabrillo expedition of two vessels was cruising northward from Navidad along the Pacific coast of California. After discovering San Diego Bay, Cabrillo moved up the coast to the vicinity of Point Reyes, a storm causing him to miss the Golden Gate. He died shortly thereafter, and Bartolomé Ferrelo assumed command. He reached the vicinity of the Oregon coast—perhaps between the 42d and 44th parallels—before returning to his home port. In 1602–3, Sebastián Vizcaíno also sailed up the coast, into Monterey and Drakes Bay, and explored the coastline of Oregon. Despite this exploration, Spain's chief interest in the area that is now the United States was focused for the next century and a half, not on California and the Pacific coast, but on Florida and the gulf coast region.

In the mid-18th century, Spain was spurred to colonize California by Russian fur-trade and exploratory intrusions on the Pacific coast, from Alaska as far south as Oregon, and the desire to provide supply and watering facilities for her Manila galleons. Colonization began in 1769 with a combined sea and land approach from Baja California. Under the leadership of Gaspar de Portolá and Father Junípero Serra, a Franciscan missionary, the overland expedition reached San Diego Bay in two stages. The sea party, consisting of two vessels of colonists and a supply ship, was less successful. The supply ship was lost at sea; the other two became separated, lost their bearings, and their passengers fell prey to scurvy before they landed. When finally assembled, the little band of California pioneers consisted of 126 persons. On July 16, Father Serra consecrated San Diego de Alcalá Mission.

Two days earlier an overland expedition commanded by Portolá had headed up the coast toward Monterey Bay, which had been discovered by Vizcaíno. Portolá failed to recognize Monterey Bay, but stumbled by accident onto "a very large and fine harbor such that not only all of the navy of our most Catholic Majesty but those of all Europe could take shelter in it." It was, of course, San Francisco Bay. And Portolá had seen only a part of it. After a brief exploration, the party turned south, identified Monterey Bay, and returned to San Diego.

Presidio of Monterey, in 1791. During the Spanish and Mexican periods Monterey was the hub of social, military, economic, and political activities in California. From a drawing by José Cardero. Courtesy, Bancroft Library, University of California.

There the men found a critical situation. Fifty men had died, the natives had become unruly, and the little colony was on the point of starvation. Most wanted to abandon the enterprise and return home, but

Father Serra vowed that he would never leave. Just when things looked the blackest, the sails of a supply ship were sighted, and the venture was saved. Quickly Portolá and Serra organized another expedition to Monterey Bay. In June 1770, to secure Spain's hold on the California coast, the Spanish founded the presidio of Monterey and the mission San Carlos de Borroméo.

During the next 2 years, as additional Franciscans and colonists arrived in California, Father Serra busied himself with establishing new missions between San Diego and Monterey. In 1771, he relocated the San Carlos mission a few miles away from the presidio at Monterey along the Carmel River, from which it took its permanent name. Traveling down the coast, in July 1771 he founded San Antonio de Padua Mission; and, in September, the mission San Gabriel Arcangel, about 9 miles east of the site of Los Angeles. A year later, he dedicated another mission, San Luis Obispo, between San Antonio and San Gabriel. In 1774, he moved the San Diego mission to a new site 6 miles away from its original location.

Two major problems yet faced the California venture: the opening of a land supply route from Spanish bases in Old Mexico and the occupation of the San Francisco Bay region. Many more colonies were needed, as well as livestock for a stable economy. The presidio and missions, remote from Spanish New World bases, were entirely dependent upon the uncertain arrival of supply ships. Father Serra returned to Mexico City, obtained the enthusiastic support of the new Viceroy, and helped plan a remarkable expedition from Sonora that was to culminate in the founding of San Francisco.

Meanwhile, Juan Bautista de Anza, the captain of the presidio at Tubac, had written the Viceroy of his proposed route to California.

Don JUAN BAUTISTA de ANZA

The Spanish explorer Juan Bautista de Anza. In 1774, he founded an overland route from Tubac, Arizona, to San Gabriel Mission, California. Subsequently he explored the San Francisco area and in 1777–78 served as Governor of New Mexico. From a conjectural painting, by an unknown artist, at Tumacacori National Monument, Arizona.

"The Mission of San Francisco, Upper California," probably San Francisco de Solano (Sonoma) Mission, in 1835. From a lithograph by Day & Haghe, published in 1839. Courtesy, Bancroft Library, University of California.

Appointed to lead the expedition being planned by Father Serra, Anza in 1774 opened the route from Tubac to Los Angeles. He traveled down the Gila to the Colorado, into the deserts and sand dunes of the California border—where his party almost lost its way—up San Felipe Creek into the Sierra Nevada, through San Carlos Pass, and then down into the valley of Los Angeles.

Returning to Tubac after a visit to Monterey Bay, Anza organized a colonizing expedition that departed in November 1775 for San Francisco Bay. With about 225 settlers, he reached Monterey in January 1776. Not Anza but his second in command actually founded a colony at the Golden Gate, in the autumn of 1776. The settlers built a presidio overlooking the harbor, and some distance from the bay, on a stream named Dolores, Father Serra erected a little mission. Anza himself left to become Governor of New Mexico and never returned to California, but his route was used to help colonize and supply the Pacific coast from Sonora. In 1776, Fathers Francisco Atanasio Domínguez and Silvestre Escalante failed in an attempt to develop an overland route from Santa Fe, New Mexico, to California.

The settlements in California grew and prospered. Monterey became the capital; in 1777, one of Anza's lieutenants established the village of San José; in 1781, the Spanish founded the pueblo of Los Angeles; and the following year, Santa Barbara Presidio. The last of the pueblos established was Villa de Branciforte (Santa Cruz), in 1797. The mission system expanded even more rapidly than the civil settlements—despite occasional Indian resistance and the martyrdom of some Franciscans. The padres founded San Juan Capistrano the same year as San Francisco Asís, 1776; Santa Clara, 1777; San Buenaventura, 1782; Santa Barbara, 1786; Purísima Concepción, 1787; Santa Cruz and Soledad, 1791; San José, San Miguel, San Fernando, and San Juan Bautista, 1797; and San Luis Rey, 1798. Three small missions were added to the chain early in the 19th century: Santa Inez, 1804; San Rafael, 1817; and San Francisco Solano, 1823.

In all, the Franciscans founded 21 missions in California—the last one, in 1823, during the Mexican administration—and small settlements grew up around most of them. The economy of Spanish California was agrarian, as in most other Spanish colonies, the missions being its chief element and forced Indian labor its main support. This economy continued for the first 12 years of the Mexican regime. In 1833, however, Mexico began secularizing the missions, despite the strenuous opposition of the padres, who had successfully forestalled similar Spanish decrees. These decrees called for the freedom of the Indians from missionary control, the granting to them of citizenship and lands, and the conversion of the missions into pueblos under civil jurisdiction.

Juan Bautista de Anza's second expedition to California, in 1775–76. Anza led about 225 colonists from Tubac to Monterey. They later settled at the site of San Francisco. From a painting, by Cal Peters, at Tumacacori National Monument.

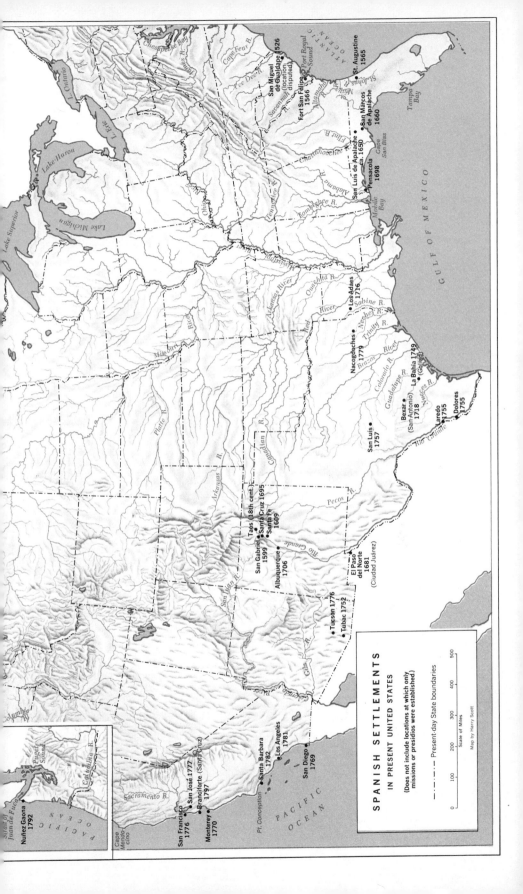

SPANISH SETTLEMENTS
IN PRESENT UNITED STATES

(Does not include locations at which only
missions or presidios were established.)

– · – · – Present-day State boundaries

Scale of Miles

0   100   200   300   400   500

Map by Harry Scott

San Miguel de Gualdape 1526

St. Augustine 1565

San Felipe 1566

Fort San Felipe (location disputed)

San Marcos de Apalache 1660

San Luis de Apalache ca. 1650

Pensacola 1698

Los Adaes 1716

Nacogdoches 1779

San Luis 1757

La Bahia 1749 (Goliad)

Bexar (San Antonio) 1718

Laredo 1755

Dolores 1755

El Paso del Norte 1681 (Ciudad Juárez)

Taos (18th cent.)

Santa Cruz 1695

Santa Fe 1609

San Gabriel 1599

Albuquerque 1706

Tucson 1776

Tubac 1752

San Diego 1769

Los Angeles 1781

Santa Barbara 1782

Branciforte (Santa Cruz) 1797

San José 1777

Monterey 1770

San Francisco 1776

Núñez Gaona 1792

GULF OF MEXICO

PACIFIC OCEAN

The Franciscans, maintaining that the Indians were not ready for freedom and not wishing to give up their temporal powers, vehemently opposed secularization. Friction and hostility with Mexican officials ensued. The Indians poorly comprehended the new measures, designed for their progress, and the missionaries influenced them against the Mexican Government. Destroying livestock and mission property, many of them fled into the wilderness. Vandals raided deserted missions and confiscated property and lands. The Mexican Government, realizing its failure, in 1845 issued a proclamation providing for the rental or sale of the missions. The result of a decade's confusion was, besides the tragic scattering of the neophytes, the destruction of most of the mission buildings.

San Luis Rey de Francia Mission, California, in 1829. From a lithograph by G. & W. Endicott, published in 1846. Courtesy, Bancroft Library, University of California.

The fortunate combination of mild climate, fertile soil, and Indian labor provided Spanish settlers in colonial California a life of leisure, ease, and even indolence. Some Spaniards and a larger number of Creoles, who had come from impoverished circumstances in Old Mexico, formed the upper layer of the socioeconomic structure and participated in the bounteous prosperity and life of idyllic graciousness. Thus California remained loyal to Spain during the first years of the independence movement in Mexico, which came to fruition in 1821, and only with some reluctance joined the Mexican Republic. Political unrest and turmoil in the 1830's and early 1840's presaged the official acquisition of California by the United States in 1848, at the end of the Mexican War.

IMPERIAL CONFLICT ON THE PACIFIC COAST

During the final decades of her tenure in North America, Spain became alarmed because of English and Russian expansion on the Pacific coast, between California and Alaska, and sought to assert her own claims in the region. Deciding to explore the area further and determine her ability to maintain her interests, she sent out a series of exploring expeditions, which also acquired much data on geology and natural history.

In 1774, Juan Peréz sailed almost to the tip of southern Alaska to observe Russian activity, but he learned nothing. The following year the Spanish dispatched Bruno Heceta and Juan Francisco de la Bodega y Quadra on a similar mission. Heceta mapped the estuary of the Columbia River and was the first European to land in the present State of Washington, at Point Grenville, where he proclaimed Spanish possession of the Pacific Northwest. He then returned to his home base. Bodega continued northward alone, landed at several points along the coast, and reached as far as Bristol Bay, in southwestern Alaska.

In 1778, Capt. James Cook of the British Navy explored the northwestern coast of the present United States in a search for the Northwest Passage. In 1789, as the Spanish set out with a similar aim, as well as to establish sovereignty over the Pacific Northwest, they were alarmed to find both British and American ships at Nootka, on the west coast of Vancouver Island, where in 1788 Capt. John Meares, an Englishman, had erected a fort. The Spanish seized the British ships, and built new fortifications. As a result, England and Spain were on the verge of war. In 1790, unable to obtain allies, Spain signed in Madrid the Nootka Sound Convention, which granted the British the right to explore, settle, and trade in the region north of San Francisco. Spain, however, did not agree to abandon her existing settlements there.

England immediately dispatched Capt. George Vancouver to reconnoiter the region. En route, in 1792, he visited Monterey, San Francisco, and various other Spanish settlements along the California coast, causing

Capt. George Vancouver's *Discovery* on the rocks, in Queen Charlotte Sound, Canada, in 1794. Its sister ship stands by. Vancouver explored the west coast of North America during the years 1791–95. From an engraving by B. T. Pouncy, after an on-the-scene drawing by Z. Mudge. Courtesy, Bancroft Library, University of California.

the Spanish to strengthen their defenses. Passing the Columbia River, he moved on to the Strait of Juan de Fuca and Puget Sound, where the Spanish expedition of Alejandro Malaspina was still exploring after its return from Lituya Bay, Alaska.

The Spanish, who had just founded a small settlement called Nuñez Gaona at Neah Bay, in the present State of Washington, moved it to Nootka. While Vancouver was probing northern Washington, Capt.

Fort Ross, California, in 1828. In 1812, the Russians founded the fort as a fur trading post and agricultural center to supply their colonies in Alaska. In 1841, they sold it to John A. Sutter. From a sketch by an unknown artist, published in 1834–35. Courtesy, Bancroft Library, University of California.

Russian house at Fort Ross, California, in 1841. From a sketch by an unknown artist, published in the year 1844. Courtesy, Bancroft Library, University of California.

Robert Gray, an American, arrived in the Pacific Northwest to search for sea-otter and other skins. In 1792, he sailed a few miles up the Columbia River, the first white man to do so, and laid the basis for later claims by the United States. The Lewis and Clark Expedition (1804–6) reinforced these claims.

In 1812, about a decade before Spain lost California and the rest of her territory in North America, the Russian-American Fur Company established Fort Ross, about 60 miles north of San Francisco, as a fur trading post and agricultural center for supplying her settlements in Alaska. The Spanish were somewhat alarmed by this new incursion of a foreign power. In only a few years, however, they lost all their possessions in North America to the United States and the newly independent Mexico.

DOWNFALL AND DEMISE

Although indeed continuous on the maps, the Spanish provinces were in no sense unified; each was a separate entity, having little political or economic connection with the others. Spanish claims in the present United States reached their maximum extent in the years between 1783 and 1803—when Spain's dominion stretched from Florida to California in one vast empire. In 1763, by the Treaty of Paris, Spain had lost Florida but 1 year earlier she had gained western Louisiana. In 1783, the treaty ending the American War for Independence restored Florida to her domain.

Surprisingly, Spain's empire in the New World reached its acme long after Spain had begun to lose her dominance in Europe—a process set in motion by the defeat of her armada by the English in 1588. By international politics, not active colonization, she obtained Louisiana and regained Florida, then but a remnant of a once lively colony. In the vast territory of Louisiana, Spanish control rested lightly on already existing French institutions. Not until more than 3 years after Spain acquired the territory did she form even a superficial government, at New Orleans. By 1800, the settlements in Texas had dwindled to a few thousand persons. The little colony along the upper Rio Grande, in New Mexico, was as dormant as ever. Southern Arizona showed even fewer signs of life, and in California the last burst of Spanish energy quickly spent itself.

Wife of a Monterey soldier. From a drawing, in 1791, by José Cardero, a member of the Malaspina expedition. Courtesy, Bancroft Library, University of California.

A Monterey soldier. From a drawing, in 1791, by José Cardero, one of several artists on the Malaspina expedition. Courtesy, Bancroft Library, University of California.

In the 19th century, disintegration and dismemberment of the empire were rapid. In 1803, France regained Louisiana and immediately sold it to the United States. In 1810 and 1812, settlers in West Florida— a few French and Spanish but mostly newcomers from the United States—revolted and sought annexation by the United States. In 1818, Gen. Andrew Jackson, directly asserting U.S. interest in Florida, marched into West Florida and captured Pensacola. Because of these troubles and her inability to control the Florida Indians, Spain, in the Adams-Onís Treaty (1819), ceded Florida to the United States and obtained a delineation of the disputed Texas boundary.

At about the same time, came the greatest blow. Imbued with the ideas of the French Revolution—liberty, equality, and fraternity—and inspired by the example of U.S. independence to the north, Spain's own colonies in North and South America began breaking away early in the 19th century. When Mexico gained independence in 1821, she acquired the Spanish possessions of Texas, New Mexico (including most of present Arizona), and California. These areas grew as restive a few years later under the despotism that evolved in Mexico, as Old Mexico had grown under Spanish rule.   Texas, colonized by many Anglo-Americans, gained independence in 1836, and 9 years later the United States annexed the Republic of Texas. New Mexico lay supine under the iron control of Manuel Armijo, a minion of the Mexican centralists, but California trembled for 15 years on the verge of open rebellion. When war broke out between the United States and Mexico in 1846, many residents of the Southwest welcomed the American troops as liberators. In 1848, by the Treaty of Guadalupe Hidalgo, the bulk of the old Spanish border-lands passed to the United States. Then the Gadsden Purchase, in 1853, added a strip of land to southern Arizona and New Mexico.

OUR SPANISH HERITAGE

Although the one-time Spanish territory gained by the United States in the trans-Mississippi West from Mexico was enormous and the gold soon discovered in California vitally affected Western development, per-haps the most rewarding and durable value of the Spanish borderlands was the heritage that lay in the land—from the Pacific to the Atlantic roughly south of the 40th parallel.

This heritage is most clearly evidenced by Spanish place names—from

Castillo de San Marcos, in Florida, to San Juan Capistrano Mission, on the Pacific coast. Florida, Colorado, Nevada, and California are Spanish names, and New Mexico is only slightly anglicized. The nomenclature of scores of cities, counties, rivers, and mountains also reveals that the Spaniards were the first Europeans to trod the land.

The language of Castile lingers not only in place names in the old Spanish borderlands, but more vividly on the tongues of men. Hundreds of words of Spanish derivation also enrich the modern English vocabulary; a few examples are lasso, calaboose, rodeo, sombrero, mesquite, and arroyo. From Florida to California, the Roman Catholic Church has thousands of adherents, and other aspects of Spanish culture are present. Architecture has the flavor of Madrid and Granada; ornamentation, of Oaxaca and Saltillo; art, of Mexico City and Guadalajara.

The origins of the cattle industry that has become the backbone of the Western economy are Spanish. The practice of working cattle from horseback, branding, trail driving, roundups, and even the cattle themselves and other livestock are all of Spanish origin. Less obvious, but

California *vaqueros* ply their trade. San José Mission is in the background. From a lithograph by L. M. Lefevre, published in 1839, after a drawing by Captain Smyth. Courtesy, Bancroft Library, University of California.

equally important, elements of the Spanish heritage are various modifications of statutory and common law that are attributable directly to the *regulamientos* of Spain. Among these are property, mining, and range laws. Also, the arid Western States have adopted the Spanish concept of prior usage rights to water in streams and rivers instead of the age-old English doctrine of riparian rights.

In all these ways, and in numerous others, Spanish conquistadors, padres, and settlers have left their mark on the American image.

The French: Trappers and Traders

Not long after the Spanish conquistadors began to move into the present Southeastern United States, the French did so in the north. The French penetration—which ultimately extended from the Great Lakes to the Gulf of Mexico—was of an entirely different nature than that of the Spanish. Generally characterized by commercial exploitation of a fruitful but cold land, except in the warmer climes of Louisiana, rather than permanent settlement of a sunny and arid one, it was a veneer over the native life, not a lasting and deep-rooted influence. The tiny, scattered, and heterogeneous French settlements also contrasted sharply with the well-ordered English, Dutch, and Swedish towns on the Atlantic coast.

Adventuresome and individualistic *coureurs de bois* and voyageurs gradually penetrated the winding waterways and the deep forests. Ultimately exploring almost two-thirds of the continent, they founded small missions and temporary posts deep in the river-threaded heartland rather than great religious edifices and cities that could be easily supplied by sea. Lonely trappers and traders, living with Indian women, used their isolated huts as bases of operations. The amenities of civilization were rare in the far reaches of New France.

The soil of the Mississippi Valley was fertile, but the restless commercial activities of the French did not encourage stable agrarian development, and they did not recognize the immense agricultural potential of the rich soil that stretched away from the rivers of the heartland. Claiming a much larger territory than her major rivals—England and Spain—and beset with European wars, France never could enforce total sovereignty over the vast wilderness. For all these reasons, she was the first of the three major European powers to be driven out of the present United States—in 1763—and few physical remains of her occupation exist today except in Louisiana, where settlement was more intensive than elsewhere.

Like the other European powers, France was impelled by a desire to spread Christianity, to find wealth, and to counter the efforts of other nations; and her New World colonies were also closely tied to her under the mercantilistic system. She, too, hoped to find a new water route to the East through the North American Continent. Her exploring expeditions naturally probed the present Northeast United States, whose shores were already known to her fishermen and were conveniently accessible from northern Europe. French explorers sailed down the St. Lawrence, across the waterways of Canada, through the Great Lakes, and finally to the Mississippi River and its vast drainage system. Instead of discovering a water passage through the continent, they found endless forests filled with fur-bearing animals and Indians eager to trade pelts for trinkets, muskets, and brandy.

The French Empire in North America thus came to be based on the trade in furs, originally controlled from permanent settlements in Canada. Intrepid frontiersmen plunged into the wilderness to barter and bargain, while the mother country tried to control the lucrative business by granting monopolies, forming companies, and utilizing other administrative devices. During the 17th century, most of the furs were brought into Montreal to a great annual fair. But both licensed traders and freelancers operated with increasing freedom as the French Empire spilled thinly into the heart of the continent. Frenchmen also did some mining for copper and lead in the upper Mississippi country, but transportation, manpower, and other problems hampered their efforts.

Side by side with the voyageurs, friars brought Christianity to the Indians. Most of them were strong-willed Jesuits, although Recollect Friars of the Franciscan Order accompanied Champlain and La Salle. French missionaries were far more mobile and had a less lasting influence on the native population than their Spanish counterparts. They founded no major missions, such as San José in Texas, San Xavier in Arizona, or San Luis Rey in California. Instead, scores of temporary mission stations, where priests read masses and performed the sacraments, dotted the forests of the northland. Nor did the French missionaries ordinarily attempt, as did the Spanish, to teach the arts of civilization to the Indians. The Spanish attitude toward the natives was paternalistic; the French, fraternalistic. The French adapted to the ways of the Indian; the Spanish "civilized" him.

With a few exceptions, mainly in Louisiana, the French settlements consisted of a few families of *habitants*, who farmed the river lands in the vicinity of the forts, trading posts, missions, and Indian villages that were the centers of frontier life. Added to this small and more or less stable population were scores of restless traders, soldiers, and missionaries, continually on the move into the wilderness.

PRELUDE: COASTAL EXPLORATION

The first Frenchmen in the New World were "summer people"—fishermen who, perhaps even before Columbus' voyage, plied from the shores of Normandy to the shoals of Newfoundland to harvest the teeming codbanks of the North Atlantic. They fished, they did some trading with the natives, and they returned to France; they maintained no logbooks of their voyages, and they were secretive about their quiet invasion of Spain's "exclusive" rights in the New World.

Francis I, however, who ascended the ancient throne of Charlemagne in 1515, was determined to challenge the ripening domination of Spain and her new Hapsburg monarch, Charles V. He contested, unsuccessfully, the election of Charles as Holy Roman Emperor; he sent troops to conquer some of Charles' territories in the north of Italy; and he brought the immortal Leonardo da Vinci to entertain his court in France.

But perhaps of the most lasting significance—determined that France would not be left behind in the race for empire—Francis sent an Italian navigator, Giovanni da Verrazano, across the seas in 1523–24 to establish a French claim to North America and find a passage to the East. After making a landfall, apparently somewhere along the Carolina coast, Verrazano turned north, hugged the coast around Cape Hatteras, sailed beyond the Chesapeake and Delaware Bays into New York Harbor and Narragansett Bay, around Cape Cod to Cape Breton Island, and finally back to France. He missed the great Gulf of the St. Lawrence and failed to find a water route to the East, but he provided France with a claim in the New World and announced her King's intentions.

OPENING THE ST. LAWRENCE

A decade later Francis turned to a hardy sailor of Brittany, Jacques Cartier, to renew his overseas ambitions. Scion of several generations of mariners, Cartier had earlier sailed to Portuguese Brazil and probably to the fishing banks off Newfoundland. In 1534, he set off in two small

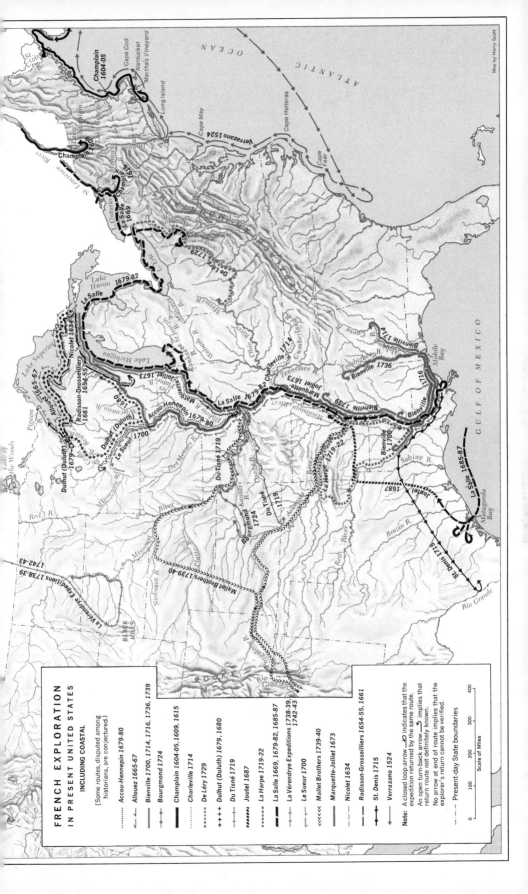

FRENCH EXPLORATION
IN PRESENT UNITED STATES
INCLUDING COASTAL

(Some routes, disputed among
historians, are conjectured.)

.... Accou-Hennepin 1679-80
⌐_⌐ Allouez 1665-67
━━━ Bienville 1700, 1714, 1716, 1736, 1739
↟ Bourgmond 1724
━━━ Champlain 1604-05, 1609, 1615
..... Charleville 1714
····· De Léry 1729
+++++ Dulhut (Duluth) 1679, 1680
⫿⫿⫿ Du Tisné 1719
▬▬▬ Joutel 1687
╪╪╪ La Harpe 1719-22
━━━ La Salle 1669, 1679-82, 1685-87
┼┼┼ La Vérendrye Expeditions 1738-39,
         1742-43
◁◁◁ Le Sueur 1700
<<<< Mallet Brothers 1739-40
—·—·— Marquette-Jolliet 1673
—··—·· Nicolet 1634
━━━ Radisson-Grossselliers 1654-55, 1661
━━━ St. Denis 1715
↓ Verrazano 1524

Note: A closed loop-arrow ⟳ indicates that the
expedition returned by the same route.
An open turn-back arrow ⟲ implies that
return route not definitely known.
No arrow at end of route implies that the
explorer's return cannot be verified.

— — — Present-day State boundaries

Scale of Miles

0   100   200   300   400

Map by Harry Scott

vessels with a royal commission to find a water route to the East—and it seemed at first as if he might have done so, for he discovered the broad waters of the St. Lawrence. After landing and planting a large cross to claim the land for his sovereign, he sailed around the perimeter of the Gulf of St. Lawrence and returned home.

Support for another voyage to the promising western waters was prompt and generous. Cartier sailed in May 1535, with three ships and a crew of more than 100, and moved across the Atlantic and up the St. Lawrence. As the river narrowed and the current to the sea flowed stronger, his earlier suspicion that he had not found a route around the continent was confirmed. Putting ashore in September at Stadacona, an Indian village (the site of Quebec), Cartier decided to spend the winter there. During the last days of autumn, however, he struck inland with his smallest vessel and reached the falls of the St. Lawrence, near the site of Montreal. From the Indians, with whom he exchanged presents, he heard tales of vast waterways to the west—the Great Lakes— and returned to Stadacona with reborn hope.

But this was the first of many harsh and trying winters that French pioneers were to spend in the ice and snow of Canada. By spring, a third of the expedition had died, and the emaciated survivors had no heart for further exploration. Abandoning one ship for want of a full crew, they headed back for France, where they arrived in July 1536. The King and many Frenchmen found Cartier's report interesting, but not sufficiently encouraging to finance another voyage. Not until 1541 could Cartier find another backer, the Sieur de Roberval, a nobleman of Picardy.

Roberval obtained from the Crown a license to explore and colonize the St. Lawrence at his own expense. He outfitted Cartier with three ships and himself with a like number. But from the beginning the expedition was plagued with bad luck, indecision, and dissension. In the spring of 1541, Cartier impatiently sailed from France ahead of his patron and pushed on to Stadacona. There he spent the winter of 1541– 42, and in June 1542 joined Roberval in St. John's Harbor, Newfoundland. Roberval, whose departure had been delayed 1 year, was anxious to continue the explorations. Cartier was not, and slipped away to France. Roberval proceeded to Stadacona, where he encamped for the winter. Perhaps it was an unduly harsh season, or the newcomers were unprepared; when spring at last arrived, the survivors could hardly wait to return home.

H U G U E N O T   S E T T L E M E N T   A T T E M P T S

France's next efforts at conquering the New World—two decades later—were motivated less by dreams of wealth and glory than by the desire of some Frenchmen to escape religious persecution. After Francis I died, civil and religious wars broke out in France that ultimately led to the downfall and expulsion of the Huguenots (Protestants). Fearing further punishment and reprisals, some Huguenots immediately emigrated elsewhere in Europe and others sought a refuge in the New World.

To establish such a refuge, the Huguenot leader, Adm. Gaspard de Coligny, in 1562 sent out Jean Ribaut, who landed at Port Royal Sound, in present South Carolina, and founded a tiny post, Charlesfort. When he returned to France, he left 30 volunteers behind to hold the post, but they bickered, abandoned the settlement, and sailed for France in a hastily constructed vessel. A passing English ship miraculously rescued the starving band, half-crazed from drinking salt water and reduced to cannibalism.

Yet the Huguenots were not disheartened. Under the leadership of

In 1564, René de Laudonnière landed with a group of Huguenot settlers along the St. Johns River, in Florida, where he built Fort Caroline. He found that the Florida Indians were worshipping a column erected 2 years earlier by Jean Ribaut during an unsuccessful colonizing attempt. From a 1591 engraving by Theodore de Bry, after an on-the-scene drawing by Jacques le Moyne de Morgues. Courtesy, Library of Congress.

René de Laudonnière, who had returned to France with Ribaut, in 1564 they made another attempt at settlement—Fort Caroline—at the mouth of the St. Johns River in Florida. This aroused the anger of Spain's Philip II. The following year, Pedro Menéndez de Avilés established St. Augustine and massacred the Huguenots, including Jean Ribaut. Thus Spain prevented French occupation of the southern Atlantic coast.

But France was not to be deterred for long from reentering the contest for empire. Early in the 17th century, two enterprising leaders took over the direction of French efforts in the New World: Pierre du Guast, Sieur de Monts, a Huguenot leader; and Samuel de Champlain, a young geographer who came to be called the "Father of New France." In 1604, De Monts received an exclusive monopoly of the fur trade, and he enlisted Champlain's aid in founding a permanent settlement in New France to serve as a trading post and a religious haven for Huguenots. Choosing an unfavorable site on St. Croix Island, near the northern boundary of Maine, Champlain's group spent a miserable winter, during which nearly half died of scurvy. When spring came, the survivors moved across the Bay of Fundy to a more suitable site at Port Royal, Nova Scotia, which they called Acadia and where they resided until returning to France in 1608. Meanwhile, in 1604–5, Champlain had explored the New England coastline as far south as Narragansett Bay and as far north as Nova Scotia.

Inland penetration

In 1608, Champlain planted a permanent settlement, called Quebec, adjacent to the Indian village of Stadacona, as a base for his explorations. The colonists survived the rigors of the winter only because of his grim determination. During the period 1609–15, Champlain struck boldly into the wilderness; he penetrated as far to the south as the southern tip of the lake that bears his name, up the Ottawa River into Canada, along the shores of Georgian Bay to Lake Huron, and back to the eastern end of Lake Ontario. Sometimes with him, and always with his encouragement and support, Jesuit fathers and some Franciscans carried the cross up the rivers and into the forests. Some successes, many disappointments, and a few failures attended their efforts.

To insure Indian acquiescence in his designs for colonization and development of the fur trade, Champlain early cultivated an alliance with the tribes that formed an unwilling buffer between French Canada and

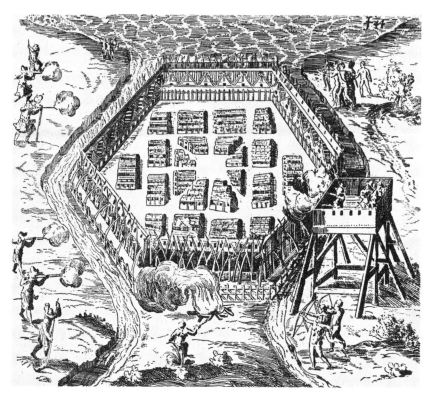

The palisaded Onondaga (Iroquois) fort, in present New York, attacked in 1615 by Samuel de Champlain and his Huron allies. From Champlain's own sketch, published in 1619. Courtesy, Smithsonian Institution.

the powerful Iroquois. In 1609, he had been persuaded by his Huron Indian friends to join them in an attack on the Iroquois near Lake Champlain—and again, in 1615, on the Oneida village south of Oneida Lake. Thus the French incurred the undying hatred of the five-nation Iroquois Confederacy, of which the Oneida were members, and this had repercussions for nearly a century. When the Iroquois finally overcame the Hurons, bands of the Confederacy—armed by Dutch traders in the Hudson Valley—spread out across southern Canada threatening to leave no Frenchman alive. In the Iroquois War (1642–53), the Indians twice nearly captured the newly founded Montreal and killed hundreds of Frenchmen, including several priests.

Indian attacks were not the only problems for the French. Several times Champlain was forced to return to France to obtain additional backing. In 1627, Cardinal Richelieu organized the Company of One Hundred Associates and took over the control of New France. When dissension rent this group, affairs in New France suffered from poor administration, as well as from Indian attacks. Following Champlain's death, in 1635, New France declined for more than two decades. In 1663, however, King Louis XIV took control away from the quibbling Associates and reorga-

Pierre Radisson and Sieur de Grosseilliers, fur traders and explorers, with Indian guides. They were among the first white men to explore and trade in the Lake Superior region. From a painting by Frederic Remington, published in 1906.

nized it under the jurisdiction of a civil administrator.

The year before Champlain's death, his lieutenant, Jean Nicolet, had traversed Lake Huron and the northern tip of Lake Michigan, and initiated trading compacts with the Indians in the Wisconsin area. In 1654 and 1655, the Sieur de Grosseilliers and his brother-in-law Pierre Radisson traced his route and established a lucrative trading post on the Wisconsin shore of Lake Michigan. Subsequently they explored Lake Superior, and in 1661 founded a post called Fort Radisson on its western shore.

"The Building of the *Griffon*." Built above Niagara Falls in 1679 by La Salle, the vessel was lost a few months later while returning, loaded with furs, from Green Bay. From an engraving in a book by Père Louis Hennepin, published late in the 17th century. Courtesy, Chicago Historical Society.

QUASHING THE INDIAN THREAT

The demise of the Associates and the arrival in New France of such powerful leaders as Jean Talon, Count Frontenac, and René Robert Cavelier, Sieur de la Salle, stimulated expansion. Under Talon, a French army of more than 1,000 troops arrived in Canada; in 1666, it defeated the aggressive Iroquois and their allies and achieved relative peace for two decades. The same year, to prevent future Indian depredations, as well as to check the incursions of English trappers, the French built Fort La Motte at the upper end of Lake Champlain; 1 year earlier, Fort Chambly had been constructed on the Richelieu River, north of the lake. Their position strengthened, Frenchmen plunged again into the forests and soon pushed the frontiers of New France all the way to the Gulf of Mexico.

TO THE MISSISSIPPI

Père Claude Jean Allouez explored Lake Superior from 1665 to 1667. At his little mission station near the western end of the lake, he heard from the Indians of a great river to the west. Père Jacques Marquette determined to investigate. In 1673, accompanied by Louis Jolliet and five others, he left St. Ignace Mission and ascended the Fox River, which flows into Green Bay, crossed over to the Wisconsin River, and followed it to the upper Mississippi. The party then descended the Mississippi to the mouth of the Arkansas. These Frenchmen were not the first Europeans to sight or travel the Mississippi; De Soto and Moscoso had done so a century and a half before.

The report of the exploration was rushed back to Quebec, where, in 1672, Count Frontenac had arrived as Governor of the province. He and his friend, the remarkable La Salle—who earlier may have penetrated the Ohio River Valley—listened with deep interest. Prior to that time, the two men had been involved in projects to open the western lake country to French trade.

PROBING THE ILLINOIS COUNTRY

In 1673, La Salle established Fort Frontenac on Lake Ontario to defend against the intrusion of English traders from the east. On two trips back to France, he obtained a title of *seignior* in the new Canadian nobility, a right to trade in furs, and authorization to erect additional posts and seek a water passage to the Gulf of Mexico. In 1678, he and his lieutenant, Henry de Tonty, and a party of Franciscans arrived at Niagara Falls. There, in 1679, above the falls they built a blockhouse fort, Fort Niagara, to guard Lake Ontario and the approaches to the west, and constructed a special boat to transport them through the Great Lakes.

Overcoming one obstacle after another, La Salle led his party to the site of Green Bay to trade, from where he sent the boat, loaded with furs, back to Fort Niagara for supplies. He then traveled by canoe down Lake Michigan and around its southern tip to the mouth of the St. Joseph River, where he built the semipermanent Fort Miami. After waiting in vain about 3 months for the supply boat to arrive, he ascended the St. Joseph to the site of South Bend, crossed to the Kankakee River, and descended it to the Illinois, which he followed to Lake Peoria. In 1680, at this lake he built Fort Crèvecoeur. After sending Michel Accou and Père Louis Hennepin to explore the upper Mississippi, he set out to return to his base at Fort Frontenac for supplies, and left Henry de Tonty in charge of Fort Crèvecoeur. Subsequently, by messenger La Salle directed Tonty to move to Starved Rock.

Disaster struck. The Sioux captured Accou and Hennepin, who had

René Robert Cavelier, Sieur de la Salle, envisioned a French empire in North America. He did much to achieve his dream by exploring and founding posts in the vast Illinois country. From an 1882 conjectural painting by G. P. A. Healy. Courtesy, Chicago Historical Society.

followed the Illinois and Mississippi up to the Wisconsin. The Frenchmen stationed at Fort Crèvecoeur pillaged and deserted it. Iroquois and Illinois hostilities in the Starved Rock area forced Tonty to withdraw to Green Bay, from where he moved to Mackinac. La Salle himself was met at Montreal by creditors, political enemies, and the news that the boatful of furs he had dispatched from Green Bay the previous year had never been heard from. Again his indomitable will prevailed. He obtained renewed backing, and in the summer of 1680 set out once more for the Illinois country, where he found that Fort Crèvecoeur had been destroyed and that Tonty had left Starved Rock. After spending the winter at Fort Miami, he returned to Mackinac and rejoined Tonty.

DESCENT OF THE MISSISSIPPI

Meanwhile, Accou and Hennepin, after wandering about Minnesota and falling captive to Indians, were rescued by another explorer, Daniel Greysolon, Sieur Dulhut (Duluth), Tonty's cousin. Dulhut traversed both the Fox-Wisconsin and St. Croix portages and renewed the fur trade with the Indians west of Lake Superior. Hennepin later made the absurd claim that he had traveled to the mouth of the Mississippi. This feat was accomplished by La Salle and Tonty and recorded by Père

Zenobius Membré, who accompanied them. The party entered the Mississippi from the Illinois River in February 1682. In April they reached the mouth of the Mississippi, where La Salle ceremoniously planted the French flag and claimed the entire drainage system for Louis XIV.

"Daniel Greysolon, Sieur Dulhut (Duluth), at the Head of the Lakes, in 1679." Dulhut, a fur trader, explored the lands west of Lake Superior. From a painting by F. L. Jaques. Courtesy, Minnesota Historical Society.

LA SALLE'S TEXAS VENTURE

La Salle returned to France to report his magnificent addition to the empire and to answer those who attempted to discredit him. In 1682–83, Tonty constructed Fort St. Louis at Starved Rock and reoccupied Fort

Indians plundering Père Hennepin's party, in 1681. From an engraving in a book by Hennepin, published in 1704. Courtesy, Library of Congress.

Miami. With renewed support from the Crown and intending to establish a colony at the mouth of the Mississippi, La Salle gathered an expedition of 4 ships and nearly 400 colonists. He sailed from France in July 1684, little realizing the disaster that lay ahead. He fell sick and almost died; the Spaniards captured one of his ships; he quarreled with his principal mariner, Captain Beaujeau; and his men almost mutinied. The three ships passed the mouth of the Mississippi, and early in 1685 sailed into Matagorda Bay, on the Texas coast. One ship foundered in the bay and was lost. Then Beaujeau treacherously sailed away in another ship, loaded with men and supplies. The remaining ship landed near the mouth of the Lavaca River, and the colonists hastily erected Fort St. Louis. A month later, they moved to a new location 5 miles away. Meanwhile, the debilitated La Salle undertook to lead overland reconnaissances to locate the Mississippi. Strangely enough, he apparently traveled westward. Was the great explorer lost? Or was he, in reality, more interested in locating Spanish mines for some secret purpose of his sovereign?

In any event, circumstances soon forced La Salle to abandon his reconnaissances. Supplies at Fort St. Louis dwindled, and he lost his last ship in eastern Matagorda Bay. Unerringly now, he set out northeast—toward the Mississippi—to return to the Illinois country for provisions.

The strength of the post had been reduced to less than 100; La Salle took 17 men with him and left the remainder behind. On this, his last trek, mutineers assassinated him, in 1687, somewhere in east Texas. They

La Salle lands in Matagorda Bay, Texas, 1685. From an engraving in a book by Père Louis Hennepin, published in 1704. Courtesy, Library of Congress.

stripped his body and left it to the wolves, divided the meager spoils, and forced the innocent members of the party to accompany them. But soon the murderers quarreled among themselves, and La Salle's friends, including Henry Joutel, escaped.

All the mutineers except the enigmatic Jean l'Archeveque, who turned up in Santa Fe years later, were lost or killed by the Indians. Ascending the Mississippi, Joutel and his party met at the mouth of the Arkansas none other than Henry de Tonty, who had floated down from Starved

Rock with a party looking for La Salle. Leaving some of his men to establish what came to be known as Arkansas Post, Tonty returned to Canada with Joutel. Arkansas Post was of intermittent value to France in the years that followed.

Back at Fort St. Louis, in Texas, after months of waiting for La Salle's return, the starving remnant of his colony despaired. Some died; the rest deserted the fort and went to live with the Indians. Fear of French encroachment in Texas stimulated Spanish efforts there. In 1689, the Spanish expedition of Capt. Alonso de León burned the French fort to the ground. La Salle was dead and his most ambitious venture a failure. But scores of intrepid trappers, traders, and missionaries followed him into the heartland of North America.

EXTENSION OF FRENCH INFLUENCE

In the mid-17th century, the French possessions lay on a chain of waterways extending from the great river system of the St. Lawrence, through the Great Lakes, and down the Mississippi Valley to the Gulf of Mexico. French claims to this vast region were announced by explorations such as La Salle's; and they were affirmed by the establishment of forts and small settlements, the extension of the fur trade and missionary efforts, and the spread of influence over the Indians. After 1670, condi-

"Shooting the Rapids." Voyageurs used the Montreal canoe, illustrated here, which was larger than the North canoe, on the Great Lakes. From a painting by Mrs. Edward Hopkins. Courtesy, Public Archives of Canada.

tions were especially favorable for the development of the frontier. The French had quelled the Iroquois in 1666. To check further Indian depredations and the incursions of English trappers, they then founded a series of forts.

Jesuits and trappers spread out into the western country. In 1668, at a well known and strategic location on the straits between Lake Superior and Lake Huron, Père Marquette had established a mission to the Chippewas. There, in 1671, the French held a grand council with the Indians of the region, and over the years a village called Sault Ste. Marie arose. An equally strategic point was the Mackinac Straits, a few miles to the south of Sault Ste. Marie, between Lakes Michigan and Huron. In 1670–71, missionaries founded St. Ignace Mission on Mackinac Island, and 2 years later relocated it at the tip of the peninsula on the north side of the straits, where soldiers built a small fort to protect the missionaries. Later, during the period 1715–20, the French erected Fort Michilimackinac on the southern shores of the straits. The straits area and Sault Ste. Marie were centers of missionary, as well as fur-trading, activity. From these and other bases, French missionaries penetrated the hinterland and carried the word of God to the Sioux, Chippewas, Illinois, Fox, and other tribes. The missionaries established small outlying stations, impermanently occupied for visitations.

Meanwhile, the fur trade expanded into the western country. Along the upper Mississippi, traders founded a number of posts, some of them temporary. Among the most prominent were Fort St. Croix (1680), near the portage to western Lake Superior; La Baye (1684), at the southern tip of Green Bay; Fort St. Antoine (1685), on the Mississippi between the St. Croix and Wisconsin Rivers; and Fort St. Nicolas (ca. 1685), at the mouth of the Wisconsin River, around which arose the settlement of Prairie du Chien. Troops occasionally occupied these posts, but they were primarily used as bases by the *coureurs de bois*—dare-devil Frenchmen who took to the forest to trade with the Indians.

The passage between Lakes Huron and Erie was the last of the connecting links in the chain of the Great Lakes that the French fortified. In 1686, they erected a small post, Fort St. Joseph, north of Lake St. Clair near the entrance to Lake Huron. Then, in 1701, Antoine de la Mothe Cadillac built Fort Pontchartrain at the southern entrance to Lake St. Clair. This fort proved to be the most important and durable of those along the Great Lakes, and around it grew up the village of Detroit. The two forts protected the water route through Lakes Ontario and Erie.

"The Buffalo." From an engraving in a book by Père Louis Hennepin, published late in the 17th century. Courtesy, Chicago Historical Society.

Previously, most of the traffic from Montreal had passed up the Ottawa River, over the portage at Nipissing, into Georgian Bay, on the northeast of Lake Huron, and then through Lake Huron to Sault Ste. Marie and Lake Superior or to the Mackinac Straits and Lake Michigan.

The growing popularity of the route through Lake Erie resulted in the opening of the Wabash portage late in the 17th century to facilitate travel to the Illinois country. To protect the route, about 1704 the French founded Fort Miami at the western end of the Maumee River; in 1719, Fort Ouiatenon, on the Wabash; and, in 1735, Fort Vincennes, also on the Wabash. Besides the Wabash River route, two other earlier portage routes, which had been used by La Salle, led into the Illinois country from southern Lake Michigan. One of these was by way of the St. Joseph River, which flows into eastern Lake Michigan, to the Kankakee River, in present Indiana; the other was via the Chicago portage to the Des Plaines and Illinois Rivers. Forts Miami, St. Joseph, and St. Louis protected these two routes.

From construction in 1683 to abandonment in 1691, Fort St. Louis was an important center of French influence in the Illinois country. Subsequent posts in the region were Cahokia, near present East St. Louis, founded in 1698; at Kaskaskia, a few miles down the Mississippi, in 1703; and at St. Denis, just above the Mississippi-Ohio juncture, in 1702. These villages, conveniently situated in a fertile area between the Great Lakes and the Mississippi Delta, were a source of agricultural produce for other settlements.

DEVELOPMENT OF LOUISIANA

Not long after La Salle's initial penetration of the lower Mississippi region in 1682 and his aborted Texas venture in 1685, the French took steps to found permanent settlements along the lower Mississippi. In 1698, the Le Moyne brothers, the Sieur d'Iberville and the Sieur de Bienville, sons of a prominent Quebec official, obtained a patent from Louis XIV to colonize the mouth of the Mississippi. Early the next year, the expedition of 4 vessels and about 200 colonists and soldiers temporarily landed at Dauphin Island, in Mobile Bay. It then moved westward in the gulf to Ship Island, just offshore from present Biloxi, Miss. Leaving the fleet and colonists at the island, Bienville and Iberville explored the lower Mississippi in small boats. Though they separated at one time,

A dance of the Natchez Indians. From an on-the-scene drawing by Antoine du Pratz, published in 1758. Courtesy, Smithsonian Institution.

they finally reunited at the island. After Iberville sailed away to Canada, the colonists and soldiers settled on the mainland at Old Biloxi, near present Ocean Springs, and constructed Fort Maurepas. Bienville continued his exploration of the region. When Iberville returned, the brothers built Fort de la Boulaye about 40 miles below the site of New Orleans and garrisoned it between 1700 and 1707.

Because of adverse conditions at Fort Maurepas, including disease, a shortage of food, and poor morale, Iberville decided to relocate most of the colonists on the Mobile River, about 30 miles above its entrance into Mobile Bay. There he built Fort Louis de la Mobile, and set up a post on Dauphin Island as port of entry to the colony. In 1710–11, after Iberville's death, Bienville moved the colony to the site of Mobile, and built a new Fort Louis, renamed Fort Condé in 1720. The Mobile settlement, despite the protests of the Spanish commander at nearby Pensacola, grew steadily and soon numbered more than 1,000. Other settlers founded New Biloxi, which became the seat of government for Louisiana, and some soon moved up the rivers and streams into present Alabama, Arkansas, Mississippi, Tennessee, and beyond. As early as 1700, Pierre Charles le Sueur had led an expedition of 20 men northward against the treacherous current of the Mississippi as far as the Minnesota River, where he set up a temporary base called Fort L'Huillier. Iberville had visited Arkansas Post, and Bienville had explored along the lower Red River.

In 1712, Louis XIV, anxious to develop Louisiana but having an empty treasury, turned to a commercial venture. He granted Sieur Antoine Crozat a trading monopoly and other rights in the province, whose boundaries were set to take in the settlements in the Illinois country, including St. Denis, Kaskaskia, Cahokia, and Starved Rock, but not those in the Wisconsin region. Crozat sent Antoine de la Mothe Cadillac to replace Bienville as Governor. Cadillac immediately invoked the enmity of the settlers by imposing a series of severe restrictions on them, paying trappers low prices for skins, and charging exorbitant prices for supplies. He also failed to maintain the good relations with the Indians that Bienville had inaugurated. In 1715, stirred by rumors of mineral wealth in Missouri, Cadillac investigated the area but found nothing. When he returned, he found that the Indians had risen against the settlers. In 1717, the disillusioned Crozat recalled him to France.

That same year, Crozat turned his patent over to one of the most amazing promotional enterprises in Western European history—the Company of the West, a stock concern headed by John Law, a glamorous

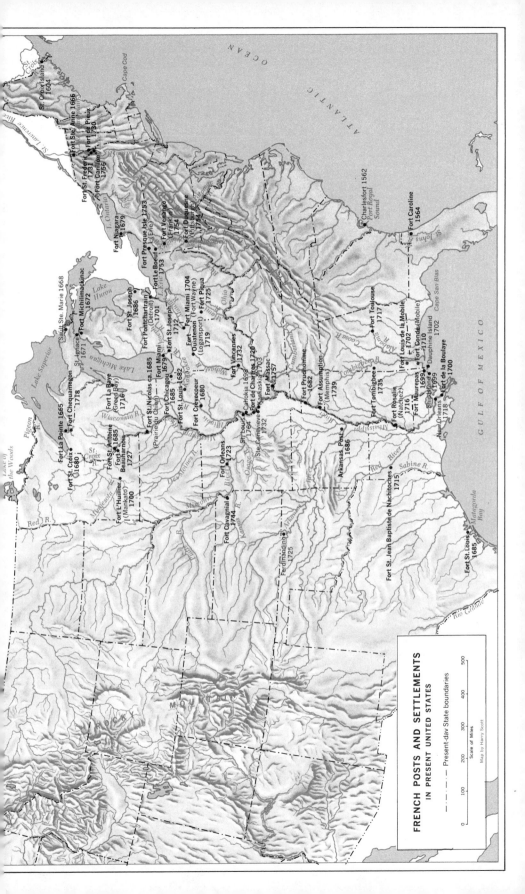

ATLANTIC OCEAN

GULF OF MEXICO

St. Croix Island 1604
St. Croix River
St. Lawrence River
Fort Ste. Anne 1666
Fort de Pieux 1730
Fort St. Frederic 1731
Fort Carillon 1756
Cape Cod
L. Ontario
Fort Niagara
Fort Presque Isle 1753 (Erie)
Fort Venango (Franklin) 1754
Fort Le Boeuf 1753
Fort Duquesne (Pittsburgh) 1754
Charlesfort 1562
Port Royal
Fort Royal Sound
Fort Caroline 1564
St. Johns R.

Sault Ste. Marie 1668
St. Ignace 1671
Fort Michilimackinac 1672
Lake Superior
Lake Huron
Lake Michigan
Fort St. Joseph 1686
Fort Pontchartrain 1701 (Detroit)
Fort Miami 1704
Fort Piqua 1725
Fort St. Joseph 1712
Fort Miami 1679
Ouiatenon (Fort Wayne) 1719
(Logansport) 1719
Fort Toulouse 1717
Coosa R.
Cape San Blas

Fort La Pointe 1665
Fort Chequamegon 1718
Fort La Baye (Green Bay) 1716
Wisconsin R.
Fort St. Nicolas ca. 1685 (Prairie du Chien)
Fort Chicagou 1679
Fort St. Louis 1682
Fort Crèvecoeur 1680
Illinois R.
Fort Vincennes 1732
Wabash R.
Cahokia 1698
Fort de Chartres 1720
Kaskaskia 1703
Fort Massac 1757
Ohio R.
Cumberland R.
Fort Prudhomme 1682
Fort Assumption (Memphis) 1739
Fort Tombigbee 1735
Tombigbee R.
Alabama R.
Fort Louis de la Mobile 1702
Fort Condé (Mobile) 1710
Dauphine Island 1702
Fort Maurepas 1699
Biloxi 1699
Fort de la Boulaye 1700
New Orleans 1718
Fort Rosalie (Natchez) 1716

Pigeon R.
Lake of the Woods
Fort St. Antoine 1685
Fort Beauharnois 1727
St. Croix R.
Fort St. Croix c. 1680
L'Huillier (Mankato) 1700
Red R.
Minnesota R.
Des Moines R.
St. Louis 1764
Ste. Genevieve 1732
Fort Orleans 1723
Missouri R.
Osage R.
Kansas R.
Fort Cavagnial 1744
Big Blue R.
Arkansas Post 1686
Arkansas R.
Ferdinandina 1725
Red River
Sabine R.
Fort St. Jean Baptiste de Nachitoches 1715
Fort St. Louis 1685
Matagorda Bay
Rio Grande

ROCKY MOUNTAINS

FRENCH POSTS AND SETTLEMENTS

IN PRESENT UNITED STATES

–·–·– Present-day State boundaries

Scale of Miles

0   100   200   300   400   500

Map by Harry Scott

Scotsman. After failing in his attempt to found a Government-sponsored national bank in his mother country, in 1716 Law had persuaded the French Crown to endorse his scheme to exploit the resources of Louisiana. The following year he formed his company, which absorbed Crozat's patent. Then, in 1718, as the speculative shares in Law's ventures soared in price, the Crown agreed to back his banknotes. Shortly thereafter, the King authorized one of Law's companies, in return for a guarantee to pay a specified portion of the national debt, to manage the mint, issue coinage, and collect all national taxes.

Based largely on rumors of wealth in the lower Mississippi region, speculation in Law's stock reached proportions unparalleled in Europe at the time. Law proposed, among other things, to settle 6,000 whites and

The Natchez Indians hunt buffalo. From an on-the-scene drawing by Antoine du Pratz, published in 1758. Courtesy, Smithsonian Institution.

3,000 Negro slaves in Louisiana. He actually settled 700 German colonists near Arkansas Post. In 1720, the "Mississippi Bubble" burst, the complex structure of Law's corporate system collapsed, and the colony near Arkansas Post was abandoned, the settlers moving to a site near New Orleans. Thousands of people who invested in Law's scheme lost money, but Louisiana enjoyed a sudden spurt of growth and publicity.

Under the impetus first of Crozat's company and then of the boom generated by John Law, the French expanded all their frontiers in Louisiana. In 1714, Bienville occupied a site just north of present Montgomery, Ala., which he fortified in 1717 and named Fort Toulouse. Only intermittently garrisoned, it served as a spearhead for French efforts to gain Indian allies in the imperial contest with the English and Spanish, as well as a defensive outpost for the protection of the settlements at Mobile Bay. In 1716, Bienville established a fort and trading post at the Natchez Indian village up the Mississippi from the site of New Orleans. Named Fort Rosalie, the post became the center of a significant settlement and was a key French post between 1716 and 1763. It was of such strategic value that over the course of time it quartered Spanish, British, and United States troops. The village on its flank became the city of Natchez, Miss.

While Bienville was thus engaged with Forts Toulouse and Rosalie, one of his young proteges, Louis Juchereau de St. Denis, had contacted the Spanish on the Rio Grande and persuaded them to reopen their mission field in east Texas. In 1717, St. Denis built a trading post at Natchitoches on the Red River in Louisiana. From this key post, the French not only smuggled goods for several decades into the Spanish Empire, but they also controlled the "northern tribes," which lived in the region of the Red and Canadian Rivers, especially the important Taovayas. In a few years, St. Denis' post grew into a prosperous village.

In 1718, Bienville at last set out to found a city on the site he had chosen almost two decades earlier. He laid out New Orleans and 4 years later moved there the seat of government for Louisiana from New Biloxi. Almost overnight, New Orleans began to rival Quebec and Montreal as the metropolis of New France. Despite a flood in 1719, it grew rapidly. In 1722, the King gave the Capuchins ecclesiastical jurisdiction over Louisiana, and 5 years later the Jesuits and the Ursuline Sisters arrived in strength. To promote the growth of New Orleans, Bienville imported from France a shipload of marriageable girls, who were chaperoned by the nuns until satisfactory mates could be found. The voyageurs and *coureurs de bois* flocked down the river to vie for their hands. Bienville also settled a small group of Germans in one section of the town, and welcomed immigrants from all nations. Into New

"The French Voyageur." From a painting by Mrs. Samuel B. Abbe. Courtesy, Minnesota Historical Society.

Orleans began to flow virtually all the commerce of the Mississippi Valley, from the Illinois country and even farther north. By 1762—when France transferred western Louisiana, including New Orleans, to Spain—the city was one of the six largest in North America.

In 1720, the French had erected Fort de Chartres, a temporary base, in the Illinois country. The fort and the nearby village of Prairie du Rocher bloomed for a brief time. The settlement, however, was never as important as its neighbors, Kaskaskia, where the Jesuits established an academy, and Cahokia, where the Sulpicians maintained an Indian school. Across the Mississippi from Kaskaskia a fourth settlement—Ste. Genevieve—joined the little cluster of Illinois villages. Originally a fur depot, by 1740 it had developed into a town. Because of its location on the west bank of the river and its ready availability to the trappers and

"French Habitation in the Country of the Illinois." From an engraving by an unknown artist, published in 1826. Courtesy, Chicago Historical Society.

traders who were penetrating deeply into the Missouri country, it soon equaled if not surpassed the other Illinois towns. Another factor promoting growth was the opening of small lead mines in the Missouri Ozarks, which also utilized it as a port.

In 1731, the 20-year monopoly granted to Crozat—transferred to Law, and thereafter owned by the bankrupt Company of the Indies—was abandoned, 1 year before it expired. Louisiana once again became a royal province. Despite the confusion of the era of commercial control, it had brought expansion and prosperity. It had also linked the Illinois country to Louisiana—a natural occurrence because of the Mississippi River connection—and fostered the growth of both areas. Because of Indian trouble and natural hazards, the northern portage route from the Illinois country to the Great Lakes was almost abandoned in favor of the river route south. Thus, most of the French communities lost their connections with the northern settlements and became identified with New Orleans and Louisiana. And it was largely from the Louisiana settlements that the great fur trade of the trans-Mississippi West developed.

THE WESTERN FUR TRADE

St. Denis' post at Natchitoches was one of the first centers of the western fur trade. From there, in 1719, Bernard de la Harpe explored the Red River and crossed the prairies to the Arkansas River just above its junction with the Canadian River. Three years later he returned to the same region and made commercial alliances with the Plains Indians that resulted in a thriving trade in buffalo robes. Thereafter, French traders followed both the Red and the Arkansas into the Plains country with increasing frequency.

Meantime, the traders Étienne Veniard de Bourgmond, during the period 1712–17, and Claude Charles du Tisné, in 1719, explored the Missouri country and traded with the Pawnee, Osage, and Arapaho tribes. In 1723, Bourgmond erected and garrisoned Fort Orleans, on the Missouri River, in present Carroll County, Mo., to exploit the trade of the region and serve as a French outpost. He maintained the fort until 1728, when he abandoned it. In 1724, illness forced him to turn back from an attempt to reach Santa Fe. Bourgmond and Du Tisné probably probed westward individually as far as the North Platte River.

It was from one of the posts in the Illinois country that a remarkable French exploration departed. In 1739, Pierre and Paul Mallet led a small trading expedition across the prairies and plains into Spanish

New Mexico. They probably followed the general route of the Santa Fe Trail of a century later, and entered Taos by way of Raton Pass. Their arrival at Santa Fe caused consternation among the Spanish officials. Already rumors of French activities had reached the Spanish through the Apache Indians; now there could be no question. Because the two nations were not at war, however, in 1740 the officials allowed the Mallets to return peaceably to New Orleans.

The aged Bienville—still the leading spirit in Louisiana—was delighted with the exploits of the Mallet brothers. Trade with the Spanish, even though illegal, was far more promising than trade with the Indians. New Mexico was an inviting prospect for French commerce. In subsequent years, Frenchmen trickled across the plains and over the mountains by various routes into New Mexico. Forbidden entry by royal decree, they nevertheless slipped surreptitiously into Taos until about 1762, when Spain assumed control of western Louisiana.

Among the last of the great French explorations were those of the Vérendryes. Though they had little bearing on the history or settlement of our Nation and the routes are disputed among historians, they have

"The Brothers La Vérendrye in Sight of the Western Mountains, New Year's Day, 1743." From a drawing by C. W. Jefferys. Courtesy, Imperial Oil Collection.

provoked the imaginations of men for more than two centuries. Pierre Gaultier de Varennes, Sieur de la Vérendrye, was commander of Fort Nipigon, on the northern shore of Lake Superior, when he obtained a monopoly of the northwestern fur trade to finance his search for the Northwest Passage. The French authorities were alarmed not only by the activities of the English Hudson's Bay Company in Canada, but also by those of the Spanish to the south. La Vérendrye established a line of posts in present Canada and Minnesota, notably Fort St. Charles on Lake of the Woods in the Northwest Angle of Minnesota, and Fort La Reine on the Assiniboine River in Manitoba.

Using Fort La Reine as a base of operations, in 1738–39 La Vérendrye and two of his sons, Louis-Joseph and Francois, penetrated the upper Missouri at a point probably near the site of Bismarck, N. Dak., where they wintered with the Mandan Indians and then returned to Fort La Reine. In 1742, the two sons and two companions traveled to the Bismarck vicinity, then set out in a southwesterly direction. On New Year's Day 1743, they sighted what were probably the Black Hills. Turning eastward, they trekked to the Missouri River, where they apparently buried a lead plate, found in 1913 near Fort Pierre, S. Dak. From this point, they likely ascended the Missouri to Apple Creek and crossed overland on their return trip to Fort La Reine.

Twilight of empire

French energies in North America were soon diverted from exploration and settlement to defense against the expanding English. As early as 1613, England had reacted to the French threat in North America by sending an expedition from Virginia under Capt. Samuel Argall to wipe out the feeble French colony at Port Royal, which had been reestablished in 1610 following the failure and abandonment of the first colony there 2 years earlier. In 1629, the English occupied Quebec itself for a short time.

When the French quelled the Iroquois in 1666, they may have had a moment of opportunity to dominate the English by moving into the Hudson Valley and New England. But they vacillated too long. England seized the initiative by capturing the Dutch settlements on the Hudson River and taking over the Iroquois fur trade, which the Dutch had found so profitable.

Three European wars between England and France were reflected in

Fort Beauharnois, a French post and site of a Jesuit mission, erected in 1727 on the west bank of the Mississippi River, in present Minnesota. From a charcoal drawing by Fletcher Sultzer. Courtesy, Goodhue County Historical Society, Minnesota.

minor struggles between their colonies: King William's War (1689–97); Queen Anne's War (1702–13); and King George's War (1745–48). Because in all of these wars French colonists suffered losses to their British counterparts, in the period of peace after 1748 France determined to so strengthen her hold on the Mississippi Valley that England could not shake it. In 1749, she dispatched Celoron de Blainville from Montreal into the Ohio Valley, occupied by Indians and English traders, to affirm French claims to the region. The principal result of his trip was increased hostility on the part of the pro-English Indians.

In the period 1750 to 1755, the French augmented the fortifications at old Fort Niagara as well as those at Fort St. Frederic, which in 1731 had been built on Lake Champlain. Also, in 1753, they rebuilt Fort de Chartres. New posts included Fort St. John (1748), on the Richelieu River north of Lake Champlain; Fort de la Presentation (1749), northeast of Lake Ontario; Fort Rouille (1749), on the western shore of Lake Ontario; Fort Presque Isle (1753), east of Lake Erie in present western Pennsylvania; Fort Le Boeuf (1753), also in western Pennsylvania; and, of primary importance, Fort Duquesne (1754), at the Forks of the Ohio.

Thus by the mid-18th century the final conflict, long deferred by the unwillingness of either side to make an all-out effort, was at hand. Englishmen were spilling over the Appalachians into the Ohio Valley, erecting trading posts and blazing trails into the heartland claimed by France.

It was the construction of Forts Le Boeuf and Duquesne that provoked the French and Indian War and brought disaster to the French in North America. Shortly after they built Le Boeuf, a small contingent of troops from its garrison seized and occupied Venango, an English trading post. Maj. George Washington, only 21 years of age, was dispatched from Virginia in the winter of 1753–54 to protest the action. His remonstrations were in vain, both at Venango and Le Boeuf, although he was courteously treated despite his youth.

To counter the rebuff, English officials in Virginia decided to drive the French out. In March 1754, Washington and 300 Virginia militia set out across the mountains to construct a defensive post at the strategically located Forks of the Ohio. A month earlier Capt. William Trent

Artist's rendition of the Battle of Monongahela, in 1755, one of the bloodiest in the French and Indian War and a major French victory. A group of Frenchmen and their Indian allies are shown here ambushing Gen. Edward Braddock's troops. From a wood engraving by John Andrew, after Billings, published in 1858. Courtesy, Library of Congress.

Louisbourg, on Cape Breton Island, Canada, in 1758, besieged by British Gen. James Wolfe. It was a major French base during the French and Indian War. From an engraving by P. Canot, after an on-the-scene drawing by Captain Ince of the 35th Regiment. Courtesy, Library of Congress.

and about 30 men had proceeded to the site. Unknown to Washington, they had been captured by an overwhelming force of French and Indian allies, who constructed Fort Duquesne as their own defensive outpost against the English. While Washington advanced steadily but slowly through the mountains, French scouts carefully watched his progress. On May 28, the first skirmish occurred.

Learning from prisoners of the strong force ensconced at Fort Duquesne, Washington attempted to provide a defense for his troops from the certain French attack. At Great Meadows he and his men hastily threw up a log palisade they called "Fort Necessity." On July 3, 1754, more than 600 French and Indians, skilled at forest combat and attacking from natural forest cover, invested the little fort. After 9 hours of heavy fighting, Washington surrendered, but he was allowed to march from the post with the "honors of war," on a date that was to prove portentous—July 4.

The martial conflagration thus ignited soon spread to most of the nations of Europe and about 100 colonial posts around the globe. The next year, the French troops successfully defended Fort Niagara and routed the proud British force under Gen. Edward Braddock that attempted to conquer Fort Duquesne. In 1756, the war, so far confined to the New World, broadened to Europe. The following year, when the British were still off balance, the French brought in fresh European troops and captured post after post along the English frontier. But in 1758 the tide of fortune turned. When Quebec fell to the British in September 1759,

"A View of the Taking of Quebeck by the English Forces Commanded by Gen. Wolfe," in 1759. Soon after Quebec capitulated, the French and Indian War ended and Canada came under British rule. From an engraving by an unknown artist, published in 1760. Courtesy, Library of Congress.

the war in America was over to all intents and purposes—even though hositilities continued for another year. In the spring of 1760, the French besieged Quebec; and, late in the summer, the British surrounded Montreal. Finally, in September, the Governor of Canada surrendered the whole of Canada to England.

As the defeat of France elsewhere in the world became assured, in 1762 she hastily consigned western Louisiana to her ally Spain by the secret Treaty of Fontainebleau. Then, in the Treaty of Paris the following year, she surrendered the rest of her North American possessions to Great Britain. Spain had to relinquish Florida in return for the restoration of her key posts of Havana and Manila, which had fallen to the British Navy. The French Empire in the New World was no more—although for a few weeks in 1803 France repossessed Louisiana from Spain, but almost immediately transferred it to the United States.

OUR FRENCH HERITAGE

Our heritage is richer because of the men of France who came to this continent and explored and settled the wilderness. The breadth of their achievements and the depth of the heritage they bequeathed to the United States transcends their small numbers. A substantial part of this heritage was mixed into the mainstream of America through 6,000 unhappy Acadians, who were expelled in 1755 from Acadia (Nova Scotia) by the British, its new rulers under the terms of the Treaty of Utrecht. The Acadians at first scattered throughout the British colonies, from Maine to Georgia, but most of them finally settled in Louisiana. Henry Wadsworth Longfellow's poem *Evangeline*, an epic about the Acadian odyssey, is the most widely known tribute to the French heritage in the United States.

Other persecuted Huguenots, also seeking refuge and religious freedom, contributed another equally important segment of our French heritage. They settled in clusters from Rhode Island to South Carolina, especially in Charleston, and enriched the cultural patterns evolving in the colonies. Therefore, much of the flavor of France in the United States today stems not from areas that once were French colonies but from French settlers in the British colonies.

In the final analysis, the city of New Orleans is the heart of French influence. The Illinois settlements quickly lost their French characteristics, but southern Louisiana clung to French customs and traditions. Today, more than a century and a half after the Louisiana Purchase, French is still spoken in New Orleans and many parts of Louisiana. Roman Catholicism remains the principal religion. Even the political subdivisions of the State are called parishes, not counties. Much of the

New Orleans, in 1803, viewed from the Plantation of Marigny. From a painting by Boqueto de Woieseri. Courtesy, Chicago Historical Society.

legal code is rooted in the Roman law of France rather than the common law of England, which prevails elsewhere in the United States. Proud Creoles have cherished their traditions, and through them a happy combination of graciousness and gaiety has filtrated into American life. Mardi Gras, first celebrated by Bienville's colonists in 1702, has been a regular part of Louisiana life ever since and has been enjoyed by many Americans.

French place names, scattered from the Rockies to the Alleghenies, are a constant reminder of the golden era of the voyageurs and *coureurs de bois,* whose songs are still sung. Evidences of French colonial architecture still remain in Louisiana and other places in the Mississippi Valley.

The Dutch and the Swedes: Patroons and Plowmen

Another European nation, newly risen to power, was not to be denied a share of the New World wealth. Holland, or the Netherlands, was almost as quick as Britain and France to seize the opportunities in North America. Dutchmen as well as Englishmen, however, clashed before long with the newly arrived Swedes, whom they felt were encroaching on their territory. New Netherland soon conquered New Sweden, only to fall itself to Britain, whose settlers surrounded it on all sides. Though the Dutch and Swedish phases of colonial history were short-lived—from about 1614 until 1664—the settlers of the two nations contributed substantially to our national heritage.

DUTCH EXPLORATION

The various provinces that comprised the Netherlands passed from the estates of the Dukes of Burgundy to the Hapsburg family in the late Middle Ages. Philip II, Hapsburg heir in the mid-16th century to most of Europe as well as Spain, ruled the Low Countries through a despotic overlord who precipitated a revolt that culminated in 1581 in the independence of Holland. The meteoric rise of the little Dutch Republic to a powerful position among the nations of Europe is one of the most dramatic in history—as well as a tribute to its form of government.

The enterprising burghers of Amsterdam soon began to seek a share in the trade of both the East Indies and the New World. In 1602, the States General (the parliament) chartered the Dutch East India Company and boldly authorized it to capture what it could of the Eastern trade from

Henry Hudson meeting with the Indians along the Hudson River. An Englishman, he probed the North American Continent for the Dutch East India Company. After exploring the coast from Newfoundland to Virginia, he sailed into New York Harbor and up the Hudson River to the site of Albany. From a painting by J. L. G. Ferris. Courtesy, William E. Ryder and the Smithsonian Institution.

other nations. In 1609, the company employed Henry Hudson, an English navigator who twice had unsuccessfully sought the Northwest Passage in northern waters for the Muscovy Company, to probe the North American Continent. On the *Half Moon,* he struck the coast of Newfoundland, turned south as far as Virginia, and then returned up the coast to Delaware Bay. He continued northward and entered New York Harbor. When he first sighted the "Great River of the Mountains," or the "Great North River," later named for him, he excited hope among the crew that the passage to the East had been found. The *Half Moon* moved upstream for 11 days, to the site of Albany, before Hudson, observing the narrow channel and shallow water, decided that he had not found the passage to the East and returned to Holland. The next year, no longer employed by the Dutch, but sponsored by a group of English adventurers, he still pursued the passage. But his crew mutinied and set him adrift to perish on the cold waters of the great northern bay that now bears his name.

Establishment of new netherland

Although the Dutch East India Company was disappointed that Hudson had not found a passage to the East, other Dutchmen grasped the opportunities presented by the discovery of the Hudson River. The Dutch Republic now had a New World claim. The year after Hudson's voyage, in 1610, Dutch traders began flocking to the Hudson Valley. They did not come to stay, but to trade with the Indians, who usually welcomed them and exchanged furs for trinkets, kettles, knives, hatchets, and guns. In repeated visits between 1610 and 1613 the traders familiarized themselves with the Hudson Valley from its mouth to the juncture of the Mohawk River. A few then apparently pushed westward to the Delaware River.

In 1613, Adriaen Block discovered Hell Gate, explored Long Island Sound and the Connecticut River, gave his name to Block Island, rounded Cape Cod, and traveled along the Massachusetts coast past the site of Boston. The same year, Cornelius May circled the southern shore of Long Island and explored Delaware Bay and the Delaware River as far as the mouth of the Schuylkill River. The next year, 1614, the merchants who had financed these explorations organized the New Netherland Company and obtained from the States General a monopoly on the fur trade in the region between the 40th and 45th parallels. Having determined that the heart of the fur trade was at the head of navigation on the Hudson, the company immediately erected Fort Nassau on Castle Island, just below the site of Albany. It never garrisoned the fort, however, which served simply as a trading post. Relations with the Iroquois bands who came to the post to trade were quite friendly. In 1614, a Dutchman erected a small trading post on the island at the mouth of the Hudson River that was inhabited by the Manhattan Indians. In 1617, a spring flood destroyed Fort Nassau.

In 1618, the States General did not renew the charter of the New Netherland Company. The last significant act of the company, that same year, was the cementing of friendship with the Iroquois by a formal treaty, which insured their continued hostility toward the French and provided a buffer for the Dutch colonists. In all likelihood, the friendship between the Dutch and Iroquois prevented the French from occupying the Mohawk and Hudson Valleys and confined them to the lake region to the west. For several years after the expiration of the New

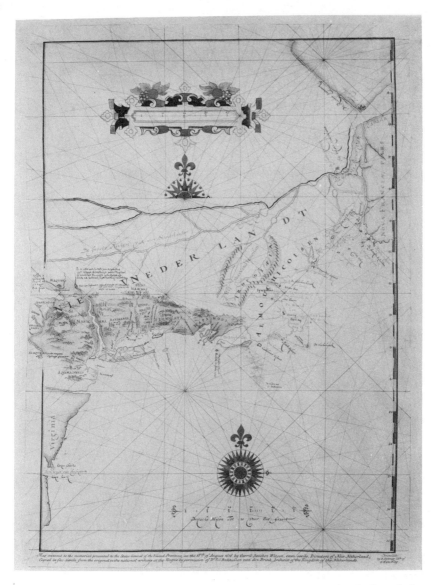

Adriaen Block's map of New Netherland, 1614. From a facsimile of the original, in the national archives of the Netherlands. Courtesy, Museum of the City of New York.

Netherland Company charter, the area was open to free traders, who apparently took advantage of the opportunity.

The success of these independent traders alone did not provoke the organization of the company that was to guide the future destinies of New Netherland. The lucrative possibility of harrying the commerce of Spain—a nation that all Dutchmen hated—was the basic reason for the charter issued by the States General in 1621 that authorized formation of the Dutch West India Company, a vast and wealthy corporation which was given a monopolistic control over New Netherland. The company's fleet consisted of more than 30 warships, 20 armed sloops, and a large fleet of merchant ships.

Although not at first intending to colonize, in the spring of 1624 the company sent out 30 families, mostly Protestant Walloons fleeing persecution in Belgium, under the leadership of Cornelius May. He located most of the settlers around Fort Orange, which was erected on the site of old Fort Nassau, and some on the Delaware River across from the mouth of the Schuylkill, where they built a new Fort Nassau. Still others he distributed around the post on Manhattan Island and on Staten Island. The handful of religious refugees was at first thinly scattered in the new land; not more than a few families were settled at any one location. When May returned to Holland in 1625, he left William Verhulst in charge.

The company organized the New Netherland government on the basis of the authority contained in its charter. It vested control in the board of directors in Holland, who represented the shareholders. The board chose a Director General to govern the colony. Given full executive and judicial authority, he was assisted by a local council that was also selected by the board of directors in Holland. At critical times, he called quasi-representative assemblies into being, but they were in no sense legislative bodies. The government was, therefore, virtually an autocracy under the Director General.

Peter Minuit was the first of these. He actually landed on Manhattan Island in May 1625, prior to his official appointment, bringing more settlers. His instructions from the company included this important injunction: "In case there should be any Indians living on the aforesaid island . . . or claiming any title to it . . . they must not be expelled with violence or threats but be persuaded with kind words . . . or should be given something . . . and a contract should be made . . . to be signed by them." For 60 guilders worth of trinkets—the traditional $24—Minuit concluded a bargain with the principal sachem of the Manhattans that permitted the Dutch to settle among them. Therewith, at the lower end of the island, in 1626, he established the village of Nieuw (New) Amsterdam, which consisted of a small fort and a cluster of homes. The company transferred the settlers at Fort Nassau and most of

New Amsterdam, in the 1650's. From a watercolor by an unknown artist, in the national archives of the Netherlands. Courtesy, Museum of the City of New York.

those from Fort Orange back to reinforce the new village, and shipped in a boatful of Negro slaves to meet the growing demand for labor.

In the colonization plan of 1624, the company created two classes of colonists: freemen, whose transportation and upkeep for 2 years the company financed, and who were eventually permitted to own homes and farms; and indentured servants, who worked on the company's farms. Colonists were not authorized to engage in the fur trade, which was reserved for licensed traders. The farms were called *bouweries.* Those owned and operated by the company were adjacent to Nieuw Amsterdam in lower Manhattan—the origin of today's "Bowery." But few Dutchmen came to live or work on the company *bouweries,* conditions at home being too peaceful and prosperous.

Most of the immigrants so far had been Walloon families. To induce further settlement, in 1629 the company devised a new scheme. In the "Charter of Privileges to Patroons," it authorized princely grants of land—16 miles along one bank or 8 miles along opposite banks of any navigable river—to "patroons," who would bear the costs of settling 50 adults on these manors within 4 years. The patroons were to enjoy the rights of feudal lords; the occupants of their land would be tenants-at-will, pay crop rents, and look to the patroon for the administration of justice.

The company directors rushed to avail themselves of this opportunity. Would-be patroons—most of whom stayed at home and managed affairs through an agent—shortly claimed some of the best lands in the Hudson Valley. One director held title to all of Staten Island, but most of the patroonships were located up the river. The most successful of these was Rensselaerswyck, near the site of Albany. Kiliaen Van Rensselaer, an Amsterdam pearl merchant, enlarged his grant by purchasing more land from the Indians, and acquired the greater part of two present counties.

Most of the patroonships were failures, primarily because of the restrictions on tenants. A short distance away, the English colonies had begun to thrive, and, as one Englishman wrote: "What man will be such a fool as to become a bare tenant . . . when for crossing Hudson's River that man can for a song purchase a good freehold." In 1640, the company modified the patroon system and 6 years later abandoned it entirely. By the end of the Dutch period, all but two of the patroonships had reverted to company ownership.

Perhaps the most significant failure among the patroonships was that of a company director named De Vries, near Cape Henlopen, at the entrance to Delaware Bay. He settled some 30 families in 1631 at the site of Lewes, Del., under the leadership of Capt. Pieter Heyes, and named the settlement Zwaanendael, or Swaanendael, meaning "Valley of the Swans." The colonists planted crops and built a palisade of upright logs to protect their huts before Heyes returned to Holland for supplies. In his absence, the colonists aroused the antagonism of the Indians in the area; a surprise attack in 1632 wiped out all the Dutchmen but one.

The same year that De Vries planted the settlement at Zwaanendael, the company recalled Minuit and discharged him as Director General. In 1633, it replaced an acting director with Wouter Van Twiller, the second Dutch Governor, an incompetent and indecisive man. Though he was a nephew of Kiliaen Van Rensselaer, the company dismissed him in 1637 and he retired to Rensselaerswyck. Van Twiller's successor was William Kieft, who was even less popular. Kieft served as Director General from 1637 to 1646. His regime is distinguished by a war with the Indians, a quarrel with the English then in Connecticut, and a clash with the citizens of New Netherland that led to his dismissal.

The Dutch only temporarily occupied the British-claimed Connecticut River Valley for trading purposes until 1633, when they bought lands—

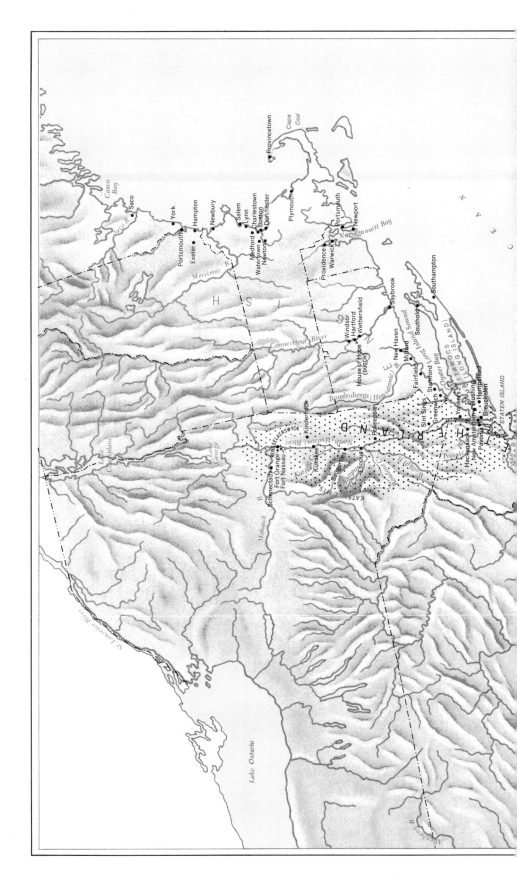

DUTCH, SWEDISH, AND ENGLISH SETTLEMENTS IN PRESENT UNITED STATES — Mid-17th Century. Map by Harry Scott

as was their regular custom—from the Pequot Indians and began a permanent settlement on the site of Hartford. They named it Fort Good Hope (House of Good Hope). Gov. John Winthrop of Massachusetts promptly notified Director General Van Twiller that the Dutch were trespassing. Van Twiller was his indecisive self, and neither Governor took further action. But a small party of Englishmen from Plymouth ignored the Dutch, sailed 10 miles up the Connecticut River, and established the town of Windsor. In 1635, three entire towns moved from Massachusetts to the Connecticut Valley, one group settling around Fort Good Hope. Kieft's querulous attempts to oust the English caused only friction.

Perhaps the Director General would have taken stronger measures in Connecticut if he had not been so involved at home with Indian troubles. Kieft tried to collect a tribute from the Indians living in the vicinity of Manhattan. His inept handling of their refusal provoked the series of attacks from 1641 to 1645 known as the Indian War, during which the natives laid waste to many of the outlying settlements of New Netherland. During the war, in 1642, Kieft called a special council of the heads of families on Manhattan Island. This meeting elected a board, called the Twelve Men, to advise the Governor. A despot errs in bringing a representative assembly into being; the Twelve Men demanded reform and a popularly elected council. Kieft angrily dismissed them, but renewed Indian attacks forced him in 1643 to call another general assembly, and he formed a council of Eight Men. Resenting Kieft's haughty arrogance and taxation measures, this council also demanded reform and appealed to the States General in Holland.

The company discharged Kieft, but the people of New Netherland found little comfort in his successor. Peg-legged Peter Stuyvesant, who had lost a leg in defense of the company's interests in the West Indies, was as autocratic as Kieft and even more hot-tempered. Royally announcing on his arrival in 1647 that he would govern the colonists "as a father his children," Stuyvesant banished Kieft's accusers and threatened to hang them if they appealed to the States General. In answer to a demand for representation, Stuyvesant replied: "We derive our authority from God and the Company, not from a few ignorant subjects. If the nomination and the election of magistrates were to be left to the populace . . . then each would vote for one of his own stamp—the thief for a thief; the rogue, the tippler, the smuggler for a brother in equity."

"King Peter's" reign was not a happy one, but he was an industrious and competent executive. The Indian troubles at an end, in 1650 he turned to settle the problem with the English. With surprising tact he

Peter Stuyvesant, last Governor of New Netherland. In spite of his unpopularity, he was a competent and industrious executive. From a painting, probably conjectural, by an unknown artist. Courtesy, New-York Historical Society.

negotiated a treaty with the New England Confederation—never ratified by either national government—to establish a boundary between New Netherland and New England. This line split Long Island in half and extended north about 20 miles east of the Hudson and parallel to it; it is approximately today's eastern boundary of New York State.

The next year, 1651, Stuyvesant turned his attention southward to face a menace to the company's domain. In 1638, Swedish settlers and traders had moved into the Delaware region. The Director General armed a fleet of 11 vessels and swept into the bay with much "drumming and cannonading" to announce the Dutch claim to the feeble Swedish settlements, whose population probably never exceeded 400. Landing near the mouth of the Delaware, he built Fort Casimir. All vessels entering or leaving New Sweden would have to pass under the Dutch guns.

FOUNDING OF NEW SWEDEN

Sweden's great King, Gustavus Adolphus, who raised his nation to a powerful position in Europe, was interested in the potential of the American fur trade. After he died, his daughter's regent continued this interest, spurred undoubtedly by William Usselinx, a merchant prince of Amsterdam who had been one of the original promoters of the Dutch West India Company. In 1637, the Swedish Government chartered the New Sweden Company, one of the directors of which was none other than Peter Minuit, late Governor of New Netherland. After being recalled to Holland from New Netherland, he had offered his services to Sweden, whose enthusiasm for New World colonization he undoubtedly stimulated.

In December 1637, Minuit sailed out of Gothenburg in 2 vessels, loaded with about 50 emigrants, bound for Delaware Bay to found New Sweden. He proceeded up the Delaware River to the site of Wilmington, where he landed in the spring of 1638. After bartering with the Indians for the land, he erected Fort Christina, which he named for the youthful Queen of Sweden.

Minuit perished at sea the following year, but his leaderless colonists fared quite well. The Indians at the head of the bay were friendly and anxious to trade. Though of motley origin, the colonists proved more than equal to subduing the wilderness. Many were petty convicts, released from Swedish prisons to serve out their terms in the New World; others were recruits from Finland; and some were Dutch who for one reason or another joined the Swedes. In 1640, Peter Ridder replaced Minuit as Governor. The following year, uninvited but not entirely unwelcome, a group of disaffected Puritans from New Haven settled among them.

Two years later, a new Governor arrived: Johan Printz. He founded about a dozen new posts and settlements along the Delaware River in a 15- to 20-mile radius around Fort Christina, and moved the capital from the fort to one of the islands at the mouth of the Schuylkill River, Tinicum Island, near the site of Philadelphia. Under his able, if autocratic, leadership, New Sweden became nearly self-sufficient. Occasionally in lean times it had to purchase supplies from New England at an exorbitant price, but on the whole it fared well during the decade of Printz's administration.

ASCENDANCY OF THE DUTCH

The most serious problem of New Sweden was that both the English and Dutch looked upon it as an intrusion on land that each of them claimed. Perhaps because of the alliance of the three nations in the Thirty Years' War against their common enemy, Spain, the Swedes were not molested until after the war ended, in 1648. William Kieft, of New Netherland, had earlier sent a formal protest about the Swedish intrusion to Governor Printz. Stuyvesant acted. After he had negotiated the boundary agreement with the stronger English, on his north, in 1651 he brought a small fleet into Delaware Bay and with much fanfare erected Fort Casimir.

Printz protested in vain that Sweden had purchased the land from the Indians. Such agreements with the natives were nominal at best. The Indians had no concept of land ownership and willingly "sold" the same land again and again—to Swedes, to Dutchmen, and to Englishmen. Often not even the same Indian band was involved in these duplicate transactions. But, even if the "deeds" were valid, it would have mattered little, for European rivalry in North America intensified.

Not receiving provisions and additional colonists he had requested from the company, Printz resigned in 1653 and sailed for home, leaving New Sweden leaderless and restive. His successor, Johan Rising, who arrived the following year, could do little to curb the inevitable trend. How much longer New Sweden would have had a nominal existence if Rising had not asserted her position will never be known. But his first action brought doom to the colony.

Finding Fort Casimir inadequately garrisoned, in 1654 Rising attacked and forced its surrender. Retaliation came 15 months later, when Stuyvesant appeared in Delaware Bay with three ships and a sizable army. Again with cannon shot, drum roll, and trumpet blast he proclaimed Dutch sovereignty. The Swedes, who had occupied Fort Casimir, hastily capitulated. One Swedish soldier, who had deserted before the surrender, was shot—the only casualty of the *opera bouffe*. Fort Christina and the other posts soon joined in the surrender, and New Sweden became a part of New Netherland.

FALL OF NEW NETHERLAND

Many of the Swedish and Finnish colonists from New Sweden, including Governor Rising himself, returned to Nieuw Amsterdam with the victorious Stuyvesant. There they joined the already heterogeneous population of the infant metropolis, which included some Negro slaves. As early

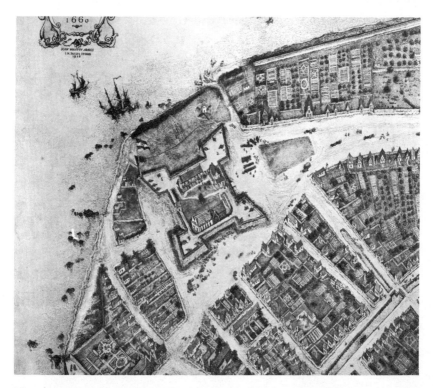

New Amsterdam, including Fort Amsterdam, in 1660. From a detail of I. N. Phelps Stokes' redraft of the Costello plan. Courtesy, Museum of the City of New York.

as 1640, the Dutch West India Company had opened New Netherland to all the peoples of Europe. A number of Europeans emigrated, many of whom sought freedom from religious persecution at home. Stuyvesant, a staunch member of the Dutch Reformed Church, insisted on religious conformity. Soon after his arrival, he initiated rigid and intolerant policies of religious enforcement that were contrary to those of the Dutch Church, though the ministers in Nieuw Amsterdam supported them. The Governor forbade Lutherans to engage in public worship, fined and banished the Baptists, and cruelly punished Quakers. Even the company's directors were embarrassed by this misplaced zeal and ordered him to permit in New Netherland the freedom of conscience that existed in Holland.

Added to this source of resentment was Stuyvesant's refusal to consider any reforms or to allow popular assemblies. Protests availed the growing population nothing. Furthermore, Stuyvesant introduced measures to curb smuggling; to regulate the fur trade; to prohibit the sale of guns, ammunition, or intoxicants to the Indians; and to collect high tariff duties. All of these, of course, were to the benefit of the company and its profit balance, but most of the settlers felt that they were detrimental and dictatorial.

In another field, Stuyvesant incurred even greater unpopularity. Intemperance was widespread in Nieuw Amsterdam; one-fourth of all the buildings were "brandy shops, tobacco or beer houses." While not at-

"The Fall of New Amsterdam, 1664." When Col. Richard Nicolls sailed into New York Harbor with four English vessels, Gov. Peter Stuyvesant prepared to fight. The citizens of New Amsterdam persuaded him to surrender. From a painting by J. L. G. Ferris. Courtesy, William E. Ryder and the Smithsonian Institution.

tempting to prohibit alcoholic beverages, Stuyvesant did restrict their sale for certain hours on Sundays. It was a decree hopeless to enforce despite its timidity. In the long run, whether Stuyvesant deserved it or not, New Netherlanders blamed him for all the dissatisfactions that they felt. When the final crisis came, they refused to support him.

Haunting all the Dutch administrators was the fact that the small colony sat in the midst of vigorous British settlements, which had a far greater population. Secondly, Dutch merchant ships had begun to carry cargoes, especially the profitable tobacco, in the New World trade—in direct violation of Britain's Navigation Acts. After the Peace of Westphalia, in 1648, Britain turned her attention to the Dutch, with whom she clashed indecisively in the first Anglo-Dutch War, 1652–54. As long as Nieuw Amsterdam was open to Dutch ships, the Navigation Acts could not be enforced. Even Massachusetts, Connecticut, and Rhode Island had rejected the mercantile theory to the point of opening their harbors to Dutch vessels.

In March 1664, the restored King Charles II acted. He granted all the region embraced by New Netherland to his brother, James, Duke of York. Parliamentary leaders assenting to an armed conquest, Charles appointed Col. Richard Nicolls as Lieutenant Governor of the province and ordered him to prepare an invasion. In August 1664, he led an English fleet of four vessels and several hundred fighting men into New York Harbor. He offered liberal terms of surrender to the inhabitants, who were given 18 months to decide whether they wanted to remain or not and were guaranteed all the rights of English citizens, including liberty of conscience and trading privileges. Furthermore, they were permitted to continue any Dutch customs not contrary to the laws of England. Impotently Stuyvesant blustered and raged. He would be "carried out dead" before he permitted surrender. But his "children" rebelled and refused to support him. With hardly a shot, on August 26, 1664, Nieuw Amsterdam capitulated and welcomed the English. Soon thereafter, the rest of New Netherland capitulated. The Treaty of Breda (1667), which ended the second Anglo-Dutch War, confirmed the loss of the colony.

OUR DUTCH AND SWEDISH HERITAGE

Ironically, it was the magnetic influence of English liberty on the Dutch and Swedes that caused the ignominious downfall of the peg-legged tyrant of New Netherland. The New Netherlanders eagerly embraced the British heritage, and New Amsterdam, already a polyglot of races and customs, quickly took on a decided English atmosphere. The Dutch, basically so much like their English cousins, became absorbed in the new way of life and did not cling tenaciously to their traditions.

Nevertheless, the influence of Holland was stamped on the province, and the language, customs, and architecture of Dutch America helped shape the city, as well as the State of New York that was later to emerge. The striking cleanliness of the Dutch villages, the style of their buildings, and their close-knit design lingered for centuries. And, as did the English, French, and Spanish in other areas, the Dutch and Swedes enriched the map with place names. Most important, the solid Dutch families who settled in Manhattan and the Hudson Valley produced an unusual number of prominent citizens and national leaders: the Rensselaers, the Cortlandts, the Schuylers, the Van Burens, and the Roosevelts, among others.

Fewer in number than the Dutch, the Swedish colonists contributed less to the developing American culture. One specific contribution of much importance attributed to them is the introduction of the art of log construction. Whether a Swede or a Finn in New Sweden built the first true log house in America may never be known. But so suitable was it to the environment that the technique spread throughout the colonies. None of the other national groups that came to the New World were familiar with log construction in their native land. Whether known later as a "cabin" or a "dog run," this style and method of construction seems clearly to have originated in New Sweden.

The British: Colonials and Progenitors

Of all the European influences on the United States, those of the English were the most substantial and enduring. British colonials were the basic progenitors of the new Nation. Many of them were escaping from the religious persecution that convulsed England in the 17th century. Indeed, the desire for religious freedom was a major factor in colonization. However, proprietors or companies, whose motives included the desire for profit, founded many of the colonies. At the same time, they also provided the outlet that many believed England needed for her surplus population.

Despite the claim in the New World provided by John Cabot's voyage in 1497, the British were the last of the three major European powers to attempt to settle. Yet, by 1700, they had established substantial colonies all along the Atlantic coast. [Development of the British colonies during the period 1700–1783 is treated in *Colonials and Patriots,* Volume VI in this series.] Though by that time the colonies had some degree of unity because of the common language and overall English control, they had made little progress toward unification. Their efforts were hampered because of the separate founding of the colonies and the lack of roads and communications. Despite the need for defense against the Indians, French, Spanish, and Dutch, six plans for union in the 17th century failed; some of these involved only two or three colonies, and the British Government sponsored some of them.

Yet colonial Englishmen, influenced by the freedom and opportunities in the New World, gradually evolved into "Americans." Their outlook and ideas began to differ from those of their compatriots in the British Isles, though they maintained strong loyalties toward their native land. The English colonies lacked the gold and silver of New Spain and the wealth in furs of New France. But, based on trade, agriculture, and fisheries, colonial wealth steadily increased. New settlers arrived to take advantage of the opportunities, and the population soon surpassed that of the French and Spanish colonies.

ESTABLISHING A CLAIM

England became unified late in the 15th century. On Bosworth Field, in 1485, Henry Tudor put an end to the civil strife of the Wars of the Roses and crowned himself Henry VII. Forcefully bringing recalcitrant

John Cabot, the English explorer, a conjectural portrait. His voyages in 1497 and 1498 laid the foundations of England's claim to North America. From a late 18th- or early 19th-century painting by an unknown artist. Courtesy, Chicago Historical Society.

nobles to heel, he strengthened his authority. For the first time in nearly a century, the country had stability in government and a considerable degree of peace and prosperity. Henry, therefore, could devote his attention to the promotion of commerce. He encouraged English merchants to enter foreign trade, supported the formation of trading companies, and restricted the activities of the foreign merchants in London and Bristol, who had monopolized trade. Columbus even sent his brother to England when he failed to obtain support from the Portuguese or Spanish Kings for his proposal that Cathay could be reached by sailing west across the Atlantic. Henry VII agreed to finance the voyage and urged Columbus to come at once to England. But, before the latter left Spain, the Spanish monarchs experienced a change of heart and supported the voyage that was to give Spain an empire.

Meanwhile, Henry VII never gave up his hope of obtaining for England a share of the rich Eastern trade. British merchants established a trade link with Iceland about 1490. And, encouraged by news of Columbus' voyage, on March 5, 1496, Henry VII granted letters-patent to the "well-beloved John Cabot" and his three sons to sail across the Atlantic to Asia. An Italian-born navigator, Cabot had lived in England since 1484. As a youth, he had visited the East, and when he arrived in London he had already decided that an all-water route could be found

John and Sebastian Cabot, English explorers, land in North America, in 1497. From a wood engraving by an unknown artist, published in 1855. Courtesy, Library of Congress.

to the trading centers there. He may have made a few trips to Iceland before the King commissioned his trans-Atlantic voyage.

In May of 1497, Cabot left Bristol with a crew of 18 and, after a voyage of 52 days across the North Atlantic, landed on Cape Breton Island and took possession of the land for Henry VII. From there, he explored several islands in the Gulf of St. Lawrence and in August returned to England and the praise of Henry VII, who granted him new letters-patent. When Cabot sailed again, in 1498, he had perhaps 5 or 6 ships, whose crews totaled some 300 men. The King personally financed a substantial portion of the expedition's cost. On his second voyage, Cabot probably explored the North American coast from Newfoundland south to the Delaware or Chesapeake Bays.

Having failed to find the shores of Cathay (China) or Cipango (Japan), the English turned in the opposite direction. Henry VII's son, Henry VIII—better known for his marital involvements and his break with the Pope—enthusiastically began to build "a fleet the like of which the world has never seen." John Cabot's son, Sebastian, became a renowned navigator. After serving Spain for a number of years, he returned to England and opened the northern sea-land route to Moscow. He also helped found the company of Merchant-Adventurers, predecessor of the Muscovy Company, and became its president for life.

Thus, for nearly a century, England's interest was diverted from the New World, and her energies were concentrated on the development of a commercial empire and a merchant fleet that became second to none in Europe. But John Cabot had given England a claim to the northern shores of the New World, and in the course of time the "sea dogs" and other English mariners were to breathe new life into it.

HARASSING THE SPANISH

When Henry VIII died, in 1547, he left his throne to his sickly son, Edward. After Edward died, in 1553, while yet a minor, the scepter passed to Mary. "Bloody" Queen Mary, half-Spanish daughter of Henry's first marriage, to Catherine of Aragon, tried with fire and sword to return England to the papal fold and against all counsel wedded her ambitious cousin Philip II of Spain. Her death, in 1558, spared the English a questionable future as Hapsburg vassals. But under Mary's half-sister, Elizabeth, the third of Henry VIII's children to ascend the Tudor throne, England entered a golden age of exploration and expansion. The Queen promptly restored the Church of England as the state religion

Queen Elizabeth was the first English monarch to encourage colonization of the New World. During her reign, England entered a golden age of exploration and expansion. From a 1596 engraving by an unknown artist.

and embarked upon a policy of ecclesiastical compromise and domestic tranquillity. Abroad, she coyly flirted with her former brother-in-law, Philip II of Spain, while secretly encouraging her admiring liegemen to enrich themselves—and her—by raiding and harassing Spanish commerce. It was a delightful game.

Shortly after Elizabeth's ascension to the throne, John Hawkins began illicitly smuggling slaves into Hispaniola. He then shifted to the plundering of Spanish treasure galleons, and ultimately to the raiding of coastal towns in Spain's colonial empire. By about 1570, usually with royal connivance, English sea rovers were regularly attacking the Spanish treasure fleets. The Queen knighted both Hawkins and Francis Drake, whose exploits are better known. Drake not only pillaged towns and ships in the Caribbean. In 1577, he also passed through the Strait of Magellan and, in a series of surprise attacks, looted Spanish settlements on the Pacific coast. While on this incredible escapade, in 1579 he landed on the California coast. Then, laden as he was with plunder that he feared Spanish men-of-war might wrest from him if he returned through the strait, he boldly struck out across the Pacific. He completed his circumnavigation of the globe in 1580, when he arrived back in England. His hold bore treasure that repaid his financial backers some 5,000 percent on their investment and added more than a quarter of a million pounds to the Queen's coffers.

SEEKING THE NORTHWEST PASSAGE

About this same time, during the period 1576–78, Martin Frobisher made three voyages to the northernmost part of the New World, exciting short-lived rumors that he had discovered gold west of Frobisher's Bay and, at long last, the Northwest Passage to the Orient. After his first exploring expedition, he and his associates organized the Company of Cathay, which went bankrupt after the failure of two subsequent expeditions. A few years later, John Davis revived his project of seeking a Northwest Passage. He, too, made three voyages into the icy waters beyond the Hudson Strait, between 1585 and 1587, the results of which were as disappointing as Frobisher's.

FIRST SETTLEMENT ATTEMPTS

An ardent advocate of the existence of a Northwest Passage and a shareholder in Frobisher's Company of Cathay, Sir Humphrey Gilbert turned the Queen's attention to colonization projects. In 1578, a royal grant in hand, he set out from Plymouth to found an English colony in some part of the new lands "not actually possessed by any Christian prince." Storms and misadventures drove him back to England, but he was undaunted. Using funds that he had solicited from his countrymen, in 1583 he left England again, with 5 ships and more than 250 colonists. But the colony that he established in Newfoundland also ended disastrously, and on the return trip he was lost at sea.

The first Englishmen arrive in "Virginia." Roanoke Island is shown in the bay. From an engraving by Theodore de Bry, after John White's on-the-scene drawing.

The following year, Elizabeth renewed Gilbert's grant in the name of his half-brother, Sir Walter Raleigh—poet, soldier, historian, and adventurer—who had invested heavily in Gilbert's second effort. Plans were again laid for an English colony in the New World. Raleigh first sent out an expedition, led by Philip Amandas and Arthur Barlowe, to make a reconnaissance of the North American coast. In 1584, sailing by way of the Canaries and the West Indies, it traveled up the coast to present North Carolina, explored the region, and returned to recommend it enthusiastically for a colony. Raleigh christened the new land "Virginia"—for the "Virgin Queen"—and appointed Sir Richard Grenville to establish a settlement. Grenville, a renowned sea rover, left in 1585 with 7 vessels and about 100 colonists. After brief exploration, the group settled on Roanoke Island. Grenville placed Ralph Lane in temporary charge and sailed away, promising to return the next year with supplies.

Obsessed with the dream that they might discover gold in the New World as the Spanish had done, the colonists were little inclined to labor at clearing fields and planting crops. By summer of the following year, they were constantly quarreling and warring with the Indians, from whom they had first obtained supplies, and were nearly out of provisions. In June a fleet approached—not Grenville but Drake, returning from a triumphant raid in the West Indies. Discouraged, Lane and his men returned to England with Drake. They had missed Grenville and the supply expedition by only a few weeks. After a brief and futile search, being "unwilling to loose possession of the countrey which Englishmen had so long held," Grenville stationed 15 of his men at the post on Roanoke Island and hastened southward to cruise for Spanish prizes. The 15 were never heard from again.

But Raleigh persisted. In 1587, he dispatched another and larger group of colonists to Roanoke under the leadership of John White. The group landed and refurbished the fort built by Lane. Among the 150 colonists were 17 women, one of whom was White's daughter, the wife of Ananias Dare. At this tiny outpost of England, she gave birth to the first English child born in America, Virginia Dare.

Late in 1587, White returned to England for supplies, and Raleigh patiently equipped another fleet to supply his colony. But destiny interfered. Philip of Spain had finally tired of Elizabeth's sport and had launched a mighty armada to destroy English seapower once and for all— even perhaps to invade England itself. During defense preparations, the Queen requisitioned Raleigh's entire supply fleet into the royal service.

Southern Algonquian Indians fishing along the coast of present North Carolina. From an on-the-scene watercolor by John White, 1585. Courtesy, Smithsonian Institution.

England's momentous victory in 1588 over the Spanish Armada in the English Channel was a major turning point in history, for Spanish seapower, as well as Spanish dominance in Europe, was dealt a severe blow. Elizabeth's grand triumph, however, meant Roanoke's demise. By the time White was able to return to the colony, in 1590, it had disappeared. The mystery of its fate has never been solved. The bare letters C-R-O-A-T-O-A-N—the name of an Indian tribe and island south of Cape Hatteras—carved in the bark of a tree were the only clue.

JAMESTOWN AND THE FOUNDING OF VIRGINIA

The defeat of the Spanish Armada made the New World safer for the English. Though the Raleigh ventures failed, they excited interest in colonization. Between 1602 and 1605, a few expeditions, including those led by Bartholomew Gosnold and Capt. George Weymouth, unsuccessfully attempted to settle groups of colonists at various points along the Atlantic coast. The next British attempts were to be made by joint-stock companies, which had emerged in the 16th century. Early successes of the Muscovy and Levant companies in Europe had led to the organization of the highly profitable East India Company, and a number of others. Chartered and loosely supervised by the Crown, these companies began to lead in the expansion of the British Empire.

In 1606, a group of merchant investors founded the joint-stock Virginia Company and obtained a charter from James I that authorized colonization of the lands claimed for England by John Cabot. From the first, the company consisted of two groups: The London Company, whose domain was the southern coast; and the Plymouth Company, the northern. The latter made the first attempt at colonization, but it was unsuccessful; in August 1606, the Spanish captured a shipload of about 30 colonists in the West Indies. Another expedition of the company, commanded by George Popham, left England in May 1607 and landed in August on the New England coast near the mouth of the Kennebec River, in present Maine. There the colonists built Fort St. George, a church, and 15 small huts. Late the following year, a shortage of supplies, the severity of the winter, and dissension and idleness brought about the end of the colony, and the survivors returned to England.

Meantime, in 1607, the London Company had established a successful settlement in Virginia. In December 1606, the company had dispatched a full-scale colonization expedition from London that consisted of 3

Capt. John Smith's map of Virginia, published in London, in 1612. Courtesy, Smithsonian Institution.

small ships—the *Susan Constant, Godspeed,* and *Discovery*—that carried about 140 men. Christopher Newport, an experienced navigator, was in command until the group landed. In a sealed box in his cabin were the names of the Governor and council of the colony.

After entering Chesapeake Bay and landing temporarily on April 26, 1607, at Cape Henry, where they stayed for 4 days, the colonists moved up the James River to find a more defensible location. On May 13, the colonists selected a site and named it James-Forte, or Jamestowne. A swampy, wooded peninsula about 30 miles from the sea, it provided good docking facilities and satisfactory defense against the Indians. But malaria-bearing mosquitoes swarmed about, fresh-water springs were insufficient, and the profuse trees were not only an obstacle to clearing the land, but also provided natural cover for the Indians.

When Newport opened the sealed instructions, the names of the seven councilors were revealed. Among them were Edward M. Wingfield, who was selected as Governor; Bartholomew Gosnold, a navigator; and Capt. John Smith, whom Newport had placed in irons during the voyage for his fractious behavior. Yet, in the long run, it was Smith who was to save the colony. From the outset, troubles and dissension plagued the governing council. Wingfield served as Governor only a few months; he was removed from the council in September and replaced as Governor by John Ratcliffe. Capt. George Kendall, another council member, was executed for treason, and Gosnold died of malaria.

Newport, who had returned to England for supplies and more settlers in June of 1607, arrived back in Jamestown in January the following year to find that only 38 of the original settlers had survived disease and Indian ambuscade. Because the colony continued to dwindle alarmingly, in April 1608 Newport set out on his second trip to England; he returned in October with supplies and about 70 settlers, including the first 2 women. The previous month, Smith, who had gained the ascendancy in the council, had succeeded Ratcliffe as Governor. Initiating rigid discipline, he directed the erection of a blockhouse fort, a score of cabins, and a well. He also forced the colonists, who traded with the Indians to obtain corn, to raise livestock and chickens, as well as to plant crops.

The plight of the colony caused so much alarm in England that in May 1609 the King issued a new charter to the London Company which placed responsibility for government of the colony solely in the hands of the directors. Confidence reinspired, shareholders raised additional funds, and in June 1609 a well equipped relief expedition of 9 ships and 500 settlers left England. Lord Delaware (de la Warr) was appointed as Governor, but delayed his departure. Sir George Somers, Sir Thomas Gates, and Christopher Newport led the expedition. Caught in a hurricane, one of the vessels foundered and another bearing Gates and Somers was wrecked in the Bermudas. In August, the remaining seven, carrying about 300 settlers, including women and children, limped into Jamestown.

Smith was in charge of the colony, but the newcomers refused to recognize his authority. Once more quarrels broke out among the colonists. Smith, badly burned by a gunpowder explosion and discouraged by the turn of events, returned to England and left Jamestown leaderless. The winter of 1609–10 was devastating. Food became so scarce that the colonists first ate their horses and dogs, then tried to catch rats and snakes. During this "starving time," the population slumped from about 500 to 60.

Meanwhile, Gates and Somers had constructed two small ships and in May 1610 reached Jamestown. Overcome by what they saw, they loaded the nearly demented survivors and turned down the James River for home. Only by coincidence was the colony saved from abandonment. Lord Delaware, aboard one of three ships commanded by Capt. Samuel Argall, put into the river's mouth just as Gates and Somers were about to sail out into the sea. The fortuitous meeting would not have occurred had young Argall not determined to "trace the ready way" straight across the mid-Atlantic, rather than sailing by way of the Canaries, the West Indies, and the Florida coast. The year before, when bringing supplies to Jamestown, he had proved the feasibility of the new route, his use of which now saved the colony.

Delaware ordered the outward-bound ship to put about and took charge of the overwhelming task of rebuilding not only the colony but also the colonists' morale. Progress was soon apparent under his wise leadership, but in the spring of 1611 he became ill and returned to England. Thereafter, he governed the colony through deputies. The first of these was Sir Thomas Dale, a strict disciplinarian but a competent leader. "Dale's Laws," as his regulations were called, were necessarily severe. However, his leadership was constructive and the colony survived. The colonists erected buildings, planted crops, established outposts, and made peace with the Indians.

Peace with the Indians was the result of the enterprise of Argall, who in 1613 met Pocahontas, the youthful daughter of the Indian chief Powhatan, along the shores of the Potomac. She was married to a neighboring chief, but Argall resolved to "possesse myself of her by any Stratagem that I could use, for ransoming of so many Englishmen as were Prisoners with Powhatan . . . as also to get such Armes and Tooles as he and other Indians had got." He had only to trade the chief a copper kettle for the girl, who was delighted to accompany the Englishman back to Jamestown. There John Rolfe became attracted to her and married her. As a result, until Powhatan died, relative peace prevailed with the Indians. Rolfe took his bride to visit London. There she gave birth to a son, but she died soon afterward.

In 1617, Rolfe returned to Virginia as secretary to Argall, who had just been appointed as Deputy Governor. Under Dale (1611, 1613–16), Gates (1611–13), and Argall (1617–19)—however strict the martial rule—the colony began to prosper. A new charter in 1612 encouraged emigration from England; the introduction that same year by Rolfe of West Indian tobacco provided Virginia with an economic base; the colonists founded a dozen or so inland settlements; and the population reached more than 1,000.

In 1618, the company decreed the end of martial rule in Virginia and

The first women arrive at Jamestown, Virginia, in 1619. Recruited by the Virginia Company to help stabilize the colony, the women became wives of the settlers. From a sketch by an unknown artist, published in 1876. Courtesy, Library of Congress.

instructed Lord Delaware to institute a popular assembly. He died en route to the colony, however, and his successor, George Yeardley, in 1619 brought into existence the first representative assembly in America, the Virginia House of Burgesses. In the same year, the first Negroes landed— apparently as indentured servants rather than slaves. And, the following year, to supplement the small group of women who had come in 1609, a group of marriageable maidens arrived.

Yet, in the years immediately following, the colony barely survived. In 1622, the Indians laid waste to the outlying settlements and killed about 350 colonists. Even more serious were the chronic problems of disease and lack of food and other necessities; many deaths resulted and numerous colonists returned to England. Between 1619 and 1624, more than 4,000 colonists joined the few hundred already in Virginia, but by the end of the period the population was only 1,275. Because of adverse conditions in the colony and political trends in England, in 1624 James I annulled the charter of the Virginia Company and made Virginia a royal colony directly under his control.

Despite all the early trials, over the years a plantation-small farm system began to extend along the coasts and rivers of Tidewater Virginia. As the colonists grew stronger, they began to assert their rights. In 1635, they temporarily deposed the royal Governor; and, in 1676, a century before the Declaration of Independence, some of them rose in open rebellion against the administration of Sir William Berkeley. Nathaniel Bacon and his followers drove Berkeley from Jamestown, which they put to the torch and almost completely destroyed because they considered it to be a "stronghold of oppression." Bacon died, Berkeley was replaced, and the rebellious spirit cooled, but Jamestown never fully recovered. In 1699, the year after the statehouse accidentally burned, the General Assembly moved the seat of government to Williamsburg. Within a few years, Jamestown was practically abandoned. About the time of the War for Independence, the isthmus connecting it with the mainland was washed out and an island created. The town ceased to exist.

THE MASSACHUSETTS SETTLEMENTS

Not long after the founding of Virginia, other Englishmen established another colony to the north. In 1620, a shipload of religious dissenters, later known as Pilgrims, debarked from the *Mayflower* on the western shore of Cape Cod Bay, on the coast of Massachusetts. The nucleus of the group were Puritan separatists, part of a congregation of nonconformists of Scrooby parish in Nottinghamshire, England. Because of the strict enforcement of the religious laws by James I, in 1608–9 the entire congregation of about 100 had moved to Holland seeking toleration. In 1620, they received permission from the Crown and financial backing from the London Company to migrate to Virginia. About 35 members of the congregation chose to do so; they first traveled to England, where they joined another group of dissenters. The *Mayflower* carried 101 passengers and a crew of 48. They were the first Englishmen—but by no means the last— to escape Stuart persecution in the New World.

The religious situation in England had grown complicated since Henry VIII separated the established church from Rome and placed himself at its head. In the last years of his reign, pressure from Protestant reformers forced him to modify much of the ecclesiastical code. After his death, the regents of his young son stimulated the Protestant movement. Mary then had attempted to reverse the tide, but Elizabeth wisely chose a middle course. She instituted moderate reforms in the Church of Eng-

A romanticized rendition of the Pilgrims signing the Mayflower Compact, in 1620, on board the *Mayflower*. The compact is a landmark in U.S. constitutional development. From an engraving by Gauthier, after T. H. Matteson. Courtesy, Library of Congress.

land and, though not disposed to tolerance of Protestants, did not rigorously enforce the regulations that restricted them.

A large group arose that wanted to continue the process of reform. Gradually they came to be called Puritans. Those Anglicans who would "purify" the church from within were known as conforming Puritans; those favoring stronger measures, as nonconformists, dissenters, or separatists. Religious disputation was the rage of the day, when translations of the Bible were first beginning to reach the hands of the people, who were also stimulated by the controversies that the Reformation had fostered. Interestingly enough, the version on which the Scrooby Pilgrims based their dissent was probably the Bishops' Bible, not the King James translation used today by most Protestant sects.

By authorizing this magnificent translation, James I undoubtedly hoped to put an end to dissent; instead, he only quickened it. His other religious policies, which grew harsher toward the end of his reign, were also designed to stamp out the heresy that was budding all over England. The King increased the pressure on nonconformists and separatists, and churchmen grew more and more intolerant, even of the conforming

Puritans. But the more vigorous the pruning, the healthier the plant became. After James died, in 1625, his son Charles I (1625–49) proved to
be even less tolerant. A bloody revolution cost Charles his throne and his
life, and the Puritan colonies in New England grew rapidly.

The Pilgrims, authorized to settle in Virginia, for some reason deviated
from their planned course—perhaps more by design than accident—
and founded a colony on land belonging to the Plymouth Company
in an area that Capt. John Smith had visited in 1614, during an
exploring expedition from Jamestown, and named "Plimouth." Realiz-

Pilgrims going to church. The lives of the Massachusetts colonists centered
around church activities. From a painting by George H. Boughton (1833–
1905). Courtesy, Library of Congress.

ing that they were outside the jurisdiction of the London Company and
seeking to control some turbulent members, before landing the leaders
drew up the Mayflower Compact. Assented to by most of the freemen
in the group, it created a sort of government by social compact. Its
signers swore to "convenant and combine ourselves together into a civill

body politick." This idea of voluntary obedience to lawful majority rule was unique in the 17th century and is a landmark in U.S. constitutional development.

The Plymouth colony was successful mainly because of the grim determination and industry of its inhabitants. The location was one of the most unfavorable for colonization on the Atlantic coast, combining as it did bitter climate and rocky, infertile soil. Furthermore, the Pilgrims arrived at the onset of winter, in November, and construction began in late December. The colonists continued to live on the ship while a meetinghouse and homes were built. The first winter was especially severe, a famine being averted only because friendly Indians supplied corn.

The stamina and fortitude of the colonists was augmented by excellent leadership: John Carver, the first Governor, who died in 1621; Miles Standish; William Brewster; and William Bradford, who had been a young boy at the time of the emigration to Holland, and who was elected Governor by popular vote in 1621 and served most of the time until 1657. In 1621 and 1630 Bradford obtained patents from the Council for New England (successor of the Plymouth Company) that permitted the Pilgrims to remain on the land that they had occupied. As the years passed, they were able to pay not only for the land but also for the costs of their migration. But at first life was a constant struggle. By 1630, the population of the Plymouth colony was only 300. Within a decade, however, because of a great migration of Puritans from England who were escaping the persecution of Charles I, it leaped to about 3,000.

In 1629, the Massachusetts Bay Company organized on a joint-stock basis and obtained from the King a charter authorizing it to establish a colony in New England and to govern it in much the same way as the Virginia Company governed Jamestown. The new company was the successor of the New England Company (1628–29), which had purchased land in the area of Massachusetts from the Council for New England (1620–35), which succeeded the Plymouth Company. In 1628–29, the New England Company had begun a settlement at present Salem. This settlement incorporated small groups of colonists from Dorchester, England, already at the site, who had moved there in 1626 from Gloucester, which they had settled in 1623.

The Massachusetts Bay Company was chartered as a commercial rather than a religious enterprise. But most of the stockholders were

Puritans. In August 1629, a significant event in U.S. constitutional development occurred: the signing of the Cambridge Agreement. This agreement marked the acceptance of the offer of John Winthrop and 11 other prominent nonconformists to migrate to America as members of the board of directors if the headquarters of the company were transferred to the New World. All company officers not willing to migrate resigned, and Massachusetts was designated as company headquarters.

The agreement had far-reaching significance because the company was authorized to govern the colony; when its headquarters, officers, directors, and principal stockholders moved to the colony itself, Massachusetts became completely self-governing and legitimately authorized by the Crown. Furthermore, the charter became the basis of the government—in essence a written constitution superior to the officers of the company themselves.

The great Puritan migration began. Winthrop was elected Governor. Carrying the charter with him, in 1630 he headed the first contingent of colonists. Before the end of the year, approximately 2,000 persons had migrated to Massachusetts. In the ensuing decade, more than 200

"The First Thanksgiving, 1621." From a painting by J. L. G. Ferris. Courtesy, William E. Ryder and the Smithsonian Institution.

ships transported about 20,000 Puritans to Massachusetts, which thrived almost from the beginning. In rapid succession, the towns of Boston, Cambridge, Watertown, Charlestown, and 18 others were founded. Other Puritans went to the West Indies in this, the largest mass exodus of Englishmen in history.

The evolution of representative self-government based on a written document is undoubtedly the most lasting contribution of the Bay Colony to American life. Initially, Winthrop and a handful of company directors attempted to keep control of the colony in their own hands, and Winthrop kept the charter locked in his trunk. Eventually, however, the free-holders demanded that the charter be produced. In time, the Puritan leaders broadened suffrage, created a representative assembly, and evolved a bicameral legislature. Yet, for the most part, the original, tightly knit, Puritan oligarchy retained close control of the government. Church and state were interwoven; personal behavior and religious practices were closely related and supervised.

For this very reason and because of the fact that the Puritans would not tolerate divergent religious views, dissenters founded other colonies in New England. Winthrop and his assistants, seeking to protect their "holy experiment," were probably more intolerant of diversity in religion than Charles I. They drove hundreds of "otherwise thinking" people out of Massachusetts—to the lasting benefit of the Nation that later emerged on the Atlantic coast.

RHODE ISLAND AND RELIGIOUS EXILES

The first serious conflict produced the colony of Rhode Island— founded by Roger Williams, champion of religious liberty and humanitarianism. Williams was a nonconforming Welsh minister who in 1631 migrated to Massachusetts. Almost immediately, he fell into disagreement with the authorities. He preached such heretical ideas as freedom of conscience in religious matters, a complete separation of civil and church laws, and Indian land ownership. He contended that the government should not compel any man to attend church services nor dictate the nature of these services, that church tithes and civil taxes were two entirely different matters, and that the King and the colonists would not have title to the land until they purchased it from the Indians.

Because of Williams' popularity, the Puritan oligarchy at first tried to quiet him by argument and reason, but finally decreed his banishment from the colony. To escape being sent back to England, in the winter

Fortifications at Oswego, New York, in 1767. In the 18th century, Oswego was of strategic importance in controlling Lake Ontario. In 1756, during the French and Indian War, the French destroyed the British fort on the site, but after the war the British rebuilt it. From an engraving by Gavit & Duthie, published in 1767. Courtesy, Chicago Historical Society.

of 1635 he fled to Narragansett Bay, where Indians befriended him. He purchased land from them and established the village of Providence as a haven for other dissenters from the Boston orthodoxy, some of whom arrived the following spring.

Subsequently, as religious unrest continued, many other dissenters emigrated from the Massachusetts Bay Colony. Anne Hutchinson, wife of a wealthy Boston Puritan, voiced religious opinions disturbingly different than those emanating from most of the pulpits. A warm personality and an excellent conversationalist, she held weekly meetings in her home to discuss the sermons and the preachers. Advocating as she did the necessity of faith alone for salvation rather than moral behavior and "good works," she minimized the role of the clergy. Her views were heretical to Winthrop and the church elders, who were committed to the Bible, as interpreted by the clergy, as the sole source of religious inspiration. But many approved of her views, and she gained a substantial following. She finally clashed with the Puritan authorities, especially Winthrop, in a power struggle to control the General Court, but they emerged victorious. They convicted her of heresy and treason, imprisoned her for a short time, and finally excommunicated and banished her.

Anne Hutchinson and her family and a large number of followers moved to an island in Narragansett Bay, where in 1638 they established the town of Portsmouth. A year later one of her followers, William Coddington, founded Newport on the southern side of Aquidneck Island, or Rhode Island, as it was later renamed. In 1638, Samuel Gorton, who had been cast out of Massachusetts and Plymouth for blasphemous opinions, was likewise rejected by the Hutchinsonians at Portsmouth. He moved to the mainland below Providence, where he started the settlement of Warwick.

Fearing persecution from Massachusetts, Williams united the towns of Providence, Portsmouth, and Newport, and in 1643 carried their petition for a separate government to England. There the outcome of the civil war between the Roundheads and the Crown was yet undecided. In 1644, Williams received from the Roundhead Parliament—what was left of it—a charter uniting the three towns into the colony of Rhode Island and authorizing self-government. Three years later, Warwick joined the union. After Charles II was restored to the throne, he issued, in 1663, a royal charter, based on the parliamentary grant. Until 1842, this document served as Rhode Island's constitution.

The government of Rhode Island was patterned after that of Massachusetts with two major exceptions: church and state were completely separated, and religious toleration was guaranteed. Rhode Island became, therefore, a haven for religious minorities and dissenters, including Jews and Quakers, although toleration of the latter strained even Roger Williams' beliefs.

CONNECTICUT AND ECONOMIC OPPORTUNITY

The movement into the fertile Connecticut River Valley was motivated less by a desire to seek religious freedom than to escape the tyranny of unproductive and rocky farmlands. It began in 1633, when a small group from Plymouth moved west into Dutch territory and settled at Windsor, some 10 miles above Fort Good Hope, a Dutch post. In 1634, a number of farmers from Massachusetts founded Wethersfield. The following year, some 60 families moved from Newtown (Cambridge) and established Hartford adjacent to Fort Good Hope. Then, in 1636, virtually the entire Massachusetts villages of Dorchester, Watertown, and Newton made a mass exodus to the new locations in Connecticut.

Thomas Hooker, pastor of the Newtown congregation, did not disagree with Winthrop in theological matters, but he did object to the oligarchical government of Massachusetts. Insisting that "the foundation of authority is laide in the consent of the governed," he opposed the re-

The British 60th Foot (Royal-American) Regiment, some of whose members are pictured here, was a regular British regiment consisting of about 4,000 men. Most of the personnel consisted of American colonists. From a drawing by Frederick E. Ray, Jr. Courtesy, the artist, the Company of Military Historians, and the Chicago Historical Society.

stricted suffrage in Massachusetts. Under his leadership, a movement to unify the Connecticut towns resulted in the Fundamental Orders of Connecticut, devised and adopted in 1639 by representatives of the towns. This document, which has been called the first written constitution in the New World, set up a government similar to that in Massachusetts except that church membership was not required for voting and the franchise was much broader. With minor modifications, until 1818 it served as Connecticut's constitution. In 1662, Connecticut received a royal charter.

THE NEW HAVEN THEOCRACY

Theophilus Eaton, a wealthy merchant of London, and John Davenport, a radical nonconforming minister, in 1637 brought a shipload of Puritans to Massachusetts. There they found the controversy between Winthrop and the Hutchinsonians at its height. Feeling that the Massachusetts authorities had not been sufficiently strict, they moved on to Long Island Sound, west of the Connecticut River, where in 1638 they founded a Bible commonwealth, New Haven. The following year its residents established a theocracy even more autocratic than that in Massachusetts.

Within a few years, emigrants from the Massachusetts Bay Colony and England founded more than a dozen settlements in the vicinity, and by 1644 these had all federated with the town of New Haven to form a colony contiguous to Connecticut. New Haven was probably the most radical of the Puritan commonwealths. It had no charter from either Parliament or the Crown, and it was accused of harboring the men responsible for the beheading of Charles I. In 1662, the royal charter of Connecticut officially joined it to Connecticut. Only with much reluctance did New Haven acknowledge this union 2 years later.

MAINE AND NEW HAMPSHIRE

The first attempts at colonizing Maine began with two ill-fated ventures, the French settlement at St. Croix Island in 1604–5 and the English Popham settlement on the Kennebec in 1607–8. Between 1622 and 1624, English colonists made permanent settlements at Monhegan, Saco, and York. During the large Puritan migration of the next decade, the Englishman Sir Ferdinando Gorges promoted colonization expeditions to Maine, and established several small, isolated farming and fishing communities along the southern coast. The English settlements were restricted primarily to the southern coastal area of Maine because of the French trading posts along the St. Croix River.

MAINE, ca. 1630
(to Mass., 1652)

NEW HAMPSHIRE 1623

MASSACHUSETTS 1623

PLYMOUTH, 1620
(to Mass., 1691)
Cape Cod

NEW YORK 1624

CONNECTICUT 1633

NEW HAVEN, 1637
(to Conn., 1665)

RHODE ISLAND 1636

LONG ISLAND

NEW JERSEY, 1629

PENNSYLVANIA 1682

DELAWARE, 1638
(to New Netherland, 1655)
(to William Penn, 1682)
(Separate Government, 1703)

MARYLAND 1632

CONFLICTING COLONIAL CLAIMS

VIRGINIA 1607

Cape Henry

NORTH CAROLINA ca. 1653

Pamlico Sound   Cape Hatteras

Cape Fear R.

Cape Fear

SOUTH CAROLINA 1669

GEORGIA 1733

St. Lawrence River

Lake Champlain

L. George

Lake Huron

Lake Ontario

Mohawk R.

Lake Erie

Juniata R.

Allegheny R.

Susquehanna R.

Ohio River

Delaware R.

Potomac R.

Chesapeake Bay

James R.

Roanoke R.

Tennessee River

Pee Dee R.

Santee R.

Savannah River

Ocmulgee R.

Oconee R.

Altamaha R.

Chattahoochee R.

Flint R.

St. Marys R.

Connecticut R.

Hudson River

ATLANTIC OCEAN

GULF OF MEXICO

BRITISH COLONIES
IN
PRESENT UNITED STATES

with date of
first permanent settlement

.... Colonial boundaries

- - - - - Earlier separate colonial boundaries

//////// Settled area as of 1700

—·—·— Present-day State boundaries

0   50   100   150   200
Scale of Miles

Map by Harry Scott

In New Hampshire, as early as 1623, a group of colonists from England had settled at Odiorne's Point, near present Portsmouth. At about the same time, another group founded Dover. New Hampshire's largest early settlement, Exeter, was established as an unorthodox Puritan settlement in 1639 by John Wheelwright, the nonconformist brother-in-law of Anne Hutchinson, who had been banished from the Massachusetts Bay Colony. Shortly thereafter, however, orthodox Puritans from the Bay Colony settled at nearby Hampton. Perhaps because of the lack of religious unanimity, but more likely because of quarrels and litigation over land ownership, the settlements in New Hampshire and Maine never formed any sort of political union as had those in Massachusetts, Connecticut, Rhode Island, and New Haven.

The Maine-New Hampshire region had been granted in 1622 to Gorges and John Mason jointly by the Council for New England. In 1629, they agreed to split their grant, Mason taking the area of present New Hampshire; and Gorges, Maine. However, the charter of the Massachusetts Bay Colony, issued the same year, included these areas. In 1641, the Bay Colony arbitrarily extended jurisdiction over the settlements in New Hampshire and Maine. The heirs of Mason and Gorges protested. After considerable legal maneuvering and delay, in 1677 the matter was finally decided against Massachusetts, which then bought Maine from the Gorges heirs. Two years later, in 1679, New Hampshire became a royal colony.

BEGINNING OF NEW ENGLAND UNITY

The need of the New England colonies for a common defense against the Indians resulted in the beginning of unity there. Throughout most of the colonial period, New England faced danger from hostile Indians. The first real trouble began in 1633, when settlers moved into Pequot country in Connecticut and alienated the Indians. Sporadic attacks occurred until 1637, when the Pequot War began with an attack on Wethersfield. Wreaking a terrible vengeance, Massachusetts and Connecticut militia burned the Pequot fort at Mystic and killed most of the 600 or so inhabitants. The militia pursued them, killed many, and captured others and made them slaves of the colonials or sold them into slavery in the West Indies. Others who later surrendered were distributed among the Mohegan, the Narragansett, and the Niantic—English allies. Thus the Pequots lost their identity as a separate tribe.

Representative uniforms and equipment of the New England Independent
Companies. For several decades, the English colonists were responsible
for their own protection. Around 1675, because of increasing Indian hostility and Anglo-Dutch rivalry, England began sending Independent Companies, the first British regulars in America. From a drawing by Eric I.
Manders. Courtesy, the artist, the Company of Military Historians, and
the Chicago Historical Society.

Fear of additional Indian attacks led in 1643 to the formation of the
New England Confederation—the first attempt at intercolonial cooperation—consisting of Massachusetts, New Haven, Plymouth, and Connecticut. Each of the four had an equal voice in the council, although Massachusetts outnumbered the others three to one in population and furnished
most of the funds. Nevertheless, the confederation was fairly active for
about two decades, though theoretically it existed until 1684.

In 1645, the confederation conducted a victorious campaign against
the Narragansett Indians; in 1650, negotiated the Hartford Treaty with

Peter Stuyvesant of New Netherland; established a system of criminal extradition; insisted that member colonies regulate church membership and exclude Quakers from their jurisdictions; and, finally, led a stumbling but ultimately victorious defense in King Philip's War (1675–76). One of the bloodiest Indian uprisings in colonial history, this war was caused by the increasing encroachment of the Puritans on Indian lands. King Philip (Metacomet), chief of the Wampanoag tribe and son of Massasoit, who originally befriended the Pilgrims, led his allies in a series of raids on New England towns and settlements. They won numerous victories and destroyed 12 towns, but confederation-sponsored troops finally defeated them.

About this time, a movement developed among the disenfranchised in Massachusetts to convert it to a royal colony. This movement coincided with growing distrust in England over the virtual independence of Massachusetts and with hostility toward her disregard of the Navigation Acts. In 1677, Massachusetts lost her claim to Maine and bought it from the heirs of Gorges; in 1679, a royal commission separated New Hampshire from Massachusetts. In 1682, Edward Randolph, who had been appointed by the Crown as surveyor and collector of customs in New England, dispatched to authorities in England a series of reports hostile to Massachusetts. Consequently, the Lords of Trade filed a suit in chancery to cancel the charter of the Massachusetts Bay Company. The charter was canceled in 1684, and Massachusetts became a royal colony.

Because of the fragmentation of New England into so many small colonies and the recalcitrant independence of the Puritans, in 1686 the Crown organized the Dominion of New England to centralize royal control over the northern colonies. The King appointed Sir Edmund Andros as Governor-General and established the capital at Boston. Within a couple of years, Andros was able to bring into the Dominion the colonies of Maine, New Hampshire, Massachusetts, Plymouth, Connecticut (already united with New Haven), Rhode Island, New York, and East and West New Jersey. His task of controlling them was an impossible one, however, and he incurred the animosity of all classes. The year after the Glorious Revolution unseated James II in 1688, because of his Catholic leanings, insurgents in Boston, declaring for the newly crowned William and Mary, imprisoned Andros and the Dominion came to an end. A similar uprising in New York squelched Andros' deputy there.

In 1691, Massachusetts was granted a new charter, as a royal colony, and to it was attached not only Maine, as formerly, but also Plymouth. The charters of Rhode Island and Connecticut were restored, and separate royal governments were reestablished in New York and New Hampshire.

THE PROPRIETARY COLONIES

After the founding of Virginia, the British Crown established all the other middle and southern colonies under the proprietary system, which it had previously used to settle Maine and New Hampshire. Under this system, which succeeded the joint-stock company as a device to build England's colonial empire, the King granted large areas and the sovereign right to rule them to proprietors, his favorites or those to whom he was indebted. The proprietors were, in essence, feudal lords, though they were sometimes required to yield to the people certain political privileges and powers. The proprietors granted land to settlers on their own terms, could mortgage their grants, or could make subgrants.

MARYLAND: ANOTHER RELIGIOUS REFUGE

Sir George Calvert was a close friend and supporter of James I. For his services, in 1617, James rewarded him with a knighthood; in 1619, named him secretary of state; in 1620, gave him a substantial annuity; in 1623, granted him lands in Newfoundland; and, in 1625, named him Baron of Baltimore and deeded him a large estate in Ireland. In 1624, Baltimore had announced his adherence to Roman Catholicism and resigned as secretary of state because of his unwillingness to take the Oath of Supremacy. In 1627, he attempted to settle the Newfoundland grant, which he called Avalon, but abandoned it because of the severity of the weather. The following year, he visited Virginia, where he found the climate favorable.

Denied permission to live in Virginia because of his religion, Lord Baltimore returned home and appealed to the King for help. Charles I, who may have had secret inclinations toward Catholicism, granted him a tract of land north of Virginia, but before the grant was consummated Lord Baltimore died, in 1632. The grant passed to his son Cecilius Calvert, second Lord Baltimore, who named the region of the grant "Maryland" and proceeded to establish a haven for English Catholics.

"*Ark* and *Dove*." These ships brought the first colonists to Maryland. From a modern watercolor by John Moll. Courtesy, Maryland Historical Society.

The grant conveyed almost absolute powers to the Baltimores. They could not only own and dispose of the land, but they could govern it with few restrictions. Their laws and decrees, however, had to be in harmony with those of England and had to be made "with the advice, assent, and approbation of the freemen or the greater part of them or their representatives."

The young Baltimore soon organized a colonizing expedition and appointed his brother, Leonard Calvert, to lead it. In 1634, more than 200 settlers, in 2 ships, landed in Maryland and established the town of St. Marys. Twenty men in the group were "gentlemen" and received feudal grants from Baltimore; the remainder were laborers and workmen. About half were Catholic, two of whom were Jesuit priests. From the beginning, the colony fared far better than any previous English settlement in the New World. The location was favorable, the Indians were friendly, and Governor Calvert made certain to profit from the mistakes that had been made in settling Virginia. Moreover, he could obtain emergency supplies from Virginia or New England instead of making a long voyage to England.

Despite the colony's prosperity, its growth was slow because, strangely enough, few English Catholics cared to migrate; and because Baltimore insisted on an obsolescent plan of land tenure, which involved the renewal

"Founding of Maryland." From a painting by Emmanuel Leutze. Courtesy, Maryland Historical Society.

of long-outmoded feudal concepts. Under this plan, in the first years some 60 manors of 1,000 acres or more were established. Yeomen farmers, however, formed the backbone of the venture.

Partially to encourage the migration of Protestant workingmen to populate his grant and partially in the spirit of religious freedom, in 1649 Baltimore—with the approval of his assembly—officially proclaimed the religious toleration that he had practiced from the beginning. He was also probably motivated by the ascendancy of the Puritans in England at the time and the threat that they posed to the continuation of his grant. The Maryland Toleration Act promised freedom of worship and assembly to all who would profess belief in the Holy Trinity.

Many Puritans had immigrated into Maryland in 1648, including a substantial group from Virginia. Within a short time, the Puritans wielded more power than the Catholics. In 1654, they gained control of the assembly; deposed Baltimore's Governor, William Stone, himself a Puritan; and amended the Toleration Act to exclude all but Puritans. Meanwhile, Lord Baltimore had been deprived by the Puritan Parliament of his rights to govern the colony. He appealed to Oliver Cromwell, who ultimately sided with him against the Puritan rebels in Maryland. In 1657, his rights were restored and the bigotry of the amended Toleration Act corrected.

In the wake of the anti-Catholicism of the Glorious Revolution in England, in 1691 the third Lord Baltimore lost his governmental privileges, and Maryland became a royal colony. His conversion to the Anglican faith in 1713, however, prompted the return of the proprietorship 2 years later, the Baltimores retaining control until the War for Independence. But intolerance of Catholicism, which had begun after 1691, continued to plague Maryland. The fear of Catholicism was not restricted to Puritans; it was present in all other Protestant groups. In England, French Catholic support for the deposed Stuart pretenders to the throne was a constant menace to the stability of the government.

THE CAROLINAS—PROPRIETORS AND THE CROWN

In the 16th century, the three major European powers all unsuccessfully tried to found permanent settlements in the Carolinas. These attempts included those of the Spaniard De Ayllón, in 1526, at two unknown sites; the Frenchman Jean Ribaut's Charlesfort, in 1562, at Parris Island; a Spanish settlement, in 1566, also at Parris Island; and Raleigh's two English settlements, between 1585 and 1590, at Roanoke Island. As elsewhere in the New World, England was later in settling than the other European powers, but more persevering. It was she who made the first permanent settlements in the Carolinas.

All of present North Carolina and approximately the northern half of

Consisting of about 600 frontiersmen, R o g e r ' s Rangers was a British-American corps that served in the French and Indian War. The rangers acted as advance scouts for the armies of British Generals Abercromby and Amherst. Shown here are an officer and two rangers. From a drawing by Frederick T. Chapman. Courtesy, the artist, the Company of Military Historians, and the Chicago Historical Society.

South Carolina were included in "Virginia" as granted by James I in 1606 to the London and Plymouth Companies. In 1624, however, when "Virginia" became a royal colony, the lands that had not been settled reverted to the King, including all the above portions of the Carolinas. Five years later, shortly after bold Virginia hunters and traders had begun probing southward into the Carolinas, Charles I granted the "Province of Carolana" to Sir Robert Heath, his Attorney General. The boundaries were defined as 31° and 36° north latitude, which extended English claims down through present Georgia, even farther into Spanish-claimed territory. The plans of Heath and his colleagues for settlement of the Carolinas came to naught.

When Charles II regained his throne in 1660, he reclaimed the Carolina grant and 3 years later reissued it to eight men who had aided in the Restoration. The charter gave them the powers of government, specified guarantees for the political rights of the settlers, and authorized the granting of toleration to religious dissenters.

Despite the powers granted the proprietors, they profited little from the Carolinas and did not contribute much to their growth. Their administration was in general marked by poor management, neglect, impractical political experimentation, a low rate of settlement, and recurrent clashes between the Governors and the settlers. The low rate of settlement was attributable in part to circumstances beyond the control of the pro-

The Southern Algonquian Indian village of Secota, situated on the north bank of the Pamlico River, in present Beaufort County, North Carolina. The letters identify parts of the town. From an engraving by Theodore de Bry, after an on-the-scene water-color by John White, 1585. Courtesy, Smithsonian Institution.

prietors. Few settlers could be induced to emigrate from England during the period of comparative religious peace that followed the great migration of Puritans to Massachusetts, in the 1630's. As a result, many of the settlers in the Carolinas came from the British West Indies, especially overcrowded Barbados. Therefore, more than any other British colonies, the Carolinas were influenced by the economic and social attitudes of West Indian planters, as manifested particularly in the adoption of a strict slave code.

The proprietors were unsuccessful in instituting workable local governments, and their theoretical ideas of government were quite impractical. For example, in 1669, they called upon John Locke, a political philosopher whose writings were markedly to influence colonial patriots a century later, to draft the "Fundamental Constitutions of Carolina." This document presented an impractical feudal scheme of polity and land tenure as the basis for proprietary government. It created a petty nobility, with such fanciful titles as landgrave, cacique, and palatine, which was to control two-thirds of the land. The lower classes were slaves, serfs, and freemen. Other provisions pertained to a popular assembly, natural rights, and religious toleration. The proprietors attempted to persuade the colonial legislatures to approve the Fundamental Constitutions, but they were never successful.

One of the first steps of the proprietors was to designate three "counties": Albemarle, north of the Chowan River, in present northeastern North Carolina; Clarendon, south of Albemarle in the Cape Fear region; and Craven, south of Cape Romain, in South Carolina. The latter county, which received the greatest attention from the proprietors, was the most successful. Albemarle progressed slowly, but Clarendon had only a short-lived existence.

A few settlers from Virginia, lured by the prospect of cheaper and better lands, began crossing over the present North Carolina boundary into the Albemarle area at least a decade prior to the charter of 1663. Even though the proprietors offered tax exemptions and generously granted lands to newcomers, the county grew slowly and proved unprofitable for the proprietors, partly because they invested little in it, in money, supplies, or direction. They also failed to institute a stable government. The agitated settlers deposed Governor after Governor.

Problems in Albemarle were soon aggravated unknowingly by the proprietors themselves. In 1665, they obtained a new charter that extended the boundaries of the Carolinas one-half degree to the north and 2 degrees to the south. The latter placed the boundary south of St. Augustine, the major settlement in Spanish Florida, and the former took still more of the lands that had originally been included in Virginia. This action, plus competition in tobacco production, created resentment on the part of Virginians toward Albemarle. Because Albemarle lacked good harbors and navigable rivers, communication with the outside world was mainly limited to land, especially with Virginia. Virginia's hostility, plus the uncertainty of land titles, high quitrents, bad government, apathy of the proprietors, and difficulties in marketing tobacco, the chief money crop, resulted in unrest, confusion, slow growth, and even armed rebellion in Albemarle. However, over the course of time the settlement expanded, particularly after the first town, Bath, was incorporated, in 1705.

Prior to the designation of Clarendon "county," some New Englanders and a group of Barbadians settled near the mouth of the Cape Fear River. Later, in 1665, another party of Barbadians made an attempt to settle in the region, but the colony failed within 2 years because of friction with the earlier settlers and Indian hostility.

Glowing reports of the Port Royal region, coupled with the abandonment of Clarendon in 1667, caused the proprietors to shift their interest to Craven "county," to which they gave their major attention and expenditures. After making plans to bring settlers from England, Ireland, Barbados, and the Bahamas, the proprietors purchased three ships, which sailed from London in August 1669. Storms wrecked two of them after they had left Barbados, and only the *Carolina* reached its destination, the following March, after being repaired at Bermuda. Instead of remaining at Port Royal as instructed, the colonists settled on Albemarle Point (Old Charles Town), at the mouth of the Ashley River. The site was low, open to attack, and infested with malaria. In 1680, the main body of settlers moved to the junction of the Ashley and Cooper Rivers, the site of Charleston.

During its first decade, the colony proved a disappointment to the proprietors. It failed to grow in population as expected, it did not return the anticipated profit, and it refused to put most of the provisions of Locke's "Fundamental Constitutions" into effect as the proprietors had directed. In 1682, the proprietors launched two campaigns, one aimed at recruiting immigrants and the other at reforming the government.

The former was very successful. To attract settlers, the proprietors revised the "Fundamental Constitutions" to allow even greater religious freedom by denying the Anglican Church the right to tax non-Anglicans and by giving each congregation, regardless of sect, the right to tax its own members. This action enticed about 500 English Presbyterians and Baptists to the colony between 1682 and 1685. Immigrants came from Scotland and France as well; in 1684, a group of Presbyterian Scots founded a colony at Stuart's Town, near Port Royal, and before 1690 at least 600 French Huguenots had settled in South Carolina. In 1686, the Spaniards destroyed Stuart's Town, and the Scots fled to Charleston.

To the settlers, the most important of the proprietors' directives for reforming the government were aimed at gaining control over the Indian trade, stopping the traffic in Indian slaves, and preventing the use of the colony as a pirate haven. To put these reforms into effect, the proprietors had to replace the Barbadians who were in control of the government, for they were involved in both the Indian and pirate trades. As a result, a decade of political chaos occurred, and the colony floundered aimlessly without effective direction. The colony's leadership divided into two bitterly opposed factions: the proprietary group, composed mainly of new immigrants; and the antiproprietary group, made up primarily of old settlers. The controversy reached a climax when the parliament demanded a government based on the charter of 1663. The proprietors ordered the parliament dissolved and all laws rescinded. By 1690, not one statute was in force. The Governor, after attempting to rule by executive decree, finally placed the colony under martial law. A revolt occurred in 1690, and one of the proprietors, a former Governor of Albemarle who had been banished in 1689, became Governor. He immediately summoned parliament and won the support of the popular party. Within a short time, however, he began disobeying instructions of the proprietary board and was recalled to England.

His banishment from Albemarle in 1689 had been followed by the appointment of a Governor of "that part of Carolina that lyes North and East of Cape Feare." This action marked the practical end of Albemarle "county" as a unit of government and the real beginning of North Carolina as a separate colony. Two years later, a "Governor of Carolina," who resided in Charleston, received a commission and authority to appoint a deputy for North Carolina. In 1694, he was empowered to appoint deputies "both in South and North Carolina." The two regions were then governed separately, but in 1712 a Governor of North Carolina was named "independent of the Governour of Carolina."

In 1729, because of the repeated failures of the proprietors and their continuing disputes with the populace, the Crown once again took over the Carolinas as royal colonies. At that time, the only major settlements were those at Albemarle and Charleston. During the century, however, settlers began to move inland into the piedmont and the mountains and help create the modern States of North and South Carolina.

THE DUKE OF YORK'S GRANT

Only a few months before the English conquered New Netherland in 1664, Charles II granted the territory as a proprietorship to his brother, James, Duke of York, to hold with all customary proprietary rights. James, keeping for himself the Hudson Valley and the islands in the harbor, renamed the province, as well as the town on Manhattan Island, New York. He conveyed the southern part of his grant, between the Hudson and the Delaware Rivers, to two loyal Stuart supporters, Lord John Berkeley and Sir George Carteret, who named it New Jersey. New York was quickly amalgamated into the English colonial system and enjoyed a continuing prosperity. When James assumed the throne, the province automatically became a royal colony. It was attached briefly to the Dominion of New England, but regained separate status after the Glorious Revolution (1688).

New Jersey had few settlements when it passed into the possession of the new proprietors. A scattering of Swedes, Dutch, and Finns had filtered into the area from New York. Almost as soon as English control was asserted, New England Puritans moved into the area. They were welcomed by the proprietors' representative, who in 1665 founded the village of Elizabethtown. Because immigration into New Jersey was encouraged by promises of religious toleration, representative government, and moderately priced land, the colony was populated rather quickly.

In 1674, Lord Berkeley sold his interest in New Jersey to two English Quakers. From them, it passed into the hands of three others, one of whom was William Penn. In 1676, Carteret agreed with them to split the colony into East and West Jersey and ceded the latter to them. In 1688, James II reasserted his governing right and brought the Jerseys into the Dominion of New England. After the collapse of the Dominion, in 1689, East and West Jersey reverted to full proprietary control. In 1702, however, the proprietors surrendered their governing power to the Crown, but retained their land titles. In 1738, New Jersey was reestablished as a separate royal colony.

In 1682, to obtain access to the seacoast, William Penn acquired Delaware from the Duke of York, who between 1664 and 1680 had taken over the area on the assumption that it was part of his grant and had divided it into three counties, or "Territories." After Penn's purchase, these counties were at first governed as part of Pennsylvania and basked in the same prosperity. In 1701, however, they were authorized to form a separate assembly, which occurred in 1704, and the colony of Delaware was born. But it remained under the jurisdiction of the Penn family until the War for Independence.

PENNSYLVANIA: A QUAKER PROPRIETORSHIP

Pennsylvania was the most successful of the proprietary colonies. Adm. Sir William Penn was a wealthy and respected friend of Charles II. His son, William, was an associate of George Fox, founder of the Society of Friends—a despised Quaker. When the senior Penn died, in 1670, his Quaker son inherited not only the friendship of the Crown but also an outstanding unpaid debt of some magnitude owed to his father by the King. In settlement, in 1681 he received a grant of land in America, called "Pennsylvania," which he decided to use as a refuge for his perse-

"The Landing of William Penn, 1682." From a painting by J. L. G. Ferris. Courtesy, William E. Ryder and the Smithsonian Institution.

cuted coreligionists. It was a princely domain, extending along the Delaware River from the 40th to the 43d parallel. As proprietor, Penn was
both ruler and landlord. The restrictions on the grant were essentially the
same as those imposed on the second Lord Baltimore: colonial laws had
to be in harmony with those of England and had to be assented to by a
representative assembly.

Penn lost little time in advertising his grant and the terms on which he
offered settlement. He promised religious freedom and virtually total self-
government. More than 1,000 colonists arrived the first year, most of
whom were Mennonites and Quakers. Penn himself arrived in 1682 at
New Castle and spent the winter at Upland, a Swedish settlement on the
Delaware that the English had taken over; he renamed it Chester. He
founded a capital city a few miles upstream and named it Philadelphia—
the City of Brotherly Love. Well situated and well planned, it grew
rapidly. Within 2 years, it had more than 600 houses, many of them handsome brick residences surrounded by lawns and gardens.

Shiploads of Quakers poured into the colony. By the summer of 1683,
more than 3,000 settlers had arrived. Welsh, Germans, Scotch-Irish,
Mennonites, Quakers, Jews, and Baptists mingled in a New World
utopia. Not even the great Puritan migration had populated a colony so
fast. Pennsylvania soon rivaled Massachusetts, New York, and Virginia.
In part its prosperity is attributable to its splendid location and fertile

A group of Cherokee Indians brought to London in 1730 by Sir Alexander
Cuming. From an engraving by Isaac Basire, after a painting by Markham,
in the British Museum. Courtesy, Smithsonian Institution.

Symbolic scene representing the various treaties William Penn negotiated with the Indians in Pennsylvania. The Indians admired Penn because he dealt fairly with them in land transactions and protected them. From an engraving by John Hall, 1775, after a painting by Benjamin West. Courtesy, Library of Congress.

soils, but even more to the proprietor's felicitous administration. In a series of laws—the Great Law and the First and Second Frames of Government—Penn created one of the most humane and progressive governments then in existence. It was characterized by broad principles of religious toleration, a well-organized bicameral legislature, and a forward-looking penal code.

Another reason for the colony's growth was that, unlike the other colonies, it was not troubled by the Indians. Penn had bought their lands and made a series of peace treaties that were scrupulously fair and rigidly adhered to. For more than half a century, Indians and whites lived in Pennsylvania in peace. Quaker farmers, who were never armed, could leave their children with neighboring "savages" when they went into town for a visit.

By any measure, Penn's "Holy Experiment" was a magnificent success. Penn proved that a state could function smoothly on Quaker principles, without oaths, arms, or priests, and that these principles encouraged in-

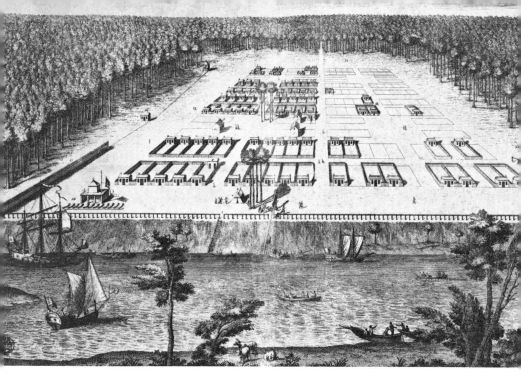

Savannah, in 1734, the year after James Oglethorpe founded the city and colony of Georgia. From an engraving by P. Fourdrinier, after an on-the-scene drawing by Peter Gordon. Courtesy, Library of Congress.

James Oglethorpe, founder of the colony of Georgia, presents Tomochichi, chief of the Yamacraws, to the Lord Trustees of the colony, in England. Oglethorpe, wearing a black suit, stands in the center. From a painting by William Verelst, 1734. Courtesy, Smithsonian Institution.

dividual morality and freedom of conscience. Furthermore, ever a good businessman, he made a personal fortune while treating his subjects with unbending fairness and honesty.

GEORGIA—EARLY PENETRATION

By 1700, the last of the British colonies in the present United States, Georgia, had not yet been founded. Not until 1733 did the philanthropist Gen. James Oglethorpe begin to settle the colony, which he had conceived as a refuge for oppressed debtors in English prisons [*Colonials and Patriots,* Vol. VI in this series, pp. 19–20]. As the 17th century neared an end, however, the British were beginning to penetrate the area. English traders set up posts on the Savannah, Oconee, and Ocmulgee Rivers and were active along the Chattahoochee and as far west as the Mississippi. Winning the friendship of two powerful Indian tribes, the Creek and the Chickasaw, they created the antagonism with the Spanish and the French that resulted in the international clashes of the early 1700's.

SOCIAL AND CULTURAL LIFE

Life in early colonial times was harsh, and the refinements of the mother country were ordinarily lacking. The colonists, however, soon began to mold their English culture into the fresh environment of a new land. The influence of religion permeated the entire way of life. In most southern colonies, the Anglican Church was the legally established church. In New England, the Puritans were dominant; and, in Pennsylvania, the Quakers. Especially in the New England colonies, the local or village church was the hub of community life; the authorities strictly enforced the Sabbath and sometimes banished nonbelievers and dissenters.

Unfortunately, the same sort of religious intolerance, bigotry, and superstition associated with the age of the Reformation in Europe also prevailed in some of the colonies, though on a lesser scale. In the last half of the 17th century, during sporadic outbreaks of religious fanaticism and hysteria, Massachusetts and Connecticut authorities tried and hanged a few women as "witches." Early in the 18th century, some other witchcraft persecution occurred, in Virginia, North Carolina, and Rhode Island. As the decades passed, however, religious toleration developed in the colonies.

Because of the strong religious influence in the colonies, especially in New England, religious instruction and Bible reading played an important part in education. In Massachusetts, for example, a law of 1647 required each town to maintain a grammar school for the purpose of providing religious, as well as general, instruction. In the southern colonies, only a few privately endowed free schools existed. Private tutors instructed the sons of well-to-do planters, who completed their educations in English universities. Young males in poor families throughout the colonies were ordinarily apprenticed for vocational education.

By 1700, two colleges had been founded: Harvard, established by the Massachusetts Legislature in 1636; and William and Mary, in Virginia, which originated in 1693 under a royal charter. Other cultural activities before 1700 were limited. The few literary products of the colonists, mostly historical narratives, journals, sermons, and some poetry, were printed in England. The *Bay Psalm Book* (1640) was the first book printed in the colonies. Artists and composers were few, and their output was of a relatively simple character.

OUR BASIC ENGLISH HERITAGE

Our American heritage is basically English, as infused through the British colonies that ultimately revolted and formed a new nation. Of all the English colonial roots of the American way of life, those concerned with government and democracy are the most basic. The distance from the mother country, the cheapness of land, and the scarcity of labor created a social and political atmosphere that was quite liberal for the times. In strong contrast to the royal autocracy that prevailed in the French and Spanish colonies, a considerable degree of self-government flourished. Social distinctions were less important than in England. Suffrage, though restricted by property and church membership qualifications, was broadened as time went on.

Arbitrary rule in the English settlements was short lived. The traditions of Parliament, trade guilds, and merchant associations encouraged the King to permit the formation of local representative assemblies, even in the proprietary colonies; the first meeting of such an assembly was the Virginia House of Burgesses, in 1619. In New England, the Congregational religious background influenced the growth of democracy, as did also the conduct of town meetings. The governments of most of the colonies were based on some form of written document, which stemmed from the issuance of charters and grants by the Crown to joint-stock companies and proprietors, and were potentially democratic in form. Conflicts between the royal Governors and the lawmaking colonial assemblies occurred early. By obtaining control of the revenue and refusing assent to unwanted taxes, the assemblies gained a measure of control over the Governors, of whose powers they were always suspicious.

Associated with our English heritage of democratic institutions and constitutional government is the emphasis placed on individual rights. Wherever the British colonists settled, they carried with them the fundamental belief that they were entitled to all the rights and freedoms of Englishmen. Not the least of these rights was that of having some representation in the branch of government that levied taxes on them. Over the breach of these rights, the colonists finally fought the War for Independence, which separated them from the British Empire. As time went on, they blended into the concept of individual rights the freedom of conscience and religious belief.

Outstanding among our other rich English legacies are those in language, literature, architecture, and common law.

Epilogue—The United States: An Amalgam

During the colonial period of U.S. history, most of the nations of Western Europe planted their seeds in the fresh soil that was to nourish the growth of the United States of America. Spain spread her blood, language, and traditions from Florida to California. France sowed a rich heritage throughout the length of the Mississippi Valley. Holland and Sweden transplanted roots to the banks of the Hudson and the Delaware. In the course of time, the offshoots of all these plantings were grafted onto the oak-solid trunks of the British colonies on the Atlantic shore. From the beginning, the hybrid was nurtured by immigrants of various races and religions from scores of other lands.

The amalgamation of such rich and diverse national, cultural, and racial elements into a free and democratic society has created the United States of America—a harmonious blending of cultures, languages, and traditions that mirrors the hopes and aspirations of all mankind.

PART II

Explorers and Settlers:

Survey of Historic

Sites and Buildings

A FULL APPRECIATION of our national historical heritage can never be gained by the reading of historical narrative or formal study alone—interesting and important though such study is. Visits to historic sites and buildings rekindle, stimulate, and broaden historical interest and knowledge; they add new dimensions to the past. The numerous sites and buildings that are described below illustrate an intriguing and vital epoch in our history: early exploration and settlement. They reveal the widespread activities of the various European nations, the clashes of imperial rivalry, and the beginnings of the amalgam of nationalities, cultures, and races that became the United States.

Sites and buildings associated with the epoch are scattered throughout the United States. They include: Missions, pueblos, presidios, houses, memorial parks, ruins, and lost sites. Spanish sites, which indicate the broad geographical extent of Spanish exploration and settlement, range from the lower Atlantic seaboard across the Southeast and the gulf coast to the Southwest and the Pacific coast. The remains or ruins of various forts, missions, and trading posts in the Great Lakes region, the

[135

Mississippi Valley, and the Southeast are remnants of the French Empire in the New World. Dutch and Swedish sites are in New York, Pennsylvania, Delaware, and New Jersey. Because sites pertaining to the later English colonial period, after 1700, are described in a separate volume of this series, *Colonials and Patriots,* those treated in this volume are proportionately fewer than those for Spain, France, Holland, and Sweden. Indian archeological sites have been included that reveal European contact and extent of exploration.

The identification, maintenance, preservation, and reconstruction of historic sites and buildings associated with the period of early exploration and settlement present some unique problems because of the passage of so much time and the paucity and obscurity of the early historical records. More sites have been "lost" than in later periods of history; some sites were definitively located only after exhaustive historical and archeological research. Also, as would be expected, more of these historic buildings are in ruins or partial ruins than are those of later times. All these problems have been encountered by the various governmental and private groups and individuals on the National, State, county, and local levels that maintain historic sites and buildings representing the period.

Some of the fruits of the National Survey of Historic Sites and Buildings program are presented in this volume, which also includes sites in the National Park System that illustrate early exploration and settlement. State universities, park departments, and historical societies throughout the Nation have done important work in this period of history, as have also many county and municipal governments. Private organizations, too, have made substantial contributions. These include, for example, on the National level, the National Trust for Historic Preservation; on the State level, in California, the Daughters of the American Revolution, the Native Daughters of the Golden West, and the Native Sons of the Golden West; on the city level, in New Mexico, the Historic Santa Fe Foundation and the Old Santa Fe Association. Examples in the East include Sleepy Hollow Restorations, Inc., in New York; the Society for the Preservation of Virginia Antiquities; the Association for the Preservation of New England Antiquities; the Antiquarian and Landmarks Society of Connecticut; the Plymouth Antiquarian Society, in Massachusetts; and the St. Augustine Historical Society, in Florida. Private local associations of historians and archeologists have also done much valuable work.

The efforts of all these organizations, as well as those of numerous others and scores of private owners, have fostered our national heritage

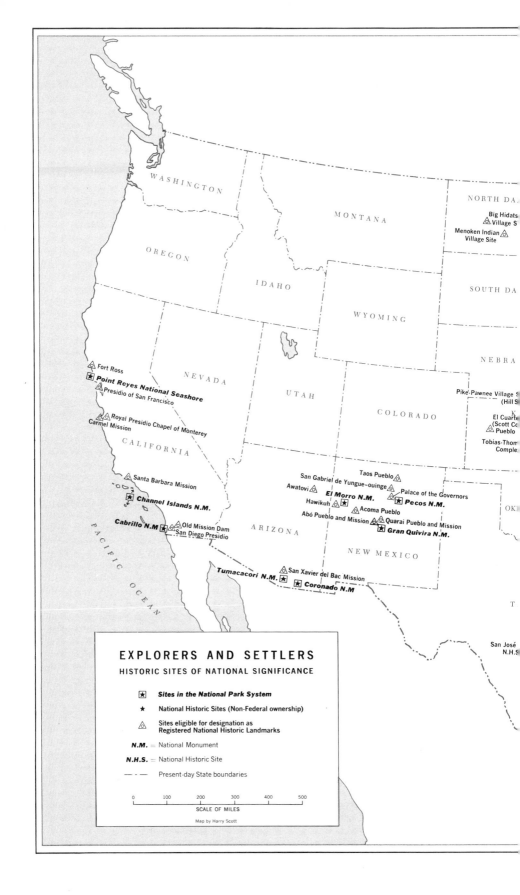

WASHINGTON

MONTANA

NORTH DA.

Big Hidats
△ Village S

Menoken Indian △
Village Site

OREGON

IDAHO

SOUTH DA

WYOMING

NEBRA

△ Fort Ross
★ Point Reyes National Seashore
△ Presidio of San Francisco

NEVADA

UTAH

Pike-Pawnee Village S
(Hill S

△△ Royal Presidio Chapel of Monterey
Carmel Mission

COLORADO

El Cuarte
(Scott Co
△ Pueblo

△ Santa Barbara Mission

CALIFORNIA

Tobias-Thom
Comple.

Taos Pueblo △

San Gabriel de Yungue-ouinge △

★ Channel Islands N.M.

Awatovi △   El Morro N.M.   Palace of the Governors △
Hawikuh △ ★   ★ Pecos N.M.
△ Acoma Pueblo

Cabrillo N.M ★ △△ Old Mission Dam
San Diego Presidio

Abó Pueblo and Mission △△ △ Quarai Pueblo and Mission
★ Gran Quivira N.M.

OK

ARIZONA

NEW MEXICO

PACIFIC OCEAN

Tumacacori N.M. ★ △ San Xavier del Bac Mission

T

★ Coronado N.M

San José
N.H.S

EXPLORERS AND SETTLERS

HISTORIC SITES OF NATIONAL SIGNIFICANCE

★ (boxed) *Sites in the National Park System*

★   National Historic Sites (Non-Federal ownership)

△   Sites eligible for designation as
Registered National Historic Landmarks

N.M. = National Monument

N.H.S. = National Historic Site

- · - · —   Present-day State boundaries

0   100   200   300   400   500
SCALE OF MILES

Map by Harry Scott

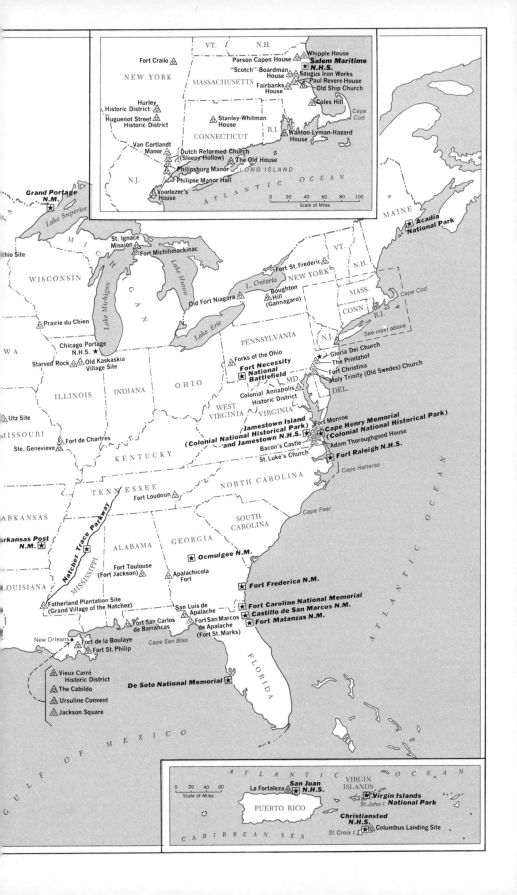

VT.   N.H.
Fort Crailo △
Parson Capen House △   △ △ Whipple House
★ Salem Maritime
N.H.S.
"Scotch"-Boardman
House △   △ Saugus Iron Works
△ Paul Revere House
Fairbanks △ △ Old Ship Church
House
△ Coles Hill
NEW YORK   MASSACHUSETTS
Hurley
Historic District △   Cape
Cod
Huguenot Street △
Historic District
Stanley-Whitman
△ House
Van Cortlandt   CONNECTICUT   R.I.
Manor △   △ Wanton-Lyman-Hazard
△ Dutch Reformed Church   House
(Sleepy Hollow) △ The Old House
Philipsburg Manor △   LONG ISLAND
△ Philipse Manor Hall
Voorlezer's △
House   A T L A N T I C   O C E A N
N.J.

0   20   40   60   80   100
Scale of Miles

Grand Portage
N.M. ★
Lake Superior   MAINE   ★ Acadia
National Park

St. Ignace
Mission △
△ Fort Michilimackinac   Fort St. Frederic △   VT.   N.H.
hio Site
WISCONSIN   Old Fort Niagara △   L. Ontario   NEW YORK   MASS.
Boughton   Cape Cod
Hill
(Gannagaro) △   CONN.   R.I.
Prairie du Chien △   WA   See inset above
Chicago Portage   N.J.
N.H.S. ★   PENNSYLVANIA   ★ Gloria Dei Church
Starved Rock △△ Old Kaskaskia   △ Forks of the Ohio   The Printzhof
Village Site   Fort Necessity   Fort Christina
National   Holy Trinity (Old Swedes) Church
Battlefield ★   DEL.
ILLINOIS   INDIANA   OHIO   Colonial Annapolis △
Historic District
WEST   MD.
A   VIRGINIA   VIRGINIA
Utz Site   Jamestown Island   Fort Monroe   Cape Henry Memorial
(Colonial National Historical Park)   (Colonial National Historical Park)
MISSOURI   Fort de Chartres △   and Jamestown N.H.S. ★   △△ Adam Thoroughgood House
Ste. Geneviève △   Bacon's Castle △   ★ Fort Raleigh N.H.S.
KENTUCKY   St. Luke's Church △

TENNESSEE   NORTH CAROLINA   Cape Hatteras
Fort Loudoun △
ARKANSAS   SOUTH
CAROLINA   Cape Fear
Arkansas Post   ALABAMA   GEORGIA   ★ Ocmulgee N.M.
N.M. ★
Fort Toulouse
(Fort Jackson) △   △ Apalachicola
Fort
LOUISIANA   ★ Fort Frederica N.M.
Fatherland Plantation Site   △ San Luis de   ★ Fort Caroline National Memorial
(Grand Village of the Natchez)   Apalache   ★ Castillo de San Marcos N.M.
△ Fort San Carlos   Fort San Marcos   ★ Fort Matanzas N.M.
de Barrancas   de Apalache
New Orleans ●   Fort de la Boulaye △   (Fort St. Marks)
△ Fort St. Philip   Cape San Blas
△ Vieux Carré
Historic District   F   L
△ The Cabildo   O   R
△ Ursuline Convent   De Soto National Memorial ★   I   D
△ Jackson Square   A

G   U   L   F   O   F   M   E   X   I   C   O

A T L A N T I C   O C E A N
VIRGIN
ISLANDS
0   20   40   60   La Fortaleza △△ ★ San Juan   ★ Virgin Islands
Scale of Miles   N.H.S.   St. John I.   National Park
PUERTO RICO   Christiansted
N.H.S.   △ Columbus Landing Site
C   A   R   I   B   B   E   A   N   S   E   A   St. Croix I. ★

by making it possible for Americans to visit and enjoy many of the historic sites and buildings illustrating early exploration and settlement that are described below. The sites and buildings are arranged alphabetically by State and Territory within the following five categories: Units of the National Park System; National Historic Sites in non-Federal ownership; sites eligible for the Registry of National Historic Landmarks; Historic Districts eligible for the Registry; and sites of sufficient importance to merit attention but which are not considered to be nationally significant when measured and evaluated by the special Landmark criteria (pp. 421–422).

A. Sites in the National Park System

The principal aim of the National Survey of Historic Sites and Buildings is to identify nationally important historic sites that are not units of the National Park System, but no such survey would be complete without mention of sites in the system. The sites described below are those administered by the National Park Service that have primary or secondary associations with the phases of history treated in this volume. Further information about a particular site may be obtained by writing directly to the superintendent at the address indicated.

1. Natchez Trace Parkway, Alabama-Mississippi-Tennessee

Location: Traverses the States of Mississippi, Alabama, and Tennessee, from Natchez to Nashville; address, P.O. Box 948, Tupelo, Miss. 38801.

Early inland explorers and settlers in the Southeastern part of the present United States discovered a network of animal trails and Indian paths that formed a wilderness road between present Natchez and Nashville. During the 18th century, Frenchmen, Englishmen, Spaniards, and Americans used the road. French explorers, missionaries, soldiers, and traders called it a "trace," a French word for "trail." Shortly after arriving at the gulf coast in 1699, the French first explored the trace area; in 1716, they established Fort Rosalie at the site of Natchez. In 1763, the French ceded the region to the English, who occupied it until 1779. The English, who used the trace mainly for the purpose of trading with the Natchez, Choctaw, and Chickasaw tribes, called it the "Path to the Choctaw Nation."

Scenic Natchez Trace Parkway generally follows the route of the old Natchez Trace. Indians, Spaniards, Frenchmen, Englishmen, and Americans used the trace. For several centuries, it was an important trade route and emigrant road in the old Southwest.

At the end of the War for Independence, in 1783, Spain claimed the territory between the Mississippi and Chattahoochee Rivers, as far north as Memphis, as a reward for her wartime aid to the colonies. This territory included Natchez, at the southern end of the trace, which remained under Spanish control until it passed to the United States in 1798, though in the interim the population had remained predominantly English-speaking. The United States immediately organized the Mississippi Territory. At the northern end of the trace, beginning about 1780, American settlers were populating Nashville. Kentucky traders and other frontiersmen rafted their goods downriver to Natchez or New Orleans, but used the trace—which they sometimes called the Chickasaw Trace—returning home. Frequently, they brought back Spanish silver. By 1800, about 1,000 made the trip each year, and mail service was initiated along the trace.

From 1800 to 1820, the trace was the most traveled road in the old Southwest. Over it passed a variety of colorful frontier characters: Missionaries, boatmen, Indian hunting parties, mounted postmen, and U.S. soldiers. A vital economic and social artery, it bound the old Southwest to the rest of the Nation. It was used for frontier defense in the "cold war" with Spain, until she abandoned all claims to Florida in 1819, and became a valuable military and post road. At the beginning of the War of 1812, between the United States and England, Andrew Jackson and his Tennessee Militia used it to travel to Natchez and after the war returned over it in triumph.

By 1820, the trace was no longer needed for frontier defense. Rivalries with Spain and England had ended, and the Indians were being forced westward. The new steamboat traffic robbed the trace of its trade. As Alabama, Mississippi, and Tennessee became more populous, sections were abandoned and others incorporated into local road systems. The trace lost its frontier character.

The Natchez Trace Parkway is still under construction and follows roughly—crossing, recrossing, and at times paralleling—the route of the old Natchez Trace. When completed, it will make possible a leisurely 450-mile drive through a protected zone of forest, meadow, and field that is rich in prehistoric and historic associations. Evidences of the aboriginal Indian inhabitants abound along the trace. Markers indicate historic sites, and interpretive exhibits point out their significance. The main visitor center is at Tupelo, Miss.

Conjectural likeness of Francisco Vásquez de Coronado, based on contemporary descriptions. From a charcoal portrait by Peter Hurd. Courtesy, the artist and Roswell Museum and Art Center, Roswell, New Mexico.

2. Coronado National Memorial, Arizona

Location: Cochise County, on Montezuma Canyon Road, about 30 miles west of Bisbee; address, Star Route, Hereford, Ariz. 85615.

This memorial is located along the United States-Mexico border near the point where the great Spanish expedition under Francisco Vásquez de Coronado entered the present United States in 1540. It commemorates the first major European exploration of the U.S. Southwest—only one-half century after Columbus' discovery of America and more than one-half century before the first permanent English settlement, at Jamestown. Coronado Peak affords a sweeping view of the country through which the expedition marched. Exhibits along the footpath to the peak provide information on the expedition and the natural features of the region. The memorial was established by Presidential proclamation in November 1952.

3. Tumacacori National Monument, Arizona

Location: Santa Cruz County, on U.S. 89, about 48 miles south of Tucson; address, P.O. Box 67, Tumacacori, Ariz. 85640.

This monument features a typical old mission church that illustrates Spanish colonial endeavor and commemorates the introduction of Christianity into what is now southern Arizona. The mission of San José de Tumacacori was a northern outpost of a mission chain constructed by Franciscan priests in the 1700's on sites established by the Jesuits in what was then the State of Sonora, New Spain.

The great Jesuit missionary-explorer Father Eusebio Francisco Kino first came into the Tumacacori region in 1691 when he visited the small Sobaipuri Indian village of San Cayetano de Tumacacori, thought to have been situated within a few miles of the present mission. By 1698, Tumacacori had an "earth-roofed house of adobe," fields of wheat, and herds of cattle, sheep, and goats. When a missionary was assigned to Guevavi, to the southeast, Tumacacori became a *visita* of that mission.

The year after the Pima Rebellion of 1751, Spanish authorities moved the village of San Cayetano de Tumacacori to the place where the mission now stands and renamed it San José de Tumacacori. They erected a small mission at the site and founded a presidio at Tubac, 3 miles to the north. In 1773, Apache raids forced the closing of Guevavi, and San José de Tumacacori Mission—then under the Franciscans—became district headquarters. Construction of the present building started around 1800, apparently, and it was in use by 1822, when the Mexican period began.

Under Mexican administration, the power of the Roman Catholic Church weakened. Missions were required to become parish churches, and the Government supplied no funds to support mission activity. As late as 1841, a priest is known to have been at Tumacacori, but in 1844 Mexico sold the mission lands to a private citizen. Four years later, when the last devout Indians left Tumacacori, they took with them to San Xavier del Bac Mission, near Tucson, certain church furnishings, including statues that are still used there. The Tumacacori church fell into ruins, but its massiveness preserved it from complete destruction.

Tumacacori National Monument, totaling 10 acres, was established in 1908. Administered by the National Park Service, it is no longer associated with any religious order. Some repair work was done to the old buildings in 1921, including a new roof over the long nave. Repair work since then has been limited entirely to preserving existing original construction. A reminder that Spain was active on the frontier in the

Modern view of San José de Tumacacori Mission, Arizona. Built by Franciscan priests on the site of an earlier mission, San José served as the northern outpost of a Sonoran mission chain.

Southwest long before the United States became a nation, this typical old mission church remains today an inspiring symbol of the faith, courage, and vigor of the early missionary priests, as well as of the great loyalty and devotion of the Indian converts.

4. Arkansas Post National Memorial, Arkansas

Location: Arkansas County, on Ark. 1 and 169, about 8 miles northeast of Gillett; address, Superintendent, Hot Springs National Park, P.O. Box 1219, Hot Springs National Park, Ark. 71902.

Arkansas Post, founded near the mouth of the Arkansas River, was the first European settlement in the lower Mississippi Valley and the territory of the later Louisiana Purchase. Established in 1686 among the friendly Quapaw Indians by Henry de Tonty, lieutenant of the famed explorer René Robert Cavelier, Sieur de la Salle, the first post was small, may not have been utilized continuously, and was probably abandoned during the period 1700–1720. As French activities increased along the lower Mississippi, especially in the decade following the establishment of John Law's colony about 1720, Arkansas Post thrived. In the last half of the century, the Spaniards and Americans took over the post. It flourished under the Americans. After the War of 1812, American settlers rapidly populated the area, and the post became the capital of Arkansas Territory. Although the capital was later moved to Little Rock, the post became a key point in steamboat traffic and a strategic Civil War military site.

Because of subsequent changes in location of Tonty's early post and the vagaries of the Arkansas River, the precise location of the site cannot be determined. Formerly a State park, the National Memorial was authorized by an act of Congress on July 6, 1960. On June 23, 1964, it was accepted by the National Park Service, which made plans to enhance the interpretive program.

5. Cabrillo National Monument, California

Location: San Diego County, on Point Loma, 10 miles southwest of downtown San Diego, via Pacific Boulevard (U.S. 101) and Rosecrans Street; address, P.O. Box 6175, San Diego, Calif. 92106.

Cabrillo National Monument commemorates the discovery of the coast of Alta California in 1542 by Juan Rodríguez Cabrillo, a Portuguese navigator in the service of Spain. Cabrillo's landing at San Diego Bay, which he called San Miguel Bay, marks the first contact of Europeans with that part of the New World. The expedition, consisting of two small vessels, the *San Salvador and Victoria,* originated at Navidad, on the west coast of present Mexico. It was the first Spanish expedition to pass beyond Cabo del Engaño (Cape Deceit).

At San Diego Bay, the ships anchored behind the high land of Point Loma. On going ashore, apparently at Ballast Point, a group of men were attacked by a small party of Indians, but land parties briefly explored the region. Cabrillo sailed northward along the California coast, and sighted or landed at many places. Unfortunately, he died, at San Miguel Island, in January 1543. His grave, the location of which is unknown and unmarked, is probably near Cuyler Harbor. Bartolomé Ferrelo, the chief pilot, who succeeded to command, again turned northward and reached the northernmost point of the expedition, probably the general area of the Rogue River in present southern Oregon.

From Cabrillo National Monument one of the outstanding seascapes of the world can be viewed: an inspiring scene comprising the ocean, bays, islands, mountains, foothills, valleys, and plains that surround the city of San Diego. Also visible are the following sites located on Ballast

Point in the Fort Rosecrans Military Reservation on Point Loma: the probable landing place of Cabrillo, September 28, 1542; the landing place of Sebastián Vizcaíno, who named the bay San Diego, in November 1602; and the former site of the Spanish coastal battery, Fort Guijarros, built in 1797.

The 81-acre National Monument, established in 1913, contains one of the first lighthouses on the Pacific coast, the San Diego Lighthouse, put into operation in 1855. A visitor center is planned that will contain exhibits relating to Spanish exploration and settlement.

6. Channel Islands National Monument, California

> *Location: Anacapa Island, 10 miles from the mainland, southwest of Port Hueneme; Santa Barbara Island, 38 miles from the mainland, southwest of Los Angeles; address, P.O. Box 6175, San Diego, Calif. 92106.*

The eight Channel Islands, from south to north, are San Clemente, Santa Catalina, San Nicolas, Santa Barbara, Anacapa, Santa Cruz, Santa Rosa, and San Miguel. Channel Islands National Monument includes the centrally located pair, Santa Barbara (650 acres) and Anacapa (700 acres). The prime aim of the National Park Service in these islands is to preserve and protect biological and geological phenomena for the benefit of the public. The islands, however, were among the first places visited and identified by the early Spanish explorers of the California coast. Juan Rodríguez Cabrillo, California's discoverer, died in 1543 on the island farthest northwest, San Miguel.

Santa Barbara and Anacapa Islands are undeveloped, having no permanent structures or accommodations of any kind. During summer months and on weekends throughout the year, boat service is available to Anacapa from Port Hueneme, Calif. A ranger is stationed on Anacapa during the summer. Boat service is not available to Santa Barbara, which has no ranger assigned. Both islands retain their pristine appearance, looking now just as they did when first seen by the Spanish more than 400 years ago.

7. Point Reyes National Seashore, California

> *Location: Marin County, on Calif. 1, about 35 miles northwest of San Francisco; address, Point Reyes, Calif. 94956.*

Point Reyes and Drakes Bay are mainly associated with the great Spanish

Drakes Bay, California, well known to Spanish explorers of the 16th and 17th centuries, may have been a landing place of the Englishman Sir Francis Drake in 1579 during his circumnavigation of the globe. It is now a part of Point Reyes National Seashore.

explorers of the Pacific coast during the 16th and 17th centuries, though Miwok Indians had lived for centuries before on the peninsula where Point Reyes is situated. Drakes Bay was then, as now, a harbor sheltered by Point Reyes from northerly winds but exposed to southern storms. Juan Rodríguez Cabrillo probably sighted the bay and the point in November of 1542. After attacking Spanish ships, Sir Francis Drake may have beached and repaired his vessel, the *Golden Hind*, at Point Reyes in 1579 before starting across the Pacific to complete the first English circumnavigation of the globe. On Point Reyes he may also have erected a temporary stone fort and taken possession of "Nova Albion" for Queen Elizabeth.

At Drakes Bay, in 1595, the Spanish explorer Sebastián Rodríguez Cermeño suffered the first recorded shipwreck in California waters when his Manila galleon, the *San Agustín*, was blown ashore near the mouth of Drakes Estero, which adjoins Drakes Bay. Archeologists have recovered from Indian mounds on the shores of the estero quantities of porcelain and iron spikes that almost surely came from the galleon. After 1 month's stay at Drakes Bay, which Cermeño called the Bay of San Francisco, he set out on a thorough exploration of the California coast.

In 1603, the Spanish explorer Sebastián Vizcaíno, coming north from Monterey, sailed into Drakes Bay, but did not land because of strong winds. He named the headland "Punta de los Reyes," or Point Reyes. The Spanish attempt to reach Monterey and Drakes Bay (at first called the Bay of San Francisco) by land led to the discovery of one of the best natural ports in the world. The Portolá expedition, traveling up the coast from San Diego in 1769, was actually seeking the ports of Monterey and the "Bay of San Francisco" (Drakes Bay) when it accidentally sighted for the first time the harbor that is now called San Francisco Bay.

Point Reyes National Seashore, authorized in 1962, will ultimately include Point Reyes and the 28 miles of beaches on Drakes Bay. These seashore areas are little changed since they were first sighted by the Spanish in 1542.

McClures Beach, Point Reyes National Seashore, California. Such seashore areas have changed little since first sighted by Spanish explorers in the 16th century.

Constructed in St. Augustine late in the 17th century by the Spanish, Castillo de San Marcos figured prominently in the Anglo-Spanish rivalry for control of the present Southeastern United States.

8. Castillo de San Marcos National Monument, Florida

Location: St. Johns County, St. Augustine; address, 1 Castillo Drive, St. Augustine, Fla. 32084.

This well-preserved fort figured prominently in the Spanish-English struggle for the present Southeastern United States during the 17th and 18th centuries. The Spanish began to construct it because of the English threat to Florida posed by the founding of Charleston, S.C., in 1670, only 2 years after the sack of St. Augustine by English pirates. As early as 1586, when Sir Francis Drake had raided St. Augustine, the English had shown their determination to destroy the Spanish monopoly in the New World.

Construction of the castillo began in 1672 and required almost 25 years. Spanish artisans and drafted Indian labor built substantial walls, 30 feet high and up to 12 feet thick, of the native shellstone called coquina, with mortar made from shell lime. The walls were built in a symmetrical design, in the style developed by Italian and Spanish engineers.

The castillo was well armed and manned, for the region was in turmoil. Spanish forays against the Carolinas and Georgia (1686, 1706, 1742) emanated from the castillo, which between 1683 and 1743 was also the target of six raids and sieges by pirates, Indians, and Englishmen. Though

England gained possession of Florida, including the castillo, at the end of the French and Indian War, in 1763, Spain regained control of Florida at the end of the War for American Independence and held it until the United States acquired it early in the 19th century. The U.S. Army renamed the castillo Fort Marion, and used it as a prison, Seminole and Southwestern Indians, among others, being imprisoned there.

During the Civil War, Confederate forces occupied the fort briefly before Federal troops assumed control in 1862. Ironically, its last military use—as a prison during the Spanish-American War (1898)—was against the nation that built it. Established in 1924 as a National Monument by Presidential proclamation, the fort was placed under the jurisdiction of the War Department, which in 1933 transferred it to the National Park Service. The original name was restored 9 years later.

9. De Soto National Memorial, Florida

Location: Manatee County, on Tampa Bay, 5 miles west of Bradenton; address, P.O. Box 1377, Bradenton, Fla. 33506.

This memorial commemorates De Soto's landing with a 600-man army in Florida on May 30, 1539. The exact site of the landing is not known, but it was probably between Tampa Bay and Estero Bay (Fort Myers). De Soto was the third Spaniard to lead an expedition into Florida. Ponce de León, as early as 1513, had accomplished some initial land and sea exploration. In 1528, Pánfilo de Narváez and 400 colonists had landed at Tampa Bay and marched overland to the vicinity of Apalachicola Bay, where they built small boats and sailed westward in the gulf.

De Soto's expedition is especially significant because—more than 60 years before the first permanent English settlement, at Jamestown—during the period 1539–43 it explored 4,000 miles of wilderness throughout the present Southeastern United States. Penetrating as far as Oklahoma and east Texas, it gained for Spain a broad and valuable knowledge of the interior lands and peoples. When De Soto died near the Mississippi River, his lieutenant, Luís de Moscoso, completed the exploration.

De Soto National Memorial was established in 1949. To commemorate the 400th anniversary of De Soto's landing, in 1939 the National Society of Colonial Dames of America erected the De Soto trail marker, located at Shaw's Point, which overlooks the mouth of the Manatee River.

10. Fort Caroline National Memorial, Florida

Location: Duval County, 10 miles east of Jacksonville, 5 miles north of Fla. 10; address, 1 Castillo Drive, St. Augustine, Fla. 32084.

This memorial commemorates a French attempt in 1564–65 to establish a colony in the present Southeastern United States, at a time when no other European colony existed in the present United States. By planting this colony, France hoped for a share of the New World, claimed by Spain. This French move forced Spain to act—by founding St. Augustine—and brought on the first decisive conflict between European powers within the area of the present United States. At Fort Caroline, the battle between France and Spain for supremacy in North America was joined.

The patron of the French colony was Adm. Gaspard de Coligny, a Huguenot who planned the colony at Fort Caroline as a haven for his persecuted coreligionists and as the basis for a French claim to counter that of Spain in the New World. In 1561, the Spanish King had forbade any further attempts by his subjects to colonize Florida because of the previous failures there and his lack of interest in the area. Thus, the time seemed ripe for the French. Following the failure of an earlier attempt at settlement, under Jean Ribaut in 1562 at Port Royal Sound, S.C., in June 1564 three vessels under the command of René de Laudonnière brought some 300 colonists, mostly Huguenots, from Havre de Grace to the St. Johns River. The colonists settled about 5 miles from the mouth of the river on a broad, flat knoll on the river shore in the midst of Timucua Indian country. With Indian help, they built a triangular fort of earth and logs that enclosed several palm-thatched buildings and named it Caroline in honor of King Charles IX. They built other houses in the meadow outside the fort. Vainly searching for gold and silver, they clashed with the Indians, upon whom they were dependent for food, and some even mutinied.

The French fort was a threat to Spanish commerce, for the Spanish treasure fleets had to sail past it on their return to Spain. It was also a potential base for attacks upon the Indies. The French asserted that it was their territory; the Spanish, that it was a pirates' nest on their land. In August 1565, Jean Ribaut brought reinforcements. Shortly thereafter, the Spaniard Pedro Menéndez de Avilés founded St. Augustine, captured and occupied Fort Caroline, killed almost all the Frenchmen, and renamed it San Mateo. In 1568, vengeful Frenchmen, who sailed from Bordeaux, with Indian allies they obtained in Florida, attacked and slaughtered most of the garrison.

The deepening of the St. Johns River in 1880 inundated the site of Fort Caroline. However, the carefully constructed replica of Fort Caroline at the National Memorial illustrates French defiance of a powerful enemy by establishing a colony on the edge of an unknown world.

11. Fort Matanzas National Monument, Florida

> *Location: St. Johns County, on Anastasia and Rattlesnake Islands, 14 miles south of St. Augustine on Fla. A1A (Ocean Shore Boulevard); accessible also by Intracoastal Waterway; address, 1 Castillo Drive, St. Augustine, Fla. 32084.*

The deciding scenes in the Spanish-French struggle for Florida, in 1565, occurred in the vicinity of Fort Matanzas National Monument, where Spain achieved potential control of the entire continent of North America and actual domination of the present Southeastern United States for nearly 200 years. During most of that period, Matanzas was a typical Florida military outpost, strategically important as a defense to the south entrance of St. Augustine, the capital of Spanish Florida.

The year after the French established Fort Caroline, in 1564, Pedro Menéndez de Avilés arrived under orders from the Spanish Crown to

Matanzas Tower, constructed by the Spanish in the years 1740–42 on the site of earlier fortifications, was a key defense of St. Augustine, capital of Spanish Florida.

drive the intruders out of Florida. He founded St. Augustine as his base of operations and seized Fort Caroline when the French commander, Jean Ribaut, and a party of some 558 who had set out from the fort to attack the Spanish were shipwrecked far south of St. Augustine. The party marched up the coast in two groups. Menéndez and about 40 men met the first group of about 208 when they were halted by their inability to cross the inlet south of Anastasia Island. Deploying his small force so that it appeared much larger, Menéndez persuaded the Frenchmen to surrender and put all but eight of them to the knife.

A week later the second group, numbering about 350, under Ribaut himself, arrived at the same place and were also met by Menéndez. Seeing evidence of the previous incident, about 200 Frenchmen fled south, but the Spanish finally captured most of them. Ribaut and the remainder surrendered, and all but 16 were promptly killed. Thus, the location was named *Matanzas,* meaning "slaughters."

Matanzas came to occupy a key position in the defenses of St. Augustine. By 1569, a blockhouse for 50 soldiers had been built. Later, a "sentinel house" was located at Matanzas, one of a system along the coast. A sentinel house consisted of a thatched palmetto hut, equipped with wooden watchtowers, which accommodated about six soldiers. When the soldiers at Matanzas sighted a ship, a runner carried the news to St. Augustine.

The present structure, called Matanzas Tower by the Spanish, was built after the English siege of Castillo de San Marcos in 1740 by Gen. James Oglethorpe, founder of Georgia. Construction on marshy little Rattlesnake Island, near the mouth of the Matanzas River, was difficult, but the tower was completed before the end of 1742 in spite of lack of royal support. The English garrisoned it during the period they held Florida, 1763–83, after which the Spanish reoccupied it. Spain, however, had little concern for her crumbling New World empire in the early 19th century, and the interior of the tower was already in ruins when Florida passed to the United States, in 1821.

Mantanzas Tower is still impressive although partially destroyed. It was designated as Fort Matanzas National Monument in 1924 by Presidential proclamation; and in 1933 transferred from the War Department to the National Park Service. A visitor center lies almost directly across from it on Anastasia Island. The monument area includes property on both sides of the inlet.

12. Fort Frederica National Monument, Georgia

Location: Glynn County, on St. Simons Island, via Brunswick-St. Simons Highway or inland waterway, 12 miles north of Brunswick; address, P.O. Box 816, St. Simons Island, Ga. 31522.

Fort Frederica was headquarters for Gen. James Oglethorpe's military operations against the Spanish in Florida during the War of Jenkins' Ear (1739–42), a part of the Anglo-Spanish struggle for control of the Southeastern part of the present United States. An old British fortification on St. Simons Island dating from the early days of Georgia history, the fort illustrates Britain's determination to hold this area of the coast—an area claimed by the Spanish, who were well entrenched at St. Augustine. Built in 1736 by a group of colonists led by Oglethorpe—who had first arrived in Georgia with a group of settlers in 1733 and founded Savannah—it was surrounded by a typical English village, the southernmost British settlement at the time. Two years later, troops from England and Gibraltar arrived.

The year after the founding of Fort Frederica, soldiers stationed at Fort Frederick, near present Port Royal, S.C., had been transferred to St. Simons Island, where they built an additional fortification, Fort St. Simons, or Delegal's Fort. The British built a series of other fortifications in the region, including Fort St. George, on Fort George Island, and Fort St. Andrew, on Cumberland Island. Fort Frederica was the headquarters and became the springboard for attack and base for defense against Spanish Florida.

Within a decade after the end of the War of Jenkins' Ear—during which Spain had futilely attacked Fort Frederica in a last attempt to gain the Georgia territory she had claimed for two-and-a-half centuries—the fort was practically abandoned. By 1756, the English had withdrawn the few soldiers stationed at the fort, removed many of the cannon and used them to fortify other parts of Georgia, and the town had fallen into ruins. Under the terms of the Treaty of Paris in 1763, which ended the French and Indian War, Britain acquired Florida and British-Spanish tensions eased in the region.

Archeological excavations at Fort Frederica National Monument have unearthed the long-buried foundations of many dwellings. Within the fort area, various buildings have been excavated, including the bastion towers and the barracks building as well as the town gate and the moat. Markers explain the excavations.

13. Ocmulgee National Monument, Georgia

Location: Bibb County, on U.S. 80 and 129, adjoining Macon; address, P.O. Box 4186, Macon, Ga. 31208.

Though this National Monument is noted chiefly for its prehistoric Indian remains, it also has close associations with the phases of history treated in this volume. An English trading post was established at this site about 1690. Soon thereafter a number of the important Creek Indian towns on the Chattahoochee River, no longer free to trade with the English because of Spanish interference, moved into the general vicinity of the English post. The people of one of these towns, Ocmulgee, settled adjacent to the post.

Archeological excavation has shown that the post consisted of several log buildings surrounded by a stockade of upright logs. The stockade had five sides. Access through the longest of these, 140 feet in length, was provided by two gates. Two of the other sides were 100 feet in length; and two, 50 feet.

The remains of a wide trail have also been found. This trail, which ran parallel to the longest wall of the stockade and extended some distance on either side of the post, was a section of the Lower Creek trading path. Crossing the present State of Georgia, the path ran along the fall line from Augusta to Columbus and was the main route followed by the English traders. It likely was used by Henry Woodward, who in 1685 opened the trade with the Creeks on the Chattahoochee, and by a Colonel Welch, who in 1698 initiated trade with the Chickasaw of northern Mississippi.

Both the trading path and the post at Ocmulgee played an important part in the expansion of English trade and in the struggle between the Spanish and the English for control of the Southeast. The combined English and Creek force that in 1702 destroyed Santa Fé, a Spanish mission in north-central Florida, probably set out from Ocmulgee, as did possibly the English and Creek war party that later in the year defeated the Spanish and Apalachee force on the Flint River.

Col. James Moore's army of 50 Carolinians and 1,000 Creeks, which in 1704 destroyed 5 of the Spanish missions in the province of Apalachee and captured more than 1,000 Apalachee Indians, formed at Ocmulgee.

The Creek war parties that destroyed two more Apalachee missions in June of that year were also likely from Ocmulgee. These campaigns forced the Spanish to abandon the province, which had supplied foodstuffs for both St. Augustine and Havana and served as a base for Spanish efforts to win over the Creeks.

The Ocmulgee trading post continued in existence until the Yamassee War (1715–17), when the Creeks, under "Emperor" Brim, killed off the traders scattered throughout their territory and attacked outlying settlements. They undoubtedly murdered the traders at Ocmulgee and destroyed the trading post. At the end of the war, the Creeks, fearing reprisal by the Carolinians, moved their towns back to the Chattahoochee River.

Ocmulgee National Monument preserves the remains of an unusual concentration of Indian villages. Excavation has indicated that the site was occupied by six successive Indian cultures, beginning about 8,000 B.C. and ending with the Creeks in A.D. 1717. Artifacts representative of all these cultures are displayed in the park's visitor center, which houses the largest archeological museum in the South. One earth lodge has been restored to appear as it did a thousand years ago, when the Indians used it and the seven mounds at the park for religious ceremonies. The outline of the trading post stockade is marked by horizontal logs.

14. Acadia National Park, Maine

> *Location: Hancock County; park headquarters at Bar Harbor, Mount Desert Island; address, P.O. Box 338, Bar Harbor, Maine 04609.*

La Cadie (Acadia) is a name derived from an Indian word meaning "the place," and was originally applied by the French to the North American coast from present Nova Scotia to New Jersey. In 1604, Pierre du Guast, Sieur de Monts, a Huguenot gentleman and soldier, undertook to establish Acadia as a New World dominion of France. Assisted by Samuel de Champlain, he founded a colony on an island in the St. Croix River; the settlers later relocated at Port Royal. Champlain then embarked upon further explorations and discovered Mount Desert Island, now in Acadia National Park. In 1613, this island became the site of the first French Jesuit mission in America, Saint Sauveur, on Fernald Point in Somes Sound. At this mission began the epic of French-English rivalry

In 1604, Samuel de Champlain, the famous French explorer, discovered and named Mount Desert Island, pictured here. In 1613, the island was the site of a Jesuit mission, but permanent occupation did not occur until just after the French and Indian War, when some New England colonists settled there.

in North America; a few weeks after its founding, Capt. Samuel Argall sailed up from Virginia and destroyed it.

For the next 150-years, the present Maine coast was a sort of no man's land. Sieur de la Mothe Cadillac, later founder of Detroit and Governor of Louisiana, owned Mount Desert Island in the late 1600's and may have resided for a time on its east shore. No permanent settlement was made there, however, until after the British victory over the French in 1763. At that time, groups from other parts of New England founded settlements. The island passed through the hands of many owners during the ensuing years: the Province of Massachusetts; Sir Francis Bernard, English Governor of the Province; Sir Francis' son; and Cadillac's granddaughter. Eventually, it was subdivided among the sturdy New Englanders who had earlier settled there and engaged in farming, lumbering, shipbuilding, and fishing.

The advent of steampower in the later 1800's resulted in drastic changes as steamboats began to bring in large numbers of summer visitors. Bar Harbor subsequently became synonymous with summertime among America's wealthier citizens. In 1916, a Presidential proclamation recognized the special scenic beauties of the area by creating Sieur de Monts National Monument; it was later called Lafayette National Park, the first National Park east of the Mississippi River. In 1929, the name was changed to Acadia. Primarily of interest for its marine scenery and its natural features, it is also historically noteworthy.

15. Salem Maritime National Historic Site, Massachusetts

Location: Essex County, Derby Street, Salem; address, Custom House, Derby Street, Salem, Mass. 01970.

Although Salem's maritime supremacy was of greater significance in later periods of history, particularly during the War for Independence, Salem has some important associations with the phases of history treated in this volume. Until the West was opened and began to yield to the pioneers after the War for Independence, most Americans lived within reach of the sea and naturally turned to it for adventure, a livelihood, and even riches. Indeed, the sea was the first frontier as well as the first highway. From the beginning, the colonists depended upon it for communication with the homeland and with other colonies.

Salem and other New England ports figured prominently in the colonial and early republican economy. Beginning soon in the 17th century, sailing vessels based at Salem plied the sealanes of the world, as they built the commerce upon which Yankee strength came to rest. Founded in 1626 by Roger Conant as the plantation of Naumkeag and established 2 years later as the first town in the Colony of Massachusetts Bay, Salem owed its prosperity to a seaboard location. From the very beginning, her colonists engaged in maritime pursuits; fishing and shipping were soon the leading industries. As early as 1643, fish, lumber, and provisions were being sent to the West Indies in exchange for sugar and molasses, staples that were brought home and made into rum. Gradually the orbit of trade was extended to Europe, for the most part to Portugal and Spain, which offered a ready market for dried fish and supplied salt, wine, fruit, iron, and Spanish dollars in return.

This trade and that with the West Indies—which after 1700 developed into the "triangular trade" between New England, the West Indies, and Africa—thrived until 1763, when the long struggle between France and England for the mastery of the American Continent finally came to an end and the English Government began to enact and enforce measures that stringently limited the commerce of the American colonies. Under these conditions, the economic life of Salem, like that of all ports along the Atlantic seaboard, came to a standstill and a discontent engendered that grew into resistance and eventually resulted in rebellion.

Designated a National Historic Site in 1938, Salem Maritime occupies an area of about 9 acres bordering on Salem Harbor. It preserves a group of structures and wharves that have survived from the period of the town's maritime greatness.

16. Grand Portage National Monument, Minnesota

Location: Cook County, on U.S. 61, about 38 miles northeast of Grand Marais and 49 miles southwest of the Canadian cities of Fort William and Port Arthur, Ontario; address, P.O. Box 666, Grand Marais, Minn. 55604.

This 9-mile portage route, connecting the Great Lakes with the interior network of waterways, was probably used by the Indians before the arrival of Europeans. The first recorded visit of a European was that of La Vérendrye, in 1731, who called it the Grand Portage and inferred that it was already well known by that name. From then until the French and Indian War, French traders pushed farther and farther into the Canadian Northwest, and practically all of the traffic passed over the Grand Portage. Voyageurs landed trade goods from large lake canoes at a post on the shore of Lake Superior and prepared them for portage to Pigeon River and conveyance into the interior in smaller canoes.

The period of most active use of Grand Portage was after 1783, when the famous North West Company was formed and some 20 years after the British had taken over Canada. The log stockade at Grand Portage was especially busy every July and August, when the brigades bringing goods from Montreal met the trappers and traders coming in from their posts scattered throughout the region. Employees received—and largely spent—their annual wages, and the company held its annual meeting.

The North West Company established Fort Charlotte where the portage came into Pigeon River, as well as a stockaded lake post that served as a central depot at Lake Superior. Other firms maintained rival posts in the vicinity, but their history is obscure. After 1803, when the North West Company established Fort William on the Kaministiquia, Grand Portage rapidly declined in importance. John Jacob Astor's American Fur Company built a post there after the War of 1812, which for a while was a central station in the Lake Superior fishing industry. Eventually proving unprofitable, it was abandoned, apparently in the 1840's.

In 1922, historians explored and mapped the portage route and discovered the remains of the principal posts. In 1936–37, the Minnesota Historical Society directed archeological work at Grand Portage, and the following year the stockaded lake post was reconstructed under the auspices of the Bureau of Indian Affairs, U.S. Department of the Interior. The National Monument was established in 1960 following conferences with the Minnesota Chippewa Tribal Council and the Grand Portage Band of the Chippewa Tribe, through whose reservation the route passes. Additional archeological investigation and restoration work was begun in 1962.

17. El Morro National Monument, New Mexico

Location: Valencia County, 42 miles west of Grants near N. Mex. 53; address, Ramah, N. Mex. 87321.

El Morro, the best-known inscription rock in the Southwest, is a massive, 200-foot-high pointed mesa of soft sandstone which, for more than three-and-a-half centuries, Spanish, Mexican, and American travelers used to record their visits. The ancient route that connected Acoma and the Rio Grande pueblos on the east with the Zuñi and Hopi pueblos on the west passed by. On the very top of the rock are ruins of Zuñi Indian pueblos that were abandoned long before the coming of the Spaniards. The rock was not only a conspicuous landmark, but its environs also provided a favorable camping and watering place in a dry region. Rain and melted snow from El Morro, which drained into a large natural basin below, provided a year-round supply of good water.

Fifteen years before the Pilgrims landed in Massachusetts, Don Juan de Oñate in 1605 etched the first identifiable Spanish inscription on El Morro. He was returning from his claimed discovery of the *mar del sur* (South Sea)—actually the Gulf of California. Coronado and other earlier Spanish explorers had almost certainly passed by El Morro, and in the 17th and 18th centuries many other important figures in the history of the Southwest inscribed their names. A number of these inscriptions can still be seen, notably that of Don Diego de Vargas, reconqueror of New Mexico. El Morro was also inscribed by the U.S. soldiers who occupied New Mexico in 1846; several years later by gold seekers and overland emigrants bound for California; and, in 1857, by members of Lt. Edward F. Beale's camel caravan.

This massive 200-foot-high mesa, El Morro, in New Mexico, is of archeological and historical interest. On its top, lie ruins of prehistoric Indian pueblos. The rock is covered with inscriptions, many of them carved by Western explorers and emigrants.

Established by Presidential proclamation in 1906, El Morro National Monument is about 2 square miles in area and lies at an elevation of more than 7,000 feet. Besides the inscriptions, Indian petroglyphs and partially excavated mesa-top Indian ruins are of interest.

18. Gran Quivira National Monument, New Mexico

Location: Torrance and Socorro Counties, off U.S. 60, on N. Mex. 10, about 26 miles south of Mountainair; address, Route 1, Mountainair, N. Mex. 87036.

The Mogollon Indian *Pueblo de las Humanas* (Gran Quivira) and two associated Spanish missions, all in ruins, are preserved in this National Monument, which commemorates 17th-century Spanish missionary activities among the Salinas pueblos of central New Mexico. Don Juan de Oñate, in 1598, was the first European known to have visited this pueblo, records of whose history are far from complete. About 1627 a missionary built a small church dedicated to San Isidro at the site, apparently a subsidiary to the mission of San Gregorio de Abó, 20 miles to the northwest.

Thirty years later another missionary enlarged the church facilities and rededicated them to San Buenaventura. His conversion efforts, however, did not flourish because the Indians, threatened by Apache raids, drought, famine, and pestilence, abandoned the pueblo sometime between 1672 and 1675. The survivors, and those from other villages of the area, moved to the Rio Grande Valley near Socorro to join their kinsmen or went down the valley to the El Paso area.

Ruins of San Buenaventura Mission, at Gran Quivira National Monument, New Mexico. These and other ruins at the site commemorate 17th-century Spanish missionary activities among the Salinas pueblos of central New Mexico.

Gran Quivira National Monument, embracing 611 acres, was established in 1909. The visitor center contains archeological and historical exhibits. From the center, a self-guided tour passes through the ruins of the old mission churches and the pueblo. Some of the ruins are completely excavated and some only partially. The tour demonstrates the evolution of pueblo life throughout many centuries, both before and after the coming of the Europeans.

19. Fort Raleigh National Historic Site, North Carolina

Location: Dare County, on N.C. 345, about 3 miles north of Manteo, on Roanoke Island; address, P.O. Box 457, Manteo, N.C. 27954.

Fort Raleigh National Historic Site, on Roanoke Island, is the scene of the earliest English colonizing attempts within the limits of the present United States and the birthplace of the first English child born in the New World, Virginia Dare, on August 18, 1587. Two attempts by Sir Walter Raleigh at settlement, in 1585–86 and 1587, failed because of supply problems and Indian attacks.

The first colony, originally consisting of 108 persons, was founded by Raleigh's cousin, Sir Richard Grenville. Settling on the north end of Roanoke Island in 1585, the colonists constructed dwellings and a fort and began to plant crops and explore the area, while Grenville returned to England for supplies. He left Ralph Lane in charge. The colony fared badly. Sir Francis Drake visited it in 1586 and took the survivors back to England. Soon afterward, Grenville returned and found the colony deserted. After searching along the coast, he left 15 men to hold the island for Queen Elizabeth and returned to England.

Restored earthen fort at Fort Raleigh National Historic Site, North Carolina. Late in the 16th century, in 1585–86 and 1587, Sir Walter Raleigh made two attempts to found a colony on Roanoke Island—the first English colonizing efforts within the present United States.

The second colony consisted of 150 settlers, who arrived at Roanoke Island in 1587, under the leadership of John White. Finding only desolation and the bones of one of Grenville's men, they began to rebuild the settlement. White returned to England for supplies, but found it in danger of an invasion by Spain. The Queen, refusing to spare a large ship, dispatched two small pinnaces to the colony, but they never reached it. When White returned to the colony in August of 1590, he found that the colonists had disappeared.

Fort Raleigh, designated a National Historic Site in 1941, consists of 144 acres. The fort, probably built by Lane, was investigated by archeologists in 1947–48 and restored in 1950. The village site, presumably close by, has not yet been located. At the Waterside Theater, the Roanoke Island Historical Association presents a noted pageant-drama, *Lost Colony* by the playwright Paul Green, during the summer months.

20. Fort Necessity National Battlefield, Pennsylvania

Location: Fayette County, on U.S. 40, about 11 miles east of Uniontown; address, Route 1, Box 311, Farmington, Pa. 15437.

At this battlefield, on July 3, 1754, occurred the opening engagement in the French and Indian War, a 7-year struggle between the French and English for control of the North American Continent. It was also George Washington's first major battle. French-English rivalry in the trans-

Reconstructed stockade at Fort Necessity National Battlefield, Pennsylvania. In 1754, at this battlefield French and English troops clashed in the first major battle of the French and Indian War, a long struggle for control of the North American Continent.

"Braddock's Retreat, July 9, 1755." Early in the French and Indian War, Gen. Edward Braddock sought to capture Fort Duquesne from the French. Wounded in the attempt, he died during his retreat. From a painting, in 1865, by Alonzo Chappel. Courtesy, Chicago Historical Society.

Allegheny territory approached a climax in the 1750's. In the spring of 1754, the British sent Lt. Col. George Washington and a small force from Virginia to contest French possession of the Forks of the Ohio, where the French had erected Fort Duquesne. After defeating a French scouting party at Great Meadows, Washington built a temporary fort there which he called "Fort Necessity." A battle ensued, after which the British were forced to surrender and then allowed to return to Virginia. The French destroyed Fort Necessity and returned to Fort Duquesne. By greater exertions later, however, the British won the war.

Fort Necessity National Battlefield became a part of the National Park System in 1933, and Fort Necessity State Park was transferred to it in 1962. The latter transfer added to the site sections of Great Meadows, where the 1754 battle was fought and part of which George Washington later owned. A stockade, storehouse, and entrenchments have been reconstructed on the exact site of the original structures. The site of Washington's skirmish with the French scouting party and the grave of Gen. Edward Braddock, commander in chief of the British forces in the Battle of Monongahela (1755), also may be seen.

21. Cape Henry Memorial (Colonial National Historical Park), Virginia

Location: Princess Anne County, on U.S. 60, about 10 miles east of Norfolk; address, Superintendent, Colonial National Historical Park, P.O. Box 210, Yorktown, Va. 23490.

Sea-weary English colonists, who were soon to found the first permanent English settlement in the New World, caught sight of Cape Henry, at the entrance to Chesapeake Bay, on April 26, 1607—their first view of Virginia. Having spent almost 5 months crammed aboard three tiny craft, they stopped off at Cape Henry for 4 days before proceeding up the James River to Jamestown, where they settled permanently.

The Cape Henry Memorial comprises a quarter acre, on which stands a memorial cross erected in 1935 by the National Society, Daughters of American Colonists, to mark the approximate site of the landing. It is completely surrounded by the Fort Story Military Reservation, of which it was formerly a part. The War Department transferred the memorial area to the Department of the Interior in 1939. The memorial is administered as part of Colonial National Historical Park, which also includes Jamestown, Yorktown Battlefield, and the Colonial Parkway.

No facilities or special services are available. Visitor passes are issued by military personnel at the entrance to the Fort Story Military Reservation. Religious and patriotic observances are held annually at the memorial, usually on the Sunday closest to April 26. These are sponsored by the Order of Cape Henry, 1607.

Nearby, and of special interest although not under National Park Service jurisdiction, is the old Cape Henry Light (1791), the first lighthouse erected by the Federal Government.

22. Jamestown Island (Colonial National Historical Park) and Jamestown National Historic Site (Non-Federal Ownership), Virginia

Location: James City County, 10 miles southwest of Williamsburg on the Colonial Parkway; address, Superintendent, Colonial National Historical Park, P.O. Box 210, Yorktown, Va. 23490.

At Jamestown Island, originally a peninsula, is commemorated the first permanent English settlement in America, in 1607. The first years at

Old Tower, in the foreground, believed to have been a part of a brick church begun in 1639, is the only standing ruin of 17th-century Jamestown, Virginia. Today it adjoins a memorial church, in the right rear background, erected in 1907 by the Colonial Dames of America on the foundations of the original church.

Jamestown were difficult for the settlers, who struggled constantly against sickness, starvation, and hostile Indians, and nine-tenths of them died. After 1699, when the seat of government was moved to Williamsburg, the settlement was virtually abandoned. About the time of the War for Independence, the isthmus connecting Jamestown with the mainland was washed out and the town ceased to exist.

In 1893, the Association for the Preservation of Virginia Antiquities acquired title to 22½ acres on Jamestown Island. In 1940, the Secretary of the Interior designated this acreage as Jamestown National Historic Site, under an agreement between the association and the Department of the Interior to provide for unified development of the whole island. Except for the association tract—now reduced to 20 acres because of donations to the park—the remainder of Jamestown Island is in Federal ownership. Visitors may take a walking tour and 3- and 5-mile driving tours of the island.

From a parking area, near the original townsite of Jamestown Island, a footbridge leads to the visitor center. From there, a walking tour extends over the townsite along the old streets and paths to the church, the statehouse sites, and the ruins of early houses, taverns, and shops. The visitor is guided along the way by various markers and recorded messages. In nearby Festival Park, the Commonwealth of Virginia maintains exhibits relating to the history of Jamestown.

23. San Juan National Historic Site, Puerto Rico

Location: City of San Juan; address, P.O. Box 712, San Juan, P.R. 00902.

The major Spanish defenses of Puerto Rico comprise the San Juan National Historic Site: the forts of El Morro, El Cañuelo, and San Cristóbal; La Casa Blanca (The White House); and the old city walls. They demonstrate Spanish power in the New World. Spain began constructing some of them in the 16th century; thus they are the oldest fortifications of European origin in present U.S. territory. Puerto Rico did not yield the gold the Spanish sought, but it served as an effective base for exploration and defense. Ponce de León established the first colony there, at Caparra, in 1509, and used it as a base from which he sailed to Florida. In 1521, the Spaniards founded San Juan, their first permanent colony in the present territory of the United States, and constructed mighty fortifications to protect their treasure fleets and new base.

La Casa Blanca was built in 1525 as a home for the Ponce de León family. Until 1779, the heirs owned it. In the early years, it was the only stronghold for protection of the townspeople against marauding Carib Indians and pirates. Located on the harbor side of San Juan Island, near historic San Juan Gate, it was the formal entrance to the city through the surrounding defensive wall, where Spanish colonial officials were ceremoniously greeted as they stepped ashore. Now occupied by the Commanding General of the Antilles Command, U.S. Army, it is not open to the public.

Castillo de San Felipe del Morro (Castle of St. Philip on the Headland) rises 140 feet above the sea at the west end of the island. Begun about 1539, it was the first authorized defensive work, but did not assume

Battery of El Morro, one of several forts preserved at San Juan National Historic Site, Puerto Rico. The Spanish constructed El Morro between 1539 and the late 1700's.

its present proportions until the late 1700's. On the landward side, beyond the moat, is a broad grassy slope. Behind the walls are storerooms, gunrooms, quarters, chapel, and prison. Huge cisterns lie beneath the spacious courtyard, from which ramps, tunnels, and stairways lead to the various parts of the complex. The windswept limestone ramparts that crown the headland were a familiar sight to seafaring men for centuries.

El Cañuelo, or San Juan de la Cruz (St. John of the Cross), is a 50-foot-square fort across the harbor entrance from El Morro. Its walls are about 15 feet high, and the flat roof provides a platform for cannon. The Spanish began construction about 1610, when 200 slaves were brought to San Juan and artisans arrived from Spain to work on the defenses.

Castillo de San Cristóbal looms grimly above the city of San Juan. Its construction began about 1633, and by 1678 it resembled its present aspect. As at El Morro, a courtyard, or *plaza de armas*, is surrounded by gunrooms and barracks. Tunnels lead up to a main gundeck. Highest of all is the Caballero de San Miguel, a massive, two-tiered gun platform 150 feet above the sea at the east end of the island.

The city wall still stands around much of the old town, including the harbor front between El Morro and La Fortaleza. Other impressive remains extend from El Morro to San Cristóbal, on the ocean front. Construction of the walls began in the 1630's and continued intermittently for more than 150 years. On the landward side, much of the wall was razed during the 1800's as the city expanded.

The fortifications of San Juan have a colorful history. In 1595, Sir Francis Drake was lured to San Juan to capture 35 tons of precious metal, awaiting shipment to Spain. His 23 ships and army of 3,000 men faced 1,500 Spaniards with 100 cannon behind the partially developed defenses. Beaten off, Drake sailed for Panama and soon died of fever. Three years later George Clifford, Earl of Cumberland, succeeded with a land attack. After a 2-week siege, Cumberland's standard rose over El Morro on June 21, 1598. Dysentery then accomplished what the Spaniards could not. Though forced to leave, the invaders tore down the land wall of El Morro and carried off 80 Spanish cannon.

In 1625, a Dutch fleet under Gen. Bowdoin Hendrick suffered little damage from El Morro's guns. After seizing the other fortifications, the Dutch threw a blockade around El Morro and began an artillery duel. But 38 days after they entered the harbor they were driven away. In 1797, the strengthened defenses of San Juan were again successful, against a much greater threat, when a British fleet of 60 vessels, bearing an army of 7,000 men, launched an attack. Gen. Ramón de Castro's defense of the eastern part of the city held firm; the Spaniards won the ensuing artillery duel and successfully counterattacked.

Adm. William Sampson, U.S. Navy, engaged the modernized batteries of San Juan with his flotilla for 2½ hours on May 12, 1898, during the Spanish-American War, but neither side suffered much damage. U.S. forces landed on the southern side of Puerto Rico, but before they reached San Juan an armistice had been signed. Spain's long rule over the island, including the fortifications that now comprise San Juan National Historic Site, came to an end in 1898, when the United States acquired it.

The National Historic Site was established in 1949, but the U.S. Army uses the forts under a cooperative agreement between the Department of the Interior and the Department of the Army. Regulated public access is permitted, under the supervision of the National Park Service.

24. Christiansted National Historic Site, Virgin Islands

Location: City of Christiansted, St. Croix Island, Virgin Islands; address, Superintendent, Virgin Islands National Park, P.O. Box 1707, Charlotte Amalie, St. Thomas, V.I. 00802.

This site includes approximately three city blocks, comprising 7½ acres, on the Christiansted waterfront, including Fort Christiansvaern, the Old Danish Post Office, Old Danish Customhouse, Steeple Building, and Government House. It commemorates the discovery of America, the European struggle for colonial empire, and especially the development of the Virgin Islands under the Danes. Seven flags have flown over Christiansted, the capital of the Danish West Indies when "sugar was king."

St. Croix Island is the first territory now under the flag of the United States to have been discovered by Columbus—on November 14, 1493, during his second voyage to the New World. Columbus named the island Santa Cruz (Holy Cross), which was inhabited by fierce Indians and unattractive to colonists during the 16th and early 17th centuries. During the period 1625–50, French freebooters and Dutch and English settlers apparently lived on the island at various times. In 1650, however, a Spanish expedition from Puerto Rico drove out all Europeans, only to be expelled itself several months later by a French force from St. Kitts Island.

Harbor and wharf of Christiansted, on St. Croix Island, Virgin Islands, probably in the first half of the 19th century. From a lithograph by an unknown artist.

The French, who called the island St. Croix, sold it in 1651 to the Knights of Malta, a private religious-military order. They later regained possession of it as a crown colony, but about 1696 the King transferred the French population, which consisted of 147 white settlers and 623 slaves, to Haiti. The island remained largely uninhabited until 1733, when the Danish West India and Guinea Company, which for some years had held neighboring St. Thomas and St. John Islands, purchased it.

Although earlier efforts had been made by other European nations to colonize St. Croix, under the Danes St. Croix boomed. It became a major sugar producer, bound to both Europe and America by close commercial, social, and cultural ties. By 1755, the population had reached 10,200, including 9,000 slaves. Some cotton was grown, but sugar was the principal crop. Despite the prosperity of the colonists, the company was almost bankrupt by 1755, and gladly sold out to the Danish King, under whose rule the three islands remained until the United States purchased them for $25 million in 1917.

Sugar production increased from $1\frac{1}{2}$ million pounds in 1755 to 46 million pounds in 1812, during a period when the Danish West Indies were near the economic center of gravity of the New World, among the "Fabulous Sugar Islands," as the Lesser Antilles were known. Their importance during the latter 18th century is difficult to conceive today. In such a stimulating environment, Alexander Hamilton, one of the Founding Fathers of the United States, lived during his youthful years. He worked for a Christiansted merchant during the period 1766–72.

Fort Christiansvaern, the first public building in Danish Christiansted, was originally the residence of the Governor. Little is known of the history of the Old Danish Customhouse, apparently erected between 1779 and 1815, and the Old Danish Post Office. The Steeple Building was the first church to be erected by the Danes, who started construction in 1750 and 3 years later first put the building to use. A conspicuous feature of Christiansted harbor today, it is an unusual representative of Danish colonial architecture. Built of rubble-masonry, it is one story high, and the four-tiered steeple is 77 feet high. John Wilhelm Schopen, a merchant and official of the Danish West India and Guinea Company, built the present Government House as his home. It has been renovated and enlarged over the years since then, and now consists of three floors, which total about 37,200 square feet. On the second floor is a ballroom about 98 by 22 feet. Most of the period furnishings in the building are the gift of the Danish Government.

Christiansted National Historic Site is administered by the National Park Service in cooperation with the Government of the Virgin Islands.

25. Virgin Islands National Park, Virgin Islands

Location: St. John Island, Virgin Islands; address, P.O. Box 1707, Charlotte Amalie, St. Thomas, V.I. 00802.

This park consists of about two-thirds of St. John Island, the most beautiful and least disturbed of the three major American Virgin Islands. A veritable island paradise, St. John is of interest chiefly because of its unique natural wonders. However, its history, as well as that of the islands, is also absorbing. Columbus discovered the islands in 1493, on his second voyage to the New World, and named them in honor of Saint Ursula and her 11,000 virgins. In the years that followed, Dutch, English, Spanish, French, and Danish adventurers came to the islands. The Danes first arrived in the 1670's, but did not found a permanent colony on St. John until 1717. Before long, the settlers took over all the land on the island that could support the cultivation of sugar and cotton, and imported slaves. Slave unrest often disturbed the peace, however, until the King of

St. John Island, about two-thirds of which comprises Virgin Islands National Park, has unique natural beauty. Although discovered by Columbus in 1493, it was not colonized until the first part of the 18th century.

Denmark abolished slavery in 1848, a move that helped bring about the end of the plantations, many of whose ruins may still be seen in the park.

The United States acquired St. John, along with the other Danish Virgin Islands, from Denmark in 1917. In 1956, Congress authorized the establishment of the park, which was dedicated on December 1, 1956, when Jackson Hole Preserve, Inc., of which Laurance Rockefeller is president, presented more than 5,000 acres of the original parkland to the people of the United States. The population of less than 1,000 that remains on the island is concentrated in the Cruz Bay and Coral Bay areas outside the park. Scheduled boat service is available at Red Hook Landing, St. Thomas Island, for the 30-minute passage to the park entrance at Cruz Bay, St. John Island.

B. National Historic Sites in Non-Federal Ownership

A few National Historic Sites in non-Federal ownership are located throughout the United States. These are not units of the National Park System but, as authorized by the Historic Sites Act of 1935, are administered under the provisions of cooperative agreements by the owners with the Department of the Interior. The owners agree to maintain the property in a manner consistent with good preservation practices, for which purpose they may receive assistance from the National Park Service as provided in the agreements. The Park Service provides bronze plaques for the sites. The following sites illustrate the phases of history treated in this volume.

1. Chicago Portage National Historic Site, Illinois

Location: Cook County, Old Chicago Portage Forest Preserve, junction of Portage Creek with Des Plaines River, just west of Harlem Avenue on the line of 47th Street.

Chicago owes its very existence to its strategic location on the Chicago-Illinois River route, one of the natural arteries leading from the St. Lawrence River system to the Mississippi. The portage at Chicago was discovered in September 1673 by Père Jacques Marquette and Louis Jolliet as they returned from their voyage of exploration down the Mississippi River. Marquette, in failing health, spent the winter of 1674–75 near the portage, and passed over it on other trips, as did also René

Site of Chicago, in 1820. The second Fort Dearborn, built in 1816, is situated to the left of the main river channel. From a lithograph by J. Gemmel, published by D. Fabronius, probably in 1857. Courtesy, Chicago Historical Society.

Robert Cavelier, Sieur de la Salle, Henry de Tonty, and many other Frenchmen until about 1700, when Indian hostility kept Europeans out of the area. The Indians continued to use the portage extensively.

During the French and Indian War and the War for Independence, the portage resumed its important position in non-Indian travel and commerce. In the Treaty of Greenville (1795), the Indians ceded to the United States "a piece of Land Six Miles Square, at the mouth of Chickago River, emptying into the southwest end of Lake Michigan, where a fort formerly stood." In 1803, U.S. soldiers erected the first Fort Dearborn at the river's mouth, and trade continued to be extensive until the beginning of the War of 1812, when the residents of the fort abandoned it. They began the trip to Fort Wayne, but before they had gone 2 miles Potawatomi Indians murdered most of them and then set fire to the fort.

In 1816, soldiers constructed the second Fort Dearborn, and trade again resumed over the portage. It diminished in importance, however, as the Illinois fur trade declined, though it continued to have commercial value into the 1830's. Work began in 1836 on the Illinois and Michigan Canal—finished in 1848—which followed the water-and-portage route, as does the present Sanitary and Ship Canal.

The western end of the Chicago portage route, where Marquette and Jolliet landed, is located in the Old Chicago Portage Forest Preserve, which is managed by the Forest Preserve District of Cook County, Ill. At the eastern end of the portage route, on the north end of Grant Park, are the sites of the two Fort Dearborns. In 1952, a cooperative agreement between the Cook County Forest Preserve District and the Department of the Interior authorized the designation of Chicago Portage as a National Historic Site.

2. Gloria Dei (Old Swedes') Church National Historic Site, Pennsylvania

Location: Philadelphia County, Delaware Avenue near Christian Street, South Philadelphia.

Only 8 years after the Swedes established the first European settlements along the banks of the Delaware River, a group of colonists at Wicaco, now South Philadelphia, began to use a small log blockhouse, originally utilized for defense against the Indians, as a mission of the state church of Sweden. In 1700, they built the present Gloria Dei, or Old Swedes', Church, on the same site.

Gloria Dei (Old Swedes') Church, constructed in 1700 by Swedish settlers, is the oldest church in Philadelphia. It is still an active church.

One of the finest public buildings and the oldest church in Philadelphia, it is an ivy-covered, red-brick building in Flemish and common bond and has glazed headers. The only touches of Swedish architecture are a steep-peaked gable over the main entrance, a square belfry, and a small spire. Some of the interior embellishments were brought from Sweden by the settlers. These include a stone baptismal font near the pulpit and a cherubim figurehead, once a decoration on the prow of a Swedish ship, which hangs below the organ loft. The church also contains many relics and documents pertaining to the English colonial and War for Independence periods.

In 1789, the church separated from the mother church in Sweden, and in 1845 was admitted into the Convention of the Protestant Episcopal Church of the Diocese of Pennsylvania. Still an active religious center, as well as an important historic site, in 1942 it was declared a National Historic Site.

3. San José Mission National Historic Site, Texas

> *Location: Bexar County, on U.S. 281, about 4 miles south of San Antonio.*

One of the finest surviving Spanish missions in North America, San José was one of a series of frontier missions that stretched across the Southwestern part of the present United States in the 17th and 18th centuries. It was named San José y San Miguel de Aguayo Mission when it was founded in 1720, at the instigation of the Franciscan Fray Antonio Margíl de Jesus, one of the greatest of the Spanish missionaries on the northern frontier of New Spain. Margíl was responsible for establishing the earlier east Texas missions of Dolores, Guadalupe, and San Miguel—all of which Spanish officials closed in 1720 because of fear of French aggression from Louisiana.

San José Mission grew rapidly and steadily, the first temporary adobe structures being replaced by stone buildings. By the middle of the 18th century, it was one of the most flourishing on the northern frontier. More than 200 Indian convert residents cared for 2,000 head of cattle and 1,000 sheep and produced 3,000 bushels of corn annually. When the Franciscans departed from the mission, after the civil authorities secularized it in 1794, diocesan priests (the secular clergy) presided until the Franciscans returned again, in 1931. The dome and roof of the central

Main entrance to San José Mission, Texas. Founded in 1720 by Fray Antonio Margíl de Jesus, the mission is a fine example of an 18th-century Spanish mission in the Southwestern United States.

Cloisters of San José Mission, Texas.

building had meanwhile caved in, and vandalism and neglect resulted in other damage. In 1912, the Catholic Church initiated a restoration program, to which the people of San Antonio contributed generously.

Grinding room in the old grist mill overlooking San José Mission, Texas.

During the period 1934–37, the program was intensified and the church was restored and rededicated to religious uses. In 1930, the San Antonio Conservation Society had bought the ruins of the granary from the descendants of Pedro Huizar, the artist responsible for the famous rose window and facade.

The entire San José Mission property was designated a National Historic Site in 1941, under an agreement with the Texas State Parks Board and the Archbishop of San Antonio, who administer the property in cooperation with the National Park Service. A special advisory board for the site provides advice on matters of preservation, development, and general administration. It is composed of representatives from the U.S. Department of the Interior, the Texas State Parks Board, the Archbishopric of San Antonio, the County of Bexar, and the San Antonio Conservation Society.

C. Sites Eligible for the Registry of National Historic Landmarks

Most of the historic sites in this group have been judged by the Advisory Board on National Parks, Historic Sites, Buildings, and Monuments to meet the criteria of "exceptional value" for commemorating or illustrating the phases of U.S. history treated in this volume. A few, however, which have primary associations with other phases of history, have been included in this section and the "Other Sites Considered" section because of their secondary or peripheral associations with the period treated in this volume. As historic sites of national importance, all of them have been declared by the Secretary of the Interior to be eligible for inclusion in the Registry of National Historic Landmarks. Some have already been designated Registered National Historic Landmarks, and others will receive the designation upon application of the owners. A few have been proposed for addition to the National Park System.

1. Apalachicola Fort, Alabama

Location. Russell County, on the west bank of the Chattahoochee River, near Holy Trinity.

Ownership and Administration. Privately owned.

Significance. The northernmost Spanish outpost on the Chattahoochee River, this fort was built by the Spanish about 1689 in an attempt to prevent the English from gaining a foothold among the Lower Creek Indians. It was a key Spanish outpost in the imperial struggle to control the Indians in the present Southeastern United States.

Beginning in 1675, Spanish missionaries attempted to convert the

Lower Creeks along the Chattahoochee, but they were unsuccessful. When the Indians came under the influence of English traders 10 years later, the Spanish retaliated with punitive raids. Despite the burning of several Lower Creek towns and the construction of Apalachicola Fort in the heart of the Indian territory, the Spaniards failed to gain control over the tribe.

The Lower Creeks moved many of their towns to the Ocmulgee and Oconee Rivers in present Georgia to be nearer the English. Aided and led by the English, the Creeks destroyed many of the Spanish missions among the Timucua Indians and seriously threatened even St. Augustine. The Spanish abandoned and destroyed Apalachicola Fort in 1691 because of the English threat.

The palisade of the fort was rectangular, roughly 61 by 53 feet, and had corner bastions. It was constructed of wattle and daub and reinforced by an exterior half-wall of clay. A moat surrounded the palisade. Limited archeological excavations at the site, conducted by the Smithsonian Institution and the University of Alabama, have uncovered evidence of the fort which agrees with the historical records. Majolica sherds and olive jar fragments, of Spanish origin and correct time period, were found.

Present Appearance. The site, on the margin of the Walter F. George Reservoir, is well preserved; the line of the moat is clearly visible. The land is now utilized for pasture.[1]

2. Fort Toulouse (Fort Jackson), Alabama

Location. Elmore County, at the junction of the Coosa and Tallapoosa Rivers, on a gravel road, 4 miles southwest of Wetumpka.

Ownership and Administration. State of Alabama; Department of Conservation.

Significance. From its construction in 1717 until the end of the French and Indian War, in 1763, this fort was the offensive-defensive eastern outpost of French Louisiana. Situated just below the southern tip of the Appalachian Highland, at the junction of the two main tributaries of the Alabama River, it protected the French settlements from Mobile Bay westward to New Orleans. It was also the spearhead of the French drive to wrest control of the present Southeastern United States from the Spanish and English. In 1814, after defeating the Creek Indians at Horseshoe

Bend, Andrew Jackson occupied the abandoned site. He constructed a new fort at the location of the old one and named it Fort Jackson, in August 1814 the scene of the treaty that officially ended the Creek War.

Present Appearance. The Coosa and Tallapoosa Rivers follow nearly parallel courses for some distance above their junction, and form a narrow peninsula a mile long and only a few hundred yards wide. A privately owned tract that extends upstream from the junction includes the site of an ancient Indian village, where one large mound is discernible and the ground is liberally sprinkled with sherds. East of this tract is the 6-acre Fort Toulouse tract, owned by the State.

Adjoining the tract on the south and east is private property containing the Isaac Ross Cemetery, which dates from at least the War of 1812. In 1897, about 200 bodies were removed from this cemetery to the national cemetery in Mobile. Most of them were the remains of men who had been assigned to Andrew Jackson's army, but some of them may have been Frenchmen. Amateur archeologists have carried on excavations at the Indian village site, but not at the State-owned Fort Toulouse tract. The fort area includes two monuments and the remains of what appears to have been a powder magazine.[2]

3. Awatovi, Arizona

Location. Navajo County, on the southern tip of Antelope Mesa, about 8 miles south of Keams Canyon.

Ownership and Administration. Hopi Indians.

Significance. Awatovi was the first of the Hopi villages to be visited by the Spanish and the first to capitulate. Then one of the largest and most important of the villages, it had been in existence for about 450 years. The first European visitor, in 1540, was Pedro de Tovar, whom Coronado dispatched to the Hopi villages a week after the capture of Hawikuh. A skirmish occurred when Tovar arrived, but the inhabitants quickly sued for peace and offered presents of cloth, skins, turquoise, and maize. The five remaining pueblos then offered fealty to the King of Spain. Tovar returned to Hawikuh and reported to Coronado what the Hopis had told him of a great river to the west where giants lived. Coronado immediately sent out a party under García López de Cárdenas, whom the Hopis provided with supplies and guides. The party visited the Colorado River, but found no giants.

The Spanish did not visit Tusayan (Hopiland) again until 1583, when the Antonio de Espejo expedition spent several days at the Hopi villages before turning southwest to the Verde Valley. Don Juan de Oñate, in

1598, found the Hopis ready to capitulate formally to the King of Spain. Oñate visited the pueblos again in 1605, and Capt. Gerónimo Márquez in 1614, but not until 1629 did the Spanish make any substantial missionary effort among the Hopis.

From then until the Pueblo rebellion of 1680, during which time Awatovi was under Franciscan tutelage, it had little contact with the Spanish military and no direct contact with Spanish settlements. The Hopis expected reprisals for participating in the 1680 rebellion, but none came. When Diego de Vargas, the reconqueror, arrived in 1692, the Hopis reswore their allegiance to Spain, and he departed without incident.

In 1699, the Christian faction among the Hopis, probably residents of Awatovi, sent a delegation to Santa Fe to ask for missionaries. They offered to rebuild their mission. Three Spanish priests then made a brief visit to Awatovi. They reported that most of the Hopis were hostile and would not listen to them, and they also recommended that a garrison be posted at Awatovi to protect the Christian Indians from the other Hopis. Soon thereafter, Fray Juan de Garaycoechéa was well received at Awatovi and baptized 73 children. He was induced not to try to visit the other villages, however, and Awatovi's reception of him marked its doom. Near the end of 1700, the other Hopis sacked and destroyed the pueblo, killed all the men, and redistributed the women and children among the other villages. The site was never reoccupied.

Present Appearance. Little remains today of the three church structures except parts of the friary associated with the second church, built of sandstone, which are visible, as are parts of the sandstone masonry pueblo. Dr. J. O. Brew, of the Peabody Museum, Harvard University, excavated the site between 1935 and 1939. He uncovered a large amount of aboriginal material—such as pottery and stone and bone artifacts—but only a few fragments of porcelain, metal, or other Spanish materials. The fields and gardens near Awatovi are cultivated today by the descendants of the women and children who survived the destruction of the village in 1700. They live at the First and Second Mesa pueblos.[3]

4. San Xavier del Bac Mission, Arizona

Location. Pima County, 2 miles west of U.S. 89, about 9 miles south of Tucson.

Ownership and Administration. Roman Catholic Church.

Significance. This is one of the finest surviving examples of Spanish mission architecture. The farthest north of the 24 Spanish missions of

San Xavier del Bac Mission, near Tucson, Arizona. Padre Francisco Kino founded the mission in 1700, but Apaches later destroyed it. In 1797, Franciscans erected the present structure, an excellent example of Spanish Renaissance architecture.

Pimería Alta, it commemorates the missionary activities of the famous Jesuit padre, Eusebio Francisco Kino, its founder. In 1700, Kino established the mission, for the Papago Indians, on a site about 2 miles from the present structure. After his death, in 1711, missionary work in most of Pimería Alta was sporadic because of a shortage of priests, but the Jesuits continued their work until the Pima Rebellion of 1751. After the Spanish Government founded the presidio at Tubac in 1752, the missionaries returned. In 1762, a number of Sobaipuri Indians, who had abandoned the San Pedro Valley to the Apaches, came to San Xavier for refuge.

In 1767, the Spanish Crown expelled all Jesuits from the missionary field. Franciscans then carried on the mission work in Pimería Alta, but soon after they occupied San Xavier the Apaches destroyed it. The Franciscans promptly began rebuilding the mission in its present location and consecrated it in 1797. In 1813, the Spanish secularized it. A decade later, when the Mexican regime took over, the few remaining padres abandoned it. In 1857, the Franciscans reoccupied it, after the lands south of the Gila River had passed to the United States under the terms of the Gadsden Purchase (1853). Early in the present century, the Catholic Church began restoration and followed the old plans to a large extent, except in the atrium and dormitories. San Xavier is still an active parish church, attended mainly by Papago Indians.

Present Appearance. San Xavier is distinguished architecturally and artistically. The well-preserved buildings are constructed of burned adobe brick and lime plaster, in Spanish Renaissance architectural style. This style is typified by the lavish baroque churches of Mexico, of which San Xavier is the only example within the United States.[4]

5. Carmel Mission, California

Location. Monterey County, Rio Road, Carmel.

Ownership and Administration. Roman Catholic Church.

Significance. Mission San Carlos de Borroméo, or Carmel Mission, was the most important of the California missions from an ecclesiastical standpoint. It was the headquarters of the two great Franciscan padres, Junípero Serra and Fermín Francisco de Lasuén, under whose guidance

Misión del Carmelo de Monterey

Mission San Carlos de Borroméo (Carmel Mission), in 1791, before construction of the present church. This mission served as headquarters of Fathers Serra and Lasuén, who founded 18 of the 21 California missions. From a drawing by José Cardero. Courtesy, Bancroft Library.

and inspiration 18 of the 21 California missions were established. Records for the missions and a library of 2,500 volumes were housed at Carmel, which served as a personnel and supply center for the founding of new missions and the strengthening of old ones. Both Serra and Lasuén are buried at the mission.

Father Serra founded Carmel Mission on June 3, 1770, at the Presidio of Monterey, as the second mission in California. In December 1771, he relocated it at the present site, 3 miles south of Monterey, to remove his Indian neophytes from the corrupting influence of the presidial garrison. Serra and his devoted companion, Father Crespi, who were based at the mission for the remainder of their lives, served not only the local area but also the other California missions. As father-president, Serra was responsible for establishing nine missions, all of which he visited frequently to provide encouragement and counsel. Ascetic, humble, and meek, yet a vigorous fighter in defense of the religious as against the political order, he rightfully earned the title of spiritual father of California.

When Serra died, in 1784, Father Lasuén succeeded him and ably continued his work. Lasuén was not only tactful in dealing with political and military authorities, but he was also a builder of architecturally sound missions. Before he died, in 1803, he founded nine missions in California. In 1793, he laid the foundations of the present Carmel Mission church, which was built of sandstone from the slopes of Carmel

Modern view of Carmel Mission, built between 1793 and 1797. A feature of its ornate facade is the star-shaped Moorish window.

Valley and lime manufactured from abalone shells. The finished church was dedicated in 1797, when the mission had a record number of Indian neophytes, 927. A decline followed, marked in part by the transfer of California mission headquarters to Santa Barbara after Lasuén's death. The number of neophytes was down to 381 in 1820 and 150 by 1834, when the Mexican Government secularized the mission.   By 1846, when Governor Pico offered the church for sale, it was almost totally destroyed, and the other buildings were also in ruins. In 1852, the church roof collapsed, and the tiles were carried off to be used in other structures.

Present Appearance. In 1859, the United States, which had acquired the mission as part of the Gadsden Purchase (1853), returned it to the Catholic Church. A new roof was built over what remained of the 1797 church, and in 1884 the structure was rededicated as a church. Full restoration of the mission, which began in the 1920's, was at first pursued with more zeal than historical precision. Since 1933, however, the work has continued on the basis of more careful research and the use of native building materials.

The facade and portions of the stone walls of the church are original. The remainder of the structure and all the other buildings are reconstructions. The most distinctive design feature is the ornate facade, which has a slightly irregular and star-shaped window of Moorish design. The church is furnished with the ancient stone font, where the Indians were baptized, as well as original paintings and statues that were returned to the building as part of the reconstruction program. Before the altar are situated the graves of Fathers Serra, Crespi, and Lasuén.[5]

6. Fort Ross, California

Location. Sonoma County, near the town of Fort Ross.

Ownership and Administration. State of California; Division of Beaches and Parks.

Significance. Fort Ross was established by the Russian-American Fur Company in 1812 for the threefold purpose of exploiting the rich fur hunting grounds of the California coast, opening trade with Spanish California, and providing an agricultural depot to supply Russian settlements in Alaska. Ivan Kuskoff, who began the construction, arrived in the spring of 1812 with 95 Russians and about 80 Aleuts. By

Commandant's House, at Fort Ross, California. Established in 1812 by the Russian-American Fur Company, Fort Ross supplied Russia's settlements in Alaska with farm produce and was a center for Russian-Spanish trade.

fall, enough progress had been made so that the fort was officially dedicated, although it was not completed until 1814.

The fort was built near the ocean on a plateau, about 1 square mile in extent, which terminates at the ocean in a precipice about 70 feet high. Redwood was used for all construction, including the stockaded walls, which measured 12 feet high. The quadrangular enclosure measured about 276 by 312 feet. Two hexagonal-shaped, two-story blockhouses at diagonally opposite corners of the stockade defended the walls. Eight cannons were mounted in 1812, and the number increased to about 50 by 1841, when more than 50 structures had been built.

Inside the walls were the commandant's house, officers' quarters, barracks for the Russian employees, a chapel, and 3 storehouses and offices; outside the wall were 37 redwood huts for the Aleuts, a windmill, farm buildings, granaries, cattle yards, a tannery, and workshops for blacksmiths, coopers, bakers, and carpenters. The population of the post, including Russians, Aleuts, and California Indians, never exceeded 400.

Fort Ross was not successful as an agricultural colony. Level land in the immediate neighborhood was scarce and not particularly fertile.

Also, the prevalent coastal fog caused the grain to rust, and rodents caused much crop damage. Farming was carried on rather ineffectively both by private individuals and by the fur company. Not until 1826 were any considerable shipments of grain made to Sitka, only 216,000 pounds being forwarded during the period 1826–33.

In 1833 the company opened a new farming center, Slavianka, near the mouth of the Russian River, midway between Fort Ross and the Russian port at Bodega Bay. The new establishment had uneven success—good at first, but disappointing between 1835 and 1840. The Russians obtained animals from the Spanish for stockraising, in which they had some success. At first, because of the scarcity of pasturage around Fort Ross, the cattle strayed over the forested mountain ranges half of the year, where many fell prey to bears and Indians.

To improve livestock management, in 1833 the company established two small ranches south of Fort Ross. The first, called the Kostromitinof Ranch, was located just south of the mouth of the Russian River and consisted of about 100 acres; the second, the Tschernick, or Gorgy's, Ranch, was about 5 miles north of Bodega Bay, at Russian Gulch. The latter also included a vineyard and some fruit trees. In the last 15 years of the fort's existence under Russian management, the managers exported some 216,000 pounds of salt beef and 18,000 pounds of butter to Sitka, as well as considerable quantities of excellent tanned leather.

As time went on, the Russian company decided to abandon its operation. In 1839, because of the great excess of costs over revenue in maintaining the fort, the company leased the southern coastal strip of southeastern Alaska to the Hudson's Bay Company, which agreed to

Russian Greek Orthodox Chapel, built about 1828, is one of several restored buildings at Fort Ross, California.

furnish the Russian Alaskan settlements with agricultural commodities produced on its Columbia River farms. In 1841, John A. Sutter purchased Fort Ross for $30,000 in cash and a specified amount of agricultural products over the succeeding 4 years. The last Russians withdrew in January 1842.

In addition to illustrating Russian activities in North America, Fort Ross exemplifies the threat of foreign intrusions into America that produced the Monroe Doctrine (1823) and heightened colonial activity on the part of certain European powers, notably the British.

Present Appearance. In 1906, the California Landmarks League donated 3.01 acres of the fort site and the Russian Chapel to the State. In 1928, Fort Ross was assigned to the Division of Beaches and Parks as a State Historical Monument, and since then has been gradually restored. The chapel, commandant's house, and part of one blockhouse—all of which were still standing in 1906—have been carefully restored, and a second blockhouse and the stockade reconstructed.[6]

7. Old Mission Dam (Padre Dam), California

Location. San Diego County, in Mission Gorge, just north of U.S. 80, 13 miles northeast of Old Town, San Diego.

Ownership and Administration. City of San Diego.

Significance. Old Mission Dam, whose associated aqueduct and flume extended about 5 miles to the Mission of San Diego de Alcalá, was one of the first major irrigation engineering projects on the Pacific coast of the United States. It impounded water from the San Diego River, and for much of the year provided an assured supply, which was released as needed for agricultural and domestic purposes.

San Diego de Alcalá Mission, founded by Father Junípero Serra July 16, 1769, on Presidio Hill, was the first of the 21 California missions. In 1774, Serra moved the mission 6 miles to its present location, both to free his Indian neophytes from the adverse influences of the presidial garrison and to obtain a location affording more water. Despite a native rebellion in 1775, the mission became one of the wealthiest and most populous in California.

New structures were erected during the period 1776–80, and by 1800 more than 1,500 Indian neophytes were attached to the mission. Earthquake damage in 1803 led to further rebuilding and enlargement. By

Old Mission Dam, a major irrigation project of the early 19th century, supplied water to the Mission of San Diego de Alcalá. A flume carried water about 5 miles from the dam to the mission grounds.

1813, the mission had assumed its present form. In 1824, the maximum population of 1,829 Indians was attained, but in 1835 they dispersed when the Mexican Government secularized the mission, after which the buildings were neglected and deteriorated rapidly.

The precise dates of construction of Old Mission Dam, as well as the aqueduct and flume, cannot be ascertained. Not likely begun before 1800, the dam was probably started in 1803, following a 2-year drought. By 1817, it had certainly assumed its final form. Of solid masonry, it was about 220 feet wide, 13 feet thick at the bottom, and 12 feet or more high. Native stone and locally produced cement were used to construct the dam, aqueduct, and flume. The flume, 2 feet wide and 1 foot deep, conducted water to the mission gardens and vineyards some 5 miles distant.

Present Appearance. By 1867, the dam and the aqueduct-flume system were reportedly in ruins. About 7 years later, they were repaired and again put to use. The remains of the dam, still impressive today, impound a small amount of water. The dam will be included in San Diego's proposed Fortuna Mountain-Mission Gorge Metropolitan Park. No substantial remains of the aqueduct or flume are visible. San Diego Mission has been largely reconstructed since 1931.[7]

8. Presidio of San Francisco, California

Location. San Francisco County, south side of Golden Gate, San Francisco.

Ownership and Administration. U.S. Government; Department of Defense.

Significance. This presidio, which guarded the finest harbor on the Pacific coast, figured prominently in the extension of Spanish settlement into northern California and was the northernmost bastion of the Spanish New World Empire and the chief barrier against British, Russian, and American expansion in California. Under its aegis, between 1776 and 1821, the Spaniards established four missions, two pueblos, a royal rancho, and an *asistencia.* In 1817 and 1821, Spanish exploring expeditions that penetrated the interior and the area above San Francisco Bay also used the presidio as a base. Between 1821 and 1836, under Mexican rule, the presidio continued to be the main military base in northern California.

In 1776, 7 years after the discovery of San Francisco Bay, Lt. Col. Juan Bautista de Anza, from Tubac, selected the site for the presidio.

Commandant's House, erected in the period 1776–78 at the presidio of San Francisco, now serves as an officers' club. It has been considerably altered throughout the years, but its front facade incorporates a large part of the original adobe walls.

Lt. José Joaquín Moraga supervised construction, which he initiated on a temporary basis. The buildings were primitive structures—palisaded walls and flat roofs covered with sod or tules. The military reservation of the presidio consisted of 1,564 acres. Construction was slow, however. In 1792, or 16 years after the establishment of the post, only three of the four exterior walls had been completed. Year after year, from 1776 to 1835, under both Spanish and Mexican administrations, adobe buildings that had replaced the original log buildings were constructed or repaired in the dry season, only to be damaged during the rainy season. A church, commandant's house, guardhouse, barracks, and warehouses were constructed over the years. Whether because of lack of suitable alternative building materials, lack of familiarity with other methods, binding instructions from officials in distant places—or a combination of all these reasons—presidial commanders continued to use building methods not suited to the climate. Earthquakes also caused damage.

Capt. George Vancouver, who visited San Francisco Bay in 1792, observed that the presidio—equipped as it was with only two cannons, one mounted on a carriage and the other on a log—was practically defenseless. His visit and other developments in the Pacific area led the Spanish to strengthen San Francisco's defenses by bringing in additional troops and weapons.

In 1793, the Spanish began to construct a new fort, Castillo de San Joaquín, located about 1⅓ miles northwest of the presidio on Punta del Cantíl (now called Fort Point). They completed the castillo in 1794, but its exact shape and dimensions are not known because it was apparently modified appreciably during later repairs and alterations. Upon its 10-foot-thick walls were mounted 12 cannons. In the center was a one-story barracks, built of adobe and roofed with tules, which contained two rooms. In 1796, about 225 persons, including families of soldiers, were reportedly living at the presidio.

In 1797, the troops erected the battery at Yerba Buena, located at Point San José (later called Black Point and then Fort Mason), to protect the anchorage at Yerba Buena Cove. Hastily thrown together of brushwood, fascines, and earthworks, it had eight embrasures and mounted five cannon. A sentinel daily visited the battery, which was not permanently garrisoned. When the battery was completed, the third fortification on the bay, San Francisco was the strongest military post in Spanish California. From an original population of 63, by 1820 the San Francisco District had grown to 670 Spaniards and 5,400 mission

Indians. At the close of the Spanish period, the next year, 134 soldiers and 20 guns defended the presidio. Its strength declined during the Mexican period. In 1836, the year after the government transferred the military headquarters of northern California to Sonoma, it withdrew all the soldiers from the presidio. Most of the remaining buildings disintegrated rapidly; only one has survived, and that only partially.

Yerba Buena Pueblo, which grew into the modern city of San Francisco, was established in 1835, not far from the presidio, by the Mexican Government.

Present Appearance. The site of the 1776 Presidio of San Francisco forms the southern portion of the present U.S. Presidio parade ground, and is situated on Moraga Avenue, between Graham and Mesa Streets. Except for the commandant's house, no surface remains are extant. The site is open and free of intrusions. Four Spanish cannon are on the parade ground, and two more are at Fort Mason. The presidio still

Aerial view of San Francisco. The Spanish presidio was located in the left foreground. Between the years 1776 and 1822, it served as a base for Spanish exploration and settlement of northern California. Courtesy, U.S. Army.

includes about 1,460 acres of the original Spanish reservation.

Though the commandant's house survives, it has been extensively altered since the original construction during the period 1776–78. This one-story adobe structure, on the south side of Moraga Avenue opposite the intersection with Graham Street, is now used as an officers' club. Its front section still incorporates about 75 percent of the original adobe walls.

Castillo de San Joaquín was located at the site now occupied by Fort Point. All traces of the castillo were destroyed in 1853, when the cliff on which it stood was lowered by some 90 feet and Fort Point erected. The present Fort Mason includes the site of the former battery at Yerba Buena. Nothing remains of the battery, but its site is identified by a historical marker in the small park north of the loop on the north end of Sheridan Road.[8]

9. Royal Presidio Chapel, California

Location. Monterey County, 550 Church Street, Monterey.

Ownership and Administration. Roman Catholic Church.

Significance. Monterey was not only the Spanish and Mexican capitals of California for most of the period between 1776 and 1848, but also the stronghold of European civilization on the Pacific coast of the present United States and the hub of social, military, economic, and political activities in California. The Royal Presidio Chapel of San Carlos de Borroméo de Monterey was closely associated with political activities in California; in addition to being used for religious services, which were attended by the Spanish Governors, it was the scene of many colorful ceremonies that were part of the affairs of state. The only remaining presidial chapel in California, it is also the sole extant structure from the Monterey Presidio of Spanish times and the only 18th-century Spanish architectural survival in the present city of Monterey.

Don Gaspar de Portolá, Governor of California, and Father Junípero Serra established the Presidio of Monterey and the San Carlos Mission on June 3, 1770. Within less than 2 weeks, the 60 Spaniards in the pioneer party had erected the rude huts that temporarily constituted the presidio and mission. They then built a stockade around them. The largest hut was utilized as the mission chapel until the next year, when Serra moved his mission to a new site at present-day Carmel, 3 miles south of Monterey; thereafter the hut and the building that replaced it came to be known as the Royal Chapel (*La Capilla Real*) of the Presidio of Monterey.

The chapel walls were composed of logs standing on end, the inter-

Royal Presidio Chapel, dating from the late 18th century, is the only extant building of the Spanish presidio of Monterey. Capital of Spanish and Mexican California, Monterey was the center of political and military activities and the scene of many colorful ceremonies of state.

stices being filled with twigs and plastered with mud. The roof was supported by a row of wooden beams, covered with layers of sticks, branches, and leaves, and topped with earth. This rude structure was replaced in 1773 by an adobe chapel located on the south side of the presidio plaza, which was used until 1787. In the meantime, Monterey had been designated as the capital of California, and the Governor rebuilt the presidio.

The new presidio consisted of a stone wall 537 yards in circumference, 12 feet high, and 4 feet thick, which enclosed 10 adobe houses and a barracks. In 1789, fire destroyed a new log chapel, along with about half the other buildings, necessitating another building program. This program was largely completed in 1791, except for the new stone Royal

Presidio Chapel, the present structure, which was not finished until 1795.

When Capt. George Vancouver visited Monterey in 1792, he estimated the garrison at about 100 men and observed that all the soldiers and their families lived within the presidio walls. During the 1800's, the presidio and nearby battery deteriorated. In 1818, Hippolyte de Bouchard, the Argentine pirate, attacked Monterey with 2 ships and 285 men. The Spanish defense force, consisting of only 40 soldiers and 8 rusty, poorly placed cannon, abandoned the presidio and retreated inland after making an initial show of resistance. Before departing, Bouchard ransacked the presidio and burned the battery, the northern side of the presidio, and three houses on the southern side. The chapel was not destroyed, but only adobe walls remained of much of the rest of Monterey. Because repair work proceeded slowly and conditions deteriorated during Mexican rule, by 1841 only the Royal Presidio Chapel remained standing.

Present Appearance. The Presidio of Monterey, active during the period 1770–1841, was bounded by present Webster and Fremont Streets, between Camino El Estero and Abrego Street. No remains are extant except for the Royal Presidio Chapel, erected in 1794–95. The original chapel was about 120 feet long and 30 wide, rectangular in shape and of the basilica type. Between 1855 and 1858, it was enlarged by 30 feet, and transepts were added at the south end, which changed the building's floor plan to that of a cross. Gothic windows with stained glass were also added, and the original flat roof of the belltower was replaced by the present peaked roof. The facade and walls of the original chapel are intact. The front faces north and features a facade of carved sandstone that has ornate columns and a massive arched doorway. The interior is plain, the whitewashed walls being decorated only by a few pictures and images of saints. The altar and the pulpit are at the south end of the building.

After the Mexican Government secularized Carmel Mission in 1834, it was abandoned and many of its relics removed to the Royal Presidio Chapel, where some may still be seen. During this period, the chapel served as a parish church. The chapel reflects the handiwork of Mexican Indians who were imported to construct the building and whose renderings of religious motifs have survived as notable examples of primitive art. The Stations of the Cross are original, as are also the statues of St. John, the Sorrowful Mother, the Spanish Madonna, and the bas-relief of Our Lady of Guadalupe, carved in chalk rock above the entrance.

An adjoining museum houses precious Catholic relics, including the iron safe used by Father Serra, a rudely carved reliquary of Indian manufacture, and Serra's chalice, cape, and dalmatics, together with his altar service of beaten silver.[9]

10. San Diego Presidio, California

Location. San Diego County, in Presidio Park near Old Town, San Diego.

Ownership and Administration. City of San Diego; Park and Recreation Department.

Significance. San Diego Presidio commemorates the beginning of mission effort and European settlement in California and on the Pacific coast of the present United States. Father Junípero Serra said mass at the site on July 1, 1769, before an assemblage of 126 persons, who were the survivors of 300 who had originally set out from Baja California by land and sea to occupy Alta California. After the *Te Deum*, Gov. Don Gaspar de Portolá ceremoniously took possession of California for Spain.

From then until 1776 the San Diego Presidio (a fort until it was legally established as a presidio in 1774) was the base of operations for expeditions that explored new routes and founded new missions and presidios; and from 1776 until 1837 it continued to be the seat of military jurisdiction in southern California. Under Mexican rule, after 1821, it was also the residence of the Governor, from 1825 to 1829.

The religious ceremony of July 1, 1769, was followed by the formal founding at the presidio, on July 16, of the first mission in Alta California, San Diego de Alcalá. The colonists suffered greatly during the first few months. After a damaging Indian attack in August, they erected a crude stockade on Presidio Hill to protect both mission and colony. By January 1770, the settlement was on the point of starvation. On March 19, just when all hope seemed lost, a supply ship sailed into the bay and saved the California venture from total ruin. By the end of the month the colonists had finished the stockade of the presidio, mounted two bronze cannon, and erected wooden houses with tule roofs.

The commandant's residence was situated in the center of the presidio. On the east side of the square were a chapel, cemetery, and storehouses; on the south side were the gate and guardhouse; and around the other two sides were barracks. To remove his Indian charges from the un-

San Diego Mission, the first of the 21 California missions, in 1853. From a
lithograph by Charles Koppel. Courtesy, Bancroft Library, University of
California.

wholesome influence of the presidial garrison and obtain a better water
supply, in 1774 Father Serra moved the mission to another site, 6 miles to
the northeast, the present site of San Diego Mission. In 1778,
the original wooden walls and buildings of the presidio began to be replaced with adobe structures.

When Capt. George Vancouver reached San Diego in 1793, in the
first foreign ship to visit the city, he was not much impressed from a
military standpoint. His visit, however, along with others, stimulated the
Spanish to strengthen it. In 1795–96, an esplanade, powder magazine,
flagpole, and several houses for soldiers were added to the presidio, and
Fort Guijarros—the first harbor defense work—was erected on Point
Loma. It included an adobe magazine, barracks, and a battery designed to
mount 10 cannon.

As the Spanish period drew to a close, the garrison of San Diego
Presidio increased, 50 cavalrymen being added in 1819 to the force of
about 100 soldiers—some of whom were detached to Los Angeles pueblo
and the four missions of the district. The total Spanish population of the
San Diego District in that year was about 450, in addition to about 6,800
Indian neophytes. Under the Mexican Government, the size of the mili-
tary force and the condition of the presidio declined rapidly after 1830.
In 1836, Richard Henry Dana found the presidio in a deplorable state

and Fort Guijarros in ruins. The following year the Mexicans sent the last of the troops north, and by 1839 the presidio was in complete ruins. Much stone and adobe were removed from it to erect houses in the new pueblo of San Diego, founded in 1835.

Present Appearance. George W. Marston saved the presidio site from complete oblivion in 1929 by donating about 37 acres, including the site, to San Diego for park purposes. The city formally accepted the gift in 1937. Presidio Park, which has been formally landscaped, includes the Serra Museum as its principal architectural feature. This museum, built in 1929, houses a large collection of archeological and historical objects related to early California and Spanish history. The museum library contains both original and published records of the history of the city and the region.

The former site of the presidio is in front of the museum. Construction of the San Diego River dike and the Mission Valley Road destroyed part of the presidio site, and another section lies beneath a park road. However, some vestiges of the structures that once formed the presidio still remain in the form of grass-covered mounds, which suggest part of the outline of former walls and buildings.

In the center of the old presidio stands the Junípero Serra Cross, erected in 1913 from bits of brick and floor tile found on the spot. It bears this inscription: "Here the First Citizen, Fray Junípero Serra, Planted Civilization in California, Here He Raised the Cross, Here Began the First Mission, Here Founded the First Town—San Diego, July 16, 1769." [10]

11. Santa Barbara Mission, California

Location. Santa Barbara County, 2201 Laguna Street, Santa Barbara.

Ownership and Administration. Roman Catholic Church.

Significance. One of the finest and most distinguished of the 21 California missions from an architectural standpoint, this "queen of the missions" is the only one to escape complete secularization throughout its long history. Its sanctuary light has never been extinguished.

Father Fermín Francisco de Lasuén consecrated it on December 16, 1786, as the 10th California mission, located at Santa Barbara Presidio. The first, temporary structure, erected in 1787, was replaced by an adobe church in 1789, and that in turn by a larger building in 1793–94, which

Santa Barbara Mission, in 1875. To the rear and left of the church are the remains of an Indian village that in the first part of the 19th century helped house some 1,800 neophytes. Photograph by C. E. Watkins. Courtesy, Bancroft Library, University of California.

the disastrous earthquakes of 1812 destroyed. In 1815, a labor force of Canalino Indians began to construct the present large stone church, completed for the most part by 1820. The design is classical.

The great church, 179 feet long and 38 feet wide, contained six chapels. The 6-foot-thick sandstone walls were heavily buttressed. The roof and floor were of tile. Two towers were located on the classic facade, the one on the left being completed in 1820 and the other by 1833. Other buildings included a residence for the priests, workshops, and storehouses. In 1803, some 234 adobe huts housing 1,792 Indian neophytes surrounded the mission.

Between 1806 and 1808, the Indians constructed a remarkable irrigation system. It included a large dam across Pedregoso Creek, 1½ miles north of the mission, and a reservoir that was later also used to operate a gristmill, erected in 1827–28. Aqueducts conducted the water first to a filter, or settling, tank and then to a large, stone-walled reservoir 500 feet from the church. The reservoir, 120 feet square and 7 feet high, had a stone fountain and long laundry trough.

In 1834, the Mexicans secularized Santa Barbara Mission and its lands and in 1846 sold them, but the Franciscan fathers continued to occupy the mission in the interim. Indeed, it became the Franciscan capital of California. It was the home of the last father-president, and in 1842

California's first bishop arrived at the mission to establish the seat of his diocese, which included all of Alta and Baja California.

In 1853, the Church founded a Franciscan missionary college at the mission to train English-speaking priests. The buildings were used, and kept in repair, unlike those at the other California missions, during the period of Mexican and early American administration. In 1865, the United States returned some 283 acres of the original mission property, including the buildings, to the Catholic Church.

Present Appearance. Santa Barbara Mission survived virtually intact until June 29, 1925, when a violent earthquake struck the area. Damage was severe, the east tower being destroyed and the interior furnishings battered by falling rock. Only the seven massive buttresses held the walls in place. The following year, restoration began, nearly half of the entire cost being subscribed by the people of California.

Original materials were used as far as possible, and the arches, columns, wall thickness, and all other details were accurately restored. When the reconstruction was completed in 1927, the rebuilt church and convent were little changed from their original construction. A further reconstruction was found necessary during the period 1950–53, when the buildings were discovered to be settling and the towers cracking because of the disintegration of cement and foundations. The facade and towers were de-

Reconstructed in 1926–27, and again in 1950–53, Santa Barbara Mission is one of the best preserved missions in California. The only one to escape complete secularization, it houses valuable Spanish and Mexican relics and documents.

molished and the entire church front carefully rebuilt to duplicate the original appearance.

The mission is not only an architectural gem but also a major museum of Spanish, Franciscan, mission, and California history. It contains a large collection of original records and objects, including the original altar, the beautiful Stations of the Cross brought from Mexico in 1797, 18th-century Mexican paintings and sculptures, and innumerable religious and secular memorabilia of the mission period. The archives contain thousands of original documents, which Father Zephyrin Engelhardt used to write his histories of the California missions.

The fountain and large reservoir near the church, parts of the original mission irrigation system, are perfectly preserved and are part of the present water system of the city of Santa Barbara. Extensive portions of the remainder of the irrigation system are also still visible in the botanic garden.[11]

12. Stanley-Whitman House, Connecticut

Location. Hartford County, 37 High Street, Farmington.

Ownership and Administration. Farmington Village Green and Library Association.

Significance. Built around 1660, apparently by John Stanley, this house is considered to be an almost perfect example of the "added lean-to house" and the New England architectural style. The open setting, tall trees, and picturesque stone wall add greatly to its charm and character. The house is one of the earliest and best preserved of the framed-overhang types, and its ornamental drops are among the finest in the country. The framed front overhang projects 1½ feet beyond the first floor, and the gabled overhang at each end measures 6 inches. The second floor has no overhang. The ornamental drops are carved from the ends of the four second-story posts that project through the overhang.

The interior is characteristic of the early central chimney plan, the parlor and hall being located on the sides of the great central chimney. The chimney below the roof is of well-selected, mostly flat fieldstone, laid in clay mixed with straw in the old English fashion. Above the roof the chimney is of red sandstone, sometimes called "brownstone," laid in small blocks, the wide joints being filled with lime mortar. The large stone fire-

Stanley-Whitman House, Connecticut, built about 1660, illustrates the New England style of architecture.

place in the hall is original, and is 7 feet wide and more than 3 feet high. The lean-to at the rear of the house is an 18th-century addition, possibly about 1760. It includes the central kitchen portion, a "buttery" room at one end and the traditional "birth and death" room at the other. The fireplace in the lean-to is backed against the original central chimney, although it has a separate flue.

In 1735 the Reverend Samuel Whitman, minister in Farmington from 1706 to 1751, purchased the house from Stanley. In 1935, its owner had the house expertly restored by the late J. Frederick Kelly, an authority on early domestic architecture in Connecticut, and then deeded it to the nonprofit association that now administers it.

Present Appearance. Preservation and maintenance of the house are of the highest order. The house is furnished in the style of the period, and in a manner characteristic of the region. Many of the furnishings came from the Farmington area, in which many other 17th- and 18th-century houses are located. A fireproof museum wing, added to the rear of the house, contains especially fine specimens of maps, manuscripts, articles of costume, musical instruments, china, and other items relating to Farmington history. A wagon shed on the grounds houses early farm implements, and the garden in the backyard contains more than 24 varieties of herbs and scented geraniums typical of colonial kitchen gardens. The house is open to visitors throughout the year.[12]

13. Fort Christina, Delaware

Location. New Castle County, near foot of East 7th Street, on Christina River, Wilmington.

Ownership and Administration. State of Delaware; Delaware State Museum.

Significance. The first Swedish expedition to the New World landed at this site about March 29, 1638. It erected the first fortification in New Sweden, Fort Christina, around which grew the first permanent white settlement in the Delaware River Valley and the nucleus of Swedish settlement. Peter Minuit, formerly of New Netherland, headed the expedition of the New Sweden Company, which sent him from Sweden in December 1637 to establish a Swedish foothold in the New World. His assigned destination was the Minquas Kill, which on his arrival he renamed the Christina River in honor of Sweden's young Queen. The expedition of 50 men, in two vessels, landed at a natural wharf of rocks that jutted into the Minquas Kill about 2 miles above its confluence with

Designed by Swedish sculptor Carl Milles, this monument stands on the site of Fort Christina, the first settlement in New Sweden, and commemorates the activities of Swedish colonists in the Delaware Valley. The ship at the top of the monument represents the *Kalmar Nyckel,* one of two vessels that brought the first Swedish colonists to America.

the Delaware. Near the rocks, Minuit erected Fort Christina to guard the settlement and serve as the administrative and commercial center of the colony.

The fort remained the principal center of Swedish settlement even during the period 1643–53, when Gov. Johan Bjornsson Printz ruled from his headquarters on Tinicum Island, some 15 miles north on the Delaware River. When New Sweden fell to the Dutch in the bloodless conquest of 1655, the Dutch posted a few soldiers at Fort Christina, which they called "Altena." Their relations with the Swedish colonists were amicable, but during the peaceful occupation the fort fell into disrepair until Gov. Peter Stuyvesant ordered it repaired for use as the New World headquarters of the Dutch West India Company. The settlement around Fort Christina remained predominantly Swedish despite the annexation to New Netherland. In 1664, when the Delaware Valley fell to the English, English soldiers garrisoned the fort, but the Swedish settlement remained the heart of the village that spread along the banks of the Christina and became the city of Wilmington.

Present Appearance. The 2 acres comprising Fort Christina State Park include the wharf of rocks that was the site of the first landing and near which was the heart of the first Swedish settlement in North America. The ledge of rocks is still partially visible, although much of the natural formation is covered by a plaza that surrounds a striking monument. The monument is a shaft designed by the late Swedish sculptor Carl Milles. It is constructed of black Swedish granite and surmounted by a stylized representation of the *Kalmar Nyckel* (the Key of Kalmar), one of the two ships used by the Minuit expedition.

Treatment of the park is formal. The high brick walls located on two sides, iron fence and ornamental iron gateway on the third, and the Christina River on the fourth separate the site from the surrounding industrial development. Archeological investigation is needed to establish specific information about the fort and surrounding buildings. The park is open to the public throughout the year.[13]

14. Holy Trinity (Old Swedes) Church, Delaware

Location. New Castle County, East 7th and Church Streets, Wilmington.

Ownership and Administration. Protestant Episcopal Church in the United States of America, Diocese of Delaware; maintained by the Holy Trinity (Old Swedes) Church Foundation, Inc., Wilmington.

Significance. This is the oldest surviving church built by a Swedish congregation in the Delaware Valley. No other structure is so closely related historically and geographically to the pioneer Swedish settlement on the Christina River, and none has retained its architectural integrity to so marked a degree. From every standpoint, Holy Trinity is a preeminent survival of the Swedish settlement on the Delaware.

The construction postdates by many years the fall of New Sweden to the Dutch in 1655; largely English in form, the church includes many additions to the original building. Nevertheless, it was built while the Swedish heritage was still a dominant influence in the Delaware Valley. For nearly a century, Swedish Lutheran missionary pastors were assigned. Beneath the church and in the venerable cemetery adjacent to it rest the remains of thousands of early Swedish settlers, many in unmarked graves.

The first churches of New Sweden were of rude log construction, a style later adopted by American frontiersmen. The earliest religious services of the colony were held in Fort Christina. Later, in 1667, the local congregation built a wooden church at Tranhook (Cranehook), on the south bank of the Christina River near its mouth. The new church received little direct supervision from the homeland for the next 32 years. Then, in 1697, three Swedish missionary pastors were sent out to revive

Although its construction postdates the fall of New Sweden by several decades, Holy Trinity (Old Swedes) Church is the oldest surviving Swedish church in the Delaware Valley. Its architecture is primarily English, but the interior contains many Swedish furnishings.

it. As the first step, a new church site was chosen, at the burial ground long used by the settlers around Fort Christina. On May 28, 1698, the builders laid the first foundation stone, and on Trinity Sunday, June 4, 1699, the church was consecrated as *Helga Trefaldighet Kyrcka* (Holy Trinity Church).

The original structure was of the utmost simplicity. Rectangular in shape, it had a brick floor, shingled roof, and gabled ends, without tower, belfry, gallery, or porch. The ceiling was plastered, the pews built of pine, and the altar railing and pulpit carved from walnut. Around 1750, the arched south porch was added; and, in 1774, the gallery, reached by outside stairs. The tower and belfry date from 1802.

After the last Swedish pastor departed, in 1791, jurisdiction over the church was transferred by the Swedish Missionary Society to the Protestant Episcopal Church. After 1830, when the congregation moved to a new building, the old church deteriorated badly. Only one service annually was held until the church was reopened in 1842. At that time, wooden benches were substituted for the pews except in the gallery, wooden flooring placed over the original bricks, and the gallery stairs moved inside. Restoration in 1899 corrected these alterations.

Present Appearance. Holy Trinity is maintained in excellent condition and is open to visitors. In 1946–47, the Garden Club of Wilmington restored the old churchyard. A short distance from the church is the restored Hendrickson House, a fine Swedish stone dwelling dating from about 1690 and recently moved from Essington, Pa. It serves as a museum and library devoted to Swedish colonial life on the Delaware.

Holy Trinity is rich in objects that date from its origin at the end of the 17th century or demonstrate its traditional Swedish ties. The original altar is preserved within a later one of marble; and the aged pulpit, carved in 1698, is still in use. Portraits of the early Swedish pastors, some of whom are buried beneath the church, are hung in the vestry. A former pastor, Eric Bjork, in 1718 donated a silver communion service, which is used upon special occasions. The altar cloth was a gift from the late King Gustav V of Sweden, in 1950. The King himself embroidered the central cross in gold thread. All these objects, displayed in the setting of the 17th-century interior, remind the visitor that this venerable church is one of the most significant and memorable links between Swedish America and the present.[14]

15. Fort San Carlos de Barrancas, Florida

Location. Escambia County, U.S. Naval Air Station, Pensacola.

Ownership and Administration. U.S. Government; Department of Defense.

Significance. Fort San Carlos de Barrancas was originally a semicircular fortification of Pensacola brick, built in 1787 during the last Spanish occupation of West Florida. The high bluff on which it was placed, called by the Spaniards "Barrancas de Santo Tomé," was the site of the earlier Fort San Carlos de Austria, which dated from the first permanent Spanish settlement on Pensacola Bay, in 1698. In 1719, a French force destroyed this first fort and nothing remains of it today. From 1763 to 1781, Pensacola was under British control, and its capture by a Spanish expedition in 1781 marked the beginning of the last period of Spanish rule. The new Fort San Carlos was a defense bastion in West Florida; and, with St. Augustine, a foothold in the Southeastern United States.

Spanish collaboration with the British forces during the War of 1812 led Andrew Jackson to move into Pensacola in 1814. The occupying British force retreated rapidly to their warships after blowing up Fort San Carlos. When Jackson withdrew to New Orleans, the Spanish returned and began to rebuild the fort. During the Seminole Indian War, 4 years later, Jackson again attacked Pensacola. In accepting the surrender of the Spanish Governor, in Fort San Carlos, he in effect seized

Fort San Carlos de Barrancas, Florida. In the late 18th century, the Spanish constructed the fort to guard Pensacola, the capital of Spanish West Florida.

control of West Florida for the United States. He returned as Provisional Governor of the new territory 3 years later.

As a part of the general tightening of coastal defenses during the years 1833–44, U.S. troops strengthened the defenses at the mouth of Pensacola Bay. They constructed a four-sided brick fortification, Fort Barrancas, immediately in the rear of and connected to Fort San Carlos; and, as part of the defensive complex, built Fort Redoubt about 1,000 yards north of Fort Barrancas. During the Civil War, Forts San Carlos and Barrancas were first in the hands of Florida State troops and then the Union forces.

Present Appearance. The forts are in poor condition at present.[15]

16. San Luís de Apalache, Florida

Location. Leon County, near U.S. 90, about 2 miles west of Tallahassee.

Ownership and Administration. Privately owned.

Significance. During the century following the founding of St. Augustine, in 1565, Spanish padres extended their mission system steadily northward along the Atlantic coast into the province of Guale, and westward into the provinces of Timucua and Apalachee. In this way, by the conversion and stabilization of the Indians, they helped make St. Augustine secure. Furthermore, the fertile soils of Apalachee supplied badly needed grain for the inhabitants of St. Augustine. In 1633, the mission system reached Apalachee. San Luís de Apalache (San Luís de Talimali), established sometime during the next two decades, became the administrative center of the province.

By 1675, when the Spanish mission system reached the height of its influence, some 8,000 persons were centered around the 14 flourishing missions of Apalachee. San Luís itself had some 1,400 inhabitants, including the Deputy Governor and a military garrison of infantry and artillery. In 1696, the Spanish built a wooden blockhouse because of the activities of British traders who were stirring up the Indians of the interior against them.

Prior to 1690 Indian war parties, armed and directed by the English, had destroyed two of the Timucua missions. In 1702, the British began a concentrated effort to destroy the Spanish mission system in Florida. A combined English and Creek force from the Ocmulgee trading post area attacked and partially destroyed two more Timucua missions; and the Spanish and Apalachee army, heading north in reprisal, was met and defeated on the Flint River by English-led Creeks. Later that month, Col. James Moore's army of Carolinians sailed south from Charleston, ravaged the Guale missions, and besieged Castillo de San Marcos. All Florida was now in a state of terror.

Only two missions, one in Apalachee and the other in Timucua, were attacked in 1703. In 1704, however, the attacks broke out with renewed fury. In January, an army of 50 Carolinians and 1,000 Creeks, led by Colonel Moore, destroyed 5 of the Apalachee missions—including San Francisco de Oconee—and captured more than 1,000 Apalachee Indians. San Luís escaped destruction, but the province was completely demoralized. Two more Apalachee missions were destroyed in June 1704 and another was attacked. In July, the Spanish evacuated and destroyed San Luís and abandoned the province of Apalachee. More than a decade passed before the Spanish again established a garrison in the province.

Present Appearance. Intermittently since 1948 excavation of the site has been carried out under the auspices of the Florida Park Service and Florida State University. The eastern moat of the fort and postholes indicating one wall of the blockhouse have been uncovered and many artifacts found. Further excavation will no doubt uncover evidence of the whole complex. The site is well preserved.[16]

17. Fort de Chartres, Illinois

Location. Randolph County, at the terminus of Ill. 155, near Prairie du Rocher.

Ownership and Administration. State of Illinois; Division of Parks and Memorials.

Significance. Fort de Chartres was one of France's most imposing fortifications in North America. Though never attacked, in the 18th century it served as the center of French civil and military government of the Illinois country and reflected the aspirations of Frenchmen in the Mississippi Valley.

The present partially reconstructed fort is on the site of the third outpost on the Mississippi to bear the name *de Chartres,* and is preserved as an Illinois State Park. A temporary fort was constructed in 1720. Construction of a permanent fort was begun in 1753 and largely completed

Reconstructed gateway and museum at Fort de Chartres, Illinois. In the 18th century, the fort was the center of French civil and military government in the Illinois country.

3 years later. The fort's massive stone walls, 18 feet high and more than 2 feet thick, enclosed two long barracks, a guardhouse, two officers' quarters, a powder magazine, a kitchen, and outbuildings—all arranged around a 4-acre parade ground. The fort could have accommodated a garrison of 400 men, but less than half that number were usually assigned.

Despite the formal ending of French sovereignty in America in 1763, a French garrison continued to occupy the fort until 1765, when British troops moved in and renamed it Fort Cavendish. It served as the center of British rule of the Illinois country until 1772, when it was evacuated and destroyed.

Present Appearance. The State of Illinois acquired the site in 1915, and since then has reconstructed parts of the fort, including the gateway and the combined guardhouse and chapel. The magazine, which is original, has also been restored. Of even more interest and importance are the extensive foundation remains that have been exposed by archeologists. They present a vivid picture of the nature of the fort when it housed French, and later English, garrisons. A small museum, on the foundations of the fort's original storehouse, displays various artifacts. Standing in a fertile valley free from modern encroachments, the lonely fort is an impressive symbol of the one-time widespread holdings of France in the heartland of North America.[17]

18. Old Kaskaskia Village Site, Illinois

Location. La Salle County, on north side of Illinois River, Utica Township, just upstream from Starved Rock State Park.

Ownership and Administration. Privately owned.

Significance. The Old Kaskaskia Village (or Zimmerman) Site is the best-documented historic Indian site in the Illinois River Valley. It is not to be confused with the Kaskaskia village of French origin below Cahokia. Louis Jolliet and Père Jacques Marquette, in the summer of 1673, as they returned from their pioneering voyage down the Mississippi, noted that it contained 74 houses and was inhabited by the Kaskaskia, a band of the Illinois tribe.

Marquette, who in 1675 established a mission at the village, was replaced 2 years later by Father Claude Jean Allouez, who found a village of 351 houses that was occupied by 7 other bands of the Illinois in addition to the Kaskaskia. René Robert Cavelier, Sieur de la Salle, accompanied by Father Louis Hennepin, visited the village in December 1679 and stated that the 460 houses then located there were "made like long arbors and covered with double mats of flat flags, so well sewed that they are never penetrated by wind, snow, or rain."

La Salle founded Fort Crèvecoeur at the southern end of Lake Peoria, downstream, and left it under the command of Henry de Tonty when he returned north. On his way up the Illinois River, he noted the natural fortification now called Starved Rock and sent Tonty a message to occupy it in case of an Iroquois attack. Tonty moved there in April 1680, but he did not fortify it. In September, a war party of 600 to 700 Iroquois arrived, causing the 7,000 to 8,000 inhabitants of Old Kaskaskia Village to flee downstream immediately. About 500 Illinois warriors fled after a few days of fruitless negotiating. Tonty, forced to leave the area, moved to Green Bay.

After La Salle and Tonty had started construction of Fort St. Louis atop Starved Rock, in December 1682, groups of Miamis and Shawnees joined them. In the latter part of 1683, the Kaskaskia and other Illinois bands returned and settled, probably at the abandoned village, the Old Kaskaskia Village site. In all, about 20,000 Indians gathered in the neighborhood, including some 3,880 warriors.

But the Iroquois attacks continued, and the Miamis and Shawnees departed from Fort St. Louis. As the confederacy fell apart, La Salle's dream of an Indian empire vanished. After a council decided in the fall of 1691 that Starved Rock could not be defended, the bands of Illinois still remaining moved to Lake Peoria. A faction of the Illinois from Lake Peoria that established a settlement near Starved Rock in 1712 and remained in this locality until 1722 probably did not occupy the Old Kaskaskia Village Site.

Archeological investigation at the site has yielded large quantities of European goods in association with Indian items, especially trade goods such as glass beads, copper and brass beads and jinglers, coiled brass wire ornaments, glass bottles, and iron knife and ax blades. Buffalo bones, extremely rare at aboriginal sites east of the Mississippi, are quite common. Either the Illinois hunted west of the Mississippi during the period of occupation, or buffalo roamed over the Eastern prairie.

Present Appearance. The site has been used for agricultural purposes for several generations, but much valuable archeological data probably lie untouched beneath the plow zone. Only a small percentage of the site has been excavated.[18]

19. Starved Rock, Illinois

Location. La Salle County, on Ill. 71, about 6 miles west of Ottawa.

Ownership and Administration. State of Illinois; Division of Parks and Memorials.

Significance. Starved Rock was the first major center of French influence in the Illinois country. La Salle, after his momentous voyage of discovery down the Mississippi to the Gulf of Mexico, in 1682, chose it as a base for his administration and development of the upper Mississippi Valley. With Henry de Tonty, in 1682–83, he constructed Fort St. Louis at Starved Rock (*Le Rocher*), about which La Salle concentrated thousands of Indians as part of his ambitious plan to protect and exploit the vast new territory that he claimed for France. At the lower rapids of the Illinois River, the fort controlled the strategic waterway that was a major connecting link between Canada and the Mississippi Valley. As pressure from their enemies mounted, the Illinois Indians finally deserted Starved Rock for safer territory. This ended the fort's usefulness to the French, who in 1691 abandoned it.

Present Appearance. Starved Rock State Park, dominated by the pin-

On the summit of Starved Rock, in Illinois country, the French explorer La Salle built Fort St. Louis to secure the vast Mississippi Valley for France.

nacle of Starved Rock itself, preserves some of the sites of the Indian communities that clustered around the fort. The pinnacle is a sheer promontory rising 115 feet above the Illinois River in a beautiful natural setting. Use of the park is primarily recreational, but the setting retains much of the feeling of the wilderness as La Salle knew it. Trails give access to various natural and historical features, and plaques on the summit describe the historical significance of the site—a reminder of the great age of French exploration and settlement.[19]

20. El Cuartelejo (Scott County Pueblo Site), Kansas

Location. Scott County, west of U.S. 83 within the boundaries of Scott County State Park, 12 miles north of Scott City.

Ownership and Administration. Kansas State Society, Daughters of the American Revolution.

Significance. This is one of the key sites indicating the far-reaching expansion of Spain beyond New Mexico and her interest in the Great Plains. It consists of the ruins of a seven-room, stone Puebloan structure, probably built by a group of Picurís Indians who in 1696 emigrated from New Mexico to live with the Cuartelejo Apaches. As early as the 1660's, friction between the Pueblo Indians of New Mexico and the Spanish rulers and priests had caused groups of Indians to migrate to El Cuartelejo.

Spanish expeditions under Archuleta (pre-1680 Pueblo Revolt) and Ulibarri (1706) probably came to El Cuartelejo to return groups of Indians to New Mexico. In 1719, Governor Valverde led an expedition northeast from Santa Fe, visited the Cuartelejo Apaches, and learned from them of French penetration into the Plains. As a result, in 1720, the Spanish sent out the Villasur expedition, which passed through El Cuartelejo but was destroyed later by the Pawnees in Nebraska.

Archeological excavation of the site has produced only a few artifacts of Southwestern origin. The pueblo ruin and its typically Southwestern appurtenances—slab-lined hearths, grinding trough, oven, and the like—were directly associated with a material culture complex that was almost entirely Plains Apache. Either the Puebloans stayed in the area only a short time, or they readily adapted themselves to the everyday implements and utensils of the local residents.

Present Appearance. The site has been well preserved, but traces of the pueblo ruin are rather obscure, as would be expected because of climatic factors and the passage of time.[20]

21. Tobias-Thompson Complex, Kansas

Location. Rice County, on the Little Arkansas River, about 4 miles southeast of Geneseo. The Tobias Site is on a ridge south of the river; the Thompson Site is about 450 yards away on a ridge north of the river.

Ownership and Administration. Privately owned.

Significance. Most historians, ethnologists, and archeologists agree that the Quiviran, or Wichita, sites visited by Coronado and later by Bonilla and Humaña were located in present Rice and McPherson Counties, Kans. Fragments of chain mail of ring diameters that fall within the 16th-century pattern have been excavated at the Thompson Site of the Tobias-Thompson Complex. European glass, copper, and iron objects have been obtained from the complex, as well as from the Malone

and Saxman Sites in Rice County, and from the Paint Creek Site in Mc-
Pherson County.

Further evidence of contact between the inhabitants of the Tobias-
Thompson Complex and the Southwest Indians has been provided by the
discovery of turquoise beads, Rio Grande glaze paint pottery, and
Chupadero black-on-white pottery. The glaze paint pottery probably
dates from about the time of Coronado's excursion onto the Great Plains,
in 1541.

Culturally, temporally, and spatially the Tobias and Thompson Sites
are parts of a single community. However, because they are separated by
a small stream and were considered separate sites prior to excavation, they
bear separate designations in archeological literature. Interesting features
of the Tobias-Thompson Complex and associated sites are the so-called
"council circles," low mounds that may have been temples or ritual centers. The "council circle" at the Tobias Site is approximately 60 feet in
diameter and is surrounded by four or possibly five elliptical basins in a
discontinuous circle. Only four similar "council circles" are known, all
in Indian sites culturally related to the Tobias-Thompson Complex.

Present Appearance. The complex is well preserved. It is chiefly in
grassland, but includes some unbroken sod.[21]

22. Cabildo, Louisiana

Location. Orleans Parish, Chartres and St. Peter Streets, on Jackson
Square, New Orleans.

Ownership and Administration. State of Louisiana; Louisiana State
Museum.

Significance. This building, also known as the *Casa Capitular,* was
erected in 1795 to house the *Cabildo* of Spanish Louisiana, the legislative and administrative council for the province. Though fire destroyed
two predecessor buildings, this structure survived during the last 8 years
of Spanish rule in Louisiana and the brief period of French rule in 1803
prior to the transfer of Louisiana Territory to the United States.

Two ceremonies within a period of 3 weeks—November 30 and December 20, 1803—were particularly notable in the Cabildo's history. In
the first, Louisiana Territory was placed under French rule after having
been under Spanish control for 40 years. During the brief period of
French rule, the building was called the *Maison de Ville* (Town Hall).

Representative of Spanish architecture in Louisiana is the Cabildo, or *Casa Capitular*. From 1795 to 1803, it housed the *Cabildo*, the legislative and administrative council for the province of Spanish Louisiana.

In the second ceremony, the transfer of sovereignty of Louisiana from France to the United States took place. For many years, the Cabildo continued to provide public offices, but in 1911 it became the Louisiana State Museum.

Present Appearance. The architectural historian Hugh Morrison has commented that the Cabildo, composed of "a full panoply of Renaissance architectural forms," shows the "most markedly Spanish influence in Louisiana." A massive structure of stuccoed brick, it was altered in the 1850's by the addition of a third floor, and a steep-sided mansard roof.[22]

23. Fort de la Boulaye, Louisiana

Location. Plaquemines Parish, about 1 mile north of Phoenix.

Ownership and Administration. Privately owned.

Significance. Fort de la Boulaye was the first French outpost in the present State of Louisiana. It was established in February 1700 to counter Spanish and English aggression in the region. Pierre le Moyne, Sieur d'Iberville, landed a party of soldiers on a low ridge along the east bank of the Mississippi River, about 18 leagues above its mouth at the "east pass," where his soldiers constructed a 28-foot-square wooden blockhouse and equipped it with six cannon. Iberville left an 18-man garrison, under the command of his brother, Bienville, to hold the fort. Little is known of their experiences, but by 1707 the Indian threat had forced the abandonment of the post. Nevertheless, one Louis Juchereau de St. Denis, who was on amicable terms with the Indians, remained there alone for several years and helped maintain friendly relations with them.

No physical traces of the fort remain above ground, and for many years it was a lost site. However, in the early 1930's four amateur historians of New Orleans achieved virtually certain identification on the basis of geographical evidence and correlation of the previous discovery of hand-hewn cypress logs. Dredging operations in 1923 had produced the hand-hewn logs, although their significance was not realized for some years. A cannonball was found in 1936, after the site had been tentatively identified.

Present Appearance. The site is nearly 1 mile east of the present channel of the Mississippi River on a low ridge surrounded by reclaimed swampland. The ridge is covered by a thick growth of trees and brush, and the site is bisected by a canal. A State historical marker has been erected on the site, but access is difficult.[23]

24. Jackson Square, Louisiana

Location. Orleans Parish, Vieux Carré, New Orleans.

Ownership and Administration. City of New Orleans.

Significance. On December 20, 1803, in this square in the heart of the French capital of Louisiana, the U.S. flag was raised for the first

774-955 O—68—17

time over the newly purchased Louisiana Territory—the greatest single accession of territory in the history of the Nation. Twice in 3 weeks during late 1803 the allegiance of the inhabitants of New Orleans was shifted, from Spain to France to the United States. At noon on November 30, when the square was known as the Place d'Armes, a crowd gathered to listen to the announcement from the balcony of the Cabildo that Louisiana had passed from Spanish into French possession. On December 20, they heard that their allegiance again had been changed; the flag of France was hauled down and replaced by the Stars and Stripes.

Present Appearance. Jackson Square, a public park, is still the hub of the French Quarter, as it has been throughout the years. It offers a fine view of the Cabildo, St. Louis Cathedral, and other historic buildings. In the center of the square, dominating the park, are the statue of Andrew Jackson and the flagpole marking the site of the symbolic transfer of sovereignty to the United States.[24]

25. Ursuline Convent, Louisiana

Location. Orleans Parish, 1114 Chartres Street, New Orleans.

Ownership and Administration. Roman Catholic Church.

Significance. This convent is not only of historical and religious importance, but is also architecturally significant as a Louis XV public building. It is one of the few remaining links with the beginnings of the great capital of French Louisiana. Shortly after New Orleans was

Ursuline Convent, in New Orleans, constructed in 1748–52, is one of the few extant buildings in the Vieux Carré dating from the French period.

founded, a group of Ursuline nuns arrived from France, in 1727, to establish a convent that would "relieve the poor and sick and provide at the same time for the education of young girls."

The first building of the Ursulines was replaced by the present one, built during the period 1748–52. The nuns abandoned it in 1824 and presented it to the Bishop of New Orleans, who used it as his residence. In 1848, a section of the building was demolished to permit construction of St. Mary's Catholic Church, but it remained the episcopal residence until 1899. Subsequently it served as offices for the archdiocese and as a seminary for priests and in 1924 was extensively remodeled.

Present Appearance. The Ursuline Convent serves today as the rectory for St. Mary's Italian Church, whose parish is responsible for its upkeep. Unfortunately, lack of funds has prevented the rector from doing little more than maintain the status quo. In 1963, some interior refurbishing was done, but no extensive restoration work is planned for the near future. The structure appears to be basically sound.[25]

26. Cole's Hill, Massachusetts

Location. Plymouth County, Carver Street, Plymouth.

Ownership and Administration. Pilgrim Society, Pilgrim Hall, Plymouth.

Significance. The settlement of the Puritans—later to be known as "Pilgrims"—at Plymouth in 1620 looms large in the development of New England and the United States. Unfortunately, virtually all the historic sites relating to the earliest period of the settlement have lost their original character and convey little impression of the colony. One exception is Cole's Hill, which is still the dominant landmark of Plymouth Harbor. The view from the hill of land and harbor and sea conveys a vivid impression of the scene that greeted the *Mayflower's* weary passengers.

The hill rises up from the shores of Plymouth Bay near the foot of Leyden Street, principal thoroughfare of the original settlement. It was the traditional burial place of the Plymouth colonists, Pilgrims, and others, who died during the "starving time," the tragic first winter of 1620–21. The dead were reportedly buried at night, and their graves disguised to prevent the Indians from learning the dangerously weakened state of the survivors. In later years, the colonists occasionally mounted cannons on the hill to ward off possible attack from the sea.

In an early assignment of land tracts, the hill became the site of the home of Deacon Samuel Fuller, the *Mayflower* Pilgrims' "physition & chirurgeon." It was named after the popular tavernkeeper who for many years after 1645 maintained his establishment on a spot overlooking the bay.

Historically, Cole's Hill is perhaps not as significant as other points in Plymouth—Burial Hill, for example, where the colony's first fort was erected, or Leyden Street, where the settlers built the first houses. Unfortunately, the historical character and integrity of these locations have been diminished or wholly obliterated with the passage of time and the growth of the city. Burial Hill, filled with the graves and monuments of many generations, is encroached upon by the present town. Cole's Hill, however, is today relatively open and affords a sweeping view of the bay into which the *Mayflower* sailed and the shore on which its passengers landed.

Present Appearance. Cole's Hill is maintained by the Pilgrim Society as a public park. On its top stands the memorial to the *Mayflower* Pilgrims, erected by the General Society of Mayflower Descendants. In a crypt beneath the monument are bones uncovered during excavations in the 18th and 19th centuries; because no burials were made on the hill after 1637, perhaps some are the unfortunates who braved the terrors of the ocean passage only to die in the first months of the colony's existence. Also located on the hill is the statue of Massasoit, the Wampanoag chief whose friendship shielded the struggling colony from Indian attack in its early years.

At the foot of Cole's Hill is Plymouth Rock, legendary landing site of the Pilgrims and steppingstone to the New World. It has rested in several places over the years, and has been venerated for more than two centuries, first by the people of Plymouth and later by the Nation. Whether or not the Pilgrims actually landed on the rock, it has deep meaning for most Americans. Cole's Hill, the nearby rock, and the curving shores of Plymouth Bay memorably evoke the time more than three centuries past when Englishmen came to the shores of New England to stay.[26]

27. Fairbanks House, Massachusetts

Location. Norfolk County, Eastern Avenue and East Street, Dedham.

Ownership and Administration. Fairbanks Family in America, Inc., Fairbanks House, Dedham.

Fairbanks House, Massachusetts, may be the oldest surviving framehouse in the United States. Jonathan Fayerbanke built the original section of the house about 1637 or 1638.

Significance. This is perhaps the oldest framehouse standing in the United States and an excellent example of the "growing house" of colonial times. The original portion of the house was built about 1637 or 1638 by Jonathan Fayerbanke, who moved to Dedham from Boston in September of 1636. The center portion of the present house is the oldest. As Fayerbanke added to his wealth and land, he added to the size of his home.

The original house consisted of a small porch, hall, and parlor downstairs, and bedchambers upstairs. A lean-to was later added at the back of the house and, perhaps in 1641, a wing on the east side. Still later, around 1654, the west wing was added. The two wings, which have typical New England gambrel roofs, were undoubtedly completed no later than the time of Fayerbanke's death, in 1668.

From the entry porch in the original portion of the house, stairs lead around the chimney to two second-floor bedrooms. The east wing is entered by a small porch in the angle where the wing joins the original house. This wing has a parlor and small bedroom on the lower floor, and a large second-floor room which is reached by a winding stairway.

The west wing, which is entered from the hall of the original house, was probably used as sleeping quarters by laborers on the farm. Some authorities believe that the original house was built with oak timbers brought from England—a custom of emigrants that originated in the need to erect houses quickly for defensive purposes.

Present Appearance. The Fairbanks House, which has always been in the possession of the Fairbanks family, is open to the public. It is furnished with family heirlooms. In spite of interior alterations occasioned by repairs, plastering, painting, and wallpapering, the antiquity and authenticity of the structure is obvious even to the casual observer. The house is excellently maintained—a labor of love on the part of the Fairbanks descendants, for whom the dwelling is a family shrine.[27]

28. Old Ship Church, Massachusetts

Location. Plymouth County, Main Street, Hingham.

Ownership and Administration. First Parish (Unitarian), Hingham.

Significance. Some authorities contend that this church, also known as the Meeting House, erected in 1681, is the oldest English church in continuous use in America. The major rival for this distinction is the Newport Parish Church (St. Luke's) in Smithfield, Va. Old Ship Church is certainly the earliest of New England's churches, and it is a striking survivor of the Puritan settlement of Massachusetts in the 17th century.

The earliest settlement within the bounds of the present town of Hingham dates from 1633, and the major period of settlement began in 1635, when a party arrived under the leadership of the Reverend Peter Hobart and soon built the first meetinghouse. The present structure was erected in 1681, according to tradition by ships' carpenters. This tradition, plus the "look-out," or "captain's walk," surrounding the belfry, and the curved roof timbers which give the interior the appearance of an inverted ship's hull, all probably contributed to the church's name.

For more than a century following its construction, the church was used for town meetings and village gatherings. In 1791, when the congregation voted to raze it and erect a new church, it narrowly escaped destruction. Fortunately, this move was reconsidered, and the church continued to serve its congregation without interruption.

Present Appearance. The plain wooden structure reflects the Puritan rejection of the Gothic architecture of the Anglican tradition and repre-

Old Ship Church, Massachusetts, an early English church. For more than a century after its construction, in 1681, the villagers of Hingham used it for town meetings and gatherings, as well as for religious purposes.

sents a style of building common to New England meetinghouses of the 17th century, for which no Old World precedent existed. The Puritans also abandoned traditional interior arrangements; the pulpit replaced the altar as the focal point of the service, and benches faced it and ran lengthwise of the church. The main entrance was in the rear of the benches, opposite the pulpit.

The church is a unique example of the primitive type of church that has been restored to its original condition. Except for the early 18th-century gallery additions, thanks to careful restoration in 1930, it stands today much as it was originally built. It is handsomely maintained by its Unitarian congregation.[28]

29. Parson Capen House, Massachusetts

Location. Essex County, off the Village Green and Mass. 97, Topsfield.

Ownership and Administration. Topsfield Historical Society, 70 Central Street, Topsfield.

Significance. This house, whose setting and interior are superb, is not only a perfect specimen of a New England colonial residence, but also of the English manor house in America. Erected in 1683, a date verified by inscriptions in two places on the oak frame, it eloquently reflects its English heritage. The skill of workmanship indicates the efforts of craftsmen trained in England. Except for the clapboards in place of half timbers, the house is a faithful counterpart of the English manor house of the 17th century. The Reverend Joseph Capen, minister at Topsfield for many years, had it built on a 12-acre plot given him by the town in 1682.

Present Appearance. The house framework consists of heavy oak timbers mortised and tenoned and held in place by wooden pins. The foundation timbers rest on an underpinning of unmortared field stones. The second story overhangs far out in the front, and the third story projects at each end, the overhangs being supported by wooden brackets. Carved pendants decorate the overhang corners of the building.

The staircase which winds up before the chimney in the entry has its original newel post and turned oaken balusters. The exposed brickwork of the chimney in the entry indicates the early construction of the house. The parlor and somewhat smaller hall, or kitchen, constitute the lower floor. The walls are wainscoted in a fashion typical of the period,

Erected in 1682 by Rev. Joseph Capen, minister at Topsfield, Massachusetts, the Parson Capen House is a noteworthy example of a New England colonial dwelling and 17th-century manor house.

and the hall is dominated by the fireplace, more than 8 feet wide, which has rounded back corners and a large flue. The floor has characteristic wide boards, sanded smooth.

Acquired by the Topsfield Historical Society in 1913, the house was restored under the direction of George F. Dow. The frame timbers are original, but much of the woodwork, inside and out, has been replaced. Furnishings are of the 17th century and include a food hutch, which antiquarians have called unique in America, and a baluster-back arm-chair inscribed "P. Capen 1708," believed to have been part of the wedding furniture of Priscilla Capen, the parson's daughter. The house is maintained in excellent fashion, and is open to visitors during the summer.[29]

30. Paul Revere House, Massachusetts

Location. Suffolk County, 19 North Square, Boston.

Ownership and Administration. Paul Revere Memorial Association, 19 North Square, Boston.

Significance. This house possesses an unusual combination of historical and architectural interest. Although extensively restored, it retains its original framework and is exceptionally significant as downtown Boston's only surviving 17th-century dwelling and as Revere's home from 1770 to 1800.

John Jeffs probably built the original portion of the house not long after the Boston Fire of 1676, on the site of the Increase Mather parsonage. The house was originally the simple and characteristic one-room type, but by the time Revere moved into it about a century later it had already been enlarged to three full stories. During the 19th century, when the house was a tenement and used as a store, it was considerably altered. An increasing regard for the old house led to its rehabilitation in the present century. In 1908, Joseph Everett Chandler, an architect, directed its careful restoration.

Present Appearance. The exterior of the house is clearly 17th-century in character, featuring typical rooflines, overhang, pendants, windows, and front door. Inside, the kitchen ell at the rear is an early section of the building. Revere probably used the back door in this kitchen when he set out on his famous ride of April 18, 1775; the front door would not have been safe because North Square was full of British soldiers.

In the hall is a recessed fireplace, and a small porch and winding stair are located in front of the chimney. Summer beams span the ceiling of the large room, or hall. The first-floor interior has been restored in 17th-century fashion, but the second-floor chamber is plastered, paneled, and painted as it might have been when occupied by the Reveres. The house is well maintained and is open to the public.[30]

31. Saugus Iron Works, Massachusetts

Location. Essex County, 10 miles north of Boston, on U.S. 1, Saugus.

Ownership and Administration. First Iron Works Association, Saugus.

Significance. The beginnings of the iron industry in the United States may best be traced to New England at Saugus, although some attempts at iron manufacture had been made in Virginia as early as 1619. In 1646, only 26 years after the first permanent settlement had been established in Massachusetts, a partnership bearing the name of the Company of Undertakers for the Iron Works in New England began the construction of an ironworks, under the direction of Richard Leader. The partnership benefited from the initiative of John Winthrop, Jr., and legal encouragement given by the Massachusetts General Court in 1641.

Saugus Iron Works, Massachusetts, in 1650. Courtesy, American Iron and Steel Institute.

The works consisted of a blast furnace, casting house, forge (with two "fineries" and a chafery), a rolling and slitting mill, and various storehouses and other buildings. The works was more than a blast fur-

Reconstructed forge building, at Saugus, Massachusetts, part of a full-scale "working" model of a 17th-century ironworks. In the building, workers reheated cast iron bars and converted them into wrought iron.

nace producing crude pig iron and castware. Its forge manufactured bars of wrought iron, from which could be made the tools and hardware that were needed by colonial farms and enterprises—hoes, shovels, hinges, and other items. Its rolling and slitting mill turned out rod iron that could be shaped into nails, which were much needed in the colonies.

The length of the works' operation (1648–70) and the migration of its workers and technicians to other ironmaking projects make it an important enterprise in U.S. history, even though as a business enterprise it eventually failed. After about 20 years of active and widely distributed production, a growing scarcity of raw materials seriously affected operations. Imported ironwares undercut Saugus iron in the market, and by 1670 the works had been abandoned and had begun falling into ruins. The iron industry did not flower in the colonies until the 18th century.

Present Appearance. The works had completely disappeared by the 1940's, when a project aimed at its reconstruction was begun. Rebuilding involved 6 years of research and construction and funds totaling $1.5 million. The works was opened to the public in 1954. Restored and supported by today's American iron and steel industry, it is a full-scale model of the original 17th-century works and has unique public interest and educational value. It is open daily except Mondays from May 15 through October 15.[31]

32. "Scotch"-Boardman House, Massachusetts

Location. Essex County, Howard Street, Saugus.

Ownership and Administration. Society for the Preservation of New England Antiquities, 141 Cambridge Street, Boston.

Significance. This house, an outstanding survivor of 17th-century New England, has been highly praised by most students of colonial American architecture, particularly because so much of its original finish is unspoiled. Few examples of the typical New England house remain so unmarred.

The exact date of construction is not known. For many years it was believed that the house had been built to shelter Scottish prisoners captured by Oliver Cromwell in the Battle of Dunbar, September 13, 1650, and transported to America to labor in the ironworks at Saugus. Recent scholarship throws some doubt on this contention and suggests that the present house stands near, but not on, the site of the original "Scotch" house and conjectures that the present house was built after 1686. The house followed the normal plan for a typical family dwelling of the period. Its fine decorative detail, characteristic of the best houses of the time, would hardly have been found in prisoners' quarters.

The original form of the present house was the usual two-room central-chimney plan, two-and-a-half stories high, under which a half-cellar was located. The lean-to was a later addition. On the west side of the ground floor is the parlor; on the east side, the hall, or kitchen. Above each of these rooms, on either side of the central chimney, is a sleeping chamber.

Present Appearance. The present exterior of the house—including the

clapboards, underboarding, roof covering, windows, and front door—
dates almost entirely from a later period than the interior. Formal restoration, during the period 1915–18, was expertly carried out. Little was
done to change the condition in which the structure was found, for fear
of damaging the integrity of its original finish, so much of which has
fortunately survived. Since the restoration, only repairs necessary to
preservation and upkeep have been undertaken. The house is open to the
public in the summer and is maintained in excellent condition.[32]

33. Whipple House, Massachusetts

Location. Essex County, 53 S. Main Street, Ipswich.

Ownership and Administration. Ipswich Historical Society, 53 S. Main
Street, Ipswich.

Significance. This house, one of the earliest surviving in New England,
clearly demonstrates the development of a 17th-century dwelling over
the centuries. Its three distinct units reflect the evolution of workmanship
and architectural detail as the Whipple descendants grew away from their
English origins. The original portion of the house may have been built
as early as 1638, but the earliest documented date is 1650, when an
earlier sale from John Fawn to John Whipple was confirmed.

The original portion of the house was a two-story, two-room structure,
which had casement windows and a thatched roof. At one end of the

This 17th-century dwelling, the Whipple House, originally had only two
rooms. As the Whipple family grew and prospered, they added to the house.

lower room are the entrance door, great chimney, and stairway to the large sleeping chamber on the upper floor. The sleeping room may have been divided originally by a partition. The original building was the lifetime home of the first John Whipple, a leader of some distinction in the settlement of Agawam, later Ipswich, and in the Massachusetts Colony. He served as deputy of the General Court in Boston, and held the offices of selectman, deacon, and ruling elder at the church in Ipswich.

Whipple's son, also named John, continued the family tradition of public service. He served as a representative to the General Court and as an officer during King Philip's War of 1675–76. In 1670, a year after his father's death, the captain added a second unit to the house, more than doubling its size, as well as a hewn overhang to each story at the east end. The rooms of the addition contained triple-light windows, fine molded framing timbers, and summer beams uniquely crossed at right angles. On the death of Capt. John Whipple, the executors of his will appraised the house, as well as 2½ acres of land, kiln, and outhouse, at £330; even at that early period, the house was an unusually valuable property. The structure assumed today's form when its next owner, still another John Whipple, added a lean-to at the back, sometime after 1700.

Present Appearance. The restoration and preservation of the Whipple House have involved a minimum of alteration. The house is in excellent condition and is exceptionally well furnished from a period standpoint. Maintained as a historic house museum, it is open to the public.[33]

34. Fort Michilimackinac, Michigan

Location. Cheboygan County, on the Straits of Mackinac at the terminus of U.S. 31, Mackinaw City.

Ownership and Administration. State of Michigan; Mackinac Island State Park Commission, Mackinac Island.

Significance. Fort Michilimackinac was an important bastion of French and English power on the Straits of Mackinac and a vital fur-trade center. French hegemony in the American heartland was closely related to its control of the highly strategic straits, the crossroads of the upper Great Lakes connecting Lakes Michigan, Huron, and Superior. In the early interior exploration of North America, the Great Lakes and their related waterways were the main routes into the continent for the French, the first Europeans to penetrate them. The importance of the straits did not escape them.

The earliest French activity on the straits centered on Mackinac Island and at St. Ignace, on their north side. In 1670–71, Père Claude Dablon founded a Jesuit mission on the island, which he named St. Ignace after the founder of his order, St. Ignatius. He was soon joined by Père Jacques Marquette, who came with his Huron flock from the upper end of Lake Superior. In 1672, the mission was moved to the mainland on the north shore of the straits, at which time Marquette took charge, and a fort was added to the mission.

For a few years after 1698, the French officially abandoned the straits, but traders maintained contact with the Indians around the Mackinac area. Early in the 18th century, the French formally returned to the straits and during the years 1715–20 erected a new fort, Fort Michilimackinac, on the south shore of the straits at the site of Mackinaw City. The British took over this fort during the French and Indian War, but the garrison was surprised and most of its occupants massacred in 1763 during the Pontiac uprising.

The British reoccupied the fort in 1764, and it was the only British-garrisoned outpost on the Great Lakes above Detroit until near the close of the War for Independence. In 1781, when U.S. attack appeared imminent, the post was relocated at Mackinac Island. The British remained in control until 1796 and between 1812 and 1815. From 1796 to 1812 and after 1815 the fort belonged to the United States. (The Straits of Mackinac and Mackinac Island are eligible for the Registry of National Historic Landmarks, primarily because of their association with the advance of the frontier, 1763–1830.)

Present Appearance. The restoration of Fort Michilimackinac effectively demonstrates the coordination of archeological and historical research. Modern restoration began in 1932, but the most important work was done after 1959, when the Mackinac Island State Park Commission floated bond issues totaling $125,000 to finance the complete restoration of the fort. In addition to the reconstructed buildings, exhibits at the park include objects found during the excavations and the uncovered foundation outlines of other structures. The park affords a superb view of the Straits of Mackinac.[34]

35. St. Ignace Mission, Michigan

Location. Mackinac County, State and Marquette Streets, St. Ignace.
Ownership and Administration. City of St. Ignace.
Significance. The establishment of St. Ignace Mission on Mackinac

Site of St. Ignace Mission, in St. Ignace, Michigan. The mission served as a base for Marquette and Jolliet's exploratory journey down the Mississippi River. The site is located in a small city park overlooking Lake Huron and Mackinac Island.

Island in 1670–71 marked the beginning of European occupation of the strategically located Straits of Mackinac area [see above description]. At this mission, in 1673, Marquette joined Louis Jolliet on their pioneering journey down the Mississippi River, as far as the Arkansas River. In 1672, the mission was moved to the mainland on the northern shore of the Straits of Mackinac, where it is now commemorated. Inactive during the period 1706–11, in 1712 it was reopened. In 1741, it was again relocated, on the southern shore of the straits, where Jesuits were in charge until 1765.

Present Appearance. The mission site is in a small, 1-acre city park, which overlooks Lake Huron and Mackinac Island. A museum adjacent to the park, maintained by the Catholic diocese of Marquette, interprets the story of Marquette and other French explorers and missionaries. It is open to the public.[35]

36. Kathio Site, Minnesota

Location. Mille Lacs County, along U.S. 169, on Mille Lacs Lake at Vineland, North Kathio Township.

Ownership and Administration. State of Minnesota; Minnesota State Historical Society.

Significance. Kathio (Izatys) was the largest of three villages occupied at the beginning of the historic period by the Mdewakanton band of the Santee (or eastern) division of the Sioux, or Dakota. The first historical mention of the Sioux occurs in Jesuit annals in 1640, at which time nothing was known of them except that they were living in the vicinity of the Winnebagos. They had numerous contacts with the French in the following several decades, but not until 1679 did Daniel Greysolon, Sieur Dulhut (Duluth), make the first definite historical record of Kathio village.

Dulhut stated that he "had the honor to set up the arms of his Majesty in the great village of the Nadouessioux called Izatys." The role of this village in early French-Sioux relations is further demonstrated by the capture of Father Hennepin by the Sioux in the same year. He was freed from another village by Dulhut in 1680, whereupon they went to Kathio and warned the Indians of the danger they faced if they should harm Frenchmen.

Intertribal warfare resulting from European trade and colonization, which produced profound changes in the history of the native peoples of America, is reflected in the subsequent history of Kathio. White settlement impinged upon the Iroquois; at the same time, English and Dutch traders furnished them with firearms. The Iroquois pressed against the Chippewas. The Chippewas in turn, who had the advantage of French arms, attacked the Sioux, farther to the west, who at that time had to rely almost entirely upon the bow and arrow.

As early as the visit of Pierre Charles le Sueur to the Sioux, in 1700, they were moving westward in the face of persistent Chippewa attacks. The showdown, apparently, came in the 3-day Battle of Kathio, about 1740, as a result of which the Sioux lost their territory to the Chippewas. The Sioux moved south and west, where they figured prominently in the history of the Plains and the Rocky Mountain States; they displaced other groups just as they had been displaced by the Chippewas, who still live near Kathio.

Aboriginal materials recovered from the Kathio Site, identified as historic Mdewakanton Dakota-Sioux, corroborate the historic identification of the site as Izatys.

Present Appearance. The site is well preserved. Adjoining it is the Mille Lacs Indian Museum of the Minnesota State Historical Society.[36]

37. Fatherland Plantation Site (Grand Village of the Natchez), Mississippi

Location. Adams County, along the banks of St. Catherine's Creek, 3 miles southeast of Natchez.

Ownership and Administration. Privately owned.

Significance. This is probably the most thoroughly documented historic Indian site in the Southeastern United States. Iberville, in 1700, provided the first description of the village, though it is mentioned in many other early 18th-century sources. Following the establishment of nearby Fort Rosalie after the "First Natchez War" of 1714, Le Page du Pratz sketched scenes of Natchez life, the fort, and the village. French maps of 1725 present detailed information about the Fort Rosalie-Grand Village area; several sources, including Du Pratz, describe the Natchez attack on the French in 1729 and the abandonment of the village in 1730. In addition to its historical significance, the site is extremely important archeologically. Its positive identification has provided a base for inferences concerning prehistoric sites of the Mississippian archeological period.

In the flat bottom land on the west side of St. Catherine's Creek are three mounds. Mound A, almost entirely destroyed by stream erosion, appears to have been a low, truncated pyramid. Mound B is also pyramidal, about 80 feet square at the base and 7 feet high. Excavations of Mound C, a platform mound with burials in the floor of the temple atop it, have yielded extremely significant Indian and European material. The village area, about 5 acres in extent, across the creek from the mounds, has been excavated on a preliminary basis.

Present Appearance. Although the site is within the city limits of Natchez and in an area that has been zoned for commercial use, no development has yet occurred in the vicinity. The site is situated in cutover timberland and covered with brush and second-growth trees. Portions of the village site east of the creek have been badly eroded, but other parts, as well as the village area around the mounds, are well preserved under a covering of alluvium.[37]

38. Ste. Genevieve, Missouri

Location. Ste. Genevieve County.

Ownership and Administration. Various.

Significance. Ste. Genevieve, one of the oldest surviving French settlements in Missouri and in the trans-Mississippi West, is the only place in the upper Mississippi Valley where several buildings of the pre-American period have survived. The oldest European settlement in the region, Cahokia (1699), suffered heavily from floods; Kaskaskia (1703) was entirely washed away by a change in the course of the Mississippi; and the remnants of colonial St. Louis were destroyed either by the fire of 1849 or by urban riverfront development.

The date of the first French settlements in the vicinity of Ste. Genevieve cannot be determined. Lead had been discovered by 1715 about 30 miles to the southwest, and was being mined by primitive means. The earliest known grants of land were made in 1752, when 27 inhabitants owned about 3 miles of Mississippi River frontage. The original site of settlement, probably in the period 1735–40, was in the river bottom on the west bank

Around 1785 Louis Bolduc, a prosperous miner, merchant, and planter, built this house in Ste. Genevieve, Missouri. It has a porch on all four sides, vertical posts on a stone foundation, and Norman roof trusses.

Janis-Ziegler House, or Green Tree Tavern, in Ste. Genevieve. Probably built in the 1790's, the house combines French and American architectural styles. It served as a tavern sometime in the 19th century.

of the Mississippi about 3 miles below the present town. The settlement was probably linked with Kaskaskia, almost directly across the river, then the metropolis of Illinois. Salt springs on Saline Creek, as well as the lead resources, were probably an important factor in the expansion of the settlement, from which shipments were made upstream to St. Louis or downstream to New Orleans. The settlers also grew foodstuffs for export.

Floods, notably one in 1785, caused repeated damage, and the town was moved gradually to the present site on high ground. By 1796, only a few huts of traders remained at the old site. Ste. Genevieve—the principal seat of government in the region for many years after western Louisiana passed from French to Spanish control in 1762—thrived under Spanish administration. It declined, however, as St. Louis gradually grew in importance. In 1803, the Louisiana Territory passed to the United States.

Present Appearance. The current population of Ste. Genevieve is about 4,000. Noteworthy historic buildings include the following:

(1) Bolduc House. Probably erected about 1785 by Louis Bolduc, prosperous lead miner, merchant, and planter, it has been carefully re-

stored by the National Society of Colonial Dames of America and opened to the public. Featuring a porch (*galerie*) on all four sides, construction of vertical posts on a stone foundation, and fine large Norman trusses supporting the roof, it is one of the least changed early French houses in the Mississippi Valley.

(2) Meilleur House, also known as the Old Convent. This two-story frame structure was built about 1815 for the private dwelling of René Meilleur, Louis Bolduc's son-in-law. Around 1837, the Sisters of Loretto bought it and conducted a school there until 1848. The walls are nogged with brick.

(3) Jean Baptiste Valle House. This one-and-a-half story Creole dwelling was the "State House" of the territory up to the time of the Louisiana Purchase and the home of the last commandant under the Spanish administration. It was probably built about 1785. The basic construction is similar to that of the Bolduc House, but it has been more altered. The heavy tapered beams supporting the second floor are exceptionally long.

(4) Mammy Shaw House. This house derives its name from the widow of one Dr. Shaw, a former occupant. Its origins are uncertain, but it is one of the oldest houses in the community. It is now used as a restaurant.

(5) Janis-Ziegler House, or Green Tree Tavern. This attractive structure represents in some respects the architectural transition in Ste. Genevieve from old French to typically American forms. It was probably built in the 1790's, but does not have the Norman roof trusses. The signboard,

Mammy Shaw House, a late 18th-century structure in Ste. Genevieve.

dating from the period sometime in the 19th century when the building was used as a tavern, may be seen in the Ste. Genevieve Museum.

These structures, along with others not listed of equal or slightly less age, constitute an important and unique survival of the French regime in the Mississippi Valley.[38]

39. Utz Site, Missouri

Location. Saline County, on Mo. 122, about 13 miles northwest of Marshall.

Ownership and Administration. Forty-two acres of this 200-acre site are owned by the University of Missouri and used for the Lyman Center for Archaeological Research. The remainder of the site, except for a small portion within Van Meter State Park, is privately owned farmland.

Significance. This site was probably the principal settlement of the Missouri Indians from approximately 1673 until 1728. In 1723, Étienne Veniard, Sieur de Bourgmond, a French trader, built Fort Orleans, a military and trading post, near the site, in present Carroll County. The Indians were apparently friendly with the French. Recovered artifacts include French trading items such as glass beads, brass ear ornaments and rings, and copper and brass for making ornaments.

The Indians probably abandoned their villages shortly after the French left Fort Orleans in 1728, for none of the larger items essential to life in Indian settlements—such as copper and iron kettles, metal knives and axes, and gun parts—have been found during excavations. Early cartography verifies the authenticity of this site. Marquette's map of his exploration of the Mississippi in 1673, as well as maps of La Salle's expedition of 1682, place the Missouri Indians in the area.

Present Appearance. The site is located on a range of low, broken hills along the flat river valley of the Missouri. The slopes, once grassy and treeless, are now covered with timber, except for a few cultivated areas. The 42 acres owned and recently excavated by the University of Missouri were formerly farmland. Excavations are conducted each summer from June through August and may be visited on weekends and holidays. Several buildings are in the area, and a small museum exhibiting excavated materials is open to the public.[39]

40. Pike-Pawnee Village Site (Hill Site), Nebraska

Location. Webster County, on a secondary road, along the south bank of the Republican River, about 7 miles east-southeast of Red Cloud.

Ownership and Administration. Privately owned.

Significance. When Capt. Zebulon M. Pike, U.S. Army, visited this Pawnee village on the Great Plains in 1806, during his famous expedition, he found that the Spanish had been there before him. Thus, the site indicates both the extent of Spanish penetration beyond New Mexico and the initial probing of the United States into the then unknown Southwest. Pike persuaded the Indians to fly the U.S. flag rather than the Spanish.

Among the articles recovered from this site are a Spanish peace medal that dates from 1797; an American peace medal of the type issued by the Government after 1801; a military button bearing the raised figure "1," the regimental number of Pike's infantry; European items such as tools, bridles and stirrups, wooden-backed mirrors, glass beads, and gun parts; and typical Pawnee bone and stone implements. The site coincides with the description in Pike's journal and the official map of his expedition.

Present Appearance. The site is cultivated farmland. All surface indications of the village have been obliterated, but discolored plowed-over areas indicate the location of earth lodges and cache pits.[40]

41. Abó Pueblo and Mission, New Mexico

Location. Torrance County, on north side of U.S. 60, about 10 miles west of Mountainair.

Ownership and Administration. State of New Mexico; Museum of New Mexico.

Significance. The ruins of Abó represent a significant and relatively little-known period in Southwestern aboriginal culture. Occupied from late prehistoric times—about 1300—through early Spanish times, they typify the period in which acculturation began in the Southwest. San Gregorio de Abó Mission was the most important, perhaps the "mother mission," of the Salinas group of pueblos, which also included Quarai, Tenabo, and Tabira. Gran Quivira was a *visita* of Abó, and was not occupied continuously by a priest.

Artist's conception of the San Gregorio de Abó Mission, in 1629. From a painting by Regina Tatum Cooke. Courtesy, Museum of New Mexico.

The first Europeans known to have visited Abó Pueblo were Antonio de Espejo and a small group of Spaniards, in 1583, when the pueblo had a population of about 800. In 1598, Juan de Oñate, first Governor of New Mexico, assigned Father San Francisco de San Miguel to Pecos Pueblo, where he also had the responsibility for neighboring pueblos, including Abó. He departed in 1601, in which year the people of Abó killed two Spanish deserters. When Oñate sent one of his lieutenants, Vicente de Zaldívar, to chastise the residents, a battle occurred.

Missionary efforts at Abó began about 1622. The missionaries brought about several changes in the Indian way of life by introducing a new religion, improving agriculture, introducing new domestic animals and plants, sponsoring new ideas in architecture, and bringing in Spanish goods. The mission and church are believed to have been constructed in 1629–30, under the guidance of Father Francisco de Acevedo. In 1641, the pueblo had a population of about 1,580. Drought and Apache attacks caused its abandonment in the early 1670's, when the inhabitants joined their Piro-speaking relatives on the Rio Grande. At the time of the Pueblo Revolt of 1680, a number of them joined the Spaniards in their southward retreat.

Present Appearance. The ruins lie on a low promontory at the junction of Barranco Arroyo and another unnamed arroyo in the center of a natural amphitheater formed by low-lying hills. They consist of extensive mounds of earth, stone, and debris which cover walls that are

Ruins of San Gregorio de Abó Mission, an influential Spanish mission in New Mexico.

probably several feet high. The mission is built of red sandstone set in adobe mortar. Portions of the church walls survive to roof height, as high as 40 feet above the ground. The *convento* was covered with debris prior to excavation, in 1938–39. The ruins of both pueblo and mission are in good condition.[41]

42. Acoma Pueblo, New Mexico

Location. Valencia County, on N. Mex. 23, about 13 miles south of U.S. 66.

Ownership and Administration. Acoma Tribal Council and Roman Catholic Church.

Significance. This pueblo, spectacularly perched on a prominent mesa

357 feet above the plains of western New Mexico, is believed to be the oldest continuously inhabited settlement in the United States. Probably occupied as early as A.D. 1200, it possesses important historic and prehistoric values. Several 16th-century Spanish exploring expeditions visited it, including Alvarado, one of Coronado's lieutenants, in 1540; Rodríguez and Chamuscado, in 1581; Espejo, in 1583; and Oñate, in 1598.

In part because of their defensible location, the Acoma Indians were persistently hostile during the Spanish period. This pueblo, probably more than any other in the Southwest except Taos, exemplifies native resistance to Spanish rule. In December 1598, the residents lured Capt. Juan de Zaldívar, one of Oñate's officers, into the pueblo and murdered him and 14 of his men. Two months later the Spanish retaliated. Capt. Vicente de Zaldívar, brother of the slain Juan, led a force of 70 soldiers against the fortress-like rock. In a bitterly fought battle, the Spaniards stormed the mesa, captured and partially burned the pueblo, and killed about 1,500 of the inhabitants.

Although Acoma was assigned a mission in 1598, the hostility of the Indians prevented its construction for 30 years. In 1629, Fray Juan Ramírez, a Franciscan, founded Estévan del Rey Mission. During the Pueblo rebellion of 1680, the Acomas murdered the resident priest, Fray

Acoma Pueblo, New Mexico, dates from prehistoric times. In the 16th and 17th centuries, it was a center of native resistance to Spanish rule. Only a handful of Indians live in the pueblo today. Courtesy, New Mexico State Tourist Bureau.

Lucas Maldonado. Following the reconquest, in 1692, they successfully resisted an attack by Don Diego de Vargas and held out until induced to surrender in 1699. The mission of San Estévan had suffered relatively little damage during the rebellion, and continued to serve the pueblo during the remainder of the Spanish period.

Present Appearance. Acoma today is nearly deserted, only a handful of people residing there; the rest of the Indians live at Acomita, 15 miles distant, and gather at Acoma for periodic festivals. The pueblo is little altered from its prehistoric character. Recent construction blends with the old. The church of San Estévan, still used at festival time, is constructed of plastered stone and adobe, as are the adjacent *convento* and other mission buildings, which are partially in ruins. San Estévan is one of the least altered of New Mexico missions. Measuring 150 by 40 feet, it is also one of the largest. The Acoma Indians keep the church and pueblo in good repair. Admission fees are charged to visit the pueblo and church and to take pictures. Guide service is provided.[42]

43. Hawikuh, New Mexico

Location. Valencia County, 12 miles southwest of Zuñi Pueblo, on a graded road, along the opposite side of the Zuñi River, northwest of the village of Ojo Caliente.

Ownership and Administration. Zuñi Indian Tribal Council; and U.S. Department of the Interior, Bureau of Indian Affairs.

Significance. The now-abandoned Zuñi pueblo of Hawikuh was once the largest of the fabled "Cities of Cíbola," at which the early Spanish explorers hoped to find wealth. Probably at Hawikuh, or possibly Kiakima, the Negro Estévan died at the hands of the Indians in May 1539, and Fray Marcos de Niza viewed one of these pueblos from a distance. In July 1540, Coronado and his army arrived at Hawikuh, the first pueblo they visited. After a sharp skirmish with the inhabitants, during which a few Spaniards were wounded and a few Indians killed, Coronado stormed the pueblo and took possession. The ill treatment that he and his men accorded the Indians set the pattern for Spanish-Indian conflict in the Southwest for the duration of Spanish rule.

From Hawikuh, Tovar and Cárdenas journeyed to the Hopi country and the Grand Canyon; Alvarado, north and east to Taos and Pecos. Coronado made his headquarters at Hawikuh for several months during the summer and autumn of 1540 before moving east to winter on the Rio Grande. Subsequent Spanish explorers, including Chamuscado and Rodríguez (1581), Espejo (1583), Oñate (1598 and 1604–05), and Zaldívar (1599), also visited the pueblo.

In 1629, the Spanish founded a mission, La Purísima Concepción de Hawikuh, at the pueblo. The Zuñis in 1632 murdered the resident priest, Fray Francisco Letrado, and fled to another pueblo. They returned in 1635, when the mission was reestablished as a *visita* of the mission at Halona Pueblo. In 1672, Apaches raided Hawikuh, killed the priest, and burned the church. The church was rebuilt, only to be destroyed during the Pueblo rebellion of 1680, in which the Zuñis participated whole-heartedly, and during which they abandoned the pueblo. When they submitted to Don Diego de Vargas during the reconquest of 1692, they returned to the Zuñi country but reoccupied only one of the six pueblos, Halona. Hawikuh has thus been abandoned since 1680.

Present Appearance. The ruins of Hawikuh cover the top of a long, low ridge on the Zuñi Indian Reservation. The site was excavated during the period 1917–23 by an expedition of the Heye Foundation under the leadership of Frederick Webb Hodge. Sandstone rock walls, in places several feet high, outline the foundations and rooms of part of the pueblo; and mounds of earth littered with rocks mark the locations of other portions. Mounds of eroded adobe, 2 or 3 feet high, are all that remain of the mission church and part of the monastery.[43]

44. Palace of the Governors, New Mexico

Location. Santa Fe County, north side of plaza, Santa Fe.

Ownership and Administration. State of New Mexico; Museum of New Mexico.

Significance. The Palace of the Governors, also known as the "Adobe Palace," is the oldest public building in the United States. It embodies much of the heritage and spirit of the historic Spanish capital of New Mexico, Santa Fe. Built about 1610, it has served as the Spanish, Mexican, and American capitols of New Mexico and the residence of its Governors. Even during the period 1680–92, when the Spaniards were ejected by the Indians from New Mexico, it apparently served as the residence and headquarters of the leaders of the Pueblo Revolt.

Don Pedro de Peralta, second royal Governor of New Mexico, had the palace constructed as part of the royal presidio of Sante Fe. The palace

Palace of the Governors, in Santa Fe, is the oldest public building in the United States. Built about 1610, for nearly three centuries it served as capitol of New Mexico and as the residence of Spanish, Mexican, and American Governors. Courtesy, New Mexico State Tourist Bureau.

housed administrative offices and living quarters of the Spanish Governors until the Indian rebellion of 1680. When the Spanish defenders abandoned the palace and broke through the Indian lines to make their escape to the south, Santa Fe fell. The Indians held it for a dozen years, until Don Diego de Vargas subjugated them once again, in 1692. The palace again became the seat of Spanish authority in New Mexico and continued to be so throughout the 18th and early 19th centuries.

Mexican Governors replaced the Spanish after the successful Mexican revolution in 1821, and resided in the building until Gen. Stephen Watts Kearny's "Army of the West" occupied Santa Fe and raised the U.S. flag in 1846. From then until 1885, except for a brief Confederate occupation during the Civil War, the palace housed the American Territorial government of New Mexico. A new State capitol building was occupied for offices and legislative uses in 1885, but until 1909 the Governors continued to use the palace as their residence.

Present Appearance. For more than 350 years, the palace has evolved through cycles of damage, repair, reconstruction, modification, and restoration. The present structure occupies the original site. Despite modern reconstruction and restoration, much of it is the original building. It occupies the entire northern side of the historic plaza of Santa Fe—end of the Santa Fe Trail and site of romance and adventure in the minds of generations of Americans who have been enthralled with the stories about Kit Carson and others associated with the American development of the Southwestern United States.

The front of the building is a block-long *portal*. Behind the palace is a large and attractive patio, fully enclosed by connecting parts of the building and walls. The pueblo architectural style—plastered adobe, flat roof, viga ceiling—is typical of the 17th century, when the palace, as an integral part of the presidio, covered and enclosed about 2 acres. Operated by the Museum of New Mexico, the palace houses an excellent display of exhibits relating to the prehistoric, Spanish, and Territorial periods of New Mexico history.[44]

45. Pecos Pueblo, New Mexico

Location. San Miguel County, on N. Mex. 63, about 4 miles north of U.S. 84–85.

Ownership and Administration. State of New Mexico; Museum of New Mexico.

Significance. The pueblo, whose ruins are among the most impressive

Ruins of Nuestra Señora de los Angeles de Porciúncula Mission, at Pecos Pueblo, New Mexico. The pueblo, visited by many Spanish explorers, figured prominently in the Pueblo Revolt of 1680. By the mid-19th century, it had fallen into ruins.

in the Southwest, is of exceptional historical importance because it was visited by many early Spanish explorers, it supported a mission for nearly the entire period of Spanish settlement, and it figured prominently in the Pueblo Revolt of 1680.

One of the largest pueblos of New Mexico in the 16th and 17th centuries, Pecos served as the gateway to the buffalo plains for several of the Spanish explorers. Plains tribes brought buffalo hides, "alibates flint," and other items to the pueblo to exchange for cloth, turquoise, and corn. Hernando de Alvarado, one of Coronado's lieutenants, and a few of his men were the first Spaniards to visit it, in 1540. At this pueblo Alvarado obtained the services of a Plains Indian slave—called "The Turk"—whose tales of wealth in a land called Quivira drew Coronado and his followers far out into the Plains, as far as present Kansas, in a fruitless quest; Ysopete, another Plains Indian who joined the Spaniards at Pecos Pueblo, denied these claims. One of Coronado's friars remained at the pueblo.

Castaño de Sosa and Oñate visited the pueblo in the 1590's. In the early 1600's, when the pueblo had about 2,000 inhabitants, the mission of Nuestra Señora de los Angeles de Porciúncula was established. Its church, on the south end of the mesa, was partially destroyed during the Pueblo uprising of 1680. The inhabitants of Pecos joined wholeheartedly in the war against the Spanish and against the Tewa and Tano people who remained too friendly to the Spanish. They also participated in the lesser rebellion of 1696.

The mission was reestablished on orders of Gov. Don Diego de Vargas, but by the middle of the 18th century the pueblo had declined notably. The attacks of the Comanches, who began moving south through eastern New Mexico in the early 1700's, were damaging, as were also the diseases that they introduced. As a result, by 1749 the population had dropped to 1,000. After further decline and especially a smallpox epidemic in 1788, only 152 inhabitants remained in 1792. The pueblo was then made a *visita* rather than a mission. In 1838, the surviving 17 residents departed to join their linguistic kinsmen at Jémez, to the west. The ruins were a well-known landmark to travelers on the Santa Fe Trail, which passed close by.

Present Appearance. In the 1500's, the pueblo was a quadrangle surrounded by houses four stories high, the upper stories of which were surrounded by covered walkways. The nearby mission church was large; even today its walls, in ruins, stand 50 feet high in places. These walls have been stabilized by the State, but heavy rains in recent years have done further damage. The church has been excavated, but adjacent mission buildings have not. Low walls, however, outline the pattern of the *convento.*

The pueblo, north of the mission, was partially excavated and stabilized during the period 1915–29. The exposed portions, of stone construction, are typical of pueblo architecture, but most of the pueblo still lies underground. Mounds indicate terraced houses, which were at one time four stories high. One large kiva has been restored and is open to visitors, and the stone defensive wall that once surrounded the entire pueblo has been rebuilt to a height of 3 or 4 feet. The ruins are open to the public.[45]

[On June 28, 1965, the President signed the act of Congress authorizing Pecos National Monument as a unit of the National Park System.]

46. Quarai Pueblo and Mission, New Mexico

Location. Torrance County, just west of N. Mex. 10, about 8 miles north of Mountainair.

Ownership and Administration. State of New Mexico; Museum of New Mexico.

Significance. The ruins of Quarai Pueblo and Nuestra Señora de la Concepción de Quarai Mission reflect the involvement of Indians in the sharp church-state rivalry of the mid-17th century in New Mexico. Like those at nearby Abó, they represent an important and relatively little-known period in Southwestern aboriginal culture, the period in which the native inhabitants began to become Europeanized.

Quarai may have been visited by Chamuscado and Rodríguez in 1581 and by Espejo in 1583. It is certain that Oñate visited it in 1598, while making a trip to the salt lakes on the west side of the Sandia Mountains. In that year, Fray Francisco de San Miguel was assigned to Pecos Pueblo, from where he also ministered to Quarai and other nearby villages. In 1628, Quarai received its first resident priest, Fray Juan Gutíerrez de la Chica. Until the 1670's, various Franciscans were in residence at the pueblo.

Serving as the seat of the Holy Inquisition in New Mexico during the 1630's, Quarai became a focus for the next several decades in the conflict of religious and secular authority in the province. In the late 1660's, its inhabitants, weary of being in the middle of the controversy, planned to revolt with Apache help. The Spanish discovered the plot, however, and executed the leader, Estévan Clemente.

The droughts of this period also weakened the pueblo, and in 1672 some 600 residents joined relatives living at Tajique, 12 miles to the north. In 1674, the residents of Tajique abandoned it in turn and moved to Isleta, another Tiwa-speaking pueblo, on the Rio Grande below present Albuquerque. At the time of the Pueblo Revolt of 1680, many Isleta residents moved south with the fleeing Spanish survivors; they settled near the site of El Paso, Tex., and established another community called Isleta. After the abandonment of Quarai in 1672, Indians never again occupied it. The only known subsequent residents were Spanish troops who were based there in the 1750's to ward off attacks launched through Abó Pass by Apaches.

Present Appearance. Like several other pueblos in the region, Quarai contains two churches: A small early one, of which only wall outlines remain; and a large structure, in ruins, whose walls still stand to a height of 40 feet in places. Dates of construction and related data are not known for either church. During the period 1934–36, the Museum of New Mexico excavated and stabilized the massive sandstone walls of the large church and monastery and in 1938 and 1939 accomplished additional work. A small amount of archeological effort had earlier been expended on the pueblo ruins in 1916 and the 1930's. Quarai became a State monument in 1935.[46]

47. San Gabriel de Yungue-ouinge, New Mexico

Location. Rio Arriba County, on San Juan Pueblo Grant, across the Rio Grande from San Juan Pueblo.

Ownership and Administration. Privately owned by Indians of San Juan Pueblo.

Significance. The ruins of San Gabriel de Yungue-ouinge mark the site of the first capital of New Mexico, established by the Spanish colonizer Don Juan de Oñate late in 1598 or early in 1599. Although French, Spanish, and English colonies in the Southeast predate San Gabriel, the San Gabriel ruins include the oldest European church and house remains yet found in the continental United States.

Just above the junction of the Rio Chama and the Rio Grande, Oñate and his party discovered two pueblos. They named the one on the east bank of the Rio Grande, San Juan de los Caballeros; the other, on the west side, was known by its Indian name of Yungue-ouinge. The party

Excavations at San Gabriel de Yungue-ouinge. Established by Don Juan de Oñate in 1598 or 1599, San Gabriel served as capital of Spanish New Mexico until about 1610. Courtesy, University of New Mexico.

occupied San Juan Pueblo, and hurriedly erected a church dedicated to St. John the Baptist. No trace of the church has ever been found.

After a few months, the Spaniards took over Yungue-ouinge from the Indians. The new site of Spanish occupation, renamed San Gabriel, had about 400 "houses," or rooms. Recent excavations by the University of New Mexico have revealed that San Gabriel de Yungue-ouinge was originally built in a large **U**-shape, the opening facing to the south. The Spaniards evidently leveled the west wing and built some rooms. To the east wing, they apparently added peripheral rooms, built over thickly studded cobblestone foundations. Near the mouth of the **U** they built a permanent church of white tufa blocks. Excavation has yielded many Spanish artifacts, including mail and armor, ceramicware, ecclesiastical furnishings, hinges, and various personal accouterments.

San Gabriel remained the capital of Spanish New Mexico until a new Governor, Don Pedro de Peralta, arrived in 1609. Probably the following year he established Santa Fe as a royal presidio and the capital of the province. Some Spaniards may well have remained in the San Gabriel area, but the pueblo seems to have been reoccupied at least in part by San Juan Indians. Eventually it fell into disuse, except for a few Spanish-American and Indian dwellings that stood on top of the old mounds. This was its condition until the recent excavations were undertaken.

Present Appearance. Some of the old mounds marking the site of San Gabriel de Yungue-ouinge have been bulldozed away for enlargement of modern fields, and a considerable section of the east mound remains unexcavated. In the southern part of the east wing, however, the foundations and lower walls of the Spanish-occupied section, as well as the church, have been excavated and stabilized by archeologists from the University of New Mexico. This area is fenced and the owner, a San Juan Indian who acts as caretaker, shows visitors through the site.[47]

48. Taos Pueblo, New Mexico

Location. Taos County, 3 miles northeast of Taos.

Ownership and Administration. Taos Tribal Council.

Significance. This famous, much-pictured, multistoried pueblo, more than any other Indian community of the Southwest, exemplifies native resistance to the Spanish and American invaders of New Mexico. From the earliest times it was of great importance because of its size, strategic location, and trading activities with the Plains Indians. It was visited by most of the Spanish explorers of New Mexico, including Hernando de Alvarado, one of Coronado's officers, in 1540; another member of his expedition, the next year; and the explorer-colonizer Oñate in 1598.

About 1620, Franciscan friars built the first church, San Gerónimo de Taos, at the pueblo, one of the earliest in New Mexico. At that time, the population of the pueblo was estimated at 2,500 persons. In 1639, the inhabitants destroyed the church, and tension mounted to the point that 2 years later the Spanish sent a punitive expedition against Taos. Almost a decade later, some Taos residents fled to the Plains, in present Scott County, Kans., where they took refuge among the Apaches, with whom they had long had trading contacts. When Spanish officials later induced many of these refugees to return from the Plains, they rebuilt the church and mission.

Popé, a medicine man, plotted and directed the Pueblo Revolt of 1680 from Taos. Before the Taos warriors descended the Rio Grande to join other Puebloans, attack Santa Fe, and drive the Spaniards out of New

Taos Pueblo exemplifies native resistance to Spanish and American invaders of New Mexico, especially during the Pueblo Revolt of 1680. Still inhabited, it has changed little throughout the years. Courtesy, New Mexico State Tourist Bureau.

Mexico, they again razed the Church of San Gerónimo de Taos and murdered the priest. Popé and other Taos Indians apparently held positions of leadership in Santa Fe during the dozen years of the Spanish expulsion, and they were among the last to submit when Don Diego de Vargas returned in 1692 to reassert Spanish authority. The Taosenos fled twice rather than submit, and De Vargas sacked the pueblo. In 1696, the Indians revolted again, but De Vargas pursued them into a nearby canyon, where finally they surrendered. The population of the pueblo declined from about 2,000 in 1680 to 505 by 1760.

Relationships improved during the 18th century, as Spaniards and Taosenos drew together for protection from Ute and Comanche raids. Something of this cooperative spirit was rekindled in 1847 when, instigated by Mexicans who resented the U.S. occupation of New Mexico, Taos led another rebellion. Governor Bent and other Americans were killed at the nearby Spanish-Mexican village of Taos. When troops arrived from Santa Fe, the Taos Indians took refuge behind the thick walls of San Gerónimo Mission, only to be blasted out by American artillery fire. The church has never been rebuilt, but has been replaced by a new structure at another site. Indian graves are located all around and within the crumbling walls of the ruined church, which has a roofless bell tower.

Present Appearance. The pueblo, still inhabited, has a population to-day of more than 1,200. It appears much the same as it always has, mainly because of the conservatism of its residents. It is divided into two compact units, northern and southern, by a small stream that flows from the nearby rugged mountains. Each unit is still five or six stories high, built now entirely of adobe and featuring many doors and windows. In earlier times, the upper stories were largely constructed of wood, and ceiling hatchways provided the only exterior entrances and illumination of the chambers. Each story is still terraced back, about 15 feet, from the story below. Few of the *portales,* or wooden porches, which formerly covered the terraces, remain.[48]

49. Boughton Hill (Gannagaro) Site, New York

Location. Ontario County, on Holcomb-Victor Road, 1¼ miles south of Victor.

Ownership and Administration. Privately owned.

Significance. Boughton Hill is the site of Gannagaro, an important 17th-century Seneca village, from which the Senecas struck at the French and their Indian allies. Braves from Gannagaro ranged as far west as the Illinois country, where they attacked Fort St. Louis and harried French traders. The Seneca Indians, the westernmost of the five-nation League of the Iroquois, were mainly dependent upon Dutch and English trade goods, although they rarely dealt directly with the traders. The Mohawks, an eastern Iroquois tribe, acted as middlemen in the extensive beaver fur trade between the Senecas and the Dutch.

After the beaver supply was exhausted in the Iroquois country about 1640, the League of the Iroquois attempted to gain control over the tribes engaged in the fur trade with the French. The French were angered, and conflict ensued for many years; in 1666, they invaded the Mohawk country twice. In 1683, a war party of Seneca braves sacked seven canoes filled with French goods and attacked Fort St. Louis. Wary of an Iroquois-English alliance, the French refrained from retribution until 1687, after the Marquis de Denonville became Governor of Canada. To further his ambition to secure New York for France, Denonville attacked the Seneca and drove them away from Gannagaro. Though weakened and defeated, they soon returned to the area but decentralized and lived in small family clusters.

Gannagaro was apparently a town of several hundred dwellings, but no definite pattern of settlement has been established. The site has yielded a large quantity of trade items and artifacts; few of the artifacts are aboriginal. No excavations have been carried out at the nearby Fort Hill Site, where the Seneca are said to have built a palisaded fort, or at the Battlefield Site, where Denonville is believed to have been ambushed.

Present Appearance. This site is located on farmland. No structural remains or evidence of Indian occupation are visible.[49]

50. Dutch Reformed (Sleepy Hollow) Church, New York

Location. Westchester County, on U.S. 9, at the northern outskirts of North Tarrytown.

Ownership and Administration. First Reformed Church of North Tarrytown.

Significance. This church, a distinguished relic of Dutch America, is notable for its architectural and historical associations with colonial life on the Hudson. The exact date of construction is not known, but it was probably between 1697 and 1699. Frederick Philipse I, Lord of Philipsburg Manor, erected the church for his tenants. The congregation had organized by 1697, when a pastor assumed his duties and the building was dedicated.

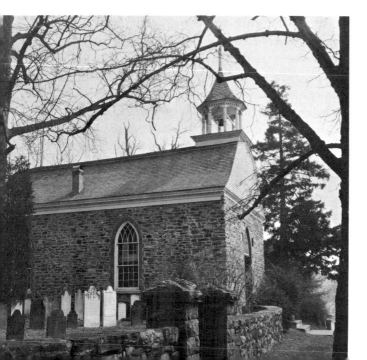

Dutch Reformed (Sleepy Hollow) Church, New York, is a notable reminder of Dutch influence in colonial America. In the late 17th century, Frederick Philipse I, Lord of Philipsburg Manor, erected the church for his tenants. It was an active church until after the Civil War.

The first significant changes in the church occurred during the War for Independence, when the special pews of the Lords of the Manor were removed, and high-backed, soft-pine pews were substituted for the plain oak tenant benches. In 1837, the building was struck by lightning and partially destroyed, and certain alterations resulted. Around 1840, the congregation built a new church in Tarrytown to serve as a branch of the old one, and after the Civil War it came to replace the original structure as the place of regular worship. From that time on, the Sleepy Hollow Church has been used only for occasional services and special programs.

Present Appearance. A partial restoration of the interior of the church—beams, quartered oak ceiling, and pulpit—was undertaken prior to the bicentennial observance; this corrected much of the 1837 alteration. The interior is barren of decoration and somewhat bleak in character. However, the charm of the original design remains, and the building and grounds are carefully maintained by the congregation of the First Reformed Church, which owns the property. The adjacent burial ground is also well kept. Included among the graves is that of Washington Irving, who perpetuated the name of "Sleepy Hollow" for the church. The church is open to the public only on special occasions.[50]

51. Fort Crailo, New York

Location. Rensselaer County, on Riverside Street south of Columbia Street, Rensselaer.

Ownership and Administration. State of New York; Department of Education, University of the State of New York, Albany.

Significance. Fort Crailo, a brick manor house on the east bank of the Hudson River, was probably built around the beginning of the 18th century. Standing near the center of what was once the 700,000-acre estate of Kiliaen Van Rensselaer, who managed the first and only successful patroonship established by authority of the Dutch West India Company, its role in Dutch life in the Albany region was a major one. The architectural changes that have taken place over the years merely emphasize the wealth of the various socially prominent Dutch owners, who enlarged and altered their residence as the need arose.

The immense Van Rensselaer estate was founded in 1630. Van Rensselaer was a wealthy diamond merchant of Amsterdam, whose agents obtained a vast tract that extended from the mouth of the Mohawk

Fort Crailo, probably built in the first part of the 18th century, was headquarters of the immense Van Rensselaer estate, at one time a 700,000-acre patroonship.

River southward for 20 miles along both sides of the Hudson, and a total width of almost 50 miles. Fort Crailo, headquarters of this empire, was built on the site of Rensselaer, known then as "Greenen Bosch"—"Pine Forest" in Dutch and corrupted later to "Green Bush."

Some authorities believe that Fort Crailo dates from 1642, but others contend that it was constructed later of material from an earlier house, or that it stands on the foundation of the 1642 residence built by Rensselaer's first agent. The State of New York, however, credits the building to Hendrick Van Rensselaer, younger brother of the patroon, and dates it about 1704. It is known that the Van Rensselaer family occupied the house as early as that year and continued to live in it until 1871.

In 1740, Col. Johannes Van Rensselaer added a cross hall and dining room, upstairs rooms, and the remainder of the ell extending behind the main building. A grandson of Johannes made other alterations early in the 19th century. In 1924, a Van Rensselaer descendant donated the old house to the State of New York. During restoration, the State eliminated most of the 19th-century alterations.

Present Appearance. Fort Crailo consists of two and one-half stories and a cellar; the earliest portion includes two rooms and a hall on the first and second floor. The heavy brick walls are laid in Dutch crossbond.

The loopholes on the lower floor indicate the original defensive nature of the house. In keeping with the house's significance as the manorial seat of a foremost Hudson Valley Dutch family, it is furnished with care. Maintained in good condition, it is open throughout the year.[51]

52. Fort St. Frederic, New York

Location. Essex County, junction of N.Y. 8 and U.S. 9N, Crown Point Reservation.

Ownership and Administration. State of New York; Department of Conservation.

Significance. This fort symbolizes the bitter struggle between France and England for mastery of North America. The French built it in 1731 to guard Lake Champlain—the key to the defense of Canada. It served in this capacity for the next 28 years, after which it was of vital importance to the British in defending the Hudson Valley and the northern colonies. Originally, it had high 18-foot-thick walls of limestone, quarried about one-half mile away. The eastern side of the four-story fort had a high watchtower that had thick walls and was equipped with a number of cannon. The fort was served by a battery of 62 guns. It was about 300 feet square and had four bastions; three were diamond-shaped, and the fourth, on the northwest, quadrangular shaped. The fort included a small church and stone quarters for officers and troops.

Some years after the fort's construction, the French erected a second fort, Carillon, 12 miles to the south to further protect the Lake Champlain approach to Canada. In 1759, British forces under Maj. Gen. Jeffrey Amherst captured Carillon and renamed it Ticonderoga. It later figured prominently in the War for Independence. At the time of Amherst's invasion, the French abandoned and destroyed Fort St. Frederic. The British did not rebuild it, but erected a new fort about 200 yards away and named it Crown Point, or Amherst.

Present Appearance. Though fragmentary, the ruins of Fort St. Frederic, consisting of walls and earthworks, make possible a mental recreation of the original stone fort. Nearby in the picturesque setting are the ruins of Fort Amherst. Chimney Point, on the opposite shore of Lake Champlain, sheltered a French settlement that was contemporary with Fort St. Frederic. An adjacent museum contains a number of relics that were found in and near the forts.[52]

53. Old Fort Niagara, New York

Location. Niagara County, on N.Y. 18, just north of Youngstown.

Ownership and Administration. State of New York; leased to the Old Fort Niagara Association, Youngstown.

Significance. At this strategic fort, in the eastern Great Lakes region, as much or more fighting occurred as at any other outpost during the colonial period and the early years of the United States. The fort was at various times controlled by the Iroquois Federation, France, England, and the United States. Situated at the mouth of the Niagara River, it commanded the Great Lakes route between Lakes Erie and Ontario and protected the approaches to New York's western frontier.

Built in 1679 by order of La Salle, the fort was rebuilt twice by the French, the last time in 1725–26. The notable Stone House, or "Castle," in reality a fort built to resemble a French provincial chateau so as to delude the Indians, was erected during this period. Between 1750 and 1759, the French enlarged the fort and converted the Stone House and temporary buildings into an elaborate stronghold with earthworks, moats, magazines, and gun emplacements. Much of this later improvement remains.

In 1759, as the struggle between England and France neared its climax in America, a British force captured Fort Niagara. William Pitt, the English Prime Minister, regarded the fort as second in importance only to Quebec. In English hands during the War for Independence, the fort was a base for combined British-Indian expeditions against the American frontier. The British held it until 1796 when, under the Treaty of 1794, the United States took it over. Recaptured by the British during the War of 1812, it was restored to the United States by the Treaty of Ghent, at the end of the conflict.

Present Appearance. The fort is today one of the best restored and preserved in America. Restored features include the famous "Stone House," moat, drawbridge, blockhouse, earthen ramparts, parade grounds, and a cross symbolic of one planted on the site in 1688 by Father Pierre Millet. Millet had accompanied a French column sent to the relief of the dozen survivors of the 100-man garrison that had been almost wiped out by hunger and disease the preceding winter. The fort is adjacent to the Fort Niagara Military Reservation, a Regular Army post. Restorations of the Old Fort Niagara Association, which were aided by the survival of several buildings and fortifications, clearly portray the fort's history.[53]

54. Old House, New York

Location. Suffolk County, on N.Y. 25, Cutchogue, Long Island.

Ownership and Administration. Congregational Society of Cutchogue.

Significance. This house, which notably commemorates English settlement on Long Island, is undoubtedly one of the most distinguished but least known examples of English domestic architecture in the United States. It was erected in 1649 by John Budd at Southold, some 10 miles northeast of its present site. A decade later, Budd built a more imposing home and gave his original house as a wedding gift to his daughter, Anna, bride of Benjamin Horton, who moved it to its present location and re-erected it. It subsequently passed into the hands of Joseph Wickham, a master tanner, who lived in it until his death, in 1734. Later, in 1784, it was confiscated from Parker Wickham, who had been a Loyalist during the War for Independence, after which its owners in turn were Jared Landon and William Harrison Case. The Case heirs donated it to the Congregational Society of Cutchogue.

Present Appearance. The house has two floors and an attic. On the first floor are the kitchen and "hall," and on the second floor are two bedrooms. The great brick chimney, whose top is pilastered, lies to the left of the center of the house. A steep winding stair leads to the second story. The stair from the second floor branches to give access to the attic, which is split in two by the great chimney.

The kitchen, on the left of the entrance, features a huge fireplace. The fireplace in the "hall," on the right of the entrance, is the same size. Both fireplaces have been somewhat reduced by the construction of smaller fireplaces inside the originals. The smaller fireplaces were added around the middle of the 18th century, probably when paneling was placed over the original walls.

The original random-width wallboards were removed and used on the exterior to replace the original hand-rived oak boards. The exterior was then lathed and plastered. Construction details throughout the house are unusually fine and reflect the work of a master builder. The three-part casement window frames on the north wall of the second floor are especially notable. Traces have also been found of the casement windows that were originally on the first floor.

The house was restored in 1940 in connection with the Southampton Old Town Tercentenary Celebration, through the efforts of the Tercentenary Committee, the Case family, and the Independent Congregational Church of Cutchogue. The church purchased the land and the Case family donated the building. Church funds and private contributions made the restoration possible. When the house was restored, the plastered walls and a saltbox roof were removed. The gunstock posts on the second floor and all interior framework were left exposed. Furnishings are of the 17th and 18th century. Among the historic items displayed is the original confiscation deed of 1784. The structure is in very good condition and is open to visitors on a regular schedule.[54]

55. Philipsburg Manor, Upper Mills, New York

Location. Westchester County, 381 Bellwood Avenue, off U.S. 9, north of intersection with N.Y. 117, North Tarrytown.

Ownership and Administration. Sleepy Hollow Restorations, Inc., Tarrytown.

Significance. This simple stone house authentically portrays a great 17th-century manor and presents a remarkable picture of Dutch settlement in the lower Hudson Valley before 1750. Frederick Philipse, First Lord of the manor of Philipsburg, built the older portion about 1683, although he used the more pretentious manor house at the site of Yonkers, a few miles south, as his main residence when away from the city of New York.

When the First Lord died, in 1702, the northern section of the manor passed to his second son, Adolphus, who made the house at North Tarrytown his permanent home. From the more imposing manor house at Yonkers, Frederick Philipse II ruled the southern section of the manor. When Adolphus died, in 1750, Frederick II inherited the northern portion of the estate and reunited the entire manor under a single owner. Frederick II continued to live in the more elaborate manor house at Yonkers, and the building at North Tarrytown fell into obscurity. In 1785, Gerard Beekman added the frame wing to the original stone structure. The house was much abused over the years until its restoration was undertaken in 1943. It is now a project of Sleepy Hollow Restorations.

Present Appearance. When all restoration work is completed and the house opened to the public, 24 rooms will be furnished in period style from the date of the earliest construction to the opening of the 19th century. These rooms will present a vivid cross section of the continuity of Dutch life and tradition on the Hudson. Further adding to the interest and historical integrity of the property is the nearby Dutch Reformed (Sleepy Hollow) Church, built around 1697 by Frederick Philipse I for his tenants.[55]

56. Philipse Manor Hall, New York

Location. Westchester County, Warburton Avenue and Dock Street, Yonkers.

Ownership and Administration. State of New York; State Education Department, University of the State of New York, Albany.

Significance. This house is an outstanding representative of the 18th-century Dutch manorial system in the lower Hudson Valley. It served as the social and administrative center of the great manor of Philipsburg, created under English rule in 1693. Governed successively by Lords of the Manor Frederick Philipse I, II, and III, the manor of Philipsburg was closer to the colonial capital of New York and was more intimately associated with its social and political institutions than any of the other Hudson River baronies.

The first Frederick Philipse came to New Netherland in 1647. Although well born, he had little more than his good name when he arrived in New Amsterdam and became a "carpenter" for the Dutch West India Company. In 1657, he acquired the "Small Burgher Right of New Amsterdam," which made him eligible to become a merchant and to occupy certain public offices in the colony. Thereafter his rise was rapid as he acquired houses and land, and profited highly in colonial trade. His marriage in 1662 to Margaret de Vries, a wealthy widow, paved the road to further advancement.

Soon Philipse was one of New Netherland's leading citizens. In 1672, he and two partners bought a large section of the former patroonship of Adriaen Van der Donck, on the site of Yonkers. Several years later Philipse bought out his partners and in succeeding years amassed holdings up the Hudson River Valley as far as the Croton River. By 1693, his estate extended more than 20 miles along the east side of the Hudson and embraced some 156,000 acres. Out of this vast empire, a royal patent in 1693 created the manor of Philipsburg and designated Frederick Philipse as its First Lord.

Philipse's domain then became an important unit in the political and

Philipse Manor Hall, New York, whose construction began in the 17th century, served as social and administrative center for the Philipse family's manor of Philipsburg. In the 19th century, it was the village and city hall of Yonkers.

social development of provincial New York. His grandson, Frederick Philipse II, inherited the manor and maintained the family's role of leadership in the colony. Frederick III, however, remained loyal to the Crown when the colonies declared for independence, and in 1776 he was arrested on orders of General Washington and the manor of Philipsburg confiscated. When Philipse and his family fled to England, a colorful chapter in the story of colonial America came to an end.

Sometime in the 1680's, perhaps before the creation of Philipsburg Manor, Frederick Philipse I built a sturdy stone house on the site of Yonkers. Many authorities have asserted that this structure is preserved today as the south wing of the present building. One expert investigator has concluded that part of the foundation may antedate 1682; that part of the southern wing dates from about the period 1682–94; and that the remainder and larger part, constructed by the Second Lord of the Manor, dates from about 1725 or 1730, or possibly as late as 1745.

After the War for Independence, Philipse Manor Hall passed through several hands. For some years following 1868, it served Yonkers as the village hall and later the city hall. Threatened with demolition at the end of the 19th century, it was saved through the efforts of local citizens and organizations. Finally, in 1908, the State of New York accepted an

endowment of the house from Mrs. William F. Cochran which specified that it be maintained by the American Scenic and Historic Preservation Society. Within 4 years, the house was completely renovated. The
notable Cochran collection of portraits of presidents and other historical
figures was also assembled and exhibited. It includes works by Stuart,
Copley, the Peales, Trumbull, and Vanderlyn.

Present Appearance. As restored, Philipse Manor Hall is an outstanding representation of the early Georgian style. The original stone portion
of the building forms the base of the L-shaped plan; the later brick addition, a long north arm. The interior is distinguished by intricate plaster-
work on the ceilings of a number of rooms in both sections. The older
portion of the house probably received this embellishment when the new
section was added by the Second Lord.

The manor hall is structurally sound and the exterior is in good condition. The interior walls and ceilings need plastering, and additional period furnishings would be highly desirable. The important Cochran
portrait collection is well displayed. The house is open to the public, and
tours are conducted. The grounds immediately adjacent to the hall are
well kept, but the setting is somewhat marred by surrounding commercial
development.[56]

57. Van Cortlandt Manor, New York

Location. Westchester County, on U.S. 9, north of intersection with
N.Y. 9A, Croton-on-Hudson.

Ownership and Administration. Sleepy Hollow Restorations, Inc.,
Tarrytown.

Significance. This stone manor house, along with its grounds and outbuildings, is the most authentic and significant survival of the 18th
century Dutch-English manor house of the Hudson Valley. Its oldest
portion was constructed between 1665 and 1681. Simplicity of line and
detail set the house apart from more pretentious manor houses such as
Philipsburg Manor, Upper Mills, at North Tarrytown, and Philipse
Manor Hall, in Yonkers. Van Cortlandt Manor was remodeled in the
mid-18th century, the period which is reflected in its recent restoration.

The Van Cortlandt family in America was founded by Oloffe Stevense
Van Cortlandt, a soldier who in 1638 came from the Netherlands. In

Representative of an 18th-century Dutch-English manor house in the Hudson Valley is the Van Cortlandt Manor, once the home of the influential Van Cortlandt family and center of their 86,000-acre estate.

1677, his son, Stephanus, started acquiring land in the lower Hudson Valley, on the Croton River. A few years later he began the construction of his country house, likely on the foundation of an earlier fort-trading post that may have been erected as early as 1665.

William III recognized Stephanus' semifeudal estate, amounting to 86,000 acres, as the Manor of Cortlandt on June 16, 1697. It was not until 1749, however, that the manor became a dwelling in fact as well as name. In that year, Pierre Van Cortlandt, Third Lord of the Manor, occupied it on a permanent year-round basis. Before moving his family to the manor, Pierre enlarged it; he added a second story and otherwise modified the earlier building to the extent seen by today's visitor.

Pierre added new lustre to the family name. A foremost leader of colonial New York, he was an active patriot in the War for Independence and became the first Lieutenant Governor of the State, 1777–95. During the war, the family abandoned the estate, which was damaged by passing troops and vandals. When it was safe for the family to return, the damage was repaired. Until 1940, the property was the home of succeeding generations of Van Cortlandts.

Present Appearance. The house and a small portion of the original manor lands were purchased in 1953 by John D. Rockefeller, Jr., and the property is now a unit of Sleepy Hollow Restorations, Inc. Under these auspices, the house and 175 acres of the original estate have been expertly restored. In addition to the manor house, the restoration includes the estate office building built by the Third Lord; the Ferry House, an 18th-century tavern that served travelers on the old Albany Post Road; and the gardens, orchards, and outbuildings of the manor. The house is furnished largely with Van Cortlandt family items, which date from the 17th to the early 19th century. Excellent guide service is provided.[57]

58. Voorlezer's House, New York

Location. Richmond County, Arthur Kill Road opposite Center Street, Staten Island.

Ownership and Administration. Staten Island Historical Society, Richmondtown, Staten Island, N.Y.

Significance. This framehouse, built before 1696, is not only the oldest known elementary school building in the United States but also one of the most important surviving relics of 17th-century Dutch settlement in New York. The earliest documented reference to it is dated 1696; and the date of the patent on which it is located is 1680. The house was probably erected some time between those dates. How long it served as a school is not known. It passed through several hands, but remained in the possession of one family for more than 150 years. Though well maintained for many years, by 1936 it had fallen into disrepair and was threatened with demolition. Fortunately, a member of the Staten Island Historical Society purchased the building and donated it to the organization.

Present Appearance. The two-story house is clapboarded. The roof has an unequal pitch because the front of the house is 2 feet higher than the rear. The foundation walls are 2 feet thick, of rough, undressed field stone laid up in mud and mortar. All timbers are of oak or white wood, cut in nearby forests and hewn to size with a broadax. A massive stone-and-brick chimney is at the northeast end of the house. Around 1800, the present staircases were substituted for the straight ladder-like stairs believed to have been used originally.

The first floor contains a small room used as living quarters and a large room for church services. The second floor has a small bedchamber and a large room, believed to be the one used for the school. The extra set of floor beams indicate that the room was designed to accommodate a large number of persons. The floors in the house are of white pine boards, 14 to 16 inches wide. The windows and doors, which have been replaced, have the low and wide proportions of the originals. The building is open by appointment; a custodian is on the premises.[58]

59. Big Hidatsa Village Site, North Dakota

Location. Mercer County, on an improved road, along the north bank of the Knife River, 2½ miles north of Stanton.

Ownership and Administration. Privately owned.

Significance. The largest of the three Hidatsa villages was located at this site, also known today as the Olds Site, from about 1740 to 1845. During that period, these villages, and two later Mandan villages nearby, were important in the Northern Plains fur trade. As early as 1738, La Vérendrye, the French fur trader and explorer, may have contacted the Hidatsas when he visited the Mandans on the Heart River. During the next decade, the French began to trade with the two tribes.

This trade flourished until the beginning of the French and Indian War, in 1754. After 1766, British traders were active in the area. Meriwether Lewis and William Clark spent the winter of 1804–5 at nearby Fort Mandan and described the Hidatsas in their journal. George Catlin, Prince Maximilian, and Karl Bodmer described and sketched the villages in the years 1832–34. These descriptions and sketches are especially valuable because the Mandans were nearly destroyed and the Hidatsas seriously weakened by a smallpox epidemic in 1837. Shortly after 1845, the surviving Hidatsas moved upstream and established a new village near the newly constructed Fort Berthold.

Archeological excavation of the site has revealed lower levels primarily of aboriginal materials and a large number of European trade items mixed with aboriginal items in the upper levels.

Present Appearance. This site, which is not open to the public, embraces approximately 15 acres. Because most of it has not been cultivated, it is exceptionally well preserved. The depressions of more than 100 circular earth lodges and several fortification trenches can be seen clearly.[59]

60. Menoken Indian Village Site, North Dakota

Location. Burleigh County, just off U.S. 10–83, about 1¼ miles north of Menoken.

Ownership and Administration. State of North Dakota.

Significance. The Mandan village located at this site was probably the one visited by the French explorer La Vérendrye in 1738. He described it as a fort built on a small hill in the open prairie. It contained about 130 dwellings and was surrounded by a palisade that had four bastions, outside of which was a defensive ditch 15 feet deep and 15 to 18 feet wide. While at the village, La Vérendyre heard of five other villages located nearby on "the river," and sent his son to visit them. After visiting only the nearest village on a 1-day trip, the son reported that it was situated "on the bank of the river," and that it was twice as big as the one they were in. He added that "the palisade and fortification there are . . . built in the same style as that in which we were."

The references are undoubtedly to the Missouri River and to the five earth lodge villages dating from the La Vérendrye period whose sites have been found at the mouth of the Heart River in North Dakota. The Menoken Indian Village is the only known fortified Mandan village of the period that is located eastward and within 1 day's journey of the Heart River villages. The ditch surrounding the site is still clearly visible, and archeological investigation has produced evidence of a palisade that had four bastions. Thus, this village was probably the one visited by La Vérendrye.

Present Appearance. The site has been well preserved by the State of North Dakota, which calls it the Menoken Indian Village Archeological Site.[60]

61. Forks of the Ohio, Pennsylvania

Location. Allegheny County, "The Golden Triangle," Point State Park, Pittsburgh.

Ownership and Administration. Commonwealth of Pennsylvania; Department of Forests and Waters.

Significance. From about 1750 until 1815 the Forks of the Ohio, where the Monongahela and Allegheny Rivers join to form the Ohio

River at Pittsburgh, was a strategic key to the Ohio Valley and the vast territory drained by the upper Mississippi River. Men of three nations fought and died struggling for control of this strategic location, where the bustling city of Pittsburgh—one of the first permanent settlements by the English west of the Allegheny Mountains—arose in the shelter of a series of fortifications. Still later, the forks was a major gateway to the West for waves of settlers pushing into the Ohio and Mississippi Valleys.

The growing French influence in the Ohio Valley region during the 1750's was incompatible with the westward thrust of England's seaboard colonies. George Washington visited the forks in November 1753, while en route to the French-held Fort Le Boeuf to warn the French away from the Ohio country. Washington strongly endorsed the forks as the most strategic position to command the rivers, and in February 1754 Englishmen began to construct the first outpost there. Two months later, however, a combined force of French and Indians seized the weak stockade. The French proceeded to build a fort, which they named after Duquesne, the Governor-General of New France. This heightened the tensions that led to the 9-year conflict known in America as the French and Indian War and abroad as the Seven Years' War.

When Washington learned that the French had seized the post at the forks, he returned with a small force, which on May 28 surprised and defeated a French scouting party near Great Meadows, 11 miles east of the present city of Uniontown. Troops from Fort Duquesne besieged the hastily built Fort Necessity and forced Washington to surrender on July 4. The French beat off a more threatening English effort the next year, when they shattered Gen. James Braddock's force several miles east of the forks. Thus, for 3 years longer, Fort Duquesne continued to serve as a French base for raids against the English frontier.

In 1758, 6,500 British and colonial troops under Gen. John Forbes made a remarkable forced march through the rugged Pennsylvania wilderness and found Duquesne destroyed and abandoned by the French because of pressures elsewhere and the desertion of their Indian allies. Col. Hugh Mercer was left with 200 men to secure the position for England. In 1759, the English began to construct a major permanent fortification, named Fort Pitt in honor of the Prime Minister of England. The exterior walls of the pentagonal fort were earthen ramparts faced with brick. Frame and brick buildings were constructed inside, parallel to the interior walls. A town that subsequently became Pittsburgh began to take shape in the surrounding vicinity as settlers, mostly Virginians, followed Braddock's trail to take advantage of whatever opportunities might be available.

Fort Pitt was one of the few English forts to withstand attack during the Pontiac uprising of 1763–64. As the French and Indian threat receded, the fort deteriorated, while the settlement of Pittsburgh prospered as a base for traders, backwoodsmen, and westward-moving settlers. The United States built a fifth and last fort, LaFayette or Fayette, at the forks in the winter of 1791–92, when war with the Indians in the old Northwest flamed anew. Located a quarter of a mile above the site of Fort Pitt, which had fallen into ruin, the fort supplied troops during the Whisky Rebellion, in 1794, and served as a supply and training depot in the War of 1812.

Present Appearance. A few years ago the point of land at the forks lay beneath a clutter of commercial structures and railroad tracks. However, development of the 36-acre Point State Park in the shadow of modern Pittsburgh's skyscrapers on the city's "Golden Triangle" has removed the most objectionable modern intrusions and will provide an eloquent historical interpretation. Archeological investigation has provided much useful information about Fort Pitt, whose flag bastion has been restored. Careful plans have been laid for rebuilding the Monongahela Bastion, including a museum under the administration of the Pennsylvania Historical and Museum Commission. The original Bouquet Blockhouse, preserved for years by the Allegheny County Chapter of the Daughters of the American Revolution, will remain at its original site. Attractive promenades have been laid out along the shores of both rivers, and stone bleachers seating 3,000 persons have been placed along the Allegheny River. In summer the city of Pittsburgh anchors a barge at the park, and free concerts and other programs are presented.[61]

62. The Printzhof, Pennsylvania

Location. Delaware County, near the junction of Pa. 291 and 420, corner of Taylor Avenue and Second Street, Essington.

Ownership and Administration. Commonwealth of Pennsylvania; Pennsylvania Historical and Museum Commission.

Significance. The site and remains of the Printzhof, home and headquarters of Gov. Johan Printz and the "capital" of New Sweden during the period 1643–53, comprise one of the most notable preservations relating to the story of Sweden in America. The site is also significant as the first permanent white settlement in what became Pennsylvania.

The first Swedish expedition to America, in 1638, planted a settlement on the banks of the Minquas Kill, now the Christina River, at the site of modern Wilmington. The infant colony of New Sweden limped along for a few years, virtually ignored by the homeland, until the energetic autocrat Johan Printz arrived in 1643 to direct affairs. After exploring the Delaware River as far north as the site of Trenton, N.J., "Big Guts," as the Indians admiringly called the Governor, chose small Tinicum Island as the best location for his dwelling place because of its fertile soil and because it was well protected by the surrounding Darby and Bow Creeks, and the Delaware itself.

Printz immediately erected a fort, New Gothenburg, and within it a commodious log house, the Printzhof, for himself and his family, as well as a log chapel, storehouse, and brewery. Two years later, in 1645, a fire and the explosion of the fort's powder magazine destroyed the buildings. With characteristic energy, Printz rebuilt the fort and the Printzhof. Until his departure from New Sweden in 1653, he ruled his struggling colony with an iron hand. At Tinicum Island he held court; acted as prosecutor, judge, and jury; and conducted a holding action against the claims to the Delaware of his Dutch counterpart in New Amsterdam, Peter Stuyvesant. At Tinicum were located the first mills, church, and school in the territory that would one day be Pennsylvania.

Present Appearance. The site of the Printzhof and a portion of the surrounding settlement has fortunately been spared from the intensive modern development on the banks of the Delaware, and is preserved in the 7 acres of Governor Printz Park. Archeological investigation in 1937 by the Pennsylvania Historical and Museum Commission disclosed the stone foundations of Printz's house, and uncovered thousands of artifacts of Swedish origin. The foundations of the Printzhof are the only visible remains of the settlement. The present park was created through the donation of land by the Swedish-Colonial Society to celebrate the 300th anniversary of the founding of New Sweden in 1938. The park was formally dedicated by Prince Bertil of Sweden on June 29, 1939.[62]

63. Wanton-Lyman-Hazard House, Rhode Island

Location. Newport County, 17 Broadway, Newport.

Ownership and Administration. Newport Historical Society, 82 Touro Street, Newport.

Significance. This house, probably built around 1695 and one of New England's best Jacobean houses, illustrates the architectural transition from the 17th to the 18th century. Its sturdy frame construction is typical of the earliest New England houses, and its elaborate structural detail and ornamentation reflect the changes that began early in the 18th century and developed into the Georgian style of the middle colonial period. Although other 17th-century structures may still stand in Newport, the Wanton-Lyman-Hazard House best reflects the architecture of the century.

The first known mention of the house dates from 1724, when Stephen Mumford transferred ownership over to Richard Ward, who in 1740 became Governor of the Colony of Rhode Island. In 1765, the house, then occupied by Martin Howard, the Tory Stamp Master of Newport, was extensively damaged during the Stamp Act riots. Subsequent repairs probably included the casing of the beams and the installation of the mantel paneling.

Present Appearance. Originally a two-and-one-half story structure, the house had rooms on both sides of the massive chimney and probably a kitchen ell on the rear. The chimney is of brick rather than stone. Because brick was not common in Rhode Island before the 18th century, the

Wanton-Lyman-Hazard House, in Newport, Rhode Island, is a combination of 17th- and 18th-century architectural styles.

chimney represents a unique example of brickwork in the colony. The characteristically steep pitch of the roof remains unchanged. The only major changes in the house's original exterior are the addition of a lean-to across the back; the installation of dormers and sash windows; and the building of the classic doorway, which dates from 1782. The huge plaster coved cornice in the front of the roof indicates an attempt on the part of the original builder to break away from the simple treatment of the 17th century.

Purchased by the Newport Historical Society from the Hazard family in 1927, the house was restored under the direction of Norman M. Isham. In the north bedchamber may be seen the original ceiling beams and the massive corner posts. The house and its garden are maintained in excellent condition. Furnishings are of the 18th century, but a few earlier pieces are included. The house is open to the public from May 15 to October 15.[63]

64. Adam Thoroughgood House, Virginia

Location. Princess Anne County, on Lynnhaven Bay, just off Va. 166, about 4 miles east of Norfolk.

Ownership and Administration. Adam Thoroughgood House Foundation, Norfolk.

Significance. This restored house, one of the oldest in Virginia, is a fine example of the central-hall house of 17th-century Virginia. Adam Thoroughgood came to Virginia in 1621 as an indentured servant. After working off his indenture, he rose rapidly in position and in 1629 became a member of the House of Burgesses. By the time of his death, in 1640, at the age of 35, he owned some 7,000 acres of land in Princess Anne County.

In 1636, Thoroughgood bought the tract on which the present house stands. The Adam Thoroughgood House Foundation does not believe that this house is the one listed in his will in 1640, but that he may have built it for one of his sons, or that it may have been built by a son or grandson. In any event, it is of authentic 17th-century design and workmanship. Of brick, it measures 45 by 22 feet. Three walls are laid in English bond and one in Flemish. The house is a low-eaved, one-and-a-half story structure and has a steep gabled roof. Of the two huge end chimneys, one is projecting and one set inside the wall. A hall, 10 feet wide, separates the two rooms below, the one to the north being the larger. The house was altered in 1745, when the original leaded glass

Adam Thoroughgood House, a fine example of a 17th-century central-hall house, is one of the oldest brick structures in Virginia.

panes in the parlor were replaced with Georgian windows; the exposed ceiling beams were covered with plaster; and paneling was added to the walls.

Present Appearance. Under the auspices of the foundation, the Thoroughgood House was restored to its 17th-century condition and opened to the public in 1957. The restoration included removal of dormers, reduction in the size of windows, return of leaded glass panes, and the removal of plaster and other later additions. In several places, glass inserts show details of the original construction. The original 5,350-acre estate has been subdivided through the years, and a recent housing development has reduced the house tract to 4½ acres. The grounds, which have been nicely landscaped, include a 17th-century garden donated by the Garden Club of Virginia.[64]

65. Bacon's Castle, Virginia

Location. Surry County, on Va. 10, between Surry and Rushmore.

Ownership and Administration. Privately owned.

Significance. Bacon's Castle is one of the most important existing buildings of 17th-century Virginia, on both historical and architectural grounds. Earliest extant example of the Virginia cross-plan houses and a remarkable architectural monument of the colonial period, it was built by Arthur Allen about 1655 and figured prominently in Bacon's Rebellion of 1676. A number of the rebel followers of Nathaniel Bacon seized Major Allen's house and fortified it; the house was thereafter known as Bacon's Castle.

This house is the earliest extant example of a 17th-century Virginia cross-plan house. In 1676, Nathaniel Bacon's rebel followers seized and fortified it for about 3 months. Thereafter it was known as Bacon's Castle.

The garrison, commanded at various times by William Rookings, Arthur Long, Joseph Rogers, and John Clements, retained control of the house for more than 3 months, but their cause was declining. The death of Bacon in October left his forces under the leadership of Joseph Ingram, who proved to be unsuited to the command. Ingram dispersed his army in small garrisons. As the demoralized troops began to plunder indiscriminately, conditions in the colony became deplorable.

Gov. William Berkeley began to conquer the isolated posts one by one, some by force and some by persuasion. A loyal force from the vessel *Young Prince* captured an unidentified "fort" on December 29 that many historians have identified as Bacon's Castle. After withstanding a brief siege early in January 1677, the Loyalists used the "fort" as a base of operations for the last engagements of the rebellion, which ended before the month was out.

Bacon's Castle is a fine extant example of the Virginia cross plan. A two-story brick structure laid in English bond, it has a 10-foot-square, two-story porch in front and a larger stair tower in the rear. The main floor originally had a great hall and smaller parlor. The stair tower afforded access to a large cellar containing several rooms and an 8-foot-wide fireplace, as well as two large bedrooms on the second floor and three more in the garret.

Exterior features of note are the Flemish gables at each end of the house; large triple chimneys stand barely free of the gables. The chimneys, set diagonally and joined only at the caps, rise from a straight stack 10 feet wide and 4 feet deep. The house is a unique example of Jacobean architecture.

Present Appearance. Bacon's Castle has been altered at various times, and until a few years ago was in poor condition. About the middle of the 19th century, a brick addition was annexed to the east side of the house; it replaced an earlier frame addition that was moved some distance away and is still standing. Many original features remain unaltered, and the present owner has renovated the house so carefully as to permit a restoration at some future time. The home is privately owned and is not ordinarily open to visitors.[65]

66. St. Luke's Church, Virginia

Location. Isle of Wight County, on U.S. 258, at Benns Church.

Ownership and Administration. Historic St. Luke's Restoration, Inc., Smithfield.

Significance. This venerable structure, originally called the "Old Brick" or "Newport Parish" Church, is probably the best surviving example of 17th-century Gothic architecture in the United States. Its construction may have begun in 1632, for that year is incised on some of the bricks. In any event, the church doubtless replaced a wooden structure built a decade earlier.

Laid in Flemish bond in a single nave plan approximately 24 by 60 feet, the brick church took about 5 years to complete. Installation of the permanent interior fittings took longer, possibly as much as 25 years. About 1657, Col. Joseph Bridger, a prominent parishioner, brought over several artisan members of the Driver family from England to complete this work. During the last quarter of the century, a third story was added to the existing church tower, possibly by second-generation members of the Driver family.

Various architectural changes were made during the 18th century. When the Anglican Church in Virginia was disestablished, in 1785, St. Luke's was used only for occasional services and was not properly maintained. Rehabilitated in 1821, it remained in use for 15 years, being abandoned a second time when Christ Church in Smithfield, 5 miles away, was completed. After a half-century of disuse, a violent storm in 1887 collapsed the roof and part of the east gable. A partial restoration was made soon after under the auspices of the Reverend David Barr, but

St. Luke's Church, Virginia, begun about 1623, is a noteworthy example of 17th-century Gothic architecture. It has been carefully restored to its original condition.

in 1953 the foundations were discovered to be crumbling. During the next 4 years, the foundations were repaired and the church was completely restored.

Present Appearance. The church has been carefully restored to its 17th-century condition, except that the commemorative stained glass windows added in the late 19th century have not been replaced. The exterior work included permanent shoring of the foundations, reopening the base of the tower, altering the east stepped gable, and repointing the masonry. Interior restoration was extensive, including a timber roof erected with Gothic tie-beams; a floor of square brick; 17th-century rood-screen, chancel rail, and pews; and a triple-decker pulpit. The church has been furnished with a number of rare items, including a pair of silver wine flagons dated 1683, a silver trencher-plate of 1696, chancel furnishings of 17th-century cut-velvet, a 17th-century Bernard Smith organ, and a font made from a tree trunk. Occasional memorial services are held at the church, which is open to visitors daily.[66]

67. La Fortaleza, Puerto Rico

Location. Between Calle Recinto Oeste and San Juan Bay, southwest side of San Juan Island, San Juan.

Ownership and Administration. Commonwealth of Puerto Rico.

Significance. La Fortaleza (The Fortress) was the first true fortification in San Juan, established in 1521. The Spanish built it between 1533 and 1540 for protection against raids by Carib Indians and by English and French freebooters. Because of its comparatively poor location, however, it soon occupied a position of only secondary importance in the defenses of San Juan. Nevertheless, at the end of the 16th century the Earl of Cumberland, who led a successful English attack on the city, described it as "a strong castle, built of stone, square, and commonly called the King's Palace . . . and where we found a great stock of ammunition." In 1625, a Dutch force under Gen. Bowdoin Hendrick captured La Fortaleza, along with the rest of the town. However, the major defensive position, El Morro, succeeded in holding out; and, when the invaders retreated, they burned everything they could, including a large part of La Fortaleza. Since reconstruction of the fortress on a larger scale, which occurred soon after, it has been used chiefly as the residence of the Governors of Puerto Rico, as well as offices of the Treasurer and Intendant.

Present Appearance. One of the oldest structures in the New World, La Fortaleza is a fine example of Spanish colonial architectural style. It has tiled roofs; galleries, staircases, and doorways liberally decorated with wrought iron; sunlit patios; and graceful arches. Originally it was a simple, two-towered fortress. By 1580, additional rooms had been erected; they were arranged to form a patio and to serve more as a residence for the military commandant and officers than as a fortification. The reconstruction in the first half of the 17th century involved a considerable enlargement of the fortress. In 1846, the Spanish thoroughly renovated La Fortaleza and altered some of the interior decorations. In 1939, the U.S. Army also thoroughly rehabilitated the structure. Many historical features were lost during these renovations, but the basic identity of the structure is intact, including elements traceable to its original construction more than 400 years ago.[67]

68. Columbus Landing Site, Virgin Islands

Location. St. Croix Island, 4 miles west of Christiansted, west side of Salt River Bay.

Ownership and Administration. Privately owned, except for 5 acres of Fort Sale site, which are owned by the Government of the Virgin Islands.

Significance. This site is the earliest one now under the U.S. flag that is associated with Columbus. On November 14, 1493, on his second voyage to the New World, Columbus discovered an island with the Indian name of *Ay Ay,* which he named Santa Cruz. Landing in a small boat from the fleet anchorage in the bay, a party of Columbus' men attacked a small group of Indians, killing one and capturing the others. This is apparently the first recorded armed conflict between Europeans and aboriginal Americans. After the men named a nearby cape the "Cape of the Arrow," the fleet sailed on.

Little is known of the subsequent history of the island until the French conquered it in 1650 and renamed it St. Croix. During their 4- to 5-year occupation of the island, they built Fort Sale on the west side of Salt River Bay. The residence of the French Governor was on the east side, as well as a small village called Bassin, on the site of Christiansted. At the time of the French exodus in 1695, the population was only 147 white persons and 623 Negro slaves.

Present Appearance. The site, a prominent knoll on the west side of the bay, is unimproved and covered with brush and some trees. It embraces the remains of Fort Sale and an aboriginal site. The latter, 6 acres covered by potsherds and shells, has been excavated extensively. Fort Sale was an earthwork fortification, and the site is now covered with sod. It has not been investigated archeologically.

In 1958, the Legislature of the Virgin Islands passed a bill providing for the acquisition of two tracts of land on Salt River Bay totaling 50.05 acres that would encompass the entire historic and archeological area. The Government of the Virgin Islands planned to develop and maintain this land as a historical and public recreational area. Five acres of land at the old fort site were purchased in 1961.[68]

D. Historic Districts Eligible for the Registry of National Historic Landmarks

In some instances, groups of historic buildings located in proximity, when considered collectively, provide outstanding illustrations of a past era. These groups are designated Historic Districts and declared eligible for the Registry of National Historic Landmarks. Such districts sometimes include individual structures that are eligible on their own merits for Landmark designation. The following Historic Districts illustrate the phases of history treated in this volume.

1. Vieux Carré Historic District, Louisiana

Location. Orleans Parish, the section of the city of New Orleans bounded by the Mississippi River, Rampart Street, Canal Street, and Esplanade Avenue.

Ownership and Administration. Various.

Significance. Covering some 85 blocks, the Vieux Carré is the nucleus of the original city of New Orleans and the scene of many historic events—from the initial French settlement through the French, Spanish, and early American eras. Many of its buildings represent a unique fusion of architectural styles, which reveal the growth of New Orleans in the late 18th and first part of the 19th centuries and the blending of diverse national influences into a cosmopolitan metropolis.

The Frenchman Jean Baptiste le Moyne, Sieur de Bienville, founded New Orleans in 1718, and 3 years later military engineers platted the town into 80 rectilinear blocks. In 1722, it became the capital of French

[282

Louisiana and, because of its location 100 miles above the mouth of the
Mississippi, thrived as a trade center. By the mid-18th century, it had
gained a reputation for glamorous living and was the cultural center of
Louisiana. In 1762, when western Louisiana passed from France to Spain,
it became the capital of Spanish Louisiana and grew rapidly. Although
fires in 1788 and 1794 nearly destroyed it, its residents erected substantial
buildings to replace the old ones.

In 1803, New Orleans officially passed from Spain back to France, and
20 days later from France to the United States. During the War of 1812,
the British failed to capture the city. After the war, it continued to prosper, particularly because it became the major port for the newly developing steamboat traffic on the Mississippi and its tributaries. The influx of
U.S. settlers and traders, Latin American political refugees, and European
immigrants made ante bellum New Orleans one of the most cosmopolitan
cities in the United States. By mid-century, it had become the commercial
and financial emporium of the entire Mississippi Valley, the fourth largest
city in the United States, and the second most active port. Today it is a
thriving port city and center of culture.

Present Appearance. Most of the buildings in the Vieux Carré date
from between 1794, when the second of two disastrous fires swept the
town, and 1850. They are a mixture of various European styles of architecture, primarily French and Spanish. To some extent, however, they
also reflect the Greek Revival style, which swept the country in the 19th
century. Sites and buildings in the Historic District dating from the French
and Spanish periods that are eligible for the Registry of National Historic
Landmarks and are described elsewhere in this volume with the other
Landmarks include: The Cabildo, Jackson Square, and the Ursuline
Convent. St. Louis Cathedral, also located in the Historic District, is described in the "Other Sites Considered" section.

Listed below are some other buildings that date back to the French and
Spanish periods:

(1) The Presbytère, 713 Chartres Street. Built between 1795 and
1813, the Presbytère was intended to be the rectory for St. Louis Cathedral, but shortly after its completion the Catholic Church rented it to the
city for a courthouse. In 1853, the city purchased it. It is now a part of the
Louisiana State Museum.

(2) Madame John's Legacy, 632 Dumaine Street. Rebuilt after a
fire destroyed the original house in 1788, this house is one of the oldest
in New Orleans. Of "brick between posts" construction on a raised base-

ment, it is typical of the French colonial period. It is owned by the Louisiana State Museum.

(3) Montegut House, 731 Royal Street. Built about 1795 and extensively remodeled about 1830, this house is a fine example of a Vieux Carré residence.

(4) Bosque House, 617 Chartres Street. Built in 1795, this residence is noted for its monogrammed balcony, one of the finest examples of Spanish colonial ironwork in the Vieux Carré.

(5) Le Petit Theatre, 616 St. Peter Street. A pink stuccoed building that is now a part of the Little Theatre, Le Petit Theatre was constructed between 1789 and 1796.

(6) Lafitte's Blacksmith Shop, 941 Bourbon Street. This building is constructed of "brick between posts," a type of architecture introduced by French builders soon after the founding of the city. The shop is mentioned in city records as early as 1772.

(7) Bank of the United States, 339 Royal Street. Probably built in 1800, this building was subsequently occupied by the Planters' Bank, a branch of the United States Bank of Philadelphia, and the New Orleans Gas Light and Banking Company. It is now owned by another private company. Its wrought-iron balconies are among the finest in New Orleans.

(8) Maspero's Exchange, 440 Chartres Street. Built in 1788, this building, originally known as the Exchange Coffee House, was a meeting place for soldiers, planters, merchants, and buccaneers. Jean and Pierre Lafitte used the second floor for their headquarters.

Many other interesting sites and buildings that pertain to later periods of history are also included in the Historic District.[69]

2. Colonial Annapolis Historic District, Maryland

Location. Anne Arundel County; the area bounded by Spa Creek, Duke of Gloucester Street, Church Circle, College Avenue, and King George, Hanover, Randall, and Prince George Streets; Annapolis.

Ownership and Administration. Various.

Significance. Though this Historic District was declared eligible for the Registry of National Historic Landmarks primarily because of its 18th-century significance, it also has important associations with the phases of history treated in this volume. In 1649, the same year that

The majority of historic buildings in Annapolis, Maryland, date from the 18th century. One exception is the Sands House, the oldest frame building in the town, built in 1690's.

Lord Baltimore's Religious Toleration Act made Maryland a haven for nonconformists, about 300 dissatisfied Puritans emigrated from Virginia to the mouth of the Severn River, near the site of Annapolis. Soon afterward, some of them settled at the site of Annapolis—which they gave various names, including Proctor's Landing, Arundelton, Severn, and Anne Arundel Town, until 1695, when they renamed it Annapolis in honor of Princess Anne, Protestant daughter of James II.

The year before, the town had been designated the capital of Maryland in place of St. Marys City. A political and mercantile center, the town also had an active social and cultural life. Merchants and planters built elegant homes and entertained legislators. Theaters, horseraces, and taverns provided entertainment. After the turn of the 18th century, the affluence of the city increased and during the War for Independence reached its pinnacle. Near the end of the war, the Continental Congress met in the Maryland State House (a Registered National Historic Landmark, relating primarily to political and military affairs, 1783–1830), where in 1783 George Washington resigned his commission. Soon after this period, Baltimore began to gain the ascendancy as the commercial center of the State of Maryland.

Present Appearance. More pre-Revolutionary brick buildings are preserved in Annapolis than in any other U.S. city. Most of the historic buildings date from the 18th century. Some of the more important are the Maryland State House, Old Treasury Building, William Reynolds Tavern, Peggy Stewart House, Christopher Hohne-Holland House, and Brice House. The few buildings remaining from the 17th century include: the Little Photo Studio, originally the Kentish Inn, constructed in 1696–1700 as a tavern; and the Sands House, the oldest frame building in the town, built in the 1690's.[70]

3. Huguenot Street Historic District, New York

Location. Ulster County, on the Walkill River, New Paltz.

Ownership and Administration. The Huguenot Historical Society, New Paltz, New York, Inc., owns the Abraham Hasbrouck House, Bevier-Elting House, Hugo Freer House, and Jean Hasbrouck House. The Daniel du Bois House is privately owned.

Significance. The settlement of Huguenots, both French and Walloons, was a significant facet of U.S. development in the 17th and 18th centuries. Nowhere is this more graphically illustrated by historic buildings than at New Paltz, where five stone houses clustered along Huguenot Street constitute a remarkable picture of an early Huguenot community. The original settlement at New Paltz was made during the latter part of the 17th century, but most of the five houses date from the first part of the 18th century, although they incorporate 17th-century elements.

Surrounded by the Dutch and friendly with them, the Huguenot settlers of New Paltz nevertheless resisted intermarriage and for many years preserved their own way of life. For all practical purposes, they were an independent, self-governing body that was tolerated by the Crown and later the State of New York. In 1785, the State legislature confirmed the ancient grants and petitions, and incorporated the town into the State government. The original system of government for New Paltz, established in 1728, consisted of a council of 12 heads of families, the *Duzine.* Descendants of the original 12 governed until 1826.

Even without its Huguenot associations, the existence of five early buildings on one continuously inhabited street would justify recognition of the New Paltz community as an outstanding survivor of colonial America. When it is also considered that Huguenot Street was a haven for European refugees, New Paltz is unique in terms of its period and historical significance.

Present Appearance. The five Huguenot houses, all strongly reflecting Dutch architectural influence, are described below:

(1) Jean Hasbrouck House (Memorial House). Built around 1712 by one of the original patentees of the settlement, it has been remarkably well preserved. Its rough stone walls, topped by a high, steep-pitched roof, give it a medieval appearance. The interior has a center-hall plan; two rooms are on each side. Over the entrance door is an early shed-stoop. The house is open to the public.

(2) Abraham Hasbrouck House. This house is also relatively unaltered. Its rough-faced stone walls and gabled roof with sloping shed dormers and three chimneys are typical Dutch colonial. The north portion dates to 1694; additions were made in 1700 and 1712.

(3) Bevier-Elting House. The center portion of this house, the home of an original New Paltz patentee, dates from the end of the 17th century, although the house was substantially enlarged around 1735.

(4) Daniel du Bois House. This house was built around 1705 on the site of a log fortress, the walls of which are said to have been incorporated in the newer dwelling. Fifty years later, the second story was added, and in the 19th century the house was enlarged and its interior altered.

(5) Hugo Freer House. In addition to thick stone walls and steep-pitched roof, this house has solid shutters on the windows and divided door with overhang hood—both common in Dutch colonial architecture. The north end was built about 1694 and the south end about 1735.

Besides these five houses, the Deyo House may be mentioned. Portions of the walls of the present house are all that remain of the original structure, built by Pierre Deyo, another of the New Paltz patentees. The house was extensively remodeled in the 19th century, little of its original construction being spared. It is also owned by the Huguenot Historical Society, New Paltz, New York, Inc.[71]

4. Hurley Historic District, New York

Location. Ulster County, on U.S. 209, about 3 miles west of Kingston and the New York Thruway.

Ownership and Administration. Privately owned houses.

Significance. Preserved in this little town, which lies between the Hudson River and the Catskills, is a collection of stone houses that still preserves the Dutch heritage of the region to an unusual degree. Ten of these houses, some still occupied by descendants of early Dutch settlers, extend along Hurley Street, the town's principal thoroughfare. Scattered nearby are other houses that have survived for two centuries and more. A few of these have characteristics more English than Dutch, attesting to the changes in settlement after the fall of New Netherland—changes that occurred despite the stubborn, if nonviolent, resistance of the original settlers to the English and their alien ways.

Hurley, or *Nieuw Dorp* (New Village), as it was then known, was founded in 1662 by a few Dutch and Huguenot settlers from nearby Wiltwyck (Kingston). With the permission of Dir. Gen. Peter Stuyvesant, the settlers laid out the new town on the fertile bottom land of Esopus Creek. Construction had scarcely started when the Esopus Indians burned it to the ground. The prisoners taken in the raid were soon released. After a short, ruthless campaign by troops of New Netherland, peace was made in May 1664.

In a matter of months, the victors were themselves conquered by the English, who seized New Netherland in the name of the Duke of York. English rule was not harsh, but the Dutch of *Nieuw Dorp* stubbornly resisted any change in their way of life. In 1669, Gov. Francis Lovelace

Ten stone houses of Dutch origin on Hurley Street and more than a dozen others in the town make Hurley, New York, an unmatched example of a Hudson Valley Dutch settlement of the 18th century. The Van Deusen House, in the foreground, built in 1723, was a temporary capitol of New York during the War for Independence.

renamed the town Hurley after his ancestral home, Hurley-on-Thames. Despite its English name, for the next century and more, Hurley remained a Dutch provincial town—in language, customs, and architecture.

During the War for Independence, the town was shaken from its accustomed serenity by the passing of the armies and the influx of refugees from Kingston, when the British set the torch to that Hudson River settlement in October 1777. The people of Hurley treasure incidents of this period, and also the town's importance as a station on the "Underground Railroad" and residence of the antislavery leader Sojourner Truth. But it is the town of Hurley, its quiet streets and sturdy houses, that is distinguished—a representative of the time when Dutch America flourished in the valley of the Hudson.

Present Appearance. All the most interesting houses except one lie along two historic roads—Hurley Street and the Hurley Mountain Road. These include the Jan Van Deusen House; the Du Mond, or Guard, House; the Houghtaling House; and the Elmendorf House, or Half Moon Tavern. The exception is the Hardenbergh House, on Schoonmaker Lane a short distance south of Hurley Street.

The old cemetery north of Hurley Street is the resting place of many of the town's earliest settlers, as revealed by the Dutch names on the worn gravestones. Not only Hurley's houses, but also the fertile flood lands of Esopus Creek, west of the town, recreate the story of the early settlers and reveal why they chose this spot for their "New Village." [72]

E. Other Sites Considered

In the process of selecting the comparatively few historic sites of such outstanding character as to merit recognition as Registered National Historic Landmarks for the phases of history treated in this volume, a great many throughout the Nation were carefully studied, compared, and evaluated. The sites described below were among those deemed by the Advisory Board to possess noteworthy historical value but not "exceptional value" (national significance) within the special Landmark criteria. Some of them, however, may satisfy the criteria for other volumes in this series. In addition to Landmark sites and those described below, many others—too numerous to list—were evaluated and judged to be of lesser importance.

1. Dauphin Island, Alabama

Location: Mobile County, at the entrance to Mobile Bay.

Pierre le Moyne, Sieur d'Iberville, sent by Louis XIV in 1699 to found a colony at the mouth of the Mississippi, was the first European known to have visited this island. He called it "Massacre Island" because he discovered a huge pile of bleaching human bones on its sandy beach. Bienville, Iberville's brother, established a post on the island in 1702, and it served as port of entry to the settlement at Fort Louis de la Mobile, 30 miles upriver, and later to the colony at the site of Mobile. A settlement grew up around the post, and in 1711 Bienville renamed the island "Dauphine" in honor of Marie Adelaide of Savoy, wife of the Dauphin Louis, Duke of Burgundy. In spite of near-destruction by hurricanes and attacks by British privateers, the colony survived.

Until about 1720, the island served as the main port of the Mobile area. In 1762, France ceded it to Spain, which retained possession until the following year, when England gained title by the Treaty of Paris. Spain reoccupied the island 20 years later and held it until 1813, when Gen. James Wilkinson, learning that a British base was located there, seized it for the United States.

The island is now connected to the mainland by an oversea highway and has undergone considerable residential development. Partially restored Fort Gaines, built in 1822 on the eastern tip of the island and prominent during the Civil War, is the most notable existing historic site today.

2. Fort Condé (Fort Charlotte) Site, Alabama

Location: Mobile County, Mobile.

In 1710, Jean Baptiste le Moyne, Sieur de Bienville, built Fort Condé on the site of Mobile. The temporary, wooden fort, first known as Fort Louis, evolved into a stone-and-brick structure that was for a time considered to be the most formidable in French Louisiana. In 1702, Bienville had moved his settlement from Fort Maurepas, near present Ocean Springs, Miss., to a site near present Mount Vernon, Ala., where he had erected Fort Louis de la Mobile, also called Fort Louis de la Louisiane. The settlers remained at this fort until floods forced them to relocate, at Fort Condé.

At the end of the French and Indian War, France yielded all territory east of the Mississippi, except New Orleans, to England. This cession included Mobile, and the English took over Fort Condé; they renamed it Fort Charlotte. They held it until 1780, when the Spanish captured it; the Spanish maintained possession until the War of 1812, when Gen. James Wilkinson of the United States ousted them. Concerned about possible attacks from the sea, the United States at this time also built defenses, such as Fort Gaines, at the entrance to the harbor. After the United States purchased Florida, in 1819, Fort Charlotte was of no further importance and gradually fell into ruins.

The site was eventually sold and used for various modern buildings. However, Fort Condé is commemorated by a bronze plaque at the rear of the Mobile County Courthouse, on Church Street, where part of an alleged original wall is also located.

3. Fort Louis de la Mobile (Fort Louis de la Louisiane) Site, Alabama

Location: Mobile County, on U.S. 43, at Twenty-Seven Mile Bluff, on the outskirts of Mount Vernon.

This fort, the second capital of French Louisiana, was established in 1702 by Jean Baptiste le Moyne, Sieur de Bienville. Also known as Fort Louis de la Louisiane, it was located on the Mobile River in the heart of the French Empire in the lower Mississippi Valley. During the first few years, the colonists were plagued by sickness, floods, and near-starvation, but by 1704 supply ships were arriving from Canada regularly. As more immigrants arrived, including brides for the colonists, the colony grew.

La Salle's lieutenant, Henry de Tonty, died at the fort during a yellow fever outbreak and was buried nearby in an unmarked grave. Most of the colonists, however, survived and stayed on until a series of floods, in 1710, forced them to abandon Fort Louis de la Mobile and move to the site of present Mobile, where they founded Fort Condé, first known as Fort Louis.

In 1902, the people of Mobile erected a monument at the site of Fort Louis de la Mobile, on property now owned by the Alabama Power Company.

4. Fort Tombigbee Site, Alabama

Location: Sumter County, on the Tombigbee River, just off U.S. 11, near Epes.

Fort Tombigbee, whose spelling varies widely in historical records, was constructed as a military-trading post by the French in 1735 above the confluence of the Tombigbee and Black Warrior Rivers, in Choctaw and Chickasaw Indian country. It served as an advanced French base during the Chickasaw War, as a base for trade with the Choctaws, and as a check against British influence in the area. After the French and Indian War, the British occupied it for 5 years and renamed it Fort York. Then abandoned, it fell into ruins. In 1794, the Spanish rebuilt and renamed it Fort Confederation. They remained until 1797, the year before Congress designated the Mississippi Territory. In 1802–3, one of a series of treaties by which the United States absorbed the Choctaw lands was negotiated at the fort. Subsequently, it was abandoned and fell into ruins. The National Society of Colonial Dames of America has placed a marker on the site.

5. Hano Pueblo, Arizona

Location: Navajo County, near Ariz. 264, north of Walpi and Sich-omovi on First Mesa, Hopi Villages.

Hano is the only pueblo inhabited today that exemplifies the shifts of the native New Mexican population resulting from Spanish pressures. During the first part of the 17th century, the Tewa-speaking people of Hano lived in the Galisteo Basin south of Santa Fe. During the Pueblo Revolt of 1680–92, they moved to a new pueblo near Santa Cruz. In 1696, they rebelled again, burned their church, killed two padres, and abandoned their pueblo, Tsanwari, as they fled west, as had other Rio Grande groups during earlier periods of unrest.

To help protect Walpi from Ute inroads, the Hopi Indians at that pueblo invited the Tewas to settle to the north, at the head of the trail leading from First Mesa. As time passed, other Rio Grande groups that had taken refuge in Hopiland returned to New Mexico, but the people of Hano remained. They still retain their language and ceremonies, although their kivas and some other aspects of their culture have been influenced by contact with the Hopis. They are noted as producers of fine pottery. Their population is more than 300 today.

6. Tubac, Arizona

Location: Santa Cruz County, on U.S. 89, about 40 miles south of Tucson.

Tubac Presidio was the most northerly Spanish military outpost of Pimería Alta between 1752 and 1776, and was the base from which Capt. Juan Bautista de Anza opened an overland route from Sonora to California and founded the colony that grew into the city of San Francisco. The Spanish established the presidio in 1752, on the site of a Pima Indian village, to protect Jesuit missionaries who had been driven from the area during a Pima rebellion the preceding year. Settlers, attracted by mining and agricultural possibilities, built the pueblo of Tubac and the church of Santa Gertrudis de Tubac.

Because of Apache depredations, in 1776 Spanish officials replaced

Ruins at Tubac, Arizona. From 1752 to 1776, Tubac Presidio was the northernmost Spanish military outpost in Pimería Alta.

the presidio at Tubac with one at Tucson. In the first years of U.S. occupation and acquisition of Arizona, Tubac and Tucson were about the only towns in the region. Until recently Tubac resembled a typical small Mexican village of adobe huts, but the present artists' colony has done much to foster interest in its early history. Tubac Presidio State Historical Monument is located in the plaza where the presidio once stood. Archeological excavation and restoration is planned at the presidio and at the nearby site of the church. The park contains an excellent museum.

7. John Law Colony (lost site), Arkansas

> Location: On Arkansas River in the general vicinity of Arkansas Post National Memorial.

John Law was an ill-starred financial wizard who, in 1717, obtained a monopoly of commerce in Louisiana from Louis XV. He also obtained a grant of about 12 square miles on the Arkansas River at Arkansas Post, where he intended to create a duchy. He agreed to settle 1,500 colonists and to provide a sufficient military force to protect them from the Indians. By April 1721, more than 700 Germans, including wives and families, had been settled and were building homes and storehouses, plowing, and sowing crops. Prospects seemed good, although there were many difficulties. Nevertheless, when news arrived that Law's

"Mississippi Bubble"—a financial house of cards—had collapsed, the colonists departed. They sailed down the Mississippi intent upon returning to Europe, but French officials persuaded them to settle along the Mississippi near New Orleans, in a district thereafter known as the "German Coast." The exact site of the colony on the Arkansas River has never been determined.

8. Menard, Wallace, and Related Sites, Arkansas

Location: Arkansas County, left bank of Arkansas River, about 5 miles below Arkansas Post National Memorial.

This extensive multicomponent group of sites has yielded increments of relatively late date, including European trade goods, and revealed native burials. One of the sites may have been that of the original Arkansas Post, the trading post founded in 1686 by Henry de Tonty on the site of an Indian village—probably Quapaw—that had contact with Europeans at an early date. Archeologists have comprehensively investigated the sites. Tonty's post was more likely at the Menard site—the Arkansas River then having had its main channel in today's Menard Bayou—but the evidence is not conclusive. The area is now mixed pastureland, orchard, cultivated acreage, and woodland.

9. Angel Island, California

Location: Marin and San Francisco Counties, in San Francisco Bay.

This island was discovered by the Portolá expedition on November 4, 1769. It was used as a base by the Ayala expedition, which in 1775 conducted the first detailed exploration of San Francisco Bay—discovered in 1769. This exploration resulted in official recognition of the bay's merits as a harbor by Spain and its first use as a port. In the early 19th century, the island was used occasionally by Russian and Aleut sea otter hunters, and also by whaling and trading vessels as a fueling and watering place. In 1839, the Mexican Government granted it to Antonio Mario Osio for use as a ranch. In 1863, the U.S. Army utilized it for harbor defense. No surviving structures date from the Spanish or Mexican periods, but much of the island is relatively unspoiled. It is being developed as a California State Historical Park.

10. Anza-Borrego Desert State Park, California

Location: Eastern side of San Diego County, extending into Imperial County; traversed by Calif. 78.

This 455,525-acre park commemorates a portion of the route twice followed during the period 1774–76 by Capt. Juan Bautista de Anza, pioneer of the 700-mile overland route from Tubac, in Pimería Alta, now in Arizona, to San Gabriel Mission, in California. Three campsites of the two expeditions are identified in the park. The desert in the region is little changed from the days of the pioneering expeditions.

Anza was commandant of Tubac in 1773, when he volunteered to find an overland route to the California missions. Accompanied by 35 volunteers, he left on January 8, 1774. Traveling by way of Caborca and Sonoita to the Yuma villages, where he crossed the Colorado River, he moved on some distance to the southwest and then turned westward into the Colorado desert. He marched south of and roughly parallel to the present international boundary until he struck the mountains on the western edge of the desert, and then turned north to Borrego Valley and traversed San Carlos Pass into the Cahuilla Valley. He then pushed on to near the site of Riverside, and reached San Gabriel Mission on March 22.

Anza's second expedition, which arrived at San Gabriel on January 4, 1776, consisted of 240 settlers, 695 horses and mules, and 355 cattle. The route was closed after the revolt of the Yuma Indians in 1781 for about 45 years, but it was used again during the period of Mexican administration; and it was followed in part by some of the gold seekers and emigrants to California in 1849 and later years.

11. Cajon Pass, California

Location: San Bernardino County, on U.S. 66–91–395, about 22 miles northeast of San Bernardino.

This pass was a major southeastern gateway into California from about 1830 to 1846. Through it passed the packhorse trail to California known as the Old Spanish Trail, which originated in Santa Fe, New Mexico. Father Francisco Garcés, who was attempting to find a California-New Mexico route, was evidently the first European to cross the San Bernardino Mountains, in 1776. He probably used an Indian trail a few miles to the east of Cajon Pass. Starting at the confluence of the Colorado and Gila Rivers, he had gone up the Colorado to the Mojave villages near the present city of Needles before turning westward across the desert.

Jedediah Smith and other American fur trappers apparently used the same Indian trail in 1826 and 1827. However, the trail over the entire distance from Santa Fe to California was not completely effective until William Wolfskill and George C. Yount utilized Cajon Pass. These well-known traders made the trip in 1830–31; they were followed by other traders, as well as by forty-niners and emigrants. The Old Spanish Trail was important, although not as heavily traveled as the more southerly Gila Trail. Cajon Pass has been substantially altered by the construction of a superhighway. The Indian trail, a Registered State Historical Landmark, is 8½ miles northwest of Crestline, on Calif. 2.

12. Dana Point, California

Location: Orange County, on U.S. 101 Alt., 7 miles south of Laguna Beach.

This point, overlooking a precipitous 400-foot-high cliff near San Juan Capistrano Mission, is one of many that were utilized in the international hide and tallow trade. Active in this trade, which flourished in the decades

Dana Point, one of many such points along the California coast, was important in the hide and tallow trade. It was named after the American author Richard Henry Dana, who participated in the trade and described it in *Two Years Before the Mast*.

just prior to the war with Mexico, were France, Russia, England, various South American nations, and the United States. Mission Indians prepared the hides and bags of tallow at the mission tanneries. The hides were soaked in salt water and brine, scraped, stretched, dried, and beaten to remove all dust. Mission Indians then transported the hides and bags on pack mules and carts to the point, from where they were thrown over the cliff to the beaches below, transported by small boats to the waiting ships, and carried to Boston, London, and other world ports.

The point was named after Richard Henry Dana, Jr., the American author who served for 2 years as a crew member on the *Pilgrim*, which was actively engaged in the hide and tallow trade. In *Two Years Before the Mast,* published in 1840, he vividly and accurately describes the trade, especially at this point.

13. De la Guerra Adobe, California

> *Location: Santa Barbara County, State and De la Guerra Streets, Santa Barbara.*

Don José Antonio Julián de la Guerra Noriega, who founded one of California's oldest and most prominent families, built this large, one-story adobe structure about 1826 during his long period of service (1815–42) as commandant of the Presidio of Santa Barbara. Because of his prominence, his home was the center of social life in the Santa Barbara region. Richard Henry Dana, Jr., who visited the home in the 1830's, described in *Two Years Before the Mast* the colorful ceremonies during the daughter's wedding. The home was built around three sides of a spacious patio, where such occasions as the wedding and state ceremonials often took place. Many of the roof timbers and door and window lintels were constructed of local sycamore, but others were probably brought in by sailing vessels.

An *altito,* a three-story, tower-like element, used for office and library purposes, has been razed. A group of other white-plastered, tile-roofed structures, which have been built around the old house, make a sizable complex that is now occupied by shops and studios and the offices of the Santa Barbara Chamber of Commerce. The local "Old Spanish Days" fiesta is held annually, the events centering around El Paseo, the "Street in Spain," which adjoins the De la Guerra Adobe.

14. Los Angeles Pueblo, California

Location: Los Angeles County, Los Angeles.

El Pueblo de Nuestra Señora la Reina de los Angeles de Porciúncula—
or Los Angeles for short—was established on September 4, 1781, by 4
soldiers, 12 settlers, and their families, who settled on a 17,500-acre tract
on the orders of Spanish Gov. Felipe de Neve. During the Spanish and
Mexican periods, the population grew slowly but steadily, totaling 1,250
in 1845. Los Angeles was the largest settlement in California when it
became a part of the United States.

The present Los Angeles plaza, laid out in 1818, replaced the 1781
plaza. The 1818 plaza survives as a city park, near which are situated
two structures dating from the Spanish period; the plaza is surrounded
by Main, Los Angeles, Arcadia, and Macy Streets. The adobe Plaza
Church (535 North Main Street) was designed by José Antonio Ramírez
and built between 1818 and 1822 by Indians under the supervision of
José Chapman. Its dimensions were originally 90 by 75 feet. It had a
choir loft, deep glassless windows, earthen floor, and tar-covered flat
roof. Little remains today of the original structure or design.

The Avila Adobe, just off the plaza at 14 Olvera Street, is the oldest
surviving house in Los Angeles. Erected in 1818 by Don José María
Avila, later mayor of the town, it contained 18 rooms in an **L**-shape and

Los Angeles, in 1853. From a lithograph by Charles Koppel. Courtesy,
Bancroft Library, University of California.

included a wing extending across present Olvera Street. The sturdy adobe walls were 2½-feet thick, the ceilings 15 feet high, and the flat roof covered with black asphalt from the Brea pits. Restored from a ruinous condition after 1930, the house is now part of the Pueblo de los Angeles State Historical Monument.

15. El Molino Viejo, California

Location: Los Angeles County, 1120 Old Mill Road, Pasadena.

El Molino Viejo (The Old Mill), probably constructed during the period 1810–12 for San Gabriel Mission by Father José María de Zaldivéa, was the first water-powered gristmill in California. The only others built there during the Spanish period were at Santa Cruz Mission and at San José Pueblo. Built with massive stone-and-adobe walls, some 5 feet thick, it measured 20 by 50 feet. It was abandoned in 1823, but the ruins provided the basis for a reconstruction in 1929. A private residence until recently, it is now owned by the California Historical Society, which plans to restore it and use it as a southern California headquarters and museum.

16. Monterey (Old Town), California

Location: Monterey County, Monterey.

Monterey abounds in historic sites and structures that illustrate the political, economic, religious, and social life of Spanish and Mexican California. Of special note is the Vizcaíno-Serra Landing Site, at the foot of Pacific Street near the entrance to the U.S. Presidio of Monterey, which commemorates Sebastián Vizcaíno's landing in 1602 and the founding of the presidio and mission of Monterey in 1770 by Fray Junípero Serra and Gov. Gaspar de Portolá. The Royal Presidio Chapel is a Registered National Historic Landmark.

Monterey as a town, or pueblo, was formally authorized in 1827 by the Mexican Government. People had already begun to construct homes outside of the walls of the presidio, and by 1830 the population was about 500. Richard Henry Dana, Jr., who visited the town a few years later, praised its appearance, especially the green lawns of the hundred or so houses.

Among the many historic sites and buildings in Monterey, in addition

Presidio and town of Monterey, California, in 1841. The town, founded in 1827 by the Mexican Government, grew up around the presidio. Courtesy, Bancroft Library, University of California.

to the Vizcaíno-Serra Landing Site and the Royal Presidio Chapel, the following are of particular interest:

(1) Site of Town Plaza, bounded by Munras, Pearl, and Tyler Streets. This is the original site of the central plaza of Monterey, a triangular area now much reduced in size and considerably altered.

(2) Old Custom House, Main and Decatur Streets. This Registered National Historic Landmark (relating primarily to the War with Mexico, 1846–48) is the oldest Government building extant in California. The original section was constructed in 1827; it was extensively enlarged during the period 1841–46. A State historical monument, it is open to the public.

(3) Larkin House, 464 Main Street. Another Registered National Historic Landmark (relating primarily to the War with Mexico, 1846–48) and a State historical monument, this two-story adobe-and-frame residence was built during the period 1835–37 by Thomas O. Larkin. It is the prototype of the architectural style known as Monterey colonial, a combination of Spanish adobe style with New England frame construction that was widely adopted in California. Larkin was the U.S. consul in California and a key figure in events of the 1830's and 1840's.

(4) Casa de Soto, 816 El Dorado Street. This residence is probably

One of many historic buildings in Monterey (Old Town), California, the Larkin House illustrates the Monterey colonial style of architecture.

the best extant architectural example of the traditional Spanish-Mexican one-story adobe residence. It was built about 1820.

(5) The French Consulate, Franklin Street and Estero. This one-story adobe, built about 1840, has been removed from its original location and restored. It is owned by the city of Monterey.

(6) The First Theater, southwest corner of Pacific and Scott Streets. Built about 1843 and used as a theater by U.S. troops in 1847, it is now owned by the State of California.

17. Placerita Canyon, California

> *Location: Los Angeles County, along an improved road, 6 miles east of Newhall.*

While looking in this canyon for stray cattle, in 1842, Francisco López y Arballo first discovered gold, near the surface, in commercial quantities in California. Fortune-seekers swarmed to the area. The placer fields were mainly worked by Francisco García, an experienced miner who brought in other miners from Sonora, Mexico. By the end of 1843, they had mined about $42,000 worth of gold nuggets from nearby San Feliciana Canyon in the San Fernando Hills, as well as an unknown amount from Placerita

Canyon. The deposits were exhausted after being worked about 5 years. The canyon is a Registered State Historical Landmark.

18. La Purísima Concepción Mission (Lompoc), California

Location: Santa Barbara County, on Calif. 1, about 4 miles northeast of Lompoc.

Of the 21 Spanish missions in California, this one is probably the most accurately restored and gives the best picture of mission life in Spanish California. Founded on December 8, 1787, by Father Fermín Francisco de Lasuén, by 1804 it had 1,520 Indian neophytes. It was destroyed by the major earthquakes of 1812, and rebuilt at its present site, 4 miles to the northeast, between 1813 and 1821. Secularized by the Mexican Government in 1834, it quickly went to ruin. During the period 1935–42 the

Ruins of the first La Purísima Concepción Mission (Lompoc), California, prior to 1925. After a disastrous earthquake in 1812, padres abandoned the mission and built a new one about 4 miles to the northwest. Courtesy, Bancroft Library, University of California.

The second La Purísima Concepción Mission (Lompoc), constructed after the 1812 earthquake. One of the most colorful missions in California, it has been carefully restored.

Civilian Conservation Corps, under the direction of the National Park Service, carefully restored most of the buildings, as well as a portion of the irrigation system. In 1941, the mission became a State historical monument, and further reconstruction has been accomplished recently.

19. La Purísima Concepción Mission Site (Fort Yuma), California

Location: Imperial County, on U.S. 80, just across the Colorado River from Yuma, Ariz.

In the fall of 1780, Padre Francisco Garcés, three other Franciscan friars, and a small band of soldiers founded on the Colorado River two new experimental colonies, combination missions-presidios-pueblos. One colony, which included Purísima Concepción Mission, was situated on the California side near the point where the Gila River enters the Colorado River. The other colony, including the San Pecho y San Pablo Mission, was 12 miles to the south in present Mexico. The experiment in combining religious, military, and civil functions did not work well because of friction among the different factions.

Anyway, not long after a fresh group of settlers arrived in June 1781, the Yuma Indians attacked and destroyed both colonies, killed all but six men, and captured the women and children. The Indians blocked travel to California by the Yuma route until 1826, when the Mexicans established a garrison at the La Purísima Concepción site to protect mail carriers and traders. The U.S. Army constructed Fort Yuma at the site in 1850, for which purpose it utilized some stones from the destroyed mission. No surface traces of the mission remain today.

20. Rancho Guajome, California

Location: San Diego County, on Calif. 76, about 8 miles east of Oceanside.

This is one of the best unaltered examples of the California rancho of the Mexican period. Many of the original outbuildings have survived, unlike those at most other ranchos, and the rural setting in the vicinity is unimpaired. The acreage, however, has been reduced in extent. The original Rancho Guajome grant comprised 1 square league, which in 1852 its two mission Indian owners, Andrés and José Manuel, sold to an American, Abel Stearns. The latter immediately presented it as a wedding gift to his sister-in-law, Ysidora Bandini, upon her marriage to a U.S. Army officer, Cave J. Couts. In 1852–53, this couple built the one-story ranchhouse.

The house is U-shaped. The doors of the approximately 20 rooms open into the inner patio. Sleeping rooms occupy one wing, and kitchen and bakehouse the other; the living quarters stretch across the front of the house. The patio, planted with flowers and orange trees, is closed on the upper side of the U by an outer courtyard surrounded by high adobe walls, which at one time had heavy wooden gates. Within the walls were a blacksmith shop, chapel, school, jail, carriage house, and other farm buildings. The house, which is not open to the public, is now privately owned.

21. Rancho Los Alamos, California

Location: Santa Barbara County, on U.S. 101, about 3 miles north of Los Alamos.

Rancho Los Alamos, in an unaltered rural setting, is probably the finest surviving example of the traditional one-story Mexican ranchhouse in

One-story Mexican ranchhouse at Rancho Los Alamos, California.

California. The original grant of 1839 to José Antonio de la Guerra y Carrillo consisted of almost 50,000 acres. In an era noted for lavish hospitality, Los Alamos was a favorite overnight stopping place for travelers between Santa Barbara and Monterey. The house, which has been carefully restored, has some American features; it has plank floors, board ceilings, paneled doors, six-paned window sashes, and central heating and electricity. The general appearance of the house, however, has not been changed greatly, and many of the original furnishings are still being used.

22. Rancho Los Cerritos, California

Location: Los Angeles County, 4600 Virginia Road, Long Beach.

The Los Cerritos ranchhouse was probably the largest and most impressive in southern California during the Mexican period, and is today the largest restored adobe house in the region. The 27,000-acre Rancho Los Cerritos was part of one of the first two provisional land grants made in California by the King of Spain in 1784 for ranching purposes. It came into the possession of John Temple, a young New Englander who married a granddaughter of the original owner and later acquired Mexican citizenship. Temple, soon a wealthy rancher, also profited in the hide trade. In the 1850's, he became an important builder in the city of Los Angeles. In 1882, the new owners subdivided the rancho for real estate and town development purposes.

The magnificent ranchhouse was built in 1844 in the Monterey colonial style. The central two-story portion, containing the family rooms, is 100 feet long, and at each end are one-story wings, each 145 feet long. A large patio is enclosed by an adobe wall, which joins the ends of the wings. In 1955, the city of Long Beach purchased the restored adobe structure and now exhibits it as a historic house and museum. The original ranch setting has been destroyed by urban growth and the intrusion of Signal Hill district oil wells.

Ranchhouse at Rancho Los Cerritos, California. The ranch figured prominently in the California cattle industry during the Mexican period.

23. Rancho Petaluma, California

> *Location: Sonoma County, near Calif. 116, about 4 miles east of Petaluma.*

The headquarters building of the former vast Rancho Petaluma is the largest adobe structure in California. Owner of the rancho was Gen.

This building, once the headquarters of Rancho Petaluma, is the largest adobe structure in California.

Mariano Guadalupe Vallejo, in the 1840's the richest man in California and one of the most powerful politically. The building from which the 67,000-acre rancho was administered—although Vallejo actually resided in Sonoma, 12 miles distant—was built between 1835 and 1844 under the supervision of the owner's younger brother, Sálvador. Oxen hauled redwood timber some 50 miles from the north, and Indians manufactured adobe bricks on the spot.

The large two-story adobe, in the Monterey colonial style, typically U-shaped, was 200 by 150 feet in size. The walls were 3 feet thick and 20 feet high, and a broad veranda ran around the interior and exterior. Iron grills and solid wooden shutters covered the windows and doors. Living quarters were on the second floor, and storerooms and Indian workshops on the ground floor. The building had fallen into a bad state of repair by 1910, when the Native Sons of the Golden West purchased it and the surrounding 5 acres. In 1951, the property became a California State Historical Monument, and is being carefully repaired and reconstructed.

24. San Antonio de Padua Mission, California

Location: Monterey County, on the Hunter Liggett Military Reservation, 5 miles northwest of Jolon.

The picturesque rural setting of this mission has remained almost unchanged since the day it was founded—the third of the California missions. Father Junípero Serra established the mission on July 14, 1771, and the following year moved it 1½ miles to the present location because of a shortage of water at the original site. At its peak in 1805, it had 1,296 Indian neophytes.

Ruins of San Antonio de Padua Mission, California, in 1875. Photograph by C. E. Watkins. Courtesy, Bancroft Library, University of California.

Construction of the present church was begun in 1810 and finished in 1813; other structures on the large adjoining quadrangle were rebuilt during the period 1813–21, including Indian quarters, workshops, walls, and storage areas. The mission's irrigation system, begun as early as 1774, ultimately consisted of several dams, reservoirs, and some 20 miles of

Chapel of San Antonio de Padua Mission, California.

open flumes and masonry conduits. In addition, wells dug near the mission supplied water for the orchard, vineyard, and gardens.

Secularized by the Mexican Government in 1834, the property was acquired by the United States Government at the end of the Mexican War, and returned to the Roman Catholic Church in 1862. Of the original buildings, only the church remained; most of the other structures were marked only by the grass-covered mounds into which the adobe structures had crumbled. Restoration, aided by the Hearst Foundation, has been underway since 1948.

Portion of restored quadrangle at San Antonio de Padua Mission, California. Restoration, aided by the Hearst Foundation, began in 1948.

Casa de Bandini, a historic structure in San Diego. Juan Bandini erected the first story in 1827–28. When the building began to be used as a hotel and stage station, in 1869, a second story was added.

25. San Diego Pueblo (Old Town), California

Location: San Diego County, west of Presidio Park and bounded approximately by Rosecrans, Frontier, and Condé Streets, San Diego.

The Mexican Government formally established San Diego Pueblo (Old Town) in 1835, although old soldiers of the Presidio of San Diego had begun to build their homes on the flats below Presidio Hill perhaps a dozen years earlier. Richard Henry Dana, Jr., who visited the town in 1836, commented: "The small settlement lay directly below the fort, composed of about 40 dark brown looking huts, or houses, and two larger ones, plastered, which belonged to two of the 'gente de razon.' The town is not more than half as large as Monterey . . . and has little or no business." The population in 1840 was only about 150, but by 1845 it had increased to about 350.

A number of Mexican sites and structures have survived, including:

(1) Old Town Plaza, bounded by Calhoun, Wallace, and Mason Streets, and San Diego Avenue. Formerly the political and social center, it is now a city park, somewhat smaller than it originally was.

(2) Casa de Bandini, 2660 Calhoun Street. This one-story residence was built in the years 1827–29 by a leading citizen, Juan Bandini. The second story and veranda were added in 1869, when the structure began to be used as a hotel and stage station.

(3) Casa de Estudillo, 4000 Mason Street between Calhoun Street and San Diego Avenue. This 12-room, one-story, U-shaped adobe was built in 1827 or 1828 by Prefect Don José Antonio Estudillo. Reconstructed from ruins in 1910, it is now a privately operated museum.

(4) Casa de Carrillo, at Presidio Hill Golf Course. The present caddy house of the golf course includes the greatly altered remnants of what is reputed to be the oldest house of San Diego Pueblo, built perhaps as early as 1824 by Don Francisco María Ruíz.

Also of interest are Casa de López (3890 Twiggs Street), Casa de Machado (2545 San Diego Avenue), Casa de Stewart (Congress Street north of Mason Street), and Casa de Pedrorena (2616 San Diego Avenue).

26. San Francisco Bay Discovery Site, California

Location: San Mateo County, on Sweeney Ridge, 4 miles west of Millbrae.

For more than 225 years, from 1542 until 1769, San Francisco Bay escaped the notice of Spanish explorers of the Pacific coast—probably because the Golden Gate is narrow and frequently obscured by fog; and islands and mountains are visible behind the low-lying bay as viewed from the ocean. It was finally discovered in 1769 by Capt. Gaspar de Portolá, whose party set out overland from San Diego for Monterey Bay. Missing that place, it pushed on to the north. Sighting Point Reyes from San Pedro Mountain, Portolá determined to move on to Drakes Bay. From a camp in San Pedro Valley, near present Shelter Cove, he sent out a scouting expedition that returned with news that a large body of water lay over the hill to the east.

The main party later followed the beach to the north and then marched to the northeast into the mountains. From a summit, the crest of present Sweeney Ridge, the men beheld San Francisco Bay, one of the great anchorages of the world. Father Juan Crespi noted in his diary: "It is a very large and fine harbor, such that not only all the navy of our most Catholic Majesty but those of all Europe could take shelter in it." After further exploration of the area in subsequent years, in 1776 the Spanish established the presidio and mission of San Francisco. The discovery site, in unaltered surroundings, is privately owned but is a Registered State Historical Landmark.

27. San Gabriel Arcángel Mission, California

> *Location: Los Angeles County, Junípero Street and West Mission Drive, San Gabriel.*

This mission was established in 1771 by a band of missionary priests sent from San Diego de Alcalá Mission by Father Junípero Serra. The present rectangular stone church, built between 1791 and 1805, replaced an earlier adobe one that had been destroyed by floods, along with other adobe mission buildings. In 1812, an earthquake severely damaged the church and other new buildings, which were subsequently repaired and restored. Much of the interior of the church is original. The church does not have front towers, like most other California mission churches. The exterior, relatively unadorned, features only the slender buttresses that line the long sidewalls, which rise above roof level to form pointed finials.

San Gabriel Mission was the western terminus of the overland trail that Capt. Juan Bautista de Anza founded from Tubac in 1776, as well as of the Old Spanish Trail and the Salt Lake-Los Angeles Trail. It was also known to Jedediah Smith in 1826–27, to many forty-niners who camped nearby, and to the patrons of the Butterfield Southern Overland Mail. The setting has been considerably altered by urban growth.

28. San José Pueblo Site, California

> *Location: Santa Clara County, Jefferson Schoolground, Hobson Street, San José.*

San José Pueblo, or village, was the first of three the Spanish founded in Alta California, the other two being Los Angeles and Branciforte. Founded in 1777 by Lt. José Moraga, who led a party of 65 soldiers and settlers, it first consisted of temporary houses of palisaded logs and earthen roofs. The next year, the residents constructed two dams for irrigation purposes. The population grew slowly; it totaled only about 80 in 1790, and about 900 by the end of the Mexican period, in the mid-19th century. About 1797, to avoid winter floods, the village had moved to an area near what is now the corner of Market and San Fernando Streets. Nothing remains today of any Spanish or Mexican house; a school is on the first site of the pueblo.

29. San Juan Bautista Pueblo, California

Location: San Benito County, San Juan Bautista.

The Mexican Government established this pueblo in 1835, just after it secularized San Juan Bautista Mission. The pueblo had a population of only about 75 at the end of the Mexican period. Grouped around the original plaza today are several structures dating from the Spanish and Mexican periods. The residence and office of Gen. José Castro is a large, well preserved, two-story adobe building, built during the period 1839–41, on the west side of the plaza. North of it is the Plaza Hotel, whose first story the Spanish built about 1814 as a barracks for the soldiers from Monterey Presidio who guarded the mission. The second floor and balcony were added in 1858, when the structure was converted to hotel use. Both of these buildings are a part of San Juan Bautista State Historical Monument, and are open to visitors.

At Third and Franklin Streets is Casa de Juan Anza, a private residence, altered but in excellent condition, believed to have been built about 1799. On the north side of the plaza is San Juan Bautista Mission. It was founded in 1797, and its church built during the period 1803–12. The church is one of the largest in California; it measures 210 by 77 feet.

San Juan Bautista Mission sits on the north side of a historic plaza in San Juan Bautista, California. Centered around the plaza are a number of structures dating from the Spanish, Mexican, and early American periods.

The outer walls are largely original. The mission, open to the public, houses a museum that contains numerous historic relics.

30. San Juan Capistrano Mission, California

Location: Orange County, just off U.S. 101 Alt., about 3 miles north of San Juan Capistrano.

This mission, named after St. John of Capistrano, was founded in 1776 by Father Junípero Serra. Until 1794, when enlargement of the mission began, a small adobe building served as a chapel. Two adobe granaries and 40 houses for neophytes were built, followed by a cruciform church. The church, a semi-Moorish stone structure, took 9 years to complete and was regarded as the finest in California. It featured a lofty tower,

Ruins of the patio at San Juan Capistrano Mission, California. In 1776, Father Junípero Serra founded the mission. In 1812, an earthquake destroyed it, but in recent years much of it has been restored. Photograph by C. E. Watkins. Courtesy, Bancroft Library, University of California.

five interior arches of irregular stone, and massive stone walls. In 1812, a major earthquake toppled the tower and killed 40 Indians. Ruined, the church was never rebuilt. Until 1834, when the Mexicans secularized the mission, the congregation used the small adobe chapel for services. The mission participated in the international hide and tallow trade that flourished just prior to the war with Mexico.

Although the great church is in ruins, the chapel, living quarters, corridors, and gardens have been restored. Owned by the Roman Catholic Church, the mission is open to the public. A museum features Spanish and Mexican artworks and artifacts.

31. San Luis Rey de Francia Mission, California

> *Location: San Diego County, just off Calif. 76, about 5 miles east of Oceanside.*

Architecturally, this mission is probably second only to Santa Barbara Mission in its design, beauty, and extent of surviving original remains. It was established in 1798 by Father Fermín Francisco de Lasuén. The church, built during the period 1811–15, combines Spanish, Moorish, and Mexican elements in a distinguished and picturesque baroque style.

One of the most beautiful missions in California—San Luis Rey de Francia, near Oceanside. Its baroque style of architecture, a combination of Spanish, Moorish, and Mexican elements, is unique.

Secularized in 1834, the mission was turned over to Capt. Pablo de la Portilla and Pío Pica, who later became Governor.

In 1865, the mission was returned to the Roman Catholic Church by the U.S. Government, which had acquired it at the end of the war with Mexico. When the Catholic Church rededicated it as a Franciscan college, in 1893, the surface remains of the church and other mission buildings were quite extensive. Since that time, a careful program of reconstruction and restoration has been carried forward.

32. Santa Barbara Presidio and Pueblo, California

Location: Santa Barbara County, Santa Barbara.

The Presidio of Santa Barbara was the fourth and last to be founded in Alta California under Spanish authority—the others being located at San Diego, Monterey, and San Francisco. Its construction was begun on April 21, 1782, by 55 soldiers under the direction of Gov. Felipe de

Presidio and pueblo of Santa Barbara, in 1829. From a lithograph by G. & W. Endicott. Courtesy, Bancroft Library, University of California.

Neve, Capt. José Francisco Ortega, and Father Junípero Serra; shortly thereafter, Santa Barbara Mission was constructed. Log huts and a stockade 80 yards square were erected first, as well as some irrigation works

Santa Barbara Mission, in 1829. From a lithograph by G. & W. Endicott. Courtesy, Bancroft Library, University of California.

in preparation for small-scale farming. Next, the temporary wooden structures and walls were replaced by adobe buildings and walls. In August 1793, the fort was finally completed. In 1826, the town, or pueblo, of Santa Barbara was established formally by the Mexican Government. The following year from 60 to 80 one-story adobe houses, each of which had its own garden, were reportedly outside the presidio walls.

The former site of the presidio is now in an area bounded approximately by Garden, Anacapa, Carrillo, and De la Guerra Streets in the heart of the modern city. Only two relics of the presidio have survived, both considerably altered: El Cuartel, 122 Cañon Perdido Street, a small one-story, two-room house erected before 1790; and El Cañada, 121 Cañon Perdido Street, another small pre-1790 structure, that was once part of the presidio wall. In addition to the two relics of the presidio, other early structures in Santa Barbara include the De la Guerra Adobe, State and De la Guerra Streets; Casa Carrillo, 11 East Carrillo Street; and the Covarrubias Adobe, 715 Santa Barbara Street.

33. Sonoma Pueblo, California

Location: Sonoma County, Sonoma.

Sonoma Pueblo was the chief military base of the Mexican Government in Alta California from 1835 to the end of the Mexican period. Established in June 1835 both to check possible Russian expansion from Fort Ross and to control the Indians, it was founded by Lt. Mariano Guadalupe Vallejo, Military Commander and Director of the Northern Frontier and Commandant of the Presidio of San Francisco, who acted under orders from Gov. José Figueroa. Transferring his garrison from San Francisco to Sonoma, Vallejo conducted a series of successful campaigns against the Indians and his force served as a buffer to Russian expansion until the Russians withdrew from California, in 1841. Promoted to colonel in 1836 and general by 1840, Vallejo was one of the most powerful figures in Alta California.

During the years 1836–41, Lt. Mariano Guadalupe Vallejo built Sonoma Barracks, shown above, at Sonoma Pueblo. The pueblo was the chief military base of the Mexican Government in Alta California from 1835 to the end of the Mexican period.

In 1846, Sonoma Plaza was the site of the raising of the Bear Flag, the beginning of the revolt of "Yankee" settlers and others against Mexican authority. It is a Registered National Historic Landmark (relating primarily to the war with Mexico, 1846–48). Near the plaza are a number of interesting Mexican-period restored buildings, including:

(1) Sonoma Barracks, northwest corner at the intersection of Spain Street and First Street East. This large, two-story adobe structure was erected during the period 1836–41 by Vallejo. It is now a part of Sonoma State Historical Monument.

(2) Site of Vallejo's Home, *Casa Grande*, north side of Spain Street west of the barracks. The home has been demolished, but behind the

San Francisco Solano (Sonoma) Mission in the 1890's, before restoration. Courtesy, De Young Museum.

modern frame buildings still stands a two-story adobe structure that was once the servant quarters.

(3) "Swiss" Hotel, 18 West Spain Street. This two-story, balconied adobe residence was built about 1840 by Vallejo's brother Sálvador, whose residence it was until about 1865. It became a hotel in 1881.

(4) Fitch House, southwest corner of plaza (First Street West and Napa Street). Jacob P. Leese built this two-story adobe house in 1841.

San Francisco Solano (Sonoma) Mission, founded in 1823, was the last of the 21 California missions to be established.

(5) San Francisco Solano (Sonoma) Mission, northeast corner of plaza. Founded in 1823, this was the last of the 21 California missions and the only one to be established during the Mexican period. As the northernmost, its purpose was to counter Russian advances. Secularized in 1834, it soon fell into ruins. The present mission "church" is actually the chapel that was built in the years 1840–43 for use as the town church. It and the nearby *convento,* or padres' residence, have been restored and are open to the public as part of Sonoma State Historical Monument.

(6) Blue Wing Inn, 133 East Spain Street. Built in 1840, this is an excellent example of a two-story adobe hotel constructed in the Monterey colonial style.

34. Trinidad Head, California

Location: Humboldt County, U.S. Coast Guard Station, just off U.S. 101, about 1½ miles from Trinidad.

The Spanish explorers Bruno Heceta and Juan Francisco de la Bodega y Cuadra visited Trinidad Bay on June 9, 1775, in their vessels, the *Santiago* and the *Sonora.* They erected a huge pine cross on the promontory and took formal possession for Charles III of Spain; they named the promontory Trinidad because it was the day following the feast of the

Holy Trinity. After briefly exploring the region and replacing a broken mast, they sailed northward. In 1793, the English explorer George Vancouver also visited the bay. The site of the original Spanish pine cross is marked by a massive granite cross, 9 feet high and weighing 2 tons, that was erected in 1913. The cross is near the lighthouse, about 400 feet above the ocean. The rugged coast area has changed little since Spanish times.

35. Villa de Branciforte (Santa Cruz), California

> Location: Santa Cruz County, along North Branciforte Street, Santa Cruz.

Villa de Branciforte was established in July 1797 at the mouth of the San Lorenzo River on its east bank by 17 colonists, 9 soldiers and their families. It was the last of the three pueblos, or villas, that the Spanish founded in Alta California—the other two being San José and Los Angeles. The site, selected by engineer Lt. Alberto Córdoba, especially because of its advantages for coastal defense, was 1 mile east of Santa Cruz Mission, on the west bank of the river. Branciforte grew slowly, and it absorbed the mission when it was secularized, in 1834. However, in 1912, Branciforte gave up its historic name when the modern city of Santa Cruz annexed it. North Branciforte Avenue, originally about 1 mile long, was the only street in the old village. No remains of original Spanish or Mexican structures are extant in Santa Cruz today.

36. Yerba Buena Pueblo, California

> Location: San Francisco County, on Kearny between Clay and Washington Streets, San Francisco.

This pueblo, on San Francisco Bay and not far from the Presidio of San Francisco, developed into the city of San Francisco after California officially became a part of the United States in 1848; its central plaza became Portsmouth Square. The Mexican Government established it in 1835, when a single settler, William A. Richardson, was residing there. After 5 years, the population was still only 50, and by 1846 only 200. By that time, a one-story adobe Custom House had been constructed to accommodate the growing commerce. Nothing remains today of pre-

Anchorage at Yerba Buena Pueblo (San Francisco), in 1846. From a lithograph by G. & W. Endicott. Courtesy, Bancroft Library, University of California.

1848 structures. The present plaza (Portsmouth Square), a small city park, replaces one that was destroyed several years ago to permit the construction of an underground public garage.

37. Buttolph-Williams House, Connecticut

Location: Hartford County, Broad and Marsh Streets, Wethersfield.

This house was erected by David Buttolph during the 1690's. The next owner, Benjamin Beldon, probably used it as a tavern. In 1721, Daniel Williams purchased it and his family retained possession for many years. Recognizing the house as a striking example of a 17th-century Connecticut home, in 1947 the Antiquarian and Landmarks Society of Connecticut acquired it. During restoration, the relatively recent clapboards were removed, and the original thin, pine clapboards were uncovered. The house features the typical large central chimney, overhangs, and small windows. Inside is an excellent collection of early colonial furniture and kitchen furnishings. The house is open to the public during the period May 15–October 15.

38. Henry Whitfield House, Connecticut

Location: New Haven County, Whitfield Street, Guilford.

This restored massive stone house dates from about 1639, 3 years after Henry Whitfield established Guilford. Whitfield erected it not only to shelter his wife and seven children but also to serve as a community meetinghouse and a garrison house during Indian attacks. Greatly damaged by fire in 1865, the house was reconstructed in 1868. However, only about a third of it is original—the rear wall, huge chimney on the north, and foundation.

The style, that of an English Midlands manor of the 16th or 17th centuries, is notable for steep roof and thick walls. On the first floor are the kitchen and a spacious hall, 33 by 15 feet, which has a large fireplace at each end. Living quarters are upstairs. The house is furnished with 17th-century pieces, and features exhibits of early weaving and metalworking. An herb garden outside the house is also of interest. Owned and operated by the State of Connecticut, the house is open to the public throughout the year except during the period December 15 to January 15.

39. Nehemiah Royce House, Connecticut

Location: New Haven County, 538 N. Main Street, Wallingford.

This house, erected in 1672, retains many of its 17th-century characteristics: Massive central chimney, gable-end overhang, and clapboarded sides. It is a sharp-peaked saltbox house, furnished with period pieces. Moved to its present location in 1924, it is owned by the Society for the Preservation of New England Antiquities and is open to the public during July and August.

40. Thomas Lee House, Connecticut

Location: New London County, west of Niantic on Conn. 156, near entrance to Rocky Ned State Park, East Lyme.

About 1660 Thomas Lee II built this single-room residence, to which additional rooms were later added—in 1695 and during the period 1730–35. It is perhaps the oldest frame building in Connecticut. The

Lee family occupied an important position in the life of the colony. Thomas Lee II served as constable and held a seat in the General Assembly in 1676; he also owned a considerable amount of land. Thomas Lee III, a justice of the peace for more than 40 years, used the house as his office.

The front of the house is dignified by a cornice and a handsome doorway, over which are five small window-lights. The east room, the original room, is sheathed with shadow-molded boards. The rooms to the west are plastered and paneled. All parts of the structure benefited from a 1914 restoration. The house, which contains period furnishings, is open to visitors between June 15 and September 15.

41. Hendrickson House, Delaware

> *Location: New Castle County, East Seventh and Church Streets, on the grounds of Holy Trinity (Old Swedes) Church, Wilmington.*

This is one of the few extant Swedish colonial houses. Erected some time before 1690 by Hendrick Johnson as a wedding present for his son Andrew, it was originally located on the father's property on Crum Creek at Essington, Pa. The property was sold in 1958 to an aircraft corporation, which offered the house to any group that would remove it. The house was later moved to the grounds of Holy Trinity Church, where it now serves as a museum and library commemorating Swedish settlement. Of stone construction, measuring 40 by 15 feet, it has one large and one small room on the first floor and a single large room with dormer windows on the second floor. A narrow, winding stairway connects the two levels. Both first-floor rooms have fireplaces. Originally, the house had 3 small windows, which contained 48 panes of glass.

42. McIntire House, Delaware

> *Location: New Castle County, 8 Strand, New Castle.*

This house is probably the oldest in New Castle, which contains many colonial buildings of historical and architectural interest. Evidently built around 1690, it is a superlative specimen of a small townhouse of the 17th century. Fortunately, it survived the disastrous New Castle fire of 1824. The design and excellence of paneling and fireplace treatment delight devotees of colonial buildings. Privately owned, the house is open only on New Castle Day, in the spring.

43. New Castle, Delaware

Location: New Castle County, on the Delaware River, 6 miles south of Wilmington.

New Castle, one of the oldest towns in the Delaware Valley, still reflects the heritage of some of its earliest citizens, the Dutch. In 1651, Peter Stuyvesant, Governor of New Amsterdam, assumed control over a Finnish and Swedish settlement farther upriver. He erected Fort Casimir—the counterpart of New Amsterdam on the Hudson—on a spit of land since carried away by the South (Delaware) River. In 1656, the fort and the surrounding settlement was renamed New Amstel. When the British

Amstel House, erected in the early 18th century, is one of many historic structures preserved in New Castle, Delaware. Courtesy, Delaware State Development Department, Dover.

captured it in 1664 and gave it its present name, it consisted of about 100 buildings. William Penn acquired the settlement as part of Delaware in 1682, and it was there that he first set foot in America. New Castle was a seat of government in Penn's colony and later briefly the capital of Delaware.

Among the historic places in New Castle are the McIntire House and the Old Dutch House [see entries directly above and below]; the Amstel House, built before 1730; Immanuel Episcopal Church, constructed between 1703 and 1710; the Gov. Gunning Bedford House of about 1730; and the Presbyterian Church, erected in 1707.

The Green—bounded by Delaware, Market, Harmony, and Third Streets—was laid out at the order of Stuyvesant when he assumed control of the settlement, and it remains the center of the historic town. One of the interesting old buildings situated on it is the Old Court House, on the north side of Delaware Street. A 20-foot section of its east wing may have existed when William Penn assumed rule of the Delaware region. One of the best times to sightsee in New Castle is on New Castle Day, on the third Saturday in May, when most of the historic buildings are open to visitors.

44. Old Dutch House, Delaware

Location: New Castle County, 32 East Third Street, New Castle.

This house is a fine example of a small, early Dutch colonial dwelling.

Old Dutch House, in New Castle, Delaware, is a charming survivor of Dutch settlement in the Delaware River Valley.

Apparently erected during the latter half of the 17th century, when New Castle was still a small village, it may be the oldest house in Delaware. The unknown builder provided exceptionally low and wide eaves, a single dormer, and a huge central chimney. Beneath the unusual front eave is a stout door, which is flanked by two shuttered, low-lying windows. The simplicity and smallness of the house contrast sharply with the grander and larger buildings of New Castle's later days. The house, which is also known as the Dutch House Museum, contains an excellent collection of Dutch furniture. Restored by the Delaware Society for the Preservation of Antiquities in 1938 and now owned by the New Castle Historical Society, it is open to the public throughout the year.

45. Swedish Blockhouse, Delaware

Location: New Castle County, on Naaman's Creek, just west of U.S. 13, about ½ mile south of Delaware-Pennsylvania boundary.

This two-story stone structure was probably erected in 1654 by the Governor of New Sweden, Johan Rising. It has a steep hip roof. The small loopholes beneath the eaves enabled muskets to be fired at attackers. A narrow stairway leads from the first to the second floor. A corner chimney and brick oven are located on the first floor. Dutch soldiers took over the blockhouse in 1655, when New Sweden fell into Dutch hands, but 6 years later it fell to the Indians. It changed hands twice during the War for Independence. During the 18th century, it was incorporated into an inn, and remains part of a public house to this day.

46. St. Augustine, Florida

Location: St. Johns County.

The first permanent European settlement within the present United States and a longtime seat of Spanish power in the New World, St. Augustine was established in 1565 by Don Pedro Menéndez de Avilés. His purpose, which was successfully executed, was to drive out the French, who had founded a settlement at Fort Caroline the previous year. From his strategically located and easily defended new base, Menéndez destroyed the fort and massacred a French force, led by Jean Ribaut, which had set out from Fort Caroline to attack the Spanish but had been shipwrecked south of St. Augustine. As a result, France lost its hold in the region.

Old Spanish Kitchen, photographed from the "Oldest House," in St. Augustine. Courtesy of J. Carver Harris, Photographer.

The Spanish controlled St. Augustine during two periods: 1565–1763 and 1783–1821. During the first period, when their power in the New World was at its zenith, the city was a vital center of imperial activity. It was the military base of operations for countering British and French influence in the region and headquarters of the missionary effort to convert the Indians, which involved the establishment of a series of missions in the present States of Georgia, South Carolina, and Florida.

As the focal point of Spanish power in the region, St. Augustine was frequently attacked—particularly by the principal antagonists of the Spanish in the region, the English. In 1586, Sir Francis Drake raided and burned the city, but the colonists returned and rebuilt it. Throughout the following century, English buccaneers, Indians, and other raiding parties harassed it; as a defense, in 1672 the authorities began to build the major fortification, Castillo de San Marcos.

The first period of Spanish influence in the region ended in effect in 1742, when Gen. James Oglethorpe, British commander in Georgia and South Carolina, who 2 years earlier had seriously threatened St. Augustine, defeated the Spanish when they tried to capture Fort Frederica. In 1763, the Treaty of Paris confirmed British control of Florida. When the British occupied St. Augustine, most of the colonists fled to Cuba, whose sovereignty had been transferred back to Spain by the British in exchange

Dining Room of "Oldest House," in St. Augustine. The house, constructed about 1703, now serves as headquarters of the St. Augustine Historical Society. Courtesy, J. Carver Harris, Photographer.

for Florida. Yet the city prospered under British rule. During the War for Independence, it was a refuge for Tories and an important base for British operations against the southern colonies.

By 1783, when Spain regained Florida, her international influence was waning, especially in the New World. In 1819, she ceded Florida to the United States by treaty; and, in 1821, the same year the treaty was finally ratified, she lost all her territory in North America because of the Mexican Revolution. For these reasons, and also because of the initial encroachment of American frontiersmen, Spanish reoccupation of St. Augustine in 1783 was little more than nominal.

St. Augustine still reveals much of its Spanish inheritance. It has many narrow, winding streets, which end abruptly in cross streets. Of particular note is the Plaza de la Constitución, which contains a public market and is lined by important civic buildings. Established in 1598, it is the oldest public square in the United States. Its name commemorates the Spanish liberal constitution of 1812. Many extant or reconstructed buildings reflect Spanish influence. Some of these are described below:

(1) The "Oldest House," 14 St. Francis Street. This house, which

features coquina walls and hand-hewn beams, was constructed about 1703 on a site occupied since at least the early 1600's. The St. Augustine Historical Society owns it and uses it for its headquarters. Adjoining the house is the Webb Memorial Library and Museum.

(2) Llambias House, 31 St. Francis Street. Built during the first Spanish occupation, this house was constructed of coquina. It is named after one of its owners, T. Llambias, one of a group of Minorcan immigrants who relocated from New Smyrna to St. Augustine during the British occupation in 1777. Now restored, it is operated by the St. Augustine Historical Society.

(3) Old Spanish Treasury, corner of St. George and Treasury Streets. This is one of the best examples of Spanish architecture of the later period. It is a flat-roofed house, which has white shutters. The first story is of yellow stuccoed stone; the second, of wood. The house is furnished with 19th-century pieces. The Woman's Exchange maintains it as a museum and operates an adjoining shop.

(4) Old Spanish Inn, 43 St. George Street. One of St. Augustine's oldest surviving buildings, it has been restored to resemble an early 18th-century inn in Spain. Nine rooms are furnished with authentic Spanish pieces brought from Madrid, Toledo, Seville, Granada, and Barcelona.

(5) Fatio House, on Aviles Street just south of the public library. This is a two-story stuccoed building of coquina which has a red tile roof. In excellent condition, it was built by Andrew Ximenez between 1806 and 1821 in a style associated with the second Spanish occupation. The old slave quarters, kitchen, patio, and balconies provide space for gift-shops, painters' studios, and apartments.

Celebrating its 400th anniversary in 1965 with special ceremonies and programs throughout the year, St. Augustine launched additional reconstruction projects.

47. San Francisco de Oconee (Scott Miller Site), Florida

> *Location: Jefferson County, about 2½ miles southeast of Wau-keenah.*

Archeological study suggests that a Spanish mission—thought to be San Francisco de Oconee—was founded at this site around 1650. About 1633, intensive Spanish mission activity began among the Indians of present northwest Florida. By 1702, when Spanish influence was at its height, the Spanish had established 14 missions in Apalachee Province, but 2 years later destroyed or abandoned all of them because of English and Creek raids. Excavation has uncovered remains of two buildings, constructed by the wattle and daub technique, which had floors of packed red clay. Items of Spanish origin were quite common, including sherds of majolica and tinaja, pistol flintlocks, a spur rowel, beads, hinges, locks, an anvil, axes, and hoes, as well as fragments of Chinese porcelain. The site is now in farmland.

48. San Marcos de Apalache (Fort St. Marks), Florida

Location: Wakulla County, on Fla. 363, about 2 miles south of U.S. 98, at the junction of the Wakulla and St. Marks Rivers, just south of the village of St. Marks.

San Marcos de Apalache was of great importance in the mid-17th century, when Spain occupied the Province of Apalachee, centered in the Florida Panhandle. Apalachee's fertile soil provided grain, sorely needed at St. Augustine, and the Wakulla-St. Marks River junction was the logical shipping point. A flimsy, wooden fortification built in 1660 at the site by the Spanish was captured in 1682 by a raiding party of French, English, and Indians. Repossessed by the Spanish, who built a stronger wooden fort, the site became the nucleus of a sizable settlement, but the Spanish abandoned it after Col. James Moore of South Carolina raided Apalachee in 1704.

In 1718, Capt. José Primo de Rivera arrived with a new force and rebuilt a third wooden fort on the site. A few years later, the Spaniards began to construct a stone fort, but it had not been completed when England acquired Florida in 1763, holding it until 1783. The British firm of Panton, Leslie & Co. established a trading center at the site and remained after the Spanish reoccupation, in 1787. San Marcos, as a result, became a thriving center of Indian trade. Gen. Andrew Jackson captured it in 1818 during the Seminole campaign and executed two British traders near the fort, one of the episodes that brought United States-Spanish relations to a crisis and influenced the Spanish to sign the Adams-Onís Treaty, by which the United States acquired Florida.

During the Civil War, the Confederates superimposed entrenchments and fortifications upon the ruins of the earlier Spanish forts. The tract, in State ownership, is heavily wooded, and only a portion of the stonework from the late Spanish fort stands above ground. The fort site is open to the public. A museum houses artifacts found in the area and exhibits prepared by the Florida State Museum.

[When this volume was in an advanced stage of publication, the Advisory Board declared Fort San Marcos de Apalache to be eligible for the Registry of National Historic Landmarks.]

49. Santa Catalina de Guale Mission Site, Georgia

Location: Liberty County, on St. Catherine's Island.

The Spanish Franciscan mission of Santa Catalina de Guale was the most important on the coast of present Georgia during the 17th century. It had been constructed by the time Gov. Pedro de Ybarra visited Guale (Georgia) in 1604, following the Guale revolt of 1597, although the precise date is uncertain. It continued to be the most significant mission in the area until its abandonment in 1686 in the face of continued English inspired and directed raids from the Carolinas. No surface indications of the mission buildings are visible today, but excavation has uncovered Spanish and Indian pottery sherds of the period and a few iron nails. The site, well preserved, is owned by a private foundation. Now in forest and underbrush, it is used for grazing.

50. Spanish Mission Site, Georgia

Location: McIntosh County, on Altamaha River, just east of Darien.

This site was probably the location of Santo Domingo de Talaje Mission, one of the Spanish missions to the Guale Indians during the period 1600–1675. Excavation of the site has revealed large, square postholes outlining a rectangular building 70 by 35 feet that was obviously not of Indian design. Three burials in the cemetery of nearby Fort King George, which was active during the period 1721–26, were superimposed over some of the postholes. Because the postholes contained only Indian and 17th-century Spanish materials, they undoubtedly were dug, used, and refilled before Fort King George was established.

A wall enclosed the rectangular building as well as a small, Indian-type house to its rear. Outside the wall to the east were shallow wall trenches and small, round postholes of 15 Indian houses. Nearly 200 sherds of Spanish majolica and tinaja, dating from the first half of the 17th century, substantiate the dating and verify Spanish occupation of the mission. Most of the site is in a State-owned tract that includes the sites of Fort King George and Fort Darien.

51. Cahokia Courthouse, Illinois

Location: St. Clair County, just off Ill. 3, Cahokia.

Capt. Jean Baptiste Saucier, the builder of Fort de Chartres, shortly after 1737 built this log-and-stone structure for his residence. It is a unique monument to the early French settlers of the Illinois country and an excellent example of French colonial architecture. The oldest house in Illinois, possibly the earliest surviving dwelling in the Midwest, and without doubt the oldest courthouse west of the Allegheny Mountains, it has been completely reconstructed.

Old Holy Family Church, Cahokia, Illinois, dates from about 1799. Restored in 1951, it is used regularly for religious services. Courtesy, *Evening and Sunday Journal,* East St. Louis.

An excellent example of French colonial architecture, Cahokia Courthouse, Cahokia, Illinois, was originally a residence. Between 1793 and 1814, it served as a U.S. courthouse.

The construction is of special interest because of the vertical placement of the wall logs; the interstices contain stone and mortar. The building measures about 35 by 43 feet—unusually large—and consists of four rooms and a large attic. The builder's son sold it to the United States in 1793, after which it served as a U.S. courthouse and a center of political activity in the old Northwest. After the county seat was moved from Cahokia in 1814, it was used as a saloon, storehouse, public hall, and finally as a home again.

In 1904, the building was exhibited at the Louisiana Purchase Exposition in St. Louis, and was then purchased by the Chicago Historical Society. Part of it was exhibited in Jackson Park, Chicago, until 1938, when Illinois State archeologists excavated the original foundation site and discovered a number of objects relating to the building. In 1939, as part of a WPA program, the building was reerected on the original site, and much of the original material employed. The State of Illinois maintains the Cahokia Courthouse as a State memorial.

52. Fort Kaskaskia State Park, Illinois

Location: Randolph County, on Ill. 3, about 5 miles north of the village of Chester.

The area memorialized by this park has been under the flags of three nations: France, Great Britain, and the United States. Kaskaskia, established by the French in 1703, prospered as an important outpost on the Mississippi and a source of agricultural commodities. During the French and Indian War, the French erected a palisaded fort on the hill across the Kaskaskia River. Apparently it was never attacked, and the inhabitants destroyed it themselves after the Treaty of Paris in 1763, when the British assumed control of the Illinois country.

During the American War for Independence, George Rogers Clark captured Kaskaskia. From 1809 to 1818, the town served as the first capital of Illinois Territory. When Illinois became a State in 1818, it served as the capital for 2 years, but after 1820 began to decline. A disastrous Mississippi flood in 1844 destroyed most of the town, and in 1910 another flood completely obliterated the site.

Fort Kaskaskia State Park includes the home of Pierre Menard, built in 1802, which stands just below the hill on which the fort stood. The home is an excellent example of French colonial architecture. Nearby, close to the fort site, is the Garrison Hill Cemetery, which contains the remains of many early settlers. Some of the ramparts of Fort Kaskaskia are still visible, and on Kaskaskia Island the State of Illinois has erected a memorial to the pioneer French settlement.

53. Fort Massac, Illinois

> *Location: Massac County, on U.S. 45, about 1 mile southeast of Metropolis*

The original Fort Massac, named Fort Ascension, was erected in 1757 by the French to thwart British encroachment into the lower Ohio Valley. The following year, the French renamed it Fort Massiac. Cherokee Indians made the only known attack upon the fort, in the fall of 1757. At the end of the French and Indian War, when the French lost the area east of the Mississippi River to England, they abandoned the fort and it steadily declined. It was soon destroyed by the Cherokees, and the ruins were left untouched by the British.

In 1794, the United States rebuilt the fort to guard against Spanish attack and renamed it Fort Massac. After the War of 1812, it was abandoned. In 1903, when little more than the site remained, the Daughters of the American Revolution preserved part of the original site and made possible some reconstruction. The State of Illinois maintains the area now as a State memorial. Wood posts outline the first fort and its buildings, and a moat has been rebuilt.

54. Père Marquette State Park, Illinois

Location: Jersey County, on Ill. 100, about 6 miles west of Grafton.

Père Marquette State Park, the largest in Illinois, commemorates the beginning of European exploration of the rich Illinois country and its subsequent settlement and development. The Illinois and Potawatomi Indians were occupying the area of the park when Père Marquette, along with Louis Jolliet and five other companions, passed by in the fall of 1673. At the confluence of the Illinois and Mississippi Rivers is located a large, plain cross in honor of Père Marquette's party. The park provides extensive accommodations for visitors, including a lodge and guesthouses, a nature museum, and interesting roadways.

55. Vincennes, Indiana

Location: Knox County.

The oldest town in Indiana, Vincennes retains to this day something of its French inheritance. The initial date of settlement is not known, but a French trading post may have been located at the site as early as 1683. Settlers were known to have been residing there by 1727, and a fort was constructed about 1732. The early settlement was called by various names, such as Au Poste, Post Ouabache (Wabash), and Post St. Francis Xavier. After Indians captured and executed the commander of the fort, Francois Marie Bissot, Sieur de Vincennes, in 1736, the settlers named the town after him. Of the three earliest French settlements in present Indiana—the other two being Fort Ouiatenon and Fort Miami—only Vincennes survived and prospered.

After the French and Indian War, the British took over the settlement and built a new fort, Fort Sackville. In 1779, George Rogers Clark, recognizing Vincennes' strategic location, captured it for the United States. When Indiana Territory was created in 1800, Vincennes became the seat of government, and William Henry Harrison was appointed Governor. In 1813, the capital was moved to Corydon.

The most tangible remaining evidence of French influence in Vincennes today is the Old French Cemetery, located on the grounds of the St. Francis Xavier Cathedral, at Second and Church Streets. This cemetery contains the remains of many early settlers; the earliest burial was in

1741. The cathedral, construction of which began in 1825, was built on or near the site of a chapel that had been erected when Vincennes was established.

56. Arkansas City Country Club Site, Kansas

> *Location: Cowley County, on the bluffs east of Walnut River, about 1 mile east of Arkansas City.*

Most historians, ethnologists, and archeologists agree that the area referred to by the early Spanish explorers as "Quivira" is the central and south-central Kansas of today, especially along the Smoky Hill and Arkansas Rivers and their immediate tributaries. Quiviran sites have been excavated in Cowley, Rice, and McPherson Counties. Coronado visited the area in 1541, Fray Juan de Padilla in 1542, the Bonilla-Humaña expedition about 1590, and the Oñate expedition in 1601.

The Arkansas City Country Club Site, one of the most interesting sites, is unique among Quiviran sites because it contains two relatively large mounds as well as smaller ones. No artifacts of European origin have been found during the limited excavations carried out to date, but other evidence reveals contact with the Pueblo Indians of the Rio Grande Valley. The Quiviran culture represented at the Arkansas City Country Club Site and at other Cowley County sites is very similar to that of the Rice and McPherson County sites. The site, located on a golf course, is well sodded and excellently preserved.

57. Fanning Site, Kansas

> *Location: Doniphan County, on a ridge between Wolf Creek and the Missouri River Valley, about 1 mile north of Fanning.*

This site, the location of a late 17th-century Kansa Indian village, reflects early contact between the Indians and European traders and trappers. Small quantities of iron, glass beads, and brass items have been discovered in trash-filled cache pits, including a few knife blades that were undoubtedly obtained from some of the small parties of French traders and trappers which ventured up the Missouri and its tributaries late in the 17th century.

The identification and significance of the Fanning Site is strengthened by its apparent relationship with the Doniphan Site, 16 miles to the north, which was the principal village of the Kansa tribe in 1724, when the French trader Étienne Veniard de Bourgmond visited them. European goods found at the Doniphan Site are believed to have come from Bourgmond's trading post, Fort Orleans, established in 1723 near present Malta Bend, Mo. The Fanning Site, now in farmland, is well preserved.

58. Fort St. Jean Baptiste de Natchitoches Sites, Louisiana

Location: Natchitoches Parish, New Second Street and vicinity, Natchitoches.

Fort St. Jean Baptiste, which the French began to construct in 1715, was the first fortified outpost on the frontier between French Louisiana and New Spain. Its location remained internationally significant for well over a century. In 1719, the garrison, commanded by Philippe Blondel, destroyed the Spanish mission at Los Adaes, 15 miles away, which had been established in 1716. As a result, in 1721–22 the Spanish founded a presidio at Los Adaes. In 1731, the Natchez Indians, fresh from slaughtering the Fort Rosalie garrison in Natchez, attacked Fort St. Jean Baptiste. With the help of friendly Indian reinforcements, the French wiped out the attackers.

In 1737, because of recurrent floods, a new fort was built on high ground, in what is now the American Cemetery, and the old fort abandoned. The latter fort is known to have been in existence in 1769. No evidence of the forts remains above ground, however, and further archeological investigation will be required to authenticate the sites and provide additional information. The earlier site, 200 yards east of the new site, is owned by the Association of Natchitoches Women for the Preservation of Historic Natchitoches, and local leaders are planning to reconstruct the original fort.

59. Fort St. Philip, Louisiana

Location: Plaquemines Parish, on the left bank of the Mississippi River, opposite Triumph.

Francisco Luís Hector, Baron de Carondelet, Governor of Louisiana and West Florida, built this fort in 1795, as a part of his plan to extend

Spain's dominion over the entire Mississippi Valley and to prevent the encroachment of American frontiersmen. His plan included the instigation of Indian attacks on the frontiersmen; a fleet of gunboats patrolling the Mississippi River; and a series of forts along the border area of the territory, including Fort St. Philip.

The fort figured prominently in the Civil War, along with Fort Jackson across the river, when Adm. David Farragut and his Union fleet bombarded the two forts in 1862 and then was able to seize the city of New Orleans. (Fort St. Philip has been designated as eligible for the Registry of National Historic Landmarks, relating primarily to the Civil War.) The Army did not garrison the fort after 1871, although it made repairs during World War I with a view to possible use. After the war, the Government sold the fort and it has remained in private ownership. The 1,100 acres of the former St. Philip Military Reservation stretch along the Mississippi River for 2 miles and are accessible only by boat. The site, covered with orange trees, is privately owned. Ruins of the early fort may be seen, along with some World War I buildings.

60. Longfellow-Evangeline State Park, Louisiana

Location: St. Martin Parish, on the Bayou Teche, 1 mile east of St. Martinsville.

This park commemorates the migration of the Acadians—now called Cajuns—who first settled in the British seaboard colonies and from 1760 on eventually settled on an irregular basis in Louisiana after being exiled from Nova Scotia because of their religious beliefs. In his poem "Evangeline," Longfellow popularized the migration and the many years of hardships the Acadians faced while searching for a homeland. The people living in the immediate vicinity of the park, and in the surrounding communities, are their direct descendants and speak with an Anglo-French dialect. The museum in the park—a house once reputedly occupied by Louis Arceneaux, the "Gabriel" of Longfellow's poem—commemorates the story of Gabriel and Evangeline and Acadian history.

61. Presidio of Los Adaes Site, Louisiana

Location: Natchitoches Parish, just north of La. 6, about 2 miles northeast of Robeline.

Concerned by the threat of French encroachment into Spanish-claimed territory, the Spaniards in 1716 established San Miguel de Linares Mission a few miles southwest of the French settlement and fort at Natchitoches. In 1719, the mission was attacked and destroyed by a French force from Fort St. Jean Baptiste de Natchitoches, but in 1721–22 the Spanish returned and rebuilt, on an adjoining hill, the Presidio of Nuestra Señora del Pilar de los Adaes (Adais).

For the next half-century, the presidio was an important outpost and the capital of the frontier province of Texas, the seat of 13 Spanish Governors down until 1773. In the last decade of its existence, it consisted only of a hexagonal fort, defended by 6 cannons and 100 soldiers, and a village of about 40 "miserable houses constructed with stakes driven into the ground."

Long after the presidio had been abandoned, in 1806, the site's strategic importance was still recognized by the signing there of a preliminary treaty between Ens. Joseph María Gonzales and Capt. Edward Turner of the U.S. Army. Gonzales agreed to retreat to Spanish-owned Texas and to cease sending Spanish patrols across the border into the United States. This treaty led to the formal establishment, a few weeks later, of "neutral ground" between Texas and the United States by Gen. James Wilkinson and Spanish Lt. Comdr. Simon de Herrera. The two nations honored the boundary for 14 years.

Only a few unidentified mounds of earth are visible today on the attractive ridge where the presidio stood. Of the 40 acres or so encompassing the presidio, mission, and village sites, about 9 acres are in public ownership as a historical park. The National Society of the Daughters of American Colonists and the State of Louisiana have commemorated the site with markers.

62. St. Louis Cathedral, Louisiana

Location: Orleans Parish, Jackson Square, New Orleans.

The site of this cathedral, facing the historic Place d'Armes, or Jackson Square, has been consecrated to the Roman Catholic Church from the earliest days of New Orleans. The stately cathedral now occupying the site honors the patron saint of Bourbon France, who was also the patron of *Nouvelle Orléans*. The first church on the site, a small adobe-wood structure called the Parish Church, was erected by Bienville soon after 1718, when he founded the city, but in 1723 a hurricane destroyed it.

Although extensive alterations have obscured its original appearance, St. Louis Cathedral, constructed between 1789 and 1794, exemplifies the Spanish period in the Vieux Carré, New Orleans.

The second church, of brick and wood, served from 1727 until destroyed in the great fire of 1788, which damaged most of the city.

The present St. Louis Cathedral, built between 1789 and 1794, originally resembled other Spanish-built churches in Mexico and South America. Extensive alterations made in 1851, however, included enlargement of the building and addition of steeples and the present columned and pilastered portico. These alterations, along with two subsequent renovations, have obscured the original appearance of the church.

63. Sang pour Sang Hill, Louisiana

Location: Natchitoches Parish, just south of Cloutierville.

This high, rocky, tree-studded hill is located adjacent to and named after a former lake called *Sang pour Sang*, which is now completely dry. In 1732, a group of Natchez Indians took refuge on the shores of this lake after fleeing down the Red River from Fort St. Jean Baptiste de Natchitoches. In 1731, they had besieged the fort unsuccessfully but burned a captive Frenchwoman alive in full view of the garrison. In retaliation, St. Denis, the commander of the fort, led 40 of his soldiers and 100 Indian allies against the Natchez and killed 92 warriors and 4 chiefs. The surviving Indians fled to the shores of the lake, where the Frenchmen found and annihilated them.

64. Norridgewock Site, Maine

Location: Somerset County, on U.S. 201 Alt., about 7 miles north of Norridgewock Town, at Old Point.

Norridgewock, or *Nanrantsouak*, is the site of an Abnaki Indian village, where a French Jesuit mission was established in 1646 and served the Indians for decades. Enmity later arose between the English and French, and in 1701 English officials ordered that the mission be closed. In 1704–5, the British destroyed the mission buildings, but Father Sebastian Rasle had a temporary structure built while work was carried forward on a new church, completed in 1718.

In 1722, however, the English returned again; 200 Englishmen under Capt. John Harmon pillaged the church and carried off the manuscript of a dictionary of the Abnaki language on which Father Rasle had been working for many years. Two years later, Father Rasle was killed during another English attack, when the church and Indian village were destroyed. In fear of further attacks, the Indians abandoned the site, part of them going to Canada. Nothing remains of the settlement today. The site is now a camping area that is owned by the State of Maine and includes some privately owned land.

65. Popham Colony Site (lost site), Maine

Location: Sagadahoc County, just off Maine 209, near Popham Beach in Phippsburg Town.

The first English colony in New England was founded at this site late in the summer of 1607 by the Plymouth Company in its effort to settle "North Virginia." Unlike the London Company's similar venture in "South Virginia," at Jamestown in the same year, this attempt was unsuccessful. The party of more than 100 colonists, led by George Popham and Raleigh Gilbert, landed on a point at the mouth of the Kennebec (then the Sagadahoc) River. They immediately constructed Fort St. George, after which they built a small ship. Severe weather and bad luck, however, plagued them. A fire during the winter destroyed most of their provisions, George Popham died, and Raleigh Gilbert had to return to England. This left the colony vulnerable and without effective leadership. Defeated, the survivors returned to England late in 1608.

The colony was located in the general area of Popham Beach on Sabino Head. The assumed site is on a 45-acre tract of land owned by the State. It is virtually unspoiled by modern intrusions, except for a few scattered framehouses and the concrete remains of Fort Baldwin, a World War I coast defense installation.

66. St. Croix Island, Maine

Location: Washington County, in the mouth of the St. Croix River.

In 1604, Pierre du Guast, Sieur de Monts, a French Huguenot, aided by Samuel de Champlain, established a colony on this island. It was one of the first French New World settlements and, though unsuccessful, was a challenge to England for the colonization of North America. The colonists suffered a disastrous winter; lack of food and water caused a scurvy epidemic, and many of them died. After a month of searching for a better site, in 1605 the leaders moved the colony across the Bay of Fundy to the site of Port Royal, Nova Scotia. In 1613, the British destroyed all of the buildings left on the island. Archeological investigation by the National Park Service has revealed burials and other traces of the original French settlement. Public Law 87, 81st Congress, approved June 8, 1949, authorized establishment of St. Croix Island National Monument.

Built in 1653 by the townspeople of York, Maine, York Gaol now serves as a museum and contains colonial and Indian relics. A portion of the original stone wall may be seen in this photograph. Photograph by Douglas Armsden. Courtesy, Old Gaol Museum Committee, York.

67. York Gaol, Maine

Location: York County, Long Lands Road, York.

This is one of the oldest public buildings in New England. York was established in 1624 by the Plymouth Company. In 1641, it formed a government and adopted a city charter, and in 1652 reorganized into a town. The townspeople then constructed many public buildings, such as the gaol, which is the oldest extant building in York. Built of stone in 1653, its walls are now covered with wood siding, and a large gambrel roof has been added. The original prisoners' cells may be seen in the old part of the structure. The gaol, now a museum containing colonial and Indian relics, is open to the public during the summer.

68. Cross Manor, Maryland

Location: St. Marys County, just off Md. 5, about 1 mile below St. Inigoes.

Built about 1643, Cross Manor is probably the oldest house in Maryland.

Constructed of brick on a 2,000-acre grant that Thomas Cornwallis obtained in 1639, it originally had a gambrel roof. The roof was later changed to a gabled design and other alterations were made. The gardens, about as old as the residence, are of interest; some of the ancient boxwood are at least 35 feet in circumference. The house is privately owned, but may be visited by appointment.

69. Hill Farm, Maryland

Location: Calvert County, just northwest of Md. 266, below Lusby.

This frame farmhouse, situated on a hill overlooking St. Leonard's Creek, is a superlative specimen of an unpretentious early farm dwelling. Dating from about 1670, it still has the original pine siding. Three small dormer windows jut from the steep roof, and brick chimneys are located at each end of the house. A log cabin, added sometime after the original construction, now forms an attractive wing. The house has been restored and furnished with period furniture. Though privately owned, it may be visited by appointment.

70. Holly Hill, Maryland

Location: Calvert County, 1½ miles from Friendship.

This is one of Maryland's most appealing and lovely early colonial houses, both on the interior and exterior. The original section of the T-shaped residence was constructed about 1667, and the most recent wing about 1720. The one-story brick house has gabled ends, a steeply pitched roof, and several imposing chimneys. Boxwood and flower borders complement the exterior. Inside, two original murals are especially noteworthy, one located over a mantel and the other over the dining room door. After the house was restored, the owners installed a collection of early 18th-century American and French antiques. The house is privately owned, but it is open by appointment.

71. St. Marys City, Maryland

Location: St. Marys County.

This city, presently the location of St. Marys College, is the site of the first English settlement in Maryland. When Leonard Calvert, brother of the Lord Proprietor of the colony, sailed into the mouth of the Potomac River and up the St. Marys River in 1634, his two ships dropped anchor near an Indian village whose inhabitants were moving away because of fear of other Indians. The 200 colonists settled in the abandoned Indian village and soon erected a fort. Later, a town evolved and grew along with other newer nearby settlements. In 1676, it was the capital of a bustling colony. In that year, a statehouse was erected for the use of the colonial assembly.

In 1694, however, the capital was moved to Anne Arundel Town, renamed Annapolis the following year, and shortly thereafter St. Marys City lost even its county seat status. As a result, it rapidly declined. No original 17th-century building has survived, though foundations of some of the 60 houses built in the 1600's lay under shallow coverings of dirt. The present reconstruction of the early statehouse, on Middle Street, was inspired by the Maryland Tercentenary Celebration of 1934. It is furnished with copies of period furniture. Nearly all the land of the old central city is privately owned. In 1965, the State was examining the possibility of reconstructing parts of the city.

72. House of Seven Gables, Massachusetts

Location: Essex County, 54 Turner Street, Salem.

Long known as the Turner House, the House of Seven Gables is now identified—perhaps inaccurately—with the novel of the same name, published in 1852, by Nathaniel Hawthorne. The earliest section of the weatherbeaten, rambling house was probably built about 1668, and it

House of Seven Gables, Massachusetts. Courtesy, Eric H. Muller, Photographer.

shows medieval influence. The house has been expanded at various times and the number of gables increased from the original four to seven. In 1910, it was restored. Numerous pieces of furniture used by various owners are exhibited, as well as items associated with Hawthorne. The House of Seven Gables Settlement Association owns the house, which is open to the public throughout the year.

73. Jethro Coffin House, Massachusetts

Location: Nantucket County, Sunset Hill Road, Nantucket Island.

This is one of the few extant 17th-century houses of the long-popular Cape Cod style and is one of the best examples. Built about 1686, it features the characteristic steeply pitched roof, having an unusually long rearward slope, and the typical massive central chimney. Small, medieval-type windows indicate the house's great age. The tall chimney has an exceptionally interesting flue device, and inverted horseshoe, which was supposed to ward off witches. In 1927, the house was completely restored. Maintained by the Nantucket Historical Society, it is open to the public between June 15 and October 1.

74. John Ward House, Massachusetts

Location: Essex County, 132 Essex Street, Salem.

This clapboard-covered house, built in 1684, reflects the architectural mode of the era. It originally had only one room, but was later expanded into a two-story structure that was distinguished by cross gables and an overhang. Moved to the present location in 1909, where it was restored and furnished, it includes colonial furnishings. The exposed beams of the kitchen and the fascinating collection of early kitchenware and utensils are of special interest. The Essex Institute owns the house, which is open to the public from June through September.

75. Peter Tufts House, Massachusetts

Location: Middlesex County, 350 Riverside Avenue, Medford.

This is probably the oldest brick house in New England. Built in 1678,

Peter Tufts House, Massachusetts, built in 1678. It is maintained by the Society for the Preservation of New England Antiquities.

it is a two-story, gambrel-roof structure that has two rooms in each story. The builders placed portholes for muskets in the front wall on both floors because Indians still posed a threat when the house was erected. Despite a remodeling of the house in the 1890's, the exterior and the great oak beams inside make it one of New England's most interesting colonial dwellings. Maintained by the Society for the Preservation of New England Antiquities, it is open to the public throughout the year on a limited schedule.

76. Plymouth Rock, Massachusetts

Location: Plymouth County, just off Water Street, Plymouth.

This great granite rock—incised with the date 1620—commemorates the landing of the Pilgrims in New England. Resting under a portico of classical design, surrounded by an iron fence, and lying two-thirds underground, it is located at the foot of Cole's Hill. Historians have not been able to determine definitely whether or not it was the actual point where the first exploring party came ashore. No mention of the

The landing of the Pilgrims in the New World is commemorated at Plymouth Rock, Massachusetts. The rock, surrounded by an iron fence, lies under this portico, at the bottom of Cole's Hill.

landing place was made in the official records of the Pilgrims. In any event, as the traditional symbol of the landing, the rock is venerated by the people of the United States.

77. Rebecca Nurse House, Massachusetts

Location: Essex County, 149 Pine Street, Danvers.

Built in 1678, this is an interesting 17th-century clapboard house whose simple lines and basic workmanship demonstrate colonial building skills. The builder was Francis Nurse, but the house derives its name from his wife Rebecca, who in 1692 was condemned and hanged as a witch during the witchcraft hysteria. She stoutly maintained her innocence, yet could not satisfy her accusers. The house has been restored and is furnished with period pieces. Owned by the Society for the Preservation of New England Antiquities, it is open to the public between June 15 and October 15. At other times, it may be visited by appointment.

78. William Harlow House, Massachusetts

> *Locqtion: Plymouth County, corner of Sandwich and South Streets, Plymouth.*

This house is one of several extant 17th-century structures in Plymouth. When Sgt. William Harlow built it in 1677, he used lumber taken from the fort on Burial Hill. Now restored, the house is owned by the Plymouth Antiquarian Society. Costumed hostesses perform spinning, weaving, candlemaking, and other household arts of the 17th century. The house is open from May 30 to September 30.

79. Fort L'Huillier Site, Minnesota

> *Location: Blue Earth County, right bank of Blue Earth River, near its junction with the Le Sueur River, just southwest of Mankato.*

Pierre Charles le Sueur established Fort L'Huillier in 1700 as a headquarters for trading and mining. The fort consisted of three or four log cabins surrounded by a palisade. When Le Sueur returned to France the following year he carried with him much geographical data—such as the location of Indian villages and streams—that were incorporated in various maps and travel accounts. He also reportedly had 2 tons of the local blue earth transported to Paris at great expense, only to find that it was merely clay instead of the valuable copper ore he believed it to be. The site of Fort L'Huillier is on a large natural mound, about 60 to 75 feet high, on the top of which are a few acres of fairly level ground. The site is in farmland, and evidence of the fort's structures has been destroyed by cultivation.

80. Fort St. Charles Site, Minnesota

> *Location: Lake of the Woods County, Magnusson Island, on the southern shore of the Northwest Angle Inlet, near Penasse.*

In 1732, Pierre Gaultier de Varennes, Sieur de la Vérendrye, established Fort St. Charles as his westernmost headquarters, and it became the focal point for French fur trade and exploration in a large region. The fort consisted of an oblong palisade of posts, about 12 to 15 feet high, within which were located several rough cabins, a missionary's residence, commandant's house, chapel, powder magazine, storehouse, and other structures. Two gates were located opposite each other, and the fort had an observation tower.

In 1736, La Vérendrye sent a relief party from the fort to Michilimackinac Island—1,500 miles away—for supplies. The party of 19 voyageurs and 3 canoes, led by La Vérendrye's son, Jean Baptiste, and Jesuit Father Aulneau, camped on a small island in the Lake of the Woods (now called Massacre Island), where Indians massacred them. The elder La Vérendrye brought the bodies back to the fort and buried them beneath the chapel. In the early 1750's, the fort was abandoned.

In 1908, an archeological expedition under the auspices of the Historical Society of St. Boniface discovered the site. Excavation revealed the ruins of a large fireplace; the locations of the chapel, the priest's house, and the commandant's quarters; remnants of the palisade; and apparently some skeletal remains of the Jean Baptiste de la Vérendrye party. In 1951, the Knights of Columbus placed a granite altar on the spot where the original chapel stood. Today, Fort St. Charles is marked by a conjecturally reconstructed stockade of cedar poles. The foundations of the original huts have been marked, and the chapel reconstructed of concrete "logs." The site is owned by the Minnesota Fourth Degree Knights of Columbus.

81. Davion's Bluff (Loftus Heights), Mississippi

Location: Wilkinson County, Fort Adams Road, Fort Adams.

In 1698, a French mission was established by Fathers Davion and Montigny at this bluff, on the bank of the Mississippi River. The site is of considerable historic interest in relation to the changing fortunes of the European powers in the lower Mississippi Valley in the 18th century, and in the later growth and development of the United States. Davion's Bluff became known as Loftus Heights following the ambush there in 1764 of an English force under Maj. Arthur Loftus.

In 1799, the United States constructed Fort Adams on the heights after the Spanish withdrew from the Natchez district. This fort helped to mark and defend the boundary between Spanish and American lands east of the Mississippi River. Aaron Burr sought to enlist the support of Gen. James Wilkinson, the fort's first commander, in his scheme to found an empire in the old Southwest. No remains are extant of the early mission and few of the fort. The town of Fort Adams, a small farming center, is now on the site of the mission. The site's historic environment has been changed by the altered course of the Mississippi River, which now lies about 1 mile away.

82. Fort Rosalie (Fort Panmure) Site, Mississippi

Location: Adams County, foot of South Broadway, Natchez.

Fort Rosalie was established in 1716 at present Natchez by the French, 3 years after a trading post was opened, for protection against the Indians. The wooden structures—officers' quarters, guardhouse, barracks, and powder magazine surrounded by a palisade—soon fell into ruin, and plans for rebuilding a permanent brick structure came to naught because in 1729 the Natchez tribe massacred most of the inhabitants. The following year, the French built another provisional post at the site.

When the British took over at the end of the French and Indian War and found the post in ruins, they rebuilt it and renamed it Fort Panmure. Seized by an American force during the War for Independence, the post was recaptured by the British, occupied by the Spanish during the period 1783–98, and then passed again into American hands. Finally, it was abandoned after Fort Adams was constructed, in 1799, nearer the crucial United States-Spanish boundary.

Peter Little built the present Rosalie Mansion in 1820 on part of the fort tract, and in 1930 the mansion was acquired by the Mississippi State Society of the Daughters of the American Revolution.

83. Old Spanish Fort, Mississippi

Location: Jackson County, on Krebs Lake, 1 mile outside of Pascagoula.

This house, known as the Old Spanish Fort, is probably the oldest in Mississippi. Yet it has changed little with the passage of time. It was built about 1718 by Joseph Simon de la Pointe on land given to his aunt, the Duchess of Chaumont, by Louis XIV. Fortified by its French occupants for defense against the Indians and Spanish, it was sturdily built of hewn timbers, shell lime, and shells. The Spanish, who took over the area in 1783, utilized it both as a fort and a chateau.

Richard Jackson House, in Portsmouth, New Hampshire, is the oldest house in the town and perhaps in the State. Its original section dates from the year 1664.

84. Richard Jackson House, New Hampshire

Location: Rockingham County, Jackson Hill Street, Portsmouth.

This two-story house is the oldest in Portsmouth, and perhaps in the State. The present central section is the original part, built in 1664. The two wings and the rear lean-to are later additions. As restored by the Society for the Preservation of New England Antiquities, which owns the property, it reflects well the architecture of its period. Plain and unpainted, the exterior is in the original state except for the casement windows. The interior also retains much of the original flavor; it has exposed beams, sheathed or crudely plastered walls, and broad floorboards. The house is open to the public from June 1 to October 15.

85. William Dam Garrison House, New Hampshire

Location: Strafford County, 182–192 Central Avenue, Dover.

This small log cabin, erected about 1675 by William Dam (Damme), is an excellent representative of the fortified residence, or garrison, that was once common in New England. It is one of the few such structures in the area that escaped destruction by the Indians. It consists of two rooms and has a central chimney. The walls are hand-hewn oak logs, some of them more than 20 feet long, which have lapped joints at the ends. The original small windows have been replaced by larger ones. The house has been preserved under a private trusteeship as a historic residence since 1915, when it was moved from its original site on Back River Road to its present location. Open to the public, it contains colonial household articles and clothing.

86. Nothnagle House, New Jersey

Location: Gloucester County, on Paulsboro-Repaupo Road, ¼ mile north of Repaupo.

A section of this house dates from the early colonial period. Evidently constructed by Swedes or Swedish-Finns, the house was originally a one-story, typical Swedish log structure, whitewashed and built of cross-piled, dovetailed logs. The fireplace was located in the corner. The date of construction cannot be determined.

87. Swedish Log Cabin, New Jersey

Location: Gloucester County, 1 mile north of Swedesboro.

This cabin, one of the few extant Swedish log cabins in the United States, stands on a plot of ground bought by Marten Martensson on March 9, 1685, some years after New Sweden had been conquered by the Dutch and then by the English. It was built in the 1680's, measures 12 by 15 feet, and is seven logs in height. The logs are dovetailed at the corners. A door, about 3 feet high, affords the only access. The cabin is located on a privately owned farm.

88. Trinity Episcopal (Old Swedes) Church, New Jersey

Location: Gloucester County, on King's Highway at Raccoon Creek, Swedesboro.

The congregation of this church consisted of some of the first Swedish settlers, who arrived in the area before 1650. Dependent at first upon occasional ministerial visits, it later obtained permission for the schoolmaster to conduct regular services in a log cabin. After the War for Independence, the congregation constructed the present handsome edifice. The date of construction, 1784, is given on a circular stone set in the wall over the entrance, below the sloping eaves of the gabled roof.

The church was constructed of brick and stone, and the facade incorporates a striking Palladian window. At the opposite end of the building is a graceful white spire. When the Swedish Lutheran mission ended in 1789, the Episcopal Church fell heir to the building and has used it ever since. The Swedish heritage is attested to by several items in the church, including the old registers, a 1730 silver communion service, and a Swedish Bible and flag. Old tombstones in the churchyard bear the names of early Swedish settlers.

89. Zabriskie-Von Steuben House, New Jersey

> Location: Bergen County, on New Bridge Road, ½ mile off N.J. 4, North Hackensack.

John and Peter Zabriskie, millers, built this interesting house between 1739 and 1752. An excellent example of early Dutch colonial construction, it is built of stone. It has a gambrel roof, front porch, and two front doors. Nine slender columns support the roof over the porch. The west wall contains a square stone plaque bearing the Zabriskies' initials, the date 1751, and a millwheel indicating the owners' business.

The house was confiscated during the War for Independence because the Zabriskies remained loyal to the Crown, and it served as headquarters for both armies during campaigns in New Jersey; it housed Gen. George Washington and Lord Charles Cornwallis. Gen. Frederick William Von Steuben, who was awarded the house and surrounding land in return for his services during the war, later sold it to the Zabriskies, after they had become citizens of the United States. The property is now owned by the State of New Jersey, and it is used as a museum and headquarters by the Bergen County Historical Society.

90. Coronado State Monument, New Mexico

> Location: Sandoval County, just off N. Mex. 44, about 5 miles northwest of Bernalillo.

This monument preserves the extensive ruins of the ancient pueblo of

Kuaua, believed to have been besieged by Coronado in the winter of 1540–41. A sister pueblo 1 mile to the south may have been the site of Coronado's winter quarters during that period. The ruins include a restored square kiva, on whose interior walls are represented prehistoric Indian murals. The murals depict masked dancers, and are based on partially preserved originals found by archeologists when the University of New Mexico excavated the kiva in the 1930's. An adjacent museum exhibits Pueblo Indian and Spanish colonial artifacts. Operated by the Museum of New Mexico, the monument is open to the public throughout the year.

91. San Felipe de Neri Church, New Mexico

> *Location: Bernalillo County, northwest side of Old Town plaza, Albuquerque.*

Construction of this church was begun by Fray Manuel Moreno, at the northwest corner of the plaza, almost as soon as Gov. Cuervo y Valdez, in 1706, established the villa of Albuquerque. The facade has been rebuilt and minor repairs have been made, but the church today differs little from the original. The most imposing and historically significant edifice in Old Town Albuquerque, it is still used by the Catholic Church for religious purposes.

92. San José de Giusewa Mission, New Mexico

> *Location: Sandoval County, on N. Mex. 4, Jémez Springs.*

This Franciscan mission was founded around 1620 at the Pueblo of Giusewa, probably by Fray Gerónimo Zarate Salmerón, and ministered actively to the Jémez Indians for at least 10 years. The pueblo sheltered some 800 inhabitants. The Jémez pueblos and missions had stormy histories—revolt, abandonments, and reestablishments at various sites. By 1658, Giusewa had definitely been abandoned, perhaps because of Navajo aggression.

The ruins of the mission church, now part of Jémez State Monument, are unusually impressive. Walls of stone, 4 to 8 feet thick, rise as high as 30 feet in places, and the ruins of an octagonal tower stand 50 feet high. Extensive remains of the *convento,* especially the monastery, adjoin the church. A small private chapel in the monastery is the best preserved room. West of the church are the ruins of the pueblo, including dwelling rooms and kivas.

93. San Juan Pueblo, New Mexico

Location: Rio Arriba County, on U.S. 64, about 27 miles north of Santa Fe.

The northernmost of the several pueblos of the Tewa group, San Juan was the first Spanish base in New Mexico, and thus the temporary first capital when Oñate occupied the region in 1598. The Spanish invaders occupied a large part of the pueblo—which they called "San Juan de los Caballeros"—while they built permanent quarters and a church across the Rio Grande at the neighboring pueblo that was known by its Indian name of Yungue-ouinge. Existence at San Juan was apparently uneventful during the 17th century until the Pueblo Revolt of 1680, in which the pueblo was deeply involved. Popé, the leader of the uprising, directed it chiefly from Taos Pueblo, but he was a native of San Juan. In 1692, the Spanish reconquered the Rio Grande Valley around San Juan.

North section of the plaza at San Juan Pueblo, the first Spanish base in New Mexico.

94. Santa Fe, New Mexico

Location: Santa Fe County.

The second oldest city in the United States, Santa Fe still reflects to a remarkable degree—in its architecture, customs, people, and language—its Indian-Spanish-Mexican heritage. Site of an ancient Indian village and since 1610 capital of New Mexico under Spain, Mexico, and the United States, *La Villa Real de la Santa Fé de San Francisco* (The Royal City of the Holy Faith of St. Francis) is truly the "Cradle of the Southwest." As in few other places in the United States, the blend of cultures that resulted from Spanish settlement can be seen and experienced.

Pueblo- and Territorial-style buildings line the narrow streets; Spanish language and customs predominate; historic sites and buildings abound. Santa Fe—also a modern art and cultural center—has made special efforts to preserve its heritage. A number of excellent museums, most of them units of the Museum of New Mexico, trace the history of this ancient city and its environs from the days of prehistoric Indians, through the Spanish and Mexican periods, to the present.

The focal point on the plaza in Santa Fe is the Palace of the Governors, a Registered National Historic Landmark. The plaza itself—also a Registered National Historic Landmark (relating primarily to the Santa Fe Trail)—has significant associations with early Indian-Spanish history. The Spanish used it for official, religious, and military functions. In fact, the entire pageantry of 17th-century Spanish conquest and settlement, Pueblo Revolt, and Spanish reconquest reached their climax in or near the plaza.

Among the many other important sites and buildings throughout the city of Santa Fe associated with the Spanish period are:

(1) Chapel of San Miguel. Originally built by Fray Alfonso de Benavides in 1626, this chapel is one of the oldest in the United States. It was partially destroyed during the Pueblo Revolt of 1680. After the reconquest, in 1692, it was rebuilt on the same site and for the next 50 years served as the military chapel of Santa Fe. Impressive carved altar decorations, historic paintings—some dating from the 13th century—and a bell said to have been cast in Spain in 1536 are interesting features. An excellent example of an 18th-century Spanish chapel, San Miguel still serves as a parish church.

(2) Rosario Chapel. Standing in the old Spanish cemetery northwest of Santa Fe, this chapel was originally built by De Vargas on the spot where his army camped while besieging Santa Fe during the reconquest of 1692. Rebuilt in 1807 and still used as a church, it is the starting point for the De Vargas procession, which commemorates the reconquest annually during Fiesta.

(3) Guadalupe Church. Built about 1795, this still-active parish church is the oldest shrine in the United States dedicated to the Virgin of Guadalupe.

(4) Barrio de Analco. This district, which surrounds the Chapel of San Miguel, was occupied by Mexican Indians who came north with the Spaniards. During the Pueblo Revolt it was razed, but after the reconquest it became the residential section for soldiers, servants, Indians, and *genízaros* (halfbreeds). Its historic buildings and narrow, winding streets make it one of the most picturesque sections of the city.

Numerous residences and commercial buildings also date from the Spanish period. Among them are the Gregorio Crespin House, the so-called "Oldest House," El Zaguan, and the Borrego House. Many of these fine old buildings have been marked with plaques by the Historic Santa Fe Foundation.

95. Billou-Stilwell-Perine House, New York

Location: Richmond County, 1476 Richmond Avenue, Dongan Hills, Staten Island.

This house is an interesting illustration of a Dutch-type house greatly modified by numerous additions in different styles, particularly in the 18th century. Pierre Billou, a Huguenot who arrived at New Amsterdam in 1661 and subsequently received a land grant on Staten Island, erected the original stone section about 1665. In 1679, Thomas Stilwell, a well-to-do landowner, enlarged the house. His descendants owned it until the mid-18th century, at which time Edward Perine acquired it. The Perine family owned it until 1913. It has a shingled, sloping roof, and an unusual jambless fireplace, which is very high and has a large stone hearth. A secret chamber opens into a room that features a ceiling with exceptionally large beams. Owned by the Staten Island Historical Society, the house is open to the public on a limited weekend schedule or by appointment.

96. Bowne House, New York

> *Location: Queens County, corner of Bowne Street and Fox Lane, Flushing, Long Island.*

John Bowne erected this simple, two-story frame residence in 1661, some 10 years after he had migrated to New Netherland from Derbyshire, England. The house not only has general historic interest but is notably associated with the growth of religious freedom in America. Bowne and his wife were jailed and deported to Holland for trial because they held Quaker gatherings in their home. Bowne pled the cause of individual freedom of worship so successfully before the court that the Bownes were permitted to return to Flushing, and the Dutch West India Company declared that henceforth freedom of worship would prevail in its New World colony.

The Bowne family occupied the house until 1946, when the Bowne House Historical Society took it over and restored it. The kitchen is of particular interest for it was the meeting place of John Bowne and his Quaker friends. It is dominated by a gigantic fireplace. The house is open to the public throughout the year for a few hours each week.

97. Brett-Teller House, New York

> *Location: Dutchess County, 50 Van Nydeck Avenue, Beacon.*

This house was erected by Catharyna and Roger Brett in 1709, the year after Catharyna inherited 28,000 acres of an 85,000-acre tract of land along the Hudson River, originally purchased from the Indians in 1663. It was a typical Dutch structure, one-and-a-half stories high, having a low gambrel roof extending downward over the porch. The original section of the house still retains some of the roundheaded shingles that were used on the exterior. Both the wing and the present kitchen were added after 1709, the latter probably after 1790. In 1790, Isaac De Peyster Teller acquired the house and it remained in the Teller family for seven generations. During the War for Independence, prominent guests included Washington, Lafayette, and Von Steuben. The house is now owned by the Melzingah Chapter, Daughters of the American Revolution, and is open daily.

98. Caughnawaga Site, New York

Location: Montgomery County, west side of Cayadutta Creek, one-quarter mile west of Fonda.

Caughnawaga, the last Mohawk village in the present United States before the tribe moved to Canada, illustrates European missionary influence on the Indians. Occupied during the period 1667–93, it was the site of a French Jesuit mission for about 10 years, 1668–79. The Indian girl Kateri Tekakwitha, known as "Lily of the Mohawks," was baptized and confirmed at this mission; she died at the age of 19. Because of her exemplary Christian life, she has gone through several stages of canonization, the first aboriginal North American to be so honored, and her influence has made the site a Catholic shrine.

Comprehensive excavation has revealed the entire circumference (1,016 feet) of the double stockade and the outlines of 12 lodges. White stakes in each of the 3,041 post molds help the visitor visualize the pattern of the village. The site is pleasantly situated on a bluff overlooking the Mohawk River. Nearby is the town of Fonda, founded in 1775 by a group of Dutchmen and named Caughnawaga until 1851.

99. Dyckman House, New York

Location: New York County, 204th Street and Broadway, New York.

This Dutch-style residence, typical of the final phase of Flemish colonial architecture, is the only 18th-century farmhouse still standing in Man-

Dyckman House, the only 18th-century framehouse extant in Manhattan, is a typical example of Flemish colonial architecture.

hattan. William Dyckman's first house on this site was burned during the War for Independence, but in 1783 Dyckman erected the one that is still carefully preserved today. The house is a white, two-story residence, the lower walls of fieldstone and the upper of clapboard. A gambrel roof in the front extends over a rail-enclosed porch. Descendants of the original owner rehabilitated the house and in 1915 presented it to New York City, which keeps it open to the public throughout the year.

100. Fort Ste. Marie de Gannentatha, New York

Location: Onondaga County, on N.Y. 57, about 1½ miles north of Syracuse.

Fort Ste. Marie de Gannentatha was erected for protection against the Dutch and Indians by 50 French colonists who in 1656 attempted to settle near the present city of Syracuse. The colony eventually failed. The present stockade is a reconstruction. The exterior is of unfinished logs and the interior of roughhewn boards; reproduced period furnishings help recreate the appearance of the original stockade. Many French and Indian relics are displayed. Near the stockade is the Jesuit Well, the site of a salt spring visited in 1654 by Father Simon le Moyne, a Jesuit missionary. The stockade is open to the public all year.

101. Lefferts Homestead, New York

Location: Kings County, on Empire Boulevard, Prospect Park, Brooklyn.

This house was built in 1777 by Lt. Peter Lefferts, descendant of a New York Dutch family, on the site of his previous home, destroyed by fire in a military action at the beginning of the War for Independence. The original site was at 563 Flatbush Avenue, from which the building was moved to the present location in 1918, when Lefferts' descendants presented it to the city of New York.

The design of the house reflects Lefferts' Dutch heritage. A low gambrel roof ends in a deep overhang in front, which is supported by several columns. The handsome front door is surmounted by a richly carved entableture of sunburst designs. Inside, an arch on the north side of the main hall separates the dining and living rooms. The parlor and bedrooms are on the south side of the hall; a children's room occupies the second floor along with a maple room and a workroom. The attic has a smokeroom. The house is furnished with period furniture and is maintained as a museum by the city of New York. It is open to the public on a limited schedule throughout the year.

102. National Shrine of North American Martyrs, New York

Location: Montgomery County, on N.Y. 58, Auriesville.

This shrine, which memorializes all Roman Catholic clerics put to death by Indians, illustrates European missionary efforts. Father Isaac Jogues, a French Jesuit missionary who first arrived in North America in 1636, was captured by the Mohawk Indians in 1642, and suffered terribly before he was helped to escape by a Dutch minister. Returning in 1646 from a voyage to France, he was again captured by unfriendly natives, who executed him on October 18, 1646, in the Mohawk village of *Osseruenon*, where the National Shrine of North American Martyrs is now located. Jogues and seven other priests who were killed by Indians were canonized in 1925. Adjoining the shrine is a statue of Kateri Tekakwitha, "Lily of the Mohawks," an Indian girl of exceptional Christian devotion, who was born in *Osseruenon*. Open from May 6 to October 28, the shrine includes an Indian museum, a cafeteria, and an inn.

103. Nichols Pond Site, New York

Location: Madison County, 10 miles south of U.S. 20, Fenner Township.

This well-preserved site is believed by some historians to have been the location of the fortified Oneida village that Champlain and his Huron allies attacked in 1615—even though pottery sherds recovered from the site are prehistoric Mohawk rather than 17th-century Oneida. The topography of the area, however, conforms generally with that described by Champlain. Excavation has revealed about 120 feet of a quadruple stockade that has ample room between the walls for the galleries mentioned by Champlain. The site has been leased to the Champlain Battle Park Association by the County of Madison and is being developed on a limited scale.

104. Old Stone Fort, New York

Location: Schoharie County, at the northern edge of Schoharie.

The Old Stone Fort was originally a church of the Reformed Protestant High Dutch Church Society. The congregation that constructed it had worshipped in two previous structures, built in 1724 and 1737, a little to the northeast of the Old Stone Fort site. The present structure was built in 1772 of local stone, hauled by the parishioners themselves. Many carved their names on the stones, but during the War for Independence the names of Tories were obliterated. In 1830, a tower and spire that had dominated the church were removed.

The church came to be called the Old Stone Fort after 1778, when the State of New York converted it into a fort by erecting a stockade around the building and blockhouses at the southwest and northeast corners. In 1780, Sir John Johnson attacked it with a force of some 800 British soldiers, Indians, and Tories, but was repulsed. The stockade was not removed until 1785. In 1844, the congregation moved to a new edifice, and in 1857 the State purchased the old church and used it as an arsenal until 1873, when it was deeded to Schoharie County. A museum today, the Old Stone Fort is administered by the County Board of Supervisors and the Schoharie County Historical Society. It is open to the public from April through October.

105. Pieter Bronck House, New York

Location: Greene County, on U.S. 9W, 1½ miles south of West Coxsackie.

This house is outstanding among Dutch colonial houses in the Hudson Valley. It was built in two sections by descendants of Jonas Bronck, who settled on Manhattan Island in 1639 and after whom the Bronx is named. In 1663, Pieter Bronck, a stepson, built a stone house on land purchased from the Indians. About 1738 his grandson, Leendert Bronck, added a larger brick house, connected to the original house by a doorway. Their descendants lived in the duplex house until 1938, when the owner presented it to the Greene County Historical Society.

The stolid, plain character of the original house exemplifies Dutch

Pieter Bronck House, New York, consists of two parts, a stone section erected in 1663 and a larger brick section erected about 1738. It is outstanding among surviving Dutch colonial houses in the Hudson River Valley.

pioneer construction. The loopholes on the second floor were used for muskets. The addition reflects the grandson's prosperity as well as more settled conditions in the area. It also consists of two stories and has a gabled roof. The living room has massive ceiling beams that are supported by nautical curved knees, a technique rather common in the area's farmhouses. This room also has a steep stairway, Dutch door, and broad floorboards, all typical of Dutch houses of the era. The house, which is open to the public throughout the year, exhibits colonial furnishings and historical memorabilia.

106. Pieter Wyckoff Homestead, New York

> Location: Kings County, southwest corner of Ralph Avenue and Canarsie Lane, Brooklyn.

Because Pieter Wyckoff, who arrived in New Amsterdam in 1637, probably built this house between 1639 and 1641, it is one of the oldest extant on Long Island. Wyckoff lived in it for 44 years, while superintendent of Peter Stuyvesant's estate and also as a large landowner in his own right. The original building was only about a little more than half as deep as the present one, and it probably had a steep roof. The existing gable roof is low and sweeping and has projecting front and rear eaves. A wing was added to the house, perhaps around 1784, and some very old shakes are still on the exterior. The house is maintained and exhibited by the Wyckoff House Foundation.

107. Senate House, New York

Location: Ulster County, 312 Fair Street, Kingston.

Erected as a residence by Col. Wessel Ten Broeck between 1676 and 1695, when Kingston was a small village called Esopus, this building remained in his family until 1888, when the State acquired it for preservation as a historic shrine. The first New York State Senate used it in 1777, soon after the State constitution was adopted, during the British occupation of New York City. The senators deliberated in the end of the building where the door opens directly onto the street. When the British subsequently burned Kingston, the building was gutted along with other structures, but it was later rebuilt. Maintained as a historic structure, it exhibits period pieces and furnishings, most of them donated by descendants of early settlers in the vicinity. An adjacent museum,

Col. Wessel Ten Broeck erected this structure in Esopus (Kingston), New York, between 1676 and 1695. During the War for Independence, when the New York State Senate met in the house, it came to be known as the Senate House. Courtesy, New York State Education Department.

erected in 1927, contains historic objects relating to the Kingston area and a collection of paintings by John Vanderlyn, a Kingston-born artist. The house and museum are open to the public throughout the year.

108. Van Alen House, New York

Location: Columbia County, on N.Y. 9H, about 6 miles east of Kinderhook.

Built by Luycas Van Alen in 1737, this house is regarded today as an exceptional example of Dutch architecture in America. The site was well situated on what later became the post road between Albany and New York. The brickwork was laid up in Dutch crossbond, on a fieldstone foundation, which enclosed a cellar. The walls were plastered and the ceilings beamed with heavy timbers. The first floor consisted of living room and kitchen, each of which had a great tiled and hooded fireplace at the gable end. A large brick wing was added to the original structure on the north end, probably before 1750. The addition had its own cellar; the first floor consisted of a hall with staircase, small bedroom or larder, and parlor; and the second floor included a hall, storage room, and bedroom.

Changes in the 19th century involved interior partitions and window and door openings, as well as the erection of a front porch across the north wing. The house is now owned by the Greene County Historical Society. Vacant since 1938, it is in poor condition; major stabilization and restoration are required to stave off imminent collapse. The outbuildings have disappeared and the grounds have become unkempt, yet the house still retains to a considerable degree the flavor of a bygone age.

109. Grand Assembly of the Albemarle (lost site), North Carolina

Location: Monument in Pasquotank County, on N.C. 170, about 1 mile north of Nixonton.

At least 100 settlers were already living in the region just north of Albemarle Sound in 1663, when Charles II granted Carolina to a group of proprietors. In 1664, they appointed William Drummond as Governor, and early the next year they promulgated the "Concessions and Agreement," which provided for a unicameral legislature having broad powers and composed of the Governor, his council, and 12 deputies. The first such legislature met early that year on Halls Creek, about 7 miles southwest of present Elizabeth City. According to tradition, it assembled beneath a large oak tree because no building was large enough to accommodate it. Among the business transacted was a petition asking that land be granted to settlers on the same terms as in Virginia—resulting in the Great Deed of Grant in 1668. The exact site of the first meeting of the Grand Assembly of the Albemarle is not known, but the stone monument adjacent to Halls Creek Church is probably not far away.

110. Cape Meares, Oregon

> *Location: Tillamook County, south side of Tillamook Bay, just west of U.S. 101.*

This rocky headland, 700 feet high, was discovered in 1778 by Capt. John Meares, an English explorer, who found the bay closed by a sand

In 1778, the English explorer Capt. John Meares discovered this headland, now Cape Meares, Oregon. It is wild and beautiful and looks today much the same as when first discovered.

barrier and called it "Quicksand Bay." The cape probably had been sighted in 1775 by the Spanish explorer Bruno Heceta. The north side is still wild and beautiful, unchanged except for an unobtrusive Coast Guard station. On the south side are a number of summer beach cottages.

111. Caleb Pusey House, Pennsylvania

Location: Delaware County, Race Street, Upland.

Built in 1683, this house is the oldest extant English-constructed house in Pennsylvania. Pusey, a Quaker, migrated from England to manage a gristmill in which William Penn was a partner. Becoming a warm friend of Penn, who apparently visited this home, he became a member of the assembly, served on the colony's Executive Council, and in 1701 sat on the Governor's Council. Selling his interest in the milling business in 1708, he moved to Chester, after which his former home had various owners. By the 1930's, the house seemed destined for eventual loss. Interest in it increased after World War II, however, and in the early 1960's the Friends of the Caleb Pusey House came to its rescue and began restoration.

112. Fort Le Boeuf, Pennsylvania

Location: Erie County, on the north bank of French Creek, Waterford.

The French built Fort Le Boeuf in the spring of 1753 as part of a major effort to strengthen their hold over the vast lands in Canada and the Mississippi-Ohio Valleys that they claimed. The fort resembled Fort Presque Isle, built a bit sooner, although it was somewhat smaller. Four log buildings stood within a log stockade. The Governor of Virginia sent a young officer, George Washington, to protest the incursion into British-claimed territory, but the French rebuffed him. During the French and Indian War, a British force laid siege to a major French stronghold, Fort Niagara, and the garrisons of Fort Le Boeuf and other minor posts were summoned as reinforcements. Fort Niagara fell, and in 1759 the French themselves destroyed Fort Le Boeuf.

Great Britain used the site of Fort Le Boeuf for a depot, and in 1794 the Americans built a blockhouse nearby, but all these buildings fell into ruins and disappeared as the area became a settled and prosperous section of modern Pennsylvania. The Commonwealth of Pennsylvania today operates a museum illustrating the history of Fort Le Boeuf on its site. Across the street are the foundations of the 1794 blockhouse. Many interesting artifacts of French, Indian, British, and American origin have been recovered in the area.

113. Fort Presque Isle Site, Pennsylvania

Location: Erie County, at 6th and Parade Streets, Erie.

In 1753, a French force under Sieur Marin from Montreal, recognizing the strategic possibilities afforded by the sheltering arm of the Presque Isle peninsula, built a fort there, about the same time as Fort Le Boeuf. The stockade of chestnut logs measured about 120 feet square and 15 feet high, and enclosed several buildings. After the British captured Fort Niagara, the French abandoned and destroyed Fort Presque Isle. The English rebuilt the fort and garrisoned it, but later abandoned it. No remains are extant today.

114. Lower Swedish Cabin, Pennsylvania

Location: Delaware County, on Creek Road, 1 mile south of Clifton Heights.

This cabin, erected during the period 1640–50, is one of the earliest extant examples of Swedish log construction in the United States. The walls

An early example of Swedish log construction, Lower Swedish Cabin, Pennsylvania, built in the period 1640–50.

consist of logs about 12 inches in diameter, notched at the corners. The cabin originally consisted of only one room, but another was added later; a low door connects the rooms. The ceiling rafters can be touched by the upraised hand. Each room contains a Swedish-style corner fireplace, above which rises a large stone chimney. The roof is gabled.

115. Pennsbury Manor, Pennsylvania

Location: Bucks County, 3½ miles east of U.S. 13, just outside of Tullytown.

This is the re-created country estate of William Penn, the founder of Pennsylvania. He purchased the lands in 1682, on his first visit to Pennsylvania, and began construction the following year. During the next 15 years, he directed the development in a stream of correspondence from England. He stayed at the manor frequently while he resided in the New World during the period 1699–1701 and entertained many colonial personages and Indian visitors. The manor fell into a deplorable state after he finally returned to England, and by the end of the century was in ruins. The Pennsylvania Historical Commission acquired it on the 250th anniversary of his first trip to America and subsequently carefully re-created the manor house, bake and brew houses, stable, other outbuildings, and gardens and grounds. The manor is open to the public all year.

116. Swedish Cabin (Morton Homestead), Pennsylvania

Location: Delaware County, on Pa. 420, near Darby Creek Bridge, about 2 miles south of Glenolden.

This hewn-log structure was probably built in 1654, a year before New Sweden fell to the Dutch, and is the best preserved and most carefully documented of the few known remains of Swedish settlement in the 17th century. About 1698, a second cabin was erected a few feet distant, and around 1806 the two structures were connected by a third one, built of stone. Marten Martensson built the original cabin shortly after he arrived in New Sweden.

The long-time tradition that the cabin was the birthplace of John Morton, a signer of the Declaration of Independence, has not been verified.

Swedish Cabin (Morton Homestead), Pennsylvania. It consists of two log cabins connected by a stone building. The three structures were built between 1654 and 1806.

Morton's great-grandfather did, however, once own the land on which the cabin stands. Since 1935, when the cabin was in a dilapidated condition and surrounded by modern framehouses, the Commonwealth of Pennsylvania has carefully restored it. It is furnished with period pieces. The setting is now preserved by a small park of approximately 3 acres, which is open to visitors throughout the year.

117. Eleazar Arnold House, Rhode Island

> *Location: Providence County, 449 Great Road, near Lincoln Woods Reservation State Park.*

This house is representative of the Rhode Island "stone-ender" type, a regional variation in construction stemming from Rhode Island's abundant supply of building stone, as compared to Massachusetts and Connecticut. When first built, it had only one room, which had a fireplace at one end. When a rear lean-to was added later, for a kitchen, a new chimney was joined to the original one; the whole was so wide that it almost covered that end of the house.

Composed of numerous pilasters, the chimney top is one of New England's most imposing. The remainder of the two-story structure is of clapboard, and features a sharp-peaked front gable and a long roof over the kitchen. The outstanding interior feature is the huge hall fireplace, which has an oak mantel more than 12 feet long. The house is owned by the Society for the Preservation of New England Antiquities, under whose aegis it was restored in the 1930's. It is open daily except Monday from June 15 to October 15; at other times, by applying to the custodian in an adjacent house.

118. Great Swamp Fight Site (lost site), Rhode Island

Location: Washington County, on R.I. 2, about 2 miles southwest of West Kingston.

This site illustrates New England's struggle with the Indians in the 17th century. On December 19, 1675, during the bloody King Philip's War, forces of the United Colonies stormed a formidable fort of the Narragansett Indians in Rhode Island's Great Swamp and crushed the Indians for all time. Many warriors escaped the disaster, but hundreds of older Indians, including women and children, were slaughtered, and the Narragansetts' winter food supply was destroyed. It was a decisive blow against King Philip's effort to overwhelm white settlements in New England. A marker on the Great Swamp indicates the approximate location of the Indian fort.

119. Roger Williams Spring and House Sites, Rhode Island

Location: Providence County, North Main Street and Alamo Lane (Spring Site), and 233 North Main Street (House Site), Providence.

These sites, which are associated with the founding of Rhode Island in 1636 by Roger Williams and a group of dissenters from the strict religious practices of the Massachusetts Bay Colony, commemorate the struggle for freedom of conscience in colonial America. The group founded the settlement of Providence near a fresh spring at the junction of the Woonasquatucket and Moshassuck Rivers, at the base of a hill. The colony was a refuge for persecuted religious groups and freedom seekers. As the colony grew, the spring provided inadequate water. In 1869, it was walled up and replaced by a pump. In 1892, the site was filled in to accommodate urban development, but in 1930 a private citizen bought it and donated it to the city, which created a small memorial park. Roger Williams' house was destroyed by fire during King Philip's War, in 1673. Excavation of the site in 1906 revealed some hearthstones, evidences of a fireplace and a wall, and a jamb. A new commercial building has since been erected on the site. It is unfortunate that no structure or site with integrity associated with the life and work of so outstanding a leader as Roger Williams is extant.

[On October 22, 1965, the President signed the act of Congress authorizing the establishment of Roger Williams National Memorial, to consist of not more than 5 acres at the Spring Site.]

120. Albemarle Point (Old Town), South Carolina

Location: Charleston County, just off S.C. 61, about 2 miles north of Charleston.

In 1670, a group of English settlers founded a colony at this point, where the seat of government remained until the founding a decade later of Charleston, originally known as Charles Town, the first permanent white settlement in present South Carolina. The colonizing expedition had left England in August 1669 in three vessels, two of which (the *Port Royall* and *Albemarle*) were lost en route. The third, the *Carolina,* was repaired at Bermuda and in March 1670 reached Port Royal Harbor. The leaders felt that the location was too exposed to Spanish and Indian attack, and sailed up the coast to Albemarle Point. They landed and erected wooden fortifications and homes. The colony's business was conducted at this location under three Governors until, in December 1679, the proprietors designated Oyster Point (Charleston), at the junction of the Cooper and Ashley Rivers, as port town for the colony. Within 1 year, Albemarle Point was deserted. All surface traces of the Albemarle settlement have disappeared. The site is included in the privately owned Old Town Plantation. A monument, erected in 1909, stands near the plantation house, which is some distance from the point.

121. Medway Plantation, South Carolina

Location: Berkeley County, 2.1 miles east of U.S. 52, at Mt. Holly.

Medway is the oldest recorded house in South Carolina. It was built of brick in 1686 by Jan Van Arrsens, Seigneur de Weirnhoudt, leader of a small group of Hollanders who came to Carolina to settle. The original

In 1686, a Dutchman built Medway, the oldest recorded house in South Carolina. The central part, featuring crow-stepped gables, is original.

house, which measured 27 by 38½ feet and had one-and-a-half stories, followed a plan described by William Penn in a 1684 broadside for prospective settlers of Pennsylvania. It had a partition near the middle and another to divide one end into two smaller rooms. Indicative of its Dutch origins, it had stepped gable ends and end chimneys.

Alterations and additions were made to the original structure. A second story was added, as well as unsymmetrical major wings on both the east and west sides and several smaller additions. Though the integrity of the original has been impaired, these changes have not spoiled the esthetic effect of the house. Consciously or otherwise, the taste of the original Dutch builder has dominated succeeding owners. None of the numerous outbuildings antedates the 19th century. The plantation, privately owned and beautifully maintained, is not open to visitors.

122. Middleburg Plantation, South Carolina

Location: Berkeley County, 2½ miles southwest of Huger.

Probably the oldest extant wooden house in South Carolina, Middleburg was built about 1699 by Benjamin Simons, whose descendants have owned it ever since. One-room deep, it resembles the distinctive Charleston "single house." The first-floor interior walls, redecorated about 1800, are finished with wide boards. In the lovely formal garden are tunneled walks of age-old camellia japonicas.

123. Parris Island, South Carolina

Location: Beaufort County, in Port Royal Sound, near Port Royal.

On this island are the sites of the first French settlement within the present United States and two later Spanish posts. In 1562, under the command of Jean Ribaut, a group of French Huguenots built a small earth-and-log post and named it Charlesfort. During Ribaut's absence in France to seek reinforcements, and lacking support from the mother country, the colonists soon abandoned the fort. After incredible hardships, they returned home.

In 1566, the Spaniards established Fort San Felipe on the island, but the Indians destroyed it about 1576. Within 1 year, the Spanish returned and built a stronger post, Fort San Marcos, which became the center of a substantial settlement of some 60 houses and the capital of the province of Santa Elena. The Spanish abandoned it in 1587 during the general retrenchment that followed Sir Francis Drake's attack on St. Augustine.

Archeological excavations under the auspices of the U.S. Marine Corps in 1923 at the southern end of the island revealed the remains of a stockade and yielded a substantial number of artifacts. The excavators identified the site as Charlesfort, and it has been so marked by a granite monument; a marker also indicates that the Spanish forts were probably on Pilot or Means Creek. However, a more recent investigator has concluded that the excavated site was probably Fort San Marcos. Owned by the U.S. Government, the island is used by the U.S. Marine Corps as a recruit depot.

124. La Vérendrye Site, South Dakota

Location: Stanley County, Third Avenue near Third Street, Fort Pierre.

On February 16, 1913, a lead plate inscribed with the names of four 18th-century French explorers, and dated March 30, 1743, was found at this site, although the location of its original placement has been questioned by some historians. Louis-Joseph and Francois de la Vérendrye and two companions, returning eastward from the Black Hills region, deposited the plate to commemorate their attempt to find a Northwest Passage to the "Western Sea." Their expedition was one of two organized and financed by Pierre Gaultier de Varennes, Sieur de la Vérendrye, the famous French explorer. The South Dakota Historical Society and the Fort Pierre Commercial Club have placed a marker at the site. The plate itself is in the possession of the society.

125. Fort Assumption Site, Tennessee

Location: Shelby County, E. H. Crump Boulevard, near the eastern end of the Mississippi River bridge, Memphis.

Fort Assumption was erected in 1739 by Jean Baptiste le Moyne, Sieur de Bienville, who landed with a French force at the Wolf River to establish a base of operations against the Chickasaw Indians, allies of the English. The fort was named in honor of the day on the church calendar that construction began. The French abandoned and destroyed it in 1740, when they made peace with the Chickasaws and Bienville disbanded the Choctaws and his other Indian allies. Though the remains have been obliterated by modern urban construction, a State historical marker indicates the site.

126. Fort Loudoun, Tennessee

Location: Monroe County, off U.S. 411, about 1 mile southeast of McGhee.

The first English settlement west of the Smoky Mountains, Fort Loudoun figured prominently in the French and Indian War. Started in 1756, the year before the French began construction of Fort Massac, near the confluence of the Ohio and Tennessee Rivers, it was completed in 1757 and occupied until 1760. Its primary purpose was to protect and support the Cherokees against the French and their Indian allies, and thus to protect the English frontier. Relations between the English and the Cherokees deteriorated, however, and in 1760 the Indians laid siege to Fort Loudoun. When Capt. Paul Demere, commander of the fort, surrendered, he obtained a promise of safe conduct to Fort Prince George, in present South Carolina, for all the soldiers and their families. Less than 15 miles from Fort Loudoun, the Indians attacked, killed 27 soldiers and 3 women, and took all the survivors as prisoners.

Extensive archeological excavations at the fort have yielded exact information on its size, shape, and construction—not only concerning the palisade but also many of the structures inside. Portions of the fort have been reconstructed, and it is open to the public daily from March through October. The site is administered by the Fort Loudoun Association. Fort Loudoun is eligible for the Registry of National Historic Landmarks (relating primarily to the development of the English colonies, 1700–1783).

127. Fort Prudhomme Site, Tennessee

> *Location: Tipton County, Second Chickasaw Bluff, just below the mouth of the Hatchie River, off Tenn. 59, between Randolph and Richardson's Landing.*

La Salle built Fort Prudhomme in 1682, on his first voyage down the Mississippi. One of the first forts or habitations of any kind built in the Tennessee country by Europeans, it was named after Pierre Prudhomme, armorer of the expedition. After Prudhomme failed to return from a hunting trip, La Salle built the fort for temporary protection during the search. After Prudhomme was found, La Salle left him in charge of the fort and continued to explore the Mississippi. On La Salle's return trip, he became ill and remained at the fort for 40 days before being able to continue upriver. The fort was then abandoned and fell into ruins. No remains are visible today.

128. Fort St. Louis Site, Texas

> *Location: Victoria County, head of Lavaca Bay, west bank of Garcitas Creek, about 10 miles east of Placedo.*

This site commemorates the first French attempt to colonize the gulf coast, which created special Spanish interest in Texas. In 1685, La Salle, intending to plant a colony near the mouth of the Mississippi, led 400 colonists and soldiers instead into present Texas, where he founded Fort St. Louis on Lavaca Bay, an inlet of Matagorda Bay. A month later, he moved it to a new location 5 miles above the mouth of Garcitas Creek. A temporary wooden structure, it served as a base for his exploration of the surrounding country.

Hunger and Indian attacks disheartened the colonists, and the venture was a failure from the beginning. La Salle, after reconnoitering to the south and west, started north, hoping to reach Fort St. Louis in Illinois country, but mutineers murdered him. Two years later, Indians attacked the fort and wiped out most of the remaining Frenchmen. The survivors were captured 3 months later by the Spanish expedition of Capt. Alonso de León, which had been sent to investigate reports of French encroachment in Texas. De León burned the fort to the ground.

The failure of La Salle's colony ended French attempts to colonize Texas. The French established themselves at the mouth of the Mississippi and continued to threaten Texas along the Louisiana frontier, but they never again seriously contested Spain's hold on Texas. In 1722, the Spanish built the mission of Nuestra Señora del Espíritu Santo de Zuñiga and the presidio of Nuestra Señora de Loreto near the site of Fort St. Louis, but abandoned them 4 years later.

Pinpointed by the late Prof. Herbert Eugene Bolton, the site has been accepted by most historians and substantially confirmed by archeological investigation. Positive proof of authenticity may never be obtained. On private ranch property, the site is marked on the surface only by traces of ancient walls constructed of adobe.

129. La Bahía (Goliad), Texas

Location: Goliad County, on U.S. 77A–183, just south of Goliad.

In the 18th century, the Goliad vicinity was known as La Bahía del Espíritu Santo. One of the oldest municipalities in Texas, La Bahía has its origins in the Spanish response to French advances into Texas beginning in 1685. In 1722, the Spanish founded the mission of Nuestra Señora del Espíritu Santo de Zuñiga and the presidio of Nuestra Señora de Loreto on Matagorda Bay near the abandoned site of La Salle's Fort St. Louis. They were commonly called the mission and presidio of La Bahía (The Bay). The settlement retained this name even after it moved inland, first to a site on the Guadalupe River, and in 1749 to its present location on the San Antonio River. The new mission and presidio attracted Spanish ranchers and farmers to the area, and a sizable colony soon grew up.

Espíritu Santo Mission, near Goliad, Texas, was a part of the Spanish settlement La Bahía, which reached its peak during the last half of the 18th century.

La Bahía reached its peak of influence during the last half of the 18th century, when hundreds of converted Indians farmed surrounding fields and tended huge herds of cattle. By 1790, however, Franciscan missionary activity in Texas began to ebb. Within a few years, La Bahía's prosperity faded and the mission Indians fled. The missions were secularized and the Franciscans returned to Mexico. In 1829, the Congress of Coahuila and Texas declared La Bahía a town and its name was changed to Goliad. A few years later, it was the site of the Goliad Massacre, during the Texas Revolution.

Espíritu Santo Mission, authentically restored under the supervision of the National Park Service, is an imposing example of 18th-century mission architecture; it resembles San Xavier del Bac, in Arizona, and San Juan Capistrano, in California. It is the central feature of Goliad State Park, which also contains a small museum illustrating Spanish colonial history. To the east, on a hill overlooking the San Antonio River, are the chapel and crumbling compound walls of La Bahía presidio. The chapel is still in use as a Catholic parish church. The compound is now being excavated and stabilized under private auspices, in cooperation with the Catholic Church, with a view toward future restoration.

West of Goliad are the ruins of the mission of Nuestra Señora del

Crumbling walls and chapel of La Bahía Presidio, Texas. It is now being accurately restored.

Rosario de los Cujanes. Twenty-nine miles south of Goliad, at the town of Refugio, is the site of the mission of Nuestra Señora del Refugio. La Bahía presidio also protected these two missions.

130. San Antonio, Texas

Location: Bexar County.

In 1718, San Antonio de Bexar was founded as part of a Spanish effort to forestall French designs on Texas. Destined to become the most important Spanish settlement in Texas, it was the capital during the latter part of Spanish rule. When it was founded, a new mission, San Antonio de Valero—which later became known as the Alamo—was established nearby. This mission carried out the first successful missionary effort in Texas. San Antonio was the political, religious, military, and population center of the Spanish province.

The rich heritage of the city has been largely preserved through the efforts of the San Antonio Conservation Society, the Daughters of the Republic of Texas, the Roman Catholic Church, the Texas State Parks Board, and the city of San Antonio. As a result, San Antonio has retained an old-world atmosphere equaled by few American cities and expressed by a wealth of significant historic sites and buildings.

The most famous historic site in Texas is the Alamo, which is eligible for the Registry of National Historic Landmarks (relating primarily to the Texas Revolution), originally known as San Antonio de Valero Mission. First of the five Franciscan missions at San Antonio, San Antonio de Valero prospered for nearly a century. At one time, members of scores of different tribes were enrolled as neophytes. Another significant mission in San Antonio, San José y San Miguel de Aguayo, is commemorated by the San José National Historic Site.

The Alamo, the most famous historic site in Texas, was originally San Antonio de Valero Mission. Courtesy, San Antonio Chamber of Commerce.

Spanish Governors Palace, in San Antonio, was the residence and headquarters of 18th-century Spanish Governors and Vice-Governors of Texas. It has been restored and now serves as a museum.

South from the central city are the other three San Antonio missions, relocated in 1731 on the San Antonio River following abandonment of the east Texas missions: Nuestra Señora de la Purísima Concepción de Acuna, San Francisco de la Espada, and San Juan Capistrano. During the middle of the 18th century, all five missions were extremely active. They were self-sufficient communities, islands of civilization in the surrounding wilderness. The Franciscans, in addition to indoctrinating Indian neophytes in the Christian religion, trained them in trades, and taught them the Spanish language.

Though the missions eventually failed, were secularized, and then abandoned, their remains are tangible evidence of Spanish colonial policy. Some are still used for special religious observances. The city of San Antonio plans a "Mission Parkway" to make the missions more accessible to visitors and students.

The Spanish Governors Palace on Plaza de las Armas was the residence and headquarters of 18th-century Spanish Governors and Vice-Governors of Texas. Over the entrance arch are the Hapsburg arms, and the date 1749 is carved on the keystone. A Spanish map, however,

Chapel of San Francisco de la Espada Mission, south of San Antonio.

shows that the palace occupied the same location as early as 1722. When Spanish sovereignty ended, it passed into private hands and was neglected. In 1929, the city of San Antonio purchased it to avert complete ruin. The present structure is an outstanding and authentic restoration. Of plastered adobe, it consists of 10 rooms, furnished with Spanish furniture. A patio in the rear, which features cobbled walks, fountain, and well, is planted with native flowers and shrubs. The palace is operated as a public museum.

Another important site, which illustrates the techniques of 18th-century mission agriculture, is the Espada Aqueduct, a Registered National Historic Landmark (relating primarily to agricultural development). Once part of an integrated irrigation system that served the five missions in the area, it is the best preserved section and is still functioning. Franciscans built the dam, aqueduct, and acequia during the period 1731–45. The most spectacular of the associated structures is the graceful, double-span aqueduct over Piedro Arroyo. The site, on Espada Road, is maintained as a park by the San Antonio Conservation Society.

Many other sites in San Antonio are associated with the Spanish period, including the restored historic district "La Villita."

Nuestra Señora de la Purísima Concepción de Acuna Mission—one of five 18th-century Franciscan missions in the San Antonio area.

131. San Francisco de los Tejas Mission (lost site), Texas

Location: Houston County, about 3 miles northwest of Weches.

This mission, the first established by Franciscans in Texas, was originally built on the west bank of the Neches River during a Spanish colonization expedition led by Alonso de León into east Texas in 1690 to discourage French encroachment. The Spanish abandoned the mission in 1693 because the Tejas Indians were uncooperative.

In 1716, the mission was reestablished at another site 8 miles away, but on the east bank of the river. It was one of seven set up by the Franciscans, again to counter a French threat, during a second expedition, led by Domingo Ramón. In 1719, the French invaded east Texas from Louisiana and forced the Spanish to again abandon the mission and retreat to San Antonio.

Two years later, after the French withdrew, the mission was again reestablished in the same location and renamed San Francisco de los Neches by Father Felix de Espinosa, who was a member of the Aguayo expedition. When the Spanish abandoned nearby Dolores presidio, the Neches mission was moved farther inland to the site of Austin and later to San Antonio.

The exact locations of the various mission sites are not known. A one-room log chapel has been constructed by the State in Davy Crockett National Forest on the approximate site of the first mission.

132. San Saba Mission and San Luís Presidio, Texas

Location: Menard County. Mission site, at the southern edge of Menard; presidio site, on Tex. 29, about 3 miles northwest of Menard.

San Sabá de la Santa Cruz Mission represents a disastrous Franciscan attempt to convert the Lipan Apache Indians. Established in 1757 by Fray Alonso Giraldo de Terreros on the south bank of the San Sabá River, it was protected by the San Luís de las Amarillas Presidio, just north of the river. The mission failed to convert the Apaches, whose only interest in it was hope of obtaining Spanish aid against their Comanche enemies. In 1758, the Comanches and their allies set fire to it; only

In 1757, the Spanish founded this presidio, San Luís de las Amarillas, to protect nearby San Sabá Mission. In 1758, Comanches destroyed the mission, and, in 1769, the Spanish abandoned the presidio. The presidio has been partially restored.

three inhabitants survived.

Although the presidio was maintained until 1769, the mission was never rebuilt. No remains of the mission are extant, but the presidio has been partially restored on the original foundations. The State of Texas is considering a proposal that the present San Sabá Historic Park, containing the ruins of the restored presidio, be connected by a scenic drive to the nearby frontier post, Fort McKavett, and redesignated the San Sabá River State Historic Park.

133. Spanish Fort Site, Texas

Location: Montague County, both sides of Red River, near village of Spanish Fort.

An important village of the Taovayas, a band of the Wichitas, was located at this site in the latter half of the 17th and most of the 18th centuries. The Wichitas were known as early as the time of Coronado, but the first known reference to the Taovayas was made in 1719 by Bernard de la Harpe, a French trader, who encountered them on the

Canadian River in present Oklahoma. They were among the tribes who in 1758 destroyed San Sabá Mission; this resulted in Diego Ortíz Parilla's retaliatory expedition the following year. The Taovaya village—protected by a stockade and moat, armed with French guns, and displaying a French flag—repulsed the Spaniards. A smallpox epidemic in 1812 decimated the village, and the survivors joined other groups of Wichitas. The site is located in privately owned cottonfields, and few surface remains are apparent. In 1936, the Texas Centennial Commission erected a marker near the site.

134. Crossing of the Fathers (lost site), Utah

> *Location: Kane and San Juan Counties, 1½ miles below Ute Ford, in Glen Canyon of the Colorado River.*

The Domínguez-Escalante expedition, consisting of the 2 fathers and 12 companions, discovered and used the ford now known as the Crossing of the Fathers on November 7, 1776, after searching 2 weeks for a way to cross the Colorado River. The party, on the trail for 5 months, had unsuccessfully attempted to blaze a trail through Colorado, Utah, and Arizona to connect New Mexico with the missions and settlements of California; and was forced to return to Santa Fe by the lateness of the season. The steps its members chiseled into the canyon wall on their return trip were still visible until recently, when completion of the Glen Canyon Dam submerged these last vestiges of an important Spanish exploration in the Lake Powell Reservoir.

135. Chimney Point, Vermont

> *Location: Addison County, at the Champlain Bridge, on Vt. 17, about 8 miles southwest of Addison.*

Chimney Point is a promontory in Lake Champlain, where Samuel de Champlain reportedly stood in 1609, after a battle with the Iroquois Indians on the western shore of the lake, and gave his name to the beautiful inland sea stretching before him. The battle marked the beginning of continued hostilities between the Iroquois and the French. In 1690, a French expedition under Jacobus de Warm built a small, temporary fort at the site, but the first important settlement was made in 1730 by some French colonists. who renovated the fort and renamed it Fort de Pieux.

The settlement that grew up around the fort became one of the most important of the French in the New World. In 1759, its inhabitants abandoned it because of a threatened Indian invasion, and in 1760 raiding Mohawks destroyed it completely. The grim picture of chimneys rising from blackened ruins gave the point its name. Many cellar holes of the ancient French town are still visible. Chimney Point is privately owned and is not open to the public.

136. Fort Ste. Anne Site, Vermont

Location: Grand Isle County, on West Shore Road, about 3 miles north of Isle La Motte Village, on Isle La Motte.

Fort Ste. Anne was the oldest European settlement in Vermont. In 1666, a group of French soldiers, led by Capt. Pierre de la Motte, built it for protection against the Mohawks. Settlers located around the fort, and the Jesuits built a chapel nearby, where the first mass in Vermont was held. The settlement proved to be a temporary one, and no remains exist. The site is outlined by cedars and spaced rock mounds.

137. Belle Air, Virginia

Location: Charles City County, on Va. 5, just east of Charles City Courthouse.

This early frame plantation house was built about 1670. Despite 18th- and 19th-century additions, it still retains its rare original structural interior framework of heart pine. Plainly visible today are the summer beams, intermediate and corner posts, and an unusual staircase. Situated on a knoll and surrounded by a 4-acre lawn and a grove of old trees, the house overlooks more than 200 acres of rolling farmland. Restored in the 1950's, it is furnished with 18th-century antiques. A smokehouse, old laundry-kitchen, and a new herb garden are interesting adjuncts to the house, which is privately owned and not open to the public.

138. Bladensfield Estate, Virginia

Location: Westmoreland County, 1.8 miles northeast of junction of Va. 3 and 203, near Warsaw.

The original Bladensfield Estate, of 1,000 acres, was patented by John

Jenkins in 1653, and the present house was built for Jenkins by Nicholas Rochester, who came from England in 1689. At Jenkins' death, in 1719,

Late in the 17th century, John Jenkins built this mansion on his 1,000-acre Bladensfield Estate, in Virginia.

Bladensfield was added to the Nomini Hall estate. The house is a large frame building on a brick basement. The walls of nogging covered with clapboards rise two stories to a gabled roof, which has several dormers. The largest of the dormers is over the entrance. Mantels and cornices are hand-carved, and the flooring is dowel-pinned. The house is privately owned and is not open to the public.

139. Fort Monroe, Virginia

> *Location: On U.S. 258, east of 64 and 60, Old Point Comfort, on the eastern outskirts of Hampton.*

Fort Monroe is located on the site of some of the first fortifications built by the English in North America. At this site, in 1609, the Jamestown settlers built Algernourne Fort, a wooden structure, against possible attack by the Spanish. This fort was occupied by 50 settlers and equipped with 7 cannon. During the period 1630 to 1632, it was reconstructed by Col. Samuel Mathews and renamed Point Comfort. It was again reconstructed, this time in brick, during the years 1728–30, and called Fort George, but in 1749 was destroyed by heavy winds. During the Siege of Yorktown, Count de Grasse strengthened his defenses by placing batteries on the point.

Construction of the present Fort Monroe was begun in 1819 and was largely completed in 1836. The fort was completely surrounded by a water-filled moat and a 40-gun water battery, which stood between the outer banks of the moat and the shore of Chesapeake Bay. In 1865, President Lincoln held an unsuccessful peace conference at the fort with Confederate commissioners. After the collapse of the Confederacy, Jefferson Davis, its President, was captured and held prisoner for 2 years at the fort, which is a Registered National Historic Landmark (relating primarily to the Civil War).

For more than 350 years, the site of Fort Monroe has been occupied continuously—having been garrisoned longer than any other Army post in the United States. Through the years the fort has grown from a crude frontier stockade to one of our major Army posts. Fort Monroe, the last and most important of the defenses built on this site, is now the headquarters for the Continental Army Command.

140. Grace Church, Virginia

Location: York County, 1 block off Main Street, Yorktown.

York-Hampton Parish was formed about 1680 by uniting the two parishes. In 1697, a new church was erected at Yorktown, the two earlier churches being abandoned. Built of native marl, it was T-shaped and had a steeple. During the War for Independence, the windows and furnishings were destroyed by fire, and the British used the church as a magazine. After being restored and used for many years, it was again burned during the War of 1812. It was then rebuilt, but the transept was pulled down, leaving the nave, the rectangular building of today.

During the Civil War, the church was used again for military purposes; the furnishings were destroyed, and the bricks from the old wall around the churchyard taken away. The old bell was removed in 1865, but in 1889 it was recast and returned. The marl walls have been hardened by the two fires that have gutted the building. The cupola and carved doorway are late additions. Services are still held every Sunday.

141. Green Spring Plantation Site, Virginia

Location: James City County, junction of Va. 5 and 415.

Sir William Berkeley, Royal Governor of Virginia during the periods 1641–52 and 1660–77, began construction of the mansion at Green Spring about 1646. When completed, it was the largest and most imposing in 17th-century Virginia and a forerunner of later pretentious colonial mansions. A road ran directly from the estate—where considerable colony business was transacted—some 3 miles to Jamestown. Unfortunately, little more than the foundations of the once great house and its dependencies now remain. Because the extensive archeological remains, complicated by later construction, are difficult to interpret, the exact outside appearance and interior arrangement of the house in Berkeley's time can only be conjectured.

Berkeley's activities at Green Spring were diverse. They included winemaking, cultivation of rice and flax, production of silk from mulberry trees, maintenance of a large fruit orchard, the raising of oranges in a hothouse, and the harvesting of timber products. Berkeley also raised livestock, including racehorses, and had a windmill and pottery kiln.

An act of Congress, approved June 5, 1936 (49 Stat. 1483), authorized the inclusion of the Green Spring site in Colonial National Historical Park.

142. Henricus (Henricopolis) Site, Virginia

Location: Henrico County, on Farrar's Island, in the James River.

In the fall of 1611, Sir Thomas Dale and 350 workmen from Jamestown, of which Dale was later Governor, built the city of Henricus about 10 miles below present Richmond at the great bend of the James River. Dale's orders were to move the inhabitants of Jamestown to the new city and to make it the capital of the colony. The proposed city was situated on 7 acres of ground in the neck of Farrar's Island, where it then joined the mainland. In 1618, Gov. Sir George Yeardley was instructed to choose a suitable site at the city for a University of Henrico, already imposed in the town's charter. Accordingly, 10,000 acres were set aside and money was collected in England to finance the college. The Indians, however, destroyed the city in 1622, and the migration from Jamestown never occurred. Nevertheless, Henricopolis marked the first notable expansion of the colony upriver from Jamestown. A small tract of the original city of Henricus is owned today by the Virginia Society of the Colonial Dames of America, and it is marked by two stone monuments.

143. Hill Farm, Virginia

> *Location: Accomack County, about 6 miles off County 661, via Va. 177, southwest of Accomac.*

This farm was patented about 1663 by Capt. Richard Hill. The well-proportioned, one-and-a-half story brick house was built in the last half of the 17th century; one of the bricks is dated 1697. Frame additions are of a later period. The first story sets on a high foundation; the half story is lighted by dormers set closely together on the tall gabled roof. In the center of the house is a wide cross hall, from which rises a fine stairway. On the left is the parlor, which has handsomely restored paneling and moldings. Privately owned, the house is not open to the public.

144. Keeling House, Virginia

> *Location: Princess Anne County, on County 615, about 5½ miles north of U.S. 58, overlooking the Lynnhaven River.*

When Adam Keeling I made his will in 1683, he bequeathed to his son Thomas the land on which this story-and-a-half house was soon built, apparently by Thomas. Especially notable is the fine colonial brickwork, which is a good example of Flemish bond. The design is worked out in the gables by the use of blue headers. The end chimneys give height, and dormers relieve the severity of the steep-pitched roof. A kitchen wing has been added to the original house. Privately owned, the house is not open to the public.

145. Merchant's Hope Church, Virginia

Location: Prince George County, on County 641, about ½ mile from Va. 10, some 6½ miles east of Hopewell.

This gaunt, rectangular church takes its name from a grant of land made in 1635 to the owners of *The Merchant's Hope*, a bark that plied between England and Virginia. The interior has been greatly altered, though the floors are still paved with the original flagstones. The year 1657, carved in one of the huge rafters of the barrel-vaulted roof, has been considered the date of construction, although the design is of a later period.

Like most of the old colonial churches, Merchant's Hope suffered depredations during later wars. The interior was destroyed during the Civil War, when the church was used as a picket station, but the beautiful colonial brick exterior is practically the same as when it was built. The church, a member of the Episcopal Diocese of Southern Virginia, holds services only during the summer months.

146. Old Mansion, Virginia

Location: Caroline County, on Va. 301, just south of Bowling Green.

Old Mansion was the seat of the original Bowling Green Estate. Maj. John Hoomes built the house on land he patented in 1670. The early brick portion of the one-and-a-half story house, built not later than 1675, has balanced dormer windows. The brick walls are in good condition, though they are somewhat concealed by a weathered coat of white paint. During the century following construction, a frame portion was added at the rear. It continues the steep-hipped gambrel roof, now covered with modern roofing. A small porch added along the side and a wide screened porch across the front further obscure the original appearance.

The grounds are distinctive. A large tree-lined oval—a well-kept bowling green—stretches from the entrance gate to near the front of the house. This is ringed by cedar trees, some of which are apparently original. An unusual walk, lined by old English boxwoods, leads from the top of the green to the house entrance. At the rear are remnants of a terraced garden. An avenue of ancient holly trees approaches the south side of the house. The house is privately owned and is not open to the public.

147. Rosegill Estate, Virginia

Location: Middlesex County, on Va. 227, about 1½ miles north of Va. 33, east of Saluda.

Ralph Wormeley patented this estate and began construction in 1649. The house contained a chapel, picture gallery, large library, and 30 guest chambers. One immense attic room provided 14 beds for bachelor guests.

This mid-17th-century mansion, at Rosegill Estate, was once the temporary seat of the colony of Virginia.

Two Governors—Sir Henry Chicheley and Lord Francis Howard—lived in the house, which was once the temporary seat of the colony. The present main house contains part of the first. The long, many-windowed building has one brick and one frame story beneath a gabled roof. Green shutters flank the numerous windows and accent the white walls. Privately owned, the house is not open to the public.

148. Sheild House, Virginia

Location: York County, Main Street, Yorktown.

Thomas Sessions built this one-and-a-half story house, an outstanding example of 17th-century brick construction, in the 1690's. Walls of large brick rise from a high basement to a gabled roof. Outside chimneys and five dormers provide character. The front door is a so-called "Christian door," although not of the same type as in the Old North Church in Boston. This one has two upright crosses, but the same tradition clung to it—that it was good for driving witches away. The house also has many HL hinges, which were chiefly used in New England. The Siege of Yorktown, in 1781, raged around the house, which was also used during the Civil War by one of Gen. George B. McClellan's staff for a headquarters. Privately owned, the house is not open to the public.

149. Smith's Fort Plantation Site (Rolfe House), Virginia

Location: Surry County, on Va. 31, about 2 miles north of Surry.

This is the site of a fortification built by Capt. John Smith on the south side of the James River as a refuge in the event that enemy attack forced evacuation of Jamestown, across the river. Constructed early in

Possibly the oldest brick residence in Virginia, the "Rolfe House," or "Warren House," dates from about 1652. It is located on the site of a fortification built in 1609 by Capt. John Smith to protect Jamestown.

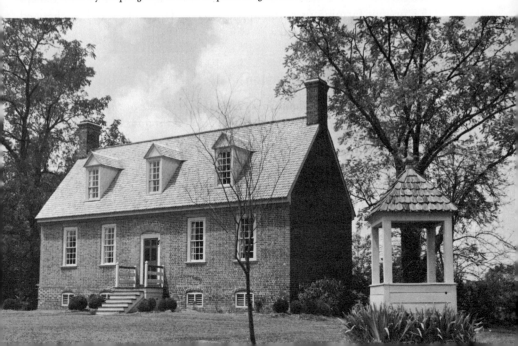

1609, the fort was the first extension of Jamestown, but was hardly used because no attacks occurred. The generally accepted site is marked by a few mounds of earth and is on property owned by the Association for the Preservation of Virginia Antiquities. The site has been called both "Smith's Fort Plantation" and "The Rolfe Property," for the site also contains a small brick residence that was built on property owned by John Rolfe. The property was part of a grant made to Rolfe by Powhatan when Rolfe married Pocahontas, Powhatan's daughter. The house, called the "Rolfe House," "Warren House," and "Fifty-Foot Brick House," was reportedly built by Thomas Warren in 1652 and is the oldest brick house in Virginia. It has been restored, furnished in 17th-century style, and is open to the public.

150. Discovery Bay, Washington

Location: Jefferson County, along U.S. 101, at the eastern entrance to the Strait of Juan de Fuca.

This bay was discovered by the Spanish explorer Alférez Manuel Quimper, on July 11, 1790, and named Bodega y Quadra Bay in honor of the famous Spanish explorer. Francisco de Eliza, another Spaniard, used it in 1791 as a temporary base of operations while he explored the San Juan Islands. The following year, during an expedition along the Pacific coast and into the Strait of Juan de Fuca, the English explorer Capt. George Vancouver anchored his vessels, including the *Discovery,* in the bay and named it Discovery Bay. After a few weeks, he set out eastward in his longboats for a 2-month exploration of the Puget Sound area. Except for present farming uses, the appearance of Discovery Bay has changed little since the 18th century.

151. Neah Bay, Washington

Location: Clallam County, on the south side of the entrance to the Strait of Juan de Fuca, at the western terminus of Wash. 9A.

The first European settlement on the present Pacific Northwest coast of the United States was made on the shores of this bay. The bay was discovered in 1790 by the Spanish explorer Alférez Manuel Quimper, who called it Bahía de Nuñez Gaona. In May 1792, the Spanish frigate *Princesa* landed on its shore a group of settlers, led by Lt. Sálvador

Fidalgo. The settlers built a fortified village of about 10 houses, which they called Nuñez Gaona, but they abandoned it after about 5 months, when Quimper moved them to Nootka.

The present settlement at Neah Bay, as the bay was later called, was initiated in 1851, when Samuel Hancock, an American wagonmaker, erected a trading post. The appearance of Neah Bay has changed little since the 18th century, except for the small village located there, which is the administrative and trading center of the Makah Indian Reservation and a fishing center. No remains of the early Spanish settlement are visible, but brick and tile used by the Spanish builders are occasionally found and are displayed by the Washington State Historical Society museum in Tacoma.

152. Point Grenville, Washington

> *Location: Grays Harbor County, 8 miles west of Wash. 9C, Quinault Indian Reservation.*

The Spanish explorers Bruno Heceta and Juan Francisco de Bodega y Quadra anchored their vessels, the *Santiago* and *Sonora,* off this point on July 13, 1775. The next day Heceta and 23 of his men landed on

Point Grenville, Washington. In 1775, the Spanish explorers Heceta and Quadra landed at the point and claimed the area for Spain. They were the first Europeans known to set foot in the State of Washington.

the promontory and claimed the area for Spain; these men were apparently the first Europeans to set foot in the present State of Washington. They were ambushed by Indians and seven of them killed. Heceta named the point "Punta de los Martires" in honor of the slaughtered sailors. In 1792, the English explorer Capt. George Vancouver sighted the promontory and renamed it Point Grenville. Little changed since 1775, the point is now utilized for a U.S. Coast Guard Station.

153. Green Bay, Wisconsin

Location: Brown County.

Green Bay, located along the banks of the Fox River, is the oldest settlement in Wisconsin. Early French voyageurs and *coureurs de bois* probably knew about the site and named it *Baye des Puants* because the Puants, a Winnebago tribe, resided there. Not until 1634, however, did Jean Nicolet, commissioned by Champlain, arrive at *La Baye* and claim the region for France. For more than 30 years little happened at *La Baye,* but in 1669 Father Claude Allouez, a Jesuit missionary, founded a mission there. In 1673, Marquette and Jolliet left St. Ignace to open up a water route to the Mississippi. They sailed from Lake Michigan to Green Bay and then went down the Fox and Wisconsin Rivers to the Mississippi. After this journey, because of its strategic position on the water route to the Mississippi, *La Baye* became an important fur trading center and rendezvous. In 1684, the French Government appointed Nicolas Perrot commandant of the region, and he built a crude frontier fort and trading post at *La Baye.* Soon, many traders, trappers, Indians, missionaries, and French soldiers settled there.

During the first half of the 18th century, the settlement was involved in constant warfare with the Fox Indians, and the French built Fort La Baye in 1716 to keep the area open for trade. In 1728, the Indians destroyed it, but the French rebuilt it 5 years later. At the end of the French and Indian War, in 1763, the British occupied Fort La Baye. They called the settlement Green Bay (*La Baye Verte*) because the water and shore assumed green tints early in the spring. During the British regime, the fur trade reached its height and Green Bay developed into a prosperous farming community. After 1783, when the United States acquired the Northwest Territory from the British, French and British traders continued to live in the settlement and opposed American interference. Not until after the War of 1812 did Americans share fully in the fur trade of the region, when John Jacob Astor's American Fur Company gained control.

Located at Green Bay is the oldest extant house in Wisconsin, the Roi-Porlier-Tank Cottage.

154. Prairie du Chien, Wisconsin

Location: Crawford County.

Located on a broad terrace overlooking the Mississippi, 3 miles north of the confluence of the Mississippi and Wisconsin Rivers, Prairie du Chien is the second oldest settlement in Wisconsin—the first being Green Bay. Prairie du Chien was a vital station on the route between Canada and the vast French-claimed heartland of North America.

Soon after Louis Jolliet and Père Jacques Marquette passed nearby in 1673 while journeying down the Wisconsin and Mississippi Rivers, the site became an important gathering place for French and Indian trappers, traders, and hunters. In the mid-1680's, Nicolas Perrot erected Fort St. Nicolas there, but a permanent French garrison was never assigned. In the mid-1700's, French stragglers may have settled at the site and named it for a Fox Indian chief whom they called *Le Chien* ("the dog"). A land claim made by three French Canadians in 1781, however, is usually considered the date of the first permanent settlement.

For more than a century, the settlement was a base for the French commercial exploitation of the entire region west of the Great Lakes. In spite of the British occupation during the War for Independence and for a short time in 1814, and subsequent American rule, no notable change occurred in commercial activities at Prairie du Chien. Both British and American trading companies prospered, even though the settlement changed hands.

No structure survives from the French period. The important surviving buildings date from the late 18th and early 19th centuries. Historical interest is centered in the older part of town, on St. Feriole Island; at Villa Louis, administered by the State Historical Society of Wisconsin; the Brisbois House; and the Astor Warehouse. Other more recent sites of interest include the second Fort Crawford, the Dousman Hotel, and the Diamond Jo Steamship Line warehouse. All of these buildings, as well as the city of Prairie du Chien, are eligible for the Registry of

National Historic Landmarks (relating primarily to the advance of the frontier, 1763–1830).

155. Roi-Porlier-Tank Cottage, Wisconsin

Location: Brown County, 10th Avenue and 5th Street, Green Bay.

This cottage in Green Bay is the oldest extant residence in Wisconsin. It is typical of those built by early fur traders in the old Northwest. The original section was built in 1776 by Francis Roi, a French trapper, several years after France had lost Wisconsin to Great Britain. Roi incorporated a huge fireplace, built of wattle and daub—an unusual method of construction in French America, but quite common in Canada. In 1805, Jacques Porlier bought the cottage and used it as his residence. During the War of 1812, English officers used it to hold conferences. Nils Otto Tank, a Norwegian, purchased it in 1850 and had it clapboarded, plastered, and painted. He also added low wings on each side. Originally located on the west bank of the Fox River, the cottage was moved to its present site by the Green Bay Historical Society and the South Side Improvement Association. It is open to the public all year.

156. Fort San Geronimo, Puerto Rico

Location: On the Boquerón, the opening into Condado Lagoon, San Juan.

This small fort occupies a strategic site that the Spanish early utilized to defend the eastern land approaches to San Juan and to support the harbor defenses. The earlier fort or forts—depending on whether or not rebuilding or new building was carried on in 1608—at this site served from the 16th through most of the 18th centuries. The Spanish designed the present masonry structure in 1791; built it in the period 1792–96; and identically reconstructed it during the years 1799–1801, after the British partially destroyed it in 1797. The fort rests on a sandstone bedrock that juts out into the sea. It has two main levels, or tiers. The upper one, the gundeck, is connected by two ramps with the forecourt. Inside are storerooms, magazines, dungeon, kitchen, and other facilities. The fort is administered by the Institute of Puerto Rican Culture, which in 1961 restored it and installed a military museum.

SUGGESTED READING

General Works

BAKELESS, JOHN E. *The Eyes of Discovery—The Pageant of North America as Seen by the First Explorers.* Philadelphia: Lippincott, 1950. Includes numerous and extensive quotations relating the marvels of discovery in the words of those who first saw the Western Hemisphere. Consists mainly of descriptions of flora, fauna, and geographical features.

BOLTON, HERBERT E. and THOMAS M. MARSHALL. *The Colonization of North America, 1492–1783.* New York: Macmillan, 1936. A concise but thorough account of the exploration and colonization of the continent and the international rivalries that were involved.

BREBNER, JOHN B. *The Explorers of North America, 1492–1806.* New York: Macmillan, 1933; reprinted in paperback 1955. A well-written work of careful scholarship that views as a whole the significant explorations of the continent. Includes quotations from contemporary narratives.

CROUSE, NELLIS M. *In Quest of the Western Ocean.* New York: Morrow, 1928. Studies European attempts to find a water passage through or around the American continental block. Also sheds light on motivations for European expansion.

DE VOTO, BERNARD A. *The Course of Empire.* Boston: Houghton Mifflin, 1952. One of a number of attempts to tie the various explorations of North America into a meaningful whole, this book is written with power and persuasion and is often considered to be De Voto's major work. It has literary merit, but its historical value has been highly praised and disparagingly criticized.

FOLMER, HENRY. *Franco-Spanish Rivalry in North America, 1524–1763.* Vol. VII of the *Spain in the West* series. Glendale: Arthur Clark, 1953. Excellent work. Stresses international rivalries and diplomatic maneuverings.

[403

NEWTON, ARTHUR P. *The Great Age of Discovery*. London: University of London, 1932. Contains monographs by various British historians on a number of explorers, from Vasco da Gama to Frobisher. Analyzes explorers against the background of their own times.

PRIESTLEY, HERBERT I. *The Coming of the White Man, 1492–1848*. Vol. I of *A History of American Life*, ed. by Arthur M. Schlesinger and Dixon R. Fox. New York: Macmillan, 1929. A history of European contacts with the New World that emphasizes social rather than military and political aspects.

The Spanish

BOLTON, HERBERT E. *Coronado, Knight of Pueblos and Plains*. Albuquerque: University of New Mexico Press, 1949. An enjoyable biography of Coronado and an extensive survey of his exploration of the Southwest.

———. *Rim of Christendom—A Biography of Eusebio Francisco Kino, Pacific Coast Pioneer*. New York: Macmillan, 1936. Not only the definitive biography of Padre Kino, the famous missionary, but also the best available account of early Spanish efforts in Arizona.

———. *The Spanish Borderlands—A Chronicle of Old Florida and the Southwest*. Vol. XXIII of *The Chronicles of America* series, ed. by Allen Johnson. New Haven: Yale University Press, 1921. A compact and readable volume that is still popular with students and laymen alike.

BOURNE, EDWARD G. *Spain in America, 1450–1580*. Vol III of *The American Nation* series, ed. by Albert B. Hart. New York: Harper, 1940; reprinted in paperback 1962. Probably the most widely read scholarly work on the foundations of the Spanish Empire in North America.

CARTER, HODDING and BETTY W. *Doomed Road of Empire—The Spanish Trail of Conquest*. American Trails series. New York: McGraw-Hill, 1963. An interesting and scholarly work on the Spanish borderlands by a Pulitzer prizewinner and his wife. Tells the stories of the Spaniards, Mexicans, and Americans who traveled the *Camino Real* (Royal Highway) from Saltillo to Natchitoches and its parallel trails in Texas between 1568 and the Battle of Buena Vista, in 1847.

CAUGHEY, JOHN W. *History of the Pacific Coast of North America*. New York: Prentice-Hall, 1938. An excellent one-volume history of the Pacific coast—from Mexico to Alaska—that emphasizes the period before 1850.

HARING, CLARENCE H. *The Spanish Empire in America.* New York: Oxford, 1947. An authoritative summary, stressing institutional development, that is equally valuable to the specialist and nonspecialist.

HORGAN, PAUL. *Great River—The Rio Grande in North American History.* 2 vols. New York: Rinehart, 1954. Vol. I, *Indians and Spain.* A Pulitzer-prize-winning history that is particularly readable. Devoted as much to life along the Rio Grande as to the river itself. Discusses various phases of Indian and Spanish life and their interrelationships.

MADARIAGA, SALVADOR DE. *The Rise of the Spanish American Empire.* New York: Macmillan, 1947. This and the following volume provide an excellent synthesis of the history of the Spanish Empire in America.

——— . *The Fall of the Spanish American Empire.* New York: Macmillan, 1948.

MORISON, SAMUEL E. *Admiral of the Ocean Sea—A Life of Christopher Columbus.* Boston: Little, Brown, 1942. A condensation of a two-volume work, published the same year, that was awarded a Pulitzer prize for biography.

SPICER, EDWARD H. *Cycles of Conquest—The Impact of Spain, Mexico, and the United States on the Indians of the Southwest, 1533–1960.* Tucson: University of Arizona Press, 1962. A comprehensive, specialized work that should nevertheless be of interest to the layman who is interested in delving beyond the surface of history. Includes the findings of recent scholarship on Indian-Spanish relationships.

The French

BISHOP, MORRIS. *Champlain—The Life of Fortitude.* New York: Knopf, 1948. A scholarly and probably the most readable biography of the famed French explorer. The author's admiration of Champlain enhances rather than detracts from the presentation.

MUNRO, WILLIAM B. and GEORGE M. WRONG. *Adventures of New France.* Vol. III of *The Chronicles of America* series, ed. by Allen Johnson. New Haven: Yale University Press, 1918. One of the better volumes of this series. Divided into two parts: "Crusaders of New France," by Munro, and "The Conquest of New France," by Wrong.

NUTE, GRACE L. *The Voyageur.* St. Paul: Minnesota Historical Association, 1931, reprint 1955. Although most of this work concentrates on the period after 1763, when the French had been driven off the continent, it is valuable for its portrayal of the French voyageur.

PARKMAN, FRANCIS. *La Salle and the Discovery of the Great West.* Vol. III of his collected *Works.* Boston: Little, Brown, 1902; available in paperback. First issued in 1869, this volume is a monument to La Salle's achievements in the Mississippi Valley. The style is somewhat more labored than usual for Parkman.

———. *Pioneers of France in the New World.* Vol. I of his collected *Works.* Boston: Little, Brown, 1902. Originally published in 1865, this classic provides a fascinating account of the activities of the early French pioneers—from Fort Caroline, in Florida, to Quebec, in Canada. It has never been surpassed as an account of the Huguenot ventures in North America, although its principal purpose is to describe the foundations of New France.

———. *The Battle for North America.* Ed. by John Tebbel. Garden City: Doubleday, 1948. A rather extensive (746 pages) condensation of Parkman's massive study of the French in North America and their struggle to hold the continent's heartland.

———. *The Jesuits in North America in the Seventeenth Century.* Vol. II of his collected *Works.* Boston: Little, Brown, 1902. This classic narrative of missionary tenacity was first published in 1867. Relates the martyrdom and zeal of the Jesuit fathers in spreading European culture and influence among the Indians and settlers in New France.

THWAITES, REUBEN G. *France in America, 1497–1763.* Vol. VII of *The American Nation* series, ed. by Albert B. Hart. New York: Harper, 1905. This book remains an outstanding summary of the French period. Like several other volumes in the series, it surpasses in literary merit and historical skill more recent works in the field.

WRONG, GEORGE M. *The Rise and Fall of New France.* 2 vols. New York: Macmillan, 1928. The story of France in America told by a Canadian historian. Neither as readable nor as perceptive as Parkman's works, but it is based on more recent scholarship and presents a different viewpoint and organization.

The Dutch and Swedes

BENSON, ADOLPH B. and NABOTH HEDIN. *Americans from Sweden. The People of America* series. Philadelphia: Lippincott, 1950. Discusses all phases of Swedish colonial history and the role of the Swedes in America, including religion and education.

NISSENSON, SAMUEL G. *The Patroon's Domain.* New York: Columbia University Press, 1937. Although this work is designed to trace the history of Rensselaerswyck and the vicinity of Albany, it is the best analysis of the patroon system available. Places colonization of New Netherland in the context of the commercial growth of the Dutch Republic.

RAESLY, ELLIS L. *Portrait of New Netherland.* New York: Columbia University Press, 1945. Originally a doctoral dissertation, this socially oriented history competently treats government, religion, culture, political ideas, literature, and other aspects of New Netherland.

The English

ANDREWS, CHARLES M. *Colonial Folkways—A Chronicle of American Life in the Reign of the Georges.* Vol. IX of *The Chronicles of America* series, ed. by Allen Johnson. New Haven: Yale University Press, 1921. Emphasizing social aspects of colonial history, this widely read book has contributed much to general understanding of the American heritage.

———. *Colonial Self-Government, 1652–1689.* Vol. V of *The American Nation* series, ed. by Albert B. Hart. New York: Harper, 1904. In the field of Andrews' specialty, this volume is still the best single one on the subject.

CHITWOOD, OLIVER P. *A History of Colonial America.* New York: Harper, 1931. One of the best works of its kind available. Presents a thorough and factual résumé of European colonization of North America, but emphasizes the area of the present United States and the activities of the English.

CRAVEN, WESLEY F. *The Southern Colonies in the Seventeenth Century, 1607–1689.* Baton Rouge: Louisiana State University Press, 1949. Vol. I of *A History of the South* series, ed. by Wendell H. Stephenson and Ellis M. Coulter. Carefully examines the cultural development of colonial Virginia, Maryland, and the Carolinas.

ELLIS, GEORGE E. *The Puritan Age and Rule in the Colony of the Massachusetts Bay, 1629–1685.* Boston: Houghton Mifflin, 1888. This study, one of the first of its kind, is still probably the most inclusive and is basically sound. Recent advances in social and intellectual history, however, have resulted in modifications of Ellis' ideas.

GREENE, EVARTS B. *The Foundation of American Nationality.* New York: American Book Co., rev. ed. 1935. A review of American colonial history as a part of that of the British Empire, from the foundations of the colonies to the adoption of the Federal Constitution. Written for laymen and students, it synthesizes modern scholarship relating to the period.

———. *Provincial America.* Vol. VI of *The American Nation* series, ed.

by Albert B. Hart. New York: Harper, 1905. Focusing on the British settlements that became part of the United States, this volume tells the story of their expansion, government, religion, culture, and commerce.

MILLER, PERRY. *The New England Mind—The Seventeenth Century.* New York: Macmillan, 1939. An intellectual history of Puritanism in New England. The theological doctrines and philosophical roots of the colonial leaders are cogently synthesized and thoroughly analyzed.

————. *Roger Williams—His Contributions to the American Tradition.* Indianapolis: Bobbs-Merrill, 1953. Of a number of biographies of Roger Williams, this one seems to present the best-rounded portrait.

MORISON, SAMUEL E. *Builders of the Bay Colony.* Boston: Houghton Mifflin, 1930. Illuminates with literary skill the lives of a number of individuals who contributed to the early development of Massachusetts—from Richard Hakluyt to Anne Bradstreet. Provides a sympathetic account of New England Puritanism.

————. *The Intellectual Life of Colonial New England.* New York: New York University Press, 2d ed. 1956. Not so much a history of ideas as a history of intellectual endeavor. It surveys such subjects as education, bookselling, libraries, sermons, political tracts, poetry, and science.

NETTELS, CURTIS P. *The Roots of American Civilization.* New York: Crofts, 1946. Crofts' *American History* series, ed. by Dixon R. Fox. Treats theoretical and practical aspects of British colonial policy from the standpoint of the British Government and the colonists. Illuminates economic, political, and social facets of the American heritage.

PEARE, CATHERINE O. *William Penn—A Biography.* Philadelphia: Lippincott, 1957. Probably the most perceptive of all the biographies of this prominent Anglo-American.

STARKEY, MARION L. *The Devil in Massachusetts—A Modern Inquiry into the Salem Witch Trials.* New York: Knopf, 1949. A modern psychological study of the witch trials. Their history is clearly told, and it is related to the social and religious background in Massachusetts. Of the numerous studies on the subject, this is probably the most interesting to the average reader.

SWEET, WILLIAM W. *Religion in Colonial America.* New York: Scribner's, 1942. The definitive general work on the subject. Examines religious motivation for colonization, the effect of the colonial experience on Old World religious thought, and the great variety and diversity of religious opinions in the colonies.

WERTENBAKER, THOMAS J. *The First Americans, 1607–1690.* Vol. II of *A History of American Life,* ed. by Arthur M. Schlesinger and Dixon R. Fox. New York: Macmillan, 1927. Like other volumes in the series, this one emphasizes social aspects, Wertenbaker's field of specialty.

——— . *The Founding of American Civilization—The Middle Colonies.* New York: Scribner's, 1938. This volume and the two listed immediately below comprise one of the finest overall studies available on our colonial heritage. Like the others, it is written from the colonial rather than the British viewpoint. Surveys the founding of New York, New Jersey, and Pennsylvania.

——— . *The Founding of American Civilization—The Old South.* New York: Scribner's, 1942. Treats the establishment of Virginia, Maryland, and the Carolinas with well-rounded historical scrutiny.

——— . *The Founding of American Civilization—The Puritan Oligarchy.* New York: Scribner's, 1947. Primarily a study of Massachusetts, but discusses the other Puritan colonies in New England. Provides an excellent analysis of the development of the Bay Colony.

WILLIAMSON, JAMES A. *The Age of Drake.* London: Black, 3d ed. 1952. Tells the tale of Drake and the "sea dogs" with vigor, taste, and authenticity. Contributes much to an understanding of the background of U.S. colonial history.

——— . *A Short History of British Expansion.* 2 vols. New York: Macmillan, 2d ed. 1931. Possibly no other single work so effectively places the development of the British seaboard colonies in the perspective of empire.

WILLISON, GEORGE F. *Saints and Strangers.* New York: Reynal and Hitchcock, 1945. A lively story of the Pilgrims and the founding of Plymouth colony. Drawn largely from original material—Bradford's journal, letters, and other manuscripts of the colonists—it is written with sympathetic understanding.

WRIGHT, LOUIS B. *The Cultural Life of the American Colonies, 1607–1763.* New York: Harper, 1957. A short but outstanding survey of our colonial cultural heritage.

NOTES

1. Apalachicola Fort, Ala.: Herbert E. Bolton, ed., *Arredondo's Proof of Spain's Title to Georgia* (Berkeley, 1925) ; Verner W. Crane, *The Southern Frontier, 1670–1732* (Durham, N.C., 1928) ; David L. DeJarnette, "Archeological Salvage in the Walter F. George Basin of the Chattahoochee River in Alabama," MS Report, National Park Service (1963).

2. Fort Toulouse (Fort Jackson), Ala.: Crane, *Southern Frontier;* Dunbar Rowland and Albert G. Sanders, *Mississippi Provincial Archives, French Dominion* (3 vols., Jackson, 1927–32) ; Daniel H. Thomas, "Fort Toulouse— In Tradition and Fact," *The Alabama Review*, XIII, 4 (October 1960).

3. Awatovi, Ariz.: Herbert E. Bolton, *Spanish Exploration in the Southwest, 1542–1706* (New York, 1916) ; R. G. Montgomery, Watson Smith, and J. O. Brew, *Franciscan Awatovi*, Papers of the Peabody Museum of Archaeology and Ethnology, XXXVI (Cambridge, 1949) ; Erik K. Reed, "Special Report on Awatovi, Arizona" and "Supplementary Report on Awatovi, Arizona," MS Reports, National Park Service (1938) ; Edward H. Spicer, *Cycles of Conquest* (Tucson, 1962).

4. San Xavier del Bac Mission, Ariz.: Herbert E. Bolton, *Rim of Christendom—A Biography of Eusebio Francisco Kino, Pacific Coast Pioneer* (New York, 1936) ; Herbert E. Bolton, *Kino's Historical Memoir of Pimería Alta* (Cleveland, 1919) ; Cleve Hallenbeck, *Spanish Missions of the Old Southwest* (New York, 1926) ; Aubrey Neasham, "Special Report on the Mission of San Xavier del Bac," MS Report, National Park Service (1940).

5. Carmel Mission, Calif.: Hubert H. Bancroft, *History of California* (7 vols., San Francisco, 1884–90), I–IV; John A. Berger, *The Franciscan Missions of California* (New York, 1941) ; Father Zephyrin Engelhardt, *Mission San Carlos Borroméo*, ed. by Father Felix Pudlowski (Santa Barbara, 1934) ; Mrs. Francis N. Smith, *The Architectural History of Mission San Carlos Borroméo* (Berkeley, 1921) ; Kurt Baer, *Architecture of the California Missions* (Berkeley and Los Angeles, 1958).

6. Fort Ross, Calif.: Bancroft, *History of California*, II and IV; Bancroft,

[411

History of Alaska (San Francisco, 1886) ; John W. Caughey, *California* (Englewood Cliffs, N.J., 1957) ; Mildred B. Hoover, Hero E. and Ethel G. Rensch, *Historic Spots in California*, rev. by Ruth Teiser (Stanford, 1958) ; Olaf T. Hagen, "Historic Sites Survey Report: Fort Ross, California," MS Report, National Park Service (1941).

7. Old Mission Dam (Padre Dam), Calif.: Bancroft, *History of California*, I and II; Father Zephyrin Engelhardt, *San Diego Mission* (San Francisco, 1920) ; Baer, *Architecture of the California Missions.*

8. Presidio of San Francisco, Calif.: Bancroft, *History of California*, I–IV; George Vancouver, *Voyage of Discovery to the North Pacific Ocean and Around the World* (6 vols., London, 1801), III.

9. Royal Presidio Chapel, Calif.: James Ladd Delkin, *Monterey Peninsula*, American Guide Series (Stanford, 1946) ; Bancroft, *History of California*, I–IV; Father Zephyrin Engelhardt, *Missions and Missionaries of California* (4 vols., San Francisco, 1908–15) ; Rexford Newcomb, *The Old Mission Churches and Historic Houses of California* (Philadelphia, 1925).

10. San Diego Presidio, Calif.: Richard F. Pourade, *The History of San Diego—The Explorers* (San Diego, 1960) ; Winifred Davidson, *Where California Began* (San Diego, 1929) ; Bancroft, *History of California*, I–III; Engelhardt, *San Diego Mission;* William E. Smythe, *History of San Diego, 1542–1907* (San Diego, 1907).

11. Santa Barbara Mission, Calif.: Father Zephyrin Engelhardt, *Mission Santa Barbara* (San Francisco, 1923) ; Bancroft, *History of California*, I–IV; John A. Berger, *The Franciscan Missions of California* (New York, 1941) ; Baer, *Architecture of the California Missions.*

12. Stanley-Whitman House, Conn.: Anthony N. B. Garvan, *Architecture and Town Planning in Colonial Connecticut* (New Haven, 1951) ; J. Frederick Kelly, *The Early Domestic Architecture of Connecticut* (New Haven, 1924) ; Hugh Morrison, *Early American Architecture—From the First Colonial Settlements to the National Period* (New York, 1952) ; Bertha C. Trowbridge and Charles M. Andrews, *Old Houses of Connecticut* (New Haven, 1923).

13. Fort Christina, Del.: Rogers W. Young, "Site of the Swedish Fort Christina, Wilmington, Delaware," MS Report, National Park Service (1940) ; Letter, Leon de Valinger, Jr., State Archivist, Dover, Del., to Northeast Regional Office, National Park Service, Mar. 24, 1961; *Delaware—A Guide to the First State*, American Guide Series (rev. ed., New York, 1955) ; Esther C. Meixner, *Swedish Landmarks in the Delaware Valley* (Bridgeport, Pa., 1960).

14. Holy Trinity (Old Swedes) Church, Del.: Letter, Rev. H. Edgar Hammond, Holy Trinity (Old Swedes) Church Foundation, Inc., Wilmington, Del., to Northeast Regional Office, National Park Service, Apr. 18,

1961; Historic American Buildings Survey, National Park Service, 7 sheets and 8 photos (1934); Meixner, *Swedish Landmarks;* Amandus Johnson, *Swedish Settlements on the Delaware—Their History and Relation to the Indians, Dutch, and English, 1638–1664* (2 vols., New York, 1911); Rogers W. Young, "Holy Trinity (Old Swedes) Church, Wilmington, Delaware," MS Report, National Park Service (1940).

15. Fort San Carlos de Barrancas, Fla.: Albert Manucy, "Report on Historic Sites at Pensacola, Florida," MS Report, National Park Service (1939); Herbert E. Bolton, *The Spanish Borderlands* (New Haven, 1921).

16. San Luís de Apalache, Fla.: Mark F. Boyd, Hale G. Smith, and John W. Griffin, *Here They Once Stood—The Tragic End of the Apalachee Missions* (Gainesville, Fla., 1951); Ralston B. Lattimore, "San Luís de Apalache," MS Report, National Park Service (1939); Venila L. Shores, "The Ruins of San Luís near Tallahassee," *Florida Historical Quarterly,* VI (1927); Mark F. Boyd, "Mission Sites in Florida," *ibid.,* XVII (1939).

17. Fort de Chartres, Ill.: *Fort de Chartres State Park,* pamphlet, State of Illinois, Division of Parks and Memorials (n.p., n.d.); Clarence W. Alvord, *The Illinois Country, 1673-1818,* Vol. I (1920), *The Centennial History of Illinois* (6 vols., Chicago, 1917–20).

18. Old Kaskaskia Village Site, Ill.: Wayne C. Temple, *Indian Villages of the Illinois Country, Historic Tribes,* Illinois State Museum Scientific Papers, Vol. II, Part 2 (Springfield, Ill., 1958); Donald E. Wray, "Archeology of the Illinois Valley, 1950," in J. B. Griffin, *Archeology of Eastern United States* (Chicago, 1952); K. G. Orr, "The Historic Upper Mississippi Phase in Northern Illinois—La Salle County Excavations, 1947," *Proceedings of the Fifth Plains Conference for Archeology,* Laboratory of Anthropology, University of Nebraska (Lincoln, 1949).

19. Starved Rock, Ill.: *Starved Rock State Park,* pamphlet, State of Illinois, Division of Parks and Memorials (n.p., n.d.); Charles W. Paape, "Starved Rock in the History of Illinois," MS Report, National Park Service (1937); Francis Parkman, *La Salle and the Discovery of the Great West* (Boston, 1903); John B. Brebner, *The Explorers of North America* (New York, 1933). *See also* Note 18.

20. El Cuartelejo (Scott County Pueblo Site), Kans.: Waldo R. Wedel, *An Introduction to Kansas Archeology,* Bureau of American Ethnology Bulletin 174 (Washington, 1959); James H. Gunnerson, "An Introduction to Plains Apache Archeology—The Dismal River Aspect," *Anthropological Papers,* Bureau of American Ethnology Bulletin 173 (Washington, 1959); A. B. Thomas, *After Coronado* (Norman, Okla., 1935).

21. Tobias-Thompson Complex, Kans.: Wedel, *Introduction to Kansas Archeology;* Waldo R. Wedel, "Archeological Remains in Central Kansas and Their Possible Bearing on the Location of Quivira," *Smithsonian Mis-*

cellaneous Collections, Vol. 101 (Washington, 1942) ; Herbert E. Bolton, Coronado, Knight of Pueblos and Plains (Albuquerque, 1949).

22. Cabildo, La.: Morrison, Early American Architecture; C. P. Dimitry, "The Story of the Ancient Cabildo," Louisiana Historical Quarterly, III (1920) ; [H. P. Dart], "The Cabildo of New Orleans," ibid., V (1922) ; J. A. Robertson, ed., Louisiana under the Rule of Spain, France, and the United States, 1785–1807 (2 vols., Cleveland, 1911).

23. Fort de la Boulaye, La.: Maurice Ries, "The Mississippi Fort Called Fort de la Boulaye," Louisiana Historical Quarterly, XIX, No. 4 (Oct. 1936) ; Dunbar Rowland and Albert G. Sanders, Mississippi Provincial Archives, French Dominion (3 vols., Jackson, 1927–32).

24. Jackson Square, La.: Stanley C. Arthur, Old New Orleans (New Orleans, 1936) ; A. P. Whitaker, The Mississippi Question, 1795–1803 (New York, 1934) ; Robertson, ed., Louisiana.

25. Ursuline Convent, La.: Samuel Wilson, Jr., "An Architectural History of the Royal Hospital and the Ursuline Convent of New Orleans," Louisiana Historical Quarterly, XXIX, No. 3 (July 1946) ; Henry C. Semple, The Ursulines in New Orleans and Our Lady of Prompt Succor— A Record of Two Centuries, 1725–1925 (New York, 1925) ; Gabriel Gravier, Relation du Voyage des Dames Religieuses Ursulines de Rouen á la Nouvelle-Orleans, avec une Introduction et des Notes (Paris, 1872).

26. Cole's Hill, Mass.: William T. Davis, Ancient Landmarks of Plymouth (Boston, 1889) ; Alvin P. Stauffer, "Historic Sites in or near Plymouth, Massachusetts, Relating to Pilgrim History," MS Report, National Park Service (1941) ; Samuel E. Morison, By Land and By Sea (New York, 1953) ; George F. Willison, Saints and Strangers (New York, 1945).

27. Fairbanks House, Mass.: Alvin L. Jones, Ye Old Fayerbanks House (Boston, 1894) ; Morrison, Early American Architecture; Harold R. Shurtleff, The Log Cabin Myth—A Study of the Early Dwellings of the English Colonists in North America (Cambridge, 1939) ; Samuel Chamberlain, Open House in New England (Brattleboro, Vt., 1937) ; Historic American Buildings Survey, National Park Service, 24 sheets (1939), 2 photos (1936).

28. Old Ship Church, Mass.: George F. Marlowe, Churches of Old New England (New York, 1947) ; Morrison, Early American Architecture; Edward F. Rines, Old Historic Churches of America (New York, 1936).

29. Parson Capen House, Mass.: George F. Dow, The History of Topsfield (Topsfield, Mass., 1940) ; Historic American Buildings Survey, National Park Service, 3 photos (1936) ; Chamberlain, Open House in New England; Fiske Kimball, Domestic Architecture of the American Colonies and of the Early Republic (New York, 1922) ; Donald Miller, "A Seventeenth Century New England House," The Architectural Record, XXXVIII, No. 3 (Sept. 1915) ; Morrison, Early American Architecture.

30. Paul Revere House, Mass.: Morrison, *Early American Architecture;* Esther Forbes, *Paul Revere and the World He Lived In* (Boston, 1942).

31. Saugus Iron Works, Mass.: *The Saugus Ironworks Restoration,* pamphlet, American Iron and Steel Institute (*ca.* 1955); E. N. Hartley, *Ironworks on the Saugus* (Norman, Okla., 1957).

32. "Scotch"-Boardman House, Mass.: Abbott Lowell Cummings, "The Scotch-Boardman House—A Fresh Appraisal," *Old Time New England,* XLIII, Nos. 3 and 4 (Winter and Spring 1953); Morrison, *Early American Architecture.*

33. Whipple House, Mass.: Thomas F. Waters, "The John Whipple House," *Publications of the Ipswich Historical Society,* XX (Ipswich, Mass., 1915); Morrison, *Early American Architecture;* Lathrop, *Historic Houses;* Dorothy and Richard Pratt, *A Treasury of Early American Homes* (New York, 1949; rev. ed. 1956).

34. Fort Michilimackinac, Mich.: Moreau S. Maxwell and Lewis R. Binford, "Excavation at Fort Michilimackinac, Mackinaw City, Michigan, 1959 Season," *Michigan State University Cultural Series,* Vol. I, No. 1; Louise P. Kellogg, *The French Regime in Wisconsin and the Northwest* (Madison, 1925); Francis Parkman, *A Half-Century of Conflict* (2 vols., Boston, 1914); Howard H. Peckham, *Pontiac and the Indian Uprising* (Princeton, 1947).

35. St. Ignace Mission, Mich.: Thomas M. Pitkin, "Mackinac Island and Associated Sites," MS Report, National Park Service, 1937; Kellogg, *French Regime;* Parkman, *Half-Century of Conflict;* Francis Parkman, *The Jesuits in North America* (2 vols., Boston, 1909).

36. Kathio Site, Minn.: Russell W. Fridley, "Preserving Historic Sites," *Minnesota History,* XXXVII, No. 2 (1960); Lloyd A. Wilford, "The Prehistoric Indians of Minnesota—The Mille Lacs Aspect," *ibid.,* XXV, No. 4 (1944); Brebner, *Explorers of North America.*

37. Fatherland Plantation Site (Grand Village of the Natchez), Miss.: James A. Ford, *Analysis of Indian Village Site Collections from Louisiana and Mississippi,* Anthropological Study No. 2, Department of Conservation, Louisiana Geological Survey (New Orleans, 1936); John R. Swanton, *Indian Tribes of the Lower Mississippi Valley and Adjacent Coast of the Gulf of Mexico,* Bureau of American Ethnology Bulletin 43 (Washington, 1911).

38. Ste. Genevieve, Mo.: John Drury, *Historic Midwest Houses* (Minneapolis, 1947); Charles E. Peterson, "Early Ste. Genevieve and Its Architecture," *The Missouri Historical Review,* XXXV, No. 2 (Jan. 1941); *Missouri: A Guide to the 'Show Me' State,* American Guide Series (New York, 1954).

39. Utz Site, Mo.: Robert T. Bray, "The Missouri Indian Tribe in Ar-

NOTES

chaeology and History," *Missouri Historical Review*, LV, No. 2 (1961); Carl H. Chapman, "A Preliminary Survey of Missouri Archaeology—Part I: Historic Indian Tribes," *The Missouri Archaeologist*, X, No. 1 (1946).

40. Pike-Pawnee Village Site (Hill Site), Nebr.: Elliott Coues, ed., *The Expeditions of Zebulon Montgomery Pike, 1805–1807* (3 vols., New York, 1895); William D. Strong, "An Introduction to Nebraska Archeology," *Smithsonian Miscellaneous Collections*, Vol. 93 (Washington, 1935); Waldo R. Wedel, *An Introduction to Pawnee Archeology*, Bureau of American Ethnology Bulletin 112 (Washington, 1936).

41. Abó Pueblo and Mission, N. Mex.: Joseph H. Toulouse, Jr., *The Mission of San Gregorio de Abó*, School of American Research Monograph No. 13 (Albuquerque, 1949); Erik K. Reed, "Special Report on Abó State Monument, New Mexico," MS Report, National Park Service (1940); George Kubler, *The Religious Architecture of New Mexico* (Colorado Springs, 1940); Paul A. F. Walter, *The Cities That Died of Fear* (Santa Fe, 1931).

42. Acoma Pueblo, N. Mex.: Leslie A. White, *The Acoma Indians*, Bureau of American Ethnology, 47th Annual Report, 1929–30 (Washington, 1932); William R. Hogan, "Brief Special Report on Acoma, New Mexico," MS Report, National Park Service (1938); Erik K. Reed, "Supplementary Report on Acoma, New Mexico," MS Report, National Park Service (1942); Stanley A. Stubbs, *Birds-Eye View of the Pueblos* (Norman, Okla., 1950); George P. Hammond and Agapito Rey, *Oñate, First Colonizer of New Mexico* (2 vols., Albuquerque, 1940); Kubler, *Religious Architecture of New Mexico*.

43. Hawikuh, N. Mex.: Frederick W. Hodge, *The History of Hawikuh* (Los Angeles, 1937); Erik K. Reed, "Special Report on Hawikuh, New Mexico," MS Report, National Park Service (1938); Herbert E. Bolton, *Coronado, Knight of Pueblo and Plain* (New York and Albuquerque, 1949); George P. Hammond and Agapito Rey, eds., *Narratives of the Coronado Expedition* (Albuquerque, 1940).

44. Palace of the Governors, N. Mex.: Clinton P. Anderson, "The Adobe Palace," *New Mexico Historical Review*, XIX (April 1944); Aubrey Neasham, "Special Report Covering the Governor's Palace in Sante Fe, New Mexico," MS Report, National Park Service (1939); Ralph E. Twitchell, ed., *The Spanish Archives of New Mexico* (2 vols., Cedar Rapids, 1914); Ralph E. Twitchell, *The Leading Facts of New Mexican History* (5 vols., Cedar Rapids, 1912); Ralph E. Twitchell, *The Palace of the Governors, the City of Sante Fe, Its Museums and Monuments*, Historical Society of New Mexico Publication No. 29 (Santa Fe, 1924); Paul A. F. Walter, *Old Sante Fe and Vicinity* (Santa Fe, 1930).

45. Pecos Pueblo, N. Mex.: Alfred V. Kidder, "The Story of the Pueblo

of Pecos," *El Palacio,* Museum of New Mexico, LVIII (1951); Kubler, *Religious Architecture of New Mexico;* Edgar L. Hewett and Reginald G. Fisher, *Mission Monuments of New Mexico* (Albuquerque, 1943); Clarence W. Hackett, *Historical Documents Relating to New Mexico, Nueva Vizcaya, and Approaches Thereto, to 1773* (Washington, 1937); Frederick W. Hodge, George P. Hammond, and Agapito Rey, eds., *Fray Alonso de Benavides' Revised Memorial of 1634* (Albuquerque, 1945).

46. Quarai Pueblo and Mission, N. Mex.: Walter, *The Cities That Died of Fear;* Kubler, *Religious Architecture of New Mexico;* Hewett and Fisher, *Mission Monuments.*

47. San Gabriel de Yungue-ouinge, N. Mex.: Hammond and Rey, *Oñate;* Hodge, Hammond, and Rey, eds., *Benavides' Memorial;* Gilberto Espinosa, *Villagra's History of New Mexico, 1610* (Los Angeles, 1933); George M. Foster, *Culture and Conquest* (New York, 1960).

48. Taos Pueblo, N. Mex.: Forrest, *Missions and Pueblos;* Frederick W. Hodge, *Handbook of American Indians* (Washington, 1910); Hewett and Fisher, *Mission Monuments;* Charles W. Hackett, "The Revolt of the Pueblo Indians of New Mexico in 1680," Texas State Historical Association *Quarterly,* XV (1911); J. Manuel Espinosa, *Crusaders of the Rio Grande: The Story of Don Diego de Vargas and the Reconquest and Refounding of New Mexico* (Chicago, 1942); Kubler, *Religious Architecture.*

49. Boughton Hill (Gannagaro) Site, N.Y.: William N. Fenton, "Problems Arising from the Historic Northeastern Position of the Iroquois," *Smithsonian Miscellaneous Collections,* Vol. 100 (1940); George T. Hunt, *The Wars of the Iroquois* (Madison, 1960); Reuben G. Thwaites, *France in America* (New York, 1905); Charles F. Wray and H. L. Schoff, "A Preliminary Report on the Seneca Sequence in Western New York, 1550–1687," *Pennsylvania Archaeologist,* XXIII, No. 2 (1953).

50. Dutch Reformed (Sleepy Hollow) Church, N.Y.: Rogers W. Young, "Dutch Reformed (Sleepy Hollow) Church, North Tarrytown, New York," MS Report, National Park Service (1940); John K. Allen, *The Legendary History of the Old Dutch Church of Sleepy Hollow, Tarrytown, N.Y.* (Tarrytown, N.Y., 1891); Helen W. Reynolds, *Dutch Houses in the Hudson Valley Before 1776* (New York, 1929).

51. Fort Crailo, N.Y.: Harold D. Eberlein and Cortlandt Van Dyke Hubbard, *Historic Houses of the Hudson Valley* (New York, 1942); Morrison, *Early American Architecture;* Reynolds, *Dutch Houses.*

52. Fort St. Frederic, N.Y.: Charles S. Marshall, "Crown Point and Plattsburg," MS Report, National Park Service (1937); "Interim Report of the Joint Legislative Committee to Study Historic Sites," Legislative Document, State of New York (Albany, 1950); Hoffman Nickerson, *The Turning Point of the Revolution* (Boston, 1928); W. Max Reid, *Lake*

George and Lake Champlain (New York, 1910).

53. Old Fort Niagara, N.Y.: Claud H. Hultzén, Sr., *Old Fort Niagara— The Story of an Ancient Gateway to the West*, pamphlet, Old Fort Niagara Association (n.p., 1933); Frank H. Severance, *An Old Frontier of France: The Niagara Region and Adjacent Lakes Under French Control* (New York, 1917); Thor Borresen, "Father Millet Cross," MS Report, National Park Service (1939).

54. Old House, N.Y.: *The Old House . . . Cutchogue, N.Y.*, pamphlet (n.p., n.d.); Letter, Mrs. Roland C. Horton, Custodian, The Old House, to Northeast Regional Office, National Park Service, Aug. 18, 1961; Dorothy and Richard Pratt, *A Guide to Early American Homes, North* (New York, 1956).

55. Philipsburg Manor, Upper Mills, N.Y.: Eberlein and Hubbard, *Historic Houses;* "Sleepy Hollow Restorations," pamphlet, Sleepy Hollow Restorations, Inc. (Tarrytown, N.Y., n.d.); Reynolds, *Dutch Houses.*

56. Philipse Manor Hall, N.Y.: Rogers W. Young, "Philipse Manor Hall, Yonkers, New York," MS Report, National Park Service (1940); Eberlein and Hubbard, *Historic Houses;* Morrison, *Early American Architecture;* Reynolds, *Dutch Houses.*

57. Van Cortlandt Manor, N.Y.: *Sleepy Hollow Restorations* and *Van Cortlandt Manor, Croton-on-Hudson*, pamphlets, Sleepy Hollow Restorations, Inc. (Tarrytown, N.Y., n.d.); Merrill Folsom, "Old Croton House Is Being Restored," *New York Times*, Aug. 11, 1958; Rogers W. Young, "Van Cortlandt Manor House, Harmon, New York," MS Report, National Park Service (1940); Eberlein and Hubbard, *Historic Houses;* Reynolds, *Dutch Houses.*

58. Voorlezer's House, N.Y.: *The Story of the Voorlezer's House*, pamphlet, Staten Island Historical Society (n.p., 1956); Loring McMillen, "The Voorlezer's House," *The Staten Island Historian*, I (Jan. 1938) and ff. *passim.*

59. Big Hidatsa Village Site, N. Dak.: Edward M. Bruner, "Mandan," in Edward H. Spicer, ed., *Perspectives in American Indian Culture Change* (Chicago, 1961); Frank G. Roe, *The Indian and the Horse* (Norman, Okla., 1955); William D. Strong, "From History to Prehistory in the Northern Great Plains," *Smithsonian Miscellaneous Collections*, Vol. 100 (Washington, 1940); George F. Will and Thad C. Hecker, "The Upper Missouri River Valley Aboriginal Culture in North Dakota," *North Dakota Historical Quarterly*, XI, Nos. 1 and 2 (1944).

60. Menoken Indian Village Site, N. Dak.: G. Hubert Smith, "Explorations of the La Vérendryes, 1738–43, With Special Reference to Vérendrye National Monument," MS Report, National Park Service (1951); Russell Reid, "Report on Vérendrye's Journey to North Dakota in 1738, With

Special Reference to the Location of the Indians and Village Sites He Visited," MS Report, National Park Service (1942); Will and Hecker, "The Upper Missouri River Valley Aboriginal Culture in North Dakota"; Strong, "From History to Prehistory in the Northern Great Plains."

61. Forks of the Ohio, Pa.: John P. Cowan, "Fort Pitt, Pittsburgh, Pennsylvania," MS Report, National Park Service (1937); Letter, John J. Grove, Coordinator, Point State Park, Pittsburgh, Pa., to Northeast Regional Office, National Park Service, Dec. 28, 1961; Alfred P. James and Charles M. Stotz, *Drums in the Forest* (Pittsburgh, 1958); "Part One of the Report of the Point Park Commission," mimeo. (Pittsburgh, 1943); *Report on Forests and Waters—Land and People,* pamphlet, Pennsylvania Department of Forests and Waters (n.p., 1958).

62. The Printzhof, Pa.: Letter, Donald H. Kent, Chief, Research and Publications Division, Pennsylvania Historical and Museum Commission, to Northeast Regional Office, National Park Service, Apr. 6, 1961; Sylvester K. Stevens and Donald H. Kent, *Conserving Pennsylvania's Historical Heritage,* pamphlet, Pennsylvania Historical and Museum Commission (Harrisburg, 1947); Johnson, *Swedish Settlements.*

63. Wanton-Lyman-Hazard House, R.I.: Maud L. Stevens and Jonas Bergner, "Two Papers on the Wanton-Lyman-Hazard House," Newport Historical Society *Bulletin,* LIX (Oct. 1926); Antoinette F. Downing, *Early Homes of Rhode Island* (Richmond, 1937); Historic American Buildings Survey, National Park Service, 6 photos (1936); Morrison, *Early American Architecture.*

64. Adam Thoroughgood House, Va.: Morrison, *Early American Architecture;* Kimball, *Domestic Architecture;* Henry C. Foreman, *The Architecture of the Old South—The Medieval Style, 1585–1850* (Cambridge, 1948).

65. Bacon's Castle, Va.: Robert H. Land, "Bacon's Castle, Surry County, Virginia," MS Report, National Park Service (1937); Kimball, *Domestic Architecture;* Morrison, *Early American Architecture;* Thomas J. Wertenbaker, *Bacon's Rebellion, 1676,* Jamestown 350th Anniversary Booklet No. 8 (Williamsburg, 1957).

66. St. Luke's Church, Va.: James G. Van Derpool, "The Restoration of Old St. Luke's," *The Commonwealth,* Sept. 1955; *Historic St. Luke's Restoration,* pamphlet, Historic St. Luke's Restoration, Inc. (n.p., n.d.); Raleigh C. Taylor, "Historic Sites Survey Report on St. Luke's Church, Isle of Wight County, Virginia," MS Report, National Park Service (1937); Henry I. Brock, *Colonial Churches in Virginia* (Richmond, 1930); Morrison, *Early American Architecture;* Historic American Buildings Survey, National Park Service, 10 sheets and 15 photos (1890–1940); George C. Mason, *Colonial Churches of Tidewater Virginia* (Richmond, 1945);

Henry C. Foreman, *Virginia Architecture in the Seventeenth Century* (Williamsburg, 1957).

67. La Fortaleza, P.R.: Ricardo T. Reyes, "The Harbor Defenses of San Juan in the Sixteenth Century," MS Report, National Park Service (1955); Adolfo de Hostos, *Ciudad Murada* (San Juan, 1948); E. A. Hoyt, *A History of the Harbor Defenses of San Juan* (San Juan, 1944); Inigo Abbad y Lasierra, *Historia Geográfica, Civil y Natural de la Isla de San Juan* ([San Juan or Madrid?], 1782); A. P. Newton, *The European Nations in the West Indies, 1493–1688* (London, 1943).

68. Columbus Landing Site, V.I.: David J. Jones and Clarence L. Johnson, "Report on Historic Sites of St. Croix, Virgin Islands, of the United States—Part Two: Salt River Bay Area," MS Report, National Park Service (1951); Samuel E. Morison, *Admiral of the Ocean Sea* (Boston, 1942); Samuel E. Morison, *The Second Voyage of Christopher Columbus from Cadiz to Hispaniola* (London, 1939); José Gonzales Ginorio, *El Descubrimiento de Puerto Rico* (San Juan, 1936); Theodoor de Booy, *Archeology of the Virgin Islands—Indian Notes and Monographs,* Vol. I, No. 1 (New York, 1919).

69. Vieux Carré, La.: Arthur, *Old New Orleans;* E. Wilson Lyon, *Louisiana in French Diplomacy, 1759–1804* (Norman, 1934); Morrison, *Early American Architecture;* Robertson, ed., *Louisiana;* Christopher Tunnard and Henry H. Reed, *American Skyline—The Growth and Form of Our Cities and Towns* (New York, 1956); Whitaker, *The Mississippi Question;* Samuel Wilson, Jr., *A Guide to Architecture of New Orleans* (New York, 1959).

70. Colonial Annapolis, Md.: Matthew P. Andrews, *The Founding of Maryland* (Baltimore, 1933); Historic Annapolis, Inc., *Three Ancient Blocks of Annapolis, Maryland's Capital City* (Annapolis, 1963); Henry P. Hopkins, pamphlet, "Colonial Houses of Annapolis, Maryland, and Their Architectural Details" (Baltimore, 1963); Newton D. Mereness, *Maryland as a Proprietary Province* (New York, 1901); Morrison, *Early American Architecture;* Lyman P. Powell, *Historic Towns of the Southern States* (New York, 1900); Thomas J. Wertenbaker, *The Old South* (New York, 1942); Paul Wilstach, *Tidewater Maryland* (Indianapolis, 1931).

71. Huguenot Street, N.Y.: Eberlein and Hubbard, *Historic Houses of the Hudson Valley;* Morrison, *Early American Architecture;* Historic American Buildings Survey, National Park Service, various sheets and photos.

72. Hurley, N.Y.: Eberlein and Hubbard, *Historic Houses; The Hurley Historian,* periodical of the Hurley-Hudson-Champlain Festival Committee, I (1959) and ff. *passim;* Reynolds, *Dutch Houses;* Augustus H. Van Buren, *A History of Ulster County Under the Dominion of the Dutch* (Kingston, 1923).

CRITERIA FOR SELECTION
OF HISTORIC SITES
OF EXCEPTIONAL VALUE

1. Structures or sites at which events occurred that have made a significant contribution to, and are identified prominently with, or which outstandingly represent, the broad cultural, political, economic, military, or social history of the Nation, and from which an understanding and appreciation of the larger patterns of our American heritage may be gained.

2. Structures or sites associated importantly with the lives of persons nationally significant in the history of the United States.

3. Structures or sites associated significantly with an important event that outstandingly represents some great idea or ideal of the American people.

4. Structures that embody the distinguishing characteristics of an architectural type specimen, exceptionally valuable for a study of a period style or method of construction; or a notable structure representing the work of a master builder, designer, or architect.

5. Objects that figured prominently in nationally significant events; or that were prominently associated with nationally significant persons; or that outstandingly represent some great idea or ideal of the American people; or that embody distinguishing characteristics of a type specimen, exceptionally valuable for study of a period style or method of construction; or that are notable as representations of the work of master workers or designers.

6. Archeological sites that have produced information of major scientific importance by revealing new cultures, or by shedding light upon periods of occupation over large areas of the United States. Such sites are those which have produced, or which may reasonably be expected to produce, data affecting theories, concepts, and ideas to a major degree.

7. When preserved or restored as integral parts of the environment, historic buildings not sufficiently significant individually by reason of historical as-

sociation or architectural merit to warrant recognition may collectively compose a "historic district" that is of historical significance to the Nation in commemorating or illustrating a way of life in its developing culture.

8. To possess national significance, a historic or prehistoric structure, district, site, or object must possess integrity:

For a historic or prehistoric structure, integrity is a composite quality derived from original workmanship, original location, and intangible elements of feeling and association. (A structure no longer on the original site may possess national significance if the person or event associated with it was of transcendent importance in the Nation's history and the association consequential.)

For a historic district, integrity is a composite quality derived from original workmanship, original location, and intangible elements of feeling and association.

For a historic or prehistoric site, integrity requires original location and intangible elements of feeling and association. (The site of a structure no longer standing may possess national significance if the person or event associated with the structure was of transcendent historical importance in the Nation's history and the association consequential.)

For a historic object, integrity requires basic original workmanship.

9. Structures or sites which are primarily of significance in the field of religion or to religious bodies but are not of national importance in other fields of the history of the United States, such as political, military, or architectural history, will not be eligible for consideration.

10. Birthplaces, graves, burials, and cemeteries, as a general rule, are not eligible for consideration and recognition except in cases of historical figures of transcendent importance. Historic sites associated with the actual careers and contributions of outstanding historical personages usually are more important than their birthplaces and burial places.

11. Structures, sites, and objects achieving historical importance within the past 50 years will not as a general rule be considered unless associated with persons or events of transcendent significance.

12. Structures, sites, and objects proposed for addition to the National Park System must also meet standards of suitability and feasibility.

ACKNOWLEDGMENTS

Advisory Board on National Parks, Historic Sites, Buildings, and Monuments (1959–61)

Stanley A. Cain, University of Michigan
Edward B. Danson, Jr., Museum of Northern Arizona
Harold P. Fabian, Utah State Park and Recreation Commission
E. Raymond Hall, University of Kansas
Walter L. Huber, San Francisco, Calif.
John A. Krout, Columbia University
Frank E. Masland, Jr., Carlisle, Pa.
John B. Oakes, New York City
Sigurd F. Olson, Ely, Minn.
Earl H. Reed, American Institute of Architects
Fred Smith, Newark, N.J.
Robert G. Sproul, Berkeley, Calif.
Robert L. Stearns, Denver, Colo.
Harold S. Wagner, Akron, Ohio
Carl I. Wheat, Menlo Park, Calif.

Consulting Committee for the National Survey of Historic Sites and Buildings (1958–61)

J. O. Brew, Peabody Museum of Archaeology and Ethnology
Eric Gugler, American Scenic and Historical Preservation Society
Richard Howland, Smithsonian Institution
Frederick Johnson, Robert S. Peabody Foundation for Archaeology, Phillips Academy
Waldo G. Leland, American Council of Learned Societies
Earl H. Reed, American Institute of Architects
S. K. Stevens, Pennsylvania Historical and Museum Commission
Louis B. Wright, Folger Shakespeare Library

[423

National Park Service

Frederick R. Bell, Picture Librarian, Office of Information

Mrs. Eleanor S. Calhoun, Publications Branch, Division of Interpretation and Visitor Services

Vincent L. Gleason, Chief of Publications, Division of Interpretation and Visitor Services

Herbert E. Kahler, Chief (retired), Division of History and Archeology

Robert E. MacKay, Student Research Assistant

Charles W. Porter III, Chief Historian (retired), Division of History Studies

Rogers W. Young, Staff Historian, Division of History Studies

Other Individuals

E. O. Baum, President, Pasquotank County Historical Society, Elizabeth City, N.C.

Mrs. H. Beal, Photographic Library, Museum of the City of New York

Mrs. Gordon C. Berryman, Directress, Thomas Rolfe Branch, Association for the Preservation of Virginia Antiquities, Surry.

Mrs. Margaret C. Blaker, Office of Anthropology, Smithsonian Institution, Washington, D.C.

Mrs. Peter Bolhouse, Executive Secretary, Newport Historical Society, Newport, R.I.

Frederick A. Bonsal, formerly Resident Director, Saugus Iron Works Restoration, Saugus, Mass.

Dr. Mark F. Boyd, Tallahassee, Fla.

Dr. Peter A. Brannon, Director, Department of Archives and History, Montgomery, Ala.

Orin M. Bullock, Jr., Supervisor of Architectural Research, Colonial Williamsburg, Williamsburg, Va.

Miss Charlotte Capers, Director, Department of Archives and History, Jackson, Miss.

Waldo S. Carrell, Pensacola Chamber of Commerce, Pensacola, Fla.

Dr. H. Bailey Carroll, Editor, *Southwestern Historical Quarterly*, University of Texas, Austin.

Robert D. Christie, Director, Historical Society of Western Pennsylvania, Pittsburgh.

Walter A. Coldwell, Assistant Director, Florida Park Service, Tallahassee.

Dr. Ernest A. Connally, Associate Professor of Architecture, University of Illinois, Urbana, Ill.

Dr. Albert B. Corey, State Historian, Division of Archives and History, New York State Education Department, Albany.

Dr. Walter L. Creese, President, Society of Architectural Historians, Urbana, Ill.

Abbott L. Cummings, Society for the Preservation of New England Antiquities, Boston, Mass.

Miss Anna K. Cunningham, Supervisor of Historic Sites, University of the State of New York, State Educational Department, Albany.

Dr. Donald C. Cutter, Department of History, University of Southern California, Los Angeles.

Miss Elizabeth Dawson, Curator, Adam Thoroughgood House Foundation, Norfolk, Va.

Leon de Valinger, Jr., State Archivist, Hall of Records, Dover, Del.

Charles L. Dufour, New Orleans, La.

Harold J. Dyer, Director of State Parks, State Park Commission, Augusta, Maine.

Jack Dyson, Historian, California Division of Beaches and Parks, Sacramento.

Thomas S. Eader, Assistant Librarian, Maryland Historical Society, Baltimore.

Claude Evanhamm, Director, Museum of Man, San Diego, Calif.

Mason Foley, Town Historian, Hingham, Mass.

Mrs. F. E. Freeman, Custodian, Fairbanks House, Dedham, Mass.

Peter Geldof, Jr., Superintendent of State Parks, Wilmington, Del.

Dr. Benjamin Gilbert, Department of History, San Jose State College, San Jose, Calif.

Mrs. Alice B. Good, Director of Library and Archives, State of Arizona, Phoenix.

E. W. Gravolet, Pointe-ala-Hache, La.

Miss Pearl V. Guyton, Natchez, Miss.

Mrs. Ethel W. Harris, Custodian, San José Mission National Historic Site, San Antonio, Tex.

J. Carver Harris, Business Manager, St. Augustine Historical Society, St. Augustine, Fla.

Dr. Emil W. Haury, Arizona State Museum, Tucson.

Miss Gertrude Hill and the staff of the Library of the Museum of New Mexico, Santa Fe.

David S. Hugg, Information Office, Delaware State Development Department, Dover.

Wesley A. Johnson, Courtaulds (Alabama), Inc., Mobile.

Rupert S. Jones, Plant Manager, Courtaulds (Alabama), Inc., Mobile.

Douglas F. Jordan, Wakefield, Mass.

Miss Elizabeth Jordan, Fort Boykin-on-the-James, Smithfield, Va.

Miss Ella Jordan, Fort Boykin-on-the-James, Smithfield, Va.

Donald H. Kent, Chief, Research and Publications Division, Pennsylvania Historical and Museum Commission, Harrisburg.

Richard G. Kimball, Minister, New North Church, Hingham, Mass.

Dr. Lawrence Kinnaird, Department of History, University of California, Berkeley.

Mrs. Walter Kyers, Whitman House–Farmington Museum, Farmington, Conn.

Mrs. Sidney J. Legendre, Medway Plantation, Mount Holly, S.C.

Miss Bessie Lewis, Pine Harbor, Ga.

Maj. Gen. R. B. Luckey, Commandant, U.S. Marine Corps Recruit Depot, Parris Island, S.C.

Thomas W. Martin, Chairman of the Board, Alabama Power Co., Birmingham.

Dr. George May, Historic Sites Specialist, Michigan Historical Commission, Lansing.

Dennis McCarthy, Director, Arizona State Parks Board, Phoenix.

James Messer, Sr., Tallahassee, Fla.

Mrs. Florence Miller, Office Manager, U.S. Capitol Historical Society, Washington, D.C.

John B. Morrill, Forest Preserve District of Cook County, River Forest, Ill.

Dr. A. Russell Mortensen, Director, Utah State Historical Society, Salt Lake City.

Dr. Aubrey Neasham, Historian, California Division of Beaches and Parks, Sacramento.

Vrest Orton, Chairman, Vermont Historic Sites, Weston.

C. H. Overman, Jr., Pensacola, Fla.

Glenn Price, Historian, California Division of Beaches and Parks, Sacramento.

Anthony Ragusin, Biloxi Chamber of Commerce, Biloxi, Miss.

Dr. Frank D. Reeve, Editor, *New Mexico Historical Review,* Albuquerque.

Mrs. Mary F. Rhymer, Curator of Prints and Photographs, Chicago Historical Society.

Dr. Rupert N. Richardson, Department of History, Hardin-Simmons University, Abilene, Tex.

Richard S. Rodney, President, New Castle Historical Society, New Castle, Del.

C. H. Schaeffer, former Director of the Florida Park Service, Tallahassee.

Henry I. Shaw, Jr., Editor-in-Chief, Company of Military Historians, Washington, D.C.

Albert Simons, F.A.I.A., Charleston, S.C.

O. K. Sistrunk, Biloxi, Miss.

Capt. Pete Skrmetta, Biloxi, Miss.

Miss Eleanor Sloan, Secretary, Arizona Pioneers Historical Society, Tucson.

Dr. S. K. Stevens, Executive Director, Pennsylvania Historical and Museum Commission, Harrisburg.

W. S. Tarlton, Historic Sites Superintendent, State Department of Archives and History, Raleigh, N.C.

John O. Theobald, Phoenix, Ariz.

William Thomas, President, Fort Toulouse Memorial Park Association, Wetumpka, Ala.

William G. Tyrrell, Historian, Division of Archives and History, New York State Education Department, Albany.

Stephen S. Waligurski, Town Historian, Hurley, N.Y.

Dr. Clyde Walton, State Historian, Illinois State Historical Library, Springfield.

Dr. Joseph Waring, Old Town Plantation, Charleston, S.C.

Mr. and Mrs. Walter P. Warren, Bacon's Castle, Smithfield, Va.

Dr. W. W. Wasley, Arizona State Museum, Tucson.

Dr. Eugene P. Watson, Librarian, Northwestern State College, Natchitoches, La.

Justin Weddell, Pensacola, Fla.

W. W. Wells, Assistant Director, State Parks and Recreation Commission, Baton Rouge, La.

Samuel Wilson, Jr., New Orleans, La.

Ted R. Worley, Executive Secretary, Arkansas History Commission, Little Rock.

Index

mapped, 114–115; Md. fares better than other colonies in, 119; mineral resources of, 93; oldest church in continuous use in, 224; outlook and ideas in, 93, 131–132; planters and plantations in, 132; political atmosphere in, 132; population of, 91, 93; ports in, 157; proprietary, *see* Proprietors, proprietary government, and proprietary colonies; prosper, 84, 93; rebel against royal Governors, 133 (*and see* Bacon's Rebellion); religion and churches in, 131–132, 395 (*and see specific religions and religious groups and sects*); revolt, *see* War for Independence; roads in, 93; separate founding of, 93; settlements in, mapped, 84–85; social, cultural, and intellectual life in, 77, 131–132; southernmost settlement in, *see* Georgia; taxation in, 133; typical village in, 153; unify, 93; university proposed in, 394; voting in, 132; wealth and resources of, 93; westward thrust and frontier of, 73, 270, 378. *See also specific cities, localities, States, regions, and colonial entities.*

English common law, 78, 133

English language, 4, 6, 46–47, 93, 133, 140, 202, 340

Episcopal Diocese of Southern Virginia, 395

Episcopalians and Episcopal Church, 177, 208, 356, 395. *See also* Religion.

Ericson, Leif, Norse explorer-colonizer, 4

Erosion, stream, 236

Escalante, Father Silvestre, Spanish missionary-explorer, 39, 389

Esopus (city), N.Y., *see* Kingston

Esopus Creek (N.Y.), 288, 289

Esopus Indians, 288

Espada Aqueduct (San Antonio), 385

Espejo, Antonio de, Spanish explorer, 26, 182, 242, 244, 246, 250; route of, mapped, 26–27

Espinosa, Father Felix de, Spanish missionary, 387

Essex Institute, 348

Essington, Pa., 208, 325

Estero Bay (Fla.), 149

Estévan, Negro slave-explorer, 16, 23, 245

Estévan del Rey Mission, N. Mex., *see* San Estévan del Rey Mission

Estudillo, José Antonio, and Casa de Estudillo, 312

Ethnologists, 216, 338

Europe, and Company of the West, 67; and Crusades, 5; and Roman Empire, 4, 6; architectural styles of, *see* European architectural styles, *and specific national architectural styles;* ascendancy and expansion of, 5–10; cities and towns in, 5; claims (to 1763) of various nations in, in present U.S., mapped, 16–17 (*and see under specific nations*); commerce, trade, economy, and trade routes of, 5, 6, 8, 66–68, 100, 157, 171; culture and civilization of, in world, 6, 195; development of, and "barbarians," 6; diplomacy of nations in, and U.S., 3; economic, political, and religious oppression and wars in, 8, 286; England last of three major powers of, to settle New World, 92; explorers of, courage and resourcefulness of, 3; feudalism in, 6; first exploration of present Southwestern United States by nation (Spain) of, 16, 141; first explorer (Spanish) from, to sight and travel Mississippi River, 57; first explorer (Spanish) from, to view Grand Canyon, 25; first nation (France) of, to penetrate to Straits of Mackinac, 232; first permanent settlement by nation (Spain) of, in New World, 11; first permanent settlement by nation (Spain) of, in present U.S., *see* St. Augustine; first settlement by nation (Sweden) of, along Delaware River, 176; first settlement by nation (France) of, in lower Mississippi Valley and later Louisiana Purchase area, 143; heritage and culture of, in U.S., *see under* United States; imperial rivalry of nations of, *see under specific nations;* intellectual movements and Renais-

INDEX

stone in, 373; cities and towns in, 85, 110, 157; commerce, trade, and industry in, 91, 157–158, 228–230; Dutch explore coast of, 80; Dutch shipping at, 91; education and schools in, 132; emigration from, 85, 110–112, 114, 115, 374–375; England distrusts, 117; farming in, 112, 224; fishing industry in, 157; founded and settled, 105–110, 157, 221–232, 347–351; general court (legislature) of, 111, 132, 228, 232; governors and government of, 85, 109, 110, 111, 112, 113–114, 132, 228, 232; historic preservation in, 136; in Dominion of New England, 117; in New England Confederation, 116; independence of, 117; Indians in, 221, 222; iron industry in, 228–230; laws in, 132; militia of, 115; Pilgrims and Puritans in, *see* Pilgrims *and* Puritans; population of, 109–110, 116; prospers, 110; religion, churches, and witchcraft in, 110–112, 114, 115, 131, 132, 224–225, 374–375 (*and see especially* Pilgrims *and* Puritans); settlements in, unite, 115; shipping industry in, 157–158; soil in, 112; town meetings in, 224; university in, 132; voting in, 110, 113, 117. *See also specific cities, localities, regions, and colonial entities.*

Massachusetts Bay Colony and Massachusetts Bay Company, *see* Massachusetts

"Massacre Island" (Ala.), *see* Dauphin Island

Massacre Island (Minn.), 352

Massanet, Father Damian, Spanish missionary, 32

Massasoit, Indian chief, 117, 222

Matagorda Bay (Tex.), 60, 379, 380; illustration of La Salle landing at, 61

Matanzas (word), 152

Matanzas, Matanzas Tower, and Fort Matanzas National Monument, Fla., 22, *151–152;* illustration of Matanzas Tower, 151

Matanzas River, 152

Mather, Rev. Increase, English clergyman, 227

Mathews, Col. Samuel, and Point Comfort, 392

Maumee River, 64

Maximilian, Prince, *see* Prince Maximilian

May, Cornelius, Dutch explorer-colonizer, 80, 82

Mayflower (ship), 105, 107–108, 221, 222; illustration of signing of compact aboard, 106

Mayflower Compact, 107–108; illustration of signing of, 106

Mdewakanton Indian band, 235, 236

Means Creek (S.C.), 377

Meares, Capt. John, English explorer, 42, 369–370

Mecca, 6

Medicine, 16, 222. *See also* Diseases; Pestilence; Sickness.

Medieval, *see* Medieval architectural style; Middle Ages

Medieval architectural style, 287, 347–348

Medway Plantation, S.C., *375–376;* illustration of house at, 376

Meeting House, Mass., *see* Old Ship Church

Meilleur, René, and Meilleur House, 239

Meilleur House (Old Convent), Mo., 239

Melzingah Chapter, Daughters of the American Revolution, 361

Membré, Père Zenobius, French missionary-explorer, 58–59

Memorial House, N.Y., *see* Hasbrouck (Jean) House

Memphis, Tenn., 140

Menard, Pierre, U.S. settler, 336

Menard, Wallace, and Related Sites, Ark., *295*

Menard Bayou, 295

Mendoza, Antonio de, Spanish official, 23–24

Mendoza, Juan Domínguez de, Spanish explorer, route of, mapped, 26–27

Menéndez de Avilés, Pedro, Spanish explorer-colonizer, 20–21, 53, 150, 151–152, 328

(Rear end paper)

New York waterfront scene, in 1679. The Dutch *Stadt Huys* (73 Pearl Street) is the dominant building. During the years 1653–1703, it served as New York City Hall. From a mid-19th-century lithograph by G. Hayward. Courtesy, New-York Historical Society.

Elizabeth Barrett Browning

Elizabeth Barrett Browning

A   LIFE

BY

DOROTHY   HEWLETT

ALFRED A. KNOPF

NEW YORK

1952

L. C. CATALOG CARD NUMBER: 51–13218

THIS IS A BORZOI BOOK,
PUBLISHED BY ALFRED A. KNOPF, INC.

COPYRIGHT *1952 by* DOROTHY HEWLETT. *All rights reserved. No part of this book may be reproduced in any form without permission in writing from the publisher, except by a reviewer who may quote brief passages and reproduce not more than three illustrations in a review to be printed in a magazine or newspaper. Manufactured in the United States of America.*

FIRST EDITION

To

Gertrude Reese Hudson,

of the University of Texas,

in affection and

gratitude

PREFACE

THIS life of Mrs. Browning was undertaken partly to please my-self and partly because it seemed to fill a need; Elizabeth has for far too many years been remembered as the wife of Robert Browning, the heroine of a romantic love story, rather than as a poet in her own right. Little of her except the lively, eloquent letters was read, though there are now signs that her poetry is attracting new attention; indeed, Mr. Gardner B. Taplin, of Indiana University, with whom I have had the advantage of discussing our respective plans, is at present writing a critical work.

In her own time, and for many years after, the world agreed with Browning in placing her, not far below, but higher than himself. Then, for some forty years or more, she was practi-cally unread, jeered at as "Victorian," "sentimental." It is prob-able that we of this generation value her with more accuracy; admitting that a lack of sustained strength is, to an appreciable extent, atoned for by the sensitive quality of her writing. In-deed, a modern poet and critic whose judgment most of us place very high in poetic perception has gone so far as to as-sert—at least in private—that Mrs. Browning is a "finer" poet than her husband. Her handicap—particularly exemplified in *Aurora Leigh*—he considers to have been an experience com-paratively narrow.

Interest in the Brownings is to-day far stronger in America than in their native land; therefore it is fitting that this book comes first before the American public.

The main book sources of my biography are given at the end of this volume: to all concerned—writers, editors, publishers, and those kind American friends who sent me the newest ones —I render grateful thanks. Mrs. Gertrude Reese Hudson has been particularly generous, not only in the provision of books difficult to obtain in England, but in answering queries and in supplying me with a whole sheaf of notes collected for her life of Robert Browning. Miss Jeannette Marks was kind enough to obtain for me a copy of her *The Family of the Barrett*. I should like particularly to mention two collections of letters which came over by gift and, by their admirable editorship, enabled me to clarify various points: Mr. Edward C. McAleer's *Dearest Isa* and his article "New Letters of Mrs. Browning to Isa Blagden" in *PMLA*, September 1951. On one point alone am I at issue with Mr. McAleer: he says that the pronunciation of Elizabeth's pet name should be "Bay," short for "baby." I have talked with members of the Barrett family, including her niece, the late Miss Mary Altham, and they all called her Aunt "Bah." And would Kenyon have spoken of Elizabeth's "bay"-lambishness?

In regard to unpublished material, Mr. and Mrs. John J. Hagedorn, of St. Louis, Missouri, most generously put at my disposal their valuable collection in the original. The Henry E. Huntington Library, the Pierpont Morgan Library, and the Henry W. and Albert Berg Collection, New York Public Library, have also allowed me to quote material in their possession. Wellesley College has delved for me into its wealth of material, and Miss Hannah French, their Research Librarian, has been both prompt and kind in answering questions. As always, I am indebted to my friends, Mr. Maurice Buxton Forman and Dr. Willard B. Pope. Mr. Buxton Forman has given me unpublished letters to Haydon. Dr. Willard B. Pope has given me others from Haydon, and has also pointed out the Marsh papers in the Wilbur Library of the University of Vermont, which I am permitted to quote. Other unpublished material in the form of letters or illustrations has been supplied by Miss Henrietta Altham, Mrs. Violet Altham, Mr. Stephen Ballard, Signor G. G. Giannini, of Florence, Mr. E. R. Moulton-Barrett, Mrs. K. J. Moulton-Barrett, Miss Winifred Myers, of Bond Street, London, Mrs. Rayner Wood, of Old Colwall; Balliol College, Oxford; the Bodleian, the National Library of Scotland, and the Torquay Natural History Society. The use of unpublished Barrett Browning material without fee has been generously conceded by the copyright owner, Sir John Murray.

Information personally given me by members of the family —Miss Henrietta Altham, the late Miss Mary Altham, the late Mr. J. A. S. Altham, and Mrs. Violet Altham, Lieutenant-Colonel E. F. Moulton-Barrett of Jamaica, Mr. E. R. Moulton-

Barrett, and Mrs. K. J. Moulton-Barrett—has been particularly helpful. In talking with them I found odd scraps of information falling into place when combined with others they were able, from family sources or tradition, to supply. They have all been extraordinarily kind and patient with an inquiring author.

For help and advice I have particularly to thank Mr. H. Phillipson, of the Tavistock Clinic, London, for clarifying a psychological problem, Dr. Maurice Campbell, of Guy's Hospital, for discussing with me Elizabeth's malady, and my husband, Norman Kilgour, whose patient help has sustained me in a long and exhausting task. Others to whom I am indebted are Mr. T. B. Layton, of Guy's, Mr. Edmund Blunden, Mlle Berthe Esseiva, of Paris, Mr. A. Farquharson, of Ledbury, Dr. G. H. Gibbens, of the Devonshire Association, Sir Frederic Kenyon, Mr. Percy Lubbock, Mr. J. W. Lucas, Miss P. Morgan, of the Malvern and the Hereford Public Libraries, Mr. F. Morley, of Malvern, Signora Franca Adamo Paoletti, of Siena, Miss Janet E. Payne, Mrs. J. Hughes Preston, Mr. Neville Rogers, Signorina Toscanella Roster, of Florence, Mrs. Rosamund Rubens, Mr. A. Stonebridge, of the St. Marylebone Public Library, Miss Signe Toksvig, the Misses Woods, Mrs. Anne Page, who found both books and manuscripts for me in London shops, and Mr. Herbert Weinstock, of Alfred A. Knopf, Inc., for detecting certain small errors and inconsistencies.

Never before in my literary career has a book of mine been published first in America; that this book so appears is to me a peculiar gratification, not only for the reason given above, but because, apart from kindnesses detailed above, and many others in the past, Americans have always been particularly generous and understanding toward my work. I can only hope that in return I may give some pleasure and profit to readers who are bodily so far away but near in spirit.

DOROTHY HEWLETT

Hampstead, London
November 1951

81
61/28

CONTENTS

ILLUSTRATIONS

Elizabeth Barrett Browning

ELIZABETH BARRETT BROWNING

C H A P T E R   1

HER FAMILY AND EARLY YEARS

IN OR ABOUT the year 1795 two Creole boys and a girl, the grand-children of Edward Barrett of Cinnamon Hill, Jamaica, came to England to be educated. The eldest, named after his grand-father, was heir through the death of his uncles to the greater part of a vast fortune.

Young Edward Barrett Moulton (soon to become by royal licence Edward Barrett Moulton Barrett) was sent to Harrow School. There, according to time-honoured custom, he had to "fag" for a senior boy; a bleak change of circumstance to a lad pampered and petted in early years by slave attendants. He who had almost certainly never done a hand's turn for himself was now expected to fetch and carry, to perform such duties as blacking boots and preparing breakfast before school began at half past seven in the morning. One can imagine him neither efficient nor resigned: soon, in the words of Robert Browning, he "received there so savage a punishment for a supposed of-fence ('burning the toast') . . . that he was withdrawn from the school by his mother, and the delinquent was expelled."

Charles Moulton, the father of the children, was still living but had early separated from his wife and children; even con-senting, though his name was ancient and honourable, to allow his sons as inheritors of their grandfather to bear the name of Barrett. When the grandfather died, in 1798, James Scarlett, later the celebrated judge Lord Abinger, became their guardian.

Elizabeth Moulton (she never resumed her maiden name of Barrett) returned to Jamaica some time before her father's death in 1798, and it was during the years of her absence that Edward stayed with the family of John Graham Clarke, a rich merchant of Newcastle-on-Tyne closely tied in friendship and business relations to the Barrett family. For the rest all we know of him at this period is that he "frequently accompanied" James Scarlett "in his post-chaise while on circuit."

At the age of eighteen Edward was entered at Trinity College, Cambridge. One of his fellow-students there was John Kenyon, a West Indian cousin who had been at school with the son of another Jamaican family, Robert Browning, the father of the poet. Edward remained only one year at Trinity.

Edward Moulton Barrett is depicted for us about this time in a miniature by Hoppner [1] as a large-eyed youth with oval face, high forehead, longish nose, short upper lip, and slightly receding chin. A strong sensibility is apparent.

John Graham Clarke had five daughters. While still at Cambridge Edward declared his love for the eldest, Mary, a beautiful gentle girl of twenty-four. Probably because of his youth and the disparity in ages, Scarlett at first made strong objections to the match, but a meeting with Mary Graham Clarke overcame them. He exclaimed: "I can hold out no longer—she is far too good for him!"

Edward Moulton Barrett's determination to have his own way, to dominate his family, has become legend, a legend unfairly distorted: that he was essentially a fine character there is no doubt. He was upright, scrupulous, and kind. His children loved and respected him. As a man and as a father he must not be judged by the standards of today. Rich and apparently little controlled from an early age, the child of long generations of arbitrary slave-owners, he married while still at a formative age and soon came to the management of a large estate: power was native to him, a power confirmed by family obligations and sanctified by religious faith. In the words of his daughter, he took "it to be his duty to rule like the Kings of Christendom, by divine right."

Perhaps James Scarlett in finally consenting had, on consider-

---

[1] Reproduced in Jeannette Marks: *The Family of the Barrett* (New York: The Macmillan Company; 1938).

ation, thought the marriage of his ward with a woman older than himself might prove a salutary check on self-will. A wife of twenty-five, even in those days of legal and approved feminine subservience, could hardly be expected to submit herself completely to the whims of a youth of nineteen. But Mary's more mature age benefited neither herself nor her future family; she being, in the words of her daughter, "one of those women who never can resist . . . too womanly she was—it was her only fault." Frequent childbearing, twelve children in nineteen years, must have helped to weaken any manifestation of resistance Mrs. Barrett might have nerved herself to make: in yielding, the gentle nature did not itself escape harm, being, her daughter added, by the "thunder a little turned from its sweetness—as when it turns milk."

So far as can be gathered from incomplete evidence, Edward Barrett was a man to be pitied rather than wholly blamed. With his own high honour, his proud rigidity and self-exaltation as an instrument of God, he must have been a lonely man; a man increasingly alone as each family loss—some later of his own making—bereft him of cherished companions. The first bereavement came early with the death of his only sister, a pretty, lively child commemorated for us in paint by Sir Thomas Lawrence as "Pinkie." Miss Marks has pointed out how, like his daughter, Mr. Barrett reacted bodily to loss, anxiety, or grief, being subject to a sharp attack of the rheumatic complaint that early plagued him. We may guess him to have been in sorrow or in personal anxiety as inarticulate as she; but unlike her Mr. Barrett was no poet with a power to relieve feeling at least partially in the written word.

Such a nature must wound itself; and perhaps there was a hidden knife for Edward Barrett to twist in his essential probity. Noncomformity, to which he leaned in religion, was an acknowledged and active accuser of the system of slavery. It was by slaves, however humanely worked, that Edward Barrett lived: by slavery his ancestors had piled up great wealth. Custom and tradition may have enabled him generally to accept the system as a natural phenomenon, but those of his religion were constantly questioning and attacking it.

Edward took his wife to Coxhoe Hall, Kelloe, Northumberland, the property of his bride's father, and there on March 6, 1806, at seven o'clock in the evening, his eldest child was born.

As first born, and in the right of her own delightful gifted little self, Elizabeth early became a child cherished and especially favoured. She had the privilege of visiting her father's room in the morning, scrambling up with an effort on to the high white bed. Laughing, she would bury her head in his pillow and whisper: "*Baisez-moi.*" She seems to have spoken French, or at least some phrases, at a very early age, talking in that language, with a "*venez ici*" or "*couchez*" to Havannah, a poodle who was supposed to understand French better than English. Elizabeth, looking back at this early and tender introduction to a foreign tongue, declared that she liked this kind of French far better than French verbs, an atrocious invention, "probably Boney's own."

To her Uncle Sam, Edward Barrett's brother, always plain Sam to her, "Dear Sam," the child was a delight: he would jealously exclaim that he loved her more than did her own father. At his comparatively early death he left to her, and to her alone in the family, investments amounting to some four thousand pounds.

Elizabeth's name, a family one, was not given her officially until after the birth of her brother Edward a year later: when Edward was six months old the two children were christened together. This was an odd custom Mr. Barrett kept up to the end of his long family. Always two at a time were dispatched at the font; perhaps in a gesture of contempt for the State religion, with which he was out of sympathy. His early attitude to the Church seems to have been a mixed one: he apparently admitted the services but repudiated her large claim. On the title page of Elizabeth's Prayer Book (dated 1813 and with her name stamped in gold on the cover) "Church of England" is altered to "Church *in* England"; in "with notes by a member of the Established Church" the word "Established" is struck through.

The little Elizabeth, affectionately called Ba in her family, was small, dark, lively, and a self-willed child. At fourteen, looking backward on her life, she wrote:

I was always of a determined and if thwarted violent disposi-
tion. My actions and temper were infinitely more inflexible at
three years than now at fourteen. At an early age I can per-
fectly remember reigning in the Nursery and being renowned
amongst the servants for self love and excessive passion.

In her paroxysms of baby rage she was given to knocking over
small articles of furniture.

To a father so young this first child may have been a pretty
toy: we hear of one trick he played, lifting her on to a high
mantelshelf and exhorting her to be a hero and stand up
straight; which she did (to quote her own words):

straighter and straighter, and then suddenly was "ware" . . .
of the walls growing alive behind me and extending two stony
hands to push me down that frightful precipice to the rug,
where the dog lay . . dear old Havannah, . . and where he
and I were likely to be dashed to pieces together and mix our
uncanonised bones.

In 1809 Henrietta (Addles in the nursery), the first of her
sisters, was born. In 1810 the family removed to Hope End,
near Ledbury in Herefordshire, their home for twenty-two
years and the birthplace of eight more of the children.

Mary, the first born at Hope End, died four years later in
tragic circumstances: during an illness leeches were put upon
her with fatal effect. It is typical of Elizabeth Barrett Browning's reticence in grief that even in her youthful reminiscences
of the nursery Mary is never mentioned. Mary was the only one
of the children to be buried with the parents at Ledbury.

There followed over the years, and up to 1824, when Eliza-
beth was eighteen, Samuel, Arabella, Charles John (Stormie),
George Goodin, Henry, Alfred Price (Daisy), Septimus James
(Sette), and Butler Octavius, the youngest, familiarly called
Occy, or Occyta.

The father of these children, himself a young man, enjoyed
among them a benevolent autocracy, perhaps at first only to a
degree common in those days, but heightened because the
mother was weak. Among the elder boys he, who retained his
youthful appearance far beyond this period, must have looked
like a brother; and as a loved elder brother he seems to have
behaved, playing cricket with them and laughing among them

in a loud boyish way. Though the tone of the birthday odes customary in this family are in his case reverential, his sons' letters from school to their "Puppy" are not constrained: to them their father was far from being an ogre. Through years of arbitrary treatment they loved and respected him. The few letters too I have seen from him to his children are friendly, affectionate—even playful. When conveying his wishes he is firm but not dictatorial, often leaving it to them to make their own decisions. There is no doubt that his anger was sometimes capricious and to be feared, but there is no hint of the physical punishment usual in those days; and where temporary injustice might be felt there were always two devoted women in the house to run to for comfort, the weak loving mother and an aunt, her sister Arabella Graham Clarke, oddly called Bummy.

The lot of these children was cast in pleasant places: set in a wooded valley within sight of Malvern Hills, the estate, though now neglected, wild, is richly beautiful. Around the old house, now pulled down, Mr. Barrett laid out gardens, one of which was reached by a subterranean passage. By 1822 at least [2] there were "some fine pieces of water" and what appears to have been a primitive rock garden, "a very large projection of rock, which the taste of the owner has highly ornamented with a fine collection of plants." At some time during Mr. Barrett's ownership a cascade was constructed.

The house, originally a farm dwelling, was not well situated, being at the narrowest part of the valley, shaded from the sun and with a restricted view. The immediate surroundings, however, were serenely beautiful. Elizabeth describes in *Aurora Leigh* what was to be seen from the window of her own room:

> *First the lime,*
> *(I had enough there, of the lime, be sure,—*
> *My morning-dream was often hummed away*
> *By the bees in it;) past the lime, the lawn,*
> *Which, after sweeping broadly round the house,*
> *Went trickling through the shrubberies in a stream*
> *Of tender turf, and wore and lost itself*
> *Among the acacias, over which you saw*

---

[2] See Mary Southall: *A Description of Malvern* (London: Longman, Hurst, Rees, Orme & Brown; 1822).

> *The irregular line of elms by the deep lane*
> *Which stopped the grounds and dammed the overflow*
> *Of arbutus and laurel.*

Above the elms and deep hidden lane there rose "the folded hills, striped up and down with hedges," planted with burly oaks and fed upon at that time by many sheep.

The children lived out of doors in fair weather:

> *If the rain fell, there was sorrow,*
> *Little head leant on the pane,*
> *Little finger drawing down it*
> *The long trailing drops upon it,*
> *And the "Rain, rain, come tomorrow,"*
> *Said for charm against the rain.*

In spring, after lovely west-country fashion, there were drifts of fruit blossom in the glades; in the grounds a fine pear and chestnuts with their fairy cones of pink and white. About Hope End there were woods and rich deep meadows, a home farm to visit, and, more immediate joy, the children's own garden, where they dug and planted their plots in long narrow beds at the end of which was an ancient thorn.

In this Eden there was a reptile; not a snake, or the little green frogs which, to the horror of her nurses, Elizabeth loved to pick up and make leap from hand to hand, but an old toad who lived in the hollow root of the thorn. Elizabeth would stoop and peep fearfully into the blackness of the hole, convinced she could see glittering there the "jewel in his head." When he chose to come out and "sate swelling his black sides" she would skirt the garden through shrubberies, nearly waist deep in wet grass and nettles, to avoid passing him; afraid that he might spit poison that would strike her dead.

The pride of these gardens was Elizabeth's own white roses, which she grew to perfection. All over the estates were trees, young ones planted by her father—among them an avenue of oaks—and giants the children could climb; Elizabeth, scorning the limitations of her sex, being foremost in the sport. In this she was more fortunate than girls later in the century, her garments being light, almost petticoatless, with probably little more than long trouser drawers and a muslin frock to tear.

The house, a spacious Georgian edifice, must have been a

delight and pride to the children: as an expression of perhaps
a smothered fantasy, a hidden luxuriance of temperament,
Edward Barrett had entirely refaced it in a "Turkish style,"
"crowded with minarets and domes, and crowned with metal
spires and crescents." But to at least one of the children when
thunder rolled among the Malvern Hills, "where great storms
most do congregate," the house was a source of fear; fear
heightened by the comments of neighbours who declared its
minarets and spires to be a provocation "to every lightning of
heaven." "Once," Elizabeth later told Robert Browning, "a
storm of storms happened," and they thought the house was
struck.

*A tree was so really, within two hundred yards of the windows
while I looked out—the bark rent from top to bottom . . torn
into long ribbons by the dreadful fiery hands, and dashed out
into the air, over the heads of other trees, or left twisted in their
branches—torn into shreds in a moment, as a flower might be,
by a child! . . . The whole trunk of that tree was bared and
peeled—and up that new whiteness of it ran the finger-mark of
the lightning in a bright beautiful rose-colour . . . the fever-
sign of the certain death—though the branches themselves were
for the most part untouched, and spread from the peeled trunk
in their full summer foliage; and birds singing in them three
hours afterwards!*

To the personal horror was added another when the girl heard
that two people had been struck dead out on the Malvern Hills.

But storms were mere interruptions in the idyll of summer at
Hope End: the serene rich beauty spreading about that fan-
tastic house lived on nostalgically, haunted with bird-song, in
Elizabeth's mind, so that she wrote lovingly of it in middle age.
At nine years old she herself added a small distinction, a giant
("Call him Hector, son of Priam!") cut in turf under the shadow
of the pear tree and picked out in flowers:

> *Eyes of gentianella azure,*
>   *Staring, winking at the skies;*
>   *Nose of gillyflowers and box;*
>   *Scented grasses put for locks,*
> *Which a little breeze at pleasure,*
>   *Set a-waving round his eyes.*

Brazen helm of daffodillies,
With a glitter toward the light;
Purple violets for the mouth,
Breathing perfumes west and south;
And a sword of flashing lilies,
Holden ready for the fight.

And a breastplate made of daisies,
Closely fitting, leaf on leaf;
Periwinkles interlaced
Drawn for belt about the waist;
While the brown bees, humming praises,
Shot their arrows round the chief.

This child of genius was precocious, but at the same time a normal little girl, loving games, climbing, riding her pony, and cherishing dolls. Out in her garden bower overhung with white roses, or in "Elizabeth's room" (probably the library), a lofty place lit by a stained-glass window, she would read Homer in the original holding the book in one hand and hugging a doll with the other. Having already formed her habit of sitting on the floor, she would lean against a wall bending over with her dark hair falling about her face.

But though Elizabeth was encouraged to, perhaps carefully nurtured for a literary life, she was not always approved. We catch hints of music studies neglected and a murmur from her grandmother, Elizabeth Moulton, a lady of the old school who would "far rather see Elizabeth's hemming more carefully finished than hear of all this Greek." Elizabeth detested the stock accomplishments of a gentlewoman, needlework, music, and drawing. She acquired enough skill in drawing, however, to be able, later on her travels, to make quite adequately those little commemorative sketches expected of ladies at that time.

In the great hall of the house there was an organ on which some member of the household regularly played, as we can learn from some verses written by Elizabeth at thirteen describing daily life at Hope End:

To school till five! & then again we fly
To play & joy & mirth & pleasures ply.
Some dance, some fight, some laugh, some play, some squall,

And the loud organ's thunder circles all.
And then at tea we snatch a short repast
As long as one large plate of toast doth last.
At nine fatigued upon the grateful bed
We stretch out weary limbs and rest our head.

These children acted plays in the nursery, some written by Elizabeth, and had their own small charitable works. Over all there hung, as we may deduce from an observation on her own boy's freer upbringing, a certain air of evangelical strictness; a strictness common to many families at that time, which a large group of children, with their private jokes and activities, could resist without too much damage to young and tender consciences. Mr. Barrett was certainly no killjoy: he dressed up as "Grand Mufti" to amuse the children [3] and may even have taken part in their performances (see Appendix 1). In summer the family, in whole or part, was taken to the seaside. Elizabeth herself, as we shall see, even made an excursion abroad.

Elizabeth was early a leader among the children. On attaining the age of six, she rejoiced that there was in the nursery "no UPSTART" to dispute her authority, Henrietta being too young and Bro a gentle child who "never allowed the rage for power to injure the endearing sweetness of his temper." Though, as they grew in size and weight, brothers less pliant probably disputed this authority in the person of an elder sister who was exceptionally small for her age, Elizabeth stood out among them by a natural supremacy of mind. Bro and Sam could write verses, and at least two of the younger boys were precocious in development, but none had the same power of learning, the same fluency of expression. And within this child's veins ran the strange ichor of genius.

At the age of four she first "mounted Pegasus" and in her sixth year, for some lines on "Virtue" carefully written out, received from her father a ten-shilling note enclosed in a letter addressed to the *Poet Laureate of Hope End.*

[3] Juvenile family letter in the possession of Mrs. K. I. Moulton-Barrett.

CHAPTER 2

THE POET LAUREATE OF HOPE END

Ah! the poor lad in yonder boat
Forced from his wife, his Friends, his home,
Now gentle Maiden how can you
Look at the misery of his doom?

THESE LINES, the earliest recorded, and written in or before her eighth year, "on the Cruelty of Forcement to Man; Alluding to the Press Gang," are of double significance in the pattern of Elizabeth Barrett Browning's life; recalling not only those strongly humanitarian poems which moved the world, "The Cry of the Children" and "The Runaway Slave at Pilgrim's Point," but also the age in which the poet was born.

War, memory of war, rumour of war and an abortive peace, unrest among the hungry workers manifest in the notorious "Peterloo," a growing feeling for individual liberty arising out of the French Revolution, abhorrence of the slave trade, and its abolishment, at least officially, in 1807; widespread misery and want, revolt physical and spiritual, all culminating in civil disturbance and in strong Government repression with, in 1817, suspension of Habeas Corpus. Though deep in the lovely retirement of Hope End, the little girl, daughter of a Liberal, could not escape the impact of this turmoil upon a sensitive spirit. The misery of the agricultural poor was only too evident around her, the poor who were taken by her father as his special province beyond the formal duties of a landowner and Justice of the Peace. It is a local tradition that he opened a school in which each of his children had his own pupils; he certainly moved among the people, giving them active sympathy, ministering to soul as well as body.

In these ministrations, these unofficial visitings of the sick, little Elizabeth often accompanied him, seeing at close range dire poverty, a rural population starving amid plenty because of bad harvests and the oppressive Corn Laws. In the neatly

written manuscript book of which the lines on the Press Gang
form the first entry we find this appeal:

> *Open, Oh Charity, thy bounteous hand!*
> *Soften the Sufferings of the tortured poor;*
> *Blow out the flame of Vice's lifted brand;*
> *To Virtue's bower shew out the golden Door!*

The children of Hope End worked actively to relieve suffering:
the set of verses, the second of which I quote, and four others
were "written for the shop to be held in the Children's Garden,
the profits of which to be charitably used." An emphasis on
virtue in the poor, on the connection between a decent standard of living and a decency of behaviour, arose probably as
much from individual observation, from parental homily, as
from a convention in the moral verse of the time. The little
poet in "To the Muse" sets out certain definite aims:

> *Come forth my Muse, and tune the lyre so bright,*
> *The darkest soul illume with purer light*
> *And pour instruction o'er the embarrassed Mind*
> *And Godly Virtue in the Wicked find:*
> *Thus like the Sun who darts his brighter beam*
> *And shines with awe, and lights the shadowed realm;*
> *So strike my muse! and through the gloomiest way*
> *Shew Virtue's path and sing beneath her Sway.*

From this purpose, culminating in *Aurora Leigh,* she never
wholly departed.

In this mood, self-conscious enough in an evangelical household where every action was probably approved, censured, or
exalted by prayer both public and private, we have a "cau-
tionary tale," that of a naughty girl eaten by a lion in a forbidden wood. To this moral work, repeated in essence more
than once, we might perhaps give a personal application: the
woods lay thick about Hope End to draw little feet astray.

Other poems in this early manuscript book, quaint and
charming enough in their degree—homilies on virtue, lines on
cottage maidens, virtuous or otherwise—are not beyond the
capacity of any clever child in stimulating surroundings, but in
"A Song," written on July 2, 1814, we have a foreshadowing of
genius:

> *Peter Quarry he called all his vices together*
> *To meet on the green field, or bright yellow meadow*
> *Says he our acquaintance I fear will be short,*
> *For of going to virtue I've a great thought.*
> > *Singing fal lal, etc.*

> *So you must begone*
> *With your weeds and your bushes,*
> *And sweet virtue must come*
> *With her larks and her thrushes.*
> > *Singing fal lal, etc.*

Elizabeth never once, so far as I am aware, mentions Blake, but surely the *Songs of Innocence* and *Songs of Experience* were on the nursery book-shelf?

Many of the poems are celebrations of nature, often in the square-toed eighteenth-century manner of personification and moral deduction, but some a direct outcome of bright-eyed observation:

> *Wild were the windings of the stream*
> *And every plant and tree looked green—*
> *The violets raised their heads so blue*
> *And grass so green around them grew—*
> *Upon a bank of roses red*
> *Laborious bees on honey fed—*
> *A boy there wasted many an hour*
> *Watching the Bees suck honey from the flower.*

"Had this portentous little girl," asked H. Buxton Forman, "an 'anticipated cognition' of Shelley's poet watching

> *'from dawn to gloom*
> *The lake-reflected sun illume*
> *The yellow bees in the ivy bloom?'*"

In this album, apart from the domestic tributes and celebrations mentioned in the previous chapter, we have certain verses of more dramatic quality, such as "On an Eruption of Mount Etna: 8th May 1814," beginning:

> *Loud blows October's chilly blast*
> *And Etna's firebrands rudely cast,*

> *Many a cottage burns upon the ground—*
> *Many a thundering hissing's heard around—*

and (with a flavour of William Cowper) "On first seeing the Sea at Tynemouth" in the summer of 1814:

> *The German Ocean rolls upon my sight,*
> *A wat'ry world of brilliant light;*
> *The proud rocks overhang the sea,*
> *The sands afford a walk for me*
> *When there, the mighty hand of God*
> *I saw in every step I trod!*

In the same year she wrote "Hannibal's Passage of the Alps," describing in such stirring lines as these the effect on the Phœnician army of attacks by stoning from above the pass:

> *Down the steep hills fell Elephants and Men,*
> *Into vast Gulphs or solitary den—*
> *Where horrid fiends were gathering far and near,*
> *Such were their feelings amid War and fear,*
> *Where ne'er was heard the blithely singing Lark,*
> *Death takes them for his bloody arrow's mark. . . .*

Of Elizabeth's lifelong interest in novels there is indication in small prose works of fiction written this year, 1814. The prose is remarkably well constructed for so young a child. We know that certain poems were composed for sale in aid of charity: perhaps a note appended to a prose work "Sebastian" was written with an agreeably childish eye upon pocket-money. The tale is dedicated to her mother:

Madam,—

> *I request you to accept this little story for three shil-lings, and to write copies to be sold to the public.*
>
> > *I am, Madam,*
> > *Your most ob't Humble Servant,*
> > *Elizabeth Barrett*

N.B. You owe me 8d. for other things:—

At the end of another tale we have a further reminder that capital, commercial or charitable, was sometimes made out of poems and stories:

ELIZABETH BARRETT AS A BABY
from the lid of a snuff-box

HOPE END
from an early photograph

EDWARD MOULTON BARRETT
probably painted about 1820

Madam,—

It would give me great pleasure if you could dispose of "The Way to humble Pride" as you have done of the other stories— I am, Madam,

> *Your most ob't Humble Serv't—*
> *Elizabeth Barrett.*

Added to these are short moral essays "Of Prophesy," "An Address to Truth," in an elevated style of copybook maxim; in the main conventional enough, though one beginning "Where can happiness be found?" having its answer in:

To rise early and to let industry have a share in your time—to open your eyes, and your ears to the voice of the beggar,— to press humanity to your breast, and at the last, to ascend to Heaven, and to receive the reward of your labors—

suggests an early conviction resolutely adhered to through years of illness and sorrow. We do not know whether Elizabeth in health willingly practised the chilly virtue of early rising, but in a life restricted by ill health she achieved much for the cause of humanity; in herself attaining at length to a degree of spirituality so fine that one who saw her a few years before her death exclaimed: "I have never seen a human frame which seemed so nearly a transparent veil for a celestial and immortal spirit."

This manuscript book extends, with few verses for the last year, to 1816, the final entries including one scene of an original tragedy upon Regulus in French excellent for her age; but Elizabeth was now turning from original work, postponing it until she was older and wiser. "I read," she tells us, "that I might write." Study became an absorption. "I felt the most ardent desire to understand the learned languages. To comprehend even the Greek alphabet was delight inexpressible." She studied Latin and Greek under Mr. McSwiney, Bro's tutor, studies rendered the more delightful because they were shared with one dearest to her in life. "Literature was the star which in prospect illuminated my future days—it was the spur which prompted me . . the aim . . the very seal of my being."

At nine years of age, though she derived much pleasure "from effusions of my imagination . . . nothing could compensate for the regret I felt in laying down a book to take up a pen." She had first felt real delight in poetry a year before; reading *Paradise Lost*, Shakespeare's plays, Pope's translation of Homer, and Beattie's *The Minstrel*. It is an instance of the remarkable sagacity of this child that at fourteen she could analyse her attitude to poetry. The greater works mainly interested her for the story. "I was then too young to feel the loveliness of simple beauty,—I required something dazzling to strike my mind. The brilliant imagery, the fine metaphors and flowing numbers of 'The Minstrel' truly astonished me."

Of particular interest to a biographer is the occasional verse of this family, mostly birthday odes and tributes, a form of compliment in which the mother herself joined. The following, written by Elizabeth on April 27th, 1814 exhibits her father in a particularly pleasant light:

TO MY DEAREST PAPA!

> *Sweet Parent! dear to me as kind*
> *Who sowed the very bottom of my mind*
> *And raised the very inmost of my heart*
> *To taste the sweets of Nature you impart!*

I hope you will let us drink tea with you, and have your fiddle to-night—

> *Your dear child Elizabeth*

An answer to the Nursery.

She writes a lively and facetious "Epistle to Dearest Papa in London," another in the same vein to her sister Henrietta suffering from a cold ("Altho' dear Addles far too much you eat"), ending:

> *And I am, dearest Henrietta!*
> *Your very dear Elizabeth Barrett*
> *Compared to you, a chatting parrott.*

More seriously, the recovery of Baby Arabella from a dangerous illness is celebrated in a birthday address to her father. A visit to Matlock is described from the carriage stop at "the neat and smiling Inn" through a climb up shaggy hills to a limestone cave with underground stream:

> *Here heedless Ba, with magic wonder struck*
> *Her eyes upraised, she gave her foot a duck;*

> *The cavern dark, Papa's laugh resounded;*
> *Mama's, Bro's, Addles's all loud rebounded;*

and the glittering beauty of petrified spars with this comment:

> *The massive rocks upon an angle rest,*
> *Nature bears all these wonders in her breast.*

Then came the return to "the morning sun," quitting "the shadowy cave with vapours hung." After running down the hill,

> *Papa, so ever kind, our joys to swell,*
> *Led us to see the petrifying well,*
> *Where heads, wigs, baskets, eggs, lie on the ground*
> *Soon turned to stone, in dropping waters drowned.*

The last poem to be quoted reminds us of a young attachment too soon to be broken by absence, that to her Uncle Sam, written on a visit to his home at Carlton, Yorkshire:

> *Dear Sam, accept my humble lay,*
> *How dear to me I need not say,*
> *And when from Carlton I am gone,*
> *I'll never cease thy love to mourn;*
> *At childhood's age these faults forgive,*
> *When I am older, if I live,*
> *I'll offer better verse to thee,*
> *Who's been so very kind to me.*

"I'll never cease thy love to mourn . . ." This is more than mere childish riming verbiage. To this remarkable girl, later to become a woman of such deep feeling, every loss was, in greater or lesser degree, a memory lifelong. When in 1860, a year before her own death, Henrietta died far from her, out of reach of an ailing woman, Browning wrote: "She has borne it, on the whole, as well as I should have thought possible, but the wounds in that heart never heal altogether, tho' they may film over."

CHAPTER   3

A TRIP TO PARIS [1815]

"I WAS VERY MUCH delighted when I set off for France, and have never repented my resolution to go."

This beginning to "Notes on a Trip to Paris, October and November 1815," comes oddly from a child of nine: the story behind it, revealed in a letter [1] written from Paris by Mrs. Barrett to her mother, Mrs. Graham Clarke, is that "after the carriage was ordered dear Ba seemed so unhappy at our going" that the parents gave way and "she jumped into the carriage with us."

This was in London at five o'clock on the evening of the 17th of October. In the carriage were Mr. and Mrs. Barrett, the triumphant child, a friend, a Mr. Wyatt,[2] and a woman servant. Elizabeth "sat quite still and contented listening to Papa's and Mr. Wyatt's discourse which pleased me much, as Mr. W. told some very entertaining Anecdotes." Later she fell asleep.

She awoke at Rochester, where they spent the night. When next day they arrived at Dover, "only just in time for the packet," our travellers "were very struck . . . with the Castle, pile on pile, heaped on chalky rocks which tell the passing stranger it is England,—England the only asylum for the forlorn and the helpless!"

The crossing took two hours, "an excellent passage," the mother says, though all were seasick; Elizabeth and her mother not seriously and "more from hunger than anything else." At Calais French boats came out to meet them and a band of noisy, quarrelling, half-naked men walked out in the sea eager "to have the honor of carrying us ashore" and looking to the child's eyes "more like monkeys than men." Mr. Barrett at first refused to be carried; "however it was all in vain, they hoisted him off on their shoulders & away we went & were set down on

[1] This has been partly drawn upon in the following narrative.
[2] Probably the artist and landscape gardener who had laid out the grounds of Hope End.

the very fine sands from whence we had to climb a ladder to
the magnificent pier."

After "an excellent supper and champagne" (the best champagne was seven shillings a bottle) at "Monsr. Quillac's fine
hotel" and a good night's rest in clean and handsome rooms,
the little student of the classics awoke "as soon as Aurora had
thrown off the veil which covered the earth" to see out of the
window preparations to drive a light vehicle out of the inn
yard. She was "much amused with the postillion's great boots,
and their thin half starved and plough tired horses with rope
harness, and nearly died of laughing at the nodding Cabriolet,
and the slow motion of the horses, as they dragged it out of the
yard." This callous laughter at the suffering beasts in one so
gentle and pitying must remind us not only of her youth but
of the age in which she was born. Horses were but a means of
locomotion: the Royal Society for the Prevention of Cruelty to
Animals was not founded until 1824.

The party set off in a hired "German barouche" drawn by
four horses. In describing the journey to Paris Elizabeth very
naturally dwells upon good and unusual food. In Abbeville at
the Hôtel de l'Europe "the dishes alone were enough to tempt
any one from America to eat them; the wine too was without
exception the most delicious I had drunk in France." At Amiens
they admired the Cathedral and at Clermont found "the country full of Prussian soldiery," a reminder to us that this was a
France occupied by the victorious Allies. Waterloo had been
fought only the previous June. Finding but poor accommodation in a town packed with troops, they did not stay to breakfast at Clermont but drove on to Chantilly, where they took the
opportunity of visiting "the remains of the magnificent stables"
of the Prince de Condé, damaged when the chateau was destroyed in the Revolution.

On the evening of the 22nd they reached Paris, having their
first view of "the superb Church of St. Denis where the King
was buried." The martyrdom of Louis XVI on the scaffold in
January 1793 was still fresh in the minds of travellers.

In Paris, the old city of ancient streets, they found "a very
disagreeable smell." As they passed Napoleon's pillar in the
Place Vendôme the wheel of the carriage came off "and obliged

us to alight." When the wheel was put on again, they drove in weary search for rooms in a Paris crowded with troops and sightseers. Much of the accommodation was *"trop cher."* They found at last top rooms five storeys up in the Hôtel de Rivoli "at seven napoleons a week" (£7). Mrs. Barrett tells us the apartment, self-contained, consisted of five rooms "magnificently furnished" self-contained, consisted of five rooms and a kitchen. Out of French windows leading on to a balcony they could see the new Bourbon King, Louis XVIII, whenever he left the Tuilleries "and when he shews himself at the windows, which is once every day after Mass." Mrs. Barrett, though the stairs put her out of breath, was "delighted with our abode," where, even from her bed, she could see the beautiful Tuileries gardens. She acted as interpreter to her husband and Mr. Wyatt, neither of whom understood a word of French.

Here was Elizabeth in Paris for the first time among the people she was to love and defend so ardently in the person of the defeated Emperor's nephew. She visited the Louvre (where much of Napoleon's loot of European art treasures was being taken down to return to its owners), the Palais Bourbon, St. Cloud, Versailles, Malmaison (seeing the room and bed in which Josephine had died the previous year), china, carpet, glass manufactories, and the Temple of mournful memory. Here, having heard an anecdote of Louis XVI in prison, she remarked in parenthesis, having apparently already a healthy suspicion of official guides: "I ought not entirely [to] believe what every body says." In the Pantheon she was most interested in the tomb of Voltaire, an author with whom this precocious little girl was perhaps already discreetly acquainted. One case in her father's library containing among other books Gibbon's *History* and *Tom Jones* was forbidden her; so, she told Robert Browning many years after, "I was very obedient and never touched the books on *that* side, and only read instead Tom Paine's 'Age of Reason,' and Voltaire's 'Philosophical Dictionary,' and Hume's 'Essays' and Werther and Rousseau and Mary Wollstonecraft . . books I was never suspected of looking towards."

Our travellers spent a busy fortnight of sightseeing in Paris, even relaxing their British and evangelical prejudices enough to go twice to Mass. Mr. Barrett and his friend spent many hours in curiosity shops, then crammed with soldiers' loot, keeping poor Costa, their *"laquais de place,"* quite "out of breath running about." Mrs. Barrett indulged in a feminine pastime later to be loved by her daughter, shopping. She bought for £2 (having been asked double at a fashionable milliner's) "a highcrowned Spanish black velvet cap" trimmed with plumes of high black feathers "as Edward could not bear the great French bonnets."

But perhaps, even more than the Jardin des Plantes with its live animals, to little Elizabeth the most stirring sight was the Elephant, some forty feet high, erected in the south-east corner of the Place de la Bastille, a preliminary model for a grandiose monument Napoleon had intended to set up to the glory of his Egyptian campaign. Its trunk, she tells us, "is to cast up water, and there is to be a staircase up one of its legs into a room for people to walk up and down in, in its body." This symbol of egomania, of a power once thought invincible, was in his crumbling old age to be immortalized at last by Victor Hugo in *Les Misérables* as the night refuge of that lively street arab *"le petit Gavroche."*

Uncle Sam, intending to spend two years abroad, arrived with friends on November 10. Elizabeth was taken twice to the theatre, to hear Talma, in whom she was disappointed, and to a ballet at the Opéra-Comique. Through a delay in getting passports, two more precious days were spent with "dear Sam," who took rooms on the ground floor of the hotel, before they set off for home. "I could not help being sorry that we left Paris so soon." This sentiment had been prospectively echoed with a qualification in Mrs. Barrett's letter to her mother: " The amusement is varied & unceasing & nothing but seeing my darlings would reconcile me to quitting France so soon as we propose to do." At home in England there were now five other children including Charles John, a baby eleven months old.

They went back through St. Germain, "where we were obliged to sleep in the same room we dined in," and on to Meulan, where again Elizabeth had the excitement of a wheel coming off the carriage: it was fastened on for a few francs, securely enough to carry them on to Vernons, by those handy men the

English soldiers, some of whom were passing. At Gaillon there was the further novelty of sleeping, when the beds were found to be damp, on an extempore couch made of four chairs. Papa and Mamma, dozing uneasily upright, did not fare so well. At Formerie, the child records, they breakfasted on honey, butter, tea, pears, and eggs.

At Port St. Omer, Papa gave money to an old beggar woman who "crossed herself, then said her prayers, crossed herself again, kissed the ground, and stood by the door curtseying—as the horses came out of the yard, she pushed them away, because she said, it was holy ground." This would seem rather excessive thanks for a sou. Papa gave her another "to try if she would repeat her devotions, which she did, and as the carriage drove off she curtseyed, saying she hoped the carriage would not tumble over before we got to the end of our journey." Elizabeth's comment, "poor thing, she was, we were told, foolish," seems superfluous.

On the road to Rouen the child admired the Seine, with its wooded islets, flowing through thick trees and hills. At Rouen they found the Hôtel de France extremely dirty, and again were obliged to sleep in the room they dined in. The inside of the Cathedral Elizabeth thought "scarcely worth seeing." She was more interested in the immense tower, which had "tumbled down three times." They saw where Joan of Arc was burned, had a bad dinner, went to bed, and set off in the dark at seven o'clock next morning for Abbeville. There, on finding the former excellent cook replaced by one decidedly inferior, the small moralist observed: "On such little causes, how much of human happiness is founded!" They sailed from Boulogne on "a fine still evening, and the translucent water reflected the sides of our ship."

"Farewell to France," the little creature exclaims, "and to a people, tho' perhaps extravagant in their praise, yet fascinating in the kindness of their manners." Soon she rejoiced to find herself "by a good comfortable English fireside which, even foreigners must allow, is preferable to all the luxuries of the world."

Elizabeth at home was perhaps confirmed in complacence: a visit to Paris, and so soon after the termination of hostilities,

must have given further distinction to the child prodigy petted
and adulated. Some of this complacence, this good conceit of
herself which she deplores on looking back from the lofty pinnacle of fourteen years, was the result perhaps of a too rapid
development of mind. We find her logical where authority demanded that she should be respectful and obedient. One day
she fell over Uncle Sam's foot and did not apologize. When
asked why, she replied: "I did not mean to do it, it was an accident—why should I beg pardon?" And on meeting her father
one morning on the stairs she merely smiled at him. "Not a
word?" he inquired. She told him she had nothing to say. "Will
you not ask me if I am well?" "No—if you had been ill, you
would have told me."

Her father led her by the hand into the breakfast room.
"Here is a little girl who thinks it too much trouble to ask her
father how he is."

"In short," commented the sage of fourteen, "I was in infinite
danger of being as vain as I was inexperienced."

The sense of superiority given by studies in Latin and Greek
—the rapid power of assimilation and possibly a daily feeling
of triumph over Bro as they worked with Mr. McSwiney—was
heightened the following summer during a visit to Ramsgate,
where "the heated imagination was perhaps increased by the
intoxicating gaieties of a watering place." Here she began her
epic poem "The Battle of Marathon." Let us continue the story
in her own words: "When we came home one day after having
written a page of poetry I considered models of beauty I ran
downstairs to the library to seek Pope's Homer in order to compare them that I might enjoy my own SUPERIORITY. . . . I read
fifty lines from the glorious Father of the lyre.—It was enough
. . . I felt the whole extent of my immense and mortifying in-
feriority."

She burst into tears of humiliation. For a time she "could find
no pleasure in any book but Homer."

CHAPTER   4

THE BATTLE OF MARATHON [1820]

"At twelve," Elizabeth tells us, looking back two years, "I enjoyed a literary life in all its pleasures. Metaphysics were my highest delight and having read a page of Locke my mind not only felt edified but exalted." It was the direct influence of Locke that led her to examine her own mind so minutely.

This exaltation led to a healthy recovery of ambition. Perhaps strengthened by the composing of an epic poem in four books, Elizabeth felt equal to dealing with the loftier subject of theology and "was in great danger of becoming the founder of a religion of my own." In the heat of imagination, an unbridled fantasy, the plain worship in her own home could not then satisfy her. "I worshipped God, heart and soul, but I forgot that my prayers should be pure and simple as the Father I adored. They were composed extempore and full of figurative and florid apostrophes to the Deity." There had been a time when this child worshipped false gods, kindling altar fires in the garden to Athena with matches stolen from the housemaid's cupboard, but now she was fervently Christian. "I shall always," she wrote at fourteen, "look back to this time as the happiest of my life."

It was perhaps inevitable, in a household where too much emphasis was openly laid upon religion for the comfort of the young, that this precocious mind in a body approaching adolescence should be painfully disturbed. A happy state of religious certainty could not endure. Having omitted a prayer one day, the little girl feared she "had so offended the God of my salvation that I hardly hoped for pardon." Her prayers were long and agonizing. "My God, my God," she cried, "why hast thou forsaken me?" It was a dark morning, "a dingy mist floated in the mid air . . . a veil of loneliness." Then a flood of sunlight illuminated the child's room. "My imagination took fire and I believed that my God had forgiven me."

This paroxysm of conscience over, Elizabeth was reading and studying to but one end: "to gain ideas, not to indulge my fancy and I studied the works of those critics whose attention was directed to my favorite authors." Milton was read all through, Shakespeare studied; Pope's Homer was still a cherished book. Her "religious enthusiasm" having subsided, she took upon herself to advocate the cause of the Church of England, but whether in the presence of her father or the seclusion of the nursery she does not say.

In this year we get a hint of wholesome discipline. A petition was put up to Papa and Mamma in neat couplets, with this argument:

> *But if a hungry chicken wants to eat*
> *The hen throws victuals close, before its feet.*
> *Then let me to the Music Meeting go—*
> *The pleasure it would give me none can know;*
> *If you are troubled for my night's repose*
> *Half of Bum's bed is open to my woes.*

The petition, though, one may guess, supported by an indulgent aunt, was refused.

By the summer of 1817, we learn from a letter to her mother, she was already at work upon the preface to *The Battle of Marathon,* but the poem was not printed until 1820, when she was fourteen.

This youthful epic is both vigorous and sonorous, though perhaps an observation of her own in the preface may serve as a major criticism: "The battle of Marathon is not, perhaps, a subject calculated to exercise the powers of the imagination, or of poetic fancy, the incidents being so limited." Two quotations may suffice, the first being the opening of Book 3:

> *When from the deep the hour's eternal sway*
> *Impels the coursers of the flaming day,*
> *The long-haired Greeks with brazen arms prepare*
> *Their freedom to preserve and wage the war.*
> *First Aristides from the couch arose,*
> *While his great mind with all Minerva glows;*
> *His mighty limbs his golden arms invest,*
> *The cuirass blazes on his ample breast,*
> *The glittering cuisses both his legs enfold,*

And the huge shield's on fire with burnished gold;
His hands two spears uphold of equal size,
And fame's bright glories kindle in his eyes;
Upon his helmet plumes of horse-hair nod,
And forth he moved, majestic as a God!

These are the last lines of the epic:

By vengeance fired, the Grecians from the deep
With rage and shouting scale the lofty ship,
Then in the briny bosom of the main
They hurl in heaps the living and the slain;
Thro' the wide shores resound triumphant cries,
Fill all the seas, and thunder thro' the skies.

It is conceivable (though I know of no example) that a clever imitative child without genius, deeply read in Homer and Pope, might accomplish such an epic, though few could stay the course through four books; but the preface, dated 1819, with its close reasoning, its clear expression and disclosure of a strong critical faculty, could only have been written by the Elizabeth Barrett who contributed so much to that important book of 1844, *A New Spirit of the Age.* After commenting that "Now, even the female may drive her Pegasus through the realms of Parnassus, without being saluted with the most equivocal of all appellations, a learned lady," she continues in the following paragraph:

In these reading days there need be little vulgar anxiety among poets for the fate of their works: the public taste is no longer so epicurean. As the press pours forth profusion, the literary multitude eagerly receive its lavish offerings, while the sublimity of Homer, and the majesty of Virgil, those grand and solitary specimens of ancient poetic excellence, so renowned through the lapse of ages, are by many read only as schoolbooks, and are justly estimated alone by the comparative few. . . .

There are real poets among these prolific rimers "though they be mingled with an inferior multitude of the common herd." Here we, with the romantic age behind us, might expect the names of Wordsworth, Coleridge, Keats, and Shelley, but in 1819 these poets, so clearly to us the great ones, were little known or respected in the average cultured home: the stars in Elizabeth's firmament were Byron, Moore, and Scott.

Of Pope, whose couplets she imitated in this work, the girl wrote:

No one who has read his translation of Homer, can refuse him the immortality which he merits so well, and for which he laboured so long. He it was who planted rime for ever in the regions of Parnassus, and uniting elegance with strength, and sublimity with beauty, raised the English language to the highest degree of smoothness and purity.

Some twenty years later, freed from the strait jacket of pseudo-classical prose and poetry, she wrote of Wordsworth:

He laid his hand on the Pegasean mane, and testified that it was not floss silk. He testified that the ground was not all lawn or bowling-green; that the forest trees were not clipped upon a pattern. He scorned to be contented with a tradition of beauty, or with an abstraction of the beautiful.

Truly in this preface to her first printed work the child was mother to the woman.

One light-hearted family criticism came from Elizabeth's grandmother, Mrs. Moulton: "Your preface my dear Elizabeth was so formidable that I expected it would end in nothing less than a call on me to pay the national debt or the seven millions which it is said will be required to build the Prince a new palace."

The volume was announced on its title page as "printed for W. Lindsell, 87, Wimpole Street, Cavendish Square," but probably the whole issue of fifty copies came down eventually, if not at first, to Hope End. There are now only seven known examples, and of these not one was of Elizabeth's own possession. Browning, indeed, doubted its existence, writing to Thomas Wise in 1888 (with, by the way, a delicious unconscious irony): "I have a doubt whether *The Battle of Marathon* . . . may not be a fabrication." Elizabeth herself, who called it in later years "Pope's Homer done over again, or rather undone," probably wished this juvenile performance to be buried and forgotten.

In 1820 when, after the publication of this ambitious piece, she wrote down those revealing "Glimpses into my own life and Literary Character" from which I have largely quoted, Elizabeth was suffering from her first loss. Bro, her constant and adored companion, was now away from her for many months of the year in London at Charterhouse School.[1] In her new loneliness the earnest child prayed for his preservation from the dangers of a public school. "Heaven knows my heart that I would unhesitatingly buy his happiness with my own misery! But oh if there is a bitterness worse than death, if there is any pang which surpasses human wretchedness in agony it would be that with which I should behold him were he ever to stray from the path of honorable rectitude!"

At this maternal anxiety in a girl of fourteen over a brother a year younger we can smile, but it must be with tenderness, commiseration: in a few years she was to know the full loss of that brother.

After dwelling in imagination on the possible behaviour of Bro "when the laugh of dissipation assails" him, she ends this remarkable document with a final self-examination. "My disposition is haughty, impatient and fiery but I trust my heart is good—I am confident it is grateful." She is "capable of patriotism, enthusiastic and sincere," and must express her anger at "the base and servile aristocracy of my beloved country"; that aristocracy which was, in 1820, trying for adultery "our magnanimous and unfortunate Queen" at the instigation of a monarch notoriously unfaithful. Like most Liberals, large and small, Elizabeth whole-heartedly supported Queen Caroline. "The dearest wish of my heart would be to serve her—to serve the glorious Queen of my native isle." Elizabeth vented indignation in dramatic form, writing a first scene in very tolerable blank verse. A line and a half of it may embody a painful personal reminiscence of the trip to France five years before: "Think of me sometimes Charlotte! . . . I must pass that terrible ocean." The scene ends with this couplet:

> And I—I go to cross the dark blue sea
> Th'abused—the desolate—but yet the free.

This recalls, both in phrase and content, another object of scandal whose affairs, amorous and matrimonial, were attract-

---

[1] He was there at the same time as Thackeray.

ing attention that year. Lord Byron's all-pervading influence is apparent in the rhapsody which follows in the "Glimpses":

I have remembered the littleness of Man when compared to the Majesty of God and my heart has throbbed almost wildly with a strange and undefined feeling!—I have gazed on the fleeting clouds which rolled their light columns over the dark blue sky and wept while I felt that such was the futility of life.

But hers was not a nature to give way more than dramatically to that cultivated melancholy, termed Byronic, which had its roots in the eighteenth-century "graveyard school" of writers. Her feelings were acute, there is too much sentiment and "too little rational reflection" in her being, but she could control herself, and so rigidly that "I often appear to my dearest friends to lack common feeling!" This restraint went deeper than mere self-control: to the end of her life and even with the supremely beloved, Mrs. Browning remained dumb in suffering, only partially able to relieve herself in poetry. She never could speak of those lost to her.

Even in Byronic mood Elizabeth was not going to admit her outlook on life to be a gloomy one: she had far too much of native high spirits for that. Although there had been moments of acute disillusionment, "my views on every subject are naturally cheerful and light as the first young vision of aerial hope."

In some notes made in maturity on her childhood (which have already been slightly drawn upon here) Elizabeth gives a less self-consciously austere picture of her young self, telling how at ten years of age she was by no means indifferent to her personal appearance, but would tiptoe to her mother's triple pier-glass to admire herself "multiplied by three." It was perhaps at this time she demanded that her hair should grow from the fashionable short crop of childhood to the long tresses we associate with her: now as she gazed the child reflected that when her hair was down to her feet, perhaps when she was fifteen ("the age when all the princesses in the fairy tales were fallen in love"), she might be as pretty as Peggy, a local rustic beauty. She intended to be very much in love. Her lover's name should be Henry—unless, of course, he happened to be Lord Byron.

But at times another dream arising out of an early dislike and contempt for femininity, a resentment she had not been born a boy, dominated Elizabeth's thoughts. She was, of course, to be a poet, among women as Homer was among men: she would wear men's clothes and live on a Greek island girt by a sea turquoise-blue, or perhaps in a cave upon Mount Parnassus, feeding on cresses and Helicon water.

This girl, later to be such an ardent friend to women, then despised them all, with the possible exception of Madame de Staël. The fashionable mincing delicacies, the tender nerves and affectations annoyed her. She herself was not "feminine." She could run fast and jump high, and though her hands were "miserably small to be sure," her wrists were strong. She could climb and slide, and liked fishing, though she didn't often catch anything. She liked bows and arrows, squirts and pop-guns; but best of all riding, "galloping till the trees raced past her and the clouds were shot over her head like arrows from a giant's bow," on her black pony, Moses, who had a tail "longer by nine times than the patriarch's beard."

At fifteen she would arm herself in complete steel and ride along the banks of the Danube, singing her own poetry as she went and collecting many warriors. At Istanbul she would be the chief of a battalion, destroy the Turkish Empire and deliver Greece. These were fine dreams, in essence not wholly abandoned: Elizabeth was to do battle, not with an army but with marshalled words, for the enslaved at home and abroad, and in later years to exhaust her frail body in excited championship of the Italian *Risorgimento*.

But by the age of fifteen this little creature's fiery energy was to receive a sobering check: some accident or illness laid her on her back for several years, driving her spirit inward on itself and making her more completely the companion of books, of the mighty dead.

C H A P T E R 5

LEARNED LADY

ELIZABETH'S FIRST PERIOD OF SERIOUS ILLNESS was attributed by Lady Ritchie (*Dictionary of National Biography*) to a fall: impatient for her ride, the girl had tried to equip a pony herself and, falling with the heavy saddle upon her, had injured her spine. Pen Browning, Elizabeth's son, however, stated that the spine injury, not suspected at first, was caused by a strain while tightening the pony's girths. Perhaps, as Elizabeth remained so small in person, this pony was still Moses, an animal fiery and impatient as his mistress; loving his freedom and escaping when he could into the Malvern Hills.

If, as Pen Browning said, the injury was not at first suspected, a derangement of the nervous system may have been wrongly and painfully treated. On March 8, 1821 we find a Dr. Carden recommending shower baths and outdoor exercise. In the following June, Dr. William Coker diagnosed "the case of Miss Barrett, that prodigy in intellectual powers and acquirements," as a serious affection of the nerves, manifesting itself in severe bouts of pain:

The suffering is agony, and the paroxysms continue from a quarter of an hour to an hour and upwards, accompanied by convulsive twitches of the muscles, in which the diaphragm is particularly concerned.

During the progress of an attack, which would cease as it reached its terrible climax, "the mind is for the most part conscious of surrounding objects, but towards its close, there is generally some, and occasionally, very considerable confusion produced by it." On looking back in 1843 to this period of torture, Elizabeth told R. H. Horne: "at fifteen I nearly died."

Elizabeth, no longer able to take an active part in the children's games, was driven in upon herself: "in a retirement happy in many ways" she read "Greek as hard under the trees as some of your Oxonians in the Bodleian; gathered visions from

Plato and the dramatists, and eat and drank Greek and made my head ache with it." Her life was, she told Browning years later, lonely, "growing green like the grass around it. Books and dreams were what I lived in—and domestic life only seemed to buzz gently around, like the bees about the grass." She was fast developing in interests, in intellectual power away from the family in general. "My sympathies drooped towards the ground like an untrained honeysuckle—and but for *one,* in my own house—but of this I cannot speak." This "one" was, of course, Bro, that loved brother finally to be lost in circumstances of bitter tragedy. Bro, however, was at this time away from home many months of the year at Charterhouse School. Sam, a lively companion too, in his way, soon joined him there.[1]

On her recovery Elizabeth seems to have led a fairly active life again, though riding is no longer mentioned. She drove fast in a pony carriage about the steep leafy Herefordshire lanes; when her father went to Ledbury on business she would accompany him. Late in the century old people remembered the young girl with the pale spiritual face sitting waiting in the carriage for her father at the toll-gate outside Ledbury. She seldom entered the busy market town.

In these years, before the illness and after, she continued her studies, not only in Greek but in Latin and Italian. Of her translations there have survived examples from Moschus, Horace, Cicero, Claudian, Anacreon, and Dante. Later she learned German, probably some Spanish, and acquired enough Hebrew to read her Old Testament through in the original from beginning to end. On looking back in 1859 Elizabeth considered this period of intensive study, although she covered "a wider surface than most scholars perhaps," as a loss of time "and life." On her Greek, which included the reading of "nearly every word extant," she commented: "never was a vainer kind of smattering!" "I *believe,*" she added, "that nothing helps the general faculties so little as the study of languages." But, even if we can accept her conclusion, surely a survey of so wide a field was a fruitful substitute for the "life" available to a young woman of her period and circumstance, one largely limited to family, drawing-room, and a remote countryside.

[1] Family letters.

Of her studies in and about 1820 I have before me evidence in the form of small exercises, Latin, Greek, French, and Italian, some in the form of letters and—more important in the development of a poet—essays in Italian verse [2] (see Appendix 1), attempts which must have gone to produce that "strange music" which haunted Robert Browning and enchanted the Rossetti brothers. These small poems, for all their necessary faults, are lively and living products of the poet. Her Italian master was quite evidently a man skilled in the practice of verse in conventional eighteenth-century metres.

The subject matter of the majority of these poems is of vital interest to a biographer: she who in her last years was to be obsessed with Italy's struggle for freedom now sang of enslaved Greece, of the bid for freedom in Spain and the death by execution of Riego, the great Spanish patriot, of tyranny in Italy and the fleeing of her patriots to Great Britain. But in 1820 the emancipation of oppressed peoples, both white and coloured, British or alien, was in the air, heralding in minds and hearts the liberal reforms of the century.

These exercises in verse and prose, the probes of a genius rather than the regular product of a student, show signs of that impatience in learning, a desire to take all knowledge too rapidly for her province, which made the Italian master call her, in an effort to convey the adjective "headlong," *"testa lunga."* The Latin of a letter [3] containing quotations that are probably hits at her brother's lessons in that language is lively but not too correct. It is addressed on its outward fold: *Puero eruditissimo et elegantissimo Bro a menu stultissimi Sam de puella impudentissima—*

> *"Scribimus docti indoctique"*   *"O tempora o mores"*
> *Horace*   *Cicero*

On four octavo sheets pinned together [4] there are, besides Anacreontic Greek verses and short translations from Greek fables, letters in lively French dated 1820, to Socrates, to Pindar, and "Au Seigneur Homère, Les Champs Elyseès, Pres du Palais de Pluton, L'Enfers." She expresses friendship, though telling Homer (with a suggestion that schoolroom hours under Mr.

---

[2] Hagedorn Collection.
[3] Hewlett Collection.
[4] Hewlett Collection.

McSwiney were not always idyllically peaceful): *"Je vous assure que vous devez etre bien poli aupres de moi car Je vous ai toujours traitée en ami et J'ai soufferte beaucoup à cause de vous et du plaisir et du douleur—par l'esprit et par les oreilles!"* Cavilling at Virgil, who, professing friendship for Homer, stole from him, she calls Virgil *"un lurion, un coquin, un lache, un poltron"* —adding: *"Je l'appellerais tous les noms dont Je peux me souvenir."* She hopes *"le Seigneur Mercure"* will be sure to deliver the letter, says she has no time to write more, and assures Homer of her *"amitie eternelle."*

The letter to Socrates is more flippant. She doesn't know him perfectly but writes with as sincere a friendship as she is capable of. She had heard he has *"les manieres bien dures"* and a grave face, and that his beard is long and majestic. Her *"discours"* may seem to him *"trop gai"* though she is trying not to laugh and make faces. She would like to compose *"une harangue philosophique sur la materialite du corps ou sur l'immortalité de l'esprit"* just to please him, but can't *"à cause de mon papier et de mon humeur que n'est pas bien adapté aux sujets philosophiques."* But her *"amour propre"* flatters her he will be charmed with her because he is not too accustomed to politeness—at any rate *"Madame notre Femme"* is not at all *"douce."* She asks him to convey her compliments to *"notre bon ami Platon,"* protests friendship, and ends in a postscript with: *"J'espere que Je vous verrai souvent quand Je viens dans l'enfer—"*

To "Electric Pindar, quick as fear," [5] she writes her last letter, telling him she loves him *"a la folie"* though she can't understand him perfectly and has to use translations. She refers to Horace's complimentary ode to him (Book IV, ii) and at the end professes her love for him in these pretty words: *"Je vous aime au tel point que la mort seroit depouilée de toutes ses terreurs, croyez moi pour le seul plaisir de vous voir—Adieu—"*

It will be seen that the French is careless, especially in point of accents, but the idiom lively and characteristic. There is genuine appreciation and understanding of these great men; understanding to be expressed tersely in poetic form some twenty years later in "A Vision of Poets." Of the depth and breadth of

[5] "A Vision of Poets."

her reading before and during those twenty years we can turn to the "Vision" and see enshrined there Homer, Æschylus, Euripides, Sophocles, Pindar, Theocritus, Sappho, Aristophanes, Virgil, Lucretius; Ariosto, Dante, Alfieri, Berni, Tasso, Petrarch; Racine, Corneille; Camoëns, Calderòn, Lope de Vega; Goethe, Schiller; and a host of English poets pseudo-classical and romantic.

Of the classical studies, vigorously pursued again later with the help of the blind scholar Hugh Boyd, evidences remain in the form of volumes with her name written in them; many of them in duodecimo because, Browning tells us, her hands were so small she could not with comfort hold larger books.

But this brilliant girl was primarily poet, not scholar. The poetic ambitions were not forgotten. By 1822 she had completed a long poem and sent it to Thomas Campbell, the popular poet and editor of the *New Monthly Magazine.*

On August 28 Campbell wrote a tactful and kindly letter [6] in which, though he held out no hope that this poem was "likely to be popularly admired," he contrived without direct praise to encourage the young author; ending with:

I trust you will believe you have a

> *Sincere & respectful well wisher*
> *Thos. Campbell.*

This very naturally elated the girl: unwisely she sent him more poems, one of which appears from the evidence of a title page and dedication [7] to have been "Leila, an Eastern Tale." This title page of "Leila" bears a quotation that in its modest humour, combined as it was with a truly handsome tribute to himself, might further have softened the poet's heart:

> *"Duke. And what's her history?*
> *Viola. A blank, my lord."*
> *Twelfth Night.*

On December 1 Campbell wrote again, this time altering his previous formal address as "Madam" to "My dear Young Lady." As he had already applauded the symptoms of promising talent, "it was very natural for your youth & ingenuousness to throw yourself again on my confidence." He liked her "nothing

---

[6] MS. 1807, f. 79. Small Collections, National Library of Scotland.
[7] Hagedorn Collection.

the worse for a mistake originating in simplicity," but he was a busy editor; far too busy to "admit of renew'd applications for criticisms on the works of young authors, however promising they may be—I have neither eye-sight nor leisure for it." There, so far as we know, the correspondence ended.

To one of these manuscripts, probably that of "Leila," there is a preface in draft [8] which shows that the young author was contemplating the publication of another volume. This, however, perhaps because of Campbell's discouragement, did not materialize: it was not until 1826 that Elizabeth published *An Essay on Mind*.

Of Elizabeth's life in the years 1822 and 1823 we have little knowledge: she was writing, while perhaps working on "An Essay on Mind," pieces in the style of Byron and Campbell. Her brother Septimus was born, and William Wordsworth visited Uvedale Price at Foxley Park, only seven and a half miles from Hope End. Uvedale Price, landscape gardener, classical scholar, and musician, may already have been a friend of the Barretts, but it is almost certain that Elizabeth did not meet Wordsworth either on this occasion or in 1827, when he came to Foxley once more; however, in verses written at the end of this year on Storm's birthday (printed among the poems appended to "An Essay on Mind" as "Memory") his influence might for the first time be apparent in such lines as

> *My Fancy's steps have often strayed*
> *To some fair vale the hills have made;*
> *Where sparkling waters travel o'er,*
> *And hold a mirror to the shore.*

But as in these verses Elizabeth says her "chatting pen runs on," it would appear that she still did not regard the easier style as more than suitable to occasional verse; indeed, the later stanzas catch up the first line's personification of Fancy with Thought and Memory, Virtue and Learning in the old Popean way.

The year 1825 marked her first entry into the public press; a form of publication she was to favour even in her days of fame. William Jerdan printed in the *Literary Gazette*, November 19, "The Rose and Zephyr," a fanciful little piece of the love of a zephyr for a faithless flower. On May 6, 1826, the *Gazette* pub-

---

[8] Hewlett Collection.

lished her "Irregular Stanzas," lines of interest to us both as an early expression of interest in Liberalism and liberty and as an involuntary prophecy:

> *Oh! should I ever live to be*
> *On the sunlit plains of Italy,*
> *I would walk as they walk beside the dead,*
> *With voiceless lips and a soundless tread!*

Italy should be for her no land of mere art, of "Pleasure, cold and light":

> *. . . Glory was her ancient spouse,*
> *And her heart remembers its early vows.*

The mind goes forward in reading these stanzas to *Casa Guidi Windows*, to the *"O bella libertà, o bella!"* the singing child outside, and to the poet's declaration:

> *And I, a singer also, from my youth,*
> *Prefer to sing with these who are awake,*
> *With birds, with babes, with men who will not fear*
> *The baptism of the holy morning dew . . .*
>
> *Than join those old thin voices with my new,*
> *And sigh for Italy with some safe sigh*
> *Cooped up in music 'twixt an oh and ah,—*
> *Nay, hand in hand with that young child, will I*
> *Go singing rather, "Bella libertà,"*
> *Than, with those poets, croon the dead or cry*
> *"Se tu men bella fossi, Italia!"*

That year of 1826 was to see the publication of her second volume of verse, *An Essay on Mind*.

CHAPTER 6

AN ESSAY ON MIND, WITH OTHER POEMS [1826]

To HER SECOND VOLUME of verse, published anonymously, Elizabeth attached a modest line from Tasso: *"Brama assai, poco spera, e nulla chiede."* [1] Perhaps the choice of this motto denoted a determination to test public opinion: *An Essay on Mind* was, priced at five shillings, obviously not intended purely for private circulation.

Whatever may have been Elizabeth's original estimate of the title work in 1843 she wrote of it to R. H. Horne as

A didactic poem . . . long repented of as worthy of all repentance. The poem is imitative in its form, yet is not without traces of an individual thinking and feeling—the bird pecks through the shell of it. With this it has a pertness and pedantry which did not even then belong to the character of the author, and which I regret now more than I do the literary defectiveness.

The "pertness" or, more strictly, mild wit of some lines leavens a heavy lump for the reader of today, revealing more than in any other work, except *Aurora Leigh,* that innate humour which makes her letters so delightful. Its main interest perhaps lies in the passages on poetry and poets. Elizabeth and her world have, by 1826, changed in poetic taste: Wordsworth has done his work. We are invited to roam with "the musing poet" and with Nature to "steal instruction from her classic tome." There is an amusing scornful passage (though prefaced by a tribute to Pope as the poet of Reason) on the pseudo-classical drama of France:

>   *—'twere mean*
> *To leave the path of Nature for Racine;*
> *When Nero's parent, 'midst her woe, defines*
> *The wrong that tortures—in two hundred lines:*
> *Or when Orestes, maddened by his crime,*
> *Forgets life, joy, and everything—but rime.*

[1] Desire much, hope for little, and demand nothing.

This girl, forestalling Victor Hugo's attack, pleaded for poetry

Not clogged by useless drapery, not beset
By the superfluous word or epithet,
Wherein Conception only dies in state,
As Draco smothered by the garments' weight—

Among the thirteen poems attached to "An Essay on Mind" we find ample evidence again of that deep interest in Continental struggles for freedom. In style a use of obsolete words and phrases points to a growing absorption in the old literature, hinting at a mediævalism that she was to be among the first to make popular in later years. We get too a touch of that nervous, almost apocalyptic mysticism which her contemporary critics stigmatized as "dreamy"; a mysticism in which there is already a vein of sad foreboding. Among these minor poems is one astonishingly mature, the beautiful "Song" beginning "Weep, as if you thought of laughter!"

When copies of *An Essay on Mind* arrived at Hope End, Elizabeth was from home: Mrs. Barrett wrote to her of the family's excitement. The copies came about dinner-time, but both parents were too excited to do justice to the dishes of a cook with the charmingly apt name of Mrs. Tuckem. When the children were in bed—having had some of the poems read to them by Arabel—Elizabeth's parents sat close to the fire turning over the leaves of this "wondrous little book."

The volume attracted little attention: William Jerdan, who had published verses of hers in the *Literary Gazette,* and to whom the secret of authorship may have been revealed, printed a short review on July 15, in which her own advice to poets was returned on her: "All that we ask of the fair author is to address herself more to nature, and undress herself from the deep *blue* in which she is now attired." H. Buxton Forman suggested that the notice was written by L. E. L., a frequent contributor to the *Literary Gazette.*

It may have been a copy of *An Essay on Mind* that drew to the learned young lady serious attention from a distinguished neighbour, Uvedale Price of Foxley Park—though Elizabeth in a birthday poem to him in 1827 suggests a longer interest.

Uvedale Price, already known as a writer upon landscape

gardening, published at the age of eighty "a most ingenious work" (to quote his friend William Wordsworth) "on ancient metres and the proper mode of reading Greek and Latin verse." "If he be right," Wordsworth added, "we have been all wrong, and I think he is." This old man, "all life and spirits," still with a heart for youth, asked the young author of *An Essay on Mind* to read and comment on the proofs of this book. Elizabeth was "greatly struck by the original chain of argument." About the chapter on hexameters, with quotations from the English poets, she made criticisms, remarking on the omission of Dante from his catalogue of poets who "have done all that was possible in less perfect languages and metres," and citing as an "instance of metrical felicity" the last line of Canto V of the *Inferno:*

E caddi come corpo morto cade

with the comment: "It is almost superfluous to observe what a different character is here given to the iambi—(no longer *celeres*)—by the monotony of consonants and vowels—how much heaviness and falling and stiffness we have instead—how much of the 'Corpo morto.' "

There ensued a long and learned correspondence [2] and the development of a stronger intellectual intimacy. "Mr. Price's friendship," Elizabeth recorded in a private memorandum, "has given me more continual happiness than any single circumstance ever did—and I pray for *him,* as the grateful pray." Uvedale Price appears to have done much to encourage the young poet, thereby poaching perhaps on a preserve the loving proud father felt to be his own: certainly from a scrutiny of the memorandum quoted above, and from other papers before him, H. Buxton Forman thought he detected distinct signs of parental jealousy. But if Price did trouble the domestic peace it was not for long. He died in 1829, one year after being created a baronet.

It is probable too that another and longer friendship arose from the publication of *An Essay on Mind.* In Malvern there lived a blind classical scholar, Hugh Stuart Boyd, with whom Elizabeth corresponded. In 1827 a meeting was discussed; but, although Boyd was a middle-aged married man with a daughter, Elizabeth's father objected. When they did meet for the

---

[2] Unpublished, in the Wellesley Collection.

first time in March 1828, it was in a somewhat violent and dramatic manner.

Boyd is known to have lived in two houses at Malvern (then but a series of villages): Ruby Cottage, Malvern Wells, and Woodland Lodge, Great Malvern. There is also a strong local tradition that he was at one time in Rose Cottage, Barnard's Green. It must, however, from the internal evidence of Elizabeth's account of their first meeting, have been Ruby Cottage, or more correctly "The Ruby," which Boyd inhabited in 1827; probably as a lodger, since many of the houses already provided apartments for the people who came to take the pure spring water of the wells.

When Boyd wrote a long reproachful letter saying that he might soon be leaving Malvern, Elizabeth went in distress to her father and begged permission to visit him. Mr. Barrett told her she might do as she liked. A few days later she set out with Bro, Arabel, and Henrietta; Bro to pay the visit with her, and the girls to await them at a house close by belonging to some friends named Trant. Elizabeth was eager but intensely nervous, expecting in the learned man's conversation "something particularly awful and abrupt."

As they came to that precipitous hill on the old road beyond the Wyche,[3] Bro noticed that there was no drag chain to the carriage; but, having been driven down without one by a friend a few days before, Elizabeth urged her brother to take the risk. The pony, with the vehicle pressing behind him, rushed down the steep. Bro cried out: "Hold tight! don't touch the reins!" but Elizabeth, losing her head, seized hold of one. Soon they were all thrown out; fortunately landing on a bank at the side of the road. Only Henrietta sustained injury, and slightly, escaping with a bumped forehead and sprained ankle.

A coach going by at that moment, Bro put Henrietta inside and set off on foot with his other two sisters. Further on they came to the carriage, but the pony seems to have been out of action, or too frightened to handle. Bro unharnessed him, tied him to a tree and took the shafts of the carriage himself. He pulled Elizabeth along until, fearing he might be tired, she was getting out when Mr. and Mrs. Boyd appeared.

[3] Cars are not now permitted to drive down it.

Poor Elizabeth, covered in dust, pelisse torn and bonnet bent, had no choice but to go up as boldly as possible to Mr. Boyd and hold out her hand. Mrs. Boyd, distressed over the accident, offered assistance at her house, but Elizabeth felt that she must deny herself the visit and go to Henrietta at the Trants' house. Mr. and Mrs. Boyd walked along with them. Boyd, a man of natural gloom, reproached himself for having been the cause of the accident. "But this is ominous, Miss Barrett—I *hope* you do not believe in omens." She assured him that "a merciful preservation could not be considered a bad omen."

Elizabeth gave an account of this adventure in a letter intended for her grandmother, Mrs. Moulton, but on second thoughts preserved by herself for future reference. Of Boyd she wrote:

My eccentric friend is a rather young looking man than otherwise, moderately tall, and slightly formed. His features are good —his face very pale, with an expression of placidity and mildness. . . . His voice is very harmonious and gentle and low— and seems to have naturally a melancholy cadence and tone!— which is affecting when you look at his quenched and deadened eyes—totally and hopelessly blind. I did not see him smile once.
Even before she had left the Trants' house a note in fervent tone came to her from Boyd.

The key of his mind, one feels, was attuned to her own. It was not the mere accident of his blindness, of a retreat from the world, that later made Hugh Boyd the only confidant in the matter of her coming marriage. This man

> *Permitted, with his wandering eyes light-proof,*
> *To catch fair visions, rendered full enough*
> *By many a ministrant accomplished ghost,—*
> *Still seeing, to sounds of softly-turned book-leaves,*
> *Sappho's crown-rose, and Meleager's spring,*
> *And Gregory's starlight on Greek-burnished eves!*
> *Till Sensuous and Unsensuous seemed one thing,*
> *Viewed from one level,—earth's reapers at the sheaves*
> *Scarce plainer than Heaven's angels on the wing!*

—this man had much of her own spirituality and mysticism: his translations of the Christian Fathers were not wholly a mere work of scholarship. Though of an older generation, bound by

classic conceptions in poetry and religious dogma of a Calvin-
istic cast, his mind could range as freely between earth and
heaven as hers.

It was on Wednesday, April 16, 1828 that Elizabeth paid her
first call in less hazardous circumstances: a month later she
came to read with her new friend "the opening of Œdipus
Tyrannus." These two facts were recorded by him in his copy of
An Essay on Mind.[4]

This man was no compromising friend: as she read Greek to
him in his learned darkness he would reprove her sharply for
speaking too low, or at too high a pitch. He was captious, hard
to please, critical of her work: perhaps a certain astringent quality in him had its value to the girl so much admired at home.
She wrote at his dictation, corrected at least one set of proofs,
exchanged books with him, and, above all, drew on the resources of his classical learning. For a while she stayed with
him at Woodland Lodge [5] working in particular upon the *Aga-
memnon,* but it would seem as if the major part of their reading
together was done at "The Ruby." Of the three houses the position of "The Ruby" fits in best with the verse in which she recalled those "golden hours" in "Wine of Cyprus":

> *When, betwixt the folio's turnings,*
> *Solemn flowed the rhythmic Greek:*
> *Past the pane the mountain spreading,*
> *Swept the sheep-bell's tinkling noise*
> *While a girlish voice was reading,*
> *Somewhat low for αι's and οι's.*

"The Ruby" is built right against a steep slope so that the sheep
—formerly so numerous as to be, in the words of the present
owner of the house, "a great nuisance"—might have come right
down outside the back windows.

The friends could not at this time have met daily, as later at
Sidmouth: there were some seven miles between them and, perhaps, certain duties and anxieties at Hope End. Mrs. Barrett
was by now an invalid. But these two, the girl of genius and
the learned man, soon became intimate. In her letters ranging
from 1828 to 1832, written in a clear hand for the easier reading

---

[4] In Wellesley College Collection.
[5] Mentioned in a family letter, undated.

aloud to one blind, but unfortunately not dated, the mode of address passed from "My dear Mr. Boyd" to " My dearest friend."
In later unhappy days when her mother was dead, the home of
childhood already threatened, and Mr. Boyd himself intending
to leave Malvern, she referred to his companionship as "the
greatest & indeed only happiness which it is possible for me
now to possess."

It was about this time that the Martins of the great banking
family, already friends of the Barretts, came to live at Old Colwall, a mile away: they and the Peytons at Barton Court were
among the closest associates of the family at Hope End. The
Martins were childless, but at Barton Court there were
children, one of whom, Harry Peyton, is thought in the family to have been attached to Elizabeth. The Barretts were
also on friendly terms with the owner of Eastnor Castle, Earl
Somers, whose estate was adjacent: at one time Elizabeth was
staying with his wife, Lady Caroline.[6] There were also those
friends, the Trants, who lived somewhere on the way to
Malvern.

It is the Martins we know most about, because Elizabeth's
letters to Mr. and Mrs. James Martin have survived. They are
published unfortunately in somewhat shortened form; as, when
the Martins were abroad, it was Elizabeth's pleasant custom to
retail the gossip of the neighbourhood, these letters in their entirety would give us a more complete picture of the Barretts' social surroundings.

Mrs. Martin, though some years older than Elizabeth, became a close friend and confidante: it is from letters to her that
we gather much of Elizabeth's emotion and thought. As her
maiden name was Julia Vignoles it seems likely she was of
French descent. Her portrait, which I have been privileged to
see at Old Colwall, shows a pretty, dark, vivacious woman. At
Old Colwall, but a mile away, Elizabeth must have spent many
happy hours; walking perhaps in the ancient yew alley or sitting in a stone summerhouse of classic design erected by Mr.
Martin.

It is from a note written by Bro to Mrs. Martin [7] that we learn
of an illness of Elizabeth's about the time of her mother's death

---

[6] Family letters.   [7] Rayner Wood Collection at Old Colwall.

in October 1827. Mrs. Barrett died not at home, but at Cheltenham Spa: Elizabeth was absent from her mother's side at the last. Mrs. Barrett had been ailing for some years, though in the spring of 1827 her health had seemed to improve.

How far Mrs. Barrett had in her quiet way fostered Elizabeth's genius after the years of precocious babyhood we do not know; but we do know her loss was a material one. A tender love for her children is mirrored in the exquisite little watercolour drawings that she made of them,[8] the beauty of which cannot be guessed at from the uncoloured portrait of Elizabeth, drawn in 1823 during her illness, given in the volume of her letters to Henrietta.

To Mr. Barrett his wife's loss was certainly a severe one though, we are told in one of Elizabeth's letters, he gave courage to his family in their grief "by his own surpassing fortitude." The bereaved husband must have been lonelier because of an intense native reserve: he took Septimus, now a lively child of six, to sleep in his room.

There were other anxieties to harass Elizabeth's father at this time: we do not know how early Mr. Barrett found himself in financial difficulties, but it is certain that not until after his wife's death did embarrassment become apparent. There had been heavy losses to the Jamaican estate through enforced litigation arising out of the grandfather's will, and perhaps Mr. Barrett had spent too much on Hope End, embellishing at a heavy cost the interior of the house, making a show garden, and extending the estate. A reverse in fortune was carefully kept from his ailing wife: it may have been to this end that the estate was heavily mortgaged.

In or about 1832 the mortgagees [9] decided to foreclose, and we find Elizabeth writing to Boyd of intruding men measuring in the estate. When her young brother Henry asked them what they were doing, he was told: "making a new map and putting down all the improvements."

The inventory of the sale, which took place in London, at Garraway's Coffee House, Change Alley, Cornhill, gives de-

---

[8] In family possession.

[9] One of them, curiously enough, bore another name destined to be known in literature: he was a London solicitor, Sacheverell Sitwell.

tails of the elaboration of house and grounds. The drawing-
room had been decorated by Italian artists and, according to a
local tradition, took seven years to complete. Many of the doors
were inlaid with mother-of-pearl. The billiards room was ornamented with Moorish views, the walls of the library stuccoed.
There were windows of stained glass. The cascade was described as "a chef d'œuvre unrivalled in this kingdom." Mr. Barrett's gardens indeed were celebrated in the neighbourhood: it
is said in the family that Princess Victoria came to visit them
when she was staying at Malvern in 1831. While she was there
the young Princess opened the new Victoria Parade, now Foley
Terrace. Mr. Boyd wrote some courtly verses on the royal presence to which Elizabeth replied in more democratic tones.[1]

Mr. Barrett remained in possession of Hope End for some period after the sale; refusing to allow the purchaser, Thomas
Heywood, to set foot in the grounds. Heywood, as a neighbour
jocularly put it, was only able to view his property with a spy
glass from the top of Herefordshire Beacon.

Mr. Barrett was so severely wounded in his pride, so hurt by
these losses, that he secluded himself, even giving up attendance on religious societies which in Ledbury, his daughter
wrote, "he was so much pledged to support, and so interested
in supporting." He no longer visited the surrounding families,
even neglecting the Martins: for this Elizabeth apologized in a
letter to Mrs. Martin after the family had left Herefordshire, remarking that "painful circumstances produce—as we have often
had occasion to observe—different effects upon different minds."
This proud withdrawal Elizabeth could not approve, though
she could understand.

There were other preoccupations to exercise the mind of
Elizabeth's harassed father, and these perhaps not entirely un-
connected with those religious societies in Ledbury he was
now avoiding. Evangelical agitation against slavery, at home in
Parliament and in Jamaica by certain earnest preachers there,
had steadily increased during the preceding twenty years. The
slave trade had been abolished as early as 1807, only to make
harder the work of those slaves remaining in Jamaica, or born

[1] In Hewlett Collection.

ELIZABETH BARRETT
from a tinted drawing by her brother Alfred

HENRIETTA MOULTON
BARRETT
from a miniature

ARABELLA MOULTON BARRETT
from a photograph

there; although good masters, such as the Barretts, treated them with humanity. Samuel Barrett provided a mission home for an ardent Presbyterian missionary, Hope Waddell, and his wife helped to educate black children. In the words of Waddell himself, Samuel tried to "improve the condition of his people both for time and eternity."

But these measures, even if known at home, could only be soothing balm to a running sore in the public conscience. The institution of slavery must go. The slaves themselves, with a hope of freedom in sight, grew restive to the point of insurrection: in February 1832 news reached London of fifty-two plantations destroyed by them. Barrett property was unharmed, but the danger signal could not be ignored. The abolition of slavery, sooner perhaps than expected, was now inevitable.

At some time after Mrs. Barrett's death, Annie Boyd entered the household in a responsible capacity; in January 1831 she left rather hurriedly. It would appear from a letter to Annie written by Henrietta that there was some sort of trouble in the house which led to a desire to part with her services. Henrietta tried to soften the matter by adding: "we did not doubt your kindness, dear Annie, we know very well however painful it would have been to yourself you would have staid with us if we had asked it." This sudden departure took place after some illness of Elizabeth's; perhaps at the time of her mother's death. On the reverse sheet she herself wrote to Mrs. Boyd:

I am afraid I must have seemed in all your opinions weak & miserable lately. Weak I know myself to be on many points—but if you knew all, you might not think the weakness on this occasion, quite inexcusable. If you knew how she has nursed me in sickness & been indulgent to me in health & loved me always—how she has been considered by us all, as a second—that which we have lost—you could not think so. I cannot recollect that she ever by one act of positive or negative unkindness—by waywardness, or neglect or any other means, ever for an instant gave me pain.

This episode is somewhat puzzling: as Annie Boyd could hardly have been more than thirty (Hugh Boyd was fifty in 1831) she would appear rather young to be regarded as a second mother by young women in their twenties. Unless, indeed, Annie was not Boyd's daughter,[2] but the child of his wife by a previous marriage.

Probably Mr. Barrett was from home when this letter was written. About January 15 his mother, Elizabeth Moulton, died at her house in Baker Street, London. Of six thousand pounds at her disposal two thousand were left to Mary Trepsack (a ward of Elizabeth's grandfather, nurse to her father in childhood and long Mrs. Moulton's companion) and four thousand to her eldest grandchild. Elizabeth, through the grandmother's benefaction and money later to come to her from her uncle, was the only member of the Barrett family financially independent of its head.

Apart from this domestic loss, Mr. Barrett must have been much away from Hope End that year: it was perhaps because of frequent absences that he put Annie Boyd in charge. Business cares were heavy and a new dwelling-place must be found. In the spring of 1832 we find him writing to his brother in Jamaica:

I expect soon to return into Herefordshire, altho' it will be for a distressing object—the packing up of all my things for removing hence; God knows where; but He knows best. I dread much the effect on my dear Children in tearing them away from their most happy associations.

Edward Barrett must bear this burden alone. His natural reticence, a self-made barrier between himself and his children, prevented confidence even to Elizabeth. But his courage was notable. When in late summer the break came, "though he had not power to say *one word,* he could play at cricket with the boys on the very last evening."

Escorted by their Aunt "Bummy," the family were to travel together to a temporary home in Sidmouth, Devon, leaving behind at Hope End only the father and Bro; but "half an hour before we set off," Elizabeth told Mrs. Martin in her first letter from Sidmouth, "papa found out that he *could not* part with Sette, who sleeps with him, and is always an amusing companion to him." Unwilling, however, to separate him "from his lit-

---

[2] In the only account (undocumented) we have of Boyd's life his daughter's name is given as Henrietta.

tle playfellows," Mr. Barrett asked the child if he very much wished to go. "Sette's heart was quite full, but he answered immediately, 'Oh, no, papa, I would *much* rather stay with *you.*'"

To Elizabeth the parting from Hope End was inexpressibly painful: she drove off in the carriage weeping bitterly. Of her grief some old servants who stayed behind spoke to a tender-hearted intelligent little girl of four, Mary Heywood, the daughter of Hope End's new proprietor. With "a sort of loyal sympathy" the child tended Elizabeth's favourite flowers in her own small garden and thought how happy she was "to live in such a lovely home while she was pining somewhere far away." [3]

The night of their departure the family slept at York House, Bath, proceeding through country that Elizabeth, with the memory of Hope End so painfully before her, could not admire. They arrived late at Sidmouth to find themselves, although it was almost dark, "besieged by a crowd of disinterested tradespeople, who *would* attend us through the town to our house, to help to unload the carriages." To their dismay they found their new home in total darkness, "not a rushlight burning," and nobody to welcome them: their arrival, which had been daily expected for three weeks, had now been despaired of.

At Sidmouth the Barretts were to live three years; years happy and unhappy to Elizabeth, but spent by a sea which could as yet bring her only joy.

[3] *Mary Sumner, her Life and Work* (1921). Mary Heywood, as Mrs. Sumner, was the founder of "The Mothers' Union."

CHAPTER 7

AT SIDMOUTH; *PROMETHEUS BOUND* [1832–5]

THE HOUSE TO WHICH the Barretts came in the dusk of a summer evening was 8, Fortfield Terrace, facing the sea; standing then on open land "with pleasant green hills and trees behind." It is singled out by a plaque on the pediment above bearing a double-headed eagle commemorating a short stay there in 1831 of the Grand Duchess Helena, a member of the Russian royal family.

All, with the exception of Aunt Arabella, took an immediate liking to Sidmouth. Elizabeth especially enjoyed the view from the drawing-room windows. "I always thought," she told Mrs. Martin, "that the sea was the sublimest object in nature. . . . *There*, the Almighty's form glasses itself in tempests—and not only in tempests, but in calm—in space, in eternal motion, in eternal regularity. How can we look at it, and consider our puny sorrows, and not say, 'We are dumb—because *Thou* didst it'?" In a few years, however, when a loss more dire than that of mother and home afflicted her, Elizabeth could derive no comfort, experience no resignation from an aspect of that sea.

She rode on a donkey sometimes at the sea's edge, slept soundly in the mild air, and admired the myrtle, the verbena, and hydrangeas tall and luxuriant in that southern climate. By the end of the month the rest of the family had joined them, "dear papa in good spirits, and not only satisfied but pleased with this place." Every day Elizabeth, on donkey-back, accompanied the children in their walks, and often the father came too. Even more than donkey rides she enjoyed a family excursion in their boat. But the memory of Hope End, or home as she was to call it yearningly in her thoughts, overshadowed these pleasures for Elizabeth; and soon there was added anxiety when sporadic but fatal cases of cholera were reported in the town.

Happily untouched by this foul result of bad drainage, the younger children tasted true seaside delights. Alfred, Sette, and Occy, in studying "the art of catching shrimps," soaked themselves up to their waists "like professors." For the older Barretts there was trout fishing in the Otter and the "noble river Sid." Although yearning for her native Herefordshire, Elizabeth had to admit the country round to be beautiful, its green shady lanes unrivalled: her own "love of water" concentrated "itself in the boat" when the sea was calm. It was here at Sidmouth that her poem "The Sea-mew," so justly admired by Miss Mitford, was written.

The more social members of the family, Sam and Henrietta among them, could enjoy intercourse with people of their own class inhabiting pretty thatched houses termed "cottages" in echo of an earlier fashionable rusticity. Elizabeth, however, tended to move, perhaps in company with her father, in a more serious circle, the centre of which was the Reverend George Barrett Hunter,[1] a Nonconformist minister.

One loss Elizabeth must have felt keenly on leaving Hope End was the learned companionship of Hugh Stuart Boyd: an intercourse with him entirely on paper was particularly unsatisfactory because her correspondent was a blind man. Boyd was able to write his own letters, but naturally he could not read them through. Her irascible friend was apt to fling his thoughts or feelings on to paper without regard to the susceptibilities of the recipient. "It has always been my habit," he had written her directly after their first meeting, "to express what I feel at the moment whether it be judicious or not." Once Boyd expressed impatience at the length of her letters from Sidmouth, making Elizabeth fear that his affection for her had cooled. She wrote humbly:

I consider the fault to be, in all probability, not yours but mine. I have observed that people in general who have liked me best, have liked me better at first than afterwards: and I used once to imagine (in my infinite modesty) that this was caused by my not being very apt to like them in return. I do not understand why people should like me better at first: for I am very certain of not pretending to be what I am not, & of there being in my

---

[1] Was he related to the Barretts?

dull shy manner, no purpureus pannus, *to catch the eye in an exordium.*

But Boyd, who appears to have left Malvern about the same time as the Barretts removed from Hope End, soon came to live at Sidmouth, and not five minutes distant from Elizabeth. Now the old communion of minds was re-established, strengthened by frequent meeting. Elizabeth would see him most days, sometimes running the short distance between their houses that she might not lose a moment of her friend's company. They resumed their Greek studies; and she had the privilege of writing down those translations of the Christian Fathers made in a learned darkness. In 1834 extracts from these translations were presented in a work published by a Sidmouth bookseller, *The Fathers not Papists, or Six Discourses by the most eloquent Fathers of the Church.* This title gives a clue to another aspect of Boyd, his passionate Protestantism.

Between the two there was friendly rivalry as to who had the best memory for classic verse: in 1832, on the anniversary of her mother's birthday, Elizabeth set down on paper the "Number of Lines which I can repeat," 3,280 in Greek prose, ranging from the Septuagint and Greek Testament through the Christian Fathers to "a few passages of Heathen writers," and in Greek verse 4,420, among which Æschylus stands first with 1,800 and the Hymns of Synesius second with 1,310.

That lines from Æschylus should be the most numerous was natural since Elizabeth was now translating, or contemplating the translation of, *Prometheus Vinctus.* This was published in 1833 by J. A. Valpy, of Red Lion Court, Fleet Street, priced five shillings, as "by the author of *An Essay on Mind.*"

In some fine verses accompanying a copy to a friend, almost certainly Hugh Boyd, she wrote:

> *To thee, acquaint with each*
> *Divinest song the Attic muses bring*
> *In golden urns from out that ancient spring*
>   *Of their own charmèd speech,*
> *How dark and dank this water will beseem*
>   *Among whose trembling reeds*
>   *A pale thin echo feeds*
> *Upon the distant tune of fairer stream.*

This modesty was to grow into positive shame: of the merits of her translation other than its accuracy, Elizabeth wrote in 1845 to another student of Greek, Robert Browning, that it was "the whole together as cold as Caucasus, and as flat as the nearest plain." The first had been hurriedly made in less than a fortnight: in 1844, or early 1845, Elizabeth was employing the long slow hours of an invalid life in a new rendering to "wash away the transgression." This fine and accurate translation admirably catches the spirit of the original: the progress she had made in handling language can be realized by comparing the two presentations of Prometheus' first great speech beginning in both versions as "O holy æther, and swift-wingèd winds."

While some ten years later Elizabeth was making this atonement the unsold copies of the 1833 edition lay "safely locked in the wardrobe of papa's bedroom, entombed as safely as Œdipus among the olives." Ultimately, one supposes they were, as Elizabeth herself wished, destroyed: the edition is very scarce today. Of original work included in this volume she wrote to Horne in 1843: "A few of the fugitive poems connected with that translation may be worth a little perhaps; but they have not so much goodness as to overcome the badness of the blasphemy of Æschylus."

The volume, like its predecessor, attracted little notice: the *Athenæum,* later to do her high honour and publish much of her work, merely advised "those who adventure into the hazardous lists of poetic translation to touch anyone rather than Æschylus; and they may take warning by the author before us." This critic ignored the 'fugitive poems'; poems that included "The Picture Gallery at Penshurst."

There is in these poems a sorrowfulness of tone, a sense of personal loss which it would be tempting, if such easy speculations were not dangerous, to attribute to frustrated love: certainly in "Idols" there is one direct expression of the unsatisfying quality of all earthly things; her "oldest worshipping" of natural beauty, that—almost as early—of "Moloch Fame," and

> *Last, human Love, thy Lares greeting,*
> *To rest and warmth I vowed my years,*
> *To rest? how wild my pulse is beating!*
> *To warmth? ah me! my burning tears.*

This surely would appear an overstatement of any purely domestic trouble or loss; unless, of course, the piece is merely dramatic, Byronic in tone. But we find the same melancholy note in a sad poem "The Autumn" where this woman nearing the age of thirty laments:

> *Youth fades; and then, the joys of youth,*
> *Which once refreshed our mind,*
> *Shall come—as, on these sighing winds,*
> *The chilling autumn wind.*

She is turning more and more to God, saying boldly that all true values are spiritual; crying out "How beautiful is earth!" but seeing it as in an apocalyptic vision. The last lines of that strong fragment "The Tempest," in which the end of the world is depicted in horrible detail, claim through the salvation of Christ a protection against natural human fear:

> *High-seeming Death, I dare thee! and have hope,*
> *In God's good time, of showing to thy face*
> *An unsuccumbing spirit, which sublime*
> *May cast away the low anxieties*
> *That wait upon the flesh; the reptile moods;*
> *And enter that eternity to come,*
> *Where live the dead, and only Death can die.*

That there was within Elizabeth at this time a deep psychological conflict is clear from a powerful and curious poem not published in her lifetime, "A True Dream." This account of a horrible nightmare she experienced in 1833 is told, significantly enough, in the verse form of "The Ancient Mariner": indeed, both the poetic narrative and the symbolism would appear to formulate a similar guilt complex to that of the killer of the Albatross. In Elizabeth's dream, after the calling up by a magic spell of sinister menacing figures, a swart man and a delusively beautiful child, three serpents "besprent with noisome poison slime" writhe before her. Here a brother comes into the dream, Bro personifying herself perhaps, and he endeavours in vain to kill the serpents by pouring on them oil of vitriol; but the serpents, as they shriek in pain, grow larger, bringing to her a personal agony. Like the Ancient Mariner, she finds herself unable to pray.

> *And in my anguish I prayed and named*
> *Aloud the holy name,*
> *The impious mocking serpent voice*
> *Did echo back the same.*

Other conflicts are apparent here, but in the main her deep trouble would appear to be an unfulfilment, symbolized by the serpents. Elizabeth was a woman of strong feeling whose dominant father would not permit his children to marry. Normal desire, thwarted, smothered in maiden ignorance, can take strange channels, and in Elizabeth's case feelings of guilt and intense conflict were surely inevitable. The strong Evangelical concept of a personal God, represented on earth in this case by a possessive father to whom she was devoted, would change natural desire into a sense of sin and a craving for death.

One factor in this disturbance—tending perhaps in Elizabeth's present state of mind to lay too strong an emphasis upon religion—was her friendship with the Reverend George Barrett Hunter; a friendship probably heightened after Boyd left Sidmouth to live in Bath. Boyd, it is true, was a religious man himself, but the main feature of her association with that older friend was a concentration on something outside herself, upon classical lore.

If we are to judge by a poem written to him eleven years later, the Nonconformist clergyman was a dominant figure in Elizabeth's life at this time. Indeed, that the thought, the memory of him even lingered on long after their lives had fallen apart is clear from verses addressed to Hunter and written on the fly leaf of a presentation copy of *Poems,* 1844, sent together with *The Seraphim* (1838). In these volumes, her only published work since Sidmouth days, Hunter's name, she pointed out, was not mentioned, but

> *There is a silence which includes*
> *Much speaking and completest,—*
> *As oft, in sylvan solitudes,*
> *Society grows sweetest.*

In poems of the country, in reference to books, to poetry itself, and to religion, his spirit, she told him, was still with her. These presentation verses end thus:

By feelings tried, by memories kept
As fervid friendship vows them, .
Accept the volumes . . and ACCEPT
The silence which endows them!

As there had been a gap of seven years since the publication
of *An Essay on Mind*, it is possible that the verses attached to
Prometheus Bound may be the outcome of earlier experience:
for work known to have been done at Sidmouth we must go
forward to 1838 and *The Seraphim*. Among poems composed
there are "An Island," "The Sleep," "The Sea-mew," "A Sabbath Morning at Sea," and "The Little Friend," the last being
written to Hunter's small daughter, Mary.

We have little knowledge of the Reverend George Hunter
beyond Elizabeth's own indirect testimony to him as a man of
strong, sensitive personality, of stern yet kindly religion. He
conserved some of her verse in manuscript. Before the Barretts
left Sidmouth he went to live in Axminster. Of correspondence
between these friends there remains, so far as I am informed,
nothing beyond that charming fanciful rimed epistle of February 22, 1837 purporting to come from Elizabeth's doves in London to Mary Hunter's canary at "Cage House, Axminster."

There is however, a letter that might by inference be ascribed
to Hunter, the signature of which is said to be indecipherable.
It was written from Axminster in September 1838 after reading
The Seraphim. The tone of this letter is rather morbidly warm,
perhaps too warm for mere friendship. The writer claims a personal association with certain poems, and especially with "A
Sabbath Morning at Sea," declaring it to be "most beautiful and
dear, and it too *is* mine. I cannot, may not tell you how & what
I feel of your kindness, while I call that and others—*Mine*—and
the feeling is so intense as it is because you taught me to call it
so." The writer speaks of her regard for "him" as "dearer to me
than of all the world besides."

"A Sabbath Morning at Sea," undoubtedly written at Sidmouth, suggests a voyage that involved a parting from one
dear to her:

For parting tears and present sleep
Have weighed mine eyelids downward.

This poem commemorates the new experience of dawn over

the water; an experience sharpened by personal emotion. In pre-railway days it was common enough for people to travel between the southern coastal parts of England by sea. Later Elizabeth herself was to make most of her journey to Torquay by water. That this particular voyage meant the loss, temporary or otherwise, of a cherished companion is clear, but who he was we can only conjecture. We can, however, be fairly certain that Hunter (if it was he who wrote the letter from Axminster) was present on board to share in a feeling of awed wonder when, as light broke,

> *Heaven, ocean, did alone partake*
> *The sacrament of morning.*

There may have been preoccupation at home further to cast a general shadow over Elizabeth's mind: financial anxiety was begining to weigh upon the family. A Bill for the abolition of slavery hung above their heads. West Indians, Mr. Barrett declared, would be irreparably ruined: "nobody in his senses would think of even attempting the culture of sugar . . . they had better hang weights to the sides of the island of Jamaica and sink it at once." At the end of August 1833 the Bill was passed. "The consternation here," Elizabeth wrote, "is very great. Nevertheless I am glad, and always shall be, that the negroes are—virtually—free!"

Edward Barrett, knowing that his brother would need help and support in the emergency, decided to send out his eldest son to Jamaica. This meant a separation of those two, twins not in the flesh but in soul, for more than a year. "Our beloved Ba," he wrote to Samuel, "upon the colour I put upon the project, namely as being profitable to Bro's interest, has consented in a spirit that has, if possible, raised her still higher in my estimation." Surely, at least in 1833, Edward Moulton Barrett was no arbitrary tyrant.

Another and more immediate danger threatened this family at Sidmouth: the house in which they were then living—not, it is thought, 8, Fortfield Terrace—was in a ruinous condition. One chimney had already been pulled down for safety. Before the winds of winter raged they must go. But where would they go? Would they leave Sidmouth? Elizabeth lived from day to day, but with faith in her father. "Of one thing," she wrote to Mrs.

Martin, "I have a comforting certainty—that wherever we may go or stay, the decree which moves or fixes us will and must be the 'wisest virtuousest discreetest best!' "

Whether they actually spent a perilous winter in this house is not known, but certainly in the autumn of next year they were established at "Belle Vue," a thatched house with a veranda, bowered in trees and "with a green lawn bounded by a Devonshire lane." [2] Here Mr. Barrett left them for some months, living in a London hotel to transact his business; perhaps that opening of an estate office or agency to which he, born a country gentleman, was soon heroically to bind himself during long hours for six days of the week. In London's damp fogs Mr. Barrett fell ill of his old rheumatic complaint. The children took a daring decision: so that he should not be suffering alone in a hotel, a brother must go to him. Bro was probably still in Jamaica: Sam, the next in age, either was not available or perhaps was not considered to be the right person. Storm and George were studying at Glasgow University. It was therefore the seventeen-year-old Henry who was sent up by coach to tend his father.

Elizabeth awaited a scolding. "We were not scolded: but my prayer to be permitted to follow Henry was condemned to silence." The unsatisfactory reports received from Henry made her "anxious and fearful." Apart from the personal loss, which would be severe, a fatal end of Mr. Barrett's illness would deprive his family, three of whom were still young, of its mainstay. "You know he is *all* left to us—" Elizabeth wrote to Mrs. Martin, "and without him we should indeed be orphans and desolate." Elizabeth's thoughts would naturally turn to the beloved uncle in Jamaica; but he was far away and necessarily occupied at such a dangerous moment in the Barrett affairs.

But happily the father recovered: by Christmas he was with his family at "Belle Vue," the pleasant house that they must soon leave. "Belle Vue" had been sold and might be handed over to a new owner in March. At least one of the family, Henrietta, was heartily tired of Sidmouth: the two months' stay first projected there had extended to three years. Elizabeth herself

___

[2] Now Cedar Shade Hotel, and in the middle of the town.

felt that she would "very much grieve to leave it." But decisions in this family rested with only one person.

It was ostensibly for George's sake that Mr. Barrett determined at least to try the experiment of settling his family in London. George, who at nineteen had become a Bachelor of Arts with distinction, was to be entered at the Bar. Charles John (Stormie) was leaving Glasgow University without a degree; not because he was less prepared than George, but because a hesitancy of speech had made him too nervous to face an oral examination.

In the late summer or autumn of 1835 the family moved to a furnished house in the London parish of St. Marylebone, an area that had already been inhabited by Barretts in several generations, including Elizabeth's grandmother, Mrs. Moulton.

CHAPTER   8

LONDON AND *THE SERAPHIM* [1835–8]

'Twas hard to sing by Babel's steam—
More hard, in Babel's street!
But if the soulless creatures deem
Their music not unmeet
For sunless walls—let us *begin,*
Who wear immortal wings within!

My Doves

THE HOUSE Mr. Barrett rented was 74 (now 99) Gloucester Place, at the end of a long row of the terrace houses. Boyd, who had preceded Elizabeth to London, was now living, a widower, in Hampstead; Mrs. Boyd had died at Bath.

The heights of Hampstead were considerably more inaccessible from Gloucester Place at that time, yet they were well within driving-distance. It is true that in London Mr. Barrett kept no carriage, but surely some vehicle might have been hired to convey Elizabeth to her old and bereaved friend; yet she did not visit him for some time. We find her writing to him that autumn: "Don't be angry because I have not visited you immediately. You know—or you *will* know, if you consider—I cannot open the window and fly."

Perhaps on first coming to London she was unwell: certainly Gloucester Place, though but on the fringe of London proper at that time, and near to Regent's Park, was a sad change to a woman country-bred. A New Year's letter to Mrs. Martin would imply, if not illness, at least in its nostalgia a physical oppression. "Half my soul . . . seems to have stayed behind on the sea-shore, which I love more than ever now that I cannot walk on it in the body. London is wrapped up like a mummy, in a yellow mist, so closely that I have had scarcely a glimpse of its countenance since we came. Well, I am trying to like it all very much." London was then for a good part of the year under a miasma of reeking chimneys, its streets covered with liquid mud, and with an odour of defective drainage too often apparent; no place for a woman weak upon the chest. When, however, Miss Mitford, introduced by John Kenyon, met Elizabeth on May 27, 1836, there was in her appearance no suggestion of invalidism.

A closer acquaintance with John Kenyon, a Jamaican cousin of Edward Barrett, was one of the immediate advantages to Elizabeth in London. Kenyon, a middle-aged wealthy man, was highly intelligent, a friend and patron of literature and himself a respectable practitioner in verse.

Kenyon, taking his old friend Mary Mitford, up from the country, to see the new giraffes at the Zoological Gardens, called first upon Elizabeth. That evening Miss Mitford wrote to her father:

A sweet young woman, whom we called for in Gloucester Place, went with us—a Miss Barrett—who reads Greek as I do French, has published some translations from Æschylus, and some striking poems. She is a delightful young creature; shy and timid and modest. Nothing but her desire to see me got her out at all.

"She is so sweet and gentle," Miss Mitford wrote the next day, "and so pretty, that one looks at her as if she were some bright flower."

Allowing for dear Miss Mitford's rose-coloured spectacles, the delightful picture of Elizabeth at this time which she later drew for a young friend seems to suggest an appearance of perfect health:

a slight, girlish figure, very delicate, with exquisite hands and feet, a round face, with a most noble forehead, a large mouth beautifully formed, and full of expression, lips like parted coral, teeth large, regular and glittering with healthy whiteness, large dark eyes, with such eyelashes, resting on the cheek when cast down; when turned upward, touching the flexible and expressive eyebrow; a dark complexion, with cheeks literally as bright as the dark China rose, a profusion of silky, dark curls, and a look of youth and of modesty hardly to be expressed. This, added to the very simple but graceful and costly dress by which all the family are distinguished, is an exact portrait of her some years ago.

Miss Mitford found her "one of the most interesting persons I had ever seen," with "a smile like a sunbeam."

Because of Miss Mitford's country residence, and also the circumstance of Elizabeth's coming illness, most of the intercourse between these two, the famous elderly writer and the younger poet on the verge of fame, must be on paper; but Miss Mitford's warm heart and intimate pen soon overcame formality. Elizabeth was to her "my dear love," "my dearest love," a being to whom she felt as a mother might to a son of genius. The friendship sprang up rapidly: during Miss Mitford's week in town that spring Elizabeth was with her a part of every day.

Having faced one pleasant literary lion, Elizabeth was emboldened to dine with Mr. Kenyon next evening and meet, among other celebrities, Landor and Wordsworth; of whom she wrote to Mrs. Martin: (Wordsworth's) "manners are very simple, and his conversation not at all *prominent*—if you quite understand what I mean by *that*. I do myself, for I saw at the same time Landor—the brilliant Landor!—and *felt* the difference between great genius and eminent talent."

Wordsworth "was very kind to me, and let me hear his conversation." The wide-eyed admiration of this girl must indeed have been balm to the aged Wordsworth, who, we know, sometimes missed the incense of the home shrine in his visits to London. As a woman friend drove him one day with Miss Mitford and Elizabeth to Chiswick, Miss Mitford took her apart to inquire whether Miss Barrett was "out," so much a child did she still look at the age of thirty.

At Kenyon's reception, Landor, "in whose hands the ashes of antiquity burn again," had talked for some ten minutes with Elizabeth and had given her two Greek epigrams lately made by himself, one being upon Napoleon. Bro, now again in England, and with whom Elizabeth had the happiness of attending this gathering, afterwards "abused Landor for '*ambitious* singularity and affectation.' "

On reading Miss Mitford's letters to her father it is strange to note that on May 26, a day before Kenyon's party, she had been dining at Serjeant Talfourd's table with Wordsworth, Landor, and other writers, among whom was the young author of "Paracelsus," a poet already hailed in that limited circle though the public would have none of him. Browning's father had been at school with John Kenyon: Kenyon's interest in his old companion's brilliant son was almost as strong as that felt for his cousin. There is indirect evidence that Elizabeth herself at once recognized the quality of "Paracelsus" "as the expression of a new mind"; but it does not appear as if she ever expressed a desire to meet Mr. Kenyon's young friend.

But this excursion into literary society at Mr. Kenyon's table appears to have been Elizabeth's first and last before marriage: her time was spent in Gloucester Place quietly at work to the background of the cooing doves in her room. She saw Boyd from time to time, letting him hear her verses. That captious old-fashioned man became, as Elizabeth developed on lines modern in her day, more and more inclined to carp and criticize: his criticisms usually provoked a lively and spirited defence.

In 1836 writings of hers appeared both in the *Athenæum* (an article in prose, "A Thought on Thoughts"), under the editorship of Charles Dilke, and in the *New Monthly Magazine,* edited by Bulwer, afterwards Lord Lytton. Dilke, as yet unaware of the identity of "E. B. B.," in his review of current magazines noted that ambitious long poem "A Poet's Vow" as "a fine almost too dreamy ballad" and exhorted "him," the author, to "greater clearness of expression and less quaintness in his choice of phraseology." To us, accustomed to the intricacies and wide word range of modern poets, it is difficult to realize that her own generation linked Elizabeth with Robert Browning as obscure. So conscious was Elizabeth of this accusation that, she told Miss Mitford, "my fear of it makes me sometimes feel quite nervous and thought-tied in composition."

In the October of 1836 Elizabeth embarked upon her most daring adventure of the mind, an exercise in sublimity itself: "The Seraphim," which was to be the title poem of her next volume. In that beautifully balanced piece of prose, her preface, she tells how even in translating *Prometheus Bound* the thought of the greatest Christian Martyrdom was with her: how from the victim of Zeus, punished for bringing benefit to man, her mind went forward "to the multitudes, whose victim was their Saviour; to the Victim, whose sustaining thought beneath an unexampled agony, was not the Titanic 'I can revenge,' but the celestial 'I can forgive!' "

If the level of the white spiritual beauty of the opening of this poem could have been sustained, surely Elizabeth Barrett Browning must have been hailed as a poet of very high rank; but always in those longer poems her hand seems to falter. Perhaps the texture of her verse is too thin, or perhaps the inhibitions of her age and sex made her self-conscious. Perhaps in this particular case the poem suffered from a broken treatment: the manuscript submitted to the *New Monthly* was lost by Colburn, its publisher. "Partly from a very rough copy, and partly from memory," Elizabeth reconstructed it, adding a second part of about twice the length.[1]

The exalted plane, the spirituality, of this work, an apex in her religious expression, can touch us perhaps more in this professedly unreligious age, when men have suffered a crucifixion of mind and body, than in her own time, when life for all but the inarticulate toiling masses was comfortable and safe. Our minds too may, because of the extent of modern outer-world discovery, be empowered to soar more easily up into space, to the lingering Seraphim momentarily disobeying a Command to follow down to the Cross those angels

> *The roar of whose descent has died*
> *To a still sound, as thunder into rain.*
>   *Immeasurable space spreads magnified*
>   *With that thick life, along the plane*
>   *The worlds slid out on. What a fall*
>   *And eddy of wings innumerous, crossed*
>   *By trailing curls that have not lost*
>   *The glitter of the God-smile shed*
>   *On every prostrate angel's head!*
>   *What gleaming up of hands that fling*
>   *Their homage in retorted rays,*
>   *From high instinct of worshipping,*
>   *And habitude of praise.*[2]

· · ·

[1] Letter to Kenyon, in Hagedorn Collection.
[2] Quoted in the later revised version.

For nearly two years more the Barrett family lived uneasily in a furnished house with dirty carpets, Elizabeth without her books and armchair, Henrietta without a pianoforte. Confidence in the house could not have been increased when, during the great storm of December 1836, a chimney-stack crashed through a skylight and, descending to ground level, broke the stone stairs; stairs on which the beloved Bro had five minutes before been standing. Sarah, the housemaid, who "looked up accidentally and saw the nodding chimneys," had run shrieking into the drawing-room where Mr. Barrett was sitting. She escaped "with one graze on the hand from one brick."

During these two years there was for Elizabeth no escape from town; but, though yearning for the lost Hope End, she now admitted to many advantages in London: "if we can't see even a leaf or a sparrow without soot on it, there are the parrots at the Zoological Gardens and the pictures at the Royal Academy; and real live poets above all, with their heads full of the trees and birds and sunshine of paradise." These poets were no new constellations in her sky, but those two she had met in 1836. Her only contact with a poet at this time, and he a very minor one, was in the increasing and fruitful friendship with her cousin, John Kenyon.

The year 1837 had, except for composition and fugitive publication, little to offer us and nothing in the way of event beyond the marriage, at which she was present, of Annie Boyd early that year or at the end of 1836. In the summer Elizabeth, to help Henry, who was going to Germany, joined with Bro in studying German. German, the last to be learned, was perhaps to be enjoyed latest in point of time: during illness towards the end of her life Elizabeth read many German books and translated a few lyrics.

1838 was, on the other hand, an outstanding year: it was to see the beginning of her long invalidism, the first publication (beyond the privately printed *Battle of Marathon*) with her name attached, and to connect her with that famous address, 50, Wimpole Street.

The family had for months been looking forward with dislike to this removal which took them to a similar house in a street parallel with Gloucester Place. But at least they had no longer to live with other people's furniture: their own came up from store in Ledbury. Elizabeth had her books back, and Henrietta a pianoforte.

Elizabeth's illness early that year began with the breaking of a blood vessel in the chest. Dr. William Frederick Chambers, physician-in-ordinary to the Queen, was called in, but though the rupture apparently healed he was unable to cure her of a persistent cough.

1838 was a year of bereavement: Samuel Moulton Barrett died at Kingston, Jamaica, on December 23, 1837. News of his death must have reached London in the February of 1838. As Elizabeth's uncle had been ill for some time, and her brother Sam was with him, the family could not have been wholly un-prepared, but her grief for the loss of him who had been "more than an uncle" was profound. His love and thought for her were expressed in a legacy that helped to make her independent. Among tokens of their mutual affection was a locket he had given her, which she habitually wore; a locket intended for per-fume, but later to contain some of Robert Browning's hair.

Although sales of *The Seraphim* were not large enough to warrant a second edition, its publication in May of this year se-cured for Elizabeth a definite place among the English poets. The *Athenæum,* though to some extent disappointed, de-clared it

an extraordinary volume—especially welcome as an evidence of female genius and accomplishment. . . . Miss Barrett's genius is of a high order; active, vigorous, and versatile, but unaccom-panied by discriminating taste. A thousand strange and beauti-ful views flit across her mind, but she cannot look at them with a steady gaze. . . .

Perhaps this criticism is just and may be partially explained by inhibitions of sex, time, and position in society. Elizabeth born and reared in the remoteness of a Haworth Parsonage might have been a stronger poet, though she could hardly have been a more sensitive one.

The *Athenæum* also spoke of a certain want "of unaffected earnestness." This accusation Elizabeth vigorously repudiated in a letter to Boyd: "I have always written too naturally (that is, too much from the impulse of thought and feeling) to have studied *attitudes.*" Later she was to write to R. H. Horne: " 'The Seraphim' has faults enough—and weaknesses, besides—but my voice is in it, in its individual tones, and not inarticulately."

The *Atlas,* a powerful newspaper whose criticisms were read with attention, laid more stress upon the faults of the volume, though admitting "occasional passages of great beauty, and full of deep poetical feeling." In considering "The Romaunt of Margret" it brought for the first time a charge which, great as was her admiration for the poet, always irritated Elizabeth: that she was strongly influenced by Tennyson. When "The Romaunt of Margret" was composed she had not yet read a line of Tennyson. "I came from the country," she told Robert Browning in 1846, "with my eyes only half open, and he had not penetrated where I had been living and sleeping."

"The Romaunt of Margret" is perhaps to a biographer the most interesting poem in the volume, embodying as it does, linked with the *Alcestis* theme, that German mystical notion of a *Doppelgänger,* a man's soul or self facing himself. It is an idea that persisted in Elizabeth's mind, growing stronger and becoming a thread in the allegory of her life.

The story, given in mediæval vein, may in its eerie atmosphere be not unfavourably compared with "Christabel":

> *The ladye doth not move—*
> *The ladye doth not dream—*
> *Yet she seeth her shade no longer laid*
> *In rest upon the stream!*
> *It shaketh without wind—*
> *It parteth from the tide—*
> *It standeth upright in the cleft moonlight—*
> *It sitteth at her side.*
>
> > *Margret, Margret!*

To Margret, sitting in happy thoughtful mood by the stream at night, her shadow announces the doom of certain death unless she can lay claim to some human being whom she loves and who loves her "more truly than the sun." The only one she can so claim is no longer living:

> *"Behold! the death-worm to his heart*
> *Is a nearer thing than* thou."
>
> > *Margret, Margret.*

Hearing that her lover is dead, the ladye casts herself into the water.

Of the other poems in this volume all are instinct with personality, all pervaded with a yearning towards God less fully expressed in previous published work. Some poems are heavily coloured with that rather self-conscious mediævalism which was to fascinate and conquer the Pre-Raphaelites: nearly all have fine opening stanzas. Her themes are striking and varied; the self-sacrifice of a poet; the beauty of motherhood in "Isobel's Child" and "To the Child Jesus"; of contemporary life in the poems of young Queen Victoria; in "The Soul's Travelling" and other poems a nostalgia for green country. Her own life is revealed to us in at least three, "The Deserted Garden," "My Doves," and "The Name." Her verse now reads more smoothly and easily to the ear. The two pieces longest to endure in popularity are "The Sea-mew" and "Cowper's Grave."

The summer of 1838 brought little improvement in Elizabeth's condition: Dr. Chambers had hoped that its warmth might prove a healing agent. In June we hear of him "shaking his head as awfully as if it bore all Jupiter's ambrosial curls." Some plan must be made for a winter abroad, a plan Mr. Barrett did not approve but which Elizabeth was for a time determined to carry out. To her brother George, now a barrister and away on circuit, she wrote:

Still it is hard to think of going out of this room to the South of Europe . . . leaving gravity in Papa's eyes, and perhaps displeasure deeper within him! If he should be displeased! But his manner *is most affectionate to me—affectionate in a marked manner & measure! which indeed was needed to stroke down & smooth a little my poor ruffled feathers, after that hard cold letter of his. Perhaps he had relented in his thoughts of me! or perhaps, George, (which I conjecture sometimes) perhaps he takes for granted that I have given up the scheme, & his good nature is meant for my compensation.*

These children might love their father, but between the typical arbitrary parent of a hundred years ago and even so affectionate and well-loved a daughter as Elizabeth there could be little real confidence. One characteristic trait of both stood, too, in the way of easy intercourse; their reticence and a difficulty in the expression of feeling in speech.

But some sort of compromise must be reached. It was decided that Elizabeth should go to Torquay, where apparently an aunt (perhaps Mrs. Hedley) was then living. In September 1838 she was taken most of the way there by sea, Bro, George, and Henrietta accompanying her. One sister was to remain at Torquay, Arabel later taking the place of Henrietta. Elizabeth wrote to Boyd on the eve of sailing:

And all this companionship is more than I hoped for, & I ought to be contented with it—& thankful for every brightness which has fallen, beyond my hope, upon my present circumstances. But still I cannot help being very sorrowful even while I write about the brightness! May God bless you. It may please Him for me to return & visit you again.

She was to return after three long, weary years, years fraught with pain, distress, and infinite sorrow.

C H A P T E R   9

TORQUAY [1838–41]

Bro had orders from his father to put Elizabeth in the care of her aunt and then return home; but Elizabeth, weakened by illness, perhaps thinking in despair that she might never see this beloved brother again, clung to him in tears. Her aunt, kissing those tears away, sat down immediately and wrote a protest to Mr. Barrett: if he should call Bro back he would break his sister's heart ("as if," Elizabeth commented bitterly seven years later to Robert Browning in a revelation of the tragedy of her life, "hearts were broken *so!*"). The father's reply, which she could never forget, was that "under such circumstances he did not refuse to suspend his purpose, but that he considered it to be *very wrong in me to exact such a thing.*"

The well-beloved brother is, oddly enough, seldom mentioned in Elizabeth's letters: we know so little about him we can only conjecture that he was, beyond the known year in Jamaica, much away from home in the 'thirties. Of what he did in town, and whether as eldest son he helped his father in business, we are quite ignorant. Perhaps Mr. Barrett's "purpose" at this time was the serious one of sending Bro out once more to Jamaica: since the death of Elizabeth's uncle, Sam, not so reliable a son, had been the only family representative there.

Of Elizabeth's first year at Torquay I can gather little except that there was a plan, of which she feared her father would disapprove, to winter abroad; that her poem "A Romance of the Ganges" was printed in *Finden's Tableaux*, edited by Miss Mitford; and that she was reading with intense enjoyment Beaumont and Fletcher.

One of her solaces in exile was frequent letters from Mary Mitford, those delightful letters full of literary gossip and containing from time to time delectable descriptions of an English countryside. In November 1839 [1] we hear of a gift of seeds from

---

[1] Wrongly dated 1838 in L'Estrange's *Friendships of Mary Mitford*.

Miss Mitford to the Barrett family, some of which came from Wordsworth's garden. Seeds from this precious packet, Elizabeth wrote her, were to be reserved by Arabel for Elizabeth's own use in a flower-pot for her window "if it should please God to permit my return to London."

In this letter Elizabeth mentions Theodosia Garrow,[2] a precocious child who, through Landor, had contributed a poem to *The Book of Beauty* edited by Lady Blessington. The Garrows, living at a house called "The Braddons" in Torquay, were friends of Mr. Kenyon. Elizabeth and Theodosia, a delicate girl, were attended by the same doctor.

Theodosia sent fruit and vegetables to the admired Miss Barrett, whom she longed to visit, but, at least in 1839, Elizabeth was too ill to admit strangers. In 1840 Theodosia contributed to a second *Book of Beauty* some verses "Presenting a Young Invalid with a Bunch of Early Violets," sending the two Annuals for Elizabeth to read. Elizabeth wrote a gracious note of thanks regretting that she could not receive Miss Garrow; anyhow "a visit to an invalid condemned to the *peine forte et dure* of being very silent, notwithstanding her womanhood" would be "a gloomy thing." Elizabeth's sense of humour, evidently not submerged by illness, may have been tickled, in the second set of verses intended for her, by a certain youthful tactlessness in such lines as "Thine innocent life, ebbing fast away . . . Innocent beings like thee fade with a gentle decay."

A record of this episode, of Theodosia, the flowers, vegetables, and verse, might not have survived the years if, in time, Theodosia had not become Mrs. Thomas Trollope, destined to meet again with Elizabeth and under happier auspices.

By November 24, 1839 Elizabeth was moved to 1, Beacon Terrace, "a still warmer nest." "Her brother," Miss Mitford wrote to Henry Chorley, "means to fold her in a cloak and carry her to the new house in his arms."

Beacon Terrace overlooks the sweep of Torbay and, in the harbour below, a bustle of business and pleasure craft. Elizabeth had long loved the sea, bitterly regretting its loss on leaving Sidmouth:

[2] Mistranscribed as "Farren" by L'Estrange.

> *. . . the glorious sea! from side to side*
> *Swinging the grandeur of his foamy strength,*
> *And undersweeping the horizon,—on—*
> *On—with his life and voice inscrutable*

was to her a living entity. Soon, however, the sea was to bring
her tragedy and a lasting grief.

That year Mr. Barrett was at Torquay in January. How long
he stayed then we do not know, but we do know that nine
months later, on November 11, there was between his daughter
and himself a parting more emotional than circumstance would
seem to warrant: he was to be absent only a fortnight. As Elizabeth let fall those tears always near her eyelids in sorrow and
in happiness, Mr. Barrett wept openly. In at least one mind,
Elizabeth's, there was a sense of ill omen, the memory of a
dream she had frequently during illness. "I used," she told Miss
Mitford,

> *to start out of fragments of dreams, broken from all parts of the*
> *universe, with the cry from my own lips, "Oh, papa, papa!" I*
> *could not trace it back to the dream behind, yet there it always*
> *was very curiously, and touchingly too, to my own heart, seem-*
> *ing scared of me, though it came from me, at once waking me*
> *with, and welcoming me to, the old straight humanities.*

In other words, and in the light of future events, sorrow was to
come through her to the beloved father. At the time Elizabeth's
interpretation of both dream and grief at parting was a fear that
she might be ill again during the fortnight's absence.

It may well be that Mr. Barrett had, in addition to the worry
of a cherished daughter's health, a more distant preoccupation:
word had come that his son's behaviour in Jamaica was not,
from his own strict standard, all that it should be. The little we
know of Sam suggests a gay, volatile spirit of some sensibility,
one who wrote verses and was fond of company. Perhaps he
found the father's control too rigid. There is a family letter [3] to
Sam with the signature torn away, obviously written from
Hope End, which suggests this artistic bias to Sam's character.
After saying that, on a question of Bro's return, "Papa's thoughts
on the subject are to us as inscrutable as if we had been all tru-
ants and adhered to the fourth form," the writer adds: "There

[3] Hewlett Collection.

is a great difference between yourself, and him, at least in *one* respect—for if your reveries are *upon* a rose, *his* are *under* it." Others, even the devoted Elizabeth herself, were, we know, exasperated by the Olympian attitude of their father towards his children.

Whatever Sam's temperament, the temptations of Jamaica and its climate to the white man appear to have been too much for him: this much we know from the account of his missionary life in the West Indies [4] written by the Reverend Hope Masterman Waddell. By February 17, 1840 the Jamaican climate had exacted a final toll. Sam was dead of the fever.

All this had been entirely forgotten, even in the family, until Miss Marks discovered it, thereby explaining the reference in a letter to R. H. Horne, on May 17, to an expression of sympathy that had touched Elizabeth "so nearly and deeply." The shock of the news, which must have come to England in the previous month, had thrown her into a fever so that she had "been too weak to hold a pen." "It was a heavy blow, for all of us—and I, being weak, you see, was struck down by a *bodily* blow, in a moment, without having time for tears." But she could find comfort in "God's will . . . manifested in Jesus Christ. Only *that* holds our hearts together when He shatters the world." But Elizabeth's world, as she was to discover in a few months' time, was not yet shattered.

The pen friendship with Horne had progressed, with her father's approval: he brought her a copy of Horne's poetic play *Gregory VII*, exclaiming at her look of pleasure: "Ah! I thought that would move you." We find her rather shyly sending Horne some Devonshire cream and, more boldly, criticizing or praising his work; praise that sounds oddly to us who have almost forgotten R. H. Horne, "the farthing poet." To Elizabeth he was at this time "one of the very first poets of the day."

At the end of May we hear in a letter to Mr. Boyd that Elizabeth was still confined to her bed and even when lifted out on to the sofa inclined to faint: she was blistered every few days. It was considered she would never again "be fit for anything like exertion."

But in spite of physical weakness mental activity continued:

[4] *Twenty-nine Years in the West Indies and Central Africa* (London, 1863).

her correspondence with Miss Mitford, Harriet Martineau,
Horne, and others was not abandoned and she was able to compose. Poems known to have been written at this period are "The
Lay of the Early Rose" (containing some beauties, especially of
rhythm, but reading too much like a metrical exercise) and
"Crowned and Buried," the subject of which was suggested by
her Torquay physician.

In this year, 1840, Napoleon's remains were brought back
from St. Helena to be given to France for more ceremonial burial: in July 1815 Napoleon had lain four days on board the
Bellerophon in the waters of Torbay. Elizabeth, though she
could not condone his crimes against humanity, felt, together
with many Liberals, that Great Britain was to be censured in
her treatment of him:

> *Because it was not well, it was not well,*
> *Nor tuneful with thy lofty-chanted part*
> *Among the Oceanides,—that Heart*
> *To bind and bare and vex with vulture fell.*
> *I would, my noble England! men might seek*
> *All crimson stains upon thy breast—not cheek!*
>
> *I would that hostile fleets had scarred Torbay,*
> *Instead of the lone ship which waited moored*
> *Until thy princely purpose was assured. . . .*

One day Elizabeth was to see the evils of arbitrary power at
close quarters; though always she was to honour the name of
Napoleon in a lesser man, his nephew.

But soon a far greater test of endurance than the second
brother's death in Jamaica was demanded of that weak body. In
the first bereavement Bro had been beside her, remaining there
though his father must have sorely needed him; declaring, as
he held his sister's hand, that he loved her better than them all
and would not leave her until she was well again. It was not
Mr. Barrett's eldest son but the third, Charles John (Stormie),
who was sent out to Jamaica after Sam's death.

On July 11 Bro went out with two friends in a sailing-boat,
La Belle Sauvage. Elizabeth, perhaps fretful at being left, let
him go "with a pettish word." The day was fine, the sea smooth,

but at the appointed hour the boat did not return. In Elizabeth's own words to Robert Browning:

For three days we waited—and I hoped while I could—oh—that awful agony of three days! And the sun shone as it shines to-day, and there was no more wind than now; and the sea under the windows was like this paper for smoothness—and my sisters drew the curtains back that I might see for myself how smooth the sea was, and how it could hurt nobody—and other boats came back one by one.

"Remember," Elizabeth continued in that account of the tragedy which unburdened her soul five years after, "how you wrote in your 'Gismond'

> *What says the body when they spring*
> *Some monstrous torture-engine's whole*
> *Strength on it? No more says the soul,*

and you never wrote anything which *lived* with me more than *that*. It is such a dreadful truth."

What remained of young Edward Barrett was thrown up by the sea and buried in Tor churchyard: the final agony remained. Face to face with her father, Elizabeth was bowed down with a load of guilt. She had robbed him of his son, his eldest son, by a selfish weakness in keeping Bro by her. Perhaps too, in the painful encounter, the father had a load on his conscience, needing all the consolation a favourite daughter might otherwise have given him: Bro had been in love, had wanted to marry, but, lacking money, could not do so against Mr. Barrett's prohibition. Elizabeth had wanted to make over to him her own income, but this was not permitted.

A great love for her father, hitherto second only in her affection, filled the wounded heart. "The crown of his house had fallen" but Edward Barrett, great in forbearance, uttered no word of reproach. "I felt," she told Robert, "that he stood nearest to me on the closed grave . . or by the unclosing sea." From the moment of loss this woman, so loving, so sensitive, ceased for many years properly to live, though the suffering lasted on.

In that fanciful poem "An Island," published with "The Seraphim," Elizabeth had pictured a solitude withdrawn from the world, alone but for a chosen few "whom dreams fantastic please as well," and beside the sea "within the sounding coral caves."

> *Choose me the loftiest cave of all,*
>   *To make a place for prayer;*
> *And I will choose a praying voice*
>   *To pour our spirits there.*
> *How silverly the echoes run—*
> Thy will be done—thy will be done!

But now, slowly emerging from the stupor into which the shock of Bro's death had first plunged her, she must drag out an existence spiritually alone by that sea, a cruel sea bringing no thought of resignation. The power of prayer might return, but even one so devout, so near to God, could no longer cry with a full heart "Thy will be done."

Only to Robert Browning could Elizabeth ever write directly of that loss so closely intertwined by a tender conscience with guilt, and even to him she never spoke of it. Her heart was too stricken for tears or lamentation. When composition was again possible she wrote in a moving sonnet:

> *I tell you, hopeless grief is passionless;*
> *That only men incredulous of despair,*
> *Half-taught in anguish, through the midnight air*
> *Beat upward to God's throne in loud access*
> *Of shrieking and reproach.*

This, "De Profundis," and other sonnets of her sorrow, are moving, but in a more dramatic presentment of misery, "The Mask," one can feel more fully the heart-break. This poem is so important in the presentment of her life that, at a risk of being overlengthy, I feel it must be quoted in full. That she herself put on this poem high value as an expression of feeling we may guess by the care lavished on it. There are three separate, widely differing, drafts extant:

> *I have a smiling face, she said,*
>   *I have a jest for all I meet,*
> *I have a garland for my head*
>   *And all its flowers are sweet,—*
> *And so you call me gay, she said.*

Grief taught to me this smile, she said,
    And Wrong did teach this jesting bold;
These flowers were plucked from garden-bed
    While a death-chime was tolled.
And what now will you say?—she said.

Behind no prison-grate, she said,
    Which slurs the sunshine half a mile,
Live captives so uncomforted
    As souls behind a smile.
God's pity let us pray, she said.

I know my face is bright, she said,—
    Such brightness, dying suns diffuse;
I bear upon my forehead shed
    The sign of what I lose,—
The ending of my day, she said.

If I dared leave this smile, she said,
    And take a moan upon my mouth,
And tie a cypress round my head,
    And let my tears run smooth,—
It were the happier way, she said.

And since that must not be, she said,
    I fain your bitter world would leave.
How calmly, calmly, smile the Dead,
    Who do not, therefore, grieve!
The yea of Heaven is yea, she said.

But in your bitter world, she said,
    Face-joy's a costly mask to wear.
'Tis bought with pangs long nourishèd,
    And rounded to despair.
Grief's earnest makes life's play, she said.

Ye weep for those who weep? she said—
    Ah fools! I bid you pass them by.
Go, weep for those whose hearts have bled
    What time their eyes were dry.
Whom sadder can I say? she said.

There were other ties to bind her, a loved father to whom she poured out gratitude, affectionate sisters and brothers: weak, arid of soul, she must forge for herself some sort of armour, a mask in which to front the world. Her natural cheerfulness, a sense of humour, enveloped the husk that remained. Feverishly she lived a life of the intellect, seeking for consolation, as the first bitterness left her, in the love of God.

But the expression of grief, a living on in profound abnegation, was for the future. Now for many months Elizabeth lay in the shadow of death. There is a gap in her correspondence: the next letter available to me, dated December 11, is to her old friend Mrs. Martin, to whom she wrote:

do believe that although grief has so changed me from myself and warped me from my old instincts, as to prevent my looking forwards with pleasure to seeing you again, yet that full amends are made in the looking back with a pleasure more true because more tender than any old retrospections.

She was thankful to be able to report that Stormie was back in England. "It is a mercy which makes me very thankful, and would make me joyful if anything could. But the meanings of some words change as we live on." After the drowning of one brother Elizabeth was to dread for those left all journeyings by sea. Indeed, she may have had to face the cruel anxiety in regard to her father at this time: from another passage in the letter we might conjecture that he found it necessary to go over to Jamaica.

The correspondence with Horne was now resumed over a bold project: to follow in the footsteps of Dryden and present Chaucer in modern language. Among others Wordsworth, Leigh Hunt, Monckton Milnes (afterwards Lord Houghton) were asked to contribute with Horne as editor. Of distinguished writers approached only Landor refused, declaring "I will have no hand in breaking his dun but richly-painted glass, to put in (if clearer) much thinner panes." All but Leigh Hunt agreed that Chaucer's language should be adhered to as closely as possible. Elizabeth modernized "Queen Annelida and False Arcite."

From a letter dated December 17, 1840 it is clear that Horne submitted preface and translations for her opinion. She considered that some of the contributors were too wide of the mark,

that "You, yourself, and Wordsworth are most devoutly near."
Though all such modernizations must lose the original in essence, Elizabeth's own rendering is perhaps as near as may be.

We also learn from this letter that Mr. Barrett, proud of the
connection, or perhaps out of gratitude to one who had helped
to rouse his ailing daughter from a lethargy of grief, had left his
card on Horne in London. Elizabeth asked Horne to pay a visit
in Wimpole Street "some day when you are in the neighbourhood—before I am there . . . it would give them such real
pleasure to know you, I am very sure." Later we hear of the gift
of a jar of West Indian tamarinds.

Another work in which she was more closely associated with
Horne at this time was a lyrical drama after the Greek manner
to be called "Psyche Apocalyptè," which they were to compose
together; he to devise the characters, interlocutors, choruses,
semi-choruses, and she to present the part of Psyche and provide the lyrical portion. As may be guessed, the theme was Elizabeth's, "the terror attending spiritual consciousness—the man's
soul to the man," exalting the *Doppelgänger* conception on to
a spiritual plane. "There are moments when we are startled at
the footsteps of our own being, more than at the thunders of
God." Perhaps the working-out of this theme on her own might
to some extent have eased Elizabeth's burdened, guilt-shad-
owed soul; but as it was, she wrote only a few isolated lyrics
after the general plan had been mapped out. The project was
never openly abandoned, though perhaps tacitly dropped. Such
a collaboration at arm's length, and on paper, seemed doomed
to failure from the start.

At the end of March 1841, Elizabeth wrote to Mrs. Martin:
*my faculties seem to hang heavily now, like flappers when the
spring is broken. My spring is broken, and a separate exertion is
necessary for the lifting up of each—and then it falls down
again. . . . Nevertheless, I don't give up much to the perni-
cious languor—the tendency to lie down to sleep among the
snows of a weary journey—I don't give up much to it.*
That she could think and write at all seems a miracle, weakened as she was by being kept in bed in a room with the windows papered up in winter to exclude every breath of fresh air
and, in addition, dosed with brandy and opium. We gather that

she was left to brood, perhaps at her own desire, many hours by herself. That spring, however, a solace was provided in her invalid life by Miss Mitford: a cocker spaniel, a faithful creature never to be forgotten. "Flush amuses me sometimes when I am inclined to be amused by nothing else," Elizabeth told her brother George.

With some slight return of bodily power, Elizabeth was now yearning to go home, to leave Beacon Terrace, where the sound of the sea was always with her. Anyhow, she wrote to her brother, Dr. Scully said she must remain in her room all the winter, so what did it matter where she lived? No decision on her future fate, however, could be obtained from Mr. Barrett. One would have thought the cruelty of keeping his daughter so long by that engulfing sea would have been evident to a father at heart so devoted, but Mr. Barrett himself made no move in the matter. Perhaps he kept Elizabeth at Torquay all that summer because his plans in life were unsettled. He was contemplating the removal of his family from London: there was even one wild scheme of a migration to the Schwarzwald in Germany. "These Black Mountains," Elizabeth commented, "are black indeed."

In June a new anxiety possessed her. Mr. Barrett talked of making Clifton, the spa near Bristol, a halting-place for a month or two before she should come home. Elizabeth was afraid a short stay there might prolong itself into the winter. "My mind," she wrote to George, "turns round & round in wondering about Papa's fancy for Clifton, that hot, white, dusty vapory place." It is possible that Mr. Barrett's fancy for Clifton originated in youthful memories: his grandmother, the wife of Edward Barrett of Jamaica, may have lived there. She certainly died at Bristol in 1804, being buried in the Cathedral.

In the meantime Elizabeth was composing: probably "The Romaunt of the Page," one of her most popular poems when it appeared, and certainly "The House of Clouds," a particular favourite with her father, were written about this time.

In early summer Elizabeth was so far improved in health as to be able to sit up out of bed for an hour without fainting: though there must necessarily be a risk, Dr. Scully pronounced her fit for travel. Patiently, "tied hand and foot and gagged" at Torquay, she awaited her release. During August her father disappeared into Herefordshire without giving a date for her departure, but at length, in September, by stages of twenty-five miles a day, she made the journey in a patent invalid carriage with "a thousand springs."

But though Torquay was left behind, although Elizabeth need no longer listen through long sleepless nights to a sound of waves on the shore, there could be no escape. An echo lingered on. "I seem now," she told Robert Browning years later, "always to hear the sea *in* the wind, voice within voice."

CHAPTER 10

A CONFIRMED INVALID [1841–3]

BACK IN WIMPOLE STREET, Elizabeth told Boyd in a letter of October 2, 1841, she was "more happy—that is, nearing to the feeling of happiness now—than a month since I could believe possible to a heart so bruised and crushed as mine. . . . To be at home is a blessing and a relief beyond what these words can say." Not only had Elizabeth escaped from that place of doom overlooking a terrible sea, but she had not now to reproach herself with tearing her family asunder, with depriving Mr. Barrett of the company and ministrations of his two younger daughters, both of whom he had lately insisted should remain with her.

An intellectual life grew daily stronger in home surroundings. "Part of me," she wrote, "is worn out; but the poetical part— that is, the *love* of poetry—is growing in me as freshly and strongly as if it were watered every day."

The exact nature of Elizabeth's illness has never been thoroughly diagnosed. I have wondered whether the first hæmorrhage came from some accidental injury to the lungs. There is, however, an interesting letter [1] written later from Italy to an old friend, Fanny Dowglass, which sheds some light. Mrs. Dowglass had been ordered to Italy because of a threat of tuberculosis. Elizabeth warned her friend not to take the prediction too seriously:

The stethoscope is not an infallible searcher—that I have "heard sain" by several medical men who trusted much to it: and I know in my own case besides several others, that differences of opinion have been elicited from the very same instrument. Congestion & tuberculation will equally produce unsatisfactory responses to an ear resting on the stethoscope—& congestion is the much less serious evil. In my own case "extensive tuberculation" was declared by one physician while by two or three oth-

[1] *c.* 1850; Huntington Library Collection.

ers the existence of anything beside congestion has been sted-
fastly denied, positively denied—& circumstances at present
seem quite to confirm the softer judgment.

By 1840 the "softer judgment" had been given by four able
physicians in the west country who pronounced the affection of
her lungs to be not tubercular consumption, but the result of a
"decline," that word which in earlier medical days so elegantly
concealed a lack of precise knowledge.

On her return to London Mr. Boyd urged that her case should
be put before a Mr. Jago, but this Elizabeth refused at first.
Later Mr. Jago was to be a trusted adviser, relied upon even in
far-away Italy.

In refusing Boyd's request Elizabeth told him that, though
unequal to meeting people in general, she would gladly see her
old friend. We have, however, no record of a visit from Boyd.
It seems likely that Boyd, now living alone, was already fast
sinking into that mood of valetudinarian apathy which was to
make his last years so tragic to beholders. He spent long hours
brooding in his chair, his ear refreshed only by the striking and
chiming of the many clocks of which he was a collector. Perhaps the marriage of his daughter in 1836, or '37, had been,
apart from the loss of her company, a serious blow to the
staunch Protestant. If "Henrietta" was in truth Annie, her husband, Henry Hayes, or Heyes, was a Roman Catholic and later
his wife became a convert.

A link with Boyd at this time was Elizabeth's work on the
Greek Christian Fathers. In January 1842 she had sent to the
Athenæum, without much hope of acceptance, translations with
a prefatory note, from Gregory Nazianzen. "You will comprehend my surprise," she wrote to Boyd, "on receiving last night
a courteous note from the editor, which I would send to you if
it were legible to anybody except people used to learn reading
from the pyramids." Those familiar with Keats's letters will remember his comment on Dilke's handwriting: "like the speaking
of a child, three years old, very understandable to its father but
to no one else."

Not only did Dilke print these translations but he welcomed
a suggestion from her that she should write an article upon the
Greek Christian Fathers (begging her to keep away from theol-

ogy). This, although it meant further hard reading, she accomplished in time for part publication in the next issue. The first instalment begins with a fine passage on the Greek language and its great exponents. I give the opening sentences:

The Greek language was a strong intellectual life, stronger than any similar one which has lived in the breath of "articulately speaking men," and survived it. No other language has lived so long and died so hard,—pang by pang, each with a dolphin colour—yielding reluctantly to that doom of death and silence which must come at last to the speaker and the speech.

Though "the instrument of the Greek tongue was, at the Christian era, an antique instrument, somewhat worn," the Christian Fathers had, as compared with the better-known Latin ecclesiastical poets, "that higher distinction inherent in brain and breast, of vivid thought and quick sensibility."

They must be estimated, however stiff and stammering, as religious poets. To Elizabeth all true poets must be in essence religious, and at this time the state of the human soul before its God was preoccupying her. She was to sing, or perhaps had already sung, in "The Soul's Travelling" of man's spirit adventuring in the world of men, but

> *. . . very vain*
> *The greatest speed of all these souls of men,*
> *Unless they travel upward to the throne,*
> *Where sittest* THOU, *the satisfying* ONE,
> *With help for sins and holy perfectings*
> *For all requirements—while the archangel, raising*
> *Unto Thy face his full ecstatic gazing,*
> *Forgets the rush and rapture of his wings.*

It is clear from a reference in "The Greek Christian Fathers" that in her preoccupation with man's soul, Goethe, in the person of his Wilhelm Meister, was impressing her mind. The wounded spirit was climbing from its abyss though its earthly shell remained weak and crushed. Boyd, perhaps fearing that her love of Greek poetry was weakening, put a direct question and received a lively answer: she had in Devonshire kept up her knowledge of Euripides, Æschylus, and Sophocles. "You know I have gone through every line of the three tragedians long ago, in the way of regular, consecutive reading." The reading of

Plato, although already extensive, she had to complete "as soon as I can take breath from Mr. Dilke." She would also round off her knowledge of Aristotle.

Mr. Kenyon, who was fast becoming a close friend, disapproved of the work on the Christian Fathers as "labour thrown away, from the unpopularity of the subject." Mrs. Jameson, however, in the first reference we have of Elizabeth's to her, although no Grecian, "read them with 'great pleasure' unconsciously of the author": "Mr. Horne the poet and Mr. Browning the poet were not behind in approbation."

Dilke had suggested that Elizabeth should also give him a series of papers on the English poets, linking it loosely as a review with a recent anthology entitled *The Book of the Poets* and rounded off with a review of Wordsworth's latest volume, *Poems, chiefly of early and late years.* This she did well enough to please even that stern critic Mr. Boyd, who, she confided delightedly to George, commented that "of the whole passage about Shakespeare, nobody can find the least sign of its being written '*by a female.*'"

Chaucer is understandingly analysed and his "true music" defended against those who still maintained that he wrote by accent only. Most interesting perhaps to modern ears is her passage on Skelton and "his influence for good upon our language. He was a writer singularly fitted for beating out the knots of the cordage, and strain the lengths to extension; a rough worker at rough work." Our modern admiration of Donne she could hardly share in 1842; Donne, "having a dumb *angel,* and knowing more noble poetry than he articulates." In a rapid survey of Elizabethan drama she asserts that, in the history of its development, "Kyd's blank verse is probably the first breaking of the true soil; and certainly far better and more dramatic than Marlowe's is—crowned poet as the latter stands before us— . . . Marlowe was more essentially a poet than a dramatist . . . Kyd . . . more essentially, with all his dramatic faults, a dramatist than a poet."

In dealing with Shakespeare and linking him with Homer, she roundly declared:
We, who have no leaning to the popular cant of Romanticism and Classicism, and believe the old Greek BEAUTY *to be both*

*new and old, and as alive and not more grey in Webster's
Duchess of Malfy than in Æschylus's Eumenides, do reverence
this Homer and this Shakespeare as the colossal borderers of
the two intellectual departments of the world's age—do behold
from their feet the antique and modern literatures sweep outwardly away.*

In speaking of the Augustan age, and the "idol-worship of
rime," Elizabeth gave a fine analysis of the earlier employment
of rime as "a felicitous adjunct, a musical accompaniment, the
tinkling of a cymbal through the choral harmonies." Dryden,
"eloquent above the sons of men," though it was then the fashion to speak of him not as a poet but an influence, "was a poet—
an excellent poet—in marble. . . . He was a poet without passion. . . . He had a large soul for a man, containing sundry
Queen Anne's men, one within the other, like quartetto tables;
but it was not a large soul for a poet. . . ." Our language and
our literature, however, remain, in certain respects, the greater
for his greatness. She could not fully join in the new fashionable
decrying of "Pope, the perfecter," the idol of her childhood, but,
with the true historic sense of a born critic, gave him his just
due, placing him as a practitioner even higher than Dryden for
*a delicate fineness of tact, of which the precise contrary is un-
pleasantly obvious in his great master . . . there is nothing of
[Dryden's] coarseness of the senses about Pope; the little pale
Queen Anne's valetudinarian had a nature fine enough to stand
erect upon the point of a needle like a schoolman's angel; and
whatever he wrote coarsely he did not write from inward impulse, but from external conventionality, from a bad social
Swift-sympathy.*

Of chief interest to a biographer in these first articles are not
only a wide understanding knowledge of the earlier poets, but
her general remarks upon poetry and nature. The true poet of
nature is not he who uses merely the language, the scenery of
nature—Nature is but "chief secretary to the creative Word."
"Nature is where God is," and so, in a larger sense, is poetry:
*In the loudest hum of your machinery, in the dunnest volume of
your steam, in the foulest street of your city—there as surely as
in the Brocken pine-woods and the watery thunders of Niagara*

*—there, as surely as He is above all, lie Nature and Poetry in full
life.*

Though she herself was to contribute largely to the fashionable
escape of a materialistic age to mediævalism, to island, to cloudy
refuge, she was also to strike the note of modernity; to culminate in *Aurora Leigh*, a story of contemporary life.

Her article on Wordsworth continued the history of poetry
into the romantic age, beginning with, in a reference to him in
a previous article, Cowper, the forerunner. Though clearly familiar with *Poems*, 1817, she did not, oddly enough to us, in
dealing with the early nineteenth-century revolt against pseudo-
classic conventions, refer to Keats's direct attack upon the
Popean school and the rules of Boileau; but Keats, awaiting the
publication of Lord Houghton's *Life and Letters* in 1848, had
not yet come into his own.

She did honour to Wordsworth for his greatness as a pioneer,
a true Christian poet and interpreter of Nature, though pointing out that in part the challenge of the *Lyrical Ballads* was
founded on a false premise: "Betty Foys of the Lake school (so
called) may be as subject to convention as Pope's Lady Bettys."
These poems of the master presented in the new volume were
not the finest of his productions. She quoted from "The Borderers," the early verse play now for the first time published,
calling it "strong black writing," though not true Wordsworth,
gave four of his sonnets, including the beautiful "Airey-Force
Valley," and in her last tribute to his greatness protested against
certain critics who

*utter melancholy frenzies, that poetry is worn out for ever. . . .
In the meantime the hopeful and believing will hope—trust on;
and better still, the Tennysons and the Brownings, and other
high-gifted spirits, will work, wait on, until as Mr. Horne has
said—*

> *Strong deeds awake,*
> *And clamouring, throng the portals of the hour.*

This, her first public mention of Browning, did singular honour
to a poet as yet unknown outside literary circles; perhaps hardly
beyond the discriminate few among which her cousin Kenyon
moved.

The footsteps are now coming nearer, only to recede. In the March of this year Mr. Kenyon wanted to bring to her sofa-side "Mr. Browning the poet . . . who was so honor-giving as to wish something of the sort: I was pleased at the thought of his wishing it—for the rest, no!" Kenyon had told her that Browning was discouraged by his reception with the public. "Poor Browning!" said Mr. Kenyon.

"And why poor Browning?"

"Because nobody reads him."

"Rather then," Elizabeth retorted, "poor readers. Mr. Carlyle is his friend—a good substitute for a crowd's shouting!"

When reporting this to George, Elizabeth commented: "you are aware how I estimate . . . admire (what is the sufficient word?) that true poet—however he may prophesy darkly." We know from Browning himself that he was physically near, at this time or another, probably for a moment or two under the same roof: Kenyon had announced him but reported her too unwell to receive him.

In the modernity of her spirit Elizabeth, in spite of enforced seclusion, kept close touch with contemporary writers. Carlyle was reverenced, and she was now reading Emerson. Novels were eagerly devoured, many of them French, her passion for French fiction being shared by Miss Mitford, with whom there was a constant exchange of recommendations. For Balzac she had, and was later to share with her husband, an immense admiration, Victor Hugo was for her far above the popular Dickens, and George Sand one of the greatest women of the age.

An interest in contemporary life had been manifest in December of the last year in verses (published in the *Athenæum*) upon the marriage of Queen Victoria with the deliberate echo-title in "Crowned and Wedded" of the previous year's "Crowned and Buried," the verses upon Napoleon Bonaparte. "Crowned and Wedded," called by the partial Miss Mitford "the most magnificent poem ever written by woman," written in a measure that does not fall too happily on modern ears, is for us redeemed from utter commonplace only by her references to the Dead "who lie in rows beneath the minster floor," the scene of the royal wedding:

The statesman whose clean palm will kiss no bribe,
                                        whate'er it be,
The courtier who for no fair queen, will rise up on his
                                        knee;
The court-dame who, for no court-tire, will leave her
                                        shroud behind;
The laureate who no courtlier rime than "dust to dust"
                                        can find;
The kings and queens who having made that vow and worn
                                        that crown,
Descended into lower thrones and darker, deep adown!

Sentiments more worthily expressed in the fine "Epitaph" beginning "Beauty who softly walkest all thy days," published with the translation of "Prometheus Bound."

To Miss Mitford Elizabeth was now writing some two or three times a week, letters of which that enthusiastic friend wrote: "Put Mdme de Sevigné and Cowper together, and you can fancy them." Though Elizabeth's letters cannot, perhaps, be placed in that high class, they are lively, penetrating, humorous, philosophic; and speak, according to the testimony of those who knew her, in her own authentic voice.

By an ever widening correspondence she kept contact with the outer world in letters to distinguished men of the day, most of whom were writers: an exception, and one of the most interesting, was the painter and priest of "high art" Benjamin Robert Haydon, with whom she had a lively exchange between 1842 and 1845. Haydon was probably put into communication with her by their common friend Miss Mitford.

A part of Elizabeth's side of this correspondence has been printed, a few letters in Haydon's *Correspondence* and some twenty by Miss Shackford, but a good number of Haydon's letters to her remain unpublished; [2] and from these I am privileged to quote.

Haydon, as natural a writer as herself, fell quickly into a tone of intimacy, commenting in his large way: "there is something so original in a couple of Geniuses corresponding, becoming acquainted, knowing each other thoroughly and yet never seeing each other, that I revelled in the Idea beyond expression."

[2] Pope Collection.

Once he had called in Wimpole Street, only to receive the usual reply that her health did not permit her to receive visitors.

He, as man of the world, an artist and a man of wide reading and interests, had much to give this recluse; perhaps more than we know in the way of drawing her back to life. He wrote lively reminiscences of illustrious people he had met twenty years before, including Keats, sent her drawings to look at, two portraits, successively, of Wordsworth upon Helvellyn to hang in her room, and his autobiography in manuscript. She on her part lent him books, including a black-letter Chaucer, helped him in the planning of his Chaucer picture, and, not the least, gave the unfortunate man sympathy, delicate feminine praise, at a time when he craved for it. When in 1843 his cartoons for the Houses of Parliament were rejected, Elizabeth tried to soften the blow, pointing out that all great men have been attacked in their generation. But it was in vain that she, the most modest of artists, combated against his overweening vanity, his enormous sense of grievance at failure.

In refusing Haydon's request that they should "change portraits royally," declaring she has no likeness to send him, Elizabeth gave, as "scanty data" to his fancy, a verbal portrait of herself that is worth quoting if only because it settles one point on which descriptions of her are at variance, the colour of her eyes:

I am "little and black" like Sappho, en attendant the immortality—five feet one high; as the latitude, straight to correspond— eyes of various colours as the sun shines,—called blue and black, without being accidentally black and blue—affidavit-ed for grey —sworn at for hazel—and set down by myself (according to my "private view" in the glass) as dark-green-brown—grounded with brown, and green otherwise; what is called "invisible green" in invisible garden-fences. . . . Not much nose of any kind; certes no superfluity of nose; but to make up for it, a mouth suitable to a larger personality—oh, and a very very little voice, to which Cordelia's was a happy medium. Dark hair and complexion— Small face and sundries.

In discussing his autobiography Elizabeth begs him to "*spare the provocative,*" to cultivate reserve, especially in regard to himself. "When the lion roars, he need not say 'I am a lion' . . .

if he SHOULD say 'I am a lion,' all the monkeys on the palm trees
are sworn to cry out . . . 'No lion! but a jackall.'" To this, in
his inflated estimate of his own genius, Haydon retorted, did
she want him to act the hypocrite?

A subject of mutual interest was Napoleon. On Elizabeth's
expression of her country's dishonour in the banishment to St.
Helena, after the Emperor had surrendered to the Prince Regent, Haydon commented: "The Rock was melancholy! but it
was poetical! It surrounded his latter days with a halo of Romance." Much as he admired Napoleon's genius, it must be admitted that security of his person was, after twenty-five years
of war, the first object. "His word of honour was nothing": at
large he must always have remained a danger. Looking at the
first Dictator with a detachment surprising in one so partial, so
emotional, Haydon added: "Napoleon threw the cause of
Genius, 100 years back, the good he did was accidental, the
Evil certain." As Elizabeth held to her point he teased her, calling her his "little Napoleonette," "You Ingenious little darling
invisible."

In this connection he gave her reminiscences of his visit to
Paris, in 1814 soon after Napoleon's abdication, where he exam-
ined "his haunts," "doating on his Genius," even seeing "the ex-
tinguisher on the last candle he read by, at Fontainebleau."
Elizabeth, always reticent about her age, did not, so far as we
know, reveal the fact that she had to some extent followed his
footsteps in 1815.

From Napoleon they passed naturally to the Empress Marie
Louise and from her, as one of two women who had left their
husbands, to Lady Byron. Elizabeth always hated Byron's wife
even after she came to know Anna Jameson, a close friend of
that unhappy lady. Haydon told her how twice he had come in
contact with Lady Byron, "that double X icicle": "and we quar-
relled without hope, the second time—the first day, I thought
Byron a brute—the second day I was convinced *she* was—a
Mathematician. The morning dress was dimity, the Evening
silk." [3]

On December 30, 1842 Haydon made a precious gift to his
"little darling invisible": the last sixty lines in holograph of "I

[3] See *Don Juan*, Canto I, st. xii.

stood tip-toe upon a little hill." Keats, loved and read then by comparatively few, Elizabeth had in 1838 already honoured in "A Vision of Poets"; later, in *Aurora Leigh*, she was to give the world an "epitaph" of him which set a seal on the new estimate of a poet who, by 1857, had entered into his kingdom.

At the end of June 1843 Haydon, rendered desperate by the rejection of his cartoons and expecting daily executions for debt, sent for safety to Elizabeth "two jars of oil (1816) twenty-seven years old," and several boxes containing papers, books, and letters. These boxes were to be, at Haydon's tragic death, a source of embarrassment and annoyance to her.

In the spring of that year Haydon, who, to do him justice, arrogant being though he was, felt to the full his high privilege in consorting with the great of his generation, sent her an urn upon which he had inscribed the names of those "immortals" who had taken tea drawn from it: though she might not drink at his own table, Elizabeth must join this illustrious band. On the 29th Elizabeth wrote, expressing both inward amusement and natural modesty: "This is my certificate, my dear Mr. Haydon that I have taken and quaffed a cup of amreeta [4] from your urn of the Immortals!" And as Flush had taken "a quaff from the lees of my cup" she made "a humble suggestion" that he "inscribe the worthy name of Flush first and my name afterwards . . we two completing together a very perfect antithesis to your *Dii Majores*."

Flush is now among the immortals and perhaps it is unnecessary to write much of him: the spaniel was her constant companion and consolation, her "loving friend." His beauty and devotion have been fitly celebrated in those well-known lines "To Flush, my Dog." A less familiar tribute is the sonnet "Flush or Faunus," which is perhaps worth quoting in full:

> *You see this dog. It was but yesterday*
> *I mused forgetful of his presence here*
> *Till thought on thought drew downward tear on tear,*
> *When from the pillow, where wet-cheeked I lay,*
> *A head as hairy as Faunus, thrust its way*
> *Right sudden against my face,—two golden-clear*

---

[4] "The Amreeta-cup of immortality." See Canto XXIV, st. 9, l. 11, Southey's *The Curse of Kehama*.

> *Great eyes astonished mine,—a drooping ear*
> *Did flap me on either cheek to dry the spray!*
> *I started first, as some Arcadian,*
> *Amazed by goatly god in twilight grove;*
> *But, as the bearded vision closelier ran*
> *My tears off, I knew Flush, and rose above*
> *Surprise and sadness,—thanking the true* PAN,
> *Who, by low creatures, leads to heights of love.*

In a letter of September 1842 we find another reference to the god Pan, who was to form the subject of two of her best-known poems: Elizabeth asked Kenyon for permission to keep a little longer his translation of Schiller's "Gods of Greece." She thanked him for two volumes of Tennyson's *Poems* recently published and, in comparing old poems with new, observed with her usual critical acumen:

nothing appears to me quite equal to "Œnone," and perhaps a few besides of my ancient favorites. . . . There is, in fact, more thought—more bare brave working of the intellect—in the latter poems, even if we miss something of the high ideality, and the music that goes with it, of the older ones.

But, though she might criticize him, Tennyson remained for Elizabeth almost an object of adoration: six months later we find her treasuring "a very kind note" from him. "I am," she wrote to George, "sensible of the honour of being written to by Mr. Tennyson, & I am ready to kiss his shoe-tyes any day. This is not in joke—it is grave, solemn, earnest." She looked eagerly for any news of Tennyson her brother might obtain. When George, on meeting the great man, reported that he wore a dirty shirt, Elizabeth countered mischievously: "I waive the dirty shirt—it is by way of lyrical transition into the society of lawyers with dirty consciences." The smoking of a pipe in society, a solecism of which Tennyson was often guilty, she was also prepared to overlook. "I envied you notwithstanding the tobacco smoke."

The summer of 1842 was a warm one, with a consequent improvement in Elizabeth's health. By the end of September she was free from the blood spittings that had been such a disturbing symptom of her illness, was able to go downstairs several times and even out in her chair. "At the end of such a double summer," she wrote to Boyd, "I might be able to go to see you at Hampstead. Nevertheless, winters and adversities are more fit for us than a constant sun."

One "adversity," if a minor one, at this time was "dearest Miss Mitford's letters from the deathbed of her father," which *make my heart ache as surely almost as the post comes. . . . If I were in her circumstances, I should sit paralysed—it would be impossible for me to write or to cry. And she, who loves and feels with the intensity of a nature warm in everything, seems to turn to sympathy by the very instinct of grief, and sits at the deathbed of her last relative, writing there, in letter after letter, every symptom, physical or moral—even to the very words of the raving of a delirium, and those, heart-breaking words!*

Practical sympathy was expressed during Dr. Mitford's illness by gifts, some West Indian in origin, of delicacies probably beyond the purse and certainly beyond the reach of his devoted daughter.

To Boyd in the December of this year Elizabeth gave, in reply to a charge of Calvinism, a clear avowal of her religious faith:

I believe simply that the saved are saved by grace, and that they shall hereafter know it fully; that the lost are lost by their choice and free will—by choosing to sin and die; and I believe absolutely that the deepest damned of all the lost will not dare to whisper to the nearest devil that reproach of Martha: "If the Lord had been near me, I had not died."

For the rest she was agnostic. "But of the means of the workings of God's grace, and the time of the formation of the Divine counsels, I know nothing, guess nothing, and struggle to guess nothing." She refuses to examine the "brickbats of controversy —there is more than enough to think of in truths clearly revealed."

It was probably at this time that she composed a group of religious sonnets. In one of the finest we get a painful glimpse into miseries silently endured in that upper room, the pains of the rack:

> *All tortured states*
> *Suppose a straitened place.*

With Mr. Boyd Elizabeth was carrying on a lively literary correspondence. Boyd in his old-fashioned way was refusing to acknowledge the merits of Wordsworth; and, curiously enough, appeared only now, in 1843, to be "discovering" Ossian, whom —more astonishingly still in a classical scholar—he claimed as superior to Homer. "The fact," Elizabeth commented succinctly, "appears to me that anomalous thing among believers —a miracle without an occasion."

About this time R. H. Horne delighted her with the loan of an original portrait of Keats, one which seems to be unrecorded. Of it she wrote: "It is a Vandyke—all but the form and color—to be sure! So, being just, I can't remonstrate against your resolution of keeping it to yourself, though I sh⁴ like very much to see your lines of correction." She noted a singular resemblance to a portrait of Horne himself.

In this letter [5] she discussed the question of euthanasia, remarking:

Intense pain & light & serenity of soul do often go together— & spectators & physicians cannot always judge of the actual condition of the patient. And pain does good to us often—& God's grace often is flowing in an undercurrent under the seemingly most rocky ground.

Elizabeth herself had, of course, known searing pain at an early age and was not now exempt from it: a bitter east wind, penetrating even to that closed room, could affect her heart.

Elizabeth had now material enough for a new volume of poems. Thinking that her literary reputation now warranted it, she offered her copyright to Saunders & Otley, the publishers of *The Seraphim*, if they would undertake publication without expense to herself. On their refusal she asked Horne to advise her as to "the most poetical bookseller" of his acquaintance. Again she was willing to surrender the copyright. It was, however, two years before "the most poetical bookseller," Edward Moxon, put out those two volumes which were to bring her both fame and happiness.

As with many English writers, and the majority of our poets in the first half of the last century, Elizabeth's reputation in

[5] Forman Collection, January 7, 1843.

America was higher than here. At the end of 1842 *Graham's Magazine* gave an enthusiastic review of her work: in the spring we find her writing to Cornelius Mathews, its editor and himself a writer of distinction, sending him poems for publication, recommending English writers, and giving the literary gossip of the day. Once in return Mathews sent her a notice of "A Blot in the 'Scutcheon," apparently not favourable, under the impression that she was personally acquainted with Browning. Elizabeth replied:

I do assure you I never saw him in my life—do not know him even by correspondence—and yet, whether through fellow-feeling for Eleusinian mysteries, or whether through the more generous motive of appreciation of his powers, I am very sensitive to the thousand and one stripes with which the assembly of critics doth expound its vocation over him, and the "Athenæum," for instance, made me quite cross and misanthropical last week.[6] The truth is—and the world should know the truth— it is easier to find a more faultless writer than a poet of equal genius.

"Don't," she added quaintly, "let us fall into the category of the sons of Noah. Noah was once drunk, indeed, but once he built the ark."

[6] In a review of *Dramatic Lyrics*.

CHAPTER 11

THE RECLUSE OF WIMPOLE STREET [1843–4]

FROM LETTERS at this time we can build up a picture of Elizabeth's surroundings in the Wimpole Street house, one of an attached row, running parallel with Gloucester Place, "whose walls look so much like Newgate's turned inside out." The house itself has been pulled down, but it can be mentally reconstructed from those remaining; with their dignified reception rooms below, the great drawing-room on the first floor and bedrooms piled above. Elizabeth's room was at the back on the second floor with Henrietta's directly above her.

That room which she hardly left for five years had a wide bay window, a window that in its noble proportions would seem to demand a fine view. It looked, however, over dark houses and chimney-pots. In a deep window box that summer of 1843 there were scarlet runners, convolvuluses, nasturtiums: a large ivy root given her by John Kenyon, and destined to veil the urban view, had recently been planted. Very soon it covered all the panes, its trailing branches even reaching up to Henrietta's window.

This greenery, these flowers brought wistful memory of gardens lost, of the countryside over which she had so freely run, ridden, or driven in and about Hope End. "I have never," she wrote Mrs. Martin, "cared so much in my life for flowers as since being shut out from gardens." But in winter this joy must be but transitory: in that close atmosphere plants and flowers quickly died.

An effort was made to disguise the fact that in this room Elizabeth slept as well as lived: the bed was "like a sofa," the wash-stand turned into a cabinet on which stood shelves home-carpentered by "Sette and Co." Similar shelves covered with crimson merino topped a chest of drawers. The wardrobe, an uncompromising piece of furniture in Victorian days, could not be disguised. In the middle of the room stood a large table to hold books and papers. Her sofa opposed an armchair, the gift of her uncle so many years before.

In the window hung an Æolian harp, given her by Mr. Barrett, of which she wrote to Boyd in friendly rivalry with his chiming clocks: "nothing below the spherical harmonies is so sweet and soft and mournfully wild." Flush was jealous of this harp, thinking it alive; always taking it "as very hard that I should say 'beautiful' to anything else except his ears!" Boyd was now living at 3, Circus Road, St. John's Wood. In attempting to induce him to walk across Regent's Park to visit her, Elizabeth told Boyd that in this retreat, her "prison," no sound should affront the over-sensitive ears of a blind man:

We live on the verge of the town rather than in it, and our noises are cousins to silence; and you should pass into a room where the silence is most absolute. Flush's breathing is my loudest sound, and then the watch's tickings, and then my heart when it beats too turbulently.

But around this quiet room, sometimes irrupting into it, was life enough in that large household. The sisters were Elizabeth's most constant companions, the lively auburn-haired Henrietta and gentler, soberer Arabel. Of these two women, neither of them girls now, Elizabeth has drawn pen portraits for us in the sonnets "Two Sketches." Henrietta, she tells us, had a Grecian profile, but a face too full at front view and rather high-coloured, her main beauty being

> *A smile that turns the sunny side o' the heart*
> *On all the world, as if herself did win*
> *By what she lavished on an open mart!*
> *Let no man call that liberal sweetness, sin,—*

Henrietta was perhaps a flirt and certainly a woman attractive to men. There was more than one eager to marry her though she was now well past the age of thirty.

Arabel, her eyes blue, dark-lashed, her head covered with fair drooping curls,

> *As many to each cheek as you might see*
> *Green leaves to a wild rose!*

was a woman born to serve, of a natural saintliness:

> *To smell this flower, come near it! such can grow*
> *In that sole garden where Christ's brow dropped blood.*

Henrietta loved balls and parties, but Arabel's deep joy was in religion, in the Paddington Chapel to which she went early each morning. She, Elizabeth's favourite sister, slept in her room.

The brothers, so far as we know, were all living at home. It is not easy to gather, except in the case of George, how they occupied themselves: Septimus later became a barrister, Occy was at one time studying architecture, and Alfred, ultimately a King's Messenger, seems in the middle forties to have had some connection with the Great Western Railway.

We are best informed about Elizabeth's relations with George because the letters written to him while he was on circuit are available. George took a lively interest in the literary society of his day and, as has been said, brought her news of Mr. Tennyson. The eldest surviving son, Charles John, or Stormie, may have helped his father at the London office, but we hear nothing of it: certainly he seems to have had enough freedom to travel in Mr. Barrett's ships when he wished. Though now the eldest, being of a softer, gentler nature than George, he tacitly ceded a place as leading spirit in the family to that more vigorous personality.

There was also in the house a pretty fair-haired girl of ten years, Elizabeth Georgina, daughter of Captain George Goodin Barrett, who, being out in Jamaica, had left her in charge of his cousin, Mr. Barrett. Elizabeth Georgina, or Lizzie, was a favourite, just the quiet kind of child to be welcome in an invalid's room:

> *Choosing pleasures, for the rest,*
> *Which come softly—just as she,*
> *When she nestles at your knee.*

Her voice murmured "lowly, as a silver stream may run." This charming child, the pet of the family, was later to become Elizabeth's sister-in-law.

At the head of this household ranging from childhood to early middle age (as age was reckoned then) was an enigmatic man who, from certain misrepresentations and a radical change in family customs, has come to be popularly regarded as one larger than life, a sinister figure: actually Mr. Barrett, though spoiled as were so many men before the emancipation of women, though arbitrary in relation to his children, seems to have been, but for one odd and distressing kink in his nature, a typical conscientious early nineteenth-century father who held firmly that a parent should command and a child obey.

In the evening, on his return after long hours in the City, Mr. Barrett liked to enjoy the society of his family, to have none else at table but his own invited guests. His nature was robust, his face and figure youthful. He took pleasure in his house, his pictures (more believed in as Old Masters by himself, it would appear, than by his children), and was not ashamed to take a feminine interest in flowers. We hear of a branch of some Australian bush (possibly wattle), sent by Mrs. Martin at Christmas, being carried by him all over the house. His laugh was frequent and hearty. When he was away from home the eldest daughter, nearest to him in spirit, felt as if some strong supporting power was withdrawn from her. As with Elizabeth, religion was in him fervent and deep-seated. Of the general influence of his strong personality, of the deep affection between Elizabeth and himself, more must be written later.

It was in 1842 that Miss Mitford gave to an enthusiastic young friend a description of Elizabeth in 1836 (see p. 63): to balance this description Miss Mitford also gave one of her as she appeared that year:

Now she has totally lost the rich, bright colouring, which certainly made the greater part of her beauty. She is dark and pallid; the hair is almost entirely hidden; the look of youth gone (I think she now looks as much beyond her actual age as, formerly, she looked behind it); nothing remaining but the noble forehead, the matchless eyes, and the fine form of the mouth and teeth; even now their whiteness is healthy . . . a symptom favourable to our beloved friend's restoration. The expression, too, is completely changed; the sweetness remains, but it is accompanied with more shrewdness, more gaiety, the look not merely of a woman of genius—that she always had—but of a superlatively clever woman.

Miss Mitford spoke of Elizabeth's ripened talent for conversation, her loss of the early shyness, "an odd effect of absence from general society":

When I first saw her, her talk, delightful as it was, had something too much of the lamp—she spoke too well—and her letters were rather too much like the very best books. Now all that is gone; the fine thoughts come gushing and sparkling as water down a hillside, clear, bright, and sparkling in the sunshine.

However slowly Elizabeth might be progressing towards that recovery her optimistic friend looked forward to (with a prescience not given to either Elizabeth herself or those about her), there was in the invalid a growing force of mind that revealed itself in her work: in the spring of 1843 she composed one of her strongest and finest poems, "The Dead Pan"; one that Kenyon, having helped to inspire, felt to be almost his own property. To him she strenuously defended a strong religious note that he thought likely to injure her popularity. "What pagan poet ever thought of casting his gods out of his poetry? And what, she asked, was popularity beside "truth and earnestness in all things?" If in "The Dead Pan" "Christ's name is improperly spoken . . . then indeed is Schiller right, and the true gods of poetry are to be sighed for mournfully." But feeling the poem to belong peculiarly to her cousin, she was willing to withhold it from publication, if he so desired. In the question of loose rimes Elizabeth was not so firm: some she altered at Kenyon's request.

Incidentally Kenyon was wrong in his estimate of injured popularity: it was in part the earnest Christian note in Elizabeth's poetry that made her so popular with a large section of the Victorian community.

Kenyon's enthusiasm for "The Dead Pan" increased Elizabeth's reputation in the literary world; he taking care to bring it to the notice of his circle, of Landor, Browning, and "several other of the demi gods." Kenyon even ventured to send several stanzas of it to Wordsworth in the hope that his appetite might be whetted for more. From what we know of the old egoist, however, it is unlikely that Wordsworth did ask for more, though he had in the previous month expressed his personal value for Elizabeth by sending her the somewhat embarrassing gift of his uninspired verses upon a heroine of the hour, Grace Darling.

Kenyon had also rendered Elizabeth a more immediately

practical service by finding in the flesh that "most poetical bookseller" she had shadowed forth to Horne a year before: Edward Moxon, lover and publisher of poets, maker of verses himself. When Moxon reported Tennyson as saying: "There is only one female poet whom I wish to see, and that is Miss Barrett," Kenyon seized the opportunity, asking: "Why, did you not once refuse a volume of Miss Barrett's poems?" In Elizabeth's light-hearted words to George, "Moxon answered pathetically in the affirmative, & went on to affirm that he had never had a night's sound sleep since for the aching of his bibliopolic heart . . . that he was suffering agonies of remorse . . . wore sackcloth under his linen and ashes in the crown of his hat." Moxon at once offered "to ruin himself for me, & me alone, by accepting any MS. I might please to send him."

Perhaps from the stimulus of a growing reputation, Elizabeth's health was improving: in the July of 1843 we hear of her again going downstairs some seven or eight times, of "meditating *the chair*" (a bath chair), when "something between cramp and rheumatism" temporarily set her back. The mind, however, was active. She told her brother:

I am in a poetical fit just now. . . . I am writing such poems—allegorical-philosophical-poetical-ethical—synthetically arranged! I am in a fit of writing—could write all day & night, & long to live by myself for three months in a forest of chestnuts and cedars, in an hourly succession of poetical paragraphs & morphine draughts.

Then perhaps with a consciousness that a resort to drugs for sleep and calm nerves was becoming with her a habit, she quickly added:

Not that I do such a thing. . . . Nota bene! You are not to say a word of morphine when you write next.

One result of this poetic activity was "The Cry of the Children," published in the August number of *Blackwood's Magazine,* the outcome of a harrowing report issued by R. H. Horne as assistant commissioner on the employment of children in mines and factories. "The Cry of the Children" both stirred and embodied public conscience.

The mental energy, even the physical labour, of this invalid was amazing. In addition to the many poems composed that

year—which included the long, finely-wrought "A Vision of
Poets"—and the letters she wrote to George, to Miss Mitford, to
Miss Martineau (most of them unhappily lost to us), to Boyd,
to Kenyon and others, Elizabeth was at work in collaboration
with Horne on a daring book to be published the following year,
A New Spirit of the Age.

CHAPTER 12

A NEW SPIRIT OF THE AGE [1844]

In 1825, Henry Colburn published *The Spirit of the Age: or Contemporary Portraits*. The work was anonymous though it must have been fairly generally known that the author was William Hazlitt.

This was an age of giants. Of the twenty-four people appraised or criticized in the second edition—writers, social theorists, reformers, or fighters for freedom of thought and expression—thirteen at least are among the great who formed the thought, modes of living, and taste of coming generations, and the rest are familiar to anyone only tolerably acquainted with the period.

Nearly twenty years later R. H. Horne, admittedly as writer and critic far below Hazlitt, set himself to prepare *A New Spirit of the Age*. Thirty-seven personalities were celebrated and others glanced at by the way: of these thirty-seven, Wordsworth, Leigh Hunt, Carlyle, Landor, Browning and Tennyson, Lord Shaftesbury and Dr. Pusey, Hood and "Thomas Ingoldsby," Macready, Dickens, Harrison Ainsworth, and Mary Shelley are the only names that ring familiarly to the plain man of this generation, and of these Wordsworth, Leigh Hunt, and Landor must more truly be said to represent the Georgian era.

The most marked difference in these analyses of two generations is the gentler, less politically biased tone of the second: when allowance has been made for Hazlitt's combative spirit and injured feelings, it must be conceded that his provocative tone towards Tory writers, Tory editors and journals was common among the Liberals. They gave as good as they got. To us, looking at the battle from afar, Hazlitt's brilliant attacks add interest to his contemporary portraits but, fine true critic though he was, they are not without an element of harsh caricature. The spirit of Rowlandson, of Gillray, informed his age; whereas

Horne's critical comments have in them the keen but more kindly humour of that new and typical voice in the land, *Punch, or the London Charivari*. In this connection it is curious to note that it was Horne, not Hazlitt, who presented the wits of twenty-five years before, Theodore Hook and Sydney Smith.

Another change in outlook, in mental atmosphere, is the more humanitarian feeling displayed, the indignation at certain social abuses, especially that of which Horne in his official capacity had first-hand knowledge: the employment of children. Emphasis, too, is laid upon the advance, the popularisation of science, the new mechanical aids to living, with a warning, in the person of Carlyle, of the dangers to the soul of material comfort, of an easiness of life. In this connection stress might have been laid on the mental and spiritual discipline called for by the High Church movement, but in dealing with Dr. Pusey the opportunity to show one clear facet of early Victorian life is missed; if indeed it was not yet too soon to realize its meaning. Dr. Pusey is represented not as a spiritual force, a man of saintly life, but as a doctrinaire, a militant theologian. It was perhaps also a natural inability always to see one's own age completely in focus that made Horne print what appears to us an entirely wrong-headed, a quite humourless criticism of another member of the Church, the Reverend R. H. Barham, "Thomas Ingoldsby." Even a stern moral outlook must, for healthiness, have its jester, and to the Victorian age at its strictest surely Thomas Ingoldsby was that jester.

There are two more differences, one being the number of women writers celebrated by Horne, and the inclusion of many novelists of both sexes: Hazlitt does not include one woman and the only two novelists he admits are Scott and Godwin, both men with a prior fame in other forms of writing.

Horne's work suffers less than one would think from a difference in method. Hazlitt's book was entirely written by himself, and anonymously, whereas Horne, though he took responsibility as editor for the whole, and wrote much himself, had collaborators, the chief being Robert Bell, once editor of the *Atlas*, a powerful London journal, and Elizabeth Barrett. The whole, however, is cleverly co-ordinated, seldom patchy in effect. The collaborators wisely remained anonymous: it was

Horne who bore the brunt of subsequent attacks from parties who felt themselves injured, by either criticism or omission.

Elizabeth's co-operation, earnest and thorough, was given selflessly, without material gain. "The most valuable friend and counsellor in a book affecting contemporaries," Horne wrote some thirty years after, is

one who, possessing a finely suitable intellect for the matter in question, and having gathered together the requisite knowledge, is dwelling comparatively out of the world and its conflicting people and opinions, yet taking a deep interest in the best things that are going on, coupled with a due indignation at the worst, and who has magnanimity to admire, as well as moral courage to demur or denounce, ever holding within, as at a shrine, an unmixed love and spirit of truth. Such a friend and counsellor . . . I had in Miss Barrett.

Another advantage to Horne, perhaps only fully realizable by one looking back on the age, is that suggested by his use of the word "shrine." Elizabeth brought to the work a spirit of religion which was also that of many of the best of her time, a spirit reverencing art as an expression of the beauty and truth of God.

Their method of collaboration, one that could only have been pursued by two persons entirely with their eye on the object and not out to ride their own particular hobby-horses, was that of separate manuscripts submitted one to the other for interpolation. The mottoes heading each article, which are beautifully apt in every case and drawn from a long range of English literature, were for the most part supplied by Elizabeth and another friend of Horne's, Robert Browning; presenting a biographer with yet another false start towards the great climax of her story. What, if only Elizabeth had not insisted on absolute anonymity, would have been more natural than that these two should have consulted one another in the delicate and important operation of choosing quotations appropriate to each author?

The article upon Landor, considered by Horne to be one of the finest, was mainly written by Elizabeth, the following extract being among the most striking:

*He writes criticism for critics, and poetry for poets: his drama,
when he is dramatic, will suppose neither pit nor gallery, nor
critics, nor dramatic laws. He is not a publican among poets—
he does not sell his Amreeta cups upon the highway. He deliv-
ers them rather with the dignity of a giver, to ticketted persons;
analysing their flavour and fragrance with a learned delicacy,
and an appeal to the esoteric. His very spelling of English is
uncommon and theoretic. He has a vein of humour which by its
own nature is peculiarly subtle and evasive; he therefore re-
fines upon it, by his art, in order to prevent anybody discovering it without a grave, solicitous, and courtly approach, which
is unspeakably ridiculous to all the parties concerned, and
which no doubt the author secretly enjoys. And as if poetry
were not, in English, a sufficiently unpopular dead language,
he has had recourse to writing poetry in Latin; with disserta-
tions on the Latin tongue, to fence it out doubly from the populace.* "Odi profanum vulgus, et arceo."

On Landor's style she commented: "In marble indeed, he
seems to work; for there is an angularity in the workmanship,
whether of prose or verse, which the very exquisiteness of the
polish renders more conspicuous. You may complain too of
hearing the chisel; but after all you applaud the work . . . his
smaller poems . . . for quiet classical grace and tenderness,
and exquisite care in their polish, may best be compared with
beautiful cameos and vases of the antique."

When one considers the influence of Landor upon the great
romantics, and his established reputation among the finer spirits of the Georgian era, it seems strange that Hazlitt did not
even mention him in *The Spirit of the Age;* perhaps because he
had in 1825 been so long out of England, or perhaps because of
his disdainful attitude towards criticism. "His feeling towards
this department of literature," wrote Elizabeth of him in a lively
account of his career, "may be estimated by his offer of a hot
penny roll and a pint of stout, for breakfast (!) to any critic
who could write one of his Imaginary Conversations—an indi-
gestible pleasantry which horribly enraged more than one critic
of the time."

The article upon Wordsworth and Leigh Hunt, largely Elizabeth's work, compares admirably with those by Hazlitt: it is typical of a change in attitude that the two veterans were linked together by Horne, whereas Hunt, known personally to Hazlitt in his younger, more volatile days, is linked in a critique with Tom Moore. Hazlitt's article on Wordsworth, though brilliant, is marred by a veiled personal attack on the man who had abandoned early revolutionary principles and accepted a Government appointment: in *A New Spirit of the Age* Wordsworth is presented reverently as accepted poet (though as sometimes dull and prolix), as father of the romantic school and an earnest Christian moralist. In her analysis of Wordsworth as poet Elizabeth surely puts a finger on the very heart of romanticism: "Chaucer and Burns made the most of a daisy, but left it still a daisy; Wordsworth leaves it transformed into *his* thoughts. This is the sublime of egotism, disinterested as extreme."

In dealing with Leigh Hunt as the founder of the so-called "Cockney School" she gives an eloquent catalogue of its illustrious members: "Lamb, who stammered out in child-like simplicity, his wit beautiful with wisdom"; "Coleridge, so full of genius and all rare acquirements"; "Hazlitt, who dwelt gloriously with philosophy in a chamber of imagery"; "Shelley with his wings of golden fire"; "Keats who saw divine visions, and the pure Greek ideal, because he had the essence in his soul"; "Leigh Hunt (now the sole survivor of all these) true poet and exquisite essayist."

In the correspondence over Leigh Hunt between Elizabeth and Horne it is interesting to note the difference in moral attitude: Horne, certainly with the advantage of a long acquaintanceship with Hunt, could, drawing from his roots in the Liberalism of the Georgian era, firmly assert that the criticism Hunt had provoked of an inability, of disinclination to draw a line between good and evil, was not a fair one: in his own lovable nature and infinite charity it was persons, not principles, Hunt was utterly unable to condemn. This, though admitting that "the cordiality and benignity of his genius are essentially Christian," Elizabeth could not admit, though she conceded that he had cancelled offending passages in later editions of his works. The general attitude of many readers in this Evangelical age is given by her in a reference to "our dear friend, Miss Mitford—no prude—no fanatic—yet one who said, or implied to me once, that a woman should not be eager to praise Leigh Hunt."

In the critique on Hunt—not, perhaps because of this outlook, so well co-ordinated as some on which they worked together— the following analysis is surely Elizabeth's:

His blank verse is the most successfully original in its freedom, of any that has appeared since the time of Beaumont and Fletcher. His images are commonly beautiful, if often fantastic—clustering like bees, or like grapes—sometimes too many for the vines—a good fault in these bare modern days. . . . His gatherings from nature are true to nature. . . . His nature, however, is seldom moor-land and mountain-land; nor is it, for the most part, English nature—we have hints of fauns and the nymphs lying in the shadow of the old Italian woods; and the sky overhead is several tints too blue for home experiences . . . it is nature by memory and phantasy; true, but touched with an exotic purple.

In the critique on Alfred Tennyson, a joint production, a lively retort is given to a reference in *The Times* of December 26, 1842 to poems of Keats as "the half-finished works of this young, miseducated, and unripe genius" which "have had the greatest influence on that which is now the popular poetry." That influence could not be denied but Keats, "divine," unique, could have no "single mechanical imitator": in regard to mere popular poetry, rather "the pure Greek wine of Keats has been set aside for the thin gruel of Kirke White."

Of the three full pages upon Keats much must have been written by Horne himself, who had walked and talked with him, but surely it was Elizabeth who wrote of his effect upon the better part of contemporary literature as:

spiritual in its ideality; it has been classical in its revivification of the forms and images of the antique, which he inspired with a new soul; it has been romantic in its spells, and dreams, and legendary associations; and it has been pastoral in its fresh gatherings from the wild forests and fields, and as little as possible from the garden, and never from the hot-house and the flower-shows.

The influence of Keats upon Tennyson might be apparent, but he was "undoubtedly one of the most original poets that ever lived." As an instance of Tennyson's "enchanted reverie," his skill in subjective scene-painting, the opening to Elizabeth's favourite poem "Œnone" is given. To most of us in the present day this critique on Tennyson will seem over-enthusiastic, over-long but, as in the case of Elizabeth herself—so soon to be accepted as a major poet—it must be remembered that this "silver-tongued romantic," as a modern poet has so happily called him, was then to be contrasted only with far lesser men and women, and in a generation that still read poetry where now only novels would be tolerated.

Elizabeth herself remained to the end of her life under the spell of Tennyson; at first as a verbal enchantment and, when she had met that large demanding personality, of a personal charm. But her intellect in regard to him was not entirely drowsed by the spell. From the first she recognized, or suspected, his lack of essential content, writing to Horne: "He is a divine poet; but I have found it difficult to analyse his divinity, and to determine (even to myself) his particular aspect as a writer. What is the reason of it?" And to another correspondent, Thomas Westwood, a literary son of Charles and Mary Lamb's landlord at Enfield: "the poet is a preacher and must look to his doctrine. Perhaps Mr. Tennyson will grow more solemn, like the sun, as his day goes on. . . . He is one of God's singers, whether he knows it or does not know it."

To us this long eulogy of Tennyson must seem out of proportion to the space given to Robert Browning, who shares attention with J. W. Marston, a poet now entirely forgotten; but it must be remembered that at this time Browning's only major works before the public were "Paracelsus," a few plays, and "Sordello" with its "broken, mazy, dancing sort of narrative no-outline, which has occasioned so much trouble, if not despair, to his most patient and pains-taking admirers." In a generation unaccustomed to trouble the intellect with its poetry it is amazing that, even among his few but fervid admirers, any were found poring over this difficult work: it is a tribute to the unique fascination of Browning, both as poet and as man.

Horne gives us no hint of how much Elizabeth contributed to this critique, nor is there in those published of the letters they exchanged any mention of this poet so soon to mingle his life

with hers. One would like to think that the climax of an affectionate and whimsical judgment of "Sordello" (unfortunately
too long to quote in its entirety) was written by Elizabeth:

*It abounds in things addressed to a second sight, and we are of-
ten required to see double in order to apprehend its meaning.
The poet may be considered the Columbus of an impossible
discovery. It is a promised land, spotted all over with disappointments, and yet most truly a land of promise, if ever so rich
and rare a chaos can be developed into form and order by revision, and its southern fulness of tumultuous heart and scattered
vineyards be ever reduced to given proportion, and wrought
into a shape that will fit the average mental vision and harmonize with the more equable pulsations of mankind.*

This revision, as we know, Browning did attempt but failed to
achieve.

Browning, his work published as yet in cheap little paper-
covered booklets paid for by his father, was a poet for the elect,
barely known to the general public, and only then as one to be
reviled and ridiculed: Elizabeth, on the other hand, though
handled in *A New Spirit of the Age* with a note of suitable con-
descension as "a poetess," had, apart from her growing popularity, a legendary existence of which the writer of the critique
upon herself and Mrs. Norton made the most. Elizabeth had
sent Horne ample details of her life on which a biographer
gratefully draws today, but this had to be embroidered upon.
In an exaltation of her learning, the composition of Latin verses
is attributed to her, and the period of seclusion of this "fair
shade" magnified into "six or seven years" of imprisonment
"during many weeks at a time, in darkness almost equal to that
of night." A human touch is added to the legend by a mention of
her love of novel-reading. With an extract from "The Seraphim," Elizabeth's poetry is characterized as "the struggles of
a soul towards heaven." "Miss Barrett often wanders amidst
the supernatural darkness of Calvary sometimes with anguish
and tears of blood, sometimes like one who echoes the songs of
triumphal quires." In comparison with Mrs. Norton "one is all
womanhood; the other all wings." As poet "Miss Barrett has
great inventiveness, but not an equal power of construction."
This incomplete picture of Elizabeth, ignoring a strong inter-

est in the world about her, was surely not written by her assiduous correspondent R. H. Horne.

The critique on Carlyle, now in full strength as a writer, was probably, though Horne does not directly state it, largely contributed by Elizabeth: certainly she wrote many letters on the subject to Horne, though only two, one of which was too late to be incorporated, are published. It is a fine analysis of this rugged rock of a writer, this Northern crag looming over the softer Southerner.

After an acknowledgment of Carlyle's own doctrine of Heroes, the article continues, I think in the words of Elizabeth:

That Mr. Carlyle is one of the men of genius thus referred to, and that he has knocked out his window from the blind wall of his century, we may add without fear of contradiction. We may say, too, that it is a window to the east; and that some men complain of a certain bleakness in the wind which enters at it, when they should rather congratulate themselves and him on the aspect of the new sun beheld through it, the orient hope of which he has so discovered to their eyes.

An integral part of this new message to mankind was the strange language in which it was couched. If not "style" and classicism, "it was something better; it was soul-language. There was a divinity at the shaping of these rough-hewn periods. . . . He uses no moulds in his modelling, as you may see by the impression of his thumb-nail upon the clay. He throws his truth with so much vehemence, that the print of the palm of his hand is left on it."

Against the charge that Carlyle brought no specific plan of action before mankind, that his was largely a philosophy of dissatisfaction, and inclined to be little material progress, the writer asserted that his teaching, however vague in import, was essentially Christian. "Life suggests to him the cradle, the grave, and eternity, with scarce a step between." Man is exhorted sometimes to work, sometimes to sit still and think. "He [Carlyle] is dazzled by the continual contemplation of a soul beating its tiny wings amidst the pale vapours of Infinity." In such a contemplation our corporeal condition, our physical wants, seem transitory, of small significance.

Carlyle, veering, to the bewilderment of the plain man, from

Tory to Radical, from Radical to Tory, was at heart a poet and therefore "*too* poetical to be philosophical . . . *so* poetical as to be philosophical in essence when treating of things." His dramatic sense too brought about a close and often misleading identification of himself with the man portrayed. His use of images was poetical. "His illustrations not only illustrate, but bear a part in the reasoning;—the images standing out, like grand and beautiful caryatides, to sustain the heights of the argument."

The most notable omission in this brave assessment of the spirit of the age is that of Miss Mitford, whose "prose-pastorals" have only passing mention; that a full-dress portrait was intended is clear from one of Elizabeth's letters. Perhaps Horne feared to embroil himself with an old and valued friend by a true estimate of those acted tragedies which the author put high above such works as *Our Village* and *Belford Regis;* perhaps he merely intended to reserve her for a future volume.

A New Spirit of the Age is illustrated by fine etched portraits, a set of which Horne gave to Elizabeth, including one from a drawing, made by his friend the Comte Amédée de Ripert-Monclar, of Robert Browning; a presentation perhaps too conventionally poetical for the Browning of 1844, but having in the eyes a direct vision, about the mouth and chin a set determination, and in the large curving nose a hint of quest, of keen scent. Browning, when Elizabeth's reply to his first letter reached him on January 11, 1845, was less informed than she: no portrait of her had appeared in *A New Spirit of the Age* or elsewhere. "There is no portrait of me at all which is considered like—except one," she told Horne, "painted in my infancy, where I appear in the character of a fugitive angel, which papa swears by all the gods is very like me to this day, and which perhaps may be like—about the wings." This charming presentation of the baby Elizabeth, on the lid of a snuff-box, we have already seen.

CHAPTER 13

BOOKS AND THOUGHTS [1843–4]

IN THE LATTER HALF of 1843 Elizabeth was actively engaged, not only on the work for Horne, but in the preparation of her new volume: at least one long poem remained to be completed.

At the end of summer an even flow of writing was interrupted by certain anxieties, the first being one which touched into life that aching memory of Torquay. George and Storm wanted to spend a holiday abroad together on the Rhine. Elizabeth took an elder-sisterly share in the diplomacy needed to gain Mr. Barrett's consent, but against her own feeling. It was, she told Mrs. Martin, "a hard, terrible struggle with me to be calm and see them go. But *that* was childish, and when I had heard from them at Ostend I grew more satisfied again, and attained to think less of the fatal influences of *my star*."

A spell of hot August weather with some dangerous drops in temperature further tried the invalid, but we hear of her being "very well for *me*" and making use of the chair for outdoor exercise. But in an enjoyment of comparative health, the happiness of knowing that her brothers were safely across the sea in enjoyment of their holiday, fresh and more immediate trouble came to her in the person of Flush. First the spaniel had been worried and wounded by another dog inmate of the house, a savage Cuban bloodhound, and then in mid-September, while out taking his exercise, he gave a sudden cry and vanished, a prey to those pests of early Victorian London, the dog-stealers.

Elizabeth spent three days without eating or sleeping, "nor could do anything much more rational than cry" amid accusations of "silliness" and "childishness" from robuster folk around her. Grief was less over the loss of Flush's companionship than from "the consideration of how he was breaking his heart, cast upon a cruel world." Even when prevented from sleeping on his mistress's bed Flush would spend the night in moaning, and often he would refuse to eat from a strange hand.

With difficulty the "dog-banditti" were hunted down and bribed into giving up the spaniel. "The audacity of the wretched men was marvellous," Elizabeth commented in anger. "They said they had been 'about stealing Flush these two years,' and warned us plainly to take care of him for the future." These scoundrels were in a strong position, and knew it. As a dog was not at that time legal property, its owner had no redress.

On his return Elizabeth wrote to Boyd:

The joy of the meeting between Flush and me would be a good subject for a Greek ode—I recommend it to you. It might take rank next to the epical parting of Hector and Andromache. He dashed up the stairs into my room and into my arms, where I hugged him and kissed him, black as he was—black as if imbued in a distillation of St. Giles's.

"You had better give your dog something to eat," said the thief who yielded up his prey to a brother, "for he has tasted nothing since he has been with us." "And yet," Flush's mistress wrote to Horne, "his heart was so full when he came home he could not eat, but shrank away from the plate and laid down his head on my shoulder. The spirit of love conquered the animal appetite even in that dog. He is worth loving. Is he not?"

All these anxieties broke in upon a period of steady work: in the letter to Boyd of September 19 quoted above, Elizabeth spoke of having just finished "A Vision of Poets," "philosophical, allegorical—anything but popular." She intended to print "as much as I can find and make room for," feeling, except in moments of bleak doubt, that she had made "some general progress in strength and expression."

But later in the autumn doubt spread about her like a seasonable London fog. "A Drama of Exile," that ambitious poem about the Expulsion from Eden, was composed rapidly from a fragment written some time before: when it was completed her mind misgave her. Was the poem worth printing, worth even preserving? She was on the point of thrusting it into the fire when her cousin Kenyon, now a privileged visitor, came in. "In the kindest way he took it into his hands, and proposed to carry it home and read it," saying: "You know I have a prejudice against these sacred subjects for poetry, but then I have another prejudice for *you*, and one may neutralise the other."

Elizabeth awaited the return of her manuscript in trepidation but, except for a few minor criticisms, Kenyon approved, considering "A Drama of Exile" "very superior as a whole to anything I ever did before—more sustained, and fuller in power."

In the spring of 1844, a short time before publication, all this was rather unwisely reported to Mr. Boyd, that older and jealous mentor. Boyd wrote immediately warning Elizabeth against taking "the man's" opinion. She told him, surely with a gleam of amusement:

The "man" is highly refined in his tastes, and leaning to the classical (I was going to say to your classical, only suddenly I thought of Ossian) a good deal more than I do. . . . If I had hesitated about the conclusiveness of his judgments, it would have been because of his confessed indisposition towards subjects religious and ways mystical, and his occasional insufficient indulgence for rhymes and rhythms which he calls "Barrettian."
Elizabeth declared to her old friend that she feared his own judgment both of this poem and of others in the new work; but clearly she no longer offered manuscripts for his old-fashioned, sweeping, and condemnatory criticism.

What Elizabeth did not tell Boyd was the depth of her despair. The supposed failure of this poem was, it is clear from a letter to Kenyon, but a passing cause, a symptom of a deeper ailment of the spirit. His encouragement saved her from a break in that high valour with which she faced life. "The book may fail signally after all—*that* is another question; but *I* shall not fail, to begin with, and *that* I owe to *you*, for I was falling to pieces in nerves and spirits when you came to help me. . . . It was a long compressed feeling breaking suddenly into words."

Elizabeth regretted a "note of weak because unavailing complaint" which she had sent him, the more so as it was accompanied by a letter from Miss Martineau "of heroic cheerfulness." That strong-hearted woman facing severe illness, the terrible threat of cancer, with great courage, had brought the power of her mind to bear upon an analysis of her condition in *Life in a Sick Room*.

It is in the November of 1843 that we first become aware of an interest in the supernatural, or extra-natural, later to become so strong a preoccupation with spiritualism. This began as a rather horrified fascination by hypnotism or "animal magnetism," soon to become a fashionable theme of the hour. The subject was, so far as I know, first discussed on paper with B. R. Haydon.[1] Haydon, "being always inclined to believe in the wonderful . . . went to ascertain the fact of Mesmerism" at the house of one John Elliotson, a physician who had been forced to resign a professorship at London University because of his avowed interest in the subject. Although the letter is unfortunately incomplete, it is obvious that Haydon considered the performance he witnessed to be fraudulent. Elizabeth's own interest in mesmerism is clearly implied.

In December a friend, accepting the current notion that "animal magnetism" could cure a variety of diseases, pressed Elizabeth to send a lock of hair to "a chief Rabbi of the magnetisers" in Paris so that he might diagnose her condition. Apart from a conviction that magnetism was of no avail in cases of the chest—that it might even be harmful—Elizabeth feared her own imagination; writing to Boyd, who urged a trial of the treatment:

If I had parted with that lock of hair, Queen Mab would have been with me day and night. I should have seen visions and dreamt dreams. And, through the thick of them, a great French disembodied spirit would have floated, peering about the room, and causing my flesh to creep with cold magnetic testimonies of a "Presence."

And then, do you remember the harm which all the old witches (whom I am beginning to believe in) did with a lock of hair?

A day's visit from Miss Mitford, that "very precious friend" and a sensible, understanding woman, must have strengthened Elizabeth's determination. Miss Mitford agreed with Kenyon that Elizabeth was wise to refuse. Mary Mitford, "sprinkled as to the soul with meadow dews," brought, with her cheerful rosy face, a taste of country joys lost, the sharp pleasure of her pointed conversation and gossip from the literary world; a salutary interlude in the long feverish preoccupation with words and books.

[1] Pope Collection, November 9, 1843.

With Miss Mitford, however, the subject uppermost in Elizabeth's mind, her work for *A New Spirit of the Age,* must be avoided. Already there had been one alarm: a Mr. Reade had informed Horne that he knew Miss Barrett was collaborating with him. To a reproachful Horne Elizabeth had protested' her entire innocence in the matter: to neither Miss Mitford, Kenyon, nor even her own father had she even mentioned the name of the book. Perhaps Miss Mitford, herself a wide correspondent, had gathered from some source that Elizabeth was to be the subject of a critique, and perhaps this information, misunderstood, had been passed on to Reade. If Mr. Reade really meant what he was reported as saying, "he must have had it from especial revelation of the angels."

On the early spring of 1844 there is little correspondence available to me except that with Horne. In one letter Elizabeth made the interesting claim that Dickens was strongly influenced by the French school of imaginative literature. She asked Horne to compare the "powerful, the wonderfully powerful" "Trois Jours d'un Condamné" with the trial of Fagin in Dickens's latest novel, *Oliver Twist.* She expressed an ever-growing admiration for French novelists:

we have no such romance-writer as Victor Hugo,—let us be as anti-Gallic as we please. . . . The indelicacy and want of elemental morality make another side of the question: but the genius is just as undeniable to me, as the sun would be in Italy. George Sand, for instance, is the greatest female genius the world ever saw—at least, since Sappho, who broke off a fragment of her soul to be guessed by—as creation did by its fossils. . . . And then Balzac—Eugene Sue—even the Soulies, and the grade lower—we cannot wish them to be popular in England, for obvious reasons, but it is melancholy to look round and see no such bloom of intellectual glory on our own literature, in shutting our doors against theirs.

In March 1844 a "painful vexation" agitated the invalid: the probable loss of a personal maid who had been with her throughout illness. Apart from a natural attachment to this woman, the idea of a stranger about her was "scarcely tolerable" to the recluse. Who this maid was and whether she now left Elizabeth's service we do not know: if she remained, and the service was unbroken, we must later acclaim her as that faithful friend Elizabeth Wilson, a young north-country woman who so cheerfully embarked with her mistress on the great adventure of 1846.

But all this was for the future: at present Robert Browning, "meditating a new poem, and an excursion on the Continent," was only a young poet of whom Elizabeth heard much that was interesting from her cousin Kenyon; a man of "many noble capabilities" at criticism of whom Elizabeth felt an oddly personal resentment; whose portrait, pronounced by Kenyon to be "rather like," hung framed on the wall of her room together with those of Carlyle, Wordsworth, Harriet Martineau, and Tennyson. But probably the most cherished of these was the portrait of Alfred Tennyson, before whom, though her intellect could not fully tell her why, she burned a delicate incense. Although Elizabeth treasured a note of Browning's written to Kenyon in praise of "The Dead Pan," she probably set higher value on one from Tennyson to herself; Tennyson of whom she demanded from George, her courier of news in the world, every fragment of "Tennysoniana" he could gather. And if any dim presage of a passionate lover, in the person of Robert Browning or any other, could have entered the mind of this invalid of thirty-eight years, she would have instantly thrust it from her.

"Books and thoughts," she wrote of herself in the autumn of 1843, "and dreams (almost too consciously *dreamed,* however, for me—the illusion of them has almost passed) and domestic tenderness can and ought to leave nobody lamenting. Also God's wisdom, deeply steeped in His love, *is* as far as we can stretch out our hands."

CHAPTER 14

POEMS [1844]

MOXON DECIDED TO PRINT an edition of fifteen hundred copies with half profits to the author; the work to begin with that poem Elizabeth had at first intended as a title piece, "A Drama of Exile," and to end with "The Dead Pan" as, she said, "a flourish of trumpets and to please Mr. Kenyon."

Her manuscript went to press at the end of March but publication was delayed: Miss Mitford is reported as saying that she "never heard of so slow-footed a book." Elizabeth, though admitting to certain alterations in proof, declared: "in my opinion, it is a good deal more the fault of Mr. Moxon's not being in a hurry, than in the excessive virtue of my patience, or vice of my indolence."

Only at the end of July were the volumes discovered to be of unequal length. "Mr. Moxon," Elizabeth told Boyd, "uttered a cry of reprehension, and wished to tear me to pieces by his printers, as the Bacchantes did Orpheus. . . . He wanted to tear away several poems from the end of the second volume, and tie them on to the end of the first!" This would mean shifting the position of "The Dead Pan," which, with the backing of her father's opinion, Elizabeth was determined not to allow. "So there was nothing for it but to finish a ballad poem called 'Lady Geraldine's Courtship,' which was lying by me, and I did so by writing, i.e. composing, *one hundred and forty lines last Saturday!*" Mr. Moxon was now as precipitous as he had once been dawdling: the *Poems* came out in the second week of August.

If, as Landor said, variety and invention are essential in any poet beyond the second-rate, *Poems*, 1844, certainly meets that qualification. There are personal utterances, ranging from sonnets to biographical poems such as "A Flower in a Letter," "The Lost Bower," to the more fanciful one of "The House of Clouds," a favourite with her father; mystical allegories such as "A Drama of Exile," "A Vision of Poets"; personal tributes to Miss

Mitford, George Sand, and to Boyd in "Wine of Cyprus"; poems
of life around her, as "The Cry of the Children," "Crowned and
Buried," "Crowned and Wedded"; poems quasi-philosophical,
quasi-religious such as "The Cry of the Human," "A Rhapsody
of Life's Progress"; the stories, all told picturesquely in styles so
different as that of "The Rime of the Duchess May" and "Lady
Geraldine's Courtship"; love poems, as that favourite with
Browning, "Caterina to Camoens" and "The Lady's Yes"; all in
forms varying from blank verse to the triple disyllabic rimed
stanzas of "A Vision of Poets."

Elizabeth was at once acclaimed, not only as an established
poet, but as first in rank among "poetesses," a compliment she
regarded as left-handed; there being in her opinion no single
poetess worthy of the name before Joanna Baillie. Chorley in
the *Athenæum* defined her position as a woman poet in declaring that between Miss Barrett's "poems and the slighter lyrics
of most of her sisterhood, there is all the difference which exists
between the putting-on of 'singing robes' for altar service, and
the taking of lute or harp to enchant an indulgent circle of
friends and kindred." In this perhaps Chorley might have excepted one woman poet who had died comparatively young
only a few years before, Felicia Hemans, who is now perhaps
undeservedly neglected: at least her "The Forest Sanctuary" is
beyond simple feminine enchantment and needs no indulgence.

Blackwood's, giving the *Poems* a whole article, found Elizabeth's poetical merits far to outweigh her defects. "Her genius
is profound, unsullied, and without a flaw." John Forster in the
Examiner boldly claimed her for posterity: the *Atlas* acknowledged extraordinary power and genius "abating the failings of
which the followers of Tennyson are guilty." This, repeated in
other reviews, annoyed Elizabeth, who, though yielding to none
in admiration of Tennyson, claimed at least her faults to be her
own. The chief peculiarity attributed to Tennyson and his
"school" was the use of compound words; a "fault," as Elizabeth pointed out, common, not only to Greek and German
poets, but to our own both in earlier times and—nearer to herself—Keats, Shelley, and Leigh Hunt.

Most of the reviews also accused her of a fault entirely her
own, that of defective or careless riming. In this Elizabeth paid

a pioneer's penalty as advocate of a freedom in verse not generally recognized until some eighty years after. She employed loose rimes and assonance with deliberate intent, asserting that in a language deficient in light end-vowels a variety in rime was needed. Her innovations were most apparent in disyllabic rimes, a fondness for which was, no doubt, a legacy from an early acquaintance with Italian literature.

"A Drama of Exile" was the poem on which Elizabeth had built a hope of enhanced reputation. She had written it at white heat, modelling her form on that of Greek tragedy. "A Drama of Exile" tells the story of Adam and Eve after they were driven into the wilderness, "with a peculiar reference to Eve's allotted grief, which, considering that self-sacrifice belonging to her womanhood, and the consciousness of originating the Fall to her offence, appeared to me imperfectly apprehended hitherto; and more expressible by a woman than a man." This is how Elizabeth phrased her intention in a preface to *Poems,* 1844, but in a letter she put it more intimately: "the subject being . . . especially the grief of Eve, under that reproach of her soul which must have afflicted her with so peculiar an agony." The personal application is implicit. No Eve could have been more tortured by remorse, could have known "so peculiar an agony" as this sensitive woman convinced that she had sent a beloved brother and treasured eldest son to his death.

"A Drama of Exile" was not, however, well received. As Browning later remarked, her individual gift in poetry was for speaking out, for that direct expression of emotion denied to himself. With the exception of the harrowing "The Mask," but slightly dramatized, it was in the most personal form, the sonnet, that Elizabeth most poignantly set down emotional statements about grief, religious feeling; sonnets which in these volumes anticipate with a sure touch the matured power of those "from the Portuguese."

Elizabeth was surprised and not a little chagrined to discover that the poem acclaimed by reviewers and public alike was not "A Drama of Exile" but that which Sir Frederic Kenyon has happily called a masterpiece of rhetorical sentimentality, "Lady Geraldine's Courtship." Amusement was added to the mixed emotion when she knew it to be an avowed favourite with

Carlyle and Miss Martineau. This unexpected popularity of "a romance of the age," "treating of railroads, routes, and all manner of 'temporalities,' and in so radical a temper," was to confirm in Elizabeth's mind that assertion of 1842 that a poet could find matter to his hand in the world around him, however drab, mundane, and industrialized that world might appear to be. A ballad poem cast in as a make-weight led clearly on to that verse novel in the thick of contemporary life, *Aurora Leigh.*

"Lady Geraldine's Courtship" has for us another significance: it was the reading of some lines in it that led directly to Robert Browning's first approach to his future wife early in 1845. Opening the first volume of *Poems* on his return from Italy he saw how Geraldine's lover would read to her:

. . . at times a modern volume,—Wordsworth's solemn-thoughted idyl,
Howitt's ballad-verse, or Tennyson's enchanted reverie,—
Or from Browning some "Pomegranate," which, if cut deep down the middle,
Shows a heart within blood-tinctured, of a veined humanity.

"The Rime of the Duchess May," a pseudo-mediæval ballad, which Elizabeth herself disliked and had considered omitting, was another favourite. This ballad is an example of how well she could tell a story, in this case a grim drama of love, revenge, and violent death; even overcoming by sheer skill in narration tiresome and sometimes strained internal rimes in two lines of each of the one hundred and twelve four-line stanzas. Of it Elizabeth wrote to Boyd:

I did not think that you would much like the "Duchess May"; but among the profanum vulgus *you cannot think how successful it has been. There was an account in one of the fugitive reviews of a lady falling into hysterics on the perusal of it, although that was nothing to the gush of tears of which there is a tradition, down the Plutonian cheeks of a lawyer unknown, over "Bertha in the Lane." But these things should not make anybody vain. It is the* story *that has power over people, just what* you *do not care for!*

"Bertha in the Lane," a vivid rather morbid delineation of two sisters, the elder dying, in love with the same man, has a Pre-Raphaelitish air of gloom.

Other favourites with the *profanum vulgus* were "The Romance of the Swan's Nest," a fanciful glimpse into the mind of a bookish romantic child, perhaps Elizabeth herself, and the highly personal "To Flush, my Dog," which the fastidious Mr. Boyd had besought Elizabeth to omit. She, though surely realizing the verses to be far from her best, protested that she could not in loyalty do this. "The Flushes have their laurels as well as the Cæsars."

Another poem of biographical interest is "The Lay of the Brown Rosary," which plays again upon the theme of "The Romaunt of Margret," though in more sinister vein. A girl is preserved from death by the powers of darkness so that she may marry her lover: the ceremony over, her husband falls dead on the altar steps. In both this poem and "The Romaunt of Margret" it is love that may preserve the woman's life, though in "The Lay of the Brown Rosary" it brings disaster to the loved one. Here, even if there may have been nothing of the shadowy prescience one is tempted to claim, is at least a clear thread in the story, the allegory of Elizabeth Barrett Browning's life. Love did pluck her back from death and, though not met by death itself, with a measure of disaster in the loss of her father's affection and the temporary alienation of her brothers:

> . . . *a mystic Shape did move*
> *Behind me, and drew me backward by the hair,*
> *And a voice said in mastery while I strove, . .*
> *"Guess now who holds thee?"—"Death," I said. But, there,*
> *The silver answer rang, . . "Not Death, but Love."*

In this ending to the first sonnet written after she knew that Robert Browning loved her is no shadowy prescience, but knowledge.

In 1844, however, this invalid, bruised by the tragedy of Bro's death, already considered at that time a middle-aged woman and solacing her "sweet sad years, the melancholy years" with poetry, with domestic affections and the comfort of God, could not foresee a miracle. Her conscious utterance of life's bitterness and loss are in the sonnets placed, perhaps with deliberate intent, after that opening "A Drama of Exile" which seems to embody her own deep-rooted sense of guilt. Of these the key-sonnet to her life is the beautiful "Past and Future":

My future will not copy fair my past
On any leaf but Heaven's. Be fully done,
Supernal Will! I would not fain be one
Who, satisfying thirst and breaking fast
Upon the fullness of the heart, at last
Says no grace after meat. My wine has run
Indeed out of my cup, and there is none
To gather up the bread of my repast
Scattered and trampled,—yet I find some good
In earth's green herbs, and streams that bubble up
Clear from the darkling ground,—content until
I sit with angels before better food.
Dear Christ! when Thy new vintage fills my cup,
This hand shall shake no more, nor that wine spill.

CHAPTER 15

MR. BARRETT OF WIMPOLE STREET

DEDICATION

TO MY FATHER

When your eyes fall upon this page of dedication, and you start to see to whom it is inscribed, your first thought will be of the time far off when I was a child and wrote verses, and when I dedicated them to you who were my public and my critic. Of all that such a recollection implies of saddest and sweetest to both of us, it would become neither of us to speak before the world; nor would it be possible for us to speak of it to one another, with voices that did not falter. Enough, that what is in my heart when I write thus, will be fully known to yours.

And my desire is that you, who are a witness how if this art of poetry had been a less earnest object to me, it must have fallen from exhausted hands before this day,—that you, who have shared with me in things bitter and sweet, softening or enhancing them, every day,—that you, who hold with me over all sense of loss and transiency, one hope by one Name,—may accept from me the inscription of these volumes, the exponents of a few years of an existence which has been sustained and comforted by you as well as given. Somewhat more faint-hearted than I used to be, it is my fancy thus to seem to return to a visible personal dependence on you, as if indeed I were a child again; to conjure your beloved image between myself and the public, so as to be sure of one smile,—and to satisfy my heart while I sanctify my ambition, by associating with the great pursuit of my life its tenderest and holiest affection.

Your

E. B. B.

ON THE 10TH OF AUGUST Elizabeth sent her *Poems* down to Mr. Barrett cut at the page of the above dedication. "When he came upstairs at one o'clock" (to continue in her own words to George), "he seemed pleased & touched by it—only the satisfaction to myself of expressing my natural feeling, is deeper (must be) certainly than any his tenderness could receive."

From the entirely personal tone of her dedication it is clear that Elizabeth's father was no longer in the old position of public and critic. As a poet she had grown from him, perhaps in imaginative power, perhaps in a fashion of poetry too new for one born in the previous century: nor did he (in her own words) "over-value poetry even in his daughter." Pride in the phenomenon he had begotten had its basis in possession, in family feeling. His measure of life was apt to be a worldly one, though deeply tinged with religion.

Mr. Barrett's strong belief in a personal God was shared by Elizabeth: it was a bond between them. It was his habit to come up to her at about eleven o'clock at night, before retiring, to pray with her. But in their religious outlook was an essential difference: Mr. Barrett's communings with his Creator produced no humility of mind. Consciously, or unconsciously, he regarded himself as His vice-regent in family affairs.

Love for his children, a native kindliness, and a certain inattention to detail made, however, that self-imposed duty "to rule like the Kings of Christendom, by divine right," less irksome than it might appear: indeed, though she might privately complain in family letters of an Olympian detachment, a reserve as to plans of life vitally affecting herself, on Elizabeth the yoke sat lightly. She had never, beyond childhood, felt a strong "will for the common things of life . . . though every now and then there must be of course a crossing and vexation—but in one's mere pleasures and fantasies, one would rather be crossed and vexed a little than vex a person one loves." In her own case, too, the word "literature" covered a certain permitted licence; and where the accepted obedience of child to father might be strained there was solemn joy in negation of self before this man whom she, by an act of weakness, had robbed of his eldest son. Not the least of her debt to him had been Mr. Barrett's tender, unreproaching kindness in her grief and during prolonged illness.

The other children of Edward Barrett, the youngest now

twenty, were, in the uncompromising words of that loving daughter, "constrained *bodily* into submission . . apparent submission at least . . by that worst and most dishonoring of necessities, the necessity of *living*"; every one of them except herself "being dependent in money-matters on the inflexible will." In the Moulton-Barrett family it is thought that Mr. Barrett was generous enough to his sons and not exigent in terms of work, but this subservience inevitably brought with it a "concealment from the heart naturally nearest to us . . . disengenuousness—the cowardice—the 'vices of slaves.' "

Yet this arbitrary rule gave the Barrett family a curious liberty: not being able to confide in the father, they took their own paths, doing in his daily absence in the City of London more or less as they wished, asking to the house whom they pleased. No friend might be invited to dinner, but before the hour of six Mr. Barrett's children were tolerably secure for six days of the week: questions were seldom asked and breaches of discipline in general not noticed unless they came directly under the paternal eye. Probably, taking the short view, this circumscribed liberty had for some of them its own fearful joy in that element of danger, of being found out, dear to a young adventurous heart. Papa might not know, or inquire, but he might from time to time guess. Mr. Barrett was not, Elizabeth told Robert, "a nice observer, but, at intervals very wide, he is subject to lightnings—call them fancies, sometimes right, sometimes wrong."

There seems to have been among the brothers and sisters little deep-seated resentment of restraint: as Elizabeth observed, "it is possible to get used to the harness and run easily in it at last." Such domestic harness was common enough in many households up to the end of the last century and beyond: children did not then expect to rule their parents. It is certain that two of the sons who lived well into living memory,[1] Octavius and Charles John, adored their father and would hear nothing against him.

But, extreme type of kindly, arbitrary old-fashioned parent though he was, Mr. Barrett differed in one strange particular. He would not have his children marry, or even discuss marriage.

[1] Charles John (Stormie) died in 1905, Octavius in 1910.

He who had taken a wife at nineteen, who came of a family so anxious to preserve the principle of primogeniture that his own surname had been changed to uphold it, would not have his children marry. In this he departed radically from the typical early Victorian parent who so valued family life that he would often himself arrange early marriages for his daughters, and sometimes even for his sons. The Barrett sons, except Alfred, remained bachelors until his death in 1857: of those children who married during his lifetime, Elizabeth, Alfred, and Henrietta, all were cast off.

Once when the daughters were discussing this strange idiosyncrasy of Mr. Barrett Elizabeth said in jest: "If a prince of Eldorado should come, with a pedigree of lineal descent from some signory in the moon on one hand, and a ticket of good-behaviour from the nearest Independent chapel in the other—?"

"Why even *then*," said her sister Arabel, "it would not *do*."

To Elizabeth, with as yet no temptation to defy him on this or any other count, her father was a comfort, a support: she felt and enjoyed his strength as father, as man. Resentments, anxieties she might feel, but these were largely vicarious; as when Arabel deprived herself of a holiday with a friend because her father had frowned when the visit was proposed; or when Henry packed his carpet bag and announced he was going to spend a day and night with friends at Dover, a journey Papa had already discountenanced. When Henry did not appear at breakfast next morning Mr. Barrett was put off with the fiction that his son was lying late abed. The rest of the story, possibly a turbulent one, is tantalizingly not given us. Henrietta's enterprises brought Elizabeth's heart into her mouth more than once; a "polka" given at the house during Mr. Barrett's absence in Cornwall, an unauthorized carriage excursion for a picnic of strawberries and cream to Three Mile Cross, the home of Miss Mitford.

All we know definitely of Mr. Barrett's activity in the City of London is that he attended at the Jamaica Coffee-house, St. Michael's Alley, Cornhill,[2] which was a subscription house for merchants and captains trading with Madeira and the West Indies, and where they could obtain accurate West Indian intelli-

[2] Family information.

gence. He had also certain enterprising side lines; having shares in a Cornish mine and, even so far back as Hope End days, a certain practical interest in shipping. Recently he had bought a craft and, under his own control, was employing her in what Elizabeth called "his favourite 'Via Lactea' of speculations." In 1844 she sailed to Alexandria with a cargo of coal. When Storm and Henry wrung from their father a reluctant permission to travel on board, nothing was said to Elizabeth of the journey until a few days before departure.

It was perhaps a sign of renewing health that Elizabeth did not, during their absence on a sea voyage, feel that gnawing anxiety of the year before when George and Storm were merely crossing the Channel. Though naturally looking forward to the travellers' return, she was not, to her own surprise, unduly worried.

One concomitant of the possessive spirit, jealousy, we can only tentatively guess at in Edward Barrett. Perhaps, knowing that her heart was his, he was content to share an influence over his daughter's mind and work; perhaps after her release from poetic leading-strings he resigned himself to a growth of mind and method beyond his scope—be it as it may, his attitude to John Kenyon, now a strong influence and an admired friend, was curious.

This kindly man, who had done so much to introduce Elizabeth to a chosen public, a cousin living near by and probably acquainted with Mr. Barrett at least from Cambridge days, never came to dine; nor was Elizabeth allowed to invite him to Mr. Barrett's table. As to Boyd, that older friend and mentor, we hear nothing of any message to him from Elizabeth's father. Apart from certain slight courtesies to R. H. Horne, Edward Barrett appears to have taken little direct interest in his daughter's growing list of literary acquaintances; her world of friends remained curiously apart from this man she so greatly loved and depended on. We never hear of him making a third in a colloquy with Miss Mitford or any other woman friend privileged to visit Elizabeth. Although Robert Browning's calls upon her, or a known proportion of them, were later allowed and even approved with some measure of pride, Mr. Barrett made no effort to meet Browning himself.

In Elizabeth, a poet of fast growing reputation, Mr. Barrett might take a healthy pride, but it was soon to appear as if he took a pride unhealthy, but typical of many of his generation, in his daughter as an incurable invalid. In a condition of helplessness there might be both an unconscious gratification and a sense of security. She, the treasure of his house, was physically dependent on him for moral support and comfort; always at home, fixed in her room, a refuge for himself, and a pivot around which family affairs could circle in the absence of that wife he had lost. With this first child, the eldest daughter, a woman with an unusual grasp of mind and a wide sympathy, perhaps this reserved man came as near to confidence as he was able. She was always there, dependable, never giving him anxiety, her heart being wholly his.

Of the second daughter Mr. Barrett might well be distrustful; that daughter whose besetting sin was, according to her sister, "an over-pleasure in pleasing; a sin made venial by a native softness of heart." Henrietta was too fond of dancing, too fond of male admiration, even going so far as to desire a husband. Mr. Barrett had had trouble with Henrietta in her youth, though certainly she had then obeyed him as a daughter should, very properly giving up her lover instantly at command. In the words of Elizabeth, "a child never submitted more meekly to a revoked holiday."

But Henrietta's submission had only seemed further to incense this man inexorable to mania on one subject. "Oh, the dreadful scenes!" Elizabeth confided to Browning in considering her own more flagrant breach of family discipline,
and only because she had seemed to feel so little. . . . I hear how her knees were made to ring upon the floor, now! She was carried out of the room in strong hysterics and I, who rose up to follow her, though I was quite well at the time and suffering only by sympathy, fell flat down upon my face in a fainting-fit. Arabel thought I was dead.

But such insubordination was not to be expected from the treasured Ba, the eldest and dearest child. Her thoughts were not of the world, not of the flesh but of the spirit. Secure in the fortress of his home, in her own weak condition and native purity, Mr. Barrett would not in the wildest flight of imagination suspect that a man unknown to him, or only slightly by reputation, could wrest his daughter from him; could within the space of a year disturb her spirit and tamper with that obedience she owed him, her father.

But any attempted portrait of Edward Barrett must be tentative, full of hesitations. Of one thing we may be certain; the depicting of this man in a certain play as a monster, a mass of cruel selfishness, was a deliberate falsification for dramatic purposes. That Mr. Barrett was arbitrary, indulged from his youth up, in possession of wealth and power too early in life, all will admit; but, however peculiar his attitude in regard to marriage within his family may appear to us of a freer generation, he could only have applauded himself in the performance of a moral duty, a duty towards his Maker. On what ground he objected to the marriage of his children none can know. No one but the ghost of himself could satisfactorily interpret that enigma; and, self-deluding as most of us are, perhaps even he in the spirit would not be equal to the task.

CHAPTER 16

ON THE THRESHOLD [1844]

IN THESE LAST MONTHS of 1844 we, who know her history, listen for coming footsteps, the steps of one privileged to release Elizabeth from bondage; a bondage of both enforced and encouraged invalidism during which limbs and heart had weakened. A bondage made more sinister by sleep and periods of false calm "red with the hood of poppies."

But, vitiated though Elizabeth inevitably was, partially drugged, sequestered in an airless room, there were signs of a lustier life: a headier draught was already taking the place of that plain water she took as her own in the sonnet quoted. The wine of success, of acclamation as a major poet of her age, was there now for her to sip, if only "like a fly." She might feel, in that cleavage of self which had distressed her so long, Elizabeth Barrett, the poet, to be but a "factitious personality" associated with her work only, but there is no doubt that there was natural gratification.

She had sung of that "Wine of Cyprus" sent her by Mr. Boyd, a wine so aromatic, so dulcet to the palate that

> . . . *the brown bees of Hymettus*
> *Make their honey not so sweet.*

Elizabeth could sip her wine, the wine of success, with pleasure, not mistaking it for a cup more sacramental; nor could she guess that God, already so near in affliction, would soon come closer to her in a gift of human love.

In this period of unconscious waiting Elizabeth's heart was warmed by the world's praise, a praise swelling to a pæan when the *Poems* were issued in America that October. One voice there was to mix criticism, some justifiable criticism, with adulation, that of Edgar Allan Poe; but he was to soften a certain harshness by a handsome dedication of his next volume to Elizabeth.

Amid the public acclamation of this already accepted but

newly popular poet several voices spoke privately, among them Miss Martineau, a public figure, and especially revered by Elizabeth as a gifted, logical, strong-minded, and courageous woman. Henry Chorley, the *Athenæum* critic, added to official praise a private letter, in his enthusiasm breaking through an unwritten law of the press.

But, though Elizabeth might in a sense be roused by success, any emotion, pleasurable or otherwise, must bring strain to a worn spirit weakened by drugs and seclusion. It was perhaps fortunate that at this time a woman came into her life who, though to prove a devoted friend, had in her something of the strength—and the resilience—of high-tempered steel. When Mrs. Jameson, who had already expressed an admiration of the *Poems*, asked for an interview, Elizabeth at first refused, but when Mrs. Jameson came to stay nearly on her own doorstep, at 51, Wimpole Street, Elizabeth wavered. A tactfully kind note left at the door finally softened her. Mrs. Jameson was admitted.

As Mrs. Jameson came upstairs Elizabeth, unused to strangers, always dreading a fresh human contact, felt her "heart beat itself almost to pieces for fear of seeing her." Perhaps Mrs. Jameson's reputation as a woman outwardly somewhat hardened by circumstance, trenchantly critical to the point of pedantry, had reached her through Kenyon, a friend of this once distinguished woman now almost forgotten but for her association with the Brownings.

Mrs. Jameson's fox-like appearance could not have soothed the nervous invalid: in Elizabeth's own words, "she is very light —has the lightest of eyes, the lightest of complexions; no eyebrows, and what looked to me like very pale red hair, and thin lips of no colour at all . . . a nose and chin projective without breadth." Elizabeth found, as she had expected, "the tone of her conversation rather analytical and critical than spontaneous and impulsive." Mrs. Jameson's acute mind would permit no vagueness of thought either in herself or in others.

But an infinite kindness towards her soon set Elizabeth at ease. Although in a letter to Horne she could not but compare Mrs. Jameson unfavourably with "our friend of Three Mile Cross who 'wears her heart upon her sleeve,' and shakes out its perfume at every moment," it is possible that Anna Jameson's sharper quality, tempered with an Irish vivacity, was just the astringent Elizabeth needed in her emotional state. Though she could not readily weep, tears always came easily to her eyes: one feels in studying the life of Mrs. Jameson that, for all her strong kindness of heart, tears were not a commodity in which she dealt.

Perhaps in comparing the two women Elizabeth had in mind that struggle common to both to maintain themselves by the pen; Miss Mitford in support of a selfish extravagant father and Mrs. Jameson of mother and sisters. Mrs. Jameson's lot was made the more bitter by the memory of a husband once loved, as selfish and unreliable as Dr. Mitford, who, after two unsatisfactory spells of life together, only unwillingly supported her.

Not without a painful travail of spirit, Anna Brownell Jameson had built up for herself a place in the world of art criticism, or rather art appreciation, and had written, among others, successful travel books, beginning eighteen years earlier with the popular *Diary of an Ennuyée*, the fruit of an excursion on the Continent as a governess. One practical aspect of her life-work was the first compilation of handbooks to Art Collections, private and public. A more idealistic aspect was an emphasis upon women in literature and society: the encouragement given by her to Bessie Rayner Parkes, Barbara Bodichon, and other pioneers of woman's emancipation was in itself a valuable contribution to the cause of human freedom. Her closest friend at this time was one whom the contemporary outlook on marriage had done much to injure, Lady Byron. She would often talk of her friend to Elizabeth, telling her that the true story of the separation reflected nothing but credit on Byron's wife, but Elizabeth, obstinate in prejudice, would not be influenced.

Whatever may have been in Elizabeth's mind at this first interview lasting nearly an hour, she at once "ran into what my sisters call 'one of my sudden intimacies' and there was an embrace for a farewell." There are indications that this early liking was later modified for a time, but soon a potent influence was brought to bear. Browning liked and admired Mrs. Jameson.

Among agitations less pleasurable this autumn was the third loss of Flush. This time he was filched away on his own doorstep while waiting with Arabel to be let into the house. So that a Jovean anger might not descend upon a favourite sister, who had taken the dog without a chain, Elizabeth was forced to conceal from her father not only Flush's absence but sleepless nights, tears, and neglect of food; by "a very convenient bad headache" avoiding contact with him when her eyes were reddest.

The thieves, yielding up Flush for six and a half guineas, announced that next time the price would be ten pounds. Part of the anxiety to keep Flush's loss from Mr. Barrett was his natural and outspoken annoyance at a member of his family being the subject of blackmail; but to one who loved the devoted animal this objection could be but a "kicking against the pricks."

Another agitation more remote, though disturbing to a sensitive secluded spirit, was the revival of interest in animal magnetism through an article in the *Athenæum* by Harriet Martineau, a firm believer in its medical efficacy and one who claimed its cure in herself of a cancerous malady. To Elizabeth, who had herself been urged to take the treatment, this apparent cure, though she could not but rejoice in it, brought a tremor of the soul. In a happier future she was, under the wing of Swedenborg, to take wondering pleasure, even delight, in supernatural questionings, but now she agreed whole-heartedly with the sturdier Mrs. Jameson who had said during their first interview "that if there was *anything* in it, there was *so much*, it became scarcely possible to limit consequences, and the subject grew awful to contemplate." "The agency," Elizabeth added for herself to Mr. Martin, who was inclined to laugh, "seems to me like the shaking of the flood-gates placed by the Divine Creator between the unprepared soul and the unseen world."

Bitter attacks were made upon Miss Martineau, who had so courageously, but not cautiously, revealed her own experiences in print. "I would rather fall into the hands of God than of man," Elizabeth told that old friend James Martin, "and suffer as she did in the body, instead of being the mark of these cruel observations." But Miss Martineau, a born fighter, took the attacks in her stride: this was not the first time she had challenged public opinion.

One lighter reference among the letters to the Martins of this autumn is perhaps worth noticing by the way; it being one to which we in this age must give hearty endorsement. "Do you take in 'Punch'? If not, you *ought*." Mr. Punch was, of course, at this time only three years old and so perhaps needing encouragement in his march forward through time. A part of Elizabeth's interest in this journal was its radical tone. In those earlier days *Punch* was a champion of the suffering poor.

That summer there had been exterior decorating at 50, Wimpole Street: Elizabeth's ivy, temporarily torn down, had been damaged. It was perhaps to replace in some measure the ivy screen that in the autumn Elizabeth added to her room a fanciful touch: a transparent green blind scene-painted, with "a castle gate-way and two walks, and several peasants, and groves of trees," all harmonizing well with new green damask curtains. "The effect is beautiful," Elizabeth told Mrs. Martin, "and the whole room catches a light from it." Mr. Kenyon joined nearly every inmate of the house in admiration of this blind: even the one dissentient, Mr. Barrett, had to give it grudging praise when the sun lit up the castle, though insulting his daughter's taste "with the analogy of a back window in a confectioner's shop." Another and more practical change in her room was a large table, the gift of Mr. Kenyon, "with a rail round it to consecrate it from Flush's paws, and large enough to hold all my variety of vanities."

In December intense cold robbed Elizabeth of her voice, forcing her to refuse, in a charming note, an interview with Mrs. Jameson: "You are not to think that I should not have been delighted to have you in a monodram, as I heard Mr. Kenyon one morning when he came and talked for an hour, as he can talk, while the audience could only clap her hands or shake her head for the yea and nay . . . but with you I was too much a stranger to propose such a thing."

In a December letter which told Mrs. Martin of a gradual recovery from this loss of voice we have our first mention of Elizabeth Wilson, that minor but important actress in the drama to come. Wilson was pleased with a pair of woollen boots sent as a present to her mistress by Mrs. Martin because "they can't be kicked off." Elizabeth adds a note of gratification: she need now not be at the trouble of pulling on her stockings in the morning.

This month two rather odd and incongruous tributes came to

Elizabeth which pleased and amused her: a "sonnet from Gutter Lane, Cheapside," and information that the fashionable "Count D'Orsay had written one of the stanzas of 'Crowned and Buried' at the bottom of an engraving of Napoleon which hangs in his room." The sonnet from Gutter Lane was followed by a highly laudatory review of her *Poems* in the *League* (the anti-Corn Law paper) praising her for "courage in opposing war and monopoly" and rumoured to have been written by Richard Cobden, "an enthusiast for poetry." "If I thought so to the point of conviction, *do you know*," Elizabeth wrote to John Kenyon, himself of advanced Liberal opinion, "*I should be much pleased?* You remember that I am a sort of (magna) chartist— only going a little farther!"

Good news had come throughout the autumn from Gibraltar, from Malta and Alexandria, to relieve an underlying anxiety: on January 12 in the new year Elizabeth told Mrs. Martin that Henry and Stormie were on the way home, "bringing with them as a companion for Flushie, a little gazelle." Elizabeth in reporting this seems to disregard the incongruity of a gazelle in Wimpole Street: perhaps she was anyhow only keeping up a humorous pretence in what was but a brotherly joke.

All that remains to us of this letter ends thus: "And I had a letter from Browning the poet last night, which threw me into ecstasies—Browning, the author of 'Paracelsus,' and king of the mystics."

CHAPTER 17

ROBERT BROWNING [1845]

I love your verses with all my heart, dear Miss Barrett,—and this is no off-hand complimentary letter that I shall write,— whatever else, no prompt matter-of-course recognition of your genius, and there a grateful and natural end of the thing. Since the day last week when I first read your poems, I quite laugh to remember how I have been turning and turning again in my mind what I should be able to tell you of their effect upon me, for in the first flush of delight I thought I would this once get out of my habit of purely passive enjoyment, when I do really enjoy, and thoroughly justify my admiration—perhaps even, as a loyal fellow-craftsman should, try and find fault and do you some little good to be proud of hereafter!—but nothing comes of it all—so into me has it gone, and part of me has it become, this great living poetry of yours, not a flower of which but took root and grew— Oh, how different this is from lying to be dried and pressed flat, and prized highly, and put in a book with a proper account at top and bottom, and shut up and put away . . . and the book called a "Flora," besides! After all, I need not give up a thought of doing that, too, in time; because even now, talking with whoever is worthy, I can give a reason for my faith in one and another excellence, the fresh strange music, the affluent language, the exquisite pathos and true brave new thought; but in this addressing myself to you—your own self, and for the first time, my feeling rises altogether. I do, as I say, love these books with all my heart—and I love you too.

THIS LETTER of January 10, 1845, written with the encouragement of her cousin, John Kenyon, continued with an account of this missed meeting three years before:

I feel as at some untoward passage in my travels, as if I had been close, so close to some world's-wonder in chapel or crypt, only a screen to push and I might have entered, but there was

*some slight, so it now seems, slight and just sufficient bar to ad-
mission, and the half-opened door shut, and I went home my
thousands of miles, and the sight was never to be?*

Elizabeth wrote back immediately expressing her delight, her
gratitude; asking that if he ever did emerge without inconvenient effort from his "passive state," would he please point out
any obvious and important faults in her work. She did not "pretend to any extraordinary meekness under criticism" but felt
that a "general observation" from such a poet on her "master-
faults" must be of value.

If he had entered that "crypt," she told him, he "might have
caught cold, or been tired to death, and *wished*" himself "a
thousand miles off": "what I have lost by one chance I may recover by some future one. Winters shut me up as they do dor-
mouse's eyes; in the spring, *we shall see:* and I am so much
better that I seem to be turning round to the outward world
again." This nervous invalid who had trembled at the advent of
Mrs. Jameson, who had so resolutely kept away from her presence older acquaintances, was eager, bold in a desire to meet
Robert Browning.

The admired and revered Tennyson had expressed a desire
through a friend to meet her, but we hear of no invitation from
Elizabeth. With Browning, however, perhaps as much admired
though with some qualification, she had long been linked; as
poets alike labelled mystical, obscure, and as the common friend
of John Kenyon. Hostile criticism of Browning as poet Elizabeth
had long resented in a curiously personal way, and of Browning
the man she had heard much, and much to his credit, from her
cousin. So linked, so familiar already to her in the mind, a step
forward to meeting was easier than in the case of others who
would seem to have had a prior claim.

She ended her letter with: "I will say that while I live to
follow this divine art of poetry, in proportion to my love for it
and my devotion to it, I must be a devout admirer and student
of your works. This is in my heart to say to you—and I say it."

Browning, himself of West Indian planter stock on his father's side, came of a family of more intellect and character
than gentle birth; such birth as Elizabeth could proudly claim
if, as a Radical, she had not discounted it as "honourable ver-

digris." The elder Robert Browning, apart from creative genius as remarkable a personality as his son, had, after a brief period in Jamaica, relinquished his inheritance there for conscience's sake. He would be no party to the institution of slavery. This man, profoundly intellectual, something of an artist, gave up the prospect of a large measure of freedom for a clerk's position in the Bank of England.

In the elder Browning, a quiet man living happily among his family and books, ambition was centred in the brilliant son who, he determined, should have that freedom necessary for the development of poetic power. Indeed, from earliest years there had been little interference with a child's natural growth: Mr. Browning himself had suffered too acutely from the tyranny of a selfish grasping father to impose even disciplinary restraint on his children.

Browning's mother, of Scottish-German stock, delicate, gentle, with a great love of flowers and music, was adored by her son: however late his engagements in Town might be, he would walk five miles to the outlying village of New Cross that he might sleep in a room beside her, with a door open between them. Browning indeed cherished a superstition that, so close was the bond between mother and son, whenever she was ill he himself was indisposed. Both mother and father were his loving, admiring friends. Unlike Mr. Barrett, they demanded no obedience: on the other hand, so great was his affection for them that in the small things of life he was content to be a child still, to fall in with their way of life.

In this idyllic home there was another intimate friend, Sarianna Browning, a clever lively girl, who, after the fashion of those days, lived in self-abnegation as daughter and sister.

Like the Barrett family the Brownings were, here through the influence of the mother, Dissenters: as with Elizabeth, Browning admitted, however, nothing of a Dissenter's narrowness of outlook: indeed, an innate catholicism of mind took him further towards agnosticism. In spiritual quality Elizabeth transcended his more worldly nature.

Browning, a monarch in the small kingdom of home, took his freedom with a proud pleasure; a freedom, with the small income allowed him by his father, to write and study untrammelled, to travel in a modest way, to lead his own life within the limits of few personal wants. Freedom, a power of self-determination, was to him infinitely dear. The Brownings, he would declare, always got what they wanted.

He was now in his thirty-second year. His worldly fame as a poet was qualified, limited, his reputation as a poetic drama-tist somewhat wider, though all ambition in the theatre had been angrily abandoned after a split with Macready. His popu-larity as an urbane, amusing, clever, well-dressed, and hand-some young man overflowed purely literary circles. Dancing, dining out, parties were becoming wearisome to him. As once he had felt impatience with the immediate narrow, suburban circle about his early Camberwell home, now he was discon-tented in a wider London world. Popularity with women had never touched his heart more than superficially: he thought that he could never fall in love, never lose a proud freedom of mind and action.

Elizabeth had on her wall a portrait which, though mislead-ing, at least gave some impression of her new correspondent: of Elizabeth Browning had but a vague notion, founded, it would seem, more upon general gossip than on any informa-tion Kenyon might have given him. His first advances were made believing her to be suffering from an incurable injury to the spine.

He followed up her reply the day after receiving it with a typical tumultuous, allusive letter, expressing joy at the thought of obtaining in spring his "Chapel-sight after all" and confess-ing himself, on consideration, unable, unwilling to find fault: *your poetry must be, cannot but be, infinitely more to me than mine to you—for you do what I always wanted, hoped to do, and only seem now likely to do for the first time. You speak out, you,—I only make men and women speak—give you truth broken into prismatic hues, and fear the pure white light, even if it is in me, but I am going to try . . . it seems bleak, melan-choly work, this talking to the wind (for I have begun)—yet I don't think I shall let* you *hear, after all, the savage things about Popes and imaginative religions that I must say.*

"What 'struck me as faults,'" he told her, "were not matters on the removal of which, one was to have—poetry, or high po-

Yours very truly,
Robert Browning.

ROBERT BROWNING

from an engraving in A New Spirit of the Age *(1844); a copy of this hung in Elizabeth's room in Wimpole Street*

ELIZABETH BARRETT BROWNING
from a daguerreotype taken at Le Havre in 1858

etry,—but the very highest poetry, so I thought, and that, to universal recognition." He seems to imply that her main fault—in itself dear to a fellow-artist because it revealed herself—was a laboured detail or method of expression; but, as so often with Browning, to whom prose was an awkward instrument, the exact meaning, only half-expressed, is hard to define.

Elizabeth, poring over this letter in her quiet room, came to a different solution; considering, wrongly as he later pointed out, that he was but renewing that charge, so often in Kenyon's mouth, of careless writing. She protested in her next letter that, though by nature headlong, impatient, there was in the pursuit of art "love strong enough, even in me, to overcome nature. . . . What no mere critic sees, but what you, an artist, know, is the difference between the idea in the writer's mind and the *eidōlon* cast off in his work." She praised his art, its "immense grasp," its power of dealing "both with abstract thought and with human passion . . . you are 'masculine' to the height— and I, as a woman, have studied some of your gestures of language and intonation wistfully, as a thing beyond me far: and more admirable for being beyond." She was delighted to be told of new work and hoped he would develop his dramatic sense in plays for the closet rather than the stage. With reference to his anticipation of a delight in her friendship she offered it "*now*, if you please, at this moment, for fear of worldly mutabilities."

It was nearly a fortnight before Browning replied. He had been trying to "find fault," but could only say that, when his head was aching from work, he would open one of her green-covered volumes at his elbow and there find "so much fresh trefoil to feel in one's hands this winter-time." He would, however, go so far as to mark in pencil passages most and least admired. Browning then went off into one of those absurd stories which pepper so pleasantly this long correspondence between them; of a man who, volunteering to criticize "a sonnet-writing somebody," had recourse in despair to "badder, badderer, badderest" and "worster, worsterer, worsterest." Of that immediate friendship she offered, he wrote "(and here Juliet's word rises to my lips)—I feel sure once and for ever."

In the last paragraph he begged Elizabeth not to write if she hated writing letters "as I hate writing to nearly everybody." In a few days she answered, protesting: "Why how could I hate to write to you, dear Mr. Browning? Could you believe in such a thing? . . . As for me, I have done most of my talking by post of late years—as people shut up in dungeons take up with scrawling mottoes on the walls." She would gladly make him one of those few regular correspondents, in company with Miss Mitford, who had "filled a large drawer in this room with delightful letters, heart-warm and soul-warm," if he would promise to do away with all ceremony as between the sexes and treat her *"en bon camarade."* "You will find me an honest man on the whole, if rather hasty and prejudging, which is a different thing from prejudice at the worst." At the end of a long letter she gives us the first example of a feature of these letters, a playful misunderstanding of his own words: "you might indeed repent your quotation from Juliet—which I guessed at once—and of course—

> *I have no joy in this contract to-day!*
> *It is too unadvised, too rash and sudden."*

At the end of January Elizabeth told Mrs. Martin: "I am getting deeper and deeper into correspondence with Robert Browning, poet and mystic, and we are growing to be the truest of friends. If I live a little longer shut up in this room, I shall certainly know everybody in the world."

Their correspondence over the next three months, so full of self-revelation, especially on her part—on his, giving many interesting stories of his friend Carlyle, and other writers of the day—can be little more than indicated in outline: indeed these amazing letters, two volumes of them, demand a separate work, so full are they of literary and classical allusions, anecdotes, thoughts on life, on poetry, and on good writing. Her letters are the finer, more lucid, more finished, but his contain, beside rich passages, a mine of unsifted wisdom, thought often incompletely, awkwardly expressed.

There was discussion of their work; his upon "Luria" and "A Soul's Tragedy," hers a new translation of *Prometheus Vinctus* to take the place of that earlier one which Elizabeth considered "the most miserable of all miserable versions of the class." She consulted him on difficult and obscure passages.

By the end of February Robert was exclaiming with impatience: "Real warm Spring, dear Miss Barrett, and the birds know it; and in Spring I shall see you, surely see you—for when did I once fail to get whatever I had set my heart upon? As I ask myself sometimes, with a strange fear." Elizabeth protested:

Yes, but, dear Mr. Browning, I want the spring according to the new "style" (mine), and not the old one of you and the rest of the poets. To me unhappily, the snowdrop is much the same as the snow—it feels as cold underfoot—and I have grown sceptical about "the voice of the turtle," the east winds blow so loud. April is a Parthian with a dart, and May (at least the early part of it) a spy in the camp. . . . A little later comes my spring; and indeed after such severe weather, from which I have just escaped with my life, I may thank it for coming at all.

On May 3 he wrote wistfully: "Surely the wind that sets my chestnut-tree dancing, all its baby-cone-blossoms, green now, rocking like fairy castles on a hill in an earthquake,—that is South West, surely!" In her reply Elizabeth made no reference to this veiled request, wishing nervously to postpone their meeting. He had asked to be allowed to collaborate with her: she told him that such an idea, though welcome to her, was impossible because the "Psyche" drama begun with his friend Horne "in my dreary Devonshire days, when I was his debtor for various little kindnesses," had never been completed.

In referring to this abortive collaboration, and the subject chosen by her, Elizabeth uncovered for this new friend a hidden place: that cleft in her nature furrowed deep by sorrow in the dark days at Torquay. "Did you ever feel afraid of your own soul, as I have done?"

In Browning, so complete a man, untouched by grief, there was already a disturbance, a weakening of self-sufficiency—a premonition. This woman with whom he was now so intimate on paper had power to move him strangely. Elizabeth's careless exaggerated invalid's statement that from the rigours of winter she had "just escaped with her life" touched a tragic chord on his "life's harp" to which, he said, she had added "octaves on octaves of new golden strings." The thought of Elizabeth Barrett was already an agitation, if a sweet one, in his planned poetic life, his life of a chartered freedom. We hear of an ache, a singing in the head, denoting nervous strain. Why will she not see him, he demanded. Did she mistrust him?

Elizabeth did not mistrust him, but she was shy: however, on a strict understanding that he kept silent about the visit, she would receive him. "I *cannot* admit visitors in a general way—and putting the question of health quite aside, it would be unbecoming to lie here on the sofa and make a company-show of an infirmity, and hold a beggar's hat for sympathy."

The only other man friend Elizabeth had consented to receive had been Horne, who, in 1844, before he went to Germany, would not take a first denial but begged for an interview in a letter "expressive of mortification and vexation." When Horne had not kept the engagement Elizabeth "clapped her hands with joy when I felt my danger to be passed"; and yet she liked, admired Horne, and had worked on familiar terms with him. Browning was but comparatively a new acquaintance and yet already he had singularly affected her. "For instance," she wrote him nine months later, "by two or three half words you made me see you, and other people had delivered orations on the same subject quite without effect. I surprised everybody in this house by consenting to see you." Most of the letters this romantic celebrity received from men anxious to get a sight of her went directly on to the fire.

He fixed a call three days ahead so that, if unequal to their meeting, Elizabeth might have time to write. A great part of this letter is taken up with a jaunty and rather tactless tale of a mythical "Simpson" who came to pay homage to a literary idol and departed ejaculating "mentally—'Well, I *did* expect to see something different from that little yellow commonplace man.'"

Browning's intention, his own apprehension, is clear to us: would she feel disappointed in one so long admired as a poet? But Elizabeth's humility, her consciousness of a lost hold on the words, led her to give a twist to the story. "I think you should have made out the case in some such way as it was in nature—viz. that you had lashed yourself up to an exorbitant wishing to see me . . . because I was unfortunate enough to be shut up in a room and silly enough to make a fuss about opening the door."

From his growing warmth, from an impatience to meet her, Elizabeth feared that Browning might expect more than he would find; that he might have to substitute for some enchanted princess poet a mere sickly invalid. And from these earlier letters, throbbing with the beat of a strong heart, we cannot doubt, I think, that Robert Browning came to Wimpole Street on May 20, 1845 ready to fall in love.

In a spasm of shyness Elizabeth had removed his portrait from where it hung under Wordsworth, pulling down Tennyson as well "in a fit of justice." The over-poetical portrait, which later she was to condemn as "a vulgarized caricature," could have given her little hint of the man who did appear; a handsome man, but with none of the traditional bearing of a poet. Even less could Elizabeth link this urbane courteous man with the writer of impulsive, affectionate letters.

Elizabeth did not, however, feel that profound disappointment Browning was to bring to many in the years of celebrity: she did not think he looked like a gentleman farmer, or a mere intelligent man of affairs. What struck her particularly was his eyes; the most serene, the most spiritual she had ever seen.

He stayed an hour and a half, and when he went a memory of him lingered in that quiet room. "I had a sense of your presence constantly," Elizabeth told him nine months later. There was, however, in her no presentiment of what was to come. Next morning she said to her father: "It is most extraordinary how the idea of Mr. Browning does beset me—I suppose it is not being used to see strangers, in some degree—but it haunts me . . . it is a persecution."

Mr. Barrett, happily for all three of them also without presentiment, smiled and told her "it is not grateful to your friend to use such a word."

On his return home Browning noted on her last letter the date and length of his visit. He then sent a note asking whether he had behaved as he should, talked softly enough, and not stayed too long. His "great happiness, such as it will be if I see you, as this morning, from time to time," must "be obtained at a cost of as little inconvenience to you as we can contrive." On his part there was one objection: "do not humiliate me—*do not* again,—by calling me 'kind' in that way."

She wrote back at once protesting. There must be no restriction on "our vocabulary." A kindness felt must be expressed. "It is hard for you to understand what my mental position is after the peculiar experience I have suffered and what τι ἐμοὶ καὶ σοί,[1] a sort of feeling irrepressible from me to you, when, from the height of your brilliant happy sphere, you ask, as you did ask, for personal intercourse with me." He was to come again in a week's time—"and again, when you like and can together—and it will not be more 'inconvenient' to me to be pleased, I suppose, than it is to people in general."

Elizabeth has written impulsively before and regretted it; yet even if in this case time had been given for consideration, she could not have thought that a sight of her, a wan invalid no longer young, could inflame any man. The next day he wrote to her "intemperate things"; an open declaration of love.

After a lapse of two days there came an agitated reply:
You do not know what pain you give me in speaking so wildly. . . . You remember—surely you do—that I am in the most exceptional of positions; and that, just because of it, I am able to receive you as I did on Tuesday. . . . Now, if there should be one word of answer attempted to this; or of reference; I must not . . . I will not see you again—and you will justify me later in your heart . . . spare me the sadness of having to break through an intercourse just as it was promising pleasure to me; to me who have so many sadnesses and so few pleasures. . . . Your mistakes in me . . which I cannot mistake (—and which have so humbled me by too much honoring—) I put away gently, and with grateful tears in my eyes. . . .
She begged him to "forget *at once*, and *for ever*" what he had written: "and which (so) will die out between *you and me alone*, like a misprint between you and the printer."

A new paragraph began on a note of calm friendship. With an excuse, perhaps to give herself time to regain composure, she put off his visit for a week because of relations now in London. On their next meeting he should criticize her "Prometheus." The end of this pitiful letter is tremulous with emotion:
You are not displeased with me? . . . I do not write as I might, of some words of yours—but you know I am not a stone, even if

---

[1] "What have I to do with thee?"

silent like one. And if in the unsilence, *I have said one word to vex you, pity me for having had to say it—and for the rest, may God bless you far beyond the reach of vexation from my words or my deeds!*

This brilliant man, Elizabeth told herself, had fallen in love, not with a worn-out woman, but with a poet romantically secluded.

Robert Browning, for a proved psychologist, acted so stupidly on receiving this that one can only suppose he lost his head; fearing to lose what had just been gained. Into her delay of a week he read an intention to deny him admittance unless "the past avowal" was "blotted out." Instead of allowing her letter to pass, as she had requested, in silence, he wrote the next day falsely, almost jauntily:

Don't you remember I told you, once on a time, that you "knew nothing of me"? whereat you demurred—but I meant what I said, and knew it was so. To be grand in a simile, for every poor speck of a Vesuvius or a Stromboli in my microcosm there are huge layers of ice and pits of black cold water—and I make the most of my two or three fire-eyes, because I know by experience, alas, how these tend to extinction—and the ice grows and grows—still this last is true part of me, most characteristic part, best part perhaps, and I disown nothing—only,—when you talked of "knowing me"! Still, I am utterly unused, of these late years particularly, to dream of communicating anything about that to another person (all my writings are purely dramatic as I am always anxious to say) that when I make never so little an attempt, no wonder if I bungle notably—"language," too, is an organ that never studded this heavy heavy head of mine. Will you not think me very brutal if I tell you I could almost smile at your misapprehension of what I meant to write?

What he had hurriedly written must "have looked absurd enough as seen apart from the horrible counterbalancing never-to-be-written *rest of me*—by the side of which, could it be written and put before you, my note would sink to its proper and relative place, and become a mere 'thank you' for your good opinion."

On this theme he embroidered rather incoherently for what fills another page of print; reproaching himself for having given her pain, assuring her that next Tuesday she will find him "precisely the same mild man-about-town you were gracious to the other morning." A postscript, written rather in the tone of a man who wants to suppress the evidence of an indiscretion, asked her to return his note that he might destroy it.

This blundering male effort to set matters right, to put Elizabeth's mind at rest, hampered his future courtship. Even when her love for him was avowed; a possibility with renewed health of marriage admitted, Elizabeth could not entirely rid herself of the feeling that it was an idea Browning worshipped, a sublimation of combined poet and woman. In her own phrase nine months later, "the lava of that letter has kept running down into my thought of you too much." This doubt was intensified by a long continued inability wholly to identify Browning, the writer of ardent letters, with the quiet, self-controlled man, declared lover though he was, who visited her.

Even in her morbid state of self-abasement Elizabeth might well have been offended by this extraordinary declaration: but, quite angelically, she wrote tendering humble apologies
*for having spent so much solemnity on so simple a matter. . . .
I am quite as much ashamed of myself as I ought to be, which
is not a little. You will find it difficult to believe me perhaps
when I assure you that I never made such a mistake (I mean of
over-seriousness to indefinite compliments), no, never in my
life before—indeed my sisters have often jested with me (in
matters of which they were cognizant) on my supernatural in-
difference to a superlative degree in general, as if it meant nothing in grammar. . . . I wrote what I wrote so unfortunately,*
through reverence for you, *and not at all from vanity on my
own account . .*
though, she added with a touch of humour, no man "who ever lived in the world (not even *you*) could be expected to believe" this "though said, sung and sworn."

She then again protested his superiority to her. This protestation, now from her, and now from him to her, becomes in these letters an almost wearisome ding-dong of self-depreciation.

After some general literary chat Elizabeth appointed a further meeting when "I, for one, shall have forgotten everything by that time; being quick at forgetting my own faults usually."

Still Browning could not leave well alone:

Nay—I must have the last word—as all people in the wrong de-
sire to have—and then no more of the subject. You said I had
given you great pain—so long as I stop that, think anything of
me you choose or can! But before your former letter came, I
saw the preordained uselessness of mine . . . since the offering
to cut off one's right-hand to save anybody a head-ache, is in
vile taste, even for our melodramas, seeing that it was never yet
believed in on the stage or off it,—how much worse to make the
ugly chop, and afterwards come sheepishly in, one's arm in a
black sling, and find the delectable gift had changed aching to
nausea! There! And now "exit prompt-side, nearest door, Luria"
—and enter Robert Browning—next Wednesday—as boldly as he
suspects most people do just after they have been soundly
frightened!

Unless in her heart Elizabeth did suspect that "ugly chop,"
the denial of his true feelings, to be a mere dramatization in a
sense other than that in which he had first presented it to her,
this letter could only have bewildered. Be it as it may, his letter and the whole painful subject were now ignored by her,
though at the next meeting embarrassment could hardly have
been confined to him. It was long before those beautiful eyes,
so admired by Miss Mitford, were again raised in Browning's
presence.

His own constraint, an effort to conceal the love that had
proved so perilous, is implied in a short note of mid-June: a request that she will not allow him to run on in conversation
about matters on which he is ignorant. "I tell you plainly I
only trench on them, and intrench in them, from gaucherie, pure
and respectable . . . I should certainly grow instructive upon
the prospects of hay-crops and pasture-land if deprived of this
resource." A safe and congenial subject, both in the mouth and
on paper, was the poems Robert was gathering together for his
next volume.

The essential nervousness of Robert Browning's temperament, bodily robust though he was, manifested itself at this
time of trial in frequent headaches. For him, a man who boasted
somewhat arrogantly that he always got what he wanted, the
first setback must have been a serious blow apart from natural
disappointment in love. Whether from accident or design—since

nothing appeals so much to an unselfish invalid as other people's symptoms—he spoke freely of these headaches. She took
them, and other signs of temporary indisposition in a healthy
man, very seriously indeed: surely he must have smiled when
she attributed a slight cold to having carried flowers to her un-
wrapped, the wet stalks in his bare hand.

Soon a fresh embarrassment was to beset Elizabeth. With the
coming of summer, friends and relations began to descend upon
Wimpole Street: there was further need for caution. So many,
friends of Browning among them, had been denied entrance
that she did not want his visits to be known. This necessity of
concealment meant an anxious watch upon dates and, from
time to time, some alterations. Only to Miss Mitford, for sheer
love of truth with an intimate friend, had Elizabeth admitted to
one single visit from Robert Browning. Kenyon soon knew of
their interviews, though from whom it is not clear: no attempt
was made to conceal the weekly calls from Elizabeth's father,
who, curiously enough, though he did not "overvalue poetry,"
appears to have taken pride in them.

In regard to a secrecy so alien to his nature Browning himself
declared:

*Indeed, though on other grounds I should be all so proud of be-
ing known for your friend by everybody, yet there's no denying
the deep delight of playing the Eastern Jew's part here in this
London—they go about . . . with the tokens of extreme desti-
tution and misery, and steal by blind ways and by-paths to
some blank dreary house, one obscure door in it—which being
well shut behind them, they grope on through a dark corridor
or so, and then, a blaze follows the lifting a curtain or the like,
for they are in a palace-hall with fountains and light, and marble and gold, of which the envious are never to dream!*

He was clearly plucking up courage in love. "Pomegranates you
may cut down the middle and see into," he had written on June
25, "but not hearts,—so why should I try and speak?" He ended
this short note with "and so your own R. B."

On July 8 Elizabeth took a first faltering step towards recovery; leaving not only her room but the house, going out for a
short carriage drive. Only her sister's prudence in this first venture prevented her from entering Regent's Park and also from

leaving a card "vaingloriously" at Kenyon's house in Harley Place. The experiment was not altogether pleasant to one so weakened with long seclusion, but Elizabeth was determined to repeat it. "I walk," she told her brother George, "as well as most children of two years old."

In the course of a long letter of July 18 Elizabeth made one of her many protests against the false position in which Robert nailed her up with his "gold-headed nails of chivalry." Perhaps with a certain dreary purpose of discouraging him, she claimed the doubtful advantage of *"being older by years."* But Elizabeth did not disclose how many years: indeed, it is thought in the family that while she lived Browning never knew her real age.

It is clear from a postscript to Browning's letter of July 22 that a plan to recover health abroad was being discussed. He was proud of her praise of his work—"when will the blame come?—at Malta?" Not "from Malta," be it noted, but "at Malta." Clearly if Elizabeth goes to Malta Robert will follow.

To Mrs. Martin on July 29 Elizabeth revealed a growing strength. "I have been *getting well*," she wrote exultantly, "—going out into the carriage two or three times a week, abdicating my sofa for my armchair, moving from one room to another now and then, and walking about mine quite as well as, and with considerably more complacency than, a child of two years old. . . . I look in the looking-glass with a better conscience." But if this summer good was not to be undone she must go abroad for the winter.

In spite of a determination not to admit Robert's love, not to be the means of ruffling his smooth path "by so much as one of my flint-stones," Elizabeth was, there is no doubt, drawing strength, deep joy, from their communion. Sure of his interest, she wrote much of her own nature, feelings, and childhood, and of her development as a poet. On both sides the friendship, the pure friendship she was determined to maintain, was quite frankly tinged with emotion. His letters fast gathered in warmth.

By August she could have been in no doubt that, even if his love might be three parts ideal worship of a dream woman, the love was there, and she returned it with all her heart. When he urged her to tell him what she was writing she mentioned casually "lyrics for the most part, which lie illegibly in pure Egyptian," but "nothing worth speaking of." "Oh, there is time enough," she exclaimed, "and too much, perhaps! and so let me be idle a little now, and enjoy your poems while I can. It is pure enjoyment and must be—" Elizabeth, one may guess, far removed as she was from girlhood, was enjoying that curious drift of emotion, that awareness of another, which is a part of undeclared love: to her was added the peculiar joy, the soul-shaking experience of a return to throbbing human life:

> . . . *a mystic Shape did move*
> *Behind me, and drew me backward by the hair,*
> *And a voice said in mastery while I strove, . .*
> *"Guess now who holds thee?"—"Death," I said, But, there,*
> *The silver answer rang, . . "Not Death, but Love."*

Robert is exhorting her to exercise, to grow stronger: "Never, pray, *pray,* never lose one sunny day or propitious hour to 'go out and walk about.'" "But do not surprise *me,*" he added boldly, "one of these mornings, by 'walking' up to me when I am introduced . . or I shall infallibly, in spite of all the after repentance and begging pardon—I shall . . ." There follow some words effaced, the purport of which it does not take an expert in love to guess.

Towards the end of August, when after a long fine summer they must look forward to the fogs and winds of autumn, Malta is again mentioned, and this time by Elizabeth: Mr. Kenyon had "talked homilies of it last Sunday and wanted to speak to Papa." On the question Mr. Barrett himself, the head of the house, the acknowledged arbiter of her fate, remained curiously, ominously silent. He had been the first to suggest that a winter spent in Malta might help to restore his daughter's health, and at a time when illness and a lack of interest in living had made her indifferent in the matter, but now he was silent. From something Elizabeth had written earlier in the summer of an angry word from her father, it looks as if at this time he was persuading himself that her continued illness was perversely due to a determination not to take nourishing food, to "obstinacy and dry toast." An excuse, albeit an unconscious one,

must be made for keeping the dearest child, his comfort, near
to him.

In a momentous letter of August 25 Elizabeth rather disin-
genuously asked Browning why, with freedom and the world
before him, he had at their last meeting declared himself weary
of the world. Perhaps it was because he was unwell.

Then, in a long passage covering some four printed pages,
there followed a confession which eased her burdened soul.
Starting off from some remark she had made to him about her
father, Elizabeth spoke of Mr. Barrett's domination, but of a
deep tender affection behind it, and of the reason why she herself should submit gladly to that imperial will. Then the whole
tragic story of Bro's death was told to this man who now possessed her heart. "I have never said so much to a living being—
I never *could* speak or write of it." This grief of her life was
never again mentioned, even to him, until the tactless words of
a friend reopened the wound years later.

To Browning this revelation, tragic though it was, brought
hope of winning her. In a short note he said: "There is a better
thing than being happy in your happiness; I feel, now that you
teach me, it is so."

Elizabeth had said at the beginning of her letter, and in solemn earnest, that she was "always expecting to hear or to see
how tired you are at last of me!" Picking up this phrase, he
wrote: "I *could* blot that out of your mind for ever by a very
few words *now*,—for you *would believe* me at this moment,
close on the other subject:—but I will take no such advantage—
I will wait." "May God bless you," he ended, "—in what is past
and to come! I pray that from my heart, being yours R. B."

To a letter crossing his, written that same day, Robert made
no reply. Three days later Elizabeth asked in an agitated note,
had she vexed him? Would he please write? In the meantime
she heard from him. Sitting alone on an autumn evening, the
sun coming golden into his room, Browning was thinking of her,
but the words would not come. "It must be for another time
. . after Monday, when I am to see you."

But a lover's impatience overcame him that night: he wrote
a second letter:

I believe in you absolutely, utterly—I believe that when you bade me, that time, be silent—that such was your bidding, and I was silent—dare I say I think you did not know at that time the power I have over myself, that I could sit and speak and listen as I have done since? Let me say now—this only once—that I loved you from my soul, and gave you my life, so much of it as you would take,—and all that is done, not to be altered now: it was, in the nature of the proceeding, wholly independent of any return on your part. . . . If I thought you were like other women I have known, I should say so much!—but—(my first and last word—I believe in you!)—what you could and would give me, of your affection, you would give nobly and simply and as a giver—you would not need that I tell you—(tell you!)— what would be supreme happiness to me in the event—however distant . . . I will never recur to this, nor shall you see the least difference in my manner next Monday.

A postscript makes it clear that now there was a project for a winter in Italy. "I trust," he wrote, "you see your . . dare I say your *duty* in the Pisa affair, as all else *must* see it—"

In reply Elizabeth asked, with some simplicity, how she could have provoked this letter?

Can I forgive myself for having even seemed to provoke it? and will you believe me that if for the past's sake you sent it, it was unnecessary, and if for the future's, irrelevant? . . . if a thousand more such words were said by you to me, how could they operate upon the future or present, supposing me to choose to keep the possible modification of your feelings, as a probability, in my sight and yours?

Clearly that first denial of love was still having an effect: it might be now a mere noble pity this chivalrous poet felt for her.

She did not deny her own feeling:

I cannot help adding that, of us two, yours has not been quite the hardest part . . I mean, to a generous nature like your own, to which every sort of nobleness comes easily. Mine has been more difficult—and I have sunk under it again and again: and the sinking and the effort to recover the duty of a lost position, may have given me an appearance of vacillation and lightness, unworthy at least of you, and perhaps of both of us.

She never could allow him to take

the step of wasting, in a sense, your best feelings . . of empty-
ing your water gourds into the sand . . . you may well trust
me *to remember to my life's end, as the grateful remember; and*
to feel, as those do who have felt sorrow (for where these pits
are dug, the water will stand), the full price of your regard.

The journey to Pisa was now arranged: if Elizabeth could
bring herself, in defiance of her father, to involve the brother
and sister needed to accompany her, she would soon be on her
way. Browning had his plans too. "You were in jest," she wrote,
"about being at Pisa *before or as soon as we were*?—oh no—that
must not be indeed—we must wait a little!—even if you determine to go at all, which is a question of doubtful expediency."
Elizabeth might have been unselfish, humble in self-abnegation,
but she was also in love. There was now no question of taking
the obvious way, by forbidding him to follow, of putting an end
to the danger of being as a flint stone in the smoothness of his
path.

This letter was not sent until well after their meeting the next
day, September 1: Elizabeth seems to have waited to be exam-
ined by Dr. Chambers before posting it. On the 3rd an anxious
Browning sent her a note: "Will you not tell me something
about you—the head; and that too, *too* warm hand . . or
was it my fancy? Surely the report of Dr. Chambers is most
satisfactory,—all seems to rest with yourself." Later that day
he received the letter and wrote again. "Before you leave
London, I will answer your letter—all my attempts end in nothing now."

Six letters passed between them, friendly, informative, before Browning wrote that one in his heart. If he could win her
affection—he did not dare to aspire to her love—Elizabeth might
be sure that he would be content:

I am not what your generous self-forgetting appreciation would
sometimes make me out—but it is not since yesterday, nor ten
nor twenty years before, that I began to look into my own life,
and study its end, and requirements, what would turn to its
good or its loss—and I know, *if one may know anything, that to*
make that life yours and increase it by union with yours, would
render me supremely happy, *as I said, and say, and feel. My*
whole suit to you is, in that sense, selfish—*not that I am ignorant*

that your *nature would most surely attain happiness in being conscious that it made another happy—but* that best, best end of all, *would, like the rest, come from yourself, be a reflection of your own gift.*

Browning's chosen way of life had included no wife in its scheme:

for my own future way in the world I have always refused to care—anyone who can live a couple of years and more on bread and potatoes as I did once on a time, and who prefers a blouse and a blue shirt (such as I now write in) to all manner of dress and gentlemanly appointment, and who can, if necessary, groom a horse not so badly . . . such an one need not very much concern himself beyond considering the lilies how they grow. But now I see you near this life, all changes—and at a word, I will do all that ought to be done . . . and let "all my powers find sweet employ" as Dr. Watts sings, in getting whatever is to be got—not very much, surely. I would print these things, get them away, and do this now, and go to you at Pisa with the news—at Pisa where one may live for some £100 a year.

Charles Kean has offered him £500 for a play, and Mr. Colburn, the publisher, wants "more than his dinner" a novel on the subject of Napoleon. "So may one make money, if one does not live in a house in a row."

On the 16th Elizabeth wrote sadly affirming the impossibility of marriage. God had put a barrier between them. "As dear Mr. Kenyon said to me to-day in his smiling kindness . . 'In ten years you may be strong perhaps.'" Browning must give up all thought of her but as a friend.

There was another obstacle, her father's implacability in the matter of marriage: "if he knew that you had written to me *so*, and that I had answered you—*so*, even, [he] would not forgive me at the end of ten years—" Poverty could be in itself no bar, since if she "*wished* to be very poor, in the world's sense of poverty," she could not be so "with three or four hundred a year of which no living will can dispossess me."

"The obstacles then are of another character, and the stronger for being so. . . . The subject will not bear consideration—it breaks in our hands."

But Browning, in his great tenderness, his innate wisdom, could handle the subject gently enough to preserve it fresh: "Those obstacles are solely for *you* to see and to declare . . . and perhaps they strike me the more from my true, honest unfeigned inability to imagine what they are. . . . Your regard for me is *all* success—let the rest come, or not come." He can hardly promise to change his affections,

put them elsewhere &c. &c. That would be pure foolish talking, and quite foreign to the practical results which you will attain in a better way from a higher motive . . . in sober earnest, it is not because I renounced once for all oxen and the owning and having to do with them, that I will obstinately turn away from any unicorn when such an apparition blesses me . . but meantime I shall walk at peace on our hills here nor go looking in all corners for the bright curved horn! . . .

One final word on the other matters—the "worldly matters"— I shall own I alluded to them rather ostentatiously because—because—that would be the one poor sacrifice I could make you— one I would cheerfully make, but a sacrifice, and the only one: this careless "sweet habitude of living" . . . I feel sure that whenever I make up my mind to that, I can be rich enough and to spare—because along with what you have thought genius in me, is certainly talent, that the world recognizes as such.

He gave her an instance of ability: at the time his "Paracelsus" was laughed to scorn in the press ten years before, an Elementary French book, on a new plan, was praised; "which I 'did' for my old French master, and he published—'that was really an useful work'!"

At the end Robert broke into the first directly tender words he had permitted himself, calling her: dearest, my dearest, dearest. "I will wait. God bless you and reward you—I kiss your hands *now*." The postscript, practical again, mentioned his inquiries into shipping to Leghorn.

A letter crossed his: "it is all over with Pisa. . . . I spoke face to face and quite firmly—so as to pass with my sisters for the 'bravest person in the house' without contestation." The next day Elizabeth wrote telling Robert that, precarious as her health must always be, she would not accept sacrifices from him, and in no case could she permit "an exchange of higher work for lower work." In the last paragraph there is a touch of bitterness. "I had done *living,* I thought, when you came and sought me out! and why? and to what end? *That,* I cannot help thinking now." The hope of Pisa was not, however, entirely extinct, though but feebly flickering. On the same day, September 18, she wrote again:

Papa has been walking to and fro in this room, looking thoughtfully and talking leisurely—and every moment I have expected I confess, some word (that did not come) about Pisa. Mr. Kenyon thinks it cannot end so—and I do sometimes—and in the meantime I do confess to a little "savageness" also—at heart! All I asked him to say the other day, was that he was not displeased with me—and he wouldn't; and for me to walk across his displeasure spread on the threshold of the door, and moreover take a sister and brother with me, and do such a thing for the sake of going to Italy and securing a personal advantage, were altogether impossible, obviously impossible! So poor Papa is quite in disgrace with me just now—if he would but care for that!

Browning, before he received this, wisely keeping that tone of sweet reason most salutary to her agitated state of mind, remarked in his letter that all he desired of life was

to live and just write out certain things which are in me, and so save my soul. . . . That you cannot dance like Cerito does not materially disarrange this plan—nor . . . the incidental, particular and unexpected happiness of being allowed when not working to rather occupy myself with watching you . . . this, also, does not constitute an obstacle, as I see obstacles.

But Elizabeth, though she may have been softened, would not relent: "we cannot see the same thing in the same light." She advised him to go, for the sake of his health, to Pisa, with some Italian friends.

Her own plan for Pisa was not yet entirely given up. George had come home: he and she would speak. Arabel had offered to go with her "at whatever hazard," but this Elizabeth could not allow. On the heels of this letter Elizabeth spoke again to her father without result, "only with bitterer feelings on one side. If I go or stay they *must* be bitter: words have been said that I cannot easily forget, nor remember without pain." Mr. Barrett had complained about the "undutifulness and rebellion" of ev-

eryone in the house. When told that she felt her prospects of
health depended on going abroad that winter

but that through my affection for him, I was ready to sacrifice
those to his pleasure if he exacted it—only it was necessary to
my self-satisfaction in future years, to understand definitely
that the sacrifice was exacted by him and was made to him,
. . and not thrown away blindly and by a misapprehension.
And he would not answer that. I might do my own way, he said
—he would not speak—he would not say that he was not dis-
pleased with me, nor the contrary:—I had better do what I
liked:—for his part, he washed his hands of me altogether.

Elizabeth might have extracted some sort of comfort from an
admission that it was his love that held her there, to the detri-
ment of health, but even this Mr. Barrett would not concede,
though she gave him an opening.

We know that Elizabeth, so lucid on paper, found it always
difficult to express feeling in words: her father had not even this
consolation, the relief of a born writer. It seems unlikely that
the case was put so clearly or so well as it was in her lettter. As
with many inarticulate people, they both probably said foolish,
hurtful, and misleading things. The tragedy between father and
daughter had begun. Mr. Barrett could not have been the more
placated if he knew that the brother who proposed to go with
her was the gentle, affectionate Stormie, now his eldest son.

George advised her to continue preparations for the voyage:
he at the last minute would again state the case to the "highest
authority" and judge whether it would be possible for her to go
with brother and sister. She asked Browning's advice. George
considered that the father's displeasure would fall upon her in
either case, whether she went or stayed.

Browning had hitherto restrained himself from comment on
Elizabeth's father but now he wrote: "I truly wish *you* may
never feel what I have to bear in looking on, quite powerless,
and silent, while you are subjected to this treatment, which I
refuse to characterize—so blind is it *for* blindness." She must
nerve herself to action:

all passive obedience and implicit submission of will and intel-
lect is by far too easy, if well considered, to be the course pre-
scribed by God to Man in this life of probation—for they evade

*probation altogether, though foolish people think otherwise.
Chop off your legs, you will never go astray. . . .*

Circumstances had now shifted, placing her in what he could
only consider the veriest slavery:

*and I who could free you from it, I am here scarcely daring to
write . . though I know you must feel for me and forgive
what forces itself from me . . what retires so mutely into my
heart at your least word. . . . Now, while I dream, let me once
dream! I would marry you now and thus—I would come when
you let me, and go when you bade me—I would be no more than
one of your brothers—"no more"— . . . when your head ached
I should be here.*

When Elizabeth again made her answer of self-abnegation,
of a determination not to take "a base advantage of certain noble extravagances," she could not, as an unmarried woman, have
realized to the full the greatness of this lover's gesture; though
perhaps, even if knowing what such a statement meant to a natural man, she might still have felt that it was made out of love
for an idea, or from pity. However Browning might protest,
that foolish letter about ice-pits and fire-eyes was still having
its effect. But this last letter, his generous offer, did move her to
promise that if God

*should free me within a moderate time from the trailing chain
of this weakness, I will then be to you whatever at that hour
you shall choose . . whether friend or more than friend . .
a friend to the last in any case . . . only in the meanwhile you
are most absolutely free . . "unentangled" (as they call it)
by the breadth of a thread . . . you cannot force me to think
contrary to my first thought . . that it were better for you to
forget me at once in one relation.*

A note came to her on that same day: "oh, do not fear I am
'entangled'—my crown is loose on my head, not nailed there—
my pearl lies in my hand—I may return it to the sea, if I will!"
One can hear a joyful laugh in the very words.

Elizabeth was now making plans to sail in almost a month's
time: but the decision to break away from her father was not
yet final. Her "foot is in the air," she told Horne, "balanced on
the probability of a departure from England." To Browning she
sent a plea not to think too hardly of "poor Papa. You have his

wrong side . . his side of peculiar wrongness . . to you just now. When you have walked round him you will have other thoughts of him."

To an expressed wish that she should take this momentous journey wrapped in a cloak of his, Elizabeth must say no: "do you remember . . do you consider . . how many talkers there are in this house, and what would be talked—or that it is not worth while to provoke it all? And Papa, knowing it, would not like it." It is clear that Mr. Barrett was aware of Browning's continued visits though probably not that they were weekly: to the end there seems to have been no suspicion that Robert was anything more than a literary acquaintance.

The plan of destination veered from Pisa to Malta, from Malta and Pisa, as steamers seemed at the moment most convenient and possible, but by October 6 Pisa was fixed upon. "Oh, to be in Pisa. Now that E. B. B. is there!" Browning wrote happily. "And I *shall* be there . ."

On October 11 Elizabeth is wavering: "no: I shall not go." It remained for George to speak to her father. Mr. Barrett was still relentless in his disapproval of insubordination. His evening visits to her room had been wholly withdrawn; those precious moments of confidence always ending with prayer offered up both together, and separately by him on his daughter's account, humbly upon his knees before God:

the thing is quite expressively significant. Not that I pretend to complain, nor to have reason to complain. One should not be grateful for kindness, only while it lasts: that would be a short-breathed gratitude. I just tell you the fact, proving that it cannot be accidental.

A new anxiety was upon her: Occy had been seized with "a fever of the typhoid character" which the doctor thought might be infectious. Browning, who robustly disbelieved in contagion from fevers, refused to forgo his next visit, scouting Elizabeth's fear for him. This scepticism showed more fortitude than it would in our own day: to the London of the 'forties, with its filthy, pullulating slums, its contaminated water and lack of sanitation, typhoid was an ugly, a terrifying word indeed.

On October 13, with an arrangement made to sail on the 17th, George spoke to his father, pressing the matter with some anger. Mr. Barrett's pronouncement settled the question; that she might go if she pleased, "but that going it would be under his heaviest displeasure." Mr. Kenyon had said one day that under her "Ba-lambishness" there was a tigress-nature "distinctly cognizable": in defence of health and happiness Elizabeth might have stood out against her father, but she could not involve Arabel and Stormie in that heaviest of displeasures. The "Ba-lambishness," family affection, must prevail. Perhaps in this decision was some measure of relief: before George had spoken Elizabeth had felt "as if the house stood upon gunpowder, and as if I had held Guy Fawkes's lantern in my right hand." The habit of years, a long obedience, was not for this frail woman, however nerved by love, easy to break through. Her brother's entreaty had not even softened Mr. Barrett into permission for at least a removal to a warmer part of England. In a man who had sacrificed domestic comfort in 1840, and allowed Bro to stay on with Elizabeth at Torquay, this decision against a compromise that would have kept her within reach seems inexplicable except by the thesis that, with advancing years, an absolute power had twisted the man's nature.

The kindness of Elizabeth's sisters, who begged her not to consider them, made Elizabeth the more determined not to embroil her family. She would take up her chain once more, a chain made heavier by Mr. Barrett's continued displeasure. His visits to her room were now confined to a hasty five minutes before dressing for dinner. "The bitterest 'fact' of all is, that I believed Papa to have loved me more than he obviously does: but I never regret knowledge . . I mean I never would *unknow* anything . . even were it the taste of the apples by the Dead sea—and this must be accepted like the rest." George went further in an estimate of his father's attitude to Elizabeth, asserting roundly more than once: "He does not love you—you need not think it."

Browning declared bravely that their disappointment would "be seen for the best in the end." With a dream of perfect happiness cruelly postponed now that Elizabeth's health was again imperilled by a London winter, he must be content with snatches of joy, the letters and many more months of those visits; visits which must secretly humiliate a proud man since they

were, and in those days of formal etiquette, made to the house
of one who would not take the trouble to receive him. Moreover, he went under a false pretence of mere friendship: if it
should come to Mr. Barrett's knowledge that Browning was his
daughter's lover he would be summarily ejected.

Elizabeth composed herself to resignation. "My cage is not
worse but better since you brought the green groundsel to it—
and to dash oneself against the wires of it will not open the
door."

Better still, the caged bird was not now an ailing one. A state
of chronic invalidism had turned to hope, and the sick soul from
the grave. With Elizabeth all was changed.

"My future will not copy fair my past"—
I wrote that once; and thinking at my side
My ministering life-angel justified
The word by his appealing look upcast
To the white throne of God, I turned at last,
And there, instead, saw thee, not unallied
To angels in thy soul! Then I, long tried
By natural ills, received the comfort fast.
While budding, at thy sight, my pilgrim's staff
Gave out green leaves with morning dews impearled.
I seek no copy now of life's first half:
Leave here the pages with long musing curled,
And write me new my future's epigraph
New angel mine, unhoped for in the world!

C H A P T E R   1 8

LOVE AND EXPECTATION [1845–6]

LOVE, NOW ACKNOWLEDGED, made Browning's visits dearer but more fearful. The one weekly visit of which Mr. Barrett knew was "a thing established," and perhaps a more frequent call might be risked now and then. But, Elizabeth wrote, "I am Cassandra, you know, and smell the slaughter in the bath-room."

Elizabeth did not stop to consider how this impulsive and sinister dramatization might agitate a lover. What sort of danger could she be in from an angry man, one of whom he, Browning, had no personal knowledge? How far would Elizabeth in her unselfishness conceal persecution, indignities from him? Not wishing perhaps further to disturb her, Robert made no direct reference to the situation but when they met, and the question of visits arose, he evidently tried cautiously to draw her. From his attitude Elizabeth thought that he had not fully grasped the implications.

On October 22 she wrote him a difficult letter; a letter tremulous with apprehension, emotion, to which she begged him not to reply. There might be an occasional second call in the week "if there is no habit . . do you understand? I may be prudent in an extreme perhaps—and certainly everybody in the house is not equally prudent!" Her father's anger at discovery of the true position "the tongue of men and of angels would not modify so as to render less full of vexations to you." Only now had she fully considered the extent to which, in the case of open conflict, Robert might suffer. Perhaps it would be better if he went abroad at once; indeed, retreat from the engagement altogether. They had been too carried away by recent events and had forgotten "the other obvious evils, which the late decision about Pisa has aggravated beyond calculation . . for as the smoke rolls off we see the harm done by the fire." For her part, she would have his letters and could hope to see him on his return. The decision must be taken for both their sakes:

*If it should be your choice not to make an end now, . . why
I shall understand that by your not going . . or you may say
"no" in a word . . for I require no "protestations" indeed—
and you may trust to me . . it shall be as you choose. You*
will consider my happiness most by considering your own . .
and that is my last word.

But Browning would never allow his woman her last word;
knowing perhaps intuitively that inarticulate people should not
be allowed to brood. Gently he wrote telling her that his concern was for her only. "In this case, knowing you, I was sure that
if any imaginable form of displeasure could touch you without
reaching me, I should not hear of it too soon—so I spoke."

With a large gesture he swept aside her scruples, "the grace
of your imaginary self-denial, and fidelity to a given word, and
noble constancy; but it all happens to be none of mine, none in
the least."

*I love you because I love you; I see you "once a week" because
I cannot see you all day long; I think of you all day long, because I most certainly could not think of you once an hour less,
if I tried, or went to Pisa, or "abroad" (in every sense) in order
to "be happy" . . a kind of adventure which you seem to suppose you have in some way interfered with. . . . Do, for this
once, think, and never after, on the impossibility of your ever
(you know I must talk your own language, so I shall say—) hin-
dering any scheme of mine, stopping any supposable advancement of mine. Do you really think that before I found you, I
was going about the world seeking whom I might devour, that
is, be devoured by, in the shape of a wife . . do you suppose
I ever dreamed of marrying?*

This virile assertion of Browning's went a long way towards
expunging the traces of doubt left by that "ice-pit" "fire-eyes"
letter of six months before: "really and truly," Elizabeth told
him, "I have sometimes felt jealous of myself . . of my own
infirmities, . . and thought that you cared for me only because your chivalry touched them with a silver sound—"

Her caution, she must repeat, referred not to her brothers
and sisters, who would "be glad if I was glad," but "to one person alone. In relation to *whom*, however, there will be no 'getting over'—you might as well think to sweep off a third of the

stars of Heaven with the motion of your eyelashes—" But, though she had been a submissive and was still a loving daughter, Elizabeth had always reserved a right over her own affections "even though I *never* thought (except perhaps when the door of life was just about to open . . before it opened) never thought it probable or possible that I should have occasion for the exercise; from without and from within at once."

One reason for hesitation over the retreat to Pisa must, though it is never mentioned in the letters, have been the serious character of her brother's illness: by the end of October, however, Occy's worst symptom was "too great an appetite . . a monster-appetite indeed." During this month of anxiety, of disappointed hope, a distraction and consolation was the preparation of Robert's proofs. The new *Bells and Pomegranates* was to present to the world many of Browning's most popular poems: "The Lost Leader," "How They Brought the Good News," "The Lost Mistress," the lovely song "Nay, but you who do not love her," "The Last Ride Together," "Saul," and "Home Thoughts from Abroad." Alterations suggested by Elizabeth for the sake of harmony and of clarity were gratefully adopted by the poet.

Browning, working with a distracted mind on the closet-drama "Luria," begged Elizabeth to make every effort to improve her health. "Why, we shall see Italy together! I could, would, *will* shut myself in four walls of a room with you and never leave you and be most of all *then* 'a lord of infinite space' —but, to travel with you to Italy, or Greece."

As always with lovers, Elizabeth's world of feeling and interest dwindled to smaller proportions: the old pleasure in a visit from Miss Mitford was marred by a new fatigue, a fear "of questions with a pair of woman's eyes behind them; and these are worse than Mr. Kenyon's, when he puts on his spectacles." To Kenyon she thought it wise to confess to "visits 'generally once a week' . . . he has looked at me with scanning spectacles already and talked of its being a mystery to him how you made your way here." Those spectacles were to become more searching, more alarming as the months went by.

In this letter of November 6 Elizabeth conquered her shyness and spoke out on a subject at which she had been hinting ever since they were betrothed: the return to her of the first rash declaration of love. But "that untoward letter" was irretrievably lost. "I burned it," Robert told her, "and cried 'serve it right!' Poor letter,—yet I should have been vexed and offended *then* to be told that I *could* love you better than I did already."

In the middle of November comes the first mention of her "amreeta draught," her "elixir," the morphine that Elizabeth took under medical orders

to keep the pulse from fluttering and fainting . . to give the right composure and point of balance to the nervous system. I don't take it for my "spirits" in the usual sense; you must not think such a thing. . . . I do not suffer from it in any way, as people usually do who take opium. I am not even subject to an opium-headache.

And even, when in despair, when a lowness of spirit might seem justified, she could always be cheerful, so cheerful that it was frequently remarked upon:

Nobody has known that it was an effort (a habit of effort) to throw the light on the outside,—I do abhor so that ignoble groaning aloud of "the groans of Testy and Sensitive" [1]—*yet I may say that for three years I never was conscious of one movement of pleasure in anything.*

This effort of will, this fortitude, is hardly the attribute of a drugged woman: if Elizabeth's words are literally true, that she took forty drops of laudanum a day, it would seem as if she had a quite exceptional constitution, an immunity found in general only among Eastern peoples. It is, however, possible that Elizabeth only thought that she habitually took so strong a dose: invalids have been deceived before in such matters by those around them. But that she had contracted a habit, and one not approved by her father, is suggested by the earlier admonition to George not to mention opium in his letters. Doctors might prescribe, might in a lesser or greater degree encourage the drug-taking, but Browning, wiser than his own generation, exhorted her to abandon it. She consulted her medical advisers and, three months later, we hear of a determination gradually to lessen the doses to that end: "after all the lotus-eaters are

---

[1] Mistranscribed as "Sensitude" in the *Letters*. See Rev. James Beresford: *The Miseries of Human Life, or The Groans of Timothy Testy and Samuel Sensitive* (1806).

blessed beyond the opium-eaters; and the best of lotuses are such thoughts as I know."

The conception of Browning as in love with an idea was not entirely done away with. Robert found it necessary to declare categorically: "if you COULD tell me when I next sit by you—'I will undeceive you, I am not *the* Miss B.—she is up-stairs and you shall see her—I only wrote those letters, and am what you see, that is all now left you,'" and if by some chance this misunderstanding could have been none of Elizabeth's doing, it would make no difference to his love. Indeed, he might love her the more, "having a right to expect more strength with the strange emergency." If he had approached her only from admiration of her work, he might have done so years before: it was the mention of himself in "Lady Geraldine's Courtship" that had led him to write that first letter:

on the whole, UNWILLINGLY . . *with consciousness of having to* speak *on a subject which I* felt *thoroughly concerning, and could not be satisfied with an imperfect expression of. As for expecting* THEN *what has followed . . I shall only say I was scheming how to get done with England and go to my heart in Italy.*

And now, my love—I am round you . . my whole life is wound up and down and over you . . I feel you stir everywhere. I am not conscious of thinking or feeling but about you, with some reference to you—so will I live, so may I die!

He had been reading her sonnet "Past and Future," which affected him more than any other poem of hers. The companion sonnet, with its deep joy in a renewal of life, Robert was not to see until three years after marriage; but that it was written now, in mute answer to the sadder lyric, is clear. In her reply Elizabeth told him: "I sate by while the angel stirred the water, and I called it *Miracle.* Do not blame me now . . *my* angel!"

At the end of November Browning complained whimsically that, although by some process she seemed to know whether he was looking well or ill, he had not had a glimpse of her eyes since the day on which they first met. "I only know yours are there, and have to use that memory as if one carried dried flowers about when fairly inside the garden-enclosure." The beauty of Elizabeth's eyes, veiled by long eyelashes, was praised by others than Miss Mitford: the brilliant look of them, redeeming a sickly face, would linger long in the memory of the beholder. So shy was Elizabeth still of Robert that on sending him a ring containing her hair she begged him not to refer to it when they met. At Browning's request she gave him too a curl of that dark hair: at his death a gold locket containing it was taken from about his neck. For this lock she demanded one of his:

> *The soul's Rialto hath its merchandise;*
> *I barter curl for curl upon that mart.*

Their letters now—soon, with few omissions, to be written every day of the week—are full of that recapitulation, so dear to lovers, of the growth of love, of a knitting together of personal relations.

Mr. Kenyon, perhaps suspecting the case, began to ask Elizabeth awkward questions about Browning's visits: Browning's name was naturally much in his mouth because of an ecstatic delight in the new *Bells and Pomegranates,* "Dramatic Romances and Lyrics," published in November 1845 and dedicated to Kenyon. "Saul," his favourite, Kenyon read every night before going to sleep "to put his dreams in order."

This little paper-covered volume, as modest as its predecessors and published again at the expense of Browning's father, strongly stimulated that lively but limited literary interest aroused by the poet; and especially among the youthful Pre-Raphaelites to whom Browning became an idol to be worshipped, conned over, illustrated in paint and pencil. The greatest honour to "Dramatic Romances," bringing particular pride and pleasure to all those in Browning's immediate circle, was a poetical tribute from the revered Landor, "There is delight in singing," printed in the *Morning Chronicle* after it had been privately circulated among friends by the elder Browning.

With Elizabeth there was, beyond the love sonnets, no composition during this period of waiting: she was content to be—perhaps for the first time in life—deliciously idle, "leaning out of some turret-window of the castle of Indolence and watching the new sunrise." Her only published work was for an annual volume that summer and some small translations from the Greek for a book of Mrs. Jameson's in the spring of 1846. When in October a request came from America that the *Athenæum* prose papers might be issued in book form, there and in England, Elizabeth could not apparently bring herself to make the revision she considered necessary: the papers were not collected together until 1862, after her death.

One of the minor miracles of love in that turret room of the Castle of Indolence was the continued life of flowers that Robert brought her; so long as the season lasted, from his mother's garden. In that close room where plants and flowers withered and died, his offerings remained fresh; perhaps because Elizabeth cared for them tenderly. There were some little blue blossoms that she particularly cherished: "while I was putting them in water," she wrote him once, "I thought your visit went on all the time."

These visits, so dear to them both, Robert had from the beginning recorded. At the end of November, putting the precious minutes together, he had spent the equivalent of two whole days with her. "I enter the room determining to get up and go sooner . . and I go away into the light street repenting that I went so soon by I don't know how many minutes."

One of Browning's minor pleasures was an acquaintance in the world outside with George, whom he met at Kenyon's and elsewhere. He liked the grave legal brother: "It comforts me that he is yours." Though there can be little space for the many good stories told in these letters by Browning, perhaps one may be mentioned here. Browning and George met at the house of Serjeant Talfourd, famous in his day for the poetic drama "Ion." On a side table they found a "portentous book lettered and thick as a law-book" of congratulatory letters upon "Ion." Browning discovered his own and two of Elizabeth's [2] bound and indexed. This piece of bad taste, though it was annoying, amused them all. George in particular enjoyed his sister's discomfiture when at first she had thought that her rather effusive girlish letters had been read by Browning. But Browning, who was very short-sighted in one eye, could not see the open page as George held the book, and a closer scrutiny of "what was so unfairly exposed to view" he had neither sought nor desired.

Browning's anxiety for Elizabeth, mutely defying her father within the castle of home, was not allayed: there seems to have

[2] One is in the Hagedorn Collection.

been within him an underlying fear that he might lose her, that she might not have strength to resist Mr. Barrett's anger. This, she assured him, could never be "since I am yours, while I am of any worth to you at all." He had suggested a certain sealed letter, perhaps to be put directly into her father's hand in case of discovery; but, Elizabeth wrote, such a note would be no defence to her. "Only one person holds the thunder—and I shall be thundered at; I shall not be reasoned with—it is impossible." And really they stood in little danger. "Let there be ever so many suspectors, there will be no informers." "Why not," she asked, "leave that future to itself? For me, I sit in the track of the avalanche quite calmly . . so calmly so as to surprise myself at intervals—and yet I know the reason of the calmness well." Browning, with a lover's apprehension, a poet's imagination, and his own vivid sense of drama could not view the position so calmly: the very contrast of the Barrett household to his own home, so free from parental tyranny, must have aggravated the sore in his mind. It is no wonder that headaches, the nervous tension, continued.

In the middle of January Robert again expressed that gnawing anxiety: "as I sate by you, so full of the truest life, for this world as for the next,—and was struck by the possibility, all that might happen were I away, in the case of you continuing to acquiesce—dearest it *is* horrible—I could not but speak." When she felt strong enough and ready to come to him he must, in their approach to her father, have "the man's right of first speech. *I* stipulate, too, and require to say my own speech in my own words, or by letter—remember! But this living without you is too tormenting now. So begin thinking,—as for Spring, as for a New Year, as for a new life."

In her reply Elizabeth disabused his mind as to any idea of a normal approach to Mr. Barrett:

from the moment of a suspicion entering one *mind, we should be able to meet never again in this room, nor to have intercourse by letter through the ordinary channel. I mean, that letters of yours, addressed to me here, would infallibly be stopped and destroyed—if not opened. Therefore it is advisable to hurry on nothing—on these grounds it is advisable. What should I do if I did not see you nor hear from you, without being able to feel that it was for your happiness? What should I do for a month even? And then, I might be thrown out of the window or its equivalent—I look back shuddering to the dreadful scenes in which poor Henrietta was involved who never offended as I have offended.*

Elizabeth then told him the story of Henrietta and the lover whom she had been forced to reject; how, suffering from sympathy, she herself, though perfectly well at the time, had fallen into a dead faint in trying to follow Henrietta from the room. Both sisters now knew of the engagement and fully approved; indeed, Henrietta was in a like position to herself.

The situation was made harder to Browning by his own inherent love of freedom, his hatred of tyranny. He told her of a familiar nightmare dream: "I stand by (powerless to interpose by a word even) and see the infliction of tyranny on the unresisting man or beast (generally the last)—and I wake just in time not to die: let no one try this kind of experiment on me or mine!" He then told her the story of a man, his host, who had insulted a meek wife before guests. Browning had bided his time, but at the first opportunity had expressed his contempt for the husband "and at the end marched out of the room." His host followed him to the front door completely bewildered. "What *can* have possessed you, my *dear* B?"

In the middle of January, on an exceptionally warm day, Elizabeth took one more step towards freedom by walking downstairs into the drawing-room, surprising her family "as much as if I had walked out of the window instead."

The naturally sanguine Robert was, by February 6, eagerly looking forward:

Then see the bright weather while I write—lilacs, hawthorn, plum-trees all in bud; elders in leaf, rose-bushes with great red shoots; thrushes, whitethroats, hedge sparrows in full song— there can, let us hope, be nothing worse in store than a sharp wind, a week of it perhaps—and then comes what shall come—

In five days winter had descended once more: the pond before Browning's window was frozen over.

It has been said that Elizabeth, feeling reserve with them and fearing questions, now found irksome the visits of friends, of Kenyon and Miss Mitford in particular. There must be restraint

ELIZABETH BARRETT BROWNING

a bust executed after her death by William Wetmore Story; an
example of it is in the Keats-Shelley Memorial House, Rome

ROBERT WIEDEMAN ("PEN") BROWNING
from a photograph taken in Rome in 1861

too in letters: to Mrs. Martin however this spring she hinted at a change of circumstance. Mrs. Martin, recovering from an illness at Hastings, wished Elizabeth could be there too. "I can lose nothing here," Elizabeth wrote to this old friend, "shut up in my prison, and the nightingales come to my windows and sing through the sooty panes." A direct reference to Browning could not be kept out: "A friend of mine too—one of the greatest poets in England—brought me primroses and polyanthuses the other day, as they are grown in Surrey!"

The cold spell did not last long: the rest of the winter and the spring were mercifully mild that year. On February 27 Elizabeth went down alone to the drawing-room and surprised Henrietta singing at the pianoforte. Henrietta tried to persuade her to remain in order to "see the great sight of Capt. Surtees Cook —*plus* his regimentals—fresh from the royal presence at St. James's." It would also be Elizabeth's first introduction to Henrietta's accepted lover, William Surtees Cook, who had, by sheer perseverance and a strong emotional appeal, ousted two other suitors. Captain Surtees Cook had one decided advantage over his rivals in being a cousin of Mr. Barrett: he had therefore a licence to come and go in the house, though hardly to pay his addresses. His courtship was necessarily as clandestine as Browning's.

A knock came at the front door. It was not the decorative Captain who was announced, but Mrs. Jameson. Elizabeth, who could not face Mrs. Jameson in the drawing-room "with the prospect of the military descent in combination," begged Henrietta to take Mrs. Jameson directly upstairs that she might follow in a minute or two: "and the corollary of all this interesting history is," she wrote to Browning, "that being able to talk at all after all that 'fuss,' and after walking 'upstairs and downstairs' . . . proves my gigantic strength—now doesn't it?"

Mrs. Jameson, "kind beyond speaking of," brought a new light to the lovers, a prospect of escape from open conflict. Might she herself take Elizabeth to Italy? Others had offered to do the same, but Elizabeth had so far hesitated that she had not revealed this to Robert. Now she wanted his opinion. To this he made no reply on paper, so we cannot tell what he thought.

At the beginning of March Mr. Barrett encountered Browning in the house one morning. Coming to Elizabeth's room for a moment before dressing for dinner, he showed a certain displeasure. "I was not *scolded,* do you understand. It was more manner, but my sisters thought as I did of the significance:— and it was enough to prove to me (if I had not known) what a desperate game we should be playing if we depended on a yielding nerve *there.*"

Robert's anger against the domineering father, held in check till now, burst out a few days later in writing:

That a father choosing to give out of his whole day some five minutes to a daughter, supposed to be prevented from participating in what he, probably, in common with a whole world of sensible men, as distinguished from poets and dreamers, consider every pleasure of life, by a complete foregoing of society— that he, after the Pisa business and the enforced continuance, and as he must believe, permanence of this state in which any other human being would go mad—I do dare say, for the justification of God, who gave the mind to be used in this world, . . . that, under these circumstances, finding . . . what, you say, unless he thinks he does find, he would close the door of his house instantly; a mere sympathizing man, of the same literary tastes, who comes good-naturedly, on a proper and unexceptionable introduction, to chat with and amuse a little that invalid daughter, once a month, so far as is known, for an hour perhaps,—that such a father should show himself "not pleased plainly," at such a circumstance . . My Ba, it is SHOCKING!

He exhorted her to take advantage of the mild weather, to get strong in expectation of going to Italy before next winter.

Elizabeth in her reply wisely ignored the anger in Robert's outburst, explaining gently that it was not his visit as such which offended.

It was a sort of instinctive indisposition towards seeing you here, unexplained to himself, I have no doubt—of course unexplained, or he would have desired me to receive you never again, that would have been done at once and unscrupulously. But without defining his own feeling, he rather disliked seeing you here—it just touched one of his vibratory wires, brushed by and touched it—oh, we understand in this house.

She did her best to explain Mr. Barrett's attitude: "after using one's children as one's chattels for a time, the children drop lower and lower towards the level of the chattels, and the duty of human sympathy to them becomes difficult in proportion."

Robert wrote back more temperately:

I dare say I am unjust—hasty certainly . . . but if I ever see it right, exercising my intellect, to treat any human beings like my "chattels"—I shall pay for that mistake one day or another, I am convinced—and I very much fear that you would soon discover what one fault of mine is, if you were to hear anyone assert such a right in my presence.

Enjoying freedom, an apostle of freedom, Robert could not know or pity the inhibited man as proud in his own way and as secure of right; a man soon to receive a harsh blow from one dearest to him. Elizabeth, near to her father, loving him in spite of tyranny, could pity his loneliness, an alienation from his own children. When he was once laying down the law "about passive obedience, and particularly in respect to marriage," one by one his sons left the room. Captain Surtees Cook alone remained: to a meek question from the young man ambitious to be Mr. Barrett's son-in-law, "if children were to be considered slaves," Mr. Barrett's reply is unfortunately not recorded.

Browning, having finished "Luria," was now at work upon "A Soul's Tragedy." The first act Elizabeth found, was bound to find, gripping: it is one of Browning's finest pieces of dramatic writing. But of the whole she evidently thought it safer to generalize:

It is a new work with your mark on it. That is . . . it would make some six or sixteen works for other people, if "cut up into little stars"—rolled out . . . diluted with rain-water. But it is your work as it is—and if you do not care for that, I care, and shall remember to care on. It is a work full of power and significance.

If she had known him only by "Luria" and "A Soul's Tragedy," although "Luria" was "the completer work," it would have been "A Soul's Tragedy" that would have led her to attribute to its author "more power and a higher faculty."

All this is true, known to posterity to be true, but Browning himself could not but be dissatisfied with that heavy-footed

"Luria" and with the ill-made "A Soul's Tragedy." Both had been written with the surface of his mind. Obsessed as he was, tormented by the thought of Elizabeth, his heart, his soul, was not free enough for composition.

Elizabeth herself, not driven by the money urge, wisely abstained from any serious work beyond those sonnets which were a direct expression, a relief to an overcharged heart. Browning, who could not express himself so, had no such relief: love poetry was not for him until he was safely married. Rather reluctantly he sent those two valuable but imperfect works, the dramas of the first year of their engagement, to Moxon. "Luria" and "A Soul's Tragedy" were published in April as the last of the series *Bells and Pomegranates*.

A cold spell at the end of March, with winds and snow, prevented Elizabeth from those strengthening walks down to the drawing-room, but her health continued good. One night a howling melancholy wind brought her the sound of the sea and old sorrow, but with a difference: in happiness and a hope for the future the old surging misery echoed more remotely now. She could even feel glad of the estrangement from her father, because if he were kind and affectionate she would be the less willing to give him pain. "Ah well!" she added, "in any case I should have ended probably, in giving up all for you."

On April 4 Elizabeth went downstairs and, finding the drawing-room empty, came up again, meeting Flush half way. Flush, who had been sleeping when she left the room, leaped up against her "in such an ecstasy of astonished joy, that I nearly fell backward down the stairs." Flush was probably at this time disturbed in his faithful dog soul: he did not like this new affectionate visitor of hers, especially as he was of the wrong sex. "He hates," his mistress told Robert, "all unpetticoated people." When, later in the year, Browning arrived with an umbrella in his hand Flush openly flew at him. His contrition afterwards, when alone with his mistress, was profound: a certain bribery with cakes helped to smooth over a difficult situation.

That same day of Flush's agitation Robert started a subject which led to their first difference of opinion, that of duelling. Curiously enough he spoke in defence of it. Elizabeth, astonished, alarmed, spoke her mind. If Robert were ever to commit such an act in a fancied defence of honour she would "just *call in the police*, though you were to throw me out of the window afterwards." "Ever dearest," she begged, "do *you* promise me that you will never be provoked into such an act—never?" The next day she wrote nervously: "So I spoke my mind—and you are vexed with me, which I feel in the air. May God bless you dearest, dearest! Forgive as you can, best, Your Ba."

Browning wrote a long reasoned defence, with exemplars, of the custom of duelling on serious counts. Though giving no specific promise to abstain from duelling, he got very neatly out of the dilemma. He did not care enough, and had often reproached himself, for the ways of the world to go to an extreme in defence of righteous opinion: "*I*, angry! oh, how you misinterpret, misunderstand the motions of my mind! In all that I said, or write here, I speak of others—others, if you please, of limited natures: I say why *they* may be excused . . that is all. . . . Now, love, let this be a moot point to settle among the flowers one day."

Elizabeth, with her clear mind, detecting certain fallacies in his argument, maintained her position, that duelling was morally wrong. "Why should we see things so differently, ever dearest? If anyone had asked me, I could have answered for you that you saw it quite otherwise." But, with sweet femininity, she yielded a point. "You may be right and I wrong, of course—I only speak as I *see*. And will not speak any more last words . . taking pardon for these."

Elizabeth took his rather perverse arguments so much to heart that, brooding on what might arise from their dangerous situation, she worried herself into the old fears. Perhaps it would be better that they should part, that he should never be placed in a position where insult would be inevitable: perhaps in her feverous cloistered mind she even envisaged a clash, demanding a trial of honour, between Browning and a brother. He could not know what insult he might have to endure: "no, you *do not understand* . . you *cannot*, perhaps!" Such was her distress that Robert begged her to marry him at once and end those despairing fears, the need on his part so constantly to reaffirm his love: in an apology she told him that "through my want of familiarity with any happiness" "these weights of flowers" would drop "again and again out of weak hands."

Elizabeth escaped from the subject into news of Mr. Kenyon, who, "with those detestable spectacles—like the Greek burning glasses" turned full on her face, had said: "I suppose now that Mr. Browning's book is done and there are no more excuses for coming, he will come without excuses."

Some comment of Kenyon's on Browning's way of living, a worldly view of his lack of prospects, led Elizabeth to request that no reference should ever be made to their mutual circumstances; as "it is not of the least importance to either of us, as long as we live, whether the sixpence, we live by, came most from you or from me . . and as it will be as much mine as yours, and yours as mine, when we are together . . why let us join in throwing a little dust in all the winking eyes around," even those of her own family. This Robert agreed for the moment to do, though reserving to himself a right to speak on the subject later: almost certainly he had already determined on that marriage settlement which was his first care once they were well settled in Italy.

On April 16 Elizabeth wrote momentous news: she had been buying a bonnet. "And having chosen one a little like a Quaker's, as I thought to myself, I am immediately assured by the learned that 'nothing can be more fashionable.' " This preparation for "going out, walking out, driving out" delighted Robert, who, as a year before when he craved for a sight of Miss Barrett, wrote happily of spring, lambs bleating in a field behind the house, "beautiful sunshine . . . and a chestnut tree leafy all over, in a faint trembling chilly way, to be sure . . . and blossomed trees over the garden wall."

Two days later Kenyon came again, "spectacles and all. He sleeps in those spectacles now, I think." His first question was:

"Have you seen Mr. Browning? And what did he come for again, pray?" Robert, fearing a more personal question to himself, wondered whether they should let Kenyon into their secret, but Elizabeth was firm. It was far better that nobody should be informed on what was strictly their own concern.

A cold wind came again, an east wind that confined Elizabeth to her room. On the 26th, in spite of a late spring, Robert was able to bring her a branch of sweetbriar to unfold its leaves in her room; by the first week of May its promise was fulfilled by a sudden warmth. On the 12th Elizabeth enclosed in her letter a laburnum blossom actually plucked by herself in Regent's Park:

we stopped the carriage and got out and walked, and I put both my feet on the grass, . . which was the strangest feeling! . . and gathered this laburnum for you. . . . . I never enjoyed any of my excursions as I did to-day's—the standing under the trees and on the grass, was so delightful. It was like a bit of that Dreamland which is your especial dominion. . . . . It seemed illogical, *not to see you close by.*

"My Ba," Robert replied, "your flower is the one flower I have seen, or see, or shall see."

Mr. Barrett, who seems to have been kinder of late, brought his daughter some flowers; flowers which quickly died while Robert's remained triumphantly blooming. The contrast, the unexpected gift, brought sadness to Elizabeth. "I cannot draw a glad omen—I wish he had not given me these." It would appear strange that the constant presence of flowers in Ba's room aroused no suspicion in the dominating father's mind.

Mrs. Jameson's visits were almost as embarrassing as Kenyon's: Elizabeth wanted to talk to her of Robert, to praise him, and yet she must dread every reference. The two were linked one day in an alarming manner. Mr. Kenyon turned "those horrible spectacles" full upon Elizabeth and asked: "Does Mrs. Jameson know that Mr. Browning comes here?" "No," said Elizabeth, "suddenly abashed." "Well, then, I advise you to give directions to the servants that when she or anyone else asks for you, they should not say *Mr. Browning is with you,*—as they did the other day to Miss Bayley, who told me of it."

It was clear that behind those spectacles there was some measure of calculation. Elizabeth did not fear that he, or any other of her friends who knew the peculiarity of the household, would disapprove her marriage, or the proposed means of attaining it, but she did not want unduly to worry Mr. Kenyon, or jeopardize his friendship with the Barrett family. Her father would, on the slightest suspicion, be only too apt to say that

Kenyon had engineered the whole affair. Later this consideration for her cousin grew into a nervous anxiety: his cautious nature might lead him to attempt to divide them.

A Miss Heaton called and talked Elizabeth into complete exhaustion. In a knowing manner she gave some information
about Browning: how he had been engaged, with a strong attachment on both sides, to a lady who had broken off the engagement on the score of religious differences. This, given with
a request for secrecy, had "helped to tire" Elizabeth. Breaking
that implied promise she at once wrote of it to Browning. He,
no doubt amused and pleased by the small twinge of jealousy
clear in her words, wrote back light-heartedly: "they used to
get up better stories of Lord Byron."

Elizabeth, already accustomed as poet and romantic recluse
to letters adulatory, half amorous, eccentric, from strangers,
was now, with the amelioration of her health, to suffer a more
determined attack from those people who had tried in vain to
penetrate the house. One lady, encamped at 16, Wimpole
Street, frightened her by writing on the card attached to a
votive rose tree: "When are you going to Italy?" However close
the lovers might wrap themselves round with their secret some
fringe of it was bound to brush the public. Perhaps even some
dim consciousness of their love, or at least a close friendship,
had escaped the enchanted circle: Elizabeth again heard that
Browning was engaged to be married, this time to a Miss Campbell.

That her brothers well knew the situation was clear. On the
occasion of her next "Sunday-levée," when she was in the habit
of receiving all her brothers and sisters at once, a remark that
Ba and Mr. Browning were such *very* intimate friends met with
a wave of laughter: "on which, without any transition and with
an exceeding impertinence, Alfred threw himself down on the
sofa and declared that he felt inclined to be very ill, . . for
that then perhaps (such things being heard of) some young
lady might come to visit *him*, to talk sympathetically on the
broad and narrow gauge!"

In this letter Elizabeth told of a walk downstairs, out of doors,
and then up again with only a few rests on the stairs—"see how
vain-glorious I am. And what a summer-sense in the air—and

how lovely the strips of sky between the houses!" In a few days
the length of her walk had so far extended that Elizabeth was
obliged to allow Stormie to carry her upstairs. These walks
were, however, never more than a very short stroll: it is a measure of Elizabeth's weakness of body only a few months before
setting out on the great adventure that it was a matter of self-
congratulation when, on May 28, she posted a letter to Browning with her own hands at the office in Great Marylebone
Street,[3] just round the corner, a matter of some seventy yards
from the house. In Great Marylebone Street, at no. 6, was
Hodgson's, the bookseller, where she often rested on her way.
A chair awaited her: Flush soon began to consider the shop
sufficiently his own to snap at the shopboy. The dog's delight at
these outings, especially in the carriage, was almost, his mistress thought, beyond a natural thing. One day, while waiting
in the back drawing-room, she said: "Flush! go and see if the
carriage is come!" He ran at once to the front window, stood on
his hind legs, and looked up and down the street.

On the 30th Elizabeth walked in the Botanical Gardens, Regent's Park, again picking a flower to send to Robert; one this
time of especial significance:

*Transie de peur, I was, . . listening to Arabel's declaration
that all gathering of flowers in these gardens is highly improper,
—and I made her finish her discourse, standing between me and
the gardeners—to prove that I was the better for it. . . .*

The flower she picked, a pansy, was one peculiarly connected
with Dr. Paracelsus, "Cintrinula (flammula) herba Paracelso
multum familiaris"; confirming Robert when he received it in a
particularly happy and hopeful mood: "all bright things seem
possible."

Elizabeth continued in her letter:

*What I enjoy most to see, is the green under the green . .
where the grass stretches under trees. . . . And to stand under
a tree and feel the green shadow of a tree! I never knew before
the difference of the sensation of a green shadow and a brown
one. I seemed to feel that green shadow through and through
me, till it went out at the soles of my feet and mixed with the
other green below. Is it nonsense, or not?*

[3] Now a continuation of New Cavendish Street.

On coming home, so tired that she had to be carried upstairs, Elizabeth found Miss Bayley, a literary friend of Kenyon's, waiting to see her. "Then she sate with me an hour—and oh, such kind, insisting, persisting plans about Italy!" Very soon it was to appear as if half the world was going to Italy and wanted to escort her there.

With summer more visitors arrived to disrupt plans of quiet meeting. Among them were relations, the Hedleys, come over from their Paris home to prepare for the wedding in London of their daughter, Arabella. It was Mrs. Hedley whom Elizabeth particularly dreaded as a potential danger to her secret. Aunt Hedley was a tactless woman ever; in her niece's words, "doing a wrong with a right intention."

Mr. Kenyon now suggested that he should bring Sarianna Browning to call upon Elizabeth. Elizabeth felt obliged to refuse: in Mr. Kenyon's presence her future sister-in-law must be treated as a mere acquaintance. She shrank from the meeting too from a fear that Sarianna might not like her enough, a nervous feeling perhaps increased by a comment Browning had passed on. Looking at a portrait of Elizabeth, considered by its subject to be both flattering and unlike, Sarianna, veiling her comment because of a third person in the room, had murmured: "*molto bella.*"

On June 3 Elizabeth paid her first visit to a friend, that old friend Miss Trepsack, or Treppy. Ba's coming was celebrated with ice cream, cakes, and cherry brandy. Ba herself was "kissed to pieces as the darlingest of children." The food, which Elizabeth and Arabel found difficult to face an hour after dinner, was welcomed by Flush, who highly approved of "that class of hospitable attentions." The visit, as a new thing, tired Elizabeth excessively.

On June 6 she set down on paper her "first word written out of my room, these five years, I think"; writing in the back drawing-room on a hot stormy evening "half out of the window for air," and curled up on the sofa. The rest of the family were at church or chapel. On June 9 she drove to Hampstead, then in open country, and pulled a dog-rose for Robert.

On June 14 Elizabeth, who had been dreading an invitation

to drive with Mr. Kenyon in his carriage, found even that frightening innovation improved upon: her cousin took her to see the Great Western train come in: "we left the carriage and had chairs—and the rush of the people and the earth-thunder of the engine almost overcame me . . not being used to such sights and sounds in this room, remember!!"

The weather remained hot and close. On the 17th, as a carriage was waiting to take Henrietta out to an evening engagement, Elizabeth took advantage of it to get into the air, driving at half past seven in the evening, with her small cousin Lizzie and Flush, into Hyde Park. On the Serpentine lake "shadows were gathering in quite fast, shade upon shade; and at last the silvery water seemed to hold all the light left, as on the flat of a hand. . . . And, as we came home, the gas was in the shops . . another strange sight for me."

On the 18th of this month, so eventful for a quiet invalid, Mrs. Jameson took her for a drive in Regent's Park. Softening as she was at every meeting to this valiant woman, Elizabeth now melted into a half confidence, telling Mrs. Jameson "what might be told," admitting at least a friendship with Robert Browning. Mrs. Jameson spoke warmly in admiration of him, delighting her companion more than she could know. It seems curious that this new friend and not the old intimate, Miss Mitford, was first confided in; but, as Elizabeth said, Miss Mitford had no sympathy with love, no knowledge of it. Her opinion too of Browning as a poet was not high. Elizabeth expected Miss Mitford to speak angrily about her marriage.

There are signs at this time in the letters that Browning was more hard pressed in spirit than his Ba, girt about though she might be with difficulty and danger: his continued headaches are a symptom. He had hesitated whether to write another poem before they should leave England, or whether he should accept a diplomatic post "Young England," in the person of Richard Monckton Milnes (afterward Lord Houghton), was offering. It is evident that the money question was weighing upon a prudent, upright mind. Ways and means were always more of a preoccupation with him than with her, and after all, it would be his wife's money on which, in present circumstances, he must live. Concealment too of the situation from his parents, requested by Elizabeth so that they should not be implicated in Mr. Barrett's wrath, was painful to the loving son. This must have weighed more heavily as his delicate mother was unwell. Later it was to be through her that he paid the only personal price for his marriage.

On the evening of the 19th, while the family were at dinner and Wilson out, Elizabeth put on her bonnet "as a knight of old took his sword," went downstairs and into the street "And, with just Flush, I walked there, up and down in glorious independence." Flush, however, who had "a very good, stout vain-glory of his own, and although adoring" his mistress, had no idea of "being ruled over" by her, chose to walk on the other side of the way. Every moment Elizabeth expected him to "disappear into some bag of the dogstealers."

On June 22 Arabel went to visit Mr. Boyd, and Elizabeth accompanied her. Hugh Boyd, always a nervous man, and now living alone, had worried himself into a state of valetudinarianism: he never went out, or left his chair. It was thought wiser, as both these old friends dreaded a first meeting after years of separation, that Arabel alone should enter the house, telling Boyd that Ba was outside in the carriage.

The next day Elizabeth had an emotional experience of a different nature; driving with Mrs. Jameson to the house of Rogers, the old poet and rich banker, to see his art treasures. Pictures and statuary, under an expert guidance, she admired in a bewildered amazement, and among them the portrait of Rembrandt by himself: "such a rugged dark, deep subterraneous face . . yet inspired—! seeming to realize that God took clay and breathed into the nostrils of it." She also saw the bookseller's agreement for the purchase of *Paradise Lost*, with Milton's signature and seal. "How was it possible not to feel giddy with such sights!" As they were leaving, Mrs. Jameson led her up to a picture of Napoleon on St. Helena by B. R. Haydon.

Next day came the news of the terrible death by his own hand. Haydon must have been in that last bloody phrenzy of despair when Elizabeth was looking at his picture. The shock was great: remorse flooded the tender heart. "Could anyone—*could my own hand even . . have averted what has hap-*

pened?" She had been told again and again that "to give money *there,* was to drop it into a hole in the ground," but "if to have dropped it so, dust to dust, would have saved a living man— when then?" Though he had written to her three times in the previous week, no suspicion of the man's state of mind had come to her: he had been bitter, but light-heartedly bitter about the grotesquerie of the Tom Thumb show that had killed his own exhibition of pictures: but in the last letter now mournfully re-read, Haydon had repeated "an old phrase of his, which I had heard from him often before, and which now rings hollowly to the ears of my memory . . that he *couldn't and wouldn't die.*" Her private epitaph on this extraordinary man is acute in its analysis:

He was a man, you see, who carried his whole being and sensibility on the outside of him; nay, worse than so, since in the thoughts and opinions of the world. All the audacity and bravery and self-exultation which drew on him so much ridicule were an agony in disguise—he could not live without reputation, and he wrestled for it, struggled for it, kicked for it, forgetting grace of attitude in the pang. When all was vain, he went mad and died.

Annoyance was added to remorse and pity: Elizabeth was given to understand—although there is no evidence available today that he did so appoint her—that Haydon had named her as literary executor, asking that she should arrange for the publication of those journals left in her care. Browning soon relieved her mind of any fancied necessity to pay serious attention to this, only "part and parcel of his insanity." Anyhow Haydon's papers were the property of his creditors. Browning thought, and others supported him in the view, that Haydon, "being quite of the average astuteness in worldly matters when his own vanity and selfishness were not concerned," had hoped that Elizabeth, in her ignorance of life, would publish the journals in their libellous entirety: Talfourd had been approached to act as literary executor, and refused.

Elizabeth herself, having felt the charm and power of the man, could not so easily dismiss Haydon as insane and selfish: *His conscience was not a sufficient witness, . . nor was God. He must also have the Royal Academy and the appreciators of*

*Tom Thumb. A "weak man," of course he was,—for all vain men
are weak men. . . . But that he had in him the elements of
greatness—that he looked to noble aims in art and life, however
distractedly, . . that his thoughts and feelings were not those
of a common man, . . it is true, it is undeniable.*

On July 1 Elizabeth drove to Boyd's house, this time to visit
him. Arabel rallied her on her nervousness. "Oh, Ba, such a
coward as *you* are, never will be . . . married while the world
lasts." The rest shall be told in her own words:

*I stood at last, at the door of poor Mr. Boyd's dark little room,
and saw him sitting . . as if he had not moved these seven
years—these seven heavy, changeful years. Seeing him, my
heart was too full to speak at first, but I stooped and kissed his
poor bent-down forehead, which he never lifts up, his chin being quite buried in his breast.*

As the two women sipped his Cyprus wine Mr. Boyd began
to talk of Ossian, proving that the Adamic fall and corruption
of human nature were "never so disgustingly exemplified" as in
the literary controversy over this work. To Elizabeth, on the
threshold of a new life, it must have been as the stirring of
dead bones.

On that same day the man who now in place of this old failing scholar, and to a greater degree, ruled her life, wrote a
laughing protest: only once had he heard her call him by his
Christian name. This Elizabeth strenuously denied. "If you
heard me say 'Robert,' it was on a stair-landing in the House of
Dreams . . . and now I have got the name, shall I have courage to say it?" To her, having known no Robert except the favourite uncle whom she called "Uncle Hedley," it was entirely
new. "So it is a white name to take into life."

All those, Uncle Hedley and other relations in Town who
might disturb hours with or thoughts of this dear Robert,
moved her now but little. A visit from Miss Mitford was not
welcomed in the old way. "Why have you turned my heart into
such hard porphyry? Once, when it was plain clay, every finger (of these womanly fingers) left a mark on it."

On July 3 Elizabeth drove out as far as Harrow, seeing London as a cloud "quite far over the tops of the trees." The lanes
and hedgerows, "so silent, so full of repose," gave her serene

pleasure. She was able to read Robert's last letter alone under the trees while Arabel took Flush for a run in a field.

Her letter of the next morning gives a contemporary view of marriage which is worth quoting, if only because it can partially explain Mr. Barrett's conduct:

I think, at least, that if I were inclined to fear for my own happiness apart from yours (which, as God knows, is a fear that never comes into my head), I should have sense to reason myself clear of it all by seeing in you none of the common rampant man-vices which tread down a woman's peace—and which begin the work often long before marriage. Oh, I understand perfectly, how as soon as ever a common man is sure of a woman's affections, he takes up the tone of right and might . . and he will *have it so . . and he* won't *have it so! I have heard of the bitterest tears being shed by the victim as soon as ever, by one word of hers, she had placed herself in his power. Of such are "Lovers' quarrels" for the most part. The growth of power on one side . . and the struggle against it, by means legal and illegal, on the other.*

Add to this that the girls of the family were expected, for the most part, to give way to, to wait on their brothers, and we have the perfect basis for a tyrannical father.

With preparations going forward for Arabella Hedley's wedding, the institution of marriage was necessarily much in Elizabeth's mind of late. The paraphernalia of a fashionable ceremony tired and disgusted her: no marriage service, she felt, should be conducted in public.

With relations constantly in the house their next meeting was postponed. Elizabeth, tried by sudden changes in the weather, from hot to sudden cold, from cold to hot, felt her old weakness upon her: on the day of writing this last letter she fainted. This indisposition made a few days of entire separation from Robert hard to bear. In spite of a determination to be prudent, to take no risk of discovery until the house should be free of these people, Elizabeth wrote on the 8th: "*I must and will see you to-morrow—*I cannot do otherwise. It is just as if Flush had been shut up in a box for so many days. My spirits flag. .*"*

One evening Aunt Hedley said to Mr. Barrett over the dinner

table: "I have not seen Ba all day—and when I went to her room a gentleman was sitting there."

Arabel, in answer to her father's look of inquiry, said: "Mr. Browning called here to-day." "And Ba bowed her head," continued the well-meaning aunt, "as if she meant to signify to me that I was not to come in." Henrietta interposed quickly. "Oh, *that* must have been a mistake of yours. Perhaps she meant just the contrary." Mr. Barrett, happily unconscious of the powder-mine under his feet, merely remarked: "You should have gone in and seen the *poet*."

This was in itself alarming; but later the affectionate Stormie added his own corollary: "Oh, Mr. Browning is a *great* friend of Ba's! He comes here twice a week—is it twice a week or once, Arabel?"

This was enough to form the basis of an innocent raillery on the part of Aunt Hedley. Introducing her future son-in-law to Elizabeth, she told him knowingly that he must consider it a great honour, "for she never lets anybody come here except Mr. Kenyon, . . and a few other gentlemen."

Mr. Barrett corrected her. "Only *one* other gentleman indeed. Only Mr. Browning, the poet—the man of the pomegranates."

These incidents, though embarrassing enough, brought a measure of relief in the knowledge of Mr. Barrett's complaisance. Robert, to whom they were reported, felt positively grateful. "I dare say he is infinitely kind at bottom—I think so, that is, on my own account,—because, come what will or may, I shall never see otherwise than with your sight."

Mr. Barrett, in high good humour, was again calling her "my love" or "my puss." Before these renewed endearments Elizabeth must quail as from "so many knife-strokes. . . . Anything but his *kindness*, I can bear now." But she was glad for Browning to have at least a glimpse of her father's other side, that not "of peculiar wrongness."

"The difficulty, (almost the despair!) has been with me, to make you understand the two ends of truth . . both that he is *not* stone . . and that he *is* immovable *as* stone. . . . We must be humble and beseeching *afterwards* at least, and try to get forgiven." An application to him before marriage might lessen her father's pain, but it would not gain consent; and she herself might not be strong enough to abide the immediate consequences. They would be "hindered from writing . . hindered from meeting."

The next day Uncle Hedley, of whom Elizabeth was particularly fond, came to sit with her. She must, he told her, make up her mind to act. "If you don't go to Italy this year, you will never go." He looked forward to receiving her in his Paris home as she went through. Elizabeth told him sadly that when the time came he might cast her off. The kind man protested, asking in vain for an explanation of her words. "Do you mean," he insisted, "because you will be a rebel and a runaway?" He laughed, promising never to cast her off.

Kenyon, though he too now accepted Browning's visits as a custom established, was pleased to joke about them. No use visiting Ba—Browning had taken his place. Elizabeth was appalled to hear he intended to stay in London the whole summer. Those spectacles, though perhaps not now as inquisitorial, were too noticing for comfort; and the visits of one now so much dearer might be interrupted.

On July 21 Robert stayed with her three whole hours, hours of fearful pleasure since Aunt Hedley was about the house. Flush, perhaps misinterpreting an embrace, again behaved badly and had to be put out of the room. On his return Elizabeth would not forgive him until late evening, and even then he did not get the placating bag of cakes Browning had left lying on the table. Poor Flush! The lot of a displaced lover is hard and beyond a dog's understanding. Even Wilson, as tender to him as his mistress, had shown no sympathy, though the "whipping" she gave him, with tears of compunction in her eyes, amounted to little more than a few soft slaps of the hand. The next morning, after sniffing the chair on which his enemy had sat, Flush was given the cakes with a scolding, and expressed his contrition in doglike manner. Elizabeth threatened him with the indignity of a muzzle, but this Browning would not permit. A muzzle in his presence would only fix a dislike in Flush.

There was another lover, or jealous old friend, who resented

Browning's visits: an old unnamed admirer whom Elizabeth called "Chiappino" [4] when writing of him. He was now so plaguing her with importunities and "insolent letters" that the angry Browning talked of interfering personally, as one who had a right to protect her. Elizabeth gave an analysis of the man: "a sort of dumb Rousseau. . . . A miserable man, first by constitution and next by fortune. . . . I have told him sometimes that he had a talent for anger!" This mysterious person, a friend of some twelve or fourteen years' standing, evidently had the right of entry to Mr. Barrett's house and even to his daughter's room. Of late, however, she had refused to receive him unless Arabel were present.

One day this unhappy man "white with passion" followed Browning upstairs. Afterwards in Elizabeth's room "there was an explosion that day among the many—and I had to tell him as a consequence, that if he chose to make himself the fable and jest of the whole house, he was the master, but that I should insist upon his not involving my name in the discussion of his violences." Though the miserable "Chiappino" was jealous of Browning, sneering at him as her "New Cross Knight," it is evident that Elizabeth feared no betrayal from that quarter.

The lovers were now discussing their future life, a life necessarily to be one of the simplicity they both preferred. One extravagance, urged by her sisters, Elizabeth did propose: the taking of Wilson with her, at least for the first year. After that she might be "rather less sublimely helpless and impotent." With Wilson's connivance, too, it might be easier to slip luggage out of the house without the knowledge of her sisters, whom she was anxious to keep ignorant of the affair. Wilson had already declared she would go anywhere with her mistress, both from devotion to her and from a desire to travel. Last year when the plan for Pisa had gone awry Wilson had seemed disappointed. One drawback was the extra expense in cost of travel and in wages, Wilson being an expensive servant—at sixteen pounds a year. Browning replied that without Wilson, or some other personal maid, he would be "simply, exactly, INSANE to move a step."

One solemn preliminary on which Robert insisted was com-

4 See "A Soul's Tragedy."

plied with, not without protest, by Elizabeth: the writing of a
formal paper expressing a wish that her future husband should,
in the event of her death before him, leave her property in
equal parts to her sisters; or, failing them, to her surviving
brothers leaving out Stormie, on whom the Jamaica estates
were entailed. Elizabeth's income, of course, before the Married Woman's Property Act, became Browning's by law on
their marriage. In acknowledging this paper Robert hinted at
a pleasing contingency that might render this paper unnecessary. "There may be even a *claimant*, instead of a recipient, of
whatever either of us can bequeath—who knows?"

Towards the end of July Kenyon was pressing Elizabeth's sisters to urge an acceptance of Mrs. Jameson's offer to escort
Elizabeth to Italy: he had himself informed Mrs. Jameson of
the position, that Elizabeth might be "'cast off' as for a crime."
The sisters, somewhat embarrassed, declared that they could
not interfere in the matter. "Ba must do everything for herself."
"But how?" Mr. Kenyon very naturally asked. "She has determination of character. She will surprise everybody some day."
Kenyon looked uneasy. This renewed offer of Mrs. Jameson's
placed Elizabeth in an awkward situation. Mrs. Jameson must
both be thanked and offered some sort of excuse for the refusal
of such a generous offer.

Kenyon's visit was doubly unwelcome that day. Robert had
been with her. Hearing of Kenyon's arrival in the house he felt
obliged to go three-quarters of an hour before his time. On the
way down he met Kenyon, who further embarrassed him by an
invitation to join himself and Landor for travel in Italy that
year. Browning, confused, resentful because his visit was cut
short, acutely aware of a half-open door near them, managed
to maintain an easy manner, joking with the intruder and telling him a good story, the purport of which he was quite unable
to recollect when Elizabeth told him how Mr. Kenyon had enjoyed the anecdote.

Browning, Mr. Kenyon told Elizabeth, when invited to Italy
with him, "did not seem to encourage the idea." Perhaps behind those spectacles, as he watched Elizabeth's conscious expression, there was a twinkle: perhaps this offer was generously
made with the idea that these two might the more easily come

together away from a home where love was forbidden. It seems unlikely that suspicion was not already aroused in that acute kindly mind.

September, and a journey to Pisa partly by water, was now fixed upon. An easy motion by river and canal boat across France would be less fatiguing for the invalid. Elizabeth made the suggestion that they should jointly accept Mrs. Jameson's offer, travelling with her; but Robert, though agreeing if Ba felt it for her own good, implied a wish that they should be alone.

In regard to Kenyon, Browning was inclined to think that he would only, if he guessed at their love, shake his head good-naturedly: Elizabeth, however, reflecting on her cousin's native caution, feared that "just in proportion to the affection he bears each of us, would he labour to drive us apart . . . *he fears like a mere man of the world.*"

On the last day of July Elizabeth had an experience that painfully exposed a continued weakness of the nerves: going for a quiet visit to Westminster Abbey she found a service was just beginning. As the great organ boomed out, after enduring the sound for a minute or so she fled in panic "being so disused to music, it affects me quite absurdly." Even a song heard in the drawing-room had lately made her weep. Music always recalled to her those lost happy days with Bro and the chasm of grief which lay between: the organ perhaps had an especial potency as a reminder of childhood when, after lessons, they had played before supper "while the loud organ's thunder circles all."

On August 2 danger seemed to threaten the lovers. A thunderstorm, exceptionally heavy, had kept Robert by Elizabeth's side for many hours. When he came to her room about seven o'clock Mr. Barrett found Elizabeth in a white dressing-gown. He "looked a little as if the thunder had passed into him, and asked, 'Has this been your costume since the morning, pray?'

"'Oh, no,' Elizabeth answered, 'only just now, because of the heat.' 'Well,' he resumed with a still graver aspect, 'it appears, Ba, that *that man* has spent the whole day with you.'

"To which I replied as quietly as I could, that you had several times meant to go away, but that the rain would not let you,—and there the colloquy ended. Brief enough—but it took my breath away."

Part of Mr. Barrett's concern had been for the storm, which he knew always frightened Elizabeth. Arabel was reproved for having left Ba, who might have been ill from fear, "with only Mr. Browning in the room."

The storm, threefold that day, had, in spite of a comforting presence during some hours of it, upset the nervous woman. She was racked by apprehension of her father, of Mr. Kenyon linking up the loose threads put into his hand by one and another, and of fate in general. Foreboding had already been with her: "I had a presentiment which oppressed me during two days . . a presentiment that it would end *ill*, through some sudden accident or misery of some kind." To Robert, impotent in his distance from her, the receipt of this letter must have brought—though her candid confessions to him were sweet—a new torture of spirit which, on second thought, she might have spared him. But his Ba was to remain headlong to the end.

When Mr. Kenyon came that day to see her "through a special interposition of guardian-angels" he had broken his spectacles and carried them in his hand. "On which I caught at the opportunity and told him they were the most unbecoming things in the world, and that fervently (and sincerely) I hoped never to see them mended." But she was not to be let off the inquisition. "Did you see Browning yesterday?" Mr. Kenyon had stayed away just because he thought Browning would be with her. Elizabeth was, however, reassured by his manner especially as, without spectacles, he could not see her confusion.

Her embarrassment was not lessened, however, by the next question: was there an attachment between her sister and Surtees Cook? She said: "Why, Mr. Kenyon? What extraordinary questions, opening into unspeakable secrets, you ask."

Mr. Kenyon did not think the question extraordinary: the Captain was so often at Wimpole Street that he thought "the affair might be an arranged one by anybody's consent."

"But you ought to know," Elizabeth answered, "that such

things are never permitted in this house." She begged him to ask no questions. Was Mr. Kenyon fumbling after another secret? All Elizabeth's nervousness returned.

Mr. Kenyon, even in his awkward questions, might well have been anxious only to give these other lovers a friendly warning to tread delicately. This Browning himself thought, declaring it "the beginning of his considerate, cautious kindness . . . his own spectacled *acumen*."

Robert was, for his part, now tormented with a new fear: that Mr. Barrett, if he made the discovery, would suddenly take Elizabeth out of London—say into Sussex, or even Devonshire. Alarmed by Elizabeth's report of her father's displeasure on the day of the storm he now took a precaution, preparing himself with a letter or parcel to leave at the door if approach were indicated as dangerous: "any man's anger to me is Flushie's barking, without the respectability of motive,—but, once the door is shut on me, if he took to biting you!" Mr. Barrett's anger towards himself might be mere clamour on the air, but the thought of a sudden suspicious return to the house on the father's part, an open scene in front of Elizabeth was unendurable: "my own tied tongue, and a system of patience I can well *resolve* upon, but not be *sure* of, as experience makes sure."

His presentiment that Elizabeth might be removed from London, and perhaps into Sussex, proved literally true: next day Elizabeth told him that, as the house was to be thoroughly cleaned, papered, and painted, a retreat to either Sussex or Kent was discussed. However, the same plans had been made for several summers back, and there they had remained in Wimpole Street; so nothing might come of it.

Aunt Hedley was the immediate threat to their comfort with her arch jokes about lovers and gentlemen visitors; jokes naturally in the air with a marriage in making. On the wedding day, August 5, the lovers fancied themselves secure as the reception was to be held at an hotel, but the bridal party came back unexpectedly "to change their costume into something wearable for comfort . . into gowns which had not a devil, torturing the wearer with a morbid sense of flounces." Browning fled, not, however, in time to prevent Aunt Hedley from knowing he had been there. He left a disappointed woman behind him, but a contented dog: Flush, heavily bribed with cakes, had graciously consented to take Robert into favour.

It being necessary to know how much money they could count upon, Stormie, the eldest brother, was asked to supply the information. Elizabeth had £8,000 in the Funds, an investment in the Eastern Railroad, a share in the ship *David Lyon* bringing a little under £200 a year, and "ten shares in Drury Lane Theatre—out of which come nothing." She drew £40 a quarter, which, Storm told her, did not represent her whole income.

Robert would wonder, Elizabeth wrote, how she could spend £40 a quarter. She did spend it, but not all on herself: her dress never exceeded £20 a year. "My greatest personal expense lately has been the *morphine*. Still the money flows out of window and door—you will understand how it flows like a stream." Browning, who kept within a limited allowance, and that a small one, must have smiled over this: his Ba had never known what it was to lack money. A natural prudence in himself was to counterbalance her heedlessness in financial matters.

The practical difficulty now, however, could not escape her attention: Mr. Barrett held a power of attorney over her income, and the allowance for that quarter was spent, or accounted for. "We might either wait on the road till the required sum be called for and sent—or get a hundred pounds advanced by someone for a few weeks until everything is settled . . what would be pleasanter, if possible. Poor Papa's first act will be to abandon his management." Elizabeth added with generous pity: "Ah, may God grant him to do it rather angrily than painfully."

"When you write so of caring to be with me," she added, "my heart seems to *rock* with pleasure."

In the midst of one of those storms which always frayed Elizabeth's nerves Mrs. Jameson came to renew her offer as escort. Had the idea been given up because Mr. Kenyon had discouraged it? When Elizabeth, faintly thanking her, begged Mrs. Jameson not to reopen the subject with her cousin, that acute woman looked at her curiously: before she went Elizabeth had to face questions more pertinent. "But you will go?" "And with efficient companionship?" "And happily and quietly?" To the last Elizabeth was unable to give a full "yes." It died away in her throat.

In spite of anxieties, Elizabeth's improvement in health was so marked that those about her noticed it. Henrietta cried out in loud astonishment to Treppy: "Did you ever see anyone looking so much better? It really is wonderful, the difference within these last few weeks." Miss Trepsack, in her ancient wisdom, had seen more than Elizabeth's improvement in health. Walking with Arabel a few days later she revealed a very shrewd guess at the real state of affairs: that Ba would marry and go to Italy. Elizabeth knew the old adoring friend would do nothing to bring one of her "children" into trouble, but officially she must know nothing. "To occasion a schism between her and this house, would be to embitter the remainder of her days."

The day Elizabeth wrote of this, Robert was employing himself in putting all her letters "into rings—twenty together—and they look now as they should—'infinite treasure in a little room.'" Not only did Browning carefully preserve these letters, a "treasure" to both himself and us, but he even kept the paper and string about parcels which her fingers had touched. No man is too great for the charming imbecilities of love.

On August 15 Kenyon, inconsiderately lingering in Town that summer, drove Elizabeth to a bridge outside London so that she might watch the Birmingham train as it came down the line. As they waited, Elizabeth cut short an observation of her cousin's upon Browning's phenomenal memory with a remark about the weather. This unadroit move brought the spectacles upon her. Arabel, moved to mischief, asked Mr. Kenyon if he did not think Elizabeth should try travelling on the railroad before she undertook a journey to Italy? Kenyon asserted that Ba would not go.

"Yes, she will, perhaps—Ba is inclined to be a great deal too wild, and now that she is getting well . . ."

"To sit on thorns," Elizabeth commented, "would express rather a 'velvet cushion' than where I was sitting, while she talked this foolishness." On their return home Arabel was well scolded.

"But we saw the great, roaring, grinding Thing . . a great,

blind mole, it looked for blackness. We got out of the carriage to see closer—and Flush was so frightened at the roar of it, that he leapt upon the coach-box." This novelty of the railroad, now cutting its way all over England, was perhaps a startling portent of the changed life to come. As they watched there was a sudden shower of rain: the experience of rain spattering upon her gown and face was not new, but so remote that it pleased Elizabeth "nearly as much as the railroad sight."

Her report of this adventure heartened Browning: "once you crossed the room to look out Shelley's age in a book, and were not tired—now you cross London to see the trains arrive and (I trust) are not tired. . So—you are stronger."

Kenyon may have had a mild suspicion, but an older friend, his curiosity roused by something Elizabeth had written, was fumbling after the truth. That something, a mere passing remark, nobody else "would have paused to think over; but he, like a prisoner in a dungeon, sounds every stone of the walls round him, and discerns a hollowness, detects a wooden beam, . . patiently pricks out the mortar with a pin—all this, in his rayless, companionless Dark—poor Mr. Boyd!"

There was to be some change in the life of this cherished disciple of his. Did she intend, Boyd asked, to become a nun? On the following visit he put a direct question. Elizabeth, secure in his love, his honour and isolation from the world, gave him the truth. Boyd, rather surprisingly in so conservative a man, expressed full approval exhorting her, with quotations from the moral philosophers, to keep to her purpose. A certain element in this approval may have been a natural gratification at having deduced so much from a trifling clue: a larger part was undoubtedly an old jealousy and dislike of Mr. Barrett. The tyranny of his refusal to allow her to go to Italy the previous year had further hardened Boyd against Elizabeth's dominating father. As to Browning, he had but barely heard his name as a poet. Elizabeth, knowing how even the now well-established Wordsworth offended his eighteenth-century ear, was content to leave it at that.

On August 19 Elizabeth drove to Finchley and there, lured by a pretty rose-covered cottage and five young children, she left the carriage to join Arabel in a visit to a married friend.

Some time spent with the eager, clamouring children, ending with the treat of a carriage ride, left Elizabeth comparatively fresh. The woman whose heart beat wildly on hearing Mrs. Jameson's foot on the stairs had travelled far towards recovery.

On the 22nd Elizabeth went to St. John's Wood, where she could enjoy the relief of talking openly. Mr. Boyd was flushed with the old enthusiasm. "The very triumph of reason and righteousness, he considers the whole affair," Elizabeth told Browning, "taking us up exactly as if we were Ossian and Macpherson, or a criticism of Porson's, or a new chapter of Bentley on Phalaris."

The following Sunday she tested her strength by attendance at a Scotch church[5] in which, as a visiting parson was preaching in French, Arabel thought they might expect a small congregation. Elizabeth should sit near the door so as to leave quietly before the singing, which would excite her too much. The church, however, filled rapidly and, with tears in her eyes, Elizabeth retreated. "One gets nervous among all these people if a straw stirs." Arabel put her in a cab and she drove back alone to Wimpole Street.

That Sunday, perhaps because George was come home from circuit, the brothers had been talking about their eldest sister: Stormie asked Arabel outright whether there was an engagement between "Mr. Browning and Ba." Arabel, taken unawares, managed to reply: "You had better ask them, if you want to know. What nonsense, Storm."

Storm said he would ask Ba when they came up to her room that evening. "George was by, looking as grave, as if antedating his judgeship." Elizabeth, informed of the conversation, awaited them nervously, but no question was put to her. Browning, alarmed on hearing this, wondered whether it would not be wiser to forgo their meetings in future. "To hazard a whole life of such delight for the want of self-denial during a little month,—that would be horrible." Elizabeth compromised by limiting his visits to "nearly a week apart, perhaps."

This self-denial did not bring a reward: the postponed meeting was interrupted by the advent of Kenyon. Browning, losing his nerve, beat so rapid a retreat as to draw the attention of

[5] Was this the Scotch Chapel in Wells Street, Tottenham Court Road?

the household upon himself. Never had he stayed for so short a time.

It was the brothers whom Browning now feared: exact knowledge on their part might bring either harm to Ba and himself or, if they were content to acquiesce, a vengeance upon themselves. Elizabeth thought none of those around her would disapprove of their marriage, though some might "be vexed at the occasion given to conversation and so on." Also, if the proposed flight were known, there were those among them who might press her to make formal application to marry, "and I might perhaps, in the storm excited among so many opinions and feelings, fail to myself and you, through weakness of body. Not of the *Will!*"

Wondering whether a sea voyage would be less dangerous to his Ba than "railroad noises and the like," Robert gave prices which are interesting to compare; £21 first-class by sea to Leghorn and £10 only as far as Pisa through France, partly along the waterways, one presumes, since it was their intention to travel on them. He reckoned out that on the total expenses a sea voyage would add quite £20. This, of course, was in the early days of distance steamers. Robert thought that, after all, the journey by sea, at least as far as Gibraltar, would be more tiring than over land.

Browning now revealed to his father, through the mediation of that more intimate friend, his mother, what must in part have been for some time an open secret. Like the perfect parents they were, Mr. and Mrs. Browning received the news of their son's coming marriage with at least outward equanimity. "They have never been used to interfere with," Browning told Elizabeth, "or act for me—and they trust me. If you care for any love, purely love,—you will have theirs—they give it to you, whether you take it or no." His father was more than willing to advance money to cover the cost of their journey.

Browning was now considering whether it might not be as well to travel at least as far as Orléans with Mrs. Jameson, who was still embarrassing Elizabeth, though in the kindest manner, with questions about the Italian journey. Elizabeth, nervous of any further disclosure, offered objections. Mr. Kenyon would think he should have been confided in—Mrs. Jameson herself might disapprove of their marriage. She postponed a decision to travel with Mrs. Jameson with an obvious sense of relief. Mrs. Jameson was to make her departure in the second week of September: perhaps they might join her at Orléans.

The kindness of relations was now more teasing to Elizabeth than their raillery. The Hedleys, both realizing that some sort of plan for a winter in Italy was made, asked no inconvenient questions but, appearing to assume that Elizabeth might be planning to join Henrietta and Surtees Cook in a flight abroad, her aunt said firmly that Henrietta should not, out of respect, marry without at least a formal request to Mr. Barrett. What, Elizabeth thought, would her aunt and uncle think of her own omission?

While they talked her father came in. Aunt Hedley commented on Elizabeth's healthy appearance. Mr. Barrett seemed surprised.

"Why," the aunt insisted, "do not *you* think so? Do you pretend to say you see no surprising difference in her?"

"Oh, I don't know," Mr. Barrett replied. "She is mumpish, I think—she does not talk." Aunt Hedley suggested, not too happily, that perhaps Ba was nervous.

"Mumpish!" Elizabeth commented. "The expression proved a displeasure. Yet I am sure I have shown as little sullenness as was possible. To be very talkative and vivacious under such circumstances as those of mine, would argue insensibility, and was certainly beyond my power."

On Sunday August 31, Elizabeth again entered a place of worship, this time sitting in the vestry of Paddington Chapel with the door ajar so that she might hear the service in private. This was but a half-hearted attempt at courage. A certain fraying of the nerves was betrayed in another and more important instance. Elizabeth now seemed inclined to postpone her marriage and flight until October.

Plainly showing that he could not endure his own hateful position much longer, Browning asked her what was to be gained by a month's delay? Indeed, with cold mornings and dark evenings, much might be lost. As delicately as possible he hinted that, if by a journey at a bad season of the year her health was "irretrievably shaken" (in plainer language, if it should prove fatal to her), "the happiest fate" he could "pray for would be to live and die in some corner where I might never hear a word of the English language, much less a comment in it on my own wretched imbecility,—to disappear and be forgotten." Elizabeth agreed to go in a few weeks' time.

On the second day of September Elizabeth's general anxiety was increased by a woeful concern for her more humble lover, Flush. This time the thieves snatched him from under the wheels of the carriage just as Elizabeth herself, having done some shopping in Vere Street, was stepping in.

Arabel, alarmed by her sudden pallor at the shock, comforted Elizabeth with a reminder that the bandits had themselves promised to secure the spaniel's return on payment of £10. But, Elizabeth commented, "*Flush* doesn't know that we can recover him, and he is in the extremest despair all this while, poor darling Flush, with his fretful fears, and pretty whims, and his fancy of being near me. All this night he will howl and lament, I know perfectly,—for I fear we shall not ransom him to-night." Elizabeth tried to console herself with the thought that Flush, who was going with them, would in Pisa be safe from the London dog-stealers.

Henry, having to deal with these vile men, was naturally angry. Elizabeth begged her brother not to haggle with the thieves: there had been a dreadful story current that a lady who demurred at the price demanded had received a parcel containing her dog's head.

Browning, rashly anticipating that Elizabeth would have Flush back when she received his letter, wrote somewhat hardly: "I would not have given five shillings on that fellow's application." He would threaten the thief with punishment, the band of thieves with extermination by all the powers he possessed. "How will the poor owners fare," he argued, "who have not enough money for their dogs' redemption?" His peevishness, his open expression of anger, might be put down to a "sick vile headache." "Dearest, I am not inclined to be even as tolerant as usual." Later in the day, being now so bilious that he had to throw himself on the bed, he wrote confirming his views, but softened them by adding: "I ought to have told you (unless you divined it, as you might) that I would give all I am ever to be worth to get your Flush back for you."

Elizabeth indeed had not taken her lover too seriously; commenting, not without mischief:

Do you mean to say that if the banditti came down on us in Italy and carried me off to the mountains, and, sending to you one of my ears, to show you my probable fate if you did not let them have . . how much may I venture to say I am worth? . . five or six scudi . . . would your answer be "Not so many crazie . . . ?" Would you, dearest? Because it is as well to know beforehand, perhaps.

Elizabeth's distress was not mitigated by the two days' yelling and moaning of some dog shut up in the mews behind Wimpole Street. "Think of Flush he seemed to say."

On September 5 she determined to interview Taylor, the captain of the banditti, in person. She found her "hero not at home." Remaining in the cab at the request of Wilson, who was terrified in that rough quarter, Elizabeth parleyed with "an immense feminine bandit." Mrs. Taylor reassured her with the most gracious of smiles. "She was sure that Taylor would give his very best attention."

Mr. Taylor came to Wimpole Street, but without Flush. He demanded six guineas and confidence in his honour. Unfortunately as the money was about to be paid over on Elizabeth's behalf Alfred met "the archfiend" in the hall and called him swindler, liar, and thief. "Which no gentleman could bear, of course." Therefore with reiterated oaths Taylor swore " 'as he hoped to be saved, we should never see our dog again'—and rushed out of the house."

Mr. Kenyon's gentle Ba-lamb became a tigress. Alfred was not spared. With the thought of that dog's head in her mind, she went downstairs determined to go in person and "save the victim at any price." It was already getting dark. The whole family cried out against her. "At last, Sette said that *he* would do it, promising to be as civil as I could wish, and got me to be 'in a good humour and go up to my room again.' "

Sette prevailed. Flush came back at eight o'clock, dashing up to her door and drinking from his cup of water, filled three times over. His joy at reunion was not so great as formerly. He seemed frightened, bewildered, and, when his mistress commiserated with him, "put up his head and moaned and yelled." Mr. Taylor had magnanimously allowed the return of the dog for no more than the six guineas: perhaps Alfred's anger had had its effect in frightening the scoundrel.

Browning was this time really unwell. On September 10 he was not able to come to her. That day she sent him serious news: the project of house painting was decided upon. George was going the next day to look for a temporary dwelling, to be hired for a month, at Dover, Reigate, or Tunbridge. The thorough cleaning of 50, Wimpole Street would probably take more than the month allotted. A matter so long delayed was now to be settled in a rush. This was Wednesday: Elizabeth might well be taken out of London on the Monday following.

Browning, having gone up to Town, did not receive her note until midday. "If you *do* go on Monday, our marriage will be impossible for another year—the misery! . . . We must be *married directly* and go to Italy."

CHAPTER   19

MARRIAGE [1846]

ON ELIZABETH'S LETTER of September 11 Browning wrote: "Saturday, Septr. 12, 1846, ¼11–11¼ A.M. (91)." At their ninety-first meeting, the only meeting away from her father's house, they had been married in St. Marylebone Parish Church with Wilson and Browning's cousin, James Silverthorne, as witnesses.

On the evening of the 11th Elizabeth had tried to make the way smooth for their secret marriage by telling Arabel of an arrangement for the next morning; probably saying that she would walk to the cabstand with Wilson, driving with her to Mr. Boyd's house, and then send Wilson home. After her visit to Boyd her sisters should pick her up in a carriage and take her for a drive. This is the story so far as one can piece it together.

Before going to bed Elizabeth took Wilson more completely into her confidence. The maid was "very kind, very affectionate."

Elizabeth could not sleep that night. Next morning, as they walked to Marylebone Street, so great was her emotion and fatigue that she fainted and had to be revived with sal volatile in a chemist's shop. She left the cab at Marylebone Church looking, in the words of her lover, "more dead than alive."

At this wedding there could be no pews filled with friends and relations, no watching eyes beyond those of maid and cousin. Elizabeth would not have had a crowd at her marriage, but there must have been some, and some perhaps not then living, with whom she might wistfully in imagination have peopled the church. This, however, could be only a passing regret as she stood there at the altar beside Browning: there came into her mind a thought of those many women "who have stood where I stood . . . not one of them all perhaps, not one perhaps, since that building was a church, has had reasons strong as mine, for an absolute trust and devotion towards the man she married,—not one!" With this strong faith in her future husband it seemed to her only simple justice that she should stand there alone, unsupported by family and friends.

At half past eleven husband and wife parted. Hardly had the wedding ring been put on Elizabeth's finger but it must be taken off. Elizabeth returned to the cab and drove to St. John's Wood.

Fortunately Mr. Boyd was engaged with his doctor; so Elizabeth, having sent Wilson back in the cab, was able to settle quietly on a sofa alone to rest and try to regain composure. When she was called up to her old friend, who was in the secret, he, perhaps not as self-centred as she thought him, had the tact to demand the effort of conversation from her as she sipped his Cyprus wine. She talked and waited, but her sisters did not come. Boyd, guessing at the pallor of those thin cheeks, insisted on a luncheon of bread and butter to put some colour into her. She must not arouse suspicion.

At Wimpole Street there was considerable alarm when mistress and maid were found to be absent: perhaps a hysterical dog betrayed them, since it does not appear that Flush attended the wedding—Flush, who was used to accompanying his mistress everywhere.

Arabel, either from genuine inattention, or from a desire to help her sister by a delay, seems to have ignored the arrangement of the night before. It is known that, if not now, certainly later that day she guessed at the marriage. Presumably it was on Wilson's return that Henrietta first knew Ba was awaiting them in St. John's Wood.

The sisters came at last to Circus Road bearing marks of agitation. The gravity of their eyes, and especially Arabel's, made Elizabeth tremble, but she maintained as bold a front as she could. These two dear beings must not be implicated in her "crime." "What nonsense," she protested as they spoke of their alarm, "what fancies you have, to be sure."

She drove with them to Hampstead, as far as the Heath, chattering of this and that with a calm that surprised herself. "How necessity makes heroes—or heroines at least!" she commented to her husband by letter that afternoon. "It seems all like a dream! When we drove past that church again, I and my sisters, there was a cloud before my eyes." Knowing by in-

tuition whom this hasty marriage might most hurt, though un-
complainingly, Elizabeth added: "Ask your mother to forgive
me, Robert. If *I* had not been there, *she* would have been there,
perhaps." A certain remorse was still touching her happiness: "if
either of us two is to suffer injury and sorrow for what happened there to-day—I pray that it may all fall upon *me!* Nor
should I suffer the most pain *that* way, as I know, and God
knows."

Browning had been right in thinking, and her condition when
he met her outside the church must have confirmed this opinion,
that Elizabeth could not have endured the fatigue and excitement of both marriage and flight on one day. When the date of
the wedding had been hastily fixed, with a threat of removal
to Little Bookham on Monday, it seemed as if the double event
might have to take place, but departure from Wimpole Street
was postponed.

The delay thus gained did not, however, prove a happy one
for Elizabeth at least, forced as she was to endure day after
day of embarrassment, living under a false guise among her
family and with no confidant beyond Wilson: it had been a
fixed condition of the marriage that Browning should not again
visit her in her father's house. We are not told how she contrived to explain the absence of so constant a visitor. Surely
questions must have been asked, if not by the sisters, by the
teasing brothers.

To Browning himself this enforced absence from his wife,
painful though it must have been, brought a sense of relief:
never could he, a man of fundamental honesty, ask for Elizabeth in her maiden name at Mr. Barrett's door. Such a false-
hood would have stuck in his throat.

It was unfortunate that the next day was a Sunday when the
family all came to Elizabeth's room. That morning her head
"seemed splitting in two (one half on each shoulder)" from
fear of arousing suspicion. The noise made by her brothers, all
excited at the prospect of the removal from Town, was torture,
but she dared not protest. Several women friends up from Herefordshire called: it seemed as if they would never go. Treppy
came too. "It was like having a sort of fever."

In the midst of all this disturbance and din some church bells

rang out. One of the provincial ladies asked: "
those?" Henrietta, standing behind Elizabeth's c
her: "Marylebone Church bells."

Later in the day, when Elizabeth was sitting
writing to her husband, Mr. Kenyon came in "w.
tacles, looking as if his eyes reached to their
way round." Almost his first question was: "Whe
see Browning?" and his last: "When do you see
again?"

In the midst of this agony of embarrassment Elizabeth was
looking with longing "over the palms to Troy—I feel happy and
exulting to belong to you, past every opposition, out of sight of
every will of man—none can put us asunder, now, at least." She
was still conscious of that enforced lack of courtesy towards
Robert's people. "I feel so as if I had slipped down over the
wall into somebody's garden—I feel ashamed."

Browning, returning to a home where there need be no concealment, wrote to Elizabeth: "my father and mother and sister love you thoroughly." His mother wished so much she had
felt well enough to write to her new daughter-in-law. She must
be content to send a message. As for himself, Browning told
her: "Dearest, I woke this morning *quite well*—quite free from
the sensation in the head. I have not woke *so*, for two years perhaps—what have you been doing to me?" The long period of
nervous tension was over. There was only pure happiness to
look forward to now. "Come what will my life has borne flower
and fruit—it is a glorious, successful, felicitous life. I thank God
and you."

The few days ahead were busy ones for Wilson and Elizabeth: there must be a careful packing of luggage so as to mini-
mize cost since at that time every ounce was charged for,
arrangements made for its private dispatch to Nine Elms Station (then the terminus of the London & South Western Railway) and, above all, there were letters to write.

While composing that difficult letter to her father Elizabeth
aroused something of the suspicion she dreaded: many tears
shed over the paper before her, as she sat with hesitant pen,
made her look so pale that the family wondered what was amiss.
In the only one of these farewell letters to survive, Elizabeth's

...agitation is manifest in the broken style and wavering blurred script:

My dearest George I throw myself on your affection for me & beseech of God that it may hold under the weight—Dearest George, go to your room & read this letter—and I entreat you by all that we both hold dearest, to hold me still dear after this communication which it remains to me to make to yourself and to leave to you in order to be communicated to others in the way that shall seem best to your judgement. And oh, love me George, while you are reading it—Love me—that I may find pardon in your heart for me after it is read.

She told of Browning's early attachment and her determination to refuse him; an attachment that she had thought "a little more light on my ghastly face" would soon bring to a natural end. But Browning's love was too strong. Upon herself she took the entire responsibility of an "omission of the usual application to my father and friends." Browning himself had been only too anxious to make a formal approach. She insisted that everyone in the house was ignorant of the whole affair "and innocent of all participation in this act of my own."

It was not to the eldest brother, the gentle, affectionate Storm, that Elizabeth entrusted a letter to her father, but to this stronger-natured George; and it was with tolerable confidence in his understanding and sympathy that she did so. George had always encouraged her to break away in search of health, had himself spoken with anger on the subject to his father and knew well that her sacrifice in forgoing the Pisa trip the previous year had brought upon her only severe and prolonged displeasure.

George, after reading through the letter enclosed "for my dearest Papa," should break the news gently before giving it. Elizabeth also begged that her father would "deign to read" this letter to her brother. The forgiving replies for which she hoped were to be directed to her at Orléans.

Elizabeth was nursing a hope of her father's forgiveness: after all, he had been kind to her of late, so kind as to fill her with remorse. But the hope was a faint one. Once he had been heard to say: "Ba is the purest woman I ever knew." At the time this had amused her: what Mr. Barrett meant to convey, she thought, was that his eldest daughter had never troubled him with love affairs "or any impropriety of seeming to think about being married," but now the words seemed of graver import: "the whole sex will go down with me to the perdition of faith in any of us. See the effect of my wickedness!—'These women!' "

She urged upon Browning a complete submission. "I will put myself under his feet, to be forgiven a little, . . enough to be taken up again into his arms. I love him—he is my father—he has good and high qualities after all: he is my father *above* all." Over that difficult, tear-blotted letter Elizabeth argued to herself: "surely I may say to him, too . . 'with the exception of this act, I have submitted to the least of your wishes all my life long. Set the life against the act, and forgive me, for the sake of the daughter you once loved.' " She would remind him of her long years of suffering.

From now until the 19th their letters are short, containing little more than the discussion of necessary details, the marriage announcements, routes, and what luggage to take. There was soon real need for haste: the family were to travel to Little Bookham, Surrey, on Monday, September 21.

One of Elizabeth's last acts in her old home, characteristically impulsive, was to bring vivid regret: remembering that *Blackwood's Magazine* had said it would welcome lyrics from her, and no doubt with the possibility of an early shortage of ready money in mind, she swept her desk clear of old unpublished pieces with hardly a glance over them. These poems *Blackwood's*, perhaps with a journalistic eye on what we should now call the "news value" of the celebrated Miss Barrett who had become Mrs. Browning in circumstances that were the talk of literary circles, published hard on the flight from home, in October. They were not poems Elizabeth would have chosen to come so soon under the eye of a father she hoped to soften.

On the afternoon of Saturday, September 19, between half past three and four, two days before the departure for Little Bookham, Elizabeth and Wilson began their journey carrying with them only small bags of necessaries. It was, fortunately for the delicate woman—as Browning lovingly recalled in after years—"a delicious day."

Their greatest embarrassment in stealing out of the house unobserved was that living piece of luggage Flush, who could not be left behind to pine his heart out, and perhaps be slightingly treated as a relic of his defecting mistress. Flush, however, who seemed to understand the situation when it was put to him, behaved admirably; entirely restraining a natural noisy excitement at the prospect of an outing.

Outside Hodgson's, that friendly bookshop in which Elizabeth had so often rested, they met Browning and entered a cab bound for Nine Elms Station. Elizabeth was soon to be on the railroad she had only viewed with interest and alarm. One wonders which of them, she or Flush, was most frightened by the bustle, din, and confusion of a railway terminus, of the flying monster that carried them to Southampton on the first stage of a journey to freedom.

At Wimpole Street Elizabeth's absence was discovered long before its reason was explained. Her letters to the family, posted that morning, either did not arrive before late evening or, if they were enclosed in one envelope to George, were deliberately held back.

Elizabeth had appealed to George in vain: his heart was hard against her. He seems to have refused the cruel task of informing Mr. Barrett. It was Henrietta who told her father of Ba's flight. Mr. Barrett was standing on the stairs with a heavy book in his hand: in angry amazement he dropped the book. Henrietta slipped and fell, so giving rise to a preposterous legend that, on hearing the news of the flight of his eldest, Mr. Barrett threw his second daughter down the stairs.

It was not long before Kenyon came to him, no doubt pressing the claim of Robert Browning to be honourably received as a son-in-law. Mr. Barrett is said to have remarked: "I have no objection to the young man, but my daughter should have been thinking of another world."

It is not clear whether Mr. Barrett accompanied his family to Little Bookham on the Monday, or whether he stayed behind, nourishing his grief and anger alone. Some sort of inquisition must have been held before their departure. George in his reply to Elizabeth's letter accused both Arabel and Minnie, the housekeeper and former nurse, of connivance. This Mrs. Browning denied, but it is hard to believe there was no one partially in their secret, or how could Wilson have smuggled their boxes out of the house?

Mr. Barrett wrote an obdurate letter, casting Elizabeth from him. On the return of his family to Wimpole Street the wounded man, embattled in strong pride, kept a bold face towards a world not yet entirely done with gossip about the marriage. In high spirits, spirits perhaps unnaturally high, he entertained friends to dinner every night. He never again referred to his daughter. She was to him as one long dead and forgotten.

A notice of the marriage, giving no date so as not unduly to embarrass the Barrett family, was inserted in leading papers. When a proof of the *Daily News* reached John Forster, its editor and Browning's friend, he took it for a hoax, some poor sort of joke. Falling into "a great passion" he called for the head compositor, telling him to bring up the manuscript. As this was in a familiar hand, that of Sarianna, Forster had to believe the evidence of his eyes. The two poets, not even known to the world as acquaintances, were, in sober fact, man and wife.

To Elizabeth's friends the news of the marriage and flight brought both astonishment and apprehension. Miss Mitford wrote to a correspondent that it was "as if I had heard that Dr. Chambers had given her over when I got the letter announcing her marriage, and found she was about to cross to France. I never had an idea of her reaching Pisa alive."

C H A P T E R   2 0

PISA [1846–7]

THE BROWNINGS ARRIVED at Southampton an hour before the boat sailed; at nine o'clock they embarked at the Royal Pier for Dieppe. It was to be five years before they returned to England.

The journey from Southampton to Paris took nineteen hours and a half. In France travel was partly by rail, partly by *diligence*. We do not know whether they rested by the way, or the exact date on which they arrived in Paris.

Mrs. Jameson was travelling too, on her way to Italy with a young niece, Gerardine Bate. She was staying in the Rue de la Ville-l'Evêque, at the Hôtel de la Ville de Paris, when an astounding piece of information reached her: Robert Browning wrote to inform her that he and his bride had just arrived from London, and that the lady was Elizabeth Barrett. Elizabeth had been wrong in thinking that her friend had divined at least part of the truth; that when, unable to bid Mrs. Jameson good-bye, she had written of herself as "forced to be satisfied with the sofa and silence," Mrs. Jameson could read a certain message in that discreet phrase. The news came like a thunderbolt.

Her aunt's astonishment, Gerardine tells us, was "something almost comical." Surprise was soon lost in delight. Mrs. Jameson hurried to the Brownings' hotel. Opening her arms to them both, calling them "children of light," she gave that instant approval for which Elizabeth, disturbed in conscience, was craving from her friends. What misgiving she had Mrs. Jameson kept to herself, reserving for a friend comment on these "two celebrities who have run away and married under circumstances peculiarly interesting, and such as to render imprudence the height of prudence." "God help them!" she added, "for I know not how the two poet heads and poet hearts will get on through this prosaic world."

Finding Elizabeth exhausted and ill, Mrs. Jameson persuaded

them to take a week's rest in Paris at her own quiet hotel. She would accompany them to Pisa and help to take care of the invalid. Robert, thoroughly frightened over his wife's condition, agreed gratefully. Elizabeth herself felt private regret that they could not hurry forward; anxious as she was to reach Orléans, where the fateful letters from father and family would be awaiting her.

It was but natural, since the party had met together in Paris, that the world should credit Mrs. Jameson with having taken a large part in the arrangement of the marriage. Her absolute denial friends took to be merely discreet, shaking their heads, as Elizabeth put it in her vivid way, "incredulously over writing paper of various sizes."

"The week at Paris!" Elizabeth wrote to Miss Mitford. "Such a strange week it was, altogether like a vision. Whether in the body or out of the body I cannot tell scarcely." In her exhaustion she had to be "satisfied with the *idea* of Paris" except for one visit to the Louvre. To Miss Mitford she talked of Balzac, that exponent of Parisian society ardently and half guiltily admired by herself and her friend. One thing she did not mention to Miss Mitford, or to any other correspondent (at least in any letter I have seen), and that was her own earlier visit so far back as 1815.

This feminine reticence may serve to remind us that, together with so many of her family, the father included, Elizabeth did not look her age in spite of frail health. Browning, too, kept an appearance of youth. We find him called a young man by people who met him years later in Italy. The little Gerardine, really young at seventeen, an age when even thirty seems mature, did not regard these two as elderly and beyond romance. True, romance was heightened by the memory of a visit to Elizabeth's secluded invalid room, and newly consummated love must have put the flushed and happy lovers in a good light; but, even so, they must have appeared nearer to Gerardine than actual years would warrant. So charming, so full of delight was the coming journey, the vicarious honeymoon through beautiful France, to a young untravelled girl, that every detail remained with her in the sterner years ahead. Of this journey she wrote in or about 1877:

. . . the temptation is great to linger upon the memory of a journey so enchanting, made in the fairest days of youth, and with such companionship. The loves of the poets could not have been put into more delightful reality before the eyes of a dazzled and enthusiastic beholder; but the recollections have been rendered sacred by death as well as by love.

They travelled partly by train and *diligence,* but also in a more leisurely way by steamer on the Loire, the Saône, and the Rhone. While Gerardine was intoxicating herself in an aura of love with the beauty of landscape, Mrs. Jameson was watching the man to whom this delicate friend had given herself; a man admired, liked, but possibly not as well known as the former Miss Barrett. Her approval was whole-hearted. She "never knew anyone of so affluent a mind and imagination combined with a nature and manner so sunshiney and captivating."

Though at times the strain of that journey must have been almost unbearable to a man functionally nervous, even though an experienced and older woman was present to watch over Elizabeth, Browning was ever thoughtful for their comfort, "witty and wise, (and foolish too in the right place)." He charmed cross old women in the *diligence,* talked "latin to the priests who enquire at three in the morning whether Newman and Pusey are likely *'lapsare in erroribus'* . . . and forgets nothing and nobody . . except himself, it is the only omission."

One criticism, and one only, Mrs. Jameson had to make as she watched this couple so perfectly fitted for one another, and that was Browning's adoption of the pet family name; but Browning, who liked "Ba" as well as Elizabeth herself, could not be talked out of it. Ba might well consider herself the Baby of early days, so carefully was she cherished, pillowed by arms and knees at night against the shaking of the *diligence;* carried, laughing, protesting, upstairs and put instantly to bed when they halted on the way. Already Elizabeth was feeling a little stronger. Travel, change of air, always did her good, and now they were journeying south in perfect sunshine.

Our two minor actors in the drama, Wilson and Flush, were both delighted with their new experience, though in one case with an important reservation. Flush, now getting almost as much attention as his mistress, was perfectly reconciled to his new master, enjoying a strange freedom, but behaving admirably so far, absorbed as he was by strange sights, sounds, and scents; but when on the railroad inexorable authority clapped him into a box, his protests were loud in wailing and moaning.

As they rushed on to Orléans by train it might have been hard to say who was the more unhappy, Flush or his mistress. Elizabeth was suffering in anticipation the first sight of those letters awaiting her, an ordeal she called her "death-warrant." The rest can be told in her own words to her sisters:

Robert brought in a great packet of letters . . and I held them in my hands, not able to open one, and growing paler and colder every moment.

He wanted to sit by me while I read them, but I would not let him. I had resolved never to let him do that, before the moment came—so, after some beseeching, I got him to go away for ten minutes, to meet the agony alone, and with more courage so, according to my old habit you know. And besides, it was right not to let him read. . They were very hard letters, those from dearest Papa and dearest George— To the first I had to bow my head—I do not seem to myself to have deserved that full cup, in the intentions of this act—but he is my father and he takes his own view, of course, of what is before him to judge of. But for George, I thought it hard, I confess, that he should have written to me so with a sword.

But her brother wrote "in excitement and ignorance."

The sisters' letters were pure balm to the wound George had inflicted. When Robert returned, Elizabeth put them in his hands. Browning, with tears in his eyes, kissing the kind words as he read them through a second time, declared his affection for Henrietta and Arabel: "I am inexpressibly grateful to them, — It shall be the object of my life to justify this trust, as they express it here."

There was the "kindest letter" from Miss Mitford and one from Mr. Kenyon. It was Kenyon's verdict on the marriage, and perhaps Kenyon's alone among his friends, that Browning personally dreaded, but to his relief it was one of complete approval. Kenyon wrote: "Nothing but what is generous in thought and action could come from you and Browning. And the very peculiar circumstances of your case have transmuted what might have been otherwise called 'Imprudence' into 'Prudence,' and apparent wilfulness into real necessity." Kenyon begged his "Ba and very dear cousin" to regard him as her banker if money should prove to be temporarily short.

Of Mr. Barrett's flint-hearted letter we know nothing, except that he accused his daughter of having sold her soul for genius. "Which I might have done," Elizabeth commented, "when I was younger, if I had had the opportunity; but am in no danger of doing now."

When Elizabeth had spoken to him of Mr. Barrett's obdurate letter, Robert, with no sign of resentment at the position into which circumstances had forced him, swept her up in a wave of tenderness, laying her down on the bed, sitting by her for hours, and promising to win back for her, with God's help, the affection of those of her family who were incensed against her.

When some months before it had appeared as if her father cared little, Elizabeth had said that she was always glad to know the worst, however bitter the pill might be: now, one may guess, once the draught was taken, she was better able to enjoy the south, sun and blue sky, the certainty of love. Life was expanding for her, who had once put it so resolutely behind her, in a warmth, a fullness, an inevitability.

Gerardine Bate, looking back on that enchanted journey, a journey almost too sacred to be spoken of, permitted herself one revelation. The party rested for a couple of days at Avignon that they might make a poetical pilgrimage to Vaucluse, the home of Laura.

There, at the very source of the "chiare, fresche e dolci acque," Mr. Browning took his wife in his arms, and, carrying her across the shallow curling waters, seated her on a rock that rose throne-like in the middle of the stream. Thus love and poetry took a new possession of the spot immortalised by Petrarch's loving fancy.

The fountain, Mrs. Browning herself wrote to Westwood, was swollen by rains, flashing and roaring in its dark prison of rocks "louder and fuller than usual . . . and Flush, though by no means born to be a hero, considered my position so outrageous that he dashed through the water to me, splashing me all over, so he is baptised in Petrarch's name."

At Avignon Elizabeth was delighted by another poetically symbolic episode, this time with the charm of complete surprise. A friendly stranger approached the party to offer a pomegranate, and of the three ladies Elizabeth was the one chosen for this significant gift. She, who had never seen the fruit before, immediately took a knife and cut it "deep down the middle." But at this point the pomegranate of happy omen dwindled to an unfamiliar fruit: Mrs. Browning found it unpalatable.

By easy stages they reached Marseilles and there took ship for Genoa. Elizabeth sat on deck enjoying a new vision of "mountains, six or seven deep" as they coasted along the Riviera. From Genoa they sailed southward to Leghorn, passing Shelley country at Viareggio and the Gulf of Spezia. On reaching the port of Leghorn Browning had an odd encounter.

There was at this time a certain eccentric exuberant personality in the world of letters, Francis Mahoney, once a Jesuit Father, and then a priest. Abandoning his clerical vocation, though still retaining "an uneradicable air of the priest and seminarist" in amusing contrast to his Bohemian way of life, Mahoney contributed to *Frazer's Magazine* learned, entertaining, and poetically charged articles as "Father Prout," a name by which he soon became generally known. Of late years he had been much in London, though with frequent excursions to the Continent. Browning had already told Elizabeth how he was always "meeting that Lion in strange out of the way places roaring wildly," and had many times encountered him abroad "whenever the sight was least expected." Let us continue the story in Elizabeth's own words:

Well—while we travelled across France, my fellow-traveller laughed a little as he told me that in crossing Poland Street with our passport, just at that crisis, he met—Father Prout—"oh, of course, he met him just then"— It was a moment worthy to be signalized! . . . On our landing at Leghorn, at nine o'clock in the morning, our boat which was rowed from the steamer to the shore, passed close to a bare jutting piece of rock on which stood a man wrapt in a cloak, he also having just landed from an English vessel bound from Southampton—Father Prout!!
Robert cried: "Good Heavens, there he is again!— There's Father Prout!" At the inn after breakfast "the reverend Lion" en-

tered and was just as amazed as Browning at the meeting; more so, surely, as the poet had a wife with him, and she one far more celebrated than himself. Feeling shy and tired, Elizabeth kept to the other side of the room sheltering behind a black veil, though a slight formal introduction had to be gone through. As Father Prout was going, or returning to Rome, where he was now acting as correspondent for Dickens's paper the *Daily News,* the Brownings were to meet him again. Once at least he was to burst in dramatically upon them, and at that time more opportunely.

At Pisa, which they reached by train, Browning, after a few days of hotel life with Mrs. Jameson, took rooms for his wife and himself in the Collegio Ferdinando, a great building erected by Vasari near the Cathedral. From their windows they could see that abiding marvel, the Leaning Tower and the Cathedral behind it, with the Baptistery and peaceful Campo Santo close at hand.

The first ten days were wet but at length the sun came out, the sky was a cloudless blue and the temperature that is a warm English June. Pisa, that ancient place from which history, almost life itself, had at this time receded, Elizabeth at first found enchanting, "full of repose, yet not desolate: it is rather the repose of sleep than of death." The Cathedral, the Baptistery, the Leaning Tower are beautiful enough against a grey sky, but now they shone out in all their candour of beauty. Never was there such a complete contrast in homes than Pisa and Wimpole Street, the southern city in its pure clean air and the sooty, foggy London of 1846. Every day Elizabeth was out walking "while the golden oranges look at me over the walls, and when I am tired Robert and I sit on a stone to watch the lizards."

Flush, too, highly approved of Pisa, "going out every day and speaking Italian to the little dogs." Flush was no longer so discreet, so well behaved as when the changing vicissitudes of a journey occupied his attention. He was vociferous, arrogant, "overbearing," tyrannizing over his new master; appearing, Robert declared, to consider him "to be created for the special purpose of doing him service."

There were expeditions to the Mediterranean shore, where,

in far mist, the island of Gorgona might be seen "beautiful and blue"; to the foot of Monti Pisani, where mountain heights could be seen reflected in the pure waters of Lake Ascuno and great pines climbed upward in the silence of the woods. Elizabeth had too the unexpected delight of meeting with camels, camels loaded with faggots. These exotic beasts were bred at the Cascine di San Rossore, a farm founded by the Medici.

Once during their stay at Pisa the Brownings visited the Lanfranchi Palace, the home of Byron, a poet admired by both. There in the garden they picked a bay leaf: this leaf Browning later had mounted with a lock of Elizabeth's hair, adding a note that it was gathered in the first year of their marriage.[1]

Over the fire found necessary morning and evening in their rather too cool rooms, husband and wife would sit day-dreaming, planning future travels over roasted chestnuts and grapes. Excellent and plentiful meals came in from the *trattoria*, of which Elizabeth ate well, drinking and enjoying too the light Chianti with which Robert would dose her until she dropped asleep. At night, in spite of an uncomfortable bed stuffed with orange-tree shavings, she slept soundly. By the end of the year she had so far progressed from the old state of nervous invalidism as to be present on Christmas Eve at midnight Mass in the Cathedral.

All the strength of a great heart and mind was concentrated on assuring Elizabeth's welfare. Browning not only surrounded her with care, but put forth his best powers of entertainment, talking wisdom or foolery as the mood of his beloved seemed to demand. Elizabeth was not now, or ever in their married life, burdened with the slightest household care; all was kept in Robert's hands. Scrupulous, fidgety as he always was over money matters, bills were cast up and settled weekly, much to the amusement of Mrs. Jameson, who declared that the married poets reminded her "of the children in a poem of Heine's who set up housekeeping in a tub, and inquired gravely the price of coffee."

Browning was prudent but not calculating. Although he had lived a good deal in Italy, a present comparative cost of living

[1] In the possession of Miss Henrietta Altham.

impressed him so that he fell an easy victim to a system of systematic extortion; foreigners, at that time, and especially the English, being considered lawful prey.

Later, at Florence, the Brownings were to discover by contrast how rough was the accommodation provided here at a high price, but now, such was their state of innocence, their *padrone* was the envy of other Pisan landlords. One living opposite, to sustain his dignity, let it be known that Mrs. Browning ("mark," Elizabeth interpolated in telling of this, "Mrs. Browning") had offered him a fabulous price for his rooms if he would break a prior engagement with a certain Major's wife. This lady, "being a woman of masculine understanding, (and superstructure besides)," walked about Pisa abusing Mrs. Browning "in good set terms." Browning felt obliged to send her a peremptory note refuting the rival landlord.

Towards the end of their stay in Pisa, a kindly English neighbour took Wilson to the shops and showed her how to avoid the most barefaced cheatings, but even so, apart from the rent, Browning was soon aware that they were living at a far higher rate than was necessary. "For two hundred and fifty pounds a year," Elizabeth commented, "we might and ought to live in excellent apartments, and keep our own carriage and two horses; and a man servant to boot."

Mrs. Jameson and Gerardine remained in Pisa three weeks, spending what leisure they had with the Brownings; but much of Mrs. Jameson's time was occupied in a close study of art treasures, drawing, arranging, and classifying sometimes far into the evening.

In this labour, Gerardine, or "Geddie" as she was familiarly called, helped her aunt, though not with the assiduity that hard-working and enthusiastic art-lover demanded. Geddie, she was constantly complaining to her friends, was indolent, preferring to lounge in bed in the morning and play with Flush at night. Mrs. Jameson adored her niece, and was sacrificing much in bringing her abroad for an art training. Elizabeth, with whom the "pretty, accomplished, gentle little girl" was a favourite, was privately of the opinion that Gerardine "was no more fitted to be what Mrs. Jameson desired, a *laborious artist*, than to fly to Heaven like a lark." As with many adoring persons, Mrs. Jameson was by turns too easy and too hard with her young niece. Browning was almost tactlessly outspoken on the subject of Geddie's defects, especially when her aunt was over-enthusiastic, but Elizabeth privately sided with the pretty mismanaged child, often making excuses for her.

Mrs. Jameson's approval of the marriage was now complete: Elizabeth, she reported to the anxious Miss Mitford, was "not merely improved but transformed." For her Elizabeth's admiration grew daily stronger. Both she and Robert were now affectionately calling her "Aunt Nina." When at the end of three weeks Mrs. Jameson decided to move on to Rome, she made Browning promise that if Elizabeth were taken ill he would at once write to her: if anywhere in Italy she could come to them immediately. This from a woman who was abroad on business, studying art with a view to making money in a new work, was no light promise. It says much for her warmth of heart, her tact, that these two, naturally absorbed in each other, found parting from Mrs. Jameson genuinely painful.

The weather turned prematurely cold, unusually cold: Pisans went about "muffled in vast cloaks, with little earthenware pots full of live embers to warm their fingers." In December snow fell, the first for five years, and the cold intensified in spite of a hot sun. Their English eyes were treated to the incongruous sight of women wrapped in furs and carrying parasols. Untouched by the sun in their shaded rooms Elizabeth was languid, feeling a touch of the old discomfort in her throat. Browning, nervous about her, heaped wood on the fire, richly-burning pine from the Grand Duke's woods. Elizabeth was almost as nervous herself: "If I were to be ill after all," she wrote home, "I feel I should deserve to be stoned for having married." Robert would hardly leave her chair, having to be driven out each day for an hour's solitary exercise.

Life, now that Mrs. Jameson had gone, was completely intimate, isolated; nor did they wish it otherwise, though they would have been glad to practice the Italian language a little. The only Italian of their acquaintance, a Professor Ferucci, who lent them books, spoke French "as by a point of honour." The English were numerous in Pisa, but Robert was determined to keep them out, even at the cost of an almost open incivility. Those many admirers in Wimpole Street days excluded from "the shrine," as Elizabeth herself light-heartedly called it, could now feel that they had an easier approach and perhaps a legitimate one, since congratulations on her marriage could be offered to the romantic celebrity. Robert dreaded too "the horrors of a mixed society," foreigners not of the best who sought the company of the English, and certain of the English themselves, lion-hunters, or refugees from conventional British morality.

Apparently neither of the Brownings was yet at work: some time of the day they spent over novels from a lending library, dull novels over which Robert yawned uncontrollably, but many hours were spent happily in talk, talk "with ever so many reflections and varieties." They laughed a good deal and chattered lovers' nonsense. They wrote long letters to family and friends.

CHAPTER 21

LETTERS, AND DEPARTURE FOR FLORENCE [1846–7]

IT IS FROM LETTERS written to her sisters from Pisa, in a correspondence kept inviolate, that we get the most intimate details of the new life. Since Browning was only to see what Elizabeth might think fit to show him, these three could still talk freely and intimately on paper. Robert's own letters to his family were kept as private, but of these we have not the benefit since they were later destroyed; but from a few of his to Arabel and Henrietta we get the tones of his voice.

Perhaps feeling on arrival "at our great journey's end" her situation to be more real, more actual, Elizabeth sat back and contemplated her marriage. "I can only wonder increasingly," she wrote, "at the fact of his selecting *me* out of the world of women." Like all sensible folk, she nerved herself to expect that a honeymoon must soon be over, that they must settle down to the more humdrum friendship of marriage, but with the Brownings this was never to happen. As she put it herself, the stars kept them in light.

Elizabeth poured out love and admiration for Robert to sisters and friends, writing in a long explanatory letter to Mrs. Martin:

Now may I not tell you that his genius, and all but miraculous attainments, are the least things in him, the moral nature being of the very noblest, as all who ever knew him admit? Then he has had that wide experience of men which ends by throwing the mind back on itself and God; there is nothing incomplete in him, except as all humanity is incompleteness.

To her sisters Elizabeth was more explicit, more rapturous, speaking of a love far deeper than "in the Wimpole Street days of adoration." With a smile she begins "to wonder naturally whether I may not be some sort of a real angel after all." Then, serious again: "It is not so bad a thing, be sure, for a woman to be loved by a man of imagination. He loves her through a lustrous atmosphere which not only keeps back the faults, but produces continual novelty, through its own changes."

Browning, in letters to his sisters-in-law, wrote of Elizabeth with an expansion rare in this reserved man:

I, however, thought I knew her, while every day and hour reveals more and more to me the divine goodness and infinite tenderness of her heart,—while that wonderful mind of hers, with its inexhaustible affluence and power, continues unceasingly to impress me. I shall not attempt to tell you what she is to me. Her entire sweetness of temper makes it a delight to breathe the same air with her—and I cannot imagine any condition of life, however full of hardship, which her presence would not render not merely supportable but delicious— It is nothing to me that my whole life shall be devoted to such a woman,—its only happiness will consist in such a devotion.

At this time he was celebrating the anniversary day of their marriage every week.

But Browning's common sense, so evident in his work and letters, saved him from fatuity. Elizabeth told a little story of a mistake made in a letter home, impetuously and rather peevishly fathered on him. When she found herself to be the culprit and made a gracious acknowledgment, instead of the pretty speech she expected, her husband answered quietly: "It is a satisfaction, at any rate that you should admit it."

This same common sense, a logicality of mind, made Browning attempt to use reason with Elizabeth's angry brothers. Taking advantage of news that England was in the grip of an abnormal cold, which had even touched Pisa with an icy finger, he tried to convince them that their marriage, and the manner of it, had been inevitable: the invalid was now out of reach of a London winter, which would seriously have harmed her. To the sisters he wrote:

if, on a consideration of all the facts, your brothers can honestly come to the opinion that, by any of the ordinary methods applicable to any other case, I could have effected the same result,—that any amount of exertion on my part, any extent of sacrifice, would have availed to render extreme measures unnecessary,—then, I will express all the sorrow they can desire—

*tho' at the same time I shall expect some forgiveness for a very
involuntary error—assuring them, as I do, that I believed—and
believe—that their sister's life depended upon my acting as I
acted.*

When at the end of January Sette wrote a letter full of affection
for Elizabeth, but unrelenting towards Robert, she wrote back
sharply, through the medium of Henrietta, that her brothers
*ought to be able to see, what every other person of sense sees
in an instant, that to have* given them my confidence *and have
destroyed their prospects in the same breath, would have been
an act of the most atrocious selfishness on my part, and impossible to one who loved them as I did and do.*

Elizabeth's strong and affectionate interest in her brothers was
not lessened by their intransigeance. Soon she was worrying
over news that Stormie might go to Jamaica; a natural destination, one would think, for a son on whom the family estates were
entailed. But Storm was the eldest son because of two losses,
the first of which had been, directly or indirectly, due to the Jamaican climate. "Dearest Storm," she wrote Henrietta with
characteristic impetuosity, should "turn his eyes another way
. . any other way in the world." Why could he not come, if
the *Statira* passed through the Mediterranean that year, to visit
her? Or could not he, George, Sette, and Occy travel up the
Rhine that summer and meet them in the Luganean mountains?
She and Robert were not rooted in Italy—indeed, they were
even talking of going to Jerusalem—and an early visit must be
made home, to England.

In this new life permeated by love, in a new liberty of action,
the rigour of her father's control of the family, his anger with
herself, seem partly to have been forgotten; perhaps appearing
almost as a bad dream. In company with her husband under an
Italian sky Elizabeth could even look hopefully towards a moment when "my dearest papa will be melted . . . into a clearer
understanding of motives and intentions; I cannot believe that
he will forget me, as he says he will, and go on thinking me to
be dead rather than alive and happy."

Her thirst for news from Wimpole Street was insatiable, even
to such detail as the colour of a fresh carpet. At first her letters

were tinged with anxiety over the welfare of her family after the marriage and sudden departure; as early as November, however, she had heard that "everybody is well and happy, and dear Papa *in high spirits* and *having people to dine with him every day,* so that I have not really done anyone harm in doing myself all this good." Some natural bitterness of soul Elizabeth must conceal from her correspondent, Mrs. Jameson, but later, writing to Henrietta of her good fortune in being out of England in a severe winter, she commented: "only this is no argument to those who wish me dead!" It is presumed, since letters to Henrietta and Arabel were addressed care of Miss Trepsack at 5, Upper Montague Street, that there was even a fear of Mr. Barrett intercepting them if they were sent direct to Wimpole Street.

It had been a pleasure to hear through the Martins in Paris that Uncle Hedley unreservedly took the lovers' part against his brother-in-law. Of other relatives "Bummy," the aunt so closely connected with childhood, still took the father's side.

One genuine twinge of conscience Elizabeth had in regard to Mr. Barrett: he might read, and regard as an impudent flouting of himself, those lyrics, the hasty sweepings of her desk before flight, which *Blackwood's* printed in October. Five of these lyrics, though all clearly written before she knew Browning, dealt with the love of man and woman and, of the other two, "Hector in the Garden" vividly recalled a happy childhood at Hope End.

By the middle of October the Brownings were wishing they had not taken their apartment for six months: there was little to see in Pisa, the country round was monotonously flat for Robert's walking, and their position near the Cathedral rather noisy. The bells, Elizabeth told Boyd, who was a connoisseur in them, beginning at four o'clock in the morning, "rang my dreams apart." The fourth bell, with a profound note, called *Pasquareccia,* which was tolled on the occasion of an execution, had a ghastly effect "dropped into the deep of night like a thought of death." Sometimes all the bells of all the churches would be shaken together in a peculiar discordance. Nor was the position of the Collegio Ferdinando of the most cheerful:

The funerals throng past our windows. The monks, sometimes all in black, and sometimes all in white (according to the order), chant in a train, carrying torches . . and on the bier comes the corpse . . openfaced . . except just a veil. At first, we both used to wish to see the sight . . but the horror (my old horror, tell Arabel) grew too strong for me soon . . and he [Robert] feels it too, and attends to me often when I say, "Oh, don't go to the window." But sometimes he cries out . . "I can't help it, Ba—it draws me." Such horrible, hoarse chanting, it is.— Like the croaking of death itself.

Pisa was too, we are told by others, full of coughing invalids come there for a supposed benefit to the chest. An Italian impression of the city was summed up in a jingling tag, *Pisa pesa a chi posa*.[1]

We may guess that to a man of Browning's essentially nervous temperament this life was, for all its perfect happiness, a considerable strain. Apart from his tendency to worry over ways and means, seclusion for most of the day in a warm room was not good for one who was a social man and a great walker. Elizabeth pressed him to a couple of small extravagances, a subscription to a good library where newspapers and French books could be obtained, and a pianoforte. To the first he conceded, but was obdurate on the second point, Elizabeth having imprudently admitted that she did not perform. "The idea of even *seeming to have anything for himself* . . (though I have talked myself hoarse about my love of music and so on) is quite enough to make Robert turn back determinedly. He calls it a foolish expense."

Some little relief from the strain of this close, concentrated life, the more exhausting because of his ardent love for the fragile woman, Browning now found in work upon a collected edition. Elizabeth, for her part, was composing an anti-slavery poem "too ferocious, perhaps, for the Americans to publish: but they asked for a poem, and shall have it." This was "The Runaway Slave at Hurst Point" ("Pilgrim's Point" in English collected editions). It was printed in the *Liberty Bell*, on sale at the Boston Anti-Slavery Bazaar of 1848.

---

[1] "Pisa weighs down upon him who stays there."

At the end of January the Brownings had their first touch of domestic trouble: Wilson was taken ill while she was attending on her mistress at bedtime. Dr. Cook, being sought by Robert, pronounced her to be suffering from delayed seasickness on a stomach already disordered. Wilson was put to bed with five leeches on her side. One guesses from the doctor's remarks, conveyed by Elizabeth to her sisters in a dramatic account of Wilson's illness, that the maid had aggravated her case by indulgence in good things from the *trattoria*.

Elizabeth, who had been sitting with her feet in hot water when Wilson collapsed, had run to Robert's room with feet bare: for this she was well scolded ("I wanted to kill him. . . . I played with his life, etc., etc!"). Now she, who perhaps had never attempted such tasks before, had to dress herself, to do her own hair and perform Wilson's household duties. The nursing and preparation of breakfast was undertaken by "The Signorina," perhaps the daughter of their landlord, who had already shown them attention in the way of gifts of fine oranges and of Italian dishes not always agreeable to the English palate; a general benevolence not uncalled for since he was so heavily overcharging them for the apartment.

Frightened by her illness, Elizabeth suggested that Wilson should return home to be nearer her own people, but Wilson wanted to remain. Apart from a devotion to her mistress, and a growing interest in this new country, the maid had an easy place with plenty of opportunity for outdoor exercise. In a few months it was to prove particularly fortunate that Wilson had decided to stay.

It was in March that the Brownings' happiness was broken into by a minor tragedy, a natural event made unnatural by the heedlessness of a woman who perhaps thought herself unlikely at her age to bear children: a miscarriage at five months' date. Wilson had suspected her condition, but she had apparently been only too zealous in predicting it since the marriage: Elizabeth had taken no notice of her. The maid too had hinted that in case of pregnancy the morphia Elizabeth continued to take, though in diminished quantity, might affect herself and the child.

Elizabeth, attacked now with pains in the night, submitted

to a doubt and, at last genuinely frightened, wrote over to Mr. Jago to ask his opinion in regard to the drug-taking. But, still convinced in her own mind that she was not pregnant, she refused to see Dr. Cook, putting off Robert in his urgency "with ever so many impertinent speeches, and obstinate ones." She had but contracted an internal chill.

The pains, however, getting more severe, Dr. Cook was summoned. He spoke sternly of a lack of precaution, of unsuitable conditions, "the room at seventy, a scandalous fire, a wrong posture"; sitting for hours at a time on a low stool before the blazing pine logs. Elizabeth still refused to believe in a patent fact. Then came the crisis, painful, but doing her no injury. Browning's agony was intense: when readmitted to her room he "threw himself down on the bed in a passion of tears, sobbing like a child . . he who has not the eyes of a ready-weeper."

Six days later Elizabeth, pronounced rather benefited than harmed by the miscarriage, was carried to her sofa in the sitting-room; by March 30 she was allowed to walk a little. They need not abandon their plan, said Dr. Cook, of joining Mrs. Jameson at Florence in a fortnight's time, but there must be no travelling northward first as had been intended.

Already Elizabeth was making projects for the autumn, projects hardly to be dreamed of a year ago, of riding up mountains, of travel north, "a week at Bologna to visit Rossini," and eventually a winter in Venice, where they might meet Mr. Kenyon. Lying in bed while she recovered, Elizabeth had been thinking with ever-increasing gratitude of Mr. Kenyon. Her cousin had not only pressed them to regard him as banker in case of need, but had praised Browning to an angry father and undertaken the task, so uncongenial to a man by temperament inclined to avoid unpleasant encounters, of arranging the transfer of investments to Elizabeth's husband.

In appearance, when again "all dressed up and ringleted," Elizabeth considered herself, though a little pale, rather improved than otherwise. Again at the open window, she could enjoy exquisite weather. "The air seems to float its balmy softness *into* you."

Browning, perhaps as a result of the strain put upon him by his wife's illness, was working himself up into a state of agita-

ⵧn. They were going to Florence where, even more than in Pisa, there was danger of being plagued by members of "a mixed society"; the English living abroad, often of doubtful reputation, and foreigners, not of the best, who courted their company. Walking up and down the room he would point out the experience of Mrs. Jameson, whose entrance into that mixed society had gained her "nothing . . except the acquaintance of two interesting foreigners" neither of whom she considered fit for Gerardine to associate with.

"Those people will spoil all our happiness, if we once let them in,—you will see— If you speak of your health and save yourself on that plea, they will seize upon *me*—oh, don't I know them!"

Elizabeth, lying placidly back in her chair, would try to turn the subject, but Browning had worked himself up into a state beyond jest or reason. "There is that coarse, vulgar Mrs. Trollope—I do hope, Ba, if you don't wish to give me the greatest pain, that you won't receive that vulgar, pushing, woman who is not fit to speak to you."

Elizabeth became more urgent. "Well . . now we are at Mrs. Trollope! you will have your headache in a minute—now do sit down, and let us talk of something else, and be quite sure that if we get into such scrapes, it won't be my fault."

Their landlord at the Collegio Ferdinando, having made such an excellent profit, was reluctant to part with the Brownings, hoping fondly to the last, Elizabeth averred, that she might have a relapse, so as not to be able to leave his rooms. Browning declared that, if they stayed much longer in this apartment, they would have "fallen fixed into barbaric habits"; would have been inviting visitors to "take a mug of coffee" or request them, in the absence of any bells, to "be so good as to thump with your fist on that door," a knock being their only means of summoning Wilson.

They set off on April 17, travelling uncomfortably in the coupé of a *diligence*. For most of the journey Elizabeth lay across her husband's knees to avoid the worst of the swaying. The Tuscan scene, soon to grow familiar, passed them by; the intensely cultivated hedgerows festooned with ropes of vine, hills topped with little ancient towns, "the abrupt black line of cypresses," the tall umbrella pines, the river Arno curling, wind-ing on its way to Florence; all, in both colour and form, in sharp contrast to the scene of childhood, the soft English green of meadow and sheep-dotted down, the gentle undulating curve of Malvern Hills.

CHAPTER 22

FLORENCE [1847–9]

THE BROWNINGS ARRIVED in Florence on April 20, settling down in an excellent apartment in the Via delle Belle Donne at £4 a month, about thirty shillings less than in Pisa for far greater comfort; a sofa, a spring chair, real cups instead of the "famous mugs of Pisa." Luxury extended to decanters and champagne glasses. Wilson's comment on the new order of things was succinct but eloquent: "It's something like!" All that remained to be hired was a pianoforte at a price surely well within even Robert's range of economy, ten shillings a month including the hire of music.

Elizabeth, still weak from the miscarriage and affected by the jolting coach, had to spend a week lying down; having caught but one tantalizing glimpse of the beautiful ancient city as they entered. It pleased her to think of "our dear old yellow Arno" flowing through Florence, a living link with Pisa.

Mrs. Jameson and Gerardine were to join them as guests on the 24th. On the evening of the 23rd, however, they arrived unexpectedly, Mrs. Jameson with a bottle of wine in her hand; having thought it appropriate that she should be with the two poets on that date to drink to the immortal memory. She found Elizabeth on a sofa listening to Robert at the pianoforte. The tune he played was "The Light of Love," an air reputed to be a favourite with Shakespeare.

"Everybody was delighted to meet everybody," Elizabeth told Mrs. Martin, "and Roman news and Pisan dullness were properly discussed on every side."

In this letter to Mrs. Martin Elizabeth gives us our first intimation of interest in the Italian struggle for freedom with which she was so closely to identify herself.

Italy was at this time a series of small states dominated by the Hapsburg and Bourbon dynasties, with one notable exception, that of the Kingdom of Sardinia, which included the ducal

crowns of Piedmont and Savoy (including Nice) and the former Republic of Genoa with its capital at Turin. The King of
Sardinia was Italy's only native ruler, and one who, with the
possession of Savoy and Piedmont, straddled the Alpine barrier
to the north, thus holding a strategic position in Europe. His
determination one day to oppose Austria in Italy was by 1846
made clear in the preparation of armies.

All these states were reactionary, priest-ridden, and seething
with discontent. "Young Italy," led by the republican patriot
Giuseppe Mazzini, had already attempted to raise a banner of
revolution in Savoy. The worst oppression was in the Neapolitan
states, which included the Sicilies, and in the Papal States.

But, curiously enough, it was in the most reactionary, the
most backward, the Papal State, that some measure of Liberal
reform began. At Rome Pope Pius IX, in his first year of office,
was now astonishing the world by a line of conduct wholly new
in Papal policy; granting an amnesty to political adversaries,
giving permission for the installation of railroads and gas in
the Papal States, and showing concern for the education of
his people. He went about daily on foot and, without a guard,
would make evening visits to the houses of the poor, "a sort of
Christian Haroun el Raschid of the nineteenth century." He
lived, Mrs. Jameson told the Brownings, "in an atmosphere of
love and admiration," and "doing *what he can*"; in other words,
combating by example the injustice, the backward social conditions in other Italian states by Austrian tyranny, but necessarily wielding a power in its essence opposed to freedom of
thought. Browning's comment on this remark of Mrs. Jameson's
is characteristic: "A dreadful situation, after all, for a man of
understanding and honesty! I pity him from my soul, for he can,
at best, only temporise with truth." That supple mind was later
to present in *The Ring and the Book* a moral dilemma of the
Vicar of Christ at once so powerful and hedged in by the rigour
of tradition. These were subtleties not at once appreciated by
his wife with her more direct vision. Elizabeth's comment here
was: "but human nature is doomed to pay a high price for its
opportunities." Where Browning could see the legitimacy of
moral doubt, she would be aware with heart and soul of a
clear duty to be performed.

Browning's interest in Pope Pius IX prepared him to go further than sympathy: already in Pisa he had written to Richard Monckton Milnes (one of the first to congratulate him on his marriage) of "this tiptoe expectation of poor Italy" and a desire to give practical help. Thinking, only too hopefully, that the British Government might send a mission to this enlightened Pope, he offered himself as secretary.

The Brownings, with Mrs. Jameson and Gerardine as their guests, were enjoying the new pleasure of hospitality, and certainly not at a cost beyond their purse: the local *trattoria* could provide an excellent dinner of five courses for the four of them, with enough left over for Wilson, at a total cost of 4*s*. 6*d*. Wine was proportionately cheap. Their only handicap as hosts was Robert's inability, neat-handed man though he was, to carve a joint. Mrs. Jameson, able to watch him in his own home, was more than ever struck with Browning's devotion and his wise care of a delicate wife. His inexhaustible spirits amazed her.

It was a disappointment that Elizabeth was unable to visit the art galleries under Mrs. Jameson's expert guidance, but her fine and stimulating talk helped to restore the invalid. Some element of vexation there was, however: Gerardine, who was in her aunt's opinions so half-hearted a student, had while in Rome "completed her offences by falling in love with a bad artist! an unrefined gentleman!! a Roman catholic! (converted from protestantism!) a poor man!! with a red beard!!! what ever Geddie could mean by it was what Mrs. Jameson in her agony couldn't divine." Indeed, Mrs. Jameson was inclined to put the blame for this mishap upon the Brownings. It was their love and happiness, the disappointed aunt decided, that had infected "the dear child who never thought in her whole life before of love and marriage."

Elizabeth, privately sympathizing, had to listen to Geddie's own version of the affair. Mr. Macpherson was so good, generous, and handsome; "likely to be a good artist *when he tries*," likely to revert to Protestantism. Mr. Macpherson had "left off smoking just to please aunt Nina, and was very firm."

Geddie and her aunt left Florence early on the 30th, kissing Elizabeth good-bye as she lay between sleeping and waking. It was the last time she was to see Mrs. Jameson before her return to England.

In Elizabeth's affection for Mrs. Jameson there was, one may guess, a certain intermingled admiration and pity; the generous pity of a happy sheltered woman and admiration for one who was a partisan of the oppressed, pioneer for the freedom of her sex. "To be a *road-maker*," Elizabeth wrote to her, "is weary work, even across the Apennines of life. We have not science enough for it if we have strength, which we haven't either." A hidden feeling for young love breaks out in this letter to Geddie's aunt: "My sympathies to go with you entirely, while I wish your dear Gerardine to be happy; I wish it from my heart." Elizabeth pressed Mrs. Jameson to come back to Italy soon and stay with Robert and herself, or near them if she preferred so. With this warm-hearted impulsive woman the Brownings were even willing to share their solitude.

Elizabeth was still not strong enough for the full enjoyment of Florence, but there had been "an inglorious glorious drive round the Piazza Gran Duca, past the Duomo, outside the walls, and in again at the Cascine. It was like the trail of a vision in the evening sun. I saw the Perseus in a sort of flash." "Oh this cathedral!" she wrote to Henrietta, "so grand it is, with its pile of tesselated domes. . . . Think of a mountainous marble Dome, veined with inlaid marbles—marble running through marble: like a mountain for size, like a mosaic for curious art—rivers of colour inter-flowing, but all dimly." They had taken two walks in the cool evening, the second "as far as the Baptistry where we sat down in the half dark and talked of Dante." And at Florence, Dante's Florence, "the river rushes through the midst of its palaces like a crystal arrow" beneath the four bridges,

> *Bent bridges, seeming to strain off like bows*
> *And tremble while the arrowy undertide*
> *Shoots on and cleaves the marble as it goes.*

She marked how at sunset the river reflects in faithful semblance churches, houses, windows, bridges, and people walking, the only difference being that "down below, there is double movement; the movement of the stream beside the movement of life."

Soon the heat increased. Elizabeth sat with doors open, French windows thrown back wide, and green blinds drawn. It was true that she had felt the heat of a London summer more oppressive, but this was as yet only May.

Every afternoon, after their three o'clock dinner, Robert would wheel a great chair into his dressing-room—the coolest in the afternoon—sit her comfortably back and apply eau-de-cologne to hands and forehead. At six in the evening, when the "muslin curtains seemed to sigh themselves out—blowing to and fro," they would walk out to enjoy sweet air blowing along the ground. In spite of the heat Elizabeth was gaining strength.

But Flush could not so soon become acclimatized: there were two days of misery while he was seriously ill. Robert declared that Elizabeth "gave up loving him and only thought of Flush." The dog had fits of screaming. If they pulled him out from some dark hiding-place he would stare wildly as if he knew none of them. He refused to drink. His human friends thought miserably of hydrophobia, but after two doses of castor oil in one day, administered by Browning while his mistress hid herself in the furthest room, their patient recovered. Flush took the nauseous draught quietly, as if he knew it would cure him; though, doglike, making capital out of sweet sympathy, moaning piteously to Elizabeth. A lump of sugar made him forget grief, and he was soon as "insolent as ever," though on the whole behaving better than at Pisa.

On May 21 Elizabeth ventured into the Tribuna, with some friends of the Barretts who were visiting Florence, and saw for the first time those "divine" Raphaels, dulcet, smooth, placed so high in the realm of art by the earlier Victorians. She drove to other shrines of historic beauty, entering the Cathedral, doing reverence at the tomb of Michelangelo in Santa Croce. These friends, the Hanfords, acted as witnesses to the Brownings' marriage settlement. Neither husband nor wife, hating such mundane detail, would read it through, though Elizabeth at a glance discovered that the document provided for "a countless progeny! and all 'future husbands'!!"

They were now admitting a few strangers within their enchanted circle, the first being, fittingly enough in view of their many friendships in the coming years, an American "on the point of leaving Florence and very tame and inoffensive" who desired to "pay his respects." Their first acquaintance was American too, Hiram Powers, the sculptor once so popular whose "tinted Venus" was so much admired, and whose "Greek Slave," later to be a major exhibit at the Great Exhibition of 1851, was (in the words of Henry James) "so undressed, yet so refined, even so pensive, in sugar-white alabaster, exposed under little domed glass covers in such American homes as could bring themselves to think such things right." Elizabeth thought Powers "of the most charming simplicity, with those great burning eyes of his . . . like a wild Indian's, so black and full of light."

The eternal charm of Florence having taken hold of them, the poets decided only to leave in full summer's heat, and to return in the autumn. Elizabeth set her heart on a retirement for the hot season to Vallombrosa, then fully occupied by the Monastery of San Guilberto, high up on a slope of the Protomagno mountains; a retreat cool in shade, rich in beauty and in association, but seemingly impossible for a woman, and a delicate one at that.

But to Vallombrosa she would go, and to no other place. When there appeared to be no chance of obtaining permission Elizabeth went on "crying for my moon like a spoilt child in a pet." After some delay however they secured a letter recommending them "for various rare and valuable qualities" to the Abbot, and requesting him to allow them to make a stay there.

In early July the heat became almost unbearable. They were "being burnt up, suffocated, exterminated." Flush, creeping under sofas, "turned his head away from warm milk, and his tail from soft cushions." The Brownings longed to leave Florence but Elizabeth, waywardly infected on a sudden by Robert's economic frame of mind, put off the decision from day to day. The Italian almanac, in which they had strong faith, prophesied rain which *mitiferà l'eccessivo caldo*—why therefore should they sacrifice three weeks' rent by leaving before their period was up, on the 22nd of the month? But a week before the 22nd Elizabeth gave in. They set off for Vallombrosa.

It would seem as if a measure of common prudence should have made Browning deny her "moon" to his wife, so frail, so impetuous, so childlike in feverish desire: the journey to Vallombrosa entailed at that time some forty miles of rough travelling, and on arrival they could not be sure of their reception. Elizabeth herself was half anticipating a rebuff. "They will take Robert into the monastery," she predicted, "and leave Wilson and me on the outside with other unclean beasts. We shall not be let dine together, even, I dare say! Perhaps we may have coffee sometimes, or walk out—but otherwise there will be a divorce." But so far as his wife's health was concerned, Robert's faith, or temerity, was justified: she survived without mishap the journey up and a return down the mountains a few days later.

They started out at three o'clock in the morning, and, happily anticipating a two months' stay, armed with a dozen of port for Elizabeth's daily fortification. At Pelago they left the road and proceeded for the last five miles up winding paths between the trees, Robert on horseback, Flush and the women in wine-basket sledges drawn by two white bullocks. This last lap of the journey lasted four hours. On arrival at the monastery, Elizabeth was so tired she had scarcely appetite for the beef and oil they were offered at the House of Strangers. Food was a first disappointment: they had hoped to live on eggs, milk, bread and butter, but found they might as well have expected manna from heaven. Bread could be got, but, with its fetid smell, it "stuck in the throat like Macbeth's amen!" This bread Elizabeth disposed of by the schoolgirl trick of slipping it under the table.

The Monastery of San Guilberto was an austere retreat: its monks, all of high birth, even mortified themselves by cleaning out the pigsties with bare hands. Its little red-faced Abbot provided the second and most severe disappointment, declaring that no permit from Authority in Florence should override his strict rule that a sojourn in the House of Strangers should be but a brief one. One concession he did make, that these visitors might remain two days beyond the allotted three, but then they must go. Up here on the holy mountain, Elizabeth commented sadly, the filth of a pigsty was less uncleanly to monkish hands than the little finger of a woman.

As a second Eve she was driven out of her Eden, that same

Vallombrosa which it is said moved Milton to his description of Paradise; from the hanging forests of chestnut and beech, the "great, silent, ink-black pine-wood" where they had walked so happily. Even she had seen eagles in flight. They went down again to Florence in the glory of an unforgettable daybreak and found their apartment stifling.

One member of the party rejoiced, however, in spite of a breathless contrast with mountain air: Flush had hated Vallombrosa, was frightened in the pine forest and, in short, preferred "civilised life, and the society of little dogs with turned-up tails." The one flaw in doggy content was the fleas that at times afflicted Flush to the verge of despair. His master and mistress would kneel patiently by him with comb and a basin of water, but with little relief to him. Elizabeth could hardly bear to watch him tearing at his pretty curls. In the end Robert was to take the drastic remedy of shaving off those curls in the hottest weather.

They spent the rest of the summer in a new apartment on the Pitti side of the Arno, close to the Grand Duke's palace, in the Via Maggio, a fashionable situation only within their means because this was the dead season in Florence. They occupied a spacious suite of well-furnished first-floor rooms in the Palazzo Guidi, later more familiar to us as Casa Guidi and their permanent home. The rent, no higher than in the Via delle Belle Donne, included admission to the large and beautiful Boboli Gardens close by.

One side of Casa Guidi faces the old grey wall of San Felice Church, so that on a balcony outside their drawing-room they could walk in the moonlit cool of the evening in absolute privacy. They were to find the nights rather noisy on the Via Maggio, but by day the position was an ideal one for the woman who was so to identify herself with the Italian people: all the processions in time of *festa* or national rejoicing passed down Via Maggio into the Pitti Square, where stood the palace of the Grand Duke of Tuscany.

Here in this lovely city, alone with her husband, Elizabeth lay back and enjoyed to the full her new existence. "I take it for pure magic, this life of mine," she told Miss Mitford. "Surely nobody was ever so happy before. I shall wake some morning with my hair all dripping out of the enchanted bucket, or if not we shall both claim the 'Flitch' next September."

Life outside the Casa Guidi seemed as yet to Elizabeth untouched by care:

For what helps to charm here is the innocent gaiety of the people, who, for ever at feast day and holiday celebrations, come and go along the streets, the women in elegant dresses and with glittering fans, shining away every thought of Northern cares and taxes, such as make people grave in England. No little orphan on a house step but seems to inherit naturally his slice of water-melon and bunch of purple grapes, and the rich fraternise with the poor as we are unaccustomed to see them, listening to the same music and walking in the same gardens, and looking at the same Raphaels even! Also we were glad to be here just now, when there is new animation and energy given to Italy by this new wonderful Pope, who is a great man and doing greatly.

"And the spark spreads!" she added happily. The Grand Duke, inspired by the Pope's example, had allowed the formation of a Civic Guard in open defiance of Austrian prohibition. Her Liberal heart rejoiced. "The world learns, it is pleasant to observe."

The celebration of their wedding day on September 12 was doubly happy: that day the world outside rejoiced too: Florence, packed with people, was celebrating in a great festa the establishment of a Civic Guard. A long procession passed down Via Maggio to the Pitti, where the Grand Duke and his family stood at a palace window to receive them. Past windows bright with silks and carpets hung out, Florence in ever dignified aspect, the Magistrates, the Priests, the Lawyers, the Artists, the Trade Guilds, marched rich with flowing banners, followed by representatives with their ensigns of each Tuscan state, and sympathizers, Greek, English, French. All this colour, this elation of spirit, went into Elizabeth's poem *Casa Guidi Windows*, treasured up now in her heart as she hung over a window draped with crimson silk waving a handkerchief until her wrist ached. For three and a half hours they marched by:

At which the stones seemed breaking into thanks
And rattling up the sky, such sounds in proof

Arose; the very house-walls seemed to bend;
   The very windows, up from door to roof,
Flashed out a rapture of bright heads.

But "on the famous evening of that famous day," an anniversary
so worthily celebrated, Flush put an end to private rejoicing.
He had been watching beside her, his paws hanging over the
window-sill, but, thinking "they were rather long about it, particularly as it had nothing to do with dinner and chicken bones
and subjects of consequence," he slipped out of doors and did
not return that night. At nine o'clock next morning he was found
waiting at the door of their apartment. "I imagine," Elizabeth
wrote, "he was bewildered with the crowd and the illumination, only as he *did* look so very guilty and conscious of evil on
his return, there's room for suspecting him of having been very
much amused, 'motu proprio,' as our Grand Duke says in the
edict."

They were meeting a few more people now, though Powers
remained their chief friend. One of them, a "vivacious little person, with sparkling talk enough," Mary Boyle, niece to the Earl
of Cork, was present with them as they watched the procession.
Mary Boyle would descend on the Brownings most evenings
before going on to late parties, and, though her society was welcome, sometimes she tired Elizabeth by staying on too long.
Miss Boyle, in her reminiscences, gives us a pleasant picture of
Mrs. Browning as she appeared during those "hours of enchantment" spent at the Casa Guidi; Elizabeth would be lying on a
sofa with Flush in her lap. "The pale thin hand of his mistress
rested on the glossy head of that 'gentle fellow-creature' like a
benediction."

I have never, in the course of my life seen a more spiritual face,
or one in which the soul looked more clearly from the windows;
clusters of long curls, in a fashion now obsolete, framed her
small delicate face, and ever shrouded its outline, and her form
was so fragile as to appear but an etherial covering.

Among the most interesting new acquaintances were the
Hoppners, Byron's friends in Venice, and the Storys. William
Wetmore Story, son of the famous Judge Story of Boston, was
himself a lawyer of note, but now hesitating on the brink of a
new career as sculptor. Story and his charming wife, strongly

attracted towards the Brownings on this first encounter, were, on their return to Italy in 1851, to become fast friends.

A two months' tenancy at Casa Guidi came to an end: as the Brownings had decided to winter in Rome it was perhaps at first only for a short period that they took a new apartment in the Via Maggio, an apartment they found both quieter and cooler. But Elizabeth was again pregnant.[1] In October, when they had decided to go, her doctor, making a mistake in the date on which the child should be born,[2] prohibited the journey. Elizabeth was very disappointed. Apart from an ardent desire to see Rome, she wished to join an old friend there, a Mrs. Fanny Dowglass; she was the more annoyed because of a conviction that the doctor was wrong. But, as she told her friend, "I made a mistake at Pisa & therefore had no right to be persistent."

The Via Maggio apartment, from being cool, proved to be cold when autumn came. At a sacrifice of six months' rent, which he could ill afford, Browning removed his wife at the end of October to "funny rabbit-hutch rooms" drenched in sunlight on the Piazza Pitti, exactly opposite the Duke's palace. There Elizabeth could enjoy a grand-stand view of Italian life and politics: it was probably there that she wrote the first part of *Casa Guidi Windows,* called at first "A Meditation in Tuscany," which *Blackwood's,* reflecting a general lack of interest in Italian politics at home, refused to publish.

Here on the Piazza Pitti their new Civic Guard, in helmets and epaulets, daily delighted crowds of admiring Florentines. Robert, looking at the Guard with more realistic eye, said musingly: "Surely after all this, they would *use* those muskets." It was rumoured that the Guard, very naturally liking its uniform to be admired, had proposed it should only do day service, leaving the unspectacular and tedious night work to the "ancient military." This "triviality and innocent vanity of children" at first only amused Elizabeth, but later she was to be exasperated by what appeared the supine attitude of her Florentines to Austrian tyranny; but Austrian though he was, tyranny in the

[1] Unpublished letter to Mrs. Fanny Dowglass, October 26, 1847, Huntington Library Collection.

[2] Unpublished letter to Fanny Dowglass, April 6, 1848, Huntington Library Collection.

person of the stupid but kindly Gran Duca, called affectionately the *"gran ciuca"* (great ass), was not unacceptable to many Tuscans. Because the Duke was a wealthy man taxes were light and the fine *mezzeria* system of agriculture in his realm made the peasants happier, more prosperous than anywhere else in Italy. Never had these people known real freedom. Besides, any gesture for freedom might entail summary punishment from Vienna, which kept close control; perhaps imprisonment in the infamous fortress of Spielberg.

Sitting together in their rooms "under the very eyelids of the sun" Robert and Elizabeth read, wrote, talked, and enjoyed music. News of the outside world, of Miss Martineau in her new Ambleside home, of Tennyson's last poems, and, above all, of family affairs, came to them mostly through letters; though they did hear of Mrs. Jameson and Geddie in Rome from Father Prout, who, being but two hours in Florence, "of course, according to contract of spirits of the air," met Robert, kissing him in the open street before he disappeared inside a *diligence*.

Florence was quiet enough that winter, but the early months of 1848 brought hope and joy to those who longed for Italian liberty: January saw risings in Falerno and Naples. In February there was revolution in Paris, overthrowing the Bourbon dynasty, a declaration of independence in Sicily, revolutions in the German states, and agitation even in Vienna itself. The Emperor of Austria abdicated, the powerful, sinister Metternich was driven into exile.

The Grand Duke of Tuscany, taking heart to oppose his masters in Vienna, granted a constitution. His popularity with the warm-hearted Florentines grew to fever pitch.

One night as Elizabeth was preparing for bed, Robert called her to the window. Through darkness below, "a great flock of stars seemed sweeping up the Piazza." The people of Florence, having recognized their Duke on a private visit to the Opera, were bringing him home in triumph amid a cluster of waxen torches. The *Evvivas* were deafening. "So glad I was," this enthusiastic childlike woman wrote to her friend Miss Mitford, "I, too, stood at the window and clapped my hands. If ever Grand Duke deserved benediction this Duke does."

During this sunny Italian winter Elizabeth was well, putting on flesh, visiting the galleries; but in early March there came an abrupt check, a second miscarriage,[3] this time partly brought about, Browning declared, by "the long, long, far too long letters that she *would* write the day before."

Elizabeth was kept in bed for a week. Again she suffered no harm, her doctor declaring that "the constitution has shown an astonishing energy." Though naturally disappointed by this further mishap, she wrote bravely to Fanny Dowglass: "the right thought suggests itself naturally, that God has blessed me so abundantly in some things, there is scarcely room for a greater weight of blessing. Children may be kept for those, who have not such a husband as I, perhaps!"

Delicious spring weather helped her to gain strength. At the first moment possible she drove out with Robert in a hired carriage "to our old Paradise—the Cascine, and saw the elms as green as ever they mean to be, and the grass like emeralds, and the pheasants all alive and flying." In order to reach the Cascine Gardens they passed by ancient buildings rich with association: "such a door where Lapo stood, and past the famous stone where Dante drew his chair out to sit. Strange, to have all this old-world life about us, and the blue sky so bright besides, and ever so much talk on our lips about the new French revolution, and the King of Prussia's cunning, and the fuss in Germany and elsewhere."

There were stirring events nearer home to discuss as they rode: the Austrians had been driven from Milan, from Venice, and the republics declared. The puppet princes of Modena and Parma had fled.

Inspired by a wave of popular enthusiasm in the north, Carlo Alberto, King of Sardinia, Duke of Savoy and Piedmont, the only active ruler in Italy, put himself at the head of an army. The Grand Duke, after a stirring proclamation, sent a contingent of his troops. There was war in Lombardy.

At the end of March Florence was illuminated, lit up in the peculiarly lovely Italian manner, "the Grand Duke throwing his Pitti palace in fire upon the sky." The Austrians had suffered an initial defeat. On the night before there had been turbulence

---

[3] Unpublished letter, April 6, 1848 to Fanny Dowglass, Huntington Library Collection.

before the Brownings' windows; a turbulence that in no wise daunted Elizabeth. Amid a "shriek of curses" the crowd had rushed to the Austrian Embassy, torn down the arms of Austria, and burnt them before the Duke's palace; afterwards giving a "*Viva Leopoldo secondo*" and dispersing peacefully.

During this time of stress foreigners, and especially the many English living in Florence, had taken flight. The Brownings were by no means disposed to follow this prudent example, but rather to identify themselves more closely with the Florentines by making a home there; a home from which they might take wing when they chose. Indeed, without acquiring a still cheaper apartment, with the additional advantage of being able to let it in their absence, a plan to spend future summers in England could not be carried out. Elizabeth's income from the ship money was already reduced by £100 a year and likely to be further lessened. Neither felt they could wait until more prosperous time to see their families again. Robert in particular yearned for his mother: not a day passed without him speaking of her. In Italy unfurnished apartments were so inexpensive that the fine suite in Casa Guidi, to which they were soon to return, only cost twenty-five guineas a year. Furniture, bought out of their two years' earnings by writing, they could acquire very cheaply now that so many people were rushing away from Florence. They decided furthermore to add to their personal comfort, probably without more expense, by engaging a man servant who would be responsible for meals in future; one Alessandro, who proved to be highly efficient, if somewhat consequential.

The suite they occupied on the first floor was that which the last Count Guidi had occupied: his arms were in scagliola on Elizabeth's bedroom floor. They had six large high-ceilinged rooms, "three of them quite palace rooms and opening on a terrace." Furniture must be antique, worthy of the place. The terrace Elizabeth determined to throng with orange trees and camellias.

Casa Guidi is now so cut up into modern flats that it is difficult to visualize these fine rooms, this spacious apartment, but the building still stands outwardly as it did, rather grim and forbidding in wedge shape against the Pitti Square.

f Browning stands in the entrance way and on the
ı a tablet placed there after Elizabeth's death by "a
Florence" and celebrating, in the words of the poet
ıseo, the woman "*che in cuore di donna conciliava sci-*
ıi dotto e spirito di poeta e fece del suo verso aureo anello
ıalia e Inghilterra.[4] Another tablet on the wall overlooking
ı / Felice Church gives the beautiful first lines of her poem
Casa Guidi Windows, commencing "I heard last night a little
child go singing."

Elizabeth's first days in the Casa Guidi were saddened by
news of the death of Hugh Boyd on May 10. Although it could
not but be felt as a merciful end to many years of patient suffering, Elizabeth must grieve over the passing of this

> Steadfast friend
> *Who never didst my heart or life misknow,*
> *Nor either's faults too keenly apprehend,—*

Her heart was further touched when later she heard he had left
to her the copies of Æschylus and Gregory Nazianzen from
which she used to read to him, and a clock

> *Chiming the gradual hours out like a flock*
> *Of stars whose motion is melodious.*

On June 20 she told Mrs. Martin: "I am very well and quite
strong again, or rather, stronger than ever, and able to walk as
far as Cellini's Perseus in the moonlight evenings, on the other
side of the Arno. Oh, that Arno in the sunset, with the moon
and evening star standing by, how divine it is! . ." The statue
of Perseus in the Loggia, springing forward with the Gorgon's
severed head in his upraised hand, was to her a symbol of that
Italy now upsurging to combat tyranny.

The furnishing of their apartment, proceeding slowly since
nothing was to be admitted unworthy of the fine rooms, was
Robert's concern: not only could he circulate more freely than
Elizabeth, but he had the more sensitive eye for surroundings
and, for all his earlier protestation of devotion to a simple life,
a greater love of luxury. So particular was Browning about ap-
pearances that Elizabeth would be admonished for wearing

---

[4] "who in her woman's heart combined learning and poetry and made of
her verse a golden ring linking Italy and England."

soiled gloves. The furniture, in the taste of the period and suiting their palatial rooms, was ornate, richly carved.

There was peace in Florence that summer, a sober peace during which the inhabitants indulged in no huzzas, illuminations, or fireworks, but concentrated on collecting all the money they could for the Army in Lombardy. The Brownings contributed according to their income.

A question was exercising Italian minds, one politically dangerous because the great patriot and prophet of Italian revolution, Mazzini, was a republican: whether the new Italy should be a kingdom under Charles Albert, or a series of federated republican states. France, their prototype in revolution, was now a Republic, but a troubled one. Some remarks on the news of a massacre there, coming to Mrs. Browning on July 4, made her reflect this indecision. Robert had belief in a French Republic though "with melancholy intermediate prospects," but Elizabeth thought the French would soon be impatient for a kingship. "How did you feel," she wrote to that other enthusiast for France, Miss Mitford, "when the cry was raised 'Vive l'Empereur'? Only Prince Napoleon is a Napoleon cut out in paper after all."

The hot season was now advancing. In July the Brownings sought change and coolness by going (deluded by Murray's Guide Book) to Fano "for the benefit of the sea air and the oysters." They found Fano unbearably hot, scorched up, "the very air swooning in the sun." Their only gains there were making the acquaintance of Mrs. Wiseman, mother of Dr. (later Cardinal) Wiseman, and seeing "a divine picture of Guercino's" which moved Browning to write "The Guardian-Angel":

> *We were at Fano, and three times we went*
> *To sit and see him in his chapel there,*
> *And drink his beauty to our soul's content*
> *—My angel with me too.*

After three days they left Fano for Ancona, "a striking sea city holding up against the brown rocks and elbowing out the purple tides, beautiful to look upon." There they stayed a week "living upon fish and cold water." The place was no cooler than Fano. All the long sun-hot hours Elizabeth lay on a sofa "with dishevelled hair at full length and 'sans gown, sans stays, sans shoes, sans everything' except a petticoat and a white dressing wrapper."

They wound up their holiday with "un bel giro," visiting Loreto, Sinigaglia, Pesaro, Rimini, Ravenna, Forli. The varied scenery drew constant admiration from every traveller except Flush, that urban dog, who had "a supreme contempt" for the beauty of landscape, only putting his head out of the window as they passed through a town or village.

Ravenna they found beautiful, "holding an atmosphere of purple glory," but oppressive: "the marshes on all sides send up stenches new and old, till the hot air is sick with them." Unarmed with a special permission, they were denied entrance to Dante's tomb: too angry to apply for one, they contented themselves with peering through the grated window. This was at an early hour, between three and four in the morning; that same night they passed on to Florence from the tomb of her exiled poet, arriving in the coolness of dawn.

After a three weeks' absence, Elizabeth was delighted to get back to Casa Guidi, now justly to be called home. "Florence seemed as cool as an oven after the fire; indeed, we called it quite cool, and I took possession of my own chair and put up my feet on the cushions and was charmed, both with having been so far and coming back so soon."

By now the forces of Charles Albert had been defeated at Custozza by Marshal Radetzky: the King had been obliged to retire beyond the Ticino and beg for an armistice. Though Garibaldi continued to harass the occupation army with his irregulars, Tuscany came again under the domination of Austria: the Pope, who had at first taken up the Liberal cause, now declared against the war.

The Florentines appeared to take their defeat tamely, "eating ices and keeping the feast of the Madonna," but putting up at a review in the Cascine Gardens a show of some 10,000 men. Mrs. Browning was bitter about an apparent lack of spirit. "Dante's soul has died out of the land."

One factor in Florentine acquiescence, apart from a natural fear of Austria's hard hand and a personal affection for the Duke, was an element in revolt of Mazzinian republicanism with its hostility to the Pope and established religion; constituting a pitiful and dangerous schism in Liberal ranks. These complications were perhaps not clear to Elizabeth, who as yet had no intimate acquaintance with Italians.

Autumn brought serious news from Rome. The Pope's support of Austrian tyranny had aroused anger in the republican party led by Mazzini. In November Count Pelligrino Rossi, a minister of Liberal tendencies appointed in Rome under the new Constitution, was foully assassinated, and there were threats of further violence if the Pope did not give in to republican terms. "The poor Pope I deeply pity," Elizabeth wrote; "he is a weak man with the noblest and the most disinterested intentions. . . . He should have gone out to them and so died, but having missed that opportunity, nothing remained but flight." Pio Nono, disguising himself, had escaped to Gaeta into the arms of the reactionary King Ferdinand of Naples, whom not long before he had denounced as a rogue.

Some Roman news was brought to them by word of mouth: William Wetmore Story had been in Rome with his wife and family. These vivacious, cultivated people had made their acquaintance during a brief visit to Florence in the spring of that year, but now an autumn there was to warm that acquaintance into the beginnings of a close friendship. It is worth perhaps regarding Robert and Elizabeth at this period with Story's keen eye.

In Elizabeth, sitting quietly deep in a large easy chair, he found "nothing of that peculiarity which one would expect from reading her poems. . . . Very unaffected and pleasant and simple-hearted is she." Robert he thought a man of "great vivacity, but not the least humour, some sarcasm, considerable critical faculty, and very great frankness and friendliness of manner and mind." It seems to us strange that anyone, especially a man so congenial, could find no humour in Browning, but perhaps at this time he was not his normal self. Story also speaks of twitching of the eyes and a general nervousness of manner. In September Robert was seriously ill.

He had been laid up for nearly a month with fever and an ulcerated sore throat; and, greatly to Elizabeth's anxiety, refused to see a doctor.

When Elizabeth was feeling particularly unhappy Father Prout made his next appearance and, ignoring the old adage about starving a fever, mixed a potion of eggs and port wine while Alessandro, the Brownings' man servant, lifted his eyes in horror, crying: "O, Inglesi, Inglesi!"

Not only this "eccentric prescription," which sent Robert off into a healing sleep, but Father Prout's own quaint and hearty manner did them both good. He called Elizabeth a "bambina" for being frightened. They were now to see him every day; "he came to doctor and remained to talk." "Not refined," Elizabeth commented on him, "in a social sense by any manner of means, yet a most accomplished scholar and vibrating all over with learned associations and vivid combinations of fancy and experience." He must also have brought them vital and intimate news from Rome, where he was closely in touch with workers for liberation; writing on their behalf for his journal, the *Daily News,* a forceful series of articles.

But the society of the unrefined Father Prout had its disadvantages: he was apt to stay too late over wine, to smoke heavily in Elizabeth's presence, and to demand a spittoon. He flourished a dubious handkerchief. His native cynicism too, and his malicious talk jarred on them both. He further offended by calling his hostess "Ba," that name the prerogative of those dearest to her.

But at length Father Prout left for Rome, though not without a threat, happily coming to nothing, of returning soon. Husband and wife settled down again to their quiet evenings of uninterrupted happiness.

Robert's devotion to his wife increased, if that were possible: Elizabeth was again with child. In order to run no risk this time she resolutely broke her long habit of taking a laudanum sedative. Apart from this effort, which must have required considerable courage and strength of mind, she had nothing to do but rest and wait, attended by her husband and Wilson.

Wilson, getting rapidly Italianized, had now an engaged lover in the rather lordly and handsome person of Mr. Righi, son of a medical man and a member of the Ducal Guard. The only flaw in Wilson's content was her fellow-servant, Alessandro, whose own efficiency made him touchy and overbearing.

On the grounds of being a travelled man, he claimed to know everything. Alessandro was graciously pleased, however, to approve his employers, whose domestic happiness appeared to him quite exceptional. The Signor was an angel "and the Signora was rather an angel too—she never spent two thousand scudi on her dress at once, as *he* had seen women do—so the Signor might well be fond of the Signora—but still for a Signor to be always sitting with his wife in that way, was most extraordinary."

The December of 1848 found Elizabeth despondent over chances of Liberal success. The Florentines around her appeared supine, effeminate; a downpour of rain seeming enough to damp revolutionary enthusiasm. France, the mother of Revolution, had now elected Prince Louis Napoleon as President on no better grounds, she considered, than that he was "*le neveu de son oncle.*" Italy was again in the grip of reaction and, although allowance must be made for the ferment of new wine, it was impossible, hearing news of anarchy in Rome, "to sympathise, to go along with the *people* to whom and to whose cause all my natural sympathies yearn"; these people who were too apt to assassinate, to destroy. "The holiness of liberty is desecrated by the sign of the ass's hoof."

One may guess that she was physically weighed down. Even that which had been earlier a pleasing interest, was now termed "the slow agonies of furnishing our apartment." Elizabeth was by nature too impatient to admire the caution with which Robert acquired belongings, keeping sternly within the limits of money earned, and the more constitutional slowness of the Italian race made her rail against delays in curtaining the windows. There was pure pleasure, however, to be got out of the news that Robert's new edition would soon be out, and that a performance by Phelps at Sadler's Wells Theatre of *A Blot in the 'Scutcheon* was a decided success. There were flowers too, about the house this December, "white roses as in June."

In January the Grand Duke, seeing that might was no longer on his side, himself fled to Gaeta, going there, ironically enough, by the aid of a free nation in the British war vessel *Bulldog*. A republican party, headed by men from Leghorn, strangers to Florence, took charge against the wishes of many Florentines who wanted their Duke back. The spirit of revolution was now abroad in Florence. The English who were still in residence packed their bags ready for instant flight.

The Brownings, however, remained both from choice and necessity: Elizabeth was not now in a condition to travel. Of those at Casa Guidi Wilson was the most disturbed since the future of her *fidanzato* depended on that of the Grand Duke. She wanted her lover to leave the Duke's service and settle down as a shopkeeper in Prato on money offered as a loan by a rich tradesman brother, but Mr. Righi seemed to be fonder of himself and his own dignity than of Wilson. Later, when the Duke's bodyguard was disbanded, Mr. Righi went to Prato.

Flush, that town dog, probably welcomed street disturbances: Elizabeth, who knew he would ultimately return, no longer worried over the dog's disappearances. With his hair grown again into glossy curls after the summer's shaving, Flush was full of insolence and liveliness, seeming with advancing age to grow "preternaturally wise." In the house he would sit apart and growl singularly, appearing to commune with himself. Robert had long been accepted, not as a rival, but a friend over whom to tyrannize: Flush could not foresee that a few months would bring another claimant on his mistress's affection.

CHAPTER 23

BIRTH AND DEATH; *CASA GUIDI WINDOWS* [1849–51]

AT A QUARTER PAST TWO in the morning of March 9, 1849, Elizabeth's son was born after some twenty-one hours of labour, a strong well-nourished child. During the long day and night of bitter pain Browning was with her whenever possible, holding her hand, and for the rest he waited in the drawing-room. To the end of his life he would point out the chair on which he sat.

To the sisters, and also presumably to his parents, though the letter has not survived, Browning wrote in the early hours of the morning. To Miss Mitford he sent the news minutely written on a scrap of paper, the whole folded up to the size of a postage stamp.

Elizabeth herself, exhausted but happy, would not see her child until Robert could bring him to her in his arms. As the doctor did not think she could feed him herself, a wet nurse had to be found. Four persons were tried, the one chosen being "a mighty woman, that would cut up into twenty Bas . . . good natured and intelligent spite of her fat cheeks which overflow her neck as she bends down." Three little tufts of hair were cut off the baby's head, one for the sisters, one for Treppy, to whom Elizabeth was "favourite child," and a third for Robert's mother.

While Elizabeth lay recovering from the birth much was happening outside Casa Guidi windows. The town was in a ferment, some calling (to the same tune, Elizabeth said) "*Viva la repubblica!*" and others "*Viva Leopoldo!*" Agitation for the return of the Duke was in part, Elizabeth declared, literally a *counter* revolution, since great indignation was aroused by the unwillingness of the Livornese, who dominated the republican party, to pay their café bills. This fact may have influenced certain waverers, but undoubtedly the peasants were wholehearted in their invitation to Duke Leopold to return: all they demanded of him was a promise to respect the new Constitution. The Duke, perhaps pardonably nervous at the general turn of events, hesitated.

In that disastrous month King Charles Albert took the offensive again, only to be overwhelmingly defeated at Novara on March 23. Out of this defeat, however, though it meant eleven more years of Austrian rule in northern Italy, a strength was to come. Convinced republicans might hold resolutely to their idea of federated states, but general opinion moved towards the more human conception of a united Italy under the House of Savoy, a conception unexpectedly strengthened by the provision of a royal martyr to the cause of freedom. Charles Albert, abdicating on the field of battle in favour of his son, the wise and intrepid Victor Emmanuel, died broken-hearted after a few months of illness. Thousands made pilgrimage to his tomb, as to that of a saint, and under a new, more severe oppression a fervour for liberty was kept up.

In Rome all at first seemed to augur well for the type of freedom favoured by the republican followers of Mazzini until, on April 25, General Oudinot landed with 8,000 men at Civitavecchia sent by Louis Napoleon to extinguish, in the name of the French Republic, all hope of Republican freedom in Rome. Garibaldi, after an heroic march into Rome at the head of a small band of irregulars, only escaped by a hairsbreadth.

This action of the First Consul, on the face of it cynical, ironic, was a severe blow to the cause of Italian freedom and a stunning shock to Liberal minds; the more so because the rise to power of a second Napoleon had heartened men to revolt, remembering as they did how in 1796 Napoleon himself had come as deliverer, though an arbitrary rapacious deliverer, from the thrall of Austria and her puppet princes. And had not this Napoleon, the nephew, himself in 1831 fought with the Carbonari against Papal troops in an abortive revolt at Città Castellana? Now French forces were arriving in his name to restore Papal dominion. But Louis Napoleon, tortuous, astute, had his reasons: ambitious for an imperial crown and the old Napoleonic power in Europe, he must conciliate French Catholic opinion and strengthen his hand against Austria.

Of the man who had used power ruthlessly to drive Liberals from Rome, Elizabeth was not yet an unqualified admirer but, though she must condemn an action that "cast Rome helpless and bound into the hands of priests," she was willing to admit his position to be a difficult one. Up to a point, in her opinion, he had shown himself "an upright man with noble impulses." Her deep-rooted affection for France had perhaps first been aroused in a heart already warm with Napoleon-worship during that childish expedition of 1815. Later, in her close room, the novels of Balzac and other French writers brought a pulsing vicarious life to the invalid; so that now, from gratitude and habit, she identified herself almost as closely with France as with her beloved Italy.

At home in England, though they must often have been disturbed at the thought of Ba being so many miles away among those excitable subversive foreigners, the sisters were rejoicing over the birth of their first nephew, though with some amusement. "Tell Arabel," Elizabeth wrote them after receiving letters from Wimpole Street, "that her insult about my carrying him by the head is quite gratuitous." But she had to acknowledge that Robert seemed the more natural baby-minder.

At Hatcham there was little rejoicing, or rather a rejoicing amid sorrow: the elder Mrs. Browning, taken suddenly ill with an unsuspected ossification of the heart, lay in an unconsciousness preceding death. She could not know of the existence of her grandson. A few days later she died.

Sarianna broke the news gently to Robert, writing twice, telling of illness, and of its increasing seriousness, when in actual fact Robert's mother was dead. Even with this preparation he fell into a state of deep anguish, the excitement of his son's birth having laid him open the more to reaction. His was at first a stony grief, unable to find relief in tears. His only consolation could be, Elizabeth wrote, if his father and Sarianna could come to him at once. This, of course, was out of the question while the elder Browning was tied to an office chair. Elizabeth decided that as soon as possible she must get a change of scene for her husband, "but where to go? England looks terrible now. He says it would break his heart to see his mother's roses over the wall, and the place where she used to lay her scissors and gloves."

Outside Casa Guidi there was now open conflict between

the two parties. Shooting began: one day Robert had barely time to escape the fray. "The tree of Liberty," Elizabeth wrote, so proudly erected by republicans, had "come down with a crash." The baby in his cradle at Casa Guidi would be startled from sleep by noisy festas, rejoicings, first about this Liberty tree and then over its fall, each accompanied by the continual firing of guns and cannon.

"For my part," Elizabeth commented in May, "I am altogether *blasée* about revolutions and invasions. . . . Oh heavens! how ignoble it all has been and is! A revolution made by boys and *vivas*, and unmade by boys and *vivas*—no, there was blood shed in the unmaking—some horror and terror, but not as much patriotism and truth as could lift up the blood from the kennel." On the behaviour of her "beloved French" in Rome, Elizabeth was resolved to withhold judgment until the facts were clearer.

At the beginning of May the Grand Duke, having decided to accept an invitation from his loving subjects, came back, but accompanied by Austrian troops. Elizabeth, who had defended him against Robert's harsher opinion, now had to admit his treachery. "I give him up, having fought for him gallantly." With Austrian soldiers in the streets of Florence she was the more inclined to take a favourable view of Louis Napoleon's action, writing to Henrietta: "The French intervention has been awkwardly managed, but the *intention* . . . is, in my opinion, noble and upright—nothing else could have saved Rome, with Austria at the doors, and Russia behind Austria." Mazzini should have welcomed the French: in that case Napoleon could not have been reproached, as representative of one republic, for having put down another.

In this letter Elizabeth described the coming of the Austrians. The nurse called: "*Signora, signora, ecco i Tedeschi!*"
We ran out on the terrace together—and up from the end of the street and close under our windows came the artillery and baggage waggons—the soldiers sitting upon the cannons motionless, like dusty statues. Slowly the hateful procession filed under our windows. The people shrank back to let them pass, in the deepest silence—not a word spoken, scarcely a breath drawn. . . . For my part I felt my throat swelling with grief

and indignation. Oh, to think of our ever seeing such a sight from these windows. I wish we were a thousand miles away.

Robert came in, telling her that the Austrian General's proclamation, posted up, began with the words "Invited by your Grand Duke."

In this atmosphere of reaction and oppression Robert's grief over the loss of his mother remained sharp. Elizabeth, while sharing it in part—with some feeling of guilt since it was she who had parted those two close friends—had her own quieter sorrow: the birth of a grandson had not softened her father.

Mr. Barrett gave no sign. The brothers too remained inexorable except one who had written kindly and sent a note on the birth of her child. As her letters to him were not returned, Elizabeth tried to nourish a hope that her father at least took enough interest in her to read them: on this point she was later to be roughly disillusioned.

The baby, now two months old, was fat and rosy, reminding his mother of the Infant Christ in a reproduction of Raphael's "Virgin and Child" which used to hang in her room at Wimpole Street. He was full of life. *"O, questo bambino,"* said his proud nurse, *"è proprio rabbioso!"* In public he drew much admiration and attention. The nurse considered him to be not at all like an English child: in English children there was always *qualche cosa di strana*—something a bit queer.

On July 25 he was christened at the French Evangelical Protestant Church, a chapel at the Prussian Legation. His names, chosen by Elizabeth, were Robert Wiedeman, the second being the maiden name of Browning's mother. As Wiedeman the little creature was to be known, thus keeping alive in a manner she herself would have liked the memory of that grandmother who never knew him.

The heats of summer were beginning: with some difficulty Elizabeth persuaded Browning to leave Florence. They retired to the Bagni di Lucca high up in the mountains, taking with them the three servants. Little Wiedeman, now short-coated, was already babbling in baby language, a smiling friendly child. Robert, away from the place where grief first overwhelmed him, began to rally.

Flush, who had been sulking over the baby's advent, now

recovered his spirits too, running about in the fresher air and bathing—perhaps getting rid thus of the tiresome fleas of summer—in the hot springs, one of which gushed up close to the house. He became gracious towards Wiedeman, though always the child's love for him, rather too demonstrative, was stronger than his for the boy. This elderly animal, though he endured it with affection, could not be expected to welcome a heavy child scrambling on his back.

The Baths of Lucca were a favourite resort for coolness in summer; sheltered as they were by even higher mountains, so that a day of normal sunshine there was curtailed by four hours. The Grand Duke did all he could to attract visitors with balls, receptions, and other attractions. The Brownings stayed in the highest of the three villages called, because the Duke's estate was there, La Villa. Their house was "a sort of eagle's nest" that only donkeys and carrying-chairs could reach, lying *at the heart of a hundred mountains sung to continually by a rushing mountain stream. The sound of the river and of the cicala is all the noise we hear. Austrian drums and carriage wheels cannot vex us; God be thanked for it; the silence is full of joy and consolation.*
The Baths, which Browning had dreaded as "a sort of wasp's nest of scandal and gaming, with everything trodden flat by the Continental English," they found pleasantly deserted in this time of political trouble. Living was even cheaper than in Florence. Chestnut forests clustered thickly on the mountain; at night, so thick were the fireflies, they seemed to be "living among the stars." We hear nothing of mosquitoes on this healthy height; those mosquitoes Elizabeth feared far more than the Austrians.

But the Brownings were not entirely free to enjoy their Eden: anxiety haunted them. Cholera was raging in and about London. Near Hatcham it was virulent. Sarianna, who had promised to visit them in the autumn, would not now leave her father. Elizabeth herself was miserably aware that no danger would deter Mr. Barrett from remaining in Town, from going daily into the crowded City then so unsanitary with its stinking alley ways and horrible piled-up graveyards. "Love," she wrote sadly to Miss Mitford, "runs dreadful risks in the world."

There was a great event over which to rejoice within their owned charmed circle: "Baby has cut a tooth." The bright, healthy laughing boy was forward for his age in every particular.

About the child's upbringing there was one dispute between husband and wife: Robert very naturally wanting his son to grow up an Englishman, reproached Ba for talking to him in Italian. But, she protested, the child heard Italian all day from his voluble nurse, and from Wilson when she talked with the other servants. To hear English spoken would only confuse his small mind. When they visited England next year he could learn his native tongue in the natural way.

Elizabeth's recovered health enabled her to walk up and down steep hillside paths and even to ride, as they did one day, five miles on donkey-back to the Prato Fiorito, a velvety dome of flower-strewn grass deep in rugged mountains. They set off at half past eight in the morning and stayed out until six, riding where at some points a single slip of a donkey's foot would have meant precipitation into a deep ravine. The baby went with them, riding in turns with Wilson and the nurse.

While the Brownings were at Lucca, Elizabeth, coming quietly behind Robert as he stood looking out of the window, slipped into his hand a small book of manuscript: her love sonnets, the last written two days before marriage. She had delayed so long in giving them because of something he had said "against putting one's loves into verse." "A strange, heavy crown, that wreath of sonnets," her poet husband called them in writing of the event three years after her death to Julia Wedgwood.

On their return to Florence in October Robert was working on "Christmas Eve and Easter Day" and Elizabeth upon a collected edition. In this edition, published in 1850, the love poems were first published, lightly veiled under the title of "Sonnets from the Portuguese," chosen because "Caterina to Camoens" was a favourite with Browning. An attempt was made further to deflect attention from the personal character of the series by banishing to the last page of Volume I the sonnet beginning:

"My future will not copy fair my past"—
I wrote that once . . .

which linked up with that quoted here on page 127. Later, in the 1856 edition, it was put back in its rightful place as Sonnet XLIV.

In this new edition, and in that of 1856, Elizabeth, assisted by Browning, made many revisions: a number of the unorthodox loose rimes, or assonances, were altered to suit conventional ears, archaisms removed and certain lines rewritten; not always, I think, improving on the original. That her second thoughts were not always best—at least to modern readers—is perhaps most evident in the love sonnets if one compares with those published a set in early manuscript form [1] where the language is more direct, less "literary," and therefore more moving. I give as an example Sonnet XVI (Appendix 3).

In late autumn there is a pause in the correspondence. Elizabeth was again ill. By December 1 she had recovered but not, to Robert's disappointment, enough to resume the "grand walking expeditions." If, said Elizabeth, her husband was vain about anything, it had been of those new walking-powers, boasting of them as if, she told him teasingly, "a wife with a pair of feet was a miracle of nature."

During this illness Elizabeth had the continued comfort of Wilson's care: the maid's engagement to Mr. Righi had been broken off. Mr. Righi had not written as often as he should, and on her return to Florence did not hasten over from Prato to see her. Wilson, convinced of his unworthiness, grieved at first, but soon recovered.

More friends were now being admitted to Casa Guidi, still in the main American. The Brownings seem to have been closer in spirit to these members of a newer nation: their early appreciation of Browning's true worth warmed Elizabeth's heart to them. Americans too paid a practical homage not generally accorded by their own countrymen. Of them Elizabeth wrote in 1860:

English people will come and stare at me *sometimes, but physicians, dentists, who serve me and refuse their fees, artists who*

---

[1] In the Pierpont Morgan Library.

*give me pictures, friends who give up their carriages and make
other practical sacrifices, are* not English—*no*—

Also, many of the English abroad kept up a style of living beyond the Brownings' means.

Among American friends was Margaret Fuller, a rather wild
woman of socialistic ideas, an advocate of women's rights, and
a convinced republican. During the siege of Rome she had
served Italy nobly in the hospitals and now, French troops being
in occupation and the forces of reaction at work, she retired to
Florence bringing with her the Marquis Ossoli, an Italian husband, and a child a year old. Until the siege of Rome was at
its height none of her friends had known of the existence of a
husband, and certainly not of a child. With the Marquis Ossoli
Mrs. Browning was not impressed, though admitting his one
important qualification as Margaret Fuller's husband, that of a
good listener.

There was another home in Florence where Americans were
welcomed, that of Miss Jane Isabella Blagden, a writer of forgotten novels and verse whose fame now rests upon her hospitality. Isa Blagden's origins were obscure: she was certainly of
mixed blood, perhaps a Eurasian. Browning called her "a
bright, delicate, electric woman." Although forced to eke out a
small income by sharing her home with a woman friend and
writing "bread-and-butter" novels, she created by her generous
and lively personality a salon rivalling that of the Trollopes. Isa
Blagden was to be closely identified with the Brownings, both
in happy and in darker hours. It was—fittingly enough as their
most intimate friend—she who gave to each of them a ring of
fine chased gold in the Etruscan style; a ring commemorated for
us in *The Ring and the Book.*

For economy's sake Isa lived outside the walls, but it was not
until 1856 that she inhabited Villa Bricchieri, that "house at
Florence on the hill of Bellosguardo." Villa Bricchieri became
almost a second home to Browning: several evenings a week,
when his wife had retired for the night, he would walk up there
to enjoy a few hours of lively conversation with Isa and her
guests.

April brought news from England. Henrietta, at the age of

forty-one, had at length summoned courage to defy her father. When asked for a formal consent Mr. Barrett had intimated that she must either give up the engagement of five years' standing or leave his house. Elizabeth, who had already written a private letter of encouragement, was delighted to hear of Henrietta's marriage. As Surtees Cook's [2] income was restricted she combined strong personal desire with prudence by advising them to come and live in Florence. But for the Barrett family, so invincibly British, the Continent was for an occasional holiday and no more.

Mr. Barrett, strongly entrenched in his own bitterness, cut this second daughter out of his heart. He would "never let her name be mentioned again in his hearing."

On April 23, 1850 Wordsworth died: a new Poet Laureate must be appointed. The *Athenæum*, anonymously but in the voice of Henry Chorley, strongly pressed Elizabeth's claim as one peculiarly appropriate because a woman sat on the Throne. Elizabeth herself wished that the aged Leigh Hunt might be appointed as some compensation for early neglect and opprobrium. It is a measure of the slightness of Browning's fame at this period that his name was not seriously put forward. When Alfred Tennyson, that poet typical of the Victorian age at its height, was appointed, approbation was general.

Elizabeth's heart and mind were turning towards England. She longed to go back on a visit, to see her sisters and to "authenticate" Wiedeman, "for, as Robert says, all our fine stories about him will go for nothing, and he will be set down as a sham child."

Elizabeth's reading in her own language was constant: with Miss Mitford she discussed such new English books as could be obtained in Florence, though with some delay. She expressed disappointment in Tennyson's *The Princess*, pronounced the author of *Jane Eyre* to be certainly a woman, found *Vanity Fair* very clever, very effective, but cruel to human nature"; praised two poems in Matthew Arnold's new volume—one of them "The Forsaken Merman"—and took a personal interest, as one who had herself long planned a verse novel, in Clough's *Bothie of Tober-na-Vuolich*. Perhaps there were moments when she

[2] Later he changed his name to Altham.

longed to encounter those literary personalities whose books she read, and who were out of reach in far Florence.

Two years before, John Kenyon had made an earnest request to his cousin to draw upon him in case of need, and now he pressed the offer again; hoping perhaps to have the comfort of their presence in England once more. After his son's birth in 1849 Browning had accepted an allowance of £ 100 a year from Kenyon, but beyond this his pride, a horror of contracting debt, would not allow him to go. Even to bring his wife pleasure, he wrote, it would be "a vile habit, to say no worse, that of looking wistfully up at the clouds, on all occasions, to see what facilities may drop down." If he and Elizabeth could not raise the money between them they must remain in Italy.

When Browning decided to postpone a long and expensive journey to England he had another and a very good reason for doing so: it might be that next year they would be living in Paris, within easy access of London. But before she left Italy, perhaps for good, Ba must see Rome. This, he told Kenyon, was well within his resources.

But plans for Paris, for Rome, must be much in the air. Soon it was clear that another child might be born in January; perhaps the girl for whom Elizabeth longed. This was, however, not to be: on Sunday, July 28, Elizabeth had a serious miscarriage with great loss of blood. "Four of these mishaps, besides the advent of our babe, amount to a serious drain on such a constitution as hers." In telling Kenyon this, and not sparing the painful detail, Robert added:

how otherwise can I put you in my place, and make you fancy that, after sitting all night by the little patient white face, that could smile so much more easily than speak, your letter and its proposal for her good reached me? You surely feel that whatever I say presently, the real business is over and indeed, in the truest sense I have, as you express it, "already accepted" this last of your kindnesses, and laid it away with its fellows in my heart forever.

Elizabeth was slow in recovery: her condition was not improved by the shock of terrible news in August about a woman who, though a recent friend, was an admired one. Margaret Fuller was dead, and she had died in a manner peculiarly agonizing to Elizabeth. In late April she and the Marquis Ossoli had sailed with their child to America. They spent their last evening in Florence at Casa Guidi. Over the friends so soon to part a sad premonition brooded. The Marquis had been warned by a fortune-teller that the sea would be fatal to him. His wife turned smiling to Mrs. Browning and said: "Our ship is called the 'Elizabeth,' and I accept the omen." Before leaving that night she inscribed a Bible, as from her child to Wiedeman, "In memory of Angelo Eugene Ossoli."

The *Elizabeth* had sunk beneath the Atlantic. Robert would have preferred to keep the news from his ailing wife, but so close was their intimacy that any reserve between them was difficult: he thought it wiser to tell her at once. In writing to Miss Mitford Elizabeth told how the loss had affected her more deeply "through association with the past, when the arrowhead of anguish was broken too deeply into my life ever to be quite drawn out." Unhappiness was deepened by a personal anxiety. For twenty-four hours her child lay ill with sunstroke. "Terrible the silence that fell suddenly upon the house, without the small pattering feet and the singing voice."

Her doctor having ordered a change of air, on August 31 the Brownings left for Siena, travelling by railroad; Elizabeth, having to be lifted on the journey, "looking ghostly rather than ghastly."

They stayed a week in a hotel, probably the Villa di Londra, and then settled in a house standing in its own grounds two miles out of Siena on the *Poggio dei Venti,* Hill of the Winds. For the seven-roomed furnished villa, a vineyard, an olive ground, an orchard, a flower garden, taken for a month, the rent worked out at 11*s.* 1½*d.* a week.

The views from that hill, at their finest from a *specola,* or belvedere at the top of the house, are magnificent and today little changed. From one window the Brownings could see the ancient city, so close in that clear air, like some bright mediæval illumination; from another over a vast sweep of marshy land to the mountains of Rome, and from a third—to quote Elizabeth's own words, as true today as a hundred years ago—"the whole country leaps under the sun, alive with verdure and vineyards." There may be more villas now on the hill of the winds, but there are still "English lanes with bowery tops of trees, and brambles and blackberries, and not a wall anywhere" except house walls. The air, too, has an English quality without its dampness.

At first Elizabeth could enjoy little more than "the enchanting silence" (perhaps even more enchanting today after the noise of modern Florence) and the magnificent views as she moved with difficulty from room to room. Wiedeman, able to get out of doors, soon got back the colour in his fat cheeks, revelling in such new delights as pigeons, a pig, a donkey, and a big yellow dog; though, his mother commented, being a town baby he really preferred a military band, even if it were Austrian.

There were certain drawbacks: the doors would not shut and the house was so small that "Robert and I had to whisper all our talk whenever Wiedeman was asleep." One unexpected pleasure, however, was a good and cheap library in Siena of which the Brownings took full advantage, though lamenting that now they could never read a new Balzac: the great novelist died on August 19, 1850.

On leaving Siena in October they grew "rather pathetical" and "shrank from parting with the pig." The road home probably included a week in Siena to enjoy the art treasures and some divergence from the straight path back to Florence. Dr. Harding had prescribed a frequent change of air for his patient. This prescription both would have willingly followed over many months of their year if their income had allowed. "Every now and then we take out the road-books, calculate the expenses, and groan in the spirit when it's proved for the hundredth time that we cannot do it." Both had a fever for roaming.

We hear this autumn little about work. Elizabeth declared that she spent half the day doing nothing but admire her boy. But visitors to Casa Guidi have recorded that, although the Brownings were busy workers, they never appeared to be so, always having leisure for friends at any hour. Elizabeth at this time must have been writing or revising the second part of *Casa Guidi Windows.*

Her attitude to the Florentines about her is clearly set out in this second part. Perhaps not realizing the effect of long oppression, of terrible odds, the rank and file of Italians,

> *those oil-eaters, with large, live mobile mouths*
> *Agape for macaroni,*

now appeared to her as cheerfully submitting to tyranny so long as they might be entertained with festas, illuminations, military reviews and bands. A rigorous domination was imposed, not only by the Austrian-controlled State, but the Church: when in profound disillusionment with the Pope many flocked to Protestant churches these churches were threatened with expulsion from Italy if they allowed Catholics within their walls.

It was all very well for Elizabeth, born in free England, to admonish that

> *Austrian Metternich*
> *Can fix no yoke unless the neck agree:*

she herself was not an Italian held in subjection for many generations by Church usurping State. Nor did she take fully into account the widespread hatred of republicanism, and the personal popularity of the Grand Duke.

But Elizabeth herself would perhaps have been the first to acknowledge a certain lack of full comprehension: as she says in her preface to the published poem, it was but "a simple story of personal impressions" of political events.

The second half of the poem seems to lack the fire of the first. Perhaps, as the outcome of disappointment, the shattering of high hopes in a woman of frail physique, it was bound to be flatter in effect: though in the part that was written in 1850 there are strong passages, such as that upon the futility of military oppression, its perverse power to arouse in the end a sense of freedom, of nationality:

> *Behold, the people waits,*
> *Like God. As He, in His serene of might,*
> *So they, in their endurance of long straits.*
> *Ye stamp no nation out, though day and night*
> *Ye tread them with that absolute heel which grates*
> *And grinds them flat from all attempted height.*
> *You kill worms sooner with a garden-spade*
> *Than you kill peoples: peoples will not die;*
> *The tail curls stronger when you lop the head;*

> *They writhe at every wound and multiply,*
> *And shudder into a heap of life that's made*
> *Thus vital from God's own vitality.*

This poem was sent in early spring for Sarianna to copy and see through the press.

In the December of 1850 Elizabeth read *In Memoriam,* a poem eagerly looked forward to, for which her appetite had been whetted by review extracts. It was inevitable, from the very theme of the work, that it should go "to her heart and soul." When Miss Mitford complained of its monotony, Elizabeth replied:

The sea is monotonous, and so is lasting grief. Your complaint is against fate and humanity rather than against the poet Tennyson. Who that has suffered has not felt wave after wave break dully against one rock, till brain and heart, with all their radiances, seemed lost in a single shadow? So the effect of the book is artistic, I think, and indeed I do not wonder at the opinion . . . that Tennyson stands higher through having written it. You see, what he appeared to want . . . was an earnest personality and direct purpose.

Elizabeth had one criticism: "All I wish away is the marriage hymn at the end, and *that* for every reason I wish away—it's a discord in the music."

There was one old friend of Miss Mitford's whom till now Elizabeth had not met in Florence; and, indeed, at Robert's wish had sedulously avoided, "that coarse, vulgar Mrs. Trollope" over whom he had so worked himself up at Pisa. His objection, still maintained, seemed to arise from "a sort of vow never to sit in the same room with the author of certain books directed against liberal institutions and Victor Hugo's poetry."

This obstinacy Elizabeth had been forced to combat, and in other directions. She who was apt to be (except in certain enthusiasms) less prejudiced, found people—as in the case of Margaret Fuller—"better than their books, than their principles, and even their everyday actions, sometimes. I am always crying out: 'Blessed be the inconsistency of men.'" She hated, besides, to seem "ungracious and unkind."

Mrs. Trollope and her daughter, at length invited to Casa Guidi, proved "very agreeable, and kind, and good-natured," with an additional charm of talking much about Miss Mitford. The Brownings were to return their visit privately, avoiding Mrs. Trollope's public days "in the full flood and flow of Florentine society."

To Miss Mitford, curiously enough, Elizabeth made no mention of Mrs. Trollope's daughter-in-law, the former Theodosia Garrow, now the wife of Thomas Trollope, whom, either in 1840, or perhaps in London in 1838, Elizabeth had met. Part of Browning's reluctance to know the Trollopes may have arisen from the effect of certain malicious gossip that at one time was circulating in Florence about the lively, impulsive Theodosia. It was inevitable, of course, that the two women should encounter one another again but, although Elizabeth appreciated Theodosia's work for Italian freedom in her news-letters to the *Athenæum,* there seems, from a few letters which have survived, little personal link beyond a childish acquaintance between her young son and Beatrice, or Bice, the Trollopes' daughter. Later the children rode together. In the reminiscences of his old age Thomas Trollope appears to lay too much emphasis on friendship between the two; perhaps because he was uneasily aware of this cloud once upon his dead wife which any sort of suggested intimacy with such a woman as Elizabeth might lift in the memory.

By April 1851 the Brownings' great plan of living in Paris, closer to their people in England, was coming at least to experiment; the Florentine apartment was, however, to be retained and only temporarily let in case the Paris winter should prove dangerous to Elizabeth. That spring, fortified with the proceeds of their books and rent from the apartment, they were to take a long, lingering farewell of Italy beginning with Rome and visiting Naples, Venice, and Milan. Across the Alps they were to reach as far north as Brussels, then to Paris and, ultimately, London.

At the end of April their luggage was actually packed and a carriage to Rome bargained for, when doubt assailed them. It was late in the season, late for the festas. Rome in May might be too hot for the boy. Two journeys, south then north again, might put too much strain on their purse. They decided instead to go, on their way north, to Venice.

CHAPTER 24

VENICE; PARIS; ENGLAND [1851–2]

TRAVEL, always a pleasure, was enhanced in 1851 by discomfort left behind, the discomfort of decorators in Casa Guidi. "My head and Robert's," Elizabeth wrote, "ring again with the confusion of it all."

Elizabeth had expected to find in Venice "a dreary sort of desolation": instead she was charmed by its "soothing, lulling, rocking atmosphere."

Never had I touched the skirts of so celestial a place. The beauty of the architecture, the silver trails of water up between all that gorgeous colour and carving, the enchanting silence, the moonlight, the music, the gondolas—I mix it all up together, and maintain that nothing is like it, nothing equal to it.

They had planned at least a fortnight there, but "alas for these mortal Venices—so exquisite and so bilious!" Robert was soon in a nervous condition, unable to eat or sleep. Wilson was plagued with headaches and continual bouts of sickness. From Venice they must go.

In the meantime they "swam in gondolas," enjoyed the opera from a box on the ground floor (at two shillings and eight-pence), sat taking excellent coffee by moonlight in the great Piazza San Marco, and went out to Chioggia for a festa.

On leaving Venice they made a short stay at Padua, visiting Arqua, where Petrarch spent his declining years. "And didn't it move you," Elizabeth wrote to Kenyon, "the sight of that little room where the great soul exhaled itself? Even Robert's man's eyes had tears in them as we stood there, and looked through the window at the green-peaked hills."

They passed through Brescia at night, under a full moon, entering Milan in the morning. During their two days there Elizabeth excelled herself in those performances on her two feet of which Robert boasted, climbing three hundred and fifty stairs to the topmost pinnacle of the Cathedral. At Milan and other places passed through they visited the galleries. At Parma they saw the "sublime" Correggios, a memory of which lingered in Browning's mind, to be immortalized in that fine poem "A Face," written in 1852 after he had met Coventry Patmore's strangely beautiful wife.

> *I know, Correggio loves to mass, in rifts*
> *Of heaven, his angel faces, orb on orb*
> *Breaking its outline. . . .*

This poem Browning did not publish until 1864, after the death of both his wife and Emily Patmore. For herself, Elizabeth found Correggio's angel faces in very likeness of her own child.

Pausing at Como to enjoy the beauties of the Italian lakes, the Brownings crossed into Switzerland through the great St. Gotthard pass. Snow was unusually thick that year: a "passage through it, cut for the carriage, left the snow-walls nodding over us at a great height on each side." Although the cold was intense Elizabeth sat out for a while in the coupé so that she might have an unimpeded view. It was overwhelming, "like standing in the presence of God when He is terrible. . . . I think I never *saw* the sublime before."

Although they found Lucerne even more beautiful than the Italian lakes, there was no time to linger. They went on, traveling from Strasbourg to Paris in twenty-four hours. Their child, already an intrepid traveller, was in no way put out by the rapid motion. Little Wiedeman, a painter in the future, had indeed appeared to take delight in the beauties of their journey, both of nature and architectural. Paris, however, was to the town baby a supreme joy. His mother wrote to Kenyon:

Well, now we are in Paris and have to forget the "belle chiese": we have beautiful shops instead, false teeth grinning at the corners of the streets, and disreputable prints, and fascinating hats and caps, and brilliant restaurants, and M. le Président in a cocked hat and with a train of cavalry, passing like a rocket along the boulevards to an occasional yell from the Red. Oh yes, and don't mistake me! for I like it all extremely, it's a splendid city—a city in the country, as Venice is a city in the sea. And I'm as much amused as Wiedeman, who stands in the streets before the printshops (to Wilson's great discomfort) and roars at the lions.

This was the Paris of Daumier and Gavarni, a Paris in which luxury, the pursuit of pleasure, was daily increasing, to reach its zenith under the Second Empire: a Paris, for all its subcurrents of revolution, more self-confident than the defeated city Elizabeth had visited in 1815. Many of the mediæval streets had gone, with their fetid smells, to make way for the boulevards. To Elizabeth's eye, accustomed to the ancient close towns of Italy, the trees and gardens of this "city in the country" were a constant delight.

The great event of their month's stay was a meeting with Tennyson and his wife. So anxious was Elizabeth to make the acquaintance of this poetic hero of long standing that, although tired "half to death" by a visit to the Louvre, she rose from her sofa "in a decided state of resurrection" to take tea with him at a near-by hotel. She found Mrs. Tennyson "a very sweet person": her reaction to the poet is not specifically given, but one gathers that she was not disenchanted. Although Tennyson had only met Browning casually in London society, he went so far in friendliness now as to offer them—if it was not already let—his Twickenham home as a refuge while in England. This, according to Miss Mitford (though Elizabeth herself does not mention it) was countered by putting at his disposal their apartment in Casa Guidi, at present unoccupied.

To this momentous tea-drinking Robert induced his wife to go without a cap, claiming a promise extracted from her in Florence "after a revolutionary scene (besides various *emeutes*)." This cap was perhaps ampler than the black net she usually wore: Elizabeth's hair had apparently been cut, or greatly thinned, in illness. It was now as thick as ever.

They crossed the Channel at the end of July. Robert was eager to join his family, looking forward after a "five years' hunger" to talk with Carlyle; but much as Elizabeth longed to see her own people again, her thoughts of England must be full of bitterness, past and present. Even the physical circumstances of a return to her native land were unpropitious. She stepped ashore "into a puddle and a fog" and began to cough before reaching London. The weather was cold and windy.

They lodged at 26, Devonshire Street, Marylebone, living in three rooms which cost them £2 a week—precisely what they had paid for a luxuriously furnished seven-roomed apartment *au premier* in the most fashionable quarter. The advantage gained, however, was nearness to both Arabella and Mr. Kenyon.

Elizabeth had proposed to live the life of a hermit, only seeing her family, Kenyon, and a few old friends, but this proved impossible. The Brownings were "overwhelmed with kindnesses, crushed with gifts, like the Roman lady." The door bell was constantly ringing.

One of their first visits was to Carlyle. Elizabeth liked Carlyle "infinitely more in his personality" than she had expected; finding him "one of the most interesting men I could imagine even, deeply interesting to me. . . . All the bitterness is love with the point reversed." Mrs. Carlyle she could meet without any preconception: that fascinating woman soon became "a great favorite of mine: full of thought, and feeling, and character, it seems to me."

Miss Mitford came up to London for a week. "A strange thing," she wrote to a friend, "it was to see Miss Barrett walking about like other people." Miss Mitford was shocked in her English soul to hear people of her own race—Robert, Elizabeth, Wilson—talking in Italian to the Brownings' "pretty little boy." "I suppose next year they will all talk to him in French, and when English will take its turn, God knows."

However uneasy Elizabeth, for reasons both personal and political, might feel in this country of hers, reunion with her sisters was undiluted joy. Arabel she saw daily; Henrietta, with her first baby, stayed near her for a week or so. The brothers, though they do not appear to have been over-attentive, made their peace. A rather emotional reconciliation with George, the strongest character among them and bitterest against her marriage, brought Elizabeth great happiness.

Another attempt was made to reconcile her father, or at least to induce him to see his first grandson. Browning wrote him "a manly, true, straightforward letter," touching to Elizabeth, "generous and conciliating."

In reply he had a very violent and unsparing letter, with all the letters I had written to papa through these five years sent back unopened, the seals unbroken. *What went most to my heart was*

that some of the seals were black with black-edged envelopes;
so that he might have thought my child or husband dead, yet
never cared to solve the doubt by breaking the seal.

It must have deepened tragedy for this warped, innately affectionate man that he, who had lived in such intimacy with his
own children when young, was too stiff in fanatic pride to receive his own grandchild.

By the other grandfather, "the dear nonno," little Wiedeman
was instantly "taken into adoration." Personal contact with the
family at Hatcham, though strengthening a new and affectionate tie, must have brought pain to Elizabeth. The simple-
hearted devotion of his father was in poignant contrast to Mr.
Barrett's possessive passion for his children.

Elizabeth was far from well, so unwell that Robert contemplated a rapid return to Paris, but soon the weather improved.
Elizabeth was forced to take a much needed rest by an event
which, paradoxically, gave her little repose. Wilson left to
spend a fortnight's holiday with her mother in the north. At
first it had been arranged that the child should go with her, but
Elizabeth decided to keep him: the maid should have leisure
to enjoy a well-earned holiday. Wiedeman, suddenly bereft of
"Lilli," fearing desperately that his mother might also be
snatched away, clung to Elizabeth "like a little old man of the
mountain." As he craved constantly to be carried, to be in her
arms for comfort, it was perhaps fortunate that the heavy baby
had fined down into a small light-boned boy. To a woman unaccustomed even to care for her own person this was, though
it must bring to a mother compensatory joy, "a dreadful state
of slavery." Elizabeth learned to value more highly the ministrations of Wilson.

Elizabeth had been constantly urging Henrietta to live in
Paris, for both cheapness and pleasure: now, seeing at close
range her sister's happiness, making acquaintance with little
Altham, the baby son who might later be a companion for her
own boy, she exercised all her power of persuasion to extract
a promise that the Surtees Cooks would come to live near her
that winter. But there were ready arguments against the
scheme, such as expense and the danger of revolution in these
disturbed times.

On Wilson's return an accumulation of engagements "broke on" Elizabeth. "I had to go here and there in all directions, and see and write and talk till I was out of breath."

One engagement, though perhaps in the period before Wilson went north, was to dine with Mr. Kenyon. Elizabeth went to Devonshire Place alone. It was a fairly general rule with Kenyon not to invite husband and wife together (the Sydney Smiths were a notable exception) because he considered that they spoilt each other's conversation.

Mrs. Andrew Crosse, wife of the electrician who had been at school with Kenyon and the elder Browning, has given us an account of the dinner party at which Elizabeth was a guest of honour. Mrs. Crosse, who looked forward perhaps too eagerly to meeting a favourite poet, found herself disappointed. To her Mrs. Browning was "hard featured," "non-sympathetic," though her brow was "a noble soul-case" and her eyes "dark and penetrating." "The mouth was hard and immobile for any play of expression, while the lower jaw showed something of the strength of obstinacy."

She wore her hair in long ringlets, which, falling very much over her face, and when seen in profile, suggested the unpleasing idea of blinkers, that harshly cut across the graceful curves of brow and cheek. It was this style of arranging the hair that made Mrs. Browning look, not old fashioned—for that would have been a touch of sentiment—but strangely out of fashion. Her slight pretty figure was rather disguised than set off by garments that fell lopping round her; but thank Heaven! she was entirely and utterly free from the bad taste of the self-styled clever women, who acknowledge themselves to be failures, as women, by aping a masculine style of dress and address.

Mrs. Crosse thought Elizabeth showed "a proud aloofness of manner." This impression, in direct contradiction to that of others who met her, was perhaps on that particular occasion inevitable. Physically oppressed by the London air, modest, shy, unused to much society even in the healthy days of youth, Elizabeth found herself the lion of the party alone, torn apart from the man who for five years had been her constant companion, her other self; a man, too, accustomed to take the lead in conversation.

She seems to have cast something of a damp on the company: "there was a listening reticence in her attitude that did not help the playful tossing to and fro of talk." What remarks Elizabeth did throw into the conversation, however, were "weighed, measured, and full of sense and purpose."

Crabb Robinson, also present, though partly in agreement with Mrs. Crosse, found Elizabeth "very interesting and pleasing." Being a persistent talker himself, he appreciated a good listener.

But though these excursions into London society were a strain upon Elizabeth, she found a distinct fascination in the new environment, in "a great dazzling heap of things new and strange." Among Browning's older friends introduced to her was Forster, who gave a dinner party in Browning's honour at Thames Ditton "in sight of the swans," B. W. Procter, and Fanny Haworth, a gifted woman Browning had fervently admired in youth. Fanny Haworth became a friend in her own right, a correspondent: it was she who introduced Elizabeth to the works of Swedenborg, that visionary thinker who so influenced her latter years. Swedenborgian doctrines, mesmerism, spiritualism, those subjects which caught Elizabeth on her "weak side" of the "love of wonder," were all equally potent with this new acquaintance.

Of old friends, Mrs. Jameson, at work upon her *Legends of the Madonna,* was met with again; and Elizabeth had the pleasure of at last meeting in the flesh R. H. Horne, that former intimate correspondent.

One lion of London in this year, and the most popular, was not a man but a building, a portent: the Great Exhibition of 1851 housed under glass in Hyde Park, promoted by Prince Albert to foster commerce, the arts, and world peace. From far-off Florence Elizabeth had guessed at its materialism, its lack of real meaning in a troubled Europe.

> *O Magi of the east and of the west,*
> *Your incense, gold and myrrh are excellent!—*
> *What gifts for Christ, then, bring ye with the rest?*

she had written in *Casa Guidi Windows*, asking pertinently, did this palace of peace and plenty shed

> *No light*
> *Of teaching, liberal nations, for the poor*
>   *Who sit in darkness when it is not night?*
> *No cure for wicked children? Christ,—no cure!*
>   *No help for women sobbing out of sight*
>   *Because men made the laws?*

But these questionings, a realization of the hollowness of this temple of peace in a world of strife and oppression, surely did not prevent Elizabeth from a childlike enjoyment of its complicated splendours. That the highly original building, then in its first glitter of beauty, fascinated her is clear from a letter to Mrs. Jameson in which she asked:

But if the Crystal Palace vanishes from the face of the earth, who shall trust any more in castles? Will they really pull it down, do you think? If it's a bubble, it's a glass bubble, and not meant, therefore, for bursting in the air, it seems to me. And you do want a place in England for sculpture, and also to show people how olives grow. What a beautiful winter garden it would be!

Mrs. Jameson had a personal contact with the Exhibition, having drawn up a Guide to the Court of Modern Sculpture; she also had other and more vital contacts in London which had led her, herself an ill-used struggling woman, to speak openly, to work for the emancipation of women. In the lines quoted above: "No help for women sobbing out of sight because men made the laws," we have Elizabeth's own first protest, soon to be in *Aurora Leigh* a clarion call, against the oppression of women in law and society. At this time, and for many years after, a married woman was merged in her husband, having no legal right even to her own child and certainly not to her income, earned or unearned. It was generally thought a moral duty of woman to conceal from the world any suffering her husband might inflict on her; if she must weep, "sobbing out of sight." Elizabeth's innate feminism, an early critical attitude to marriage, a pity for those cringing women who put up a silent prayer at meal time that the chops might be well done, was given full play by Browning, a husband who so abhorred the exercise of power by one individual over another that, as has been said, it was the basis of a vivid and distressing night-mare. Any suggestion of submission to his will on Elizabeth's part hurt and excited him.

With this mutual concern for human freedom it is more than likely that the Brownings desired to meet, through Mrs. Jame-son, Barbara Leigh Smith, that intrepid young pioneer of wom-an's rights and cousin to Florence Nightingale. Better known now as Madame Bodichon, she was soon to make, with John Stuart Mill as willing instrument and mouthpiece, a first pro-test in the House of Commons against the power of a husband to confiscate his wife's earnings. Later we hear of Elizabeth collecting signatures for this petition in Paris.

One of their last evenings in London was spent with the poet Rogers, now nearly ninety and confined to his armchair as the result of an accident a year before. Elizabeth would infinitely have preferred to be with Arabel, since time was so short, but could not refuse a particular request to meet her from a man of Rogers's age. On "the last melancholy packing-up evening" she did have Arabel with her, and Treppy too.

The Brownings left London on September 25, driving from their lodgings, for a few moments poignant to Elizabeth, through Wimpole Street. There was now no hope of softening her father. The house itself she had found on her return to be, except for Arabel's own room, dismal in effect, the old familiar drawing-rooms appearing smaller, darker, with a general lack of comfort; "bachelor-looking" in appearance. The whole house needed a thorough cleansing.

At the station they met Carlyle, who, having been invited to join the Ashburtons in Paris, had not, helpless being as he was, known how to arrive there unaided. He put himself entirely into Browning's hands, sitting back to admire that energetic poet's capacity for dealing with porters, passports, and custom-houses. To both fellow-travellers, however, Carlyle made the journey wholly delightful "except the sea-part which was horrible"; rough, stormy, and lasting eight hours. All were sick including Elizabeth, who was considered a good sailor. "As to baby, he rather liked it, and rose in conscious dignity when he had used the basin." Flush, a victim too, was ordered off the deck. This is Elizabeth's first mention of Flush—at least in the letters available to me—during the whole three months of their travel; Flush, who, before the advent of a child, was constantly referred to on their journeyings.

Elizabeth set foot in France with a lighter heart in spite of seasickness:

Leaving love behind is always terrible, but it was not all love that I left, and there was relief in the state of mind with which I threw myself on the sofa at Dieppe—yes, indeed. Robert felt differently from me for once, as was natural, for it had been pure joy to him with his family and friends. . . . Oh England! I love and hate it at once. Or rather, where love of country ought to be in the heart, there is the mark of the burning iron in mine, and the depth of the scar shows the depth of the root of it.

"After all," she added, "I wasn't made to live in England, or I should not cough there perpetually." In the light, cleaner air of Paris the cough at once left her.

It would seem as if Kenyon either was in Paris, or expected there: "to please Mr. Kenyon and to be near his hotel" Browning looked for apartments near the Madeleine but, Paris being very full, sunny rooms in that quarter were both scarce and dear. He found at the suburban end of the Champs-Elysées an apartment on the second floor, "bathed in the sun and comfortably furnished, with a large Terrace and beautiful view upon the great avenue, and all for two hundred francs a month, about the same as they paid in London for "miserable accommodation" out of season.

True, the situation of 138, Champs-Elysées, now one of a row of busy shops, was then a retired one outside Paris itself, but opposite them was a stand for fiacres, any of which would carry them to the other end of Paris for half-a-crown including a generous tip. In addition there was a continual stream of omnibuses on which you could travel the same distance for six sous. In trying to persuade her sister to come over and settle in the same house Elizabeth mentioned these humble vehicles rather apologetically: Henrietta was always more fashionably inclined than herself. The cost of a journey from London to Paris, first class, was then twenty-two shillings.

Elizabeth had the delight of finding her Aunt Jane, the fa-vourite Uncle Hedley, and a cousin settled in the Faubourg St. Honoré. It was perhaps through Aunt Jane that an invitation came from Lady Elgin, which the Brownings gladly accepted, knowing that at her house they would meet many French ce-lebrities: Elizabeth was determined to make the best of the re-maining fine weather before winter shut her up again.

They found society in Paris delightfully informal and frugal, a cup of weak tea being the usual evening refreshment. "Lady Elgin was prodigal and gave us bread and butter." Soon they were visiting Madame Mohl, an Englishwoman reared in France whose *salon* was famous.

It was but natural that Henrietta should soon be asking her sister about Paris fashions. Elizabeth had bought a bonnet of drawn maroon satin trimmed with velvet and with purple flowers inside the brim; a bonnet approved even by the critical Robert. As she was imprudent enough to go to a fashionable milliner it cost her sixteen shillings. "Polkas" were the latest mode and basqued dresses a good deal worn. Wiedeman—whom now we may call by his more familiar name of Penini, his own attempt to pronounce this rather outlandish name—was wearing "trowsers" now, trousers to the knee and long white knitted gaiters. His costume was completed by a white felt hat, white satin ribbons, and feathers with a trimming of blue satin inside at each cheek. "It's a beautiful costume," Elizabeth assured her sister, "and he is much admired." Penini was soon chattering French to Désirée, the *femme de service*.

With an appetite whetted by a long study of Balzac's novels, Elizabeth perhaps expected more from French society than she found: men of letters, the writers and journalists "of all colours, from white to red," she thought much more interesting and amusing. Mazzini having, through the Carlyles, promised them a letter of introduction to George Sand, Elizabeth was now looking forward with excitement to a meeting with that remark-able and notorious woman of genius.

Paris, seething below the surface with political excitement, was bright with emotional colour. Troops passed down the Champs-Elysées every few days to be reviewed: it was ex-pected they would soon be bringing the President back with them as Emperor. Napoleon's popularity had enormously increased after the Assembly had defied him in May when he demanded the restoration of universal suffrage: so had a potential despot confused the real issue in the eyes of people only too ready, remembering old glory, to cry "*Vive l'Empereur!*" Elizabeth, for all her liberal leanings, was ready to echo that cry.

A personal gratification had been a laudatory article on Browning in the *Revue des Deux Mondes* for August, second in a series on English poetry since Byron, by Joseph Milsand, soon to become a close friend. After the mixed reception of Browning's work in his own country this understanding appreciation by a Frenchman was particularly gratifying to both husband and wife; and especially, one may guess, to Elizabeth, who from the first had, in spite of the popular suffrage, been under no illusion as to which was the greater poet.

In October they had the pleasure of a three weeks' visit from Browning's father and sister. Perhaps the elder Browning had already decided to make a future home in Paris. "They are an affectionate family," Elizabeth told Miss Mitford, "and not easy when removed one from another." Sarianna she admired for her cleverness, sense, and even temper: "devoted to her father as she was to her mother: indeed, the relations of life seem reversed in their case, and the father appears the child of the child."

By December 1 an intense and abnormal cold had shut Elizabeth up in their rooms. The cough returned and she lost flesh, but the lighter air of Paris secured her from actual illness. The warmth of a French apartment, with its lack of draughty passages and staircases, was a comfort. Paris was still a delight to her, but one can detect a certain yearning for Florence. "I love Italy, and like Paris—there's the difference."

She would not permit Robert to immure himself with her: he must visit Lady Elgin, Madame Mohl, and others, in a lively social intercourse "which really is good for him, with his temperament." Browning, the widower in London, the inveterate diner-out, was no new Browning but an intensification in loneliness of the old.

Elizabeth herself received but little. One evening when Lady Elgin and Madame Mohl were both present, she enjoyed "a great long talk about Shelley and the poets generally." Shelley was now a familiar topic in this household. Moxon was bringing out an edition of "Shelley" letters which proved to be forgeries by George Byron and were withdrawn; but not before the completion by Browning of a fine preface, both a contribution to literature and a pronouncement of his own poetic faith.

On December 2 Louis Napoleon executed his *coup d'état,* promulgating a sham constitution that enormously pleased the majority of Parisians, so they were willing to overlook the illegality of his action and the breaking of that solemn oath to the French Republic he had taken on being elected President. Elizabeth, though not yet so whole-heartedly for the future Emperor of the French as she was later to be, exonerated him on the score of expediency:

The situation was in a deadlock, and all the conflicting parties were full of dangerous hope of taking advantage of it; and I don't see, for my part, what better could be done for the French nation than to sweep the board clear and bid them begin again. . . . He [Napoleon] has broken, certainly, the husk of an oath, but fidelity to the intention of it seems to me reconcilable with the breach; and if he had not felt that he had the great mass of the people to back him, he is at least too able a man, be certain, if not too honest a man, to have dared what he has dared.

But in France there can be no political change without bloodshed. The army, that more tangible backing to a new power, had to kill citizens and disfigure buildings with cannon shot. Elizabeth, too excited to go to bed, sat up until one o'clock listening to the sound of firing.

To his elders the thought of "Frenchman against Frenchman" must bring pain, but to little Penini all was pure joy. On the fatal second day of December he had watched the entrance of troops into Paris, screaming and shouting with delight. Elizabeth wrote to her sister:

the military music and the shouting of the people, as the president rode under our windows, the manœuvring of the splendid cavalry, the white horses, glittering helmets, all the "pomp and circumstance," might well move older children than our babe. Though the author of the *coup d'état* rode in their midst, Elizabeth would not admit this parade of soldiers to be a symbol of military despotism. Was not the French army, she wrote to Mrs. Martin, "eminently *civic,* flesh of the people's flesh? . . . Every man is a citizen, and every citizen is or has been a soldier."

Repressive measures there must be in a state of emergency but, she urged, "grant the righteousness of the movement, and you must accept its conditions." Elizabeth in 1851 could not know the full danger of this plea, this unrighteous cloak of a rebel strong enough to impose his will on a nation.

Robert, though he did not reveal until long after Elizabeth's death his full hatred of Louis Napoleon and all he stood for, held his own in domestic argument, but he too was a little dazzled; confessing to his wife that "the excessive and contradictory nonsense he had heard among Legitimists, Orleanists and *English*" against the movement inclined him almost to a revulsion of feeling. As the President rode under their windows that 2nd of December "through a shout extending from the Carrousel to the Arc de l'Etoile," even his keen mind might well have been deluded into thinking this was a popular movement.

The disturbances in Paris, magnified as they so often are in foreign presses as bloody revolutions, effectively frightened the Surtees Cooks into a definite and final decision not to come to Paris. This disappointment to Elizabeth was followed by the minor one of missing her literary heroine, George Sand, during a short, private visit to the capital.

There followed on the *coup d'état* a period of material prosperity. Trade increased. In January the sun shone and festivities of the first of the year filled the city with fairs and fine things to buy. Penini was all the more charmed with Paris, "its magnificent Punches, and roundabouts, and balloons." Unconsciously expressing his mother's attitude of mind, one day he shouted "Viva Peone" (Napoleone) in at the President's carriage window.

In the middle of January the clumsy but well-meant action of one of Elizabeth's dearest friends brought her infinite pain: Miss Mitford's *Recollections of a Literary Life,* out at last, contained a long detailed passage revealing the loss of Bro. Miss Mitford, with her sturdy common sense and a certain lack of perception, had considered that grief must now be softened after a lapse of eleven years; that a woman so domestically happy could not be unduly distressed by this revelation, private though it might be. "Now," wrote Elizabeth in great distress to Mrs. Martin, "I shall be liable to see recollections dreadful to me, thrust into every vulgar notice of my books." Indeed, the *Athenæum* had already repeated the story in a long extract.

Elizabeth's letter on the subject to Miss Mitford was tender, generous, and forgiving, but did not disguise her pain. The *Athenæum* extract she could not herself read, but Robert had assured her that the facts "could not possibly be given with greater delicacy. . . . And I will add for myself, that for them to be related by anyone during my life, I would rather have *you* to relate them than another." But even so she was badly hurt. "See what a deep wound I must have in me, to be pained by the touch of such a hand."

George Sand was now making one of her infrequent returns to Paris: the letter of introduction from Mazzini having arrived, means had to be found of conveying it. They were told that Madame Sand never received strangers, that she was only in Paris for a few days "and under a new name to escape the plague of notoriety." Browning himself did not show much energy in trying to deliver the letter; seeming inclined rather to "sit in his chair and be proud a little." Nor did he approve of his wife, a woman of utter purity, coming in contact with George Sand, the freedom of whose life was common knowledge.

Mazzini's introduction was at length sent under cover of a personal note signed by both, passed mysteriously by a friend to a friend who knew where Madame Sand was concealing herself. There was an immediate reply with an invitation for the following Sunday night. Elizabeth, though this was February, determined to muffle herself up, head and all, proceeding to 3, Rue Racine in a closed carriage and armed with a respirator.

She approached her literary lioness with a beating heart, stooped, and kissed her hand. George Sand raised her quickly with a *"Mais non, je ne veux pas,"* and kissed Elizabeth on the lips. Every detail of the famous writer's appearance was noted and reported to that lover of celebrities John Kenyon. Her rather disdainful manner, "a scorn of pleasing," at first repelled Elizabeth. "But I liked her. I did not love her, but I felt the burning soul through all that quietness, and was not disappointed in George Sand."

They found her sitting in a circle of eight or nine young men, giving them directions and quiet advice; obviously "*the man* in that company." During the three-quarters of an hour the Brownings spent with her, there was little conversation. Madame Sand sat "at a corner of the fire, and warming her feet quietly, in a general silence of the most profound deference." Browning was impressed in spite of himself, saying afterwards: "If any other mistress of a house had behaved so, I would have walked out of the room." But this was George Sand. At parting she gave them, after a little indirect prompting from Elizabeth, an invitation to come again next Sunday.

To Mrs. Martin, Elizabeth commented freely on French characteristics, the love of pure ideas, and of the socialists, so strong in Paris:

I quite agree with you that various of them, yes, and some of their chief men, are full of pure and noble aspiration, the most virtuous of men and the most benevolent. Still, they hold in their hands, in their clean hands, ideas that kill, ideas which defile, ideas which, if carried out, would be the worst and most crushing kind of despotism. I would rather live under the feet of the Czar than in those states of perfectibility imagined by Fourier and Cabet, if I might choose my "pis aller."

A hundred years have not yet fully brought home to mankind this dreadful truth.

At this time the Brownings were worried about Penini, now nearly three years old: the child was too excitable, too intense. Lately he had "been attacked at night with a sort of slight hysterical seizure . . involuntary laughter & spasmodic thrills through the frame." [1] Though his parents professed to do all they could to keep him back, Penini was for ever "drawing, writing, singing, dancing." It was perhaps this early drain on vitality, living with such gifted, vivacious parents, travelling, speaking three languages, that helped to make Pen Browning the indolent man he undoubtedly was in middle life; a man who wasted a decided talent as a painter.

---

[1] Unpublished letter to Fanny Dowglass, March 5, 1852, Huntington Library Collection.

A second visit to George Sand brought to Browning an increased disgust, but to Elizabeth a lively sense of pity:

She seems to live in the abomination of desolation, as far as regards society—crowds of ill-bred men who adore her à genoux bas, *betwixt a puff of smoke and an ejection of saliva. Society of the ragged Red diluted with the lower theatrical. She herself so different, so apart, as alone in her melancholy disdain! I was deeply interested in that poor woman, I felt a profound compassion for her.*

They were both well aware that, for all her protestations, Madame Sand had no real interest in them. "Perhaps she doesn't care for anybody by this time—who knows? . . . we always felt that we couldn't penetrate—couldn't really *touch* her—it was all in vain."

By the second week in April Elizabeth was able to walk about with her husband enjoying the sunshine, the beauty of Paris, "the sentiment of southern life" as she watched men, women, and children, all classes mixing as in Italy, sitting out of doors enjoying their coffee or wine. She went to the Vaudeville to see *La Dame aux Camélias* and found it not immoral, but moral and human; moving her to the point of distress. Even Robert, "who gives himself out for *blasé* on dramatic matters," shed some tears.

In May Elizabeth caught cold, a cold that led unhappily to "*an attack* after the ancient fashion," considerably weakening her, but by mid-June all that remained, in beautiful summer weather, was a slight cough. That month Mrs. Jameson came to stay with them, perhaps to enjoy a well-earned rest: not only did her *Legends of the Madonna* come out that year but also an early travel book in second edition and heavily revised. Mrs. Jameson never really liked Paris, and took none of Elizabeth's eager interest in what she termed "vile French politics." Her social interests were more general: within the circle about Lady Byron Mrs. Jameson was becoming more and more active in the advocacy of legal and social reform to benefit women and children.

By July 23 the Brownings were in England again, this time in more comfortable rooms at a moderate price, in Welbeck Street. Henrietta was in London too, staying some twenty doors off.

The one drawback at 58, Welbeck Street was a screaming baby in the house.

There was a notable encounter this year with Giuseppe Mazzini, whom his friend Mrs. Carlyle brought to visit them. Mazzini, now working on behalf of his country's freedom as president of the National Italian Committee in London, made a profound impression "with that pale spiritual face of his, and those intense eyes full of melancholy illusions." Telling Miss Mitford of the meeting Elizabeth added:

I was thinking, while he sate there, on what Italian turf he would lie at last with a bullet in his heart, or perhaps with a knife in his back, for to one of those ends it will surely come.

At this time Mazzini had not only Austrian antagonists: he was under sentence of death pronounced in 1833 by Italy's only Italian ruler, the King of Sardinia, for having stirred up active revolution within the Sardinian army.

Mrs. Carlyle, who, though she had a strong affection for Mazzini, knew as a close friend his whims and oddities, commented tartly on the occasion: "Oh, such a fuss the Brownings made over Mazzini the other day! My private opinion of Browning is, in spite of Mr. C.'s favour for him, that he is 'nothing,' or very little more 'but a fluff of feathers!' *She* is *true* and *good,* and the most *womanly* creature." Elizabeth wrote to Miss Mitford of Jane Carlyle: "She is a great favorite of mine: full of thought, and feeling, and character, it seems to me." How valuable, how entertaining a correspondence we might have had between these two fine letter-writers; but Mrs. Carlyle's antipathy for Browning, which increased when they met again that summer, touched his wife also. In September Mrs. Carlyle declared to her husband "even she does not grow on me."

Again the Brownings had a multiplicity of engagements, engagements that kept them tied to London; though they did manage a visit to Farnham and an encounter with Charles Kingsley. On Elizabeth, though she might disapprove his theories, Kingsley made a strong impression as a man of pure ideals and good heart. Later she met another friend of Miss Mitford's, young Mr. Ruskin, whom the Brownings soon counted as "among the valuable acquaintances made this year in England." The inevitable Father Prout was in London and found them out in Welbeck Street.

By the middle of September chilly days were already warning Elizabeth that she must take care: "the horrible climate is beginning to put out its gripes." She was again cherishing a plan to winter in Rome.

Business, however, unpleasant business, detained Browning in London. A "strange and calamitous visitation," evidently some form of blackmail, was cruelly disturbing his father's quiet scholarly life. By the middle of January 1853 the elder Browning was driven into retiring from the bank, accepting a two-thirds pension, and exiling himself in Paris. There he settled down to reading at the Library, book-hunting, drawing at the Louvre, and, said his son, " 'shaping his old course in a country new,' like Lear's Kent."

Browning, having done what he could for the moment to help his father, determined to take Elizabeth away from London cold and fog on October 5, but the journey was again delayed and this time by a pleasanter cause: Tennyson wanted the Brownings to be present at the christening of his son Hallam. Elizabeth accepted the invitations for both with pleasure, but perhaps it was fortunate that she was unable to go. Tennyson was reported by Robert as "talking vehemently against the French President and the French."

On September 28 another child, the niece Elizabeth had predicted, was born to Henrietta. "Since she is yours," Elizabeth wrote, "I won't covet her—and you must accept that abnegation as a proof of love." The child, christened Mary, survived until June 7, 1951, to the end taking an interest in her famous aunt, though she barely remembered her.

In mid-October the Brownings left London at six in the morning for Paris, where they stayed for a while in the Rue de la Ville-l'Evêque. Elizabeth's cough persisted: it was soon evident that she could not pass a winter there this year. By November they had decided to return to Florence.

While in Paris Elizabeth was able to indulge Napoleonic fervour by being present on a boulevard balcony as, under a bright sun, Louis Napoleon, now the future Emperor, swept by with "all military and civil pomp" amid a crowd of admirers. On the balcony with them was the American actress Charlotte Cushman, who, although disapproving of Louis Napoleon, was startled into exclaiming: "That's fine, I must say!" when "Napoleon showed his usual tact and courage by riding on horseback quite alone, at least ten paces between himself and his nearest escort, which of course had a striking effect, taking the French on their weak side." Penini "in a state of ecstasy" called out: *"Vive Napoleon!"* and boasted that the hero took off his hat to him.

CHAPTER 25

BACK IN FLORENCE: BAGNI DI LUCCA; ROME [1852–4]

ELIZABETH did not reach home without mishap: wanting to take the shortest route, the Brownings crossed by the Mont Cenis pass, where the cold was extreme. At Genoa she was unwell "to the extent of almost losing heart and hope," but exquisite weather, warm as June, restored her. At the end of a week she was able to spend two days in sightseeing, she told Kenyon:

my "unconquerable mind" even carried me halfway up the lighthouse for the sake of the "view," only there I had to stop ingloriously, and let Robert finish the course alone while I rested on a bench: aspiration is not everything, either in literature or lighthouses, you know. . . .

In Florence they found the people crushed, demoralized: "trodden flat in the dust of the vineyards by these mules of Austria,[1] and these asses of the Papacy."

Although she regretted having to leave Paris, and at a time of political excitement, Elizabeth was pleased to find herself at home, "everything looking exactly as if we had left it yesterday." Robert, however, found Florence "all as dull as possible" after the palpitating life of the Parisian boulevards. Admitting herself that the beloved city was dead by comparison, Elizabeth added: "but it's a beautiful death, and what with the lovely climate, and the lovely associations, and the sense of repose, I could turn myself on my pillow and sleep on here to the end of my life; only be sure that I *shall do no such thing.*"

Browning's early restlessness soon left him: they subsided happily into their "former soundless, stirless hermit life" with a few visitors dropping in for tea and talk. One resident in Florence, Frederick Tennyson, a poet obscured by his younger brother, was a particular favourite with both and became a close friend of Robert. In November Elizabeth had the pleasure of meeting a cousin, Robin Hedley, and his bride: it was

[1] For a small human sidelight on the Austrian occupation see Appendix 2.

probably he who introduced into Casa Guidi a Miss Jane Wills Sandford, a woman of means who placed no undue value on money. With Miss Sandford Elizabeth fell "into a sudden intimacy."

One interesting new acquaintance was Robert Lytton, son of Edward Bulwer Lytton and himself a poet known as "Owen Meredith." Young Lytton shared to the full Elizabeth's interest in the supernatural. Powers, the sculptor, an older friend, had also by this time "made up his mind . . . upon the truth of the American rapping spirits." Elizabeth's own attitude to spiritualism is defined in a letter to Isa Blagden of March 1853:

Profane or not, I am resolved on getting as near to a solution of the spirit question as I can, and I don't believe in the least risk of profanity, seeing that whatever is, must be permitted; and that the contemplation of whatever is, must be permitted also, where the intentions are pure and reverent. I can discern no more danger in psychology than in mineralogy, only intensely a greater interest. As to the spirits, I care less about what they are capable of communicating, than of the fact of their being communications. . . . They seem abundantly foolish, one must admit. There is probably, however, a mixture of good spirits and bad, foolish and wise, of the lower orders, perhaps in both kinds. . . .

A winter was spent indoors revising for the third edition of her collected poems, and at work upon a new one; "meditating Socialism and mysticism of very various kinds," reading French novels, and eagerly listening to accounts of "my rapping spirits, of whom our American guests bring us relays of witnesses."

Among American guests was George Perkins Marsh, American Minister at Constantinople, in Florence because of a change in Presidency. Hearing that Mrs. Marsh, although an invalid and almost blind, had travelled to Jerusalem—even being carried to the top of Mount Horeb—there was a revival of that old dream of visiting the Holy Land. But it could be but a dream: even an invitation from their new friends to visit Constantinople as their guests had to be refused that year. No money was to be expected from their books for a while: until the new edition was ready Elizabeth's collected poems were out of print. *Casa Guidi Windows* had proved less popular than former works.

The winter was warm: Elizabeth was so well, busy, and happy that spring surprised her almost with regret at having to emerge from retirement. Two subjects of great interest at this moment were the French situation and a new attack on the American institution of slavery.

Elizabeth's admiration for Louis Napoleon—though still with some qualification—was rapidly growing. That astute man, elected Emperor by plebiscite in the previous November, had sealed his popularity by marriage with a beautiful girl, Eugénie de Montijo, Countess of Téba. Elizabeth "as a democrat to the bone" could still see the danger of despotism in a continued censorship of the press, but felt convinced that it was but a temporary measure. This optimism proved false: later, because of Louis Napoleon's need for Church support, severe censorship was extended to books, involving, as we know, a public prosecution of the author of *Madame Bovary.*

The new attack on slavery came in fictional form with *Uncle Tom's Cabin,* the instant and immense popularity of which soon spead from America across Europe. Rather surprisingly Mrs. Jameson appears to have shown some disapproval of its author, Harriet Beecher Stowe, and her choice of subject. Elizabeth protested:

Oh, and is it possible that you think a woman has no business with questions like the question of slavery? Then she had better use a pen no more. She had better subside into slavery and concubinage herself, I think, as in the times of old, shut herself up with the Penelopes in the "women's apartment," and take no rank among thinkers and speakers. Certainly you are not in earnest in these things. A difficult question—yes! All virtue is difficult. England found it difficult. France found it difficult. But we did not make ourselves an arm-chair of our sins. As for America, I honor America in much; but I would not be an American for the world while she wears that shameful scar upon her brow.

Penini, now four years old, was beginning to have his social successes; and Elizabeth wrote to his Aunt Henrietta: "Penini is extremely fond of society, you must understand." Robert, having more good sense in the matter than the adoring mother, would not allow Elizabeth to take the child with them on morning visits, but Elizabeth was not inclined to acquiesce in this decision, writing to her sisters:

See if I won't have my own way and work my vanity into light just as I please. Penini, too, who is just made to be carried about and shown off, with his long purple feather shaking over his trailing golden ringlets, and the small black silk jacket I have just finished embroidering for him! He does look like a fairy king of a child—and is intended to be looked at accordingly.

This feminine garb for a small boy was by no means unpermissible in the middle of the last century, though Elizabeth in her fondness (and perhaps subconsciously from a frustrated desire for a girl child) kept up this custom rather beyond the usual age, decking Penini in feathers, velvet, and embroidery up to the time of her death in 1861. It seems unlikely that the virile Browning approved: indeed, in less than a month after her death Browning reported to his sister that "the golden curls and fantastic dress, is gone just as Ba is gone: he has short hair, worn boy-wise, long trousers, is a common boy all at once"; alleging the difficulty of keeping Pen in his old garb without the assistance of a maid.

Penini would insist on being dressed up in the evening in a hope that he could keep awake long enough to help receive his mother's visitors; visitors who increased in number as the spring advanced. There was a greater influx of Americans, "a sort of fluent society," Elizabeth told her sister, "which comes and passes."

These Americans stimulated an interest in "table-tapping," which, in the spring of 1853, became a veritable rage in Florence. "When people gather round a table it isn't to play whist." Robert remained obstinately a sceptic as Elizabeth's faith in spiritualism grew, though even he was forced to admit that some evidence appeared valid; as when several clairvoyants, unknown to one another, predicted an accident to Robert Lytton's father.

In July the Brownings retired again to La Villa, Bagni di Lucca, taking Casa Tolomei, a pleasant house with a *specola* facing the village green and embowered in trees. For the next three months they worked hard to earn their holiday and perhaps a winter in Rome.

Elizabeth carried with her to Lucca a particularly happy memory, which is best told in her own words:

The evening before our last at Florence, we had tea and straw-berries on the terrace of Mr. Lytton's villa, on the heights of Bellosguardo; meeting there our friends, Mr. Powers and Mr. Tennyson. It was a bachelor's party, and I made tea like a bachelor, in an awkward way I believe, but nobody minded it between the fireflies and the stars, and Florence dissolving in the valley beneath us in that seething, purple light which had run down from the hills. Seldom have I enjoyed anything so much.[2]

This passage we may perhaps link up with one in that book on which Elizabeth was at work, *Aurora Leigh*. She described the seething purple light filling up the valley below, flooding the city; and, as the darkness deepens:

> *The duomo-bell*
> *Strikes ten, as if it struck ten fathoms down,*
> *So deep; and twenty churches answer it*
> *The same, with twenty various instances.*
> *Some gaslights tremble along squares and streets;*
> *The Pitti's palace front is drawn in fire.*

But here, deep in the mountains, were few lights beyond the village except those of

> *fireflies, that suspire*
> *In short soft lapses of transported flame*
> *Across the tingling Dark, while overhead*
> *The constant and inviolable stars*
> *Outburn those light-of-love:*

The large solitude these two claimed for work at Lucca was soon interrupted, pleasantly interrupted by the advent of Mr. and Mrs. Story, with whom a friendship had been prosperously begun in 1848. The Storys, staying at the Bagni Caldi, took them by surprise one day. Up to their house higher in the mountain Elizabeth would go on donkey-back, Robert holding the reins, "to tea-drinking and gossiping." The Storys had two children, Edith, nine years of age, and Joe, six. With Edith little Pen soon fell in childish love. Later he was to take lessons with her from an Italian tutor.

[2] Unpublished letter, July 19, 1853, from the Marsh papers in the Library of the University of Vermont.

Through the Storys the Brownings came to visit others, to join in "omnivorous teas—of hams and tarts and fruits and cakes, and coffee etc." With their American friends they rode, drove, walked, and took meals in the open.

For a fortnight Robert Lytton stayed with them at Casa Tolomei. While he was there Elizabeth wrote a poetical tribute to him so adulatory in tone that it is difficult to accept it as from a famous woman to a young man, however promising he might be as poet and seer. She called him "our leader and king of us all," declaring "There is none we can honor above you," and "We'd die for you gladly, if need be":

> *All that strength! all that power! yet so pliant!*
> *You're so great we could never come near you,*
> *Were it not that the child with the giant*
> *Is mixed—and we honor—not fear you.*

One can only suppose—if, indeed, this piece was meant to be taken seriously—that Lytton's youthful charm, his curly hair, intensely blue eyes, combined with an active interest in spiritualism to blur true vision. In later years Browning himself showed a strong dislike for Lytton and it was not long before Elizabeth was to disagree with the young diplomat on a question of Austrian power politics. Also it seems likely that there was some sort of love affair between Lytton and Isa Blagden in which the Brownings considered that he had not behaved well: certainly while in Florence Lytton was suffering from an attachment he felt to be hopeless. For a young diplomat, one destined eventually to become Viceroy of India, union with a Eurasian (if so Isa Blagden was) would have been impossible. Isa too was some ten years older than he.

But, however it might be in the future, Lytton was now a highly valued companion, with his "wit that walks forth silver-shod," his smile like "a rainbow that arches the deeps."

One day he accompanied them, with the Storys, on a long expedition to the Prato Fiorito. They went, led by guides, on horse- or donkey-back. "It was like going up and down a wall, without the smoothness." On their return all were tired out, though Robert refused to admit his fatigue. No wonder Elizabeth "could not stir for days after." But, she added with spirit to Mrs. Martin, "who wouldn't see heaven and die? Such a vision of divine scenery . . ." The Italian countryside that July was, we learn from a letter of Browning's to Allingham, peculiarly beautiful, vivid in colour, after a mild winter and heavy rains in spring.

There was one alarming incident which is best told in Elizabeth's own words:

The other day we were walking, and I, attracted by a picturesque sort of ladder-bridge of loose planks thrown across the river, ventured on it, without thinking of venturing. Robert held my hand. When we were in the middle the bridge swayed, rocked backwards and forwards, and it was difficult for either of us to keep footing. A gallant colonel who was following us went down upon his hands and knees and crept. In the meantime a peasant was assuring our admiring friends that the river was deep at that spot, and that four persons had been lost from the bridge. I was so sick with fright that I could scarcely stand when all was over, never having contemplated an heroic act. "Why, what a courageous creature you are!" said our friends. So reputations are made. . . .

When October came, with broken weather, the Brownings were glad at last to leave their mountain paradise. "This poor place," Robert wrote to Story, who had preceded them to Florence, "has given up the ghost now."

From Casa Guidi we have in a letter to Thomas Westwood one of Elizabeth's acute criticisms, this time of Coventry Patmore's early work. She found him defective "in the intellectual part of poetry."

His images are flowers thrown to him by the gods, beautiful and fragrant, but having no root either in Enna or Olympus. There's no unity and holding together, no reality properly so called, no thinking of any kind.

In this letter we find her recommending *Villette* as a "strong book."

That autumn the visit to Rome, so long desired, so often delayed, seemed at last possible: after a few weeks in Florence they set out on November 12, being eight days on the road, pausing at Assisi and having a vision of the Torni fall, "that passion of the waters which makes the heart seem so still." Excited, exalted, they entered Rome in the highest spirits, "Robert and Penini singing actually; for the child was radiant and flushed with the continual change of air and scene."

It was in the dusk they entered: at their apartment, 43, Bocca di Leone, they found "lighted fires and lamps as if coming home" and the smiling faces of friends, the Storys, who had prepared this welcome.

Happiness, however, was delusory, short-lived: in Elizabeth's own words, their "first step into Rome was a fall, not into a catacomb but a fresh grave."

The next morning, their first in Rome, had begun badly with a distinct shock for Elizabeth. Browning, who had woken in a state of bilious irritability, probably from over-exposure to the sun on their journey,

in a fit of suicidal impatience shaved away his whole beard, whiskers and all! I cried when I saw him, I was so horror-struck. I might have gone into hysterics and still been reasonable; for no human being was ever so disfigured by so simple an act. Of course I said when I recovered breath and voice, that everything was at an end between him and me if he didn't let it grow again directly.

As a "just punishment of the gods" Robert's beard grew, not the old full rich black, but grey; though Elizabeth thought "the argentine touch" becoming enough.

That morning, begun so inauspiciously, ended in anxiety and grief: a servant came from the Storys' apartment bringing little Edith to them. Her brother had been taken with convulsions. The Brownings hurried to their friends. Their first day in Rome was spent by a deathbed: that evening the boy died of gastric fever.

While they were away Edith Story had been taken ill: because space was wanting in the apartment she was taken down to another below, where Page, the American artist, another friend of Story's, lived. To add to horror and confusion, the Storys' nurse was taken seriously ill of the same fever, and soon Page's youngest daughter sickened.

Elizabeth, distraught with sympathy and shock, was in deadly fear for her own loved ones, although the physicians, among them the great Roman doctor Panteleoni, assured her that there was no danger through contagion. Though the other patients soon recovered, it was January before Edith was well again, a feverish ague following on the original gastric trouble.

Elizabeth's first drive out in the city she had so longed to visit was with Mrs. Story to the Protestant Cemetery,

where poor little Joe is laid close to Shelley's heart (Cor cordium, *says the epitaph), and where the mother insisted on going. . . . I am horribly weak about such things. I can't look on the earth-side of death; I flinch from corpses and graves, and never meet a common funeral without a sort of horror. When I look deathwards I look over death, and upwards, or I can't look that way at all. So that it was a struggle with me to sit upright in that carriage in which the poor stricken mother sat so calmly —not to drop from the seat, which would have been worse than absurd of me.*

Well, all this has blackened Rome to me. I can't think about the Cæsars in the old strain of thought; the antique words get muddled and blurred with warm dashes of modern every-day tears and fresh grave-clay.

It is possible that, whether she realized it or no, Rome was blackened for her by another aspect of that ancient city: travellers tell us that even when Tuscany was most oppressed under Austrian grand-ducal rule, a crossing over the frontier into the Papal States revealed oppression, social conditions far worse. As one put it in a *Cornhill* article (December 1860): "With quiet, almost stealthy pace, downcast look, and submissive bearing, the native Roman creeps noiselessly along the thoroughfares of his city; his gait and appearance harmonize in sad sort with the death-stricken aspect of the morally and physically dilapidated world around him." French soldiers in occupation were the only cheerful bustling people.

By the end of December Elizabeth's naturally good spirits were beginning to rise again. The invalids were convalescent and there were many visitors in the Bocca di Leone. Rome suited her: their rooms, high up in the building, were flooded with sun even in that narrow street. On Christmas morning she attended mass at St. Peter's, with an excellent view of "pope and cardinals and all"; giving herself without reserve to the beauty of service, music, and the "sight of the crowding multitudes."

Among new friends in Rome were the fascinating Mrs. Sartoris, formerly the singer Adelaide Kemble, and her more famous sister Fanny, a woman of fine intellect and majestic mien; one of those who had suffered in a miserable marriage by the law as it then stood. Staying with Mrs. Sartoris was that ancient enemy of romantic poets John Lockhart, now old and ill, near to death. Lockhart liked Browning; declaring that he wasn't in the least like "a damned literary man." And, Elizabeth told Miss Mitford, "if anybody wants small-talk by handfuls of glittering dust swept out of salons, here's Mr. Thackeray besides."

Although there was never complete ease between Elizabeth and Thackeray, they had one interest in common. Lady Ritchie has given us a picture of the two talking of spiritualism, Mrs. Browning very small, very brown, quiet, smiling, with a manner full of charm and kindness, and dressed in soft-falling flounces of black silk, a thin gold chain about her neck. Thackeray's huge bulk loomed over the dark head with its heavy curls dropping about an eager face. As they talked Browning would interrupt in his loud resonant voice, sweeping away arguments. His wife would protest, "her own weak voice in a faint minor chord, slightly lisping, 'Robert!'"

Lady Ritchie, then Annie Thackeray, would often be invited with her sister to spend an evening with Mrs. Browning while Browning and her father were out visiting: Annie conceived a profound admiration for Elizabeth, recording in her diary: "I think Mrs. Browning the greatest woman I ever knew in my life."

At a children's party given by Thackeray he drew for his fortunate little guests pictures to illustrate *The Rose and the Ring*. By the bedside of Edith Story, now slowly recovering, he would sit, soft-hearted man as he was under a crust of worldliness, reading to her from the manuscript of that book which was soon to delight in print children of many generations.

Isa Blagden was in Rome that spring, staying at 28, Corso: in the apartment above was what Story flippantly termed a "harem (scarem)" of young American women, "emancipated," artists and writers. Through them and Isa, Elizabeth came to know Hatty Hosmer, a young sculptress of great promise who lived alone, dined and breakfasted "at the *cafés* precisely as a young man would," worked at her art from morning till night "and this with an absence of pretension and simplicity of manners which accord rather with the childish dimples in her rosy cheeks than with her broad forehead and high aims." The diminutive, merry, gallant little creature became "a great pet" of the Brownings. Hatty Hosmer was the more welcome to Elizabeth because she was a visionary and a writing medium.

In March Elizabeth wrote to Sarianna: "I don't like Rome, I never shall; and as they have put it in the English newspapers that I don't, I might as well acknowledge the barbarism." One aspect, however, of Roman society which pleased her was Penini's undoubted social success. Her son was "generally acknowledged as the king of the children here." Mrs. Page, of the apartment below, gave a party, perhaps on his birthday, in Penini's honour. The self-possessed, precocious child would even talk on equal terms with that queen of tragedy Mrs. Kemble, who, his mother said, " 'dashes' most people."

Elizabeth's dislike for Rome was soon deepened by a loss of colour and vitality in her child, who was affected, in the increasing warmth of spring, by the climate of a city pervaded by miasma from the Campagna marshes, which had perhaps brought Joe Story to untimely death. It was with relief that she left for home on May 22, intending to stay there a few weeks and then set off for England.

England, and particularly London, had lately been present to Elizabeth under its grimmest aspect: she had written, for sale at a bazaar in aid of Arabel's particular work, "A Plea for the Ragged Schools of London." The "Plea" is not imbued with the direct passion of "The Cry of the Children," but its best verses are affecting enough to those who know from harrowing research the plight of many homeless waifs in Victorian England:

> *Ragged children, hungry-eyed,*
> *Huddled up out of the coldness*
> *On our doorsteps, side by side,*
> *Till your footman damns their boldness.*

To this Browning added his singular and attractive piece "The Twins" (Date and Dabitur): the two were sold on a leaflet for sixpence.

One of their first evenings in Florence was spent like the last, at Lytton's villa on Bellosguardo:

We walked home to the song of nightingales by starlight and firefly light. Florence looks to us more beautiful than ever after Rome. I love the very stones of it, to say nothing of the cypresses and river.

Hampered by lack of money, they lingered on in Florence: it soon became evident that there could be no visit to England, or even to Paris, this summer. The ship shares were yielding no income, but loss. By June the Brownings had only £100 to cover the next six months.

About June 17 Elizabeth lost her oldest companion, the comfort of unhappy years. In one sense Flush's death, however, was a relief. He had scarcely a hair on his back and the odour of him was far from pleasant. To her sister Elizabeth wrote:

dear Flush. He is gone, Arabel— He died quite quietly— I am sorry to say Penini found him, & screamed in anguish. There was no pain, nothing to regret in that way—and our grief for him is the less that his infirmities had become so great that he lost no joy in losing life. He was old you know—though dogs of his kind have lived much longer—and the climate acted unfavourably upon him . . . it has been quite a shock to me & a sadness—a dear dog he was.[3]

Flush lies buried in a cellar beneath Casa Guidi. So far as we know, his place was never taken by another animal.

In August the Brownings were really anxious about money: Mr. Kenyon had forgotten to pay the half-yearly instalment on his allowance. Chapman & Hall's accounts that summer showed little balance in their favour. *Casa Guidi Windows* was selling but slowly. They must perforce remain in Florence that summer.

In late August or early September news reached Elizabeth of an accident to her father. Mr. Barrett was knocked down by a cab [4] with a resultant lameness that, the doctors said, might be permanent; a serious blow to a man of active habits. Elizabeth wrote a letter expressing her sorrow and solicitude, taking the precaution of having it posted in London. The envelope was

[3] Unpublished letter, June 17–18, 1854, New York Public Library.
[4] Family information.

addressed by Pen. Thus his daughter's message of love must
have been received and opened by Mr. Barrett, who, however,
made no sign.

It would seem as if by the wedding anniversary, on September 12, the Brownings' temporary embarrassment was at an
end: Robert celebrated their eight years of happiness by the
gift of "a beautiful malachite brooch . . . mystically marked
and of as deep a green as the Elysian ghosts walk in when the
poets guide them." Wilson too, who was in a sense part of their
marriage, received a present.

In the autumn of 1854 a general gloom began to overshadow
the British, whether at home or abroad; a shadow familiar in
our time, but strangely heavy upon a generation of which only
the older members could have lively memories of war. War and
revolution were to the younger subjects of Queen Victoria only
for backward foreigners. There was war in the Crimea, war
against Russia. News was bad, culminating in November with
tidings of the bloody battle of Inkerman. Elizabeth had two
cousins at the front.

There were, however, aspects of the war which Elizabeth
must rejoice in; first, the alliance between France and England,
which she hoped might cure her country of the growing fear of
French aggression, and, secondly (though curiously enough
she does not mention it), Vittorio Emmanuele's decision to send
a large army of troops to the Crimea. This bold move brought
Sardinia in on the side of two major powers at the later Congress of Paris, and gave the astute Cavour an opportunity to
make public protest against conditions in Italy under Austrian
rule. Participation in the Crimean War, where the Sardinians
acquitted themselves well, also brought compensatory renown
to an army that had been so thoroughly routed at Novara.

Indeed, perhaps the only benefits of this cruel conflict came
to the minor participant: Louis Napoleon, for some reason
never fully explained, threw away the full fruit of victory by
bringing the war to an abrupt end.

Penini, of course, took a small boy's delight in war, pretending to read from the newspaper about *"bellissimi regimenti"*
and how his friend Napoleon had sent 80,000 men to Turkey.
Pen was progressing well with pianoforte-playing under his fa-

ther's strict tuition, and developing a love for opera. Finding himself unable to accompany his own rendering of "La Donna è mobile" he found compensation in making an opera of his own about Napoleon and the milkman, "an intimate enemy" who always when he called pretended to take away the child's favourite gun. From his mother's description it would seem that Penini had the right idea:

In the opera the milkman brings bad cream and milk for the "soldati francesi" in arms against the Russians, and so Napoleon comes out against him in vengeance! "è fusillato—è morto!" . . . and then comes the burial—"misericordia," "campo santo" —and all—and an immense noise of "pieti" and bells.

The year wore on to a close, darkly enough for English minds. 1855 opened with frost, snow, and a bitter wind even in Florence. Elizabeth was taken ill, seriously ill for the first time since her marriage, of the old chest complaint. Recovery was slow, leaving a depression of spirit.

Early in the year, news came of Miss Mitford's death after a long martyrdom of illness heroically borne. Never again would Elizabeth receive another of those letters full of pleasant gossip, redolent of the English countryside and full of affection; letters which came so regularly—one, indeed, arriving just before Miss Mitford's death—that any omission on a certain date of the month caused some alarm for the writer's well-being. A minor consolation for this loss, a link snapped with the old life, was a letter from a man who had been Miss Mitford's good friend in her last years, John Ruskin. Between Elizabeth and Ruskin a correspondence was to be agreeably though fitfully carried on to the end of her life.

News from the Crimea, of the sufferings of men neglected by their own rulers in an exceptionally severe winter, continued to reach shocked English ears: the sending out of Florence Nightingale with the first contingent of women nurses was of personal interest to Elizabeth, who had met her in London and remembered clearly "her face and her graceful manner, and the flowers she sent me afterwards."

With Mrs. Jameson's happy assertion that Florence Nightingale's appointment meant a distinct advance in the position of their sex, Elizabeth did not agree:

Every man is on his knees before ladies carrying lint, calling them "angelic she's," whereas, if they stir an inch as thinkers or artists from the beaten line (involving more good to general humanity than is involved in lint), the very same men would curse the impudence of the very same women and stop there. . . .
Apart from the exceptional miseries of the war . . . I do not consider the best use to which we can put a gifted and accomplished woman is to make her a hospital nurse.

Elizabeth could not then know of Florence Nightingale's administrative powers, forcefully though tactfully used to penetrate an obstinate male stronghold for the benefit of humanity as a whole.

The miseries, the cruelties and blunders of the Crimean War do not appear in themselves to have shocked Elizabeth greatly: she took them to be but a small and symptomatic part of general misery, stupidity, and corruption. "This and that poisonous berry is pulled off leisurely," but the root of it all, the system, remained. "I begin to think that nothing will do for England but a good revolution and a 'besom of destruction' used dauntlessly." She denounced the evils of nepotism:

we have soldiers, and soldiers should have military education as well as red coats, and be led by properly qualified officers, instead of Lord Nincompoop's youngest sons. As it is in the army, so it is in the State. Places given away, here and there, to incompetent heads; nobody being responsible, no unity of idea and purpose anywhere—the individual interest always in the way of the general good.

This year travel was no longer impossible: at the beginning of May both the Brownings were working hard in preparation for a journey to London, and later Paris. Each determined to take at least eight thousand lines for the printer, entering into a playful rivalry as to who should complete them first. Robert won, but Elizabeth pleaded the feminine cares of the wardrobe; especially in regard to Penini, whose "little trowsers" must be "creditably frilled and tucked." There were visits to pay after the seclusion of winter, many letters to write, and Penini's lessons to be attended to. Altogether, Elizabeth wrote, "my head swims and my heart ticks before the day's done, with positive weariness."

The serious illness of that winter had left its mark: Elizabeth had, with the warmth of spring, appeared to gain strength, but already in her letters we begin to detect a certain failing of powers so valiantly recovered nine years before. This year Elizabeth left Casa Guidi with reluctance and a certain pain. "I do love Florence so! When Penini says 'Sono Italiano, voglio essere Italiano,'[5] I agree with him perfectly." And this time Italy was to be left for a long absence, for another experiment of wintering in Paris: perhaps indeed Casa Guidi might no longer be called home.

[5] "I'm Italian—I want to be Italian."

CHAPTER 26

PARIS; LONDON [1855–6]

THE BROWNINGS TRAVELLED by sea to Marseilles and thence to Paris, arriving in June. At Marseilles a box was lost containing "all Penini's pretty dresses, trowsers, collars," everything Elizabeth had been so diligently collecting in Florence so that she might present her son worthily to his uncles and aunts; that this box also contained the manuscript of *Aurora Leigh* Elizabeth did not mention in writing of the disaster to Arabel.

In Paris Elizabeth had the pleasure of meeting her brother Alfred, there perhaps as a lover: in two months' time he was to marry his cousin, Elizabeth Georgina (Lizzie) Barrett, at the British Embassy in Paris. It was Alfred who later found the precious box at Marseilles lying in the custom-house.

In Paris there was another marriage nearer in view: Ferdinando, Robert's servant, and Peni's particular friend, had been courting Wilson for two years. In May they had become engaged. The Brownings approved though they saw legal difficulties. Ferdinando was a foreigner and a Catholic: the marriage must be perfectly in order for Wilson's sake. In Paris Ferdinando tried to press on the ceremony, but it was difficult to find a priest sufficiently unorthodox to perform it. But somehow the problem was solved to the satisfaction of master and mistress. In July 1855 Wilson became Elizabeth Romagnoli.

In July the Brownings left France, arriving in London very early on the 12th after a rough crossing that upset them all. Seasickness, however, was but a passing physical disability: to Henrietta Elizabeth wrote: "there's always a weight on my heart when I arrive. The land-sickness is worse than the sea's."

Arabel, always her chief darling among the family, she found "wonderfully well—quite brilliant" and wearing a Parisian bonnet. This bonnet, worn "dropping off behind," was not comfortable or of the most becoming: when Robert insisted on his wife "wearing hats like other people" and Elizabeth reluctantly wore one, she felt "an immense grudge" towards the Empress Eugénie, arbitress of women's fashions, "for tormenting me so, just because she likes to show her own beautiful face!"

Penini, to his mother's joy, took "a great passion of love" for her favourite sister. Nine years later his Aunt Arabel was to act in part as mother to a bereaved child.

The Brownings took comfortable lodgings at 13, Dorset Street, Baker Street, where they were at once overwhelmed with visitors, people who "want to see," Elizabeth wrote, "if Italy has cut off our noses, or what!" Two days after arrival they breakfasted with Mr. Kenyon—"to meet half America and a quarter of London."

There was one man in London, a man causing considerable sensation, whom Elizabeth particularly wanted to meet. Daniel Dunglas Home (pronounced "Hume" and always spelt so by Mrs. Browning) was a Scot brought up in America. His great mediumistic powers are, I believe, no longer disputed, but in 1855 a battle of opinion raged about his head.

An opportunity came: stimulated by tales of manifestations witnessed by Lytton and his father, the Brownings went out to Ealing, where, through Home's able guidance, the spirits were singularly courteous to Elizabeth. After such general manifestations as table-rappings and the touch of ghostly fingers,

at the request of the medium, the spiritual hands took from the table a garland which lay there, and placed it upon my head. The particular hand which did this was of the largest human size, as white as snow, and very beautiful. It was as near to me as this hand I write with, and I saw it as distinctly. I was perfectly calm! not troubled in any way, and felt convinced in my own mind that no spirit belonging to me was present on the occasion. The hands which appeared at a distance from me I put up my glass to look at—proving that it was not a mere mental impression. . . . These hands seemed to Robert and me to come from under the table, but Mr. Lytton saw them rise out of the wood of the table—

In telling Henrietta of this phenomenon Elizabeth asked her not to mention it in her reply; spiritualism being "a *tabooed* subject in this house—Robert and I taking completely different

views." Browning openly alleged trickery: it was probably this
year that Home had the temerity to call upon him and was
threatened with forcible ejection. In revenge Home sedulously
fostered a ridiculous rumour that Browning was jealous of the
wreath that had crowned his wife's head; had even moved behind her chair in the hope that it might descend on his own
brow. Later Browning was to pillory Home as "Mr. Sludge,
'The Medium.'"

Elizabeth had to admit that at the conclusion of the séance
Home, in a trance, "talked a great deal of much such twaddle as
may be heard in any fifth rate conventicle."

Henrietta, out of health this year because of the coming of a
child, Elizabeth was destined not to see: lack of means prevented the Brownings from going to her in Somerset. Mr. Barrett, still resolute in a determination not to receive his daughter,
sent the family off to Eastbourne: again shortage of money prevented the Brownings from following them. Bereft of her family, and especially of Arabel, Elizabeth felt London to be "an
empty nutshell—just to be thrown away." Even Mr. Kenyon, occupied at his Isle of Wight home with a brother recently come
from Austria, they did not see again until October, just on the
point of their departure for France.

An invitation came from Mrs. Martin but, apart from the
cost of a journey west, Elizabeth, her mind haunted by ancient
memory, felt unequal even to set foot in Herefordshire; much
less to stay at Old Colwall, so near to Hope End:

*I could as soon open a coffin as do it: there's the truth. The place
is nothing to me, of course, only the string round a faggot burnt
or scattered. But if I went there, the thought of one face which
never ceases to be present with me (and which I parted from
for ever in my poor blind unconsciousness with a pettish word)
would rise up, put down all the rest, and prevent my having one
moment of ordinary calm intercourse with you, so don't ask me;
set it down to mania or obstinacy, but I never could go into that
neighbourhood, except to die, which I think sometimes I should
like.*

There was an added note of apology to her old friend:

*Foolish to write all this! As if any human being could know
thoroughly what he was to me. It must seem so extravagant, and*

perhaps affected, even to you, *who are large-hearted and make allowance. After these years!*

The weather that summer was dull and wet. Elizabeth felt breathing difficult. But there were compensations in meeting people unattainable in far Florence: Ruskin, the Carlyles, Thackeray, Monckton Milnes, Leigh Hunt, Kinglake, the Procters, and above all, Tennyson. One memorable evening she had an experience unforgettable to more than herself.

Tennyson was now enjoying success: "Maud," published earlier that year, though unfavourably received by the critics, was ardently welcomed in the Victorian home. In a few months five thousand copies were sold. Morbidly sensitive as he was to criticism, Tennyson's enjoyment was to some extent marred: a need for personal reassurance was felt. Elizabeth admired the poem with some qualification, bewailing the earlier Tennyson, but her devotion to the poet himself was unwavering.

Tennyson, up a few days from the Isle of Wight, spent two of them with the Brownings, dining, smoking, drinking port; and, on September 27, ended their communing with a magnificent and emotional declamation of "Maud." Elizabeth, enduring tobacco smoke for love of the man, was charmed with "his frankness, confidingness, and unexampled *naïveté!*" Tennyson would now and then pause in his reading to remark: "There's a wonderful touch!" "That's very tender," or "How beautiful that is!" The Rossetti brothers were present: as Tennyson was reading Dante Gabriel made two sketches of him, one of which he gave to Elizabeth.

When Tennyson had finished, Browning took his place, giving, in strong contrast to the heavy romanticism of "Maud," his own "Fra Lippo Lippi" with (said William Rossetti) "as much of sprightly variation as there was in Tennyson of sustained continuity. Truly a night of the gods, not to be remembered without pride or pang." The friends parted at half past two in the morning.

At the beginning of October, Robert's *Men and Women* being now in print, the Brownings decided to leave England, but were delayed by the return of Mr. Kenyon, who pressed them to stay a few days longer so that he might enjoy their company. Arabel risked the parental displeasure by coming up to Town.

She begged that her nephew might return with her for a few days at Eastbourne: with some heart-searching Elizabeth consented to part with her child for the first time. Penini himself at first refused but, changing his mind at the last minute on account of "a little dog which was going to Eastbourne, and which he was wanted to take care of—some temptation about shells and the sea," he set out with Arabel "in the greatest state of excitement and dignity of a carpet bag."

While still in London Elizabeth embarked upon a small adventure of her own; going out to shop unaccompanied. In this congenial occupation time slipped by until she had been out a full hour. Robert worked himself up into a frenzy of fright: as she came back Wilson was just putting on her hat to go out in search of "the stray Ba-lamb."

On October 18 the Brownings left for Paris, where they lodged at first in unsuitable apartments at 102, Rue de Grenelle, near the elder Browning's home. After six weeks of discomfort, during which Elizabeth was far from well, they moved to 3, Rue du Colysée, a turning off the Champs-Elysées. To Mrs. Jameson Elizabeth gave a lively account of her transference on a cold December day:

That darling Robert carried me into the carriage, swathed past possible breathing, over face and respirator in woollen shawls. No, he wouldn't set me down even to walk up the fiacre steps, but shoved me in upside down, in a struggling bundle—I struggling for breath—he accounting to the concierge for "his murdered man" (rather woman) in a way which threw me into fits of laughter afterwards to remember. "Elle se porte très bien! elle se porte extrêmement bien. Ce n'est rien que les poumons." Nothing but lungs! No air in them, which was the worst! Think how the concierge must have wondered ever since about "cet original d'Anglais," and the peculiar way of treating wives when they are in excellent health. "Sacre."

In London there had been little time for writing: now, in retirement for the winter, Elizabeth was working hard to complete *Aurora Leigh*. Although the winter was mild her health was affected, partly through lack of air. In Florence she remained cloistered for months, but in apartments large and lofty. These rooms in the Rue du Colysée were small, low-ceilinged. It was April before she was fit enough to go driving in the Bois de Boulogne.

In that letter always written on March 4, Henrietta's birthday, Elizabeth spoke with envy of the coming of her sister's third child, hoping again for a niece. On April 11 she wrote to Arabel of another baby, the Emperor's son, born on March 16, 1856. Tales of Napoleon's tears and refusal to eat during the birth Arabel, probably representing the majority of her countrymen, refused to believe. To the British Louis Napoleon was a hard-hearted, treacherous intriguer.

At the beginning of May news came from England both good and bad. Henrietta's second son, Edward Altham, was born, and John Kenyon was seriously ill.

On the choice of a name for Henrietta's son Elizabeth would not comment, merely saying that for her part she didn't much care to use beloved names over again, having even a sort of regret at having called her own child Robert. Henrietta's decision to name her son Edward touched an old wound: it was not his grandfather who was commemorated, but the lost Bro.

When news came of Kenyon's illness Browning's impulse was to go over at once to the childless man; but his scrupulous nature held him back from one who was already a benefactor. He had already asked twice for permission to go, receiving the first time "a kind negative" and to the second request no answer. "It is easier for a rich man to enter, after all, into the kingdom of heaven than into the full advantages of real human tenderness," Elizabeth commented sadly.

A certain weakening of the nerves now begins to be evident in Elizabeth's letters: if Arabel neglected to write she worried unduly. Arabel, she told herself, was overworked, slaving at the Refuge and at organizing bazaars. Mr. Barrett too had never fully recovered from his accident. Liable now to asthma, he was a good deal confined to the house. Anxiety over the beloved cousin was constant. "I get so frightened by silences," Elizabeth wrote to Henrietta. Concentrated work on *Aurora Leigh* was tiring her too.

Although, apart from French celebrities she liked and admired, there were interesting people in Paris that spring—

among them Cavour, Monckton Milnes, Dickens, Macready, and, on the stage, Madame Ristori—Elizabeth appears to have gone out in public little, or not at all.

The Brownings returned to London at the end of June, to cold weather and a house full of sad association because of its owner's illness: at Mr. Kenyon's invitation they stayed at his new home, 39, Devonshire Place. As Elizabeth was working against time on her poem few invitations were accepted, but "bells ring and knockers knock." Browning was now something of a lion in his own right, at least with one advanced set of young men, the Pre-Raphaelites.

In London, Wimpole Street must be Elizabeth's chief centre of interest, but that was now an anxiety. Her father was far from well, Arabel so obviously overworked and getting rapidly set in the ways of charity and self-denial. Much as Elizabeth admired her saintlike devotion to a chosen duty, she felt that "a new set of mental associations" would greatly benefit Arabel; something less dreary than constant good works to compensate for a lack of society at home.

During a hot spell in August, "heavy stifling English heat," Elizabeth was detained in Town by the necessity of proof-reading the 11,000 lines of *Aurora Leigh*. Another trial not long to be avoided was the "heavy, damp, stifling English dinners"—at that time portentously lengthy functions. One of their pleasantest evening visits was to the Hallés' house in Bryanston Square, where they heard the musician himself "play Beethoven divinely" and the singing of their friend Adelaide Sartoris.

It was some while this summer before Mr. Barrett discovered the presence of that first offending daughter; once aware of it he sent Arabel, in early September, with some of her brothers to Ventnor, Isle of Wight. But Mr. Barrett's object was defeated: the Brownings at once followed, joining in a happy family party. Penini especially enjoyed himself by the sea in the unaccustomed company of indulgent uncles. A move to Mr. Kenyon's quiet house at West Cowes was a sad change for the child; and sadder still for his parents, who saw their cousin and friend lying dangerously ill.

When an invitation came from the Surtees Cooks at Taunton,

Somerset, Elizabeth was overjoyed and determined to go as soon as it was at all safe to leave Mr. Kenyon. The only blot on her happiness was the dismal fact that Arabel could not join them "for fear of an arrival from London." Arabel, angry at having been sent to Ventnor, disliked the place and longed to get away. Elizabeth, though Robert told her she was very wrong even to wish it, was inclined to press her to take the risk.

Elizabeth bore with her more than one burden as she crossed the Solent towards her sister's home. Apart from the heavy task of proof-reading, which must accompany her, and anxiety about Mr. Kenyon, there was that sorrow, always deeper when in England, over her father's attitude; humiliation too in her child's wonder at the estrangement. Pen, now seven years old, had come to a conclusion that his mother must "have done something very wicked to make my father what he is." Once he came to her and said earnestly: "Mama, if you've been very, very naughty—if you've *broken china*, I advise you to go into the room and say, 'Papa, I'll be dood.'" Pen's idea of a heinous crime, his mother told Mrs. Martin, was breaking china. Elizabeth felt almost inclined to take the child's advice, but on consideration decided there was much against it.

Elizabeth, after enjoying to the full a week or so of serene family life, left Taunton at the end of September. There was between the sisters a final parting, though neither of them could then suspect that they were never to meet again in life.

It was now October: fog was touching London with a damp and chilly finger. An east wind blew. Elizabeth was coughing half the night.

The remaining three weeks in England were busy and not too cheerful. There was anxiety, over not only Mr. Kenyon but her father, now with his family in the Isle of Wight. Ventnor was too damp for him. Laborious days were spent in proof-reading and, having put off the painful task as long as possible, looking through her dear Miss Mitford's letters to see what might be given to the world in a collected edition. It was probably at this time that Elizabeth recovered a box of papers left behind at Wimpole Street in 1846.

Aurora Leigh being now made ready for her launching in England and America, the Brownings set out for Florence on

October 23. A perilous ship indeed Elizabeth felt her new poem to be, containing as it did so many challenges to public opinion, decorum, and accepted religion; or, as she put it in that dedication to John Kenyon he was not to see, her "highest convictions upon Life and Art."

CHAPTER 27

AURORA LEIGH [1857]

THE POETICAL NOVEL planned by Elizabeth as far back as 1844 was to be more than a mere story; it was to comprehend "the aspect and manners of modern life, and flinching at nothing of the conventional." This representation of life around him was, she considered, the true vocation of a modern poet, who must "never flinch" but

> . . . *catch*
> *Upon the burning lava of a song*
> *The full-veined, heaving, double-breasted Age:*
> *That, when the next shall come, the men of that*
> *May touch the impress with reverend hand, and say*
> *"Behold,—behold the paps we all have sucked!*
> *This bosom seems to beat still, or at least*
> *It sets ours beating. This is living art,*
> *Which thus presents, and thus records true life."*

How far does this ambitious poem fulfil that aim? To the next generation it was indeed living art, but a later tendency was to regard *Aurora Leigh* as a mere museum specimen. In our time, however, high praise from that delicate, perceptive critic Mr. Clifford Bax has led to a new evaluation. "Period piece" the poem undoubtedly is, but one which has much in it to interest and delight us in a changed world.

Readers may, it is true, be at first repelled by a story in some respects banal, faded enough to a generation nurtured on Trollope and Jane Austen; though at the time this was no stumbling-block: it was the daring thought and expression, much to us now long accepted, that brought down a hail of criticism.

It has been stated that as a result of this criticism Elizabeth altered, softened much in the fourth [1] edition (1859), but this is not so. Apart from obvious corrections, a few verbal changes were made—not always for the better—and the system of punc-

---

[1] Given wrongly as 5th edition, 1860, by Wise.

tuation revised; but that was all. No concession was made to mealy-mouthed readers that I can discover except perhaps the altering of "chaste wife" to "perfect wife," "right damnable" to "unmerciful," and "appetite" (a man's physical appetite in marriage) to "fantasy." "Coarse" references to "the stews," street-walkers, the coupling of beasts, sweat, such verbs as "stink," all remain to shock contemporary "over-delicate ears." No bold statement or thesis is abandoned either. Elizabeth, already thoughtful in social matters, was, after her marriage with Browning, in touch with many advanced and outspoken people in her life on the Continent: it is herself she echoes in putting into the mouth of Aurora Leigh: "I've known the pregnant thinkers of my time."

The intertwined themes of Elizabeth's greatest poem are important, both for themselves and as illustration for her life and character; a strong firm claim for woman's freedom, a passionate avowal of the true artist's integrity of mind and purpose, dedicated to God's service, and the supreme importance of married love.

Aurora Leigh is perhaps no longer a living influence, but once it was a direct inspiration to women sighing out their lives in close parental drawing-rooms, longing to escape; proving to them that there were other duties beyond submission. To illustrate this point I quote from an unpublished lecture by that distinguished educationalist the late Miss Alice Woods, who died at the age of ninety-one in 1941. Miss Woods, after telling how what she and her sisters longed for, above all, was work, so that they envied girls who had to gain a living, continued:

Few writers did more to strengthen the desire than Elizabeth Barrett Browning. Aurora Leigh *had been published as early as 1856 but did not fall into my hands until about 1873, when I found the poem had living expression to my longing.*

> . . . *get leave to work*
> *In this world—'t is the best you get at all*
> *For God in cursing gives us better gifts*
> *Than men in benediction.* . . .

> . . . *get work, get work.*
> *Be sure 'tis better than what you work to get.*

And again:

> *The honest earnest man must stand and work.*
> *The woman also,—otherwise she drops*
> *At once below the dignity of man*
> *Accepting serfdom. Free men freely work.*

Only those partly enfranchised can speak on behalf of slaves: Elizabeth was more fortunate than most girls of the early nineteenth century. She was highly educated, had freedom to work on her own lines, and, in spite of a strict upbringing, was apparently subject to few of the restrictions that hampered and intimidated little girls well into living memory. She worked and played on equal terms with her brothers, climbed trees, rushed about on her pony. When comparatively late in life marriage came to her it was not as bondage, but release.

Aurora Leigh is written in blank verse, flowing verse the technical skill of which can be appreciated by a comparison with that of "A Drama of Exile," written in 1843. Dialogue, that pitfall of the novelist in verse, is on the whole well managed, particularly in the masterly church scene where fashionable folk are occupying the pews on one side and denizens of the slum of St. Giles on the other; all assembled to witness the deliberate marriage of socialistic Romney Leigh to Marian Erle, a woman of the people. The men and women of fashion twitter gossip:

> —*"Yes, really, if we need to wait in church*
> *We need to talk there." "She? 't is Lady Ayr,*
> *In blue—not purple! that's the dowager."*
> —*"She looks as young"—"She flirts as young, you mean!"*

When after a lengthy wait the bride does not appear, Romney tells the slum folk to go off and enjoy the marriage-feast prepared for them on Hampstead Heath. After an ominous moment of sullen silence a man speaks gratingly:

> *"Now, look to it, coves, that all the beef and drink*
> *Be not filched from us like the other fun.*
> *For beer's spilt easier than a woman's lost!*
> *This gentry is not honest with the poor;*
> *They bring us up, to trick us."*

Suspecting that some trick has been played on Marian, determined to "see her righted," the angry mob rise up and rush at

Romney. As an example of vivid presentment I give the ensuing panic:

> From end to end, the church
> Rocked round us like the sea in storm, and then
> Broke up like the earth in earthquake. Men cried out
> "Police"—and women stood and shrieked for God,
> Or dropt and swooned; or, like a herd of deer,
> (For whom the black woods suddenly grow alive,
> Unleashing their wild shadows down the wind
> To hunt the creatures into corners, back
> And forward) madly fled, or blindly fell,
> Trod screeching underneath the feet of those
> Who fled and screeched.

Beauty of description, the evocation of an atmosphere, was
already familiar in Elizabeth's work, but these swift, direct, concrete living pictures, heightened by metaphor, were something
new. In Elizabeth's later work the influence of her husband is,
of course, apparent, but may I also suggest that of one greater
than he, the Florentine Dante?

The degraded condition of common people, people such as
we can only imagine now in England, is vividly presented and,
from what we can read elsewhere, there is no exaggeration in
the following:

> Those, faces? 't was as if you had stirred up hell
> To heave its lowest dreg-fiends uppermost
> In fiery swirls of slime,—such strangled fronts,
> Such obdurate jaws were thrown up constantly,
> To twit you with your race, corrupt your blood,
> And grind to devilish colours all your dreams
> Henceforth. .

Elizabeth would not have to go as far as St. Giles in the London of her day to see such faces peering out of waterless, un-
drained courts, faces gaunt with hunger, swollen with cheap
drink, or covered in sores.

One offspring of this legion of the damned, the secondary
heroine of this book, is, however, unacceptable enough to a
modern reader. Marian Erle, the tramp's child, in her native
purity, her innocence and beauty of mind, her literary speech,
is to us too false a figure to stir our pity even when she is be-

trayed and hounded by respectable society; but a generation accustomed in novels to the sentimentalizing of a type of noble poor accepted Marian. Robert Lytton considered the history of Marian Erle "a sublime episode." To those not determined to bury their heads in the sand, refusing to see or hear the evil in their midst, the story of this girl, prey to a heartless woman, a procuress and a foul man, was the most moving, the most beautiful thing in the poem; the more so as they could enjoy pity with an easy conscience. Elizabeth makes it quite clear in the person of Aurora Leigh that she would in no circumstances sanction unmarried love.

The heartless woman, Lady Waldemar, who betrays Marian out of jealousy and possessive love for Romney, is also to us theatrical, unbelievable, but here again her type appears in many Victorian novels, to descend within the memory of older people to penny novelettes and Lyceum melodrama; though few authors, even at the franker end of the nineteenth century, would have had the courage to make her, knowingly or unknowingly, abet a procuress.

Romney Leigh, whose heart is governed by his head, who tries to prove his faith by marrying a girl of the people, and later by setting up in his ancestral home a "phylanstery" or communal settlement, was a type familiar in early Christian socialism, a follower, as was the father of Louisa Alcott, of François Fourier. We, who have suffered so much in this age from impractical idealists and the men in wait to exploit them, can feel the full force of this man's tragedy better perhaps than the sheltered Victorians. Elizabeth, declaring she "would rather live under the feet of the Czar than in those states of perfectibility imagined by Fourier and Cabet," was wiser in future events than she knew.

Romney's ancient home, his reputation, his sight, all perish in the vindictive flames that consume this ill-advised colony at Leigh Hall: out of a man's bloodless idealism an historic house and treasures of art are destroyed, a girl's life degraded, an illegitimate boy born, begot by a scoundrel. It is with marriage to Marian Erle that Romney proposes to atone, by a warm act of human compensation, for the failure of cold philanthropy. Perhaps if the main purpose of the theme had not been the triumph of love, it would have been more fitting, more dramatic if Aurora's cousin had made that sacrifice.

But Marian Erle, "the very lamb left mangled by the wolves" through Romney's "bad shepherding," shows more pride, more self-respect than to take the conventional course of being made an "honest woman." "Here's a hand shall keep," she declared boldly, and to the scandal of many a Victorian home, "for ever clean without a wedding-ring."

Aurora Leigh, taking to her heart that Romney she had once scornfully refused, partly in order to live her own life, to fulfil a poetic destiny, now confessed that:

> Passioned to exalt
> *The artist's instinct in me at the cost*
> *Of putting down the woman's, I forgot*
> *No perfect artist is developed here*
> *From any imperfect woman. Flower from root,*
> *And spiritual from natural, grade by grade*
> *In all our life. . . .*
>   *Art is much, but love is more.*
> *O Art, my Art, thou'rt much, but Love is more!*
> *Art symbolises heaven, but Love is God*
> *And makes heaven.*

Aurora is perhaps a little hard on herself: it was not love, the burning, selfless love of a Robert Browning, that the dismal Romney had offered her, and which she had scornfully refused. Romney had offered the poet-woman, much as St. John Rivers offered Jane Eyre, a service to humanity not her own, telling her not to "play at art." His wife was to be a little beyond the child-bearing toy of a dominant type of wealthy Victorian, but still an appanage, a chattel.

The bold and ardent feminism of *Aurora Leigh* led to much direct denunciation; the Roman Catholic *Tablet* going so far as to call the heroine "a brazen-faced woman," further implying that the story was grossly indecent. Other critics thought the language coarse. Thinkers, those more enlightened, claimed the poem as a masterpiece. Rossetti, Swinburne, and Ruskin were loud in its praise. It was soon bought up by those who admired, those who blamed or enjoyed being shocked: a second edition was called for within the fortnight and there was a steady demand throughout the century. I have before me the nineteenth edition, dated 1885; the last was, I think, that of 1898 with a preface by Swinburne.

The first book is particularly good reading in its description of Aurora's Italian home, the shock of coming on her father's death to an austerer England and a rigid, virtuous aunt. It is full of a quiet humour, the description of Miss Leigh being particularly happy:

> *The poor-club exercised her Christian gifts*
> *Of knitting stockings, stitching petticoats,*
> *Because we are of one flesh after all,*
> *And need one flannel (with a proper sense*
> *Of difference in the quality)—and still*
> *The book-club, guarded from your modern trick*
> *Of shaking dangerous questions from the crease,*
> *Preserved her intellectual. She had lived*
> *A sort of cage-bird life, born in a cage,*
> *Accounting that to leap from perch to perch*
> *Was act and joy enough for any bird.*
> *Dear heaven, how silly are the things that live*
> *In thickets, and eat berries!*

Her training of this uncongenial niece, the romantic girl half-Italian, gives a lifelike picture of the lot of many girls at this time with "instructed piety" its inculcation of "useful facts," its minimum of mathematics, science, and languages, its showy music

> *. . . shuffling off*
> *The hearer's soul through hurricanes of notes*
> *To a noisy Tophet;*

its drawing in pencil and washy water-colours, its ballroom dancing, the spinning of glass, stuffing birds, modelling flowers in wax, and hours of unlovely, feeble needlework. How many frustrated intellectual girls (if allowed to read this dangerous book) must have felt the bitterness of this passage so deeply that the humour was lost on them:

> *I read a score of books on womanhood*
> *To prove, if women do not think at all,*
> *They may teach thinking, (to a maiden-aunt*
> *Or else the author)—books demonstrating*

Their right of comprehending husband's talk
When not too deep, and even of answering
With pretty "may it please you," or "so it is,"—
Their rapid insight and fine aptitude,
Particular worth and general missionariness,
As long as they keep quiet by the fire
And never say "no" when the world says "ay,"
For that is fatal,—their angelic reach
Of virtue, chiefly used to sit and darn,
And fatten household sinners,—their, in brief,
Potential faculty in everything
Of abdicating power in it: she owned
She liked a woman to be womanly,
And English women, she thanked God and sighed,
(Some people always sigh in thanking God)
Were models to the universe.

It is on record that the girl Elizabeth hated those womanly accomplishments, needlework, music, and drawing; but for her there were compensatory hours with Mr. McSwiney, and alone with books. To the dominant father she must often have said "may it please you," but one feels that "so it is" came less frequently from the lips of Mr. Barrett's headstrong opinionated young daughter.

Aurora's young nature is Elizabeth's, in both poetic aspiration, ambition, and an absorption in books. Her own development is shadowed out, its imitations and its high-strained tones. One aspect of her own early work is given in a passage partly known to many of those who, dismissing her—unread—as Victorian, pious, sentimental, have no use for Mrs. Browning:

By Keats's soul, the man who never stepped
In gradual progress like another man,
But, turning grandly on his central self,
Ensphered himself in twenty perfect years
And died, not young—(the life of a long life
Distilled to a mere drop, falling like a tear
Upon the world's cold cheek to make it burn
For ever;) by that strong excepted soul,
I count it strange and hard to understand
That nearly all young poets should write old,

> *That Pope was sexagenary at sixteen,*
> *And beardless Byron academical,*
> *And so with others.*

Aurora, her aunt dead, living in London poor and alone, working by day and night at her art, is not in physical circumstance the sheltered Miss Barrett, but she is the poet in essence. Faced with Lady Waldemar and her selfish love for Romney, her plotting to sever him from Marian, Aurora cries:

> *"I love love: truth's no cleaner thing than love.*
> *I comprehend a love so fiery hot*
> *It burns its natural veil of august shame,*
> *And stands sublimely in the nude, as chaste*
> *As Medicean Venus. But I know,*
> *A love that burns through veils will burn through masks,*
> *And shrivel up treachery. What, love and lie!*
> *Nay—go to the opera! your love's curable."*

To many a Victorian reader this was shameless: love in its bodily manifestation was to be hidden behind drawn bed-curtains, an affair of man imposed on quiescent woman, a woman who must never speak of, or indeed was hardly expected to enjoy, the physical side of love.

Was there in the subsequent visit to Marian's lodging a memory of that shuddering adventure into Seven Dials after the lost Flush?

> *Two hours afterward,*
> *Within St. Margaret's Court I stood alone,*
> *Close-veiled. A sick child, from an ague-fit,*
> *Whose wasted right hand gambled 'gainst his left*
> *With an old brass button in a blot of sun,*
> *Jeered weakly at me as I passed across*
> *The uneven pavement; while a woman, rouged*
> *Upon the angular cheek-bones, kerchief torn,*
> *Thin dangling locks and flat lascivious mouth,*
> *Cursed at a window both ways, in and out,*
> *By turns some bed-rid creature and myself,—*
> *"Lie still there, mother! liker the dead dog*
> *You'll be to-morrow. What we pick our way,*
> *Fine madam, with those damnable small feet!*

> *We cover up our face from doing good,*
> *As if it were our purse! What brings you here,*
> *My lady? is't to find my gentleman*
> *Who visits his tame pigeon in the eaves? . . ."*

Aurora, after Marian's disappearance before the marriage, finds the betrayed girl with her child in Paris, takes the two in her care, and carries them off to Italy. They go down through France by train. The train in a tunnel was as new an experience to many at this time as going up in an aeroplane is now:

> *Athrob with effort, trembling with resolve,*
> *The fierce denouncing whistle wailing on*
> *And dying off smothered in the shuddering dark,*
> *While we, self-awed, drew troubled breath, oppressed*
> *As other Titans underneath the pile*
> *And nightmare of the mountains.*

On to Marseilles

> *With all her ships behind her, and beyond,*
> *The scimitar of ever-shining sea*
> *For right-hand use, bared blue against the sky!*

Then, on board ship, recalling Elizabeth's journey to Pisa those many years back, "The old miraculous mountains heaved in sight."

The house Aurora takes on Bellosguardo is thought to have Isa Blagden's home as its prototype; that villa overlooking Florence, the valley of the Arno, and facing the mountains of Vallombrosa.

> *No sun could die nor yet be born unseen*
> *By dwellers at my villa: morn and eve*
> *Were magnified before us in the pure*
> *Illimitable space and pause of sky,*
> *Intense as angels' garments blanched with God,*
> *Less blue than radiant.*

Here, as was fitting, Romney came, a new Romney in humility and despair, to regenerate himself in love. Here was a new dawn to an Aurora so happily named; an Aurora called so, not by happy chance, but trial and error. The heroine was at first to be Laura Leigh, then (as it appears on the manuscript) Aurora Vane; but at length Elizabeth attained to perfection in Aurora

Leigh, with its bright glow of morning, its high aspiring last vowel.

There is much more of interest in this long poem than the working-out of main themes, the enunciation of ideas, a beauty of scenic description, and a boldness in presentment: of interest too are the minor portraits of people in society; the theoretical Christian socialist, Lord Howe, Grimwald, the bilious literary critic, and Sir Blaise Delorme with so high and narrow a forehead that

> *a strong wind,*
> *You fancy, might unroof him suddenly,*
> *And blow that great top attic off his head*
> *So piled with feudal relics.*

The poem ends, as I have said, in the happiness of lovers, but a happiness which Elizabeth knew could not exist in unequal relations, that of the owner and the owned; nor in selfish absorption. These two, one an acknowledged poet and the other a man vowed to work directly for human happiness, are to experience to the full "a love of wedded souls" sanctified by God:

> *Which still presents that mystery's counterpart.*
> *Sweet shadow-rose, upon the water of life,*
> *Of such a mystic substance, Sharon gave*
> *A name to! human, vital, fructuous rose,*
> *Whose calyx holds the multitude of leaves,*
> *Loves filial, loves fraternal, neighbour-loves*
> *And civic—all fair petals, all good scents,*
> *All reddened, sweetened from one central Heart!*

The climax of this huge and intricate work, though it may make us smile rather bitterly in these days of war, frustration, and lack of faith, still has its message:

> *The world's old,*
> *But the old world waits the time to be renewed:*
> *Toward which, new hearts in individual growth*
> *Must quicken, and increase to multitude*
> *In new dynasties of the race of men,—*
> *Developed whence, shall grow spontaneously*
> *New churches, new œconomies, new laws*
> *Admitting freedom, new societies*
> *Excluding falsehood: HE shall make all new.*

My Romney!—Lifting up my hand in his,
As wheeled by Seeing spirits toward the east,
He turned instinctively, where, faint and far,
Along the tingling desert of the sky,
Beyond the circle of the conscious hills,
Were laid in jasper-stone as clear as glass
The first foundations of that new, near Day
Which should be builded out of heaven, to God.

CHAPTER 28

FLORENCE; FRANCE; WAR IN ITALY [1856–9]

THEY RETURNED TO FLORENCE in the late autumn of 1856 to find exceptionally cold weather, a bitter wind and snow already on the mountains; but, her cough having "dropped off somewhere on the road," Elizabeth felt little more than "discomfort and languor." She busied herself with the furnishing of a second drawing-room and anxiously awaited the reception of *Aurora Leigh*.

News from the Isle of Wight was "strange and sad": not only was Kenyon suffering from a relapse, but his brother had died suddenly. On December 3 Kenyon himself died. Elizabeth wrote to Mrs. Martin:

This Christmas has come to me like a cloud. I can scarcely fancy England without that bright face and sympathetic hand, that princely nature, in which you might put your trust more reasonably than in princes. These ten years back he has stood to me almost in my father's place; and now the place is empty —doubly. Since the birth of my child (seven years since) he has allowed us—rather, insisted on our accepting (for my husband was loth)—a hundred a year, and without it we should have often been in hard straits. His last act was to leave us eleven thousand pounds.

£6,500 was left to Robert and £4,500 to Elizabeth: these bequests (apart from the cousinship) were part of a general benevolence to literary people. Henrietta was left £100. Mr. Barrett, much to his annoyance, was not mentioned in the will. "If the principle of relationship had been recognised *at all*," Elizabeth wrote to her sister, "(*which it was not*) he had his undoubted claim." Because of the wealthy brother's death so near to his own some £80,000 was left unaccounted for in Kenyon's will, all of which went, as the law ordained in those days, to the residuary legatees. The trustees were dilatory: it was a full

year before the Brownings benefited by their legacies. In the
meantime Elizabeth's feelings were harrowed by many letters
of congratulation. Although she herself might materially gain
by it, the death of so loved a relative and friend could hardly
be a matter for rejoicing. In the few years remaining to her she
could never trust herself to speak of Kenyon, or even write his
name without tears. When *Aurora Leigh* came out just before
the New Year, pleasure at its immediate success was marred by
a thought that he to whom the book was dedicated could no
longer read it, or enjoy the fame it brought.

After her experience at the séance in Ealing Elizabeth's letters contain more frequent reference to Home and to spiritualism. During her absence in 1855, Home had given demonstra-
tions in Florence which had stirred society. Although he had
enemies, especially among Roman Catholics—and a certain
weakness of moral character gave them a convenient handle—
among the many who were convinced by him was Mrs. Kinney,
wife of the American chargé d'affaires at Turin, whom Elizabeth regarded as particularly "veracious and just." In 1856
Home was in Paris, not, however, holding séances: his power
had departed from him during that year. Elizabeth heard of his
presence near her husband with a certain horror: Browning had
quite worked himself up into a state of hatred of the man. He
had to promise her to be as "meek as a maid" and, if he encountered Home in the street, to pass him without recognition.

Story too was encouraging Elizabeth in her belief, writing
from America that even in "a cold conventional place like
Boston" there was enthusiasm for the spirits. Back in Florence,
Elizabeth, who had there only maintained a mild interest in
table-turning and automatic writing (of which Wilson was a
weak exponent), now heard with ever-increasing awe and interest of more thorough manifestations. To her, as to many people
in the early days of spiritualism, these manifestations were held
to be the sign of a new Revelation, of the gradual passing of human kind into a higher state of being.

In Florence there was an old and simple Englishman, Seymour Kirkup, an artist and archæologist, whose chief fame now
rests upon his discovery of Giotto's portrait of Dante in the
Bargello. Kirkup, credulous to a degree, brought marvellous

tales to Casa Guidi. Elizabeth did not always believe in his visions and spirit voices, but she did not go so far as Robert in declaring Kirkup an old humbug.

One striking case of psychometry (though it may well have been thought-transference) did, however, come to Browning's notice that year through the agency of a Count Ginnasi. Holding in his hand a gold wrist-stud of Browning's the Count declared that a voice was crying in his ear "Murder! Murder!" No one but Browning knew that the stud had been taken from the dead body of a great-uncle who had been violently killed on his estate at St. Kitts.

Life presented itself in a more frivolous aspect that spring: the February carnival of 1857 was a particularly gay one, the wearing of masks being allowed after a prohibition of some years. Peni was wholly absorbed by it, thought of nothing but carnival, and demanded a blue domino trimmed with pink. Robert prepared a domino of black silk (later made into a dress for Elizabeth) and invited friends to supper in a box at the Opera House ball. It had not been thought possible that Elizabeth should act as hostess but, the evening being exceptionally mild, she determined to be present, going out at the last minute to hire domino and mask. Let us hear the rest of the story from herself:

Do you think I was satisfied with staying in the box? No, indeed. Down I went, and Robert and I elbowed our way through the crowd to the remotest corner of the ball below. Somebody smote me on the shoulder and cried "Bella mascherina!" and I answered as imprudently as one feels under a mask.

She was much struck by the "refinement and gentleness" of these people so essentially civilized, "where no excess, no quarrelling, no rudeness nor coarseness can be observed in the course of such wild masked liberty." The Grand Duke went down among the crowd, a crowd consisting of all classes; though, uneasy in conscience as the man must have been, he did not stay long.

In Lent that year Elizabeth wrote in her usual letter to Henrietta on March 4: "everybody now is fasting and sighing,—and enlarging their petticoats." The crinoline was advancing to its final huge encirclement while Elizabeth herself was still hesitating about the mere insertion of whalebone hoops in her skirt. This curious fashion, seeming to us now an encumbrance, brought a certain freedom to women in its very lightness, discarding as they could a dragging weight of many petticoats. Elizabeth stood "lingering by that species of crinoline-petticoat called 'the tower of Malakoff.'"

In giving Henrietta this frivolous detail Elizabeth commented:

What nonsense one talks! when one has talked it, it's impossible to expect that one should be thought of except in the gayest spirits,—and yet really, Henrietta, I have had many sad and heavy thoughts this winter, many.

In March news came of the death of Miss Trepsack, the beloved "Treppy" with whom Elizabeth had been as a favourite daughter. Since this old friend was ninety years of age, tidings of her death could not come as a grievous shock, but Elizabeth was again occupied with thoughts of the past and of death. Though the trappings, the graveyard element, were abhorrent to her, of death itself Elizabeth had no fear. "Death," she wrote to Arabel, "is a bridge to cross and no more."

In the middle of March, looking forward to release from winter bondage in a burst of fine weather, Elizabeth's spirits lightened a little: by the first of April she was driving out in the Cascine Gardens and to Bellosguardo. "Beautiful, beautiful Florence. How beautiful at this time of year! The trees stand in their 'green mist' as if in a trance of joy."

The latest acquisition to Florentine society was Harriet Beecher Stowe of *Uncle Tom's Cabin* fame. Elizabeth had not thought she should like Mrs. Stowe, but found her "very simple and gentle, with a sweet voice. . . . Never did lioness roar more softly." Although Elizabeth could not admire her books "the fact is, that she above all women (yes, and men of the age) has moved the world—and *for good*." To Elizabeth's surprise she preferred her to Mrs. Gaskell, who was also in Florence.

In 1857 Victor Hugo, from his exile in Jersey, published his *Contemplations*. Elizabeth was profoundly moved by them. Grieving for Hugo, she wrote a letter to Napoleon III pleading that he, "a great poet of France," might obtain pardon.

*ire, what was written on "Napoleon le Petit" does not
h your Majesty; but what touches you is, that no historian
the age should have to write hereafter, "While Napoleon the
hird reigned, Victor Hugo lived in exile."*

This plea, covering four pages, began humbly with "I am only a woman," and designated the writer modestly as "the wife of an English poet." Her emotional appeal was not, however, actually sent to Napoleon; perhaps as the result of an intervention on Browning's part.

Elizabeth's passionate interest in the Emperor had grown considerably since the day when she had written that he was "a Napoleon cut out of paper after all." Her stout defence, to Mrs. Jameson and others, of him and his actions fills many letter pages in the future: one can only wonder that a being so clear-sighted in her invalid days, shut away from personal contact with the world in Wimpole Street, was now, with a greater knowledge of it, so prejudiced.

On April 17, 1857, Edward Moulton Barrett died of erysipelas, held to be a result of his accident in the autumn of 1854. He was buried in the vault of Ledbury Church, which held the remains of his wife and infant daughter. All Ledbury, with closed shops and drawn curtains, honoured him who had been a distinguished member of the congregation, a local philanthropist, and High Sheriff of the County.[1]

A few months before his death Mrs. Martin had attempted to bring about a reconciliation between Mr. Barrett and his daughters, only to meet with a firm refusal. The proud man went to his death still in a spirit, at least outwardly, of conscious rectitude.

Elizabeth was deeply affected by the news, unable to write of it to anyone outside her own family. An alleged spirit message sent her in July by Fanny Haworth reopened the wound. Elizabeth, for all her faith in spiritual communications, resolutely refused to believe in this one which touched her nearly. That it purported to be from or related to her father is not directly stated, but may well be assumed.

She was very weak now, lying much on the sofa, finding it hard to force herself into daily occupation, even though it might

[1] Family information.

be the teaching of her child: "I take up books—but my heart goes walking up and down constantly through that house in Wimpole Street, till it is tired, tired." The shock of her father's death brought with it a return of old grief over his relentlessness. Robert had written to Mrs. Martin soon after the news reached them:

So it is all over now, all hope of better things, or a kind answer to entreaties such as I have seen Ba write in the bitterness of her heart. There must have been something in the organisation, or education, at least, that would account for and extenuate all this; but it has caused grief enough, I know; and now here is a new grief not likely to subside very soon. Not that Ba is other than reasonable and just to herself in the matter: she does not reproach herself at all; it is all mere grief, as I say, that this should have been so.

There could be, apart from Elizabeth's weakened condition, no visit to England this year. England would arouse too many memories. Arabel's own wish that the Brownings should come to stay with her, Elizabeth herself swept aside as impossible in any case; writing to Henrietta:

There would be gêne on both sides. The irregularities of our house are scandalous—not immoral, observe, but scandalous. From morning till night people are running out and in—all sorts of people; and when we are in London we can't help it. There are men who come and talk—talk, some of them did last summer, till one in the morning—and the freest sort of philosophy is talked. Robert would be in agonies of annoyance even if Arabel could bear it.

The sisters, both children of an Evangelical home but different in outlook, had now drifted widely apart with circumstance; Arabel to become perhaps narrower, more devoted to bleak duty, and Elizabeth confirmed in Liberal tendencies, less consciously religious in tone of mind.

As summer advanced, the heat became seething, "a composition of Gehenna and Paradise." The only relief was evening visits to the Bellosguardo heights and the cool villa of Isa Blagden, now an intimate and loved friend who had a particular affection for Penini. One delightful evening was spent on her terrace listening, with Mrs. Jameson, to new poems of Robert Lytton's

(Owen Meredith's) read by himself, "which seemed to receive modulation from the divine stars and ringing mountains." Lytton had but newly returned to Florence after nearly four years out of Italy, plunging into an atmosphere like "a perpetual vapour bath."

Another pleasure at this time was the presence of Mrs. Jameson, who had come over to the Continent in search of health after years of worry and hard work. In 1854 her dearly loved mother had died, and later that year her husband out in Canada; a husband unlamented, but whose death meant the cessation of his annual allowance of £300 a year. Nothing had been left to her. As soon as he realized her plight Thackeray had exerted himself to obtain for her in 1851 a Civil Pension of £100, a regular yearly income that was doubled by the generosity of certain friends. Mrs. Jameson came now to Florence from Rome, where Geddie lived, married to her artist and in no very flourishing circumstance although he had become a photographer—one of the first in that city.

At the end of July the Brownings again fled from the heat to La Villa, Bagni di Lucca, staying in Casa Betti, a small house in a large garden rather too closed in by trees. Soon they were followed by friends, Isa Blagden and Lytton among them, who stayed at the Pelicano opposite. In the coolness and quiet of La Villa Elizabeth found the repose she needed. "You don't know this place" she wrote, "nor how sublimely the mountains look their serenity into you." [2]

But serenity was soon darkened: Lytton, never strong, affected by the July heat in Florence, developed a serious gastric fever. Isa Blagden cared for him, refusing to hire a nurse: Browning, although he privately thought her decision a foolish one, took his share, sitting up night after night with the invalid. For six weeks there was constant anxiety until he was convalescent and able to return to Florence.

In the meantime little Pen was taking his enjoyment, riding donkeys and mountain ponies with his father and bathing in the river Lima. His mother, too weak now for much walking, went about in a *portatina*, a kind of Sedan chair. One day, run-

---

[2] Unpublished letter to Jane Wells Sandford, October 4, 1857, Hewlett Collection.

ning too fast and too far by her side, the boy too was struck
down with fever, gastric fever. While he was ill his precious
"Lili," the devoted Wilson, who was about to bear a child, had,
after a week spent in bed, to return to Florence for her confine-
ment. "She went all in tears, poor thing."

Oh, to see that angel face on the pillow, in the midst of its
golden curls, with its scarlet cheeks and poor patient eyes! and
to hear his cry of pain in the night, as I did once! It was almost
more than I could bear.[3]

To add to the frail mother's difficulties the new Italian maid,
Annunziata, whom Pen liked, soon went down with the fever,
though not seriously. There had also been an accident to
Browning, which, in his fortunate escape, helped to bring Elizabeth back to reality and present blessings. His horse had fallen
over a precipice sixty feet deep, head over heels. He saved his
life by catching at a crag of rock. "I might be writing to you,"
she told Arabel in September, "(or rather not writing to you)
without a husband and without a child! . . . I feel a good deal
stricken altogether."

It is possible that Elizabeth was further disturbed at this
time of anxiety by a certain cooling in her friendship with Isa
Blagden. We know, since Eckley had been riding with Robert
at the time of his accident, that new friends were also with them
at Lucca, rich Bostonians who lived in Europe for many years.
The wife, Sophia Eckley,[4] was a sweet woman with a delusive
air of innocence, a "white rose" of such apparent purity that,
Elizabeth wrote in a poem on her, one "dared not name a sin
In her presence." It was perhaps a certain gift for flattery that
made Browning suspicious of her from the first. Elizabeth, however, accepted Mrs. Eckley at face value, becoming perhaps
more swiftly intimate because of a mutual interest in the oc-
cult. Isa Blagden was very naturally hurt and jealous.

By October Peni was able to go out in the carriage; his
mother was already making plans to travel in winter, even
thinking of Egypt and the Holy Land. On their return to Florence before the 12th, the child was fully recovered and in high
spirits.

[3] Hewlett Collection.
[4] She was second cousin to Louisa Alcott.

Elizabeth, to her husband's satisfaction, but Mrs. Jameson's disapproval, had now forsaken her "tower of Malakoff" to "sweep out in an excess of majestic circumference" in a hoop-petticoat: "but after all it is not an ungraceful fashion." The crinoline was, indeed, very becoming to a short woman. Elizabeth found it delightfully cool too in an Italian summer. "A hoop and a dress equips you."

There is little record of the autumn of 1857. Christmas Day found them dining at home with friends, and Penini on the verge of his own particular "festa," a festa that was to combine the typical Italian illumination, with many wax torches, and a boy's military dream in a display of toy soldiers, drums, guns, and swords.

In February came news of Felice Orsini's attempt to assassinate Napoleon III by bombs placed in his carriage. Orsini, an Italian patriot, was an agent of Mazzini. In Florence there seems to have been an almost general condemnation of Orsini's act. This episode proved to be important: it would seem as if a letter written to Napoleon by Orsini in prison finally persuaded that wayward man to intervene in Italian affairs.

The winter of 1857–8 was miserably cold even in Italy: Elizabeth was far from well but, as usual in Florence, she had no cough. A cloud hung over her spirits. "Brooding, brooding, brooding, and reading German, are not the ends of life after all—" she wrote in a fit of self-reproach to Arabel. "I must do some work this year at least, and get out of the cloud, if God lets me."

But, as usual, the sunshine of spring livened her thoughts again: plans were formed for meeting members of her family that summer on the Normandy coast, and again she dreamed of a winter in Egypt. A small but vivid interest was aroused when Home returned to Italy, though he was only a day in Florence. She reported that the manners and morals of her "*protegé prophet*" were much improved: debts previously contracted in Florence were now settled from an annuity left to him by an Englishwoman whose infidel opinions had been changed by his manifestation. Soon Elizabeth was to be amused by tidings of Home's marriage. "Think," she wrote, "of the conjugal furniture floating about the room at night."

In April we hear of a passing malady new to her, an eye inflammation "making the *white*, one red." She was shut up in the dark for a while "with lotions instead of literature." But by April 28 she had been out driving three times.

In June we hear of Elizabeth surviving without undue fatigue the combined visits of the American poet William Cullen Bryant (with "a magnificent head and a long beard like snow") and his fellow-countryman Nathaniel Hawthorne. The impression Elizabeth and her child made on such a sensitive recorder as Hawthorne is perhaps worth quoting:

. . . *a pale, small person, scarcely embodied at all; at any rate, only substantial enough to put forth her slender fingers to be grasped, and to speak with a shrill, yet sweet tenuity of voice. . . . It is wonderful to see how small she is, how pale her cheek, how bright and dark her eyes. There is not such another figure in the world; and her black ringlets cluster down into her neck, and make her face the whiter by their sable profusion.*

Both mother and son seemed "of the elfin race," with a strangely strong resemblance between them. Penini, he thought, was at once less childlike and less manly than a boy of nine years old should be. Hawthorne's son, Julian, nearer to Pen in age, set down his impression more bluntly: "I had the contempt for him which a philistine boy feels for a creature whom he knows he can lick with one hand tied behind his back, and I had nothing whatsoever to say to him."

"There is not such another figure in the world. . . ." This remark of Hawthorne's agrees with the general, the unique impression made by Elizabeth on those who met her. Though so little impressive physically, her radiant intellect, a faculty for coming at once to the point, and, above all, her spirituality, gave her a quiet power. Thomas Trollope, looking back in old age, said of her "in mind and heart she was *white*—stainless." Always he was conscious of coming away from Casa Guidi a better man, with higher views and aims. Lytton, a closer friend, a more imaginative man, wrote at her death to Forster: "a lovelier life never went back to God."

At the beginning of July the Brownings went by water to Marseilles and then on to Paris, able now to take express trains up through France. As usual travelling benefited Elizabeth in spite of seasickness. Avidly gathering together French novels and periodicals, she rejoiced in the swift isolated life of trains with "no possibility of unpleasant visitors. No fears of horrible letters. . . . Quite out of reach of the telegraph even, which you mock at as you run alongside the wires."

In Paris they stayed for a fortnight at the Hôtel Hyacinthe, Rue St. Honoré. Sarianna and "the dear nonno" were to accompany them to the sea: Elizabeth was ardently hoping that Arabel might join them and return for a short stay in Paris. Opera, theatres would be out of the question for one so strict, but there was much the sisters might enjoy together without moral questioning.

Elizabeth could no longer freely enjoy the delights of Paris. "I break suddenly like a stick," she told Henrietta, "at a certain point and it comes early." In general she contented herself with dining out with Robert and driving in the Bois de Boulogne. But change of scene and travel had so far restored her looks that Robert playfully set her down as a humbug.

Gloom was never far from Elizabeth in these late years: Lady Elgin, with whom Robert was such a favourite, was struck down by a third stroke of paralysis. She recovered enough to be sitting out in her garden before he left Paris, but entirely bereft of speech.

Two people encountered in Paris were the inevitable Father Prout "in great force and kindness," and the American Abolitionist and ex-Congressman Charles Sumner, come over in the hope of recovery from a physical assault made on him because of his opinions.

For the Brownings' seaside visit they first tried Etretat, but found accommodation there both bad and dear; soon they were "ignominiously settled at Havre, yes, at Havre, the name of which we should have scorned a week ago as a mere roaring commercial city." There they stayed in the Maison Versigny, 2, Rue de Perry, facing the sea and set in a pleasant garden.

At Le Havre Elizabeth had the experience, perhaps new to her, of being photographed (see Plate 6) so that a portrait might be engraved for the fourth, revised edition of *Aurora Leigh*. The engraving was supervised, with many letters of detailed criticism and advice from Browning, by D. G. Rossetti; to the partial satisfaction only of both. Of her face, not good in feature, William Rossetti observed: "it was a countenance of April shine and shower to which full justice could only be done by its own varying and exceptional play of expression." To us, however, who never saw Elizabeth, the engraving seems a remarkably accurate reproduction except, perhaps, about the mouth, where it is a little flattering.

Elizabeth could do little at Le Havre but drive and walk down to the shore, "sit on a bench and get strength, if it so pleased God." Soon she was delighted by the coming of Arabel, George, Henry and Henry's wife, whom he had married in the previous April. Joseph Milsand, a friend of both Browning households, joined the party for ten days in September.

They left Le Havre for Paris on September 20th with little regret, especially on Browning's part. He had found the place dull; moreover, a working-fit was upon him, and naturally there was among the family group but scant opportunity for composition. The weather too had been unkind. In Paris they stayed at 6, Rue de Castiglione, Place Vendôme. George and Arabel were with them. We hear nothing of the impact of Paris on Elizabeth's gentle Puritan sister, nor how long she remained there. The parting between them was to prove final.

William Allingham visited the Brownings in Rue de Castiglione; that their lodging was not of the best is indicated by a subsequent letter to him in which Elizabeth made whimsical apology for the fare set before him:

I often think how you consented to be starved, for the sake of our make-believe dinners, by our wicked French cook, who had been used to cook for Barmecide and to put the money in her pocket—and then I sigh and consider in myself how, in spite of your good-nature, you must have softly moralised on a certain friend's unfortunate destiny in having married a mere rhyming woman instead of an "angel in the house" capable of looking after the chops.

As Elizabeth's health was already affected by the chills of autumn, even in Paris, the Brownings left for Florence in the middle of October, taking nine days on the journey, one of which was spent

*at Chambéry, for the sake of Les Charmettes and Rousseau.
Robert played the "Dream" on the old harpsichord, the keys of
which rattled in a ghastly way, as if it were the bones of him
who once so "dreamed." Then there was the old watch hung up,
without a tick in it.*

From Chambéry the journey was difficult. Elizabeth suffered
much in crossing the Alps. On their journey from Genoa to Leghorn by sea in a wretched craft they ran into a *burrasca*, a painful combined disturbance of wind and undersea currents. So exhausted was she that they were obliged to stay the night at
Leghorn.

A consultant was evidently called in by her Florentine doctor: both advised a winter farther south. Unexpectedly severe
weather, however, delayed them in Florence. While still there,
Elizabeth was delighted with a gift from her husband of a bust
of Penini. There had been some debate over the cost: "I would
rather have given up Rome and had the bust," she told Sarianna. The sculptor, Alexander Munro, however, would only accept what the bust had cost him to make, twenty-five guineas.
And, after all, their journey to Rome cost them nothing, since
they were conveyed in the Eckleys' second carriage, and with
every comfort and personal attention. They had the carriage to
themselves and carried plenty of books.

There were, however, some frightening incidents: narrow es-
capes from spills, one over a mountain precipice, and a threatened knife-duel between two oxen-drivers whom Browning separated with only an injury to his trousers.

Weather on the week's journey was variable but they entered
Rome on a beautiful day. In their old sunny rooms high up in
the Bocca di Leone they met many friends, among them Charlotte Cushman, Hatty Hosmer, the painter Leighton, William
Page, "the American Titian," the sculptor Gibson, who had befriended Severn when he came with Keats to Italy, and, dearer
than them all, the Storys returned from America.

This time the omen of a sunny entrance was fulfilled. Elizabeth was well and happy in Rome. On Christmas morning, in
spite of intense cold, a heavy frost that hung the fountains with
icicles, she was able to hear the silver trumpets sound in St. Peter's. "I never once thought," she told Ruskin, "of the Scarlet

Lady." Her enjoyment of High Mass was complete "both æs-
thetically and devotionally, putting my own words to the music.
Was it wise, or wrong?"

In February 1859 Elizabeth wrote to Henrietta of a new hope
in Italy: "we Italians (such as Pen and I) are all trembling with
expectation. The great marriage in Piedmont . . ." This marriage between the Emperor's cousin, Prince Napoleon, and Vittorio Emmanuele's daughter was the outward symbol of a private meeting between Napoleon and the statesman Cavour, at
Plombières in the autumn of 1858. The alliance formed between
them against Austria was not divulged, but enough news of it
seeped through for the Tuscans to take fresh heart. In Florentine theatres (taking advantage of the composer's popularity)
there were shouts of *"Viva Verdi!"* That enthusiast Pen was
heard, much to the horror of his parents, instructing Romans
in the open street as to the meaning of *"Viva Verdi"* : *"Vittorio
Emmanuele Re d'Italia."*

While in Rome the Brownings were gratified by a visit from
Massimo D'Azeglio, Prime Minister of Piedmont before Cavour,
and an ardent patriot. D'Azeglio was, to Mrs. Browning's gratification, entirely on the side of Louis Napoleon, completely ex-
onerating that individual of any desire for territorial aggran-
dizement. As for Italy, he said, "it is '48 over again, with
matured actors." He spoke bitterly of British policy, and of the
European balance of power "as belonging to a past age, the rags
of old traditions."

This British policy, looking backward and forward to the
menace of Russia, of maintaining the balance of power, had perhaps more sense in it than Elizabeth and many of her *Italianissimi* friends could know. The official view was perhaps given
to Motley, the historian, by Robert Lytton in 1860:

*Austria is a slow power, moved by mediocre minds and always
behind the time, but she acts on the movements of the European machine, as the lead in the timepiece, regulating and bal-
ancing the motion of the whole; take away the weight and how
will the clock go?*

To Mrs. Browning he wrote in that year: "I think a wide distinction should be drawn between the moral support volunteered
by the public opinion of a free people and the material support

afforded by a responsible Government to conflicting parties abroad." No one could deny Lytton's own enthusiasm for Italian liberation, nor the help and support given to patriots by private British citizens and, unofficially, at times by Her Majesty's Navy. But to ardent, impatient Elizabeth, to the patriot D'Azeglio, such a distinction as Lytton's could carry little weight.

But, however anti-British Elizabeth might feel, she could not but express a feeling of delight at an honour done by the Crown to her husband. In February Edward, Prince of Wales, was in Rome with his tutor, Colonel Bruce. Colonel Bruce himself called to say that as "the society of the most eminent men in Rome" was desired for the Prince, it would "gratify the Queen that the Prince should make the acquaintance of Mr. Browning." Browning dined, apparently in public, with the Prince, "a fair, gentle youth, with a frank open countenance." Exhorted by his wife to take this golden opportunity (not knowing, perhaps, how little Her Majesty heeded the opinions of the heir to the Throne,) Robert talked, on the encouragement of a few questions, "quite naturally of the wrongs of Italy to an evidently sympathetic audience": though the well-primed Prince did not commit "his royal youthfulness in the least degree."

Another eminent man commanded to meet the Prince was Mr. Lear. Urged on by Mrs. Tennyson, who had written to him of "those wonderful spirit eyes" of Elizabeth's, Lear called in the Bocca di Leone. Elizabeth was receiving only for an hour each day, between four and five o'clock. He "thought her very nice" but too surrounded by people to make any real contact with. And, whether on any real basis, or whether because at this time he was not in a mood for society, Lear considered those people who had come to pay court to this celebrity a collection of flatterers, snobs, and bores. He occasionally met the Brownings in society, but never became more than a casual acquaintance. This we must regret; lacking as we do a lively description from Elizabeth of this odd being whom it was "pleasant to know."

Elizabeth now visited very little. Browning, however, though at first he tried to avoid it, was soon heavily involved, "some-

times two or three times deep in one night's engagements." Elizabeth having "no vocation for receiving alone" and finding
books hard to procure, perhaps found her evenings a little long,
but she went to bed early and consoled herself with Swedenborg. There was regret that Robert was not writing: "no Men
and Women. Men and women from without instead!"

Peni was enjoying society in Rome; being petted and admired. Robert encouraged his growing love of music by allowing him to go to day-concerts. An Italian version of *Monte
Cristo* was enthralling him in leisure hours.

For a woman whose physical powers were rapidly declining
it was probably not good that Elizabeth should be left to brood
in the quiet of solitary evenings on those Italian affairs taken so
much to heart. To Mrs. Jameson she wrote: "What I have endured in the last three or four months you might think I exaggerated if I told you—really physical palpitations in reading the
newspapers, or reading any thing." [5] The honour of her favourite Napoleon was, too, so much involved. When in April Austria demanded immediate disarmament of the growing forces of
Sardinia and Piedmont, and Napoleon appeared to be in agreement, she was "in anguish—I felt the sobs of rage in my throat—
Robert kept saying, 'I fear he has receded a step,' and I could
not say a word."

But when on April 29 Austria declared war on Victor Emman-
uel and crossed the river Ticino—a crossing that Napoleon had
declared would be considered as an act of aggression towards
France herself—the Emperor, to Elizabeth's supreme joy, acted.
In May he himself went to the front of battle, side by side with
King Victor Emmanuel. Italian feeling rose to a delirium. Even
in Rome, where the hand of oppression was strong, there was
a demonstration, which the Brownings witnessed, about the
French Ambassador's carriage. At cries of *"Viva la Francia,
Viva l'Italia, Viva l'Imperatore del Francesi!"* the Ambassador
"stood up in his carriage, took off his hat, and answered diplo-
matically, '*Pace ed allegria.*'" [6] The leaders of this minor demonstration of patriotism were arrested and imprisoned at the
demand of the Austrian Ambassador.

[5] Unpublished letter, postmarked May 4, 1859, Hagedorn Collection.
[6] See unpublished letter, May 14, 1859, Hagedorn Collection, as above.

In Florence that veiled *"Viva Verdi"* now rose into an open shout for a King of Italy. After a "rose-water revolution," with "an enormous amount of talking and shouting," Leopoldo, Grand Duke of Tuscany, was deposed. The *gran ciuca* went in peace, through a large crowd, this time never to return. It was, fortunately for him, not until after his departure that Florentines learned of an order he had issued: in the event of a popular movement, both fortresses should fire down on the city, and troops advance along the main thoroughfares in triple file, with fixed bayonets, those nearest the pavements firing at the windows of the houses. This order the officers in the fortresses had refused to carry out.

Naturally the Brownings' relations were worried about them: to Henrietta the intrepid Elizabeth wrote that, although steamers were crowded with English and Americans in flight from Italy, they intended to remain. "You know we are apt to flourish rather in a revolutionary atmosphere." They determined to stay in Rome until the end of May and then return to Florence by rail and *vetturino* through Siena.

Although invasion of the Sienese area was threatened, the travellers crossed it without incident "if only by a scratch." Their journey, a very pleasant one, was through "an almost absolute solitude."

C H A P T E R   2 9

FLORENCE, SIENA, AND ROME [1859–60]

BY THE TIME Elizabeth reached Florence at the beginning of June French troops had arrived there. National fervour was at its height. Florentines were admiring their allies, encamped in the Cascine Gardens, to heartfelt cries of *"La Guerra!"* Men poured in from unliberated states to join the forces. Funds for the prosecution of the war were rapidly collected. The Brownings contributed their quota, and little Penini, ardently wishing himself old enough to fight, earned his contribution of half a paul[1] a day by a good showing at lessons. He hung out two tricolour flags over the balcony, one French, one of the new Italy.

Although there was real danger of an Austrian attack the Brownings decided to remain in Florence "as long as the sun lets us." Elizabeth was naturally triumphant: Louis Napoleon was proving himself the great man she held him to be. Feeling against her own country grew more bitter as a British cry grew louder for stronger defences against possible French aggression. Even her beloved Tennyson urged on in popular verses the growth of a Volunteer movement.

On June 4 the French and Italian armies were victorious at Magenta: on the 8th they entered Milan. After the 20th patriots were sickened, disheartened by news of a terrible sack of Perugia by Papal troops; but on June 25 the fortress guns of Florence boomed out to announce victory for the combined arms at Solferino and San Martino. Excitement rose high: what was there now to stand in the way of total deliverance from foreign domination? Had not the Emperor of the French declared he would not rest until all Italy was liberated?

But Louis Napoleon was not made of the stuff of heroes: on July 8 he suddenly concluded an armistice with Austria. Various reasons have been given for this resolve not to press home the victory: a failure of nerve after witnessing the terrible car-

[1] About 2¾d.

nage of Solferino, a reluctance to endanger certain advantages for France by prosecuting the war in the difficult Venetian territory that lay ahead, and (the reason Mrs. Browning put forward) a fear of Prussia, which, disliking a possible access of power to the French, was already massing armies on her frontier.

The Italians very naturally took the move as pure betrayal. In Florence the many busts of this new Napoleonic "liberator" disappeared overnight: Penini was told sorrowfully by his mother that it would be wiser to take the French tricolour down from their balcony.

In the principal cities of the north there was widespread and angry agitation. Cavour, furious, thunderstruck, resigned his ministry. Victor Emmanuel himself submitted with as good a grace as possible, counting his certain gains. As yet there was no hint of a price to be paid.

In the preliminaries of peace, signed at Villafranca on July 11, Lombardy was assigned to Sardinia but the fate of Tuscany, Parma, Modena, and the Roman Legations was to be decided by plebiscite. On July 12 Pio Nono, heartened by the cessation of hostilities, appealed to Europe against Vittorio Emmanuele.

To Elizabeth, who "had been walking among the stars so many months," the news came like a physical blow, reaching her in a weakened condition: going out one very hot afternoon to the Trollopes' to see "the famous Ducal orders about bombarding Florence," she came home ill. "Violent palpitations and cough; in fact the worst attack on the chest I ever had in Italy." She would cough all the night long.

Now the little sleep she could snatch was disturbed by "political dreams . . . in inscrutable articles of peace and eternal provisional governments." To Isa Blagden she wrote of one dream of exaltation, and perhaps of prophecy:

I dreamed lately that I followed a mystic woman down a long suite of palatial rooms. She was in white, with a white mask, on her head the likeness of a crown. I knew she was Italy, but I couldn't see through the mask. . . . Walking upon the mountains of the moon, hand in hand with a Dream more beautiful

*than them all, then falling suddenly on the hard earth-ground
on one's head, no wonder that one should suffer.*

There was further torment to a fevered mind in a determination to justify Napoleon. Others must be blamed, those "selfish,
inhuman, wicked" nations which had forced his hand and
"truncated his great intentions." England, she declared, had
been in league with Prussia to "prevent the perfecting of the
greatest Deed given to men to do in these latter days."

Browning, tending his wife at night, having little sleep for
three weeks and taking over Penini's lessons by day, now shoul-
dered another and unexpected burden, the charge of an aged
and irascible genius. Walter Savage Landor, eighty-three years
of age, had of late been living with his family at the Fiesole
villa he had made over to them, together with what remained
of his income. One intensely hot day, after many violent quarrels, his wife and children turned him out of the house with
only some small change in his pocket. Either Browning found
him in a state of collapse on the road into Florence (there are
two differing accounts) or he appeared at Casa Guidi appealing
to one who had long been his ardent admirer.

Robert took Landor under his protection. Soon, however, the
wayward old man expressing a determination to go to Siena,
Browning was able temporarily to hand over charge of him to
Story, who was spending the summer in a villa outside the city.
With the help of Seymour Kirkup, Browning secured Landor's
clothes from a vindictive family and took him there in person.

Though he arrived half-crazed, his white hair streaming, in
Story's words "a case of old Lear over again," Landor soon recovered his old intellectual fire and gallantry. Back in Florence,
Browning had the unpleasant task of interviewing Mrs. Landor,
who proposed to do nothing for her aged husband. His brothers, however, stepped into the breach. Remittances amounting
to £200 a year were to be made from England to Browning for
Landor's support.

Elizabeth was now attended by Dr. Grisanowski, a German
who seems to have been on friendly terms with the Brownings
and others of their circle. He pronounced change of air as the
only hope for recovery. In early August, too weak to set foot on

the ground, she was taken like a baby in arms to Siena, where, Browning being determined not to pay the heightened price demanded for the villa he had fixed upon, they stayed a few days at the hotel. Dr. Grisanowski, refusing to accept any additional fee, had followed them by the next train. He remained with his patient for two days, "most kind and zealous."

Browning decided to rent the Villa Alberti, a house on the same hill, Poggio dei Venti, on which they had stayed in 1850, and less than a mile from Story's villa. Story was present when Browning carried his wife in from the carriage looking "like a dark shadow."

From the high *specola* of Villa Alberti, now Villa Marciano, there are the same fine wide views over hill, valley, and bright mediæval city which had delighted the Brownings nine years before. They occupied the first floor, where today, nearly one hundred years on, the furniture remains the same and frescoed walls, untouched, look as fresh in that clean dry air as they did when Elizabeth's own eye was upon them. Behind the house a garden and a small plantation of trees and bushes (*boschetta inglese*) are full of bird life. The quiet, the utter peace of the place could well bring balm to a wounded mind and spirit.

Although the heat was intense that year, even on the "windy hill," by the second week in August Elizabeth was sufficiently recovered to walk about the rooms on Robert's arm, though she remained in strict seclusion. News of Florence elections heartened her, the first election for a Tuscan parliament. Though Austria had appointed "Ferdinand IV" ruler of Tuscany, and even put ambassadors for her in Rome, Naples, and Vienna, he had little hope of entering his "Dukedom." The Liberal triumph was overwhelming. On August 16 the Assembly voted unanimously for annexation to Piedmont and adherence to King Victor.

In Italy there was still war. Garibaldi, who had fought in Tuscany, was by no means willing to accept foreign domination over other states. By July 19 he had been exhorting Italy to arm. North, in the free port of Venice, a stout resistance under siege ended in a defeat, which nevertheless demonstrated the bravery of a people long designated as soft, effeminate.

Elizabeth, remaining quiet in her lofty shaded rooms, or later

out under her favourite fig tree, occupied herself wi
and newspapers, English and Italian. Robert and Pe
much with the Storys. Peni rushed about those little leaf
which so reminded his mother of England, on a pony "t
our of his curls," a yellow Sardinian pony soon to be hi.
Landor in a cottage near by was sufficiently himself n
write Latin alcaics upon Italy's hero of the hour, Garibaldi ...c
harvest came. Penini rode "in the oxen carts, between heaps of
pomi d'oro" chattering happily with the peasants. In her villa
Elizabeth enjoyed "sunsets red as blood, seen every evening
over deep purple hills, with intermediate tracts of green vineyards."

In the silence and repose of that leafy countryside Elizabeth
recovered spirits and a measure of health, though she was never
again to be active. Driving out in a hired carriage, one day
Browning took her into Siena, that treasure-house of art, where
in the picture gallery she looked once more on "the divine Eve
of Sodoma." A visit to the Cathedral, however, proved beyond
her. She could not climb the steps before it and had to be content with "the vision of it safe within me since nine years ago."

But during these months of anxiety, illness, and slow recovery, Elizabeth had not been wholly idle. On September 24 there
came out in the *Athenæum* the first published of those poems
written on the Italian struggle for freedom, "A Tale of Villafranca." In it she defended the action of Napoleon, postulating
for him an attitude of grieved resignation:

> But HE stood sad before the sun
> (The peoples felt their fate).
> "The world is many,—I am one;
> My great Deed was too great.
> God's fruit of justice ripens slow:
> Men's souls are narrow; let them grow.
> My brothers, we must wait."

Towards the end of their stay at Villa Alberti Elizabeth had
the pleasure of receiving guests. Isa Blagden came with her
young American friend Kate Field, who lived with her and was
studying art; a girl of strong feminist views who became a favourite with both the Brownings. Odo Russell, the diplomat,
was a particularly interesting visitor who had much to tell Eliz-

abeth about Napoleon and the Italian situation. Russell confirmed a rumour that the Emperor was intriguing to secure Tuscany for his cousin, Prince Napoleon. This astute move which, if successful, would have strengthened France both against the Teutonic powers and against a possible fresh rival in the new Italy, Elizabeth was unwilling to credit, though the authority for the truth of it made her waver.

Before she left Siena Elizabeth was delighted by a presentation copy of *Idylls of the King* but, on reading the work, had to admit disappointment in spite of some "exquisite things." She wrote to Allingham:

Perhaps we had been expecting too long—had made too large an idea to fit a reality. Perhaps the breathing, throbbing life around us in Italy, where a nation is being new-born, may throw King Arthur too far off and flat. But, whatever the cause, the effect was so. The colour, the temperature, the very music, left me cold. . . . I would rather have written Maud, *for instance, than half a dozen of such* Idylls.

Surely most modern critics would agree in preferring *Maud* to Tennyson's romanticized but watered-down version of old Malory.

When their time came to an end Elizabeth clung to Siena and the Villa Alberti, not wanting to leave; perhaps divining that here she had enjoyed her last untouched period of personal tranquillity. Since all desire for travel had now left her, she might have gone more happily if there had been a prospect of remaining at Casa Guidi: the condition of her lungs, however, did not permit another winter in Florence. She must flee before the tramontana, that sharp wind from mountains, southward to Rome.

But in Florence, to which they returned in November, the Brownings were detained so long that there seemed a chance that cold weather might prevent the journey: Browning's "adopted son" must be arranged for, and this took longer than they expected. When Wilson was forced by the birth of her first child to leave the Brownings' service, although Ferdinando remained with them, she took a lodging-house in the Via Nunziatina. There the Brownings settled Landor under her care. Although the arrangement would materially benefit Wilson and her husband, Elizabeth could not help feeling for her former maid: the charge was no light one. Of Landor Elizabeth wrote to her sister-in-law from Siena:

A most courteous and refined gentleman he is, of course, and very affectionate to Robert (as he ought to be) but of self-restraint he has not a grain, and of suspiciousness many grains. . . . What do you say to dashing down a plate on the floor when you don't like what's on it? And the contadini at whose house he is lodging now have been already accused of opening desks.

The "old Lion" had sharpened his teeth again. At Siena, before they left, he had been "roaring softly, to beguile the time, in Latin alcaics against his wife and Napoleon." When Elizabeth told him that one day he must write an ode to Napoleon to please her, he "laughed carnivorously." In irritable explosions of temper, in bouts of acute suspicion of those around him, Robert, whose long admiration of Landor gave him admirable patience, could calm the old man. Wilson too seems to have managed him tolerably well though once, in attempting to prevent him throwing his dinner out of the window, she was violently accused of flinging a dish in his face. As Wilson soon proved to be a victim of religious mania, partly arising from a jealousy of Elizabeth's Italian maid, Annunziata, the tiresome old man could hardly have improved her condition; unless, indeed, he proved a salutary counter-irritant.

In October Garibaldi had appealed to the Neapolitans to revolt against their Bourbon King. By November 10, when by the Treaty of Zurich Central Italy was formally established as a confederacy of states with the Pope as President, a clash of patriots and Papal troops seemed inevitable: yet the intrepid Brownings travelled south to Rome, Elizabeth declaring that "the great guns of the revolution (and even the small daggers) will be safer to encounter than any sort of tramontana."

On November 27 they started for Rome, taking six days on the road; Pen often riding triumphantly beside them on his pony, which was fastened to the carriage horses. Elizabeth, always a good traveller, was benefiting, Robert declared, by "long doses of fresh open air which she would have made no attempt to swallow in Florence." They established themselves in a sunny apartment at 28, Via del Tritone (now demolished), an apartment which, if most of the foreign population had not left Rome for fear, would have been quite beyond their means. Elizabeth was amused to find that the Pope, though fully aware of his "alarming position" (the possibility of French troops being withdrawn), yet found it in his heart to publish an edict against "crinolines, the same being forbidden to sweep the sacred pavement of St. Peter's."

At first Elizabeth rejoiced in Roman sunshine and a new well-being, at work in her sunny rooms preparing for the press that "thin slice of a wicked book," as she called it, *Poems Before Congress.* Robert too was at work that winter, both on lyric verse, which Elizabeth did see, and a long poem he did not show her; and for a very good reason, since it was the first draft of *Prince Hohenstiel-Schwangau* under the more direct title of "Napoleon Fallen."

Elizabeth's interest in Italian politics, the struggle for freedom, continued, and in a form more active. From Isa Blagden, through Odo Russell, the diplomat, she was apparently receiving news-letters, which she seems to have returned in kind. Once she felt real alarm at the non-arrival of one of Isa's letters, telling her that even Russell's correspondence, if it went through the post, was opened and scrutinized. But this in no way daunted her: at the same time a banned newspaper, the *Monitore,* was being sent to the Brownings from Florence, through Odo Russell, and was read by Tuscan exiles with whom Ferdinando, a patriot and former Garibaldian soldier, was in touch. These men, afraid to borrow the paper because of the many spies in Rome, came to read it at 28, Via del Tritone. "We keep a sort of café in Rome," Elizabeth told Miss Blagden, "and your 'Monitore' is necessary to us." When the authorities, noting that Russell received a *Monitore* beyond the one allowed him as a diplomat, stopped the Brownings' copy, Robert arranged that it should be sent to them direct in a plain wrapping.

In January 1860 Elizabeth's enthusiasm for her adopted land led again to illness. Swords for presentation to Napoleon and Victor Emmanuel, subscribed for by twenty thousand patriotic Romans, were ready for dispatch; a dispatch sudden and secret, as the Pope had recently denounced "all such givers as traitors to the See." One wet evening at five o'clock someone came to the Via del Tritone in a closed carriage. Late though it was, Elizabeth went with Robert to view the swords at the shop of their designer, Castellani, the famous Roman jeweller:

we were received at Castellani's most flatteringly as poets and lovers of Italy; were asked for autographs; and returned in a blaze of glory and satisfaction, to collapse (as far as I'm concerned) in a near approach to mortality. You see I can't catch a simple cold. All my bad symptoms came back. Suffocations, singular heart-action, cough tearing one to atoms.

But a "gigantic blister" and the Roman climate brought about recovery at the end of a week, though the attack left her seriously debilitated. Soon, however, she was well enough to receive two interesting visitors, both American, one a spiritualist named Thomas Hazard and the other the Unitarian minister and Abolitionist Theodore Parker. Parker, already in bad health, was soon to die. The Unitarian's lack of belief in the Godhead of Christ was to Elizabeth in bleak contrast with the fervent faith, amounting to credulity, of Hazard, but at Parker's death in May she felt a measure of sorrow. "There was something high and noble about the man—though he was not deep in proportion."

In the spring of 1860 that "thin slice of a wicked book" was published, arousing in the press much expected criticism, but with an additional sting, presenting to Elizabeth and her husband a cup of bitterness undeserved.

CHAPTER 30

POEMS BEFORE CONGRESS [1860]

MISS MITFORD had dismissed *Casa Guidi Windows*, unjustly one must own, as mere pamphleteering: this accusation can be, I think, more accurately brought against *Poems Before Congress*. The emotion is there, the intense feeling for Italy, but Elizabeth was perhaps too near the events, too implicated in feeling and yet not closely enough involved, to bring a clear mind to bear.

And, although she was still to write a few fine pieces, mind and body were considerably weakened a year before death. There are flashes of poetry, some of the old bold metaphor, but on the whole, even with a strong interest in the historic and emotional background, the verses are hard to read. Contemporary critics in England less familiar with the story of Italy's struggle from day to day could feel little sympathy, accepted though Mrs. Browning was then as a major poet. And the addition, at her husband's particular request, conspicuously at the end of the volume, of one poem extraneous to the general matter completely alienated most of them, confirming the impression that Elizabeth was now openly anti-British.

In a rather natural misconception Chorley, of the *Athenæum*, leapt to a conclusion that "A Curse for a Nation," wholehearted, deep-throated, was directed against Elizabeth's native land on account of Great Britain's official attitude towards Napoleon III and the Italian struggle for freedom. No clear indication was given that in

> *Because ye have broken your own chain*
> *With the strain*
> *Of brave men climbing a Nation's height,*
> *Yet thence bear down with brand and thong*
> *On souls of others,—for this wrong*
> *This is the curse . . .*

Elizabeth was admonishing not England but America on the count of slavery. The accusation of unpatriotism was taken up by other journals.

Elizabeth, expecting "a storm of execration," was not unduly disturbed by this injustice, but Browning was enraged; declaring (not without basis in fact) that Chorley, now a bitter, disappointed man, was having his revenge for Elizabeth's criticism in a letter to himself of his novel *Roccabella*, which he had dedicated to her. Elizabeth herself was angry when the *Athenæum*, on its mistake being pointed out, did not print her letter but put in, as journals are apt to do, a correction in an inconspicuous corner; one that might well be overlooked. On finding that Chorley was not responsible for this act of discourtesy she wrote him a generous letter, adding: "I never wrote to please any of you, not even to please my own husband." She must present truth as it appeared to her. "It is one of the beatitudes of art, and attainable without putting off the flesh."

In America, where this strong piece had already appeared in the *Liberty Bell* for 1856, there was no such misconception. There *Poems Before Congress* received the respectful homage always accorded to this favourite poet. "I have," Elizabeth told a disapproving Mrs. Jameson, "extravagant praises and *prices* offered to me from 'over the western sun,' in consequence of these very 'Poems Before Congress.'" Theodore Tilton of the New York *Independent* was now offering a hundred dollars for any poem she might choose to send him; a poem that by the lack of copyright law he could have printed for nothing.

The attacks upon *Poems Before Congress* in the London press were, Elizabeth bravely considered, a justification of the poems themselves. Certainly this view was supported by Odo Russell, who held that the general censure was due solely to her support of Napoleon: for the rest, her work had succeeded in heightening sympathy for struggling Italy. *Poems Before Congress* had been published on March 17: by June Chapman & Hall were preparing to bring out a second edition.

In a letter to Chorley on May 2 Elizabeth wrote of her hero: "Observe, I may be wrong about Napoleon. He may be snake, scoundrel, devil, in his motives." "But the thing he did," she added loyally, "was done before the eyes of all." What had occurred after the French invasion might well have shaken her allegiance: Louis Napoleon had presented his bill for the partial liberation of Italy, demanding the surrender to France of Nice and Savoy, the very cradle of Italian freedom under Victor Emmanuel and his father.

This demand, held by many at the time as geographical and political common sense, was naturally to those *Italianissimi* a pure betrayal. Browning's comment was trenchant: the Emperor's intervention in Italy "was a great action; but he has taken eighteenpence for it, which is a pity." On paper, in that long poem his wife did not see, he relieved his feelings in the first draft of *Prince Hohenstiel-Schwangau.*

In Italy the political situation in early 1860 was both nebulous and critical. In only two cases were the northern Italian states definitely held; Lombardy becoming part of the Kingdom of Sardinia and Piedmont, and Venetia, including Peschiera and Mantua, to remain directly in the grip of Austria. The central states, nominally to be a separate kingdom under the presidency of the Pope, with the old Austrian rulers to return, were determined to annex themselves to Piedmont; indeed, they had direct orders from Cavour to prepare Liberal governments and acts of union. The parliament held at Turin in January included deputies from Lombardy, Tuscany, and Emilia. To the great European powers Cavour made it clear by a circular letter to agents and diplomats that, as the Italian question had not been settled satisfactorily at Zurich, Italy was now entitled to deal with internal problems herself. To Louis Napoleon he privately intimated that Nice and Savoy would be surrendered after a plebiscite judiciously arranged, and with consent of parliament, if Napoleon would support him in regard to the central states. Napoleon's reply was to march French troops into Savoy.

Elizabeth, in her Roman apartment, followed these moves, probably hearing more from diplomatic friends than the general public, with a heart "beating uncomfortably." The rushing of French troops into Savoy she was forced to stigmatize as "a haste somewhat indelicate."

March brought a personal sorrow: Mrs. Jameson died on the 17th after a short illness. The news came to Elizabeth, not gently through her husband, but thoughtlessly, abruptly in a note from Gerardine enclosed in a parcel of photographs. She could manage no more than a few agitated words in reply: Gerardine could not know to the full what she felt in "losing (as far as the loving can lose those whom they love, as far as death brings loss) that great heart, that noble human creature." In Elizabeth's frail organism the veil between life and death was becoming ever thinner. The loss of Mrs. Jameson deepened a growing depression of spirit. To Sarianna she wrote: "It's a blot more on the world to me."

A blot on Elizabeth's world at this time, and one that seriously damaged her in spirit, was the break between herself and Sophia Eckley. We do not know the actual cause of Elizabeth's disillusionment with her "white rose," but whatever it was she felt it bitterly; so bitterly that she put her emotion into that strangely harsh poem "Where's Agnes?" As for Browning, he nursed an animosity towards Mrs. Eckley for the rest of his life, writing strongly about her to Isa Blagden especially when, after his wife's death, the unworthy friend paraded affectionate letters from Elizabeth.

In March the northern states (except Venice) were annexed to Sardinia after universal plebiscite: in May, Nice and Savoy were formally ceded and French troops, except for the Roman garrison, retired from Italy. The Pope, who had lost the greater parts of his domains, was naturally enraged, excommunicating both Napoleon and Victor Emmanuel. Pen, that ardent politician, found it difficult to control his tongue; having to be "restrained into politeness and tolerance towards ecclesiastical dignitaries." To his tutor, the Italian Abbé, Pen rather neatly explained a day's bad weather "in choice Tuscan": "Of course it's the excommunication. The prophet says that a curse begins with the curser's own house; and so it is with the Holy Father's curse." The Abbé, fond of the child and secretly in sympathy, as were many priests, with the Italian struggle for freedom, found it hard to keep a straight face.

The eyes of Napoleon and Cavour were now uneasily upon Naples, that most misgoverned of kingdoms in Italy. Cavour's offer of an alliance in 1859 had already been refused: in March he heard of a plot to recover the Romagna for the Pope with Neapolitan arms. Napoleon on his side feared the annexation of Naples by Sardinia. In this event any chance of French influence in Italy might vanish. The Plenipotentiaries in Zurich were still desultorily considering the Italian situation in the light of events. Cavour felt it difficult to make an open move.

In early May, however, the question was taken out of his hands by a powerful, eccentric, and uncontrollable force. Encouraged by insurrections in Sicily, Garibaldi sailed south with his irregulars, having appealed to Cavour for open support in vain, but supplied secretly by King Victor Emmanuel with money. Napoleon, though persuaded by England not to intervene, patrolled the Sicilian straits in an effort to prevent Garibaldi from landing. It was under the unofficial cover of a British warship that the irregulars landed on the beach from their crazy old craft at Marsala on May 11.

Elizabeth watched the movements of the Sicilian expedition with a beating heart. "Garibaldi's hardy enterprise may be followed by difficult complications." Cavour too viewed the situation with alarm as Garibaldi proclaimed himself Dictator and went from triumph to triumph. That simple-hearted old warrior was under the influence of republican Mazzini: his anger over the cession of Nice, his native province, his fury against the "vulpine knave" Napoleon III might well endanger all Cavour's carefully laid plans for the uniting of Italy under his King.

Elizabeth, following the fate of her beloved Italy from day to day, had to husband a failing strength. Letter-writing, once so pleasurable to her, so active an occupation, became a weariness. For the rest, she composed a few lyrics on Italy and spent much time helping Pen with the heavy tasks set him by the Abbé. "When the sun goes down," she told her friend Isa, "I am down. At eight I generally am in bed, or little after." Visitors she found very tiring, though some were welcome. One in whom she took a strong interest was Lady Annabella Noel, granddaughter of that early hero Byron; "very quiet, and very intense, I should say." The little sculptress Hatty Hosmer remained a favourite and was often with Elizabeth.

Another visitor on intimate terms with Elizabeth this winter was Harriet Beecher Stowe. Elizabeth was amazed to find in one "coming out of a clerical and puritan *cul-de-sac* . . . a largeness and fearlessness of thought" and a strong interest in spiritualism. Perhaps when these two women, both of whom

had written on the side of human freedom, came to say good-
bye, there was a premonition that they would never meet again
on earth, Mrs. Stowe's parting words being: "Those who love
the Lord Jesus Christ never see one another for the last
time."

As she came nearer to her own end Elizabeth's interest in
spiritualism grew deeper. We find her asking news of London
activities, telling Fanny Haworth that even Robert's heart had
softened "to the point of letting me have 'The Spiritual Magazine' from England." She spoke sharply of Charles Dickens's refusal to investigate the truth of spiritualism. "This is a moral
lachêté, hard for my feminine mind to conceive of. Dickens, too,
who is so fond of ghost-stories, as long as they are impossible. ."

On June 4 the Brownings left Rome; Elizabeth with a sense
of real relief since Pen was suffering from a mild attack of fever, and there were two other cases close to their lodging. They
were four days on the road, travelling through Orvieto and
Chiusi. In spite of beautiful scenery, "interesting pictures and
tombs," the journey wearied Elizabeth. Her days of pleasure in
travel were over.

The Brownings found Landor well, living in "a chronic state
of ingratitude to the whole world except Robert, who waits for
his turn." The old man was enjoying life in the present while he
could: "he had 'quite given up thinking of a future state—he had
had thoughts of it once, but that was very early in life.'"
Though Landor was "a man of great genius, and we owe him
every attention on that ground," Elizabeth could not help confessing to her sister-in-law that "to me he is eminently unsympathetic," though she could admire his handsome person, his
"most beautiful sea-foam of a beard you ever saw, all in a curl
and white bubblement of beauty."

From Browning's letter to the Storys of June 19 [1] we learn
that not before this date did Elizabeth venture to leave the
house, having only now recovered from the journey. Her visits
were few, even to Villa Bricchieri in a carriage.

In Florence they were "all talking and dreaming Garibaldi
just now in great anxiety."

[1] Unpublished letter in Keats-Shelley Memorial House, Rome.

Scarcely since the world was a world has there been such a feat of arms. All modern heroes grow pale before him. It was necessary, however, for us all even here, and at Turin just as in Paris, to be ready to disavow him. The whole good of Central Italy was hazarded by it. If it had not been success it would have been an evil beyond failure. The enterprise was forlorner than a forlorn hope. The hero, if he had perished, would scarcely have been sure of his epitaph even.

Garibaldi, by dint of hard fighting against great odds, was now practically in possession of Sicily. Cavour tried to claim it for Victor Emmanuel, but Garibaldi was too incensed against him for the loss of Nice to consent. But there was nothing to fear of Garibaldi as a Republican. That intrepid, obstinate man had now but one aim in view; that of prosecuting a long war until he should reach Rome, eject the French garrison, and crown Victor Emmanuel on the Campidoglio. As to the political complications, he cared little or nothing.

At this time George Eliot and her Mr. Lewes were in Florence; those lovers who flouted the Victorian view of marriage. They came and went, but would return. Elizabeth declared to her sister-in-law that, out of admiration for her books, she would certainly receive "Miss Evans," but there is no record, so far as I am aware, of the two writers ever meeting.

It was during this interval of a month in Florence that Browning met with the literary adventure of his life, the discovery on a stall in Piazza San Lorenzo of the "square yellow book" for which he gave a lira, "eightpence English just"; that bound record of the Franceschini case which was to provide a story for his greatest work. Vividly he tells us how he started reading leaning against the fountain, and then took his way home

> *Through fire-irons, tribes of tongs, shovels in sheaves,*
> *Skeleton bedsteads, wardrobe-drawers agape,*
> *Rows of tall slim brass lamps with dangling gear,—*
> *And worse, cast clothes a-sweetening in the sun:*

out of the market, still reading "At the Strozzi, at the Pillar, at the Bridge," until by the time he was

> *In Casa Guidi by Felice Church,*
> *Under the doorway where the black begins*
> *With the first stone-slab on the staircase cold,*

he had mastered the contents, "knew the whole truth gathered there." Startled, obsessed as he was by the story, it must have been a disappointment to find that Elizabeth took not the slightest interest in what appeared to her merely a sordid account of crime. It was eight years before the first instalment of *The Ring and the Book* appeared: Browning did not embark upon the writing of it until three years after Elizabeth's death.

On July 7 the Brownings left Florence for Siena, probably taking with them Landor and his dog, Can 'Giallo. They stayed again in the Villa Alberti with Landor in a cottage close by, Story a mile off, and Isa Blagden but half a mile. There, in the quiet familiar house with its splendid views, Elizabeth might have attained to some measure of peace if the news had not come that Henrietta was seriously ill of a painful and fatal disease.

She fell into a melancholy state; going about her work as usual, writing, teaching Pen,
but with a sense of a black veil between me and whatever I did, sometimes feeling incapable of crawling down to sit on the cushion under my own fig-tree for an hour's vision of this beautiful country—sometimes in "des transes mortelles" of fear.
Henrietta had always seemed so strong, the most robust of the three: the more delicate Arabel was to outlive her by eight years.

Elizabeth's first impulse had been to rush over to England, but a little persuasion soon convinced her of the folly of this proceeding. All she could do was to "keep quiet and try not to give cause for trouble on my own account, to be patient and live on God's daily bread from day to day." The summer was the coolest they had known in Italy. Elizabeth added sadly: "I *could* have been very happy."

Even the news of triumphs from the south must be tempered with "a certain melancholy," since now Italian was fighting Italian. By July 20 Garibaldi's victory at Melazzo put the whole of Sicily in his hands. Another anxiety now harassed Elizabeth's tired mind: the decision of Central Italy to unite under Victor Emmanuel would lead, everyone felt sure, to a fresh war with Austria. She, who had braved war and revolutions in the past, scorning the English who had fled away, now advised against visiting Italy until the situation should clear.

One thing pleased her, that Thackeray, in that new magazine the *Cornhill,* was putting the Italian situation clearly in informed articles. Among the brilliant array of writers, Anthony Trollope, Ruskin, and Thackeray himself among them, only the poets were not anonymous, and among those poets was Elizabeth with a war poem, "The Forced Recruit, Solferino, 1859," and that fine piece "A Musical Instrument."

A later contribution sent to Thackeray in the spring of 1861 put that astute editor in a difficult position. It is a curious corollary to the success of *Aurora Leigh* that when the author of that outspoken work sent him "Lord Walter's Wife," a highly moral piece dealing with a man who tried in vain to lure away a friend's wife, Thackeray felt obliged to reject it. To write and say so to the celebrated Mrs. Browning was not easy: he put it off as long as possible. "You see," he wrote, "that our Magazine is written not only for men and women but for boys, girls, infants, sucklings almost . . . there are things *my* squeamish public will not hear on Monday, though on Sundays they listen to them without scruple."

Elizabeth's reply was gracious, generous in tone: she agreed that Thackeray as editor was probably right, but put her own point of view:

I don't like coarse subjects, or the coarse treatment of any subject. But I am deeply convinced that the corruption of our society requires not shut doors and windows, but light and air: and that it is exactly because pure and prosperous women choose to ignore *vice, that miserable women suffer wrong by it everywhere.*

As a token of forgiveness she sent him another contribution, the highly innocuous "Little Mattie Dead."

CHAPTER 31

THE LAST YEAR

THAT AUTUMN ELIZABETH, waiting with a sick heart for news of her sister, watched events in the south with feverish interest.

Progress was rapid. On September 7 Garibaldi entered Naples as a deliverer, without opposition. The Bourbon King fled before him. Cavour decided it was now time for him to move: having gained Napoleon's consent, he marched an army through the Papal States, lying between Tuscany and the Kingdom of Naples.

Encouraged by the near presence of Sardinian forces, Liberals within the Papal States rose in revolt. On September 11 the Sardinians crossed, facing and defeating at Castelfidardo Papal troops under that French General, Lamorcière, whom Napoleon had placed at their head. After laying siege to the city, Sardinian forces entered Ancona on the 29th.

On October 4 Victor Emmanuel took personal command of his army, and defeated the Neapolitans at Isernia on the 17th. Garibaldi was fighting on the Volturno front, but his victory on the 1st had proved too costly in men for the direct advance upon Rome he had planned. Resistance was stiff: Catholics from all over the world had naturally rushed to defend their Pope. On the 26th Garibaldi joined Victor Emmanuel at Teano, hailing him "King of Italy." After the conquerors had entered Naples in state Garibaldi sailed to his island home on Caprera, refusing all reward beyond Victor Emanuel's simple but heartfelt "I thank you." The Roman provinces, now freed, voted for annexation.

The one Neapolitan stronghold which held out was Gaeta, that ancient refuge of the Pope and Austrian puppet rulers. A siege was prolonged by the action of Napoleon, who prevented the Italian fleet from investing by sea; an action even such an ardent supporter as Elizabeth found difficult to explain, except that it must be for the good of France. The opposition to King Victor's forces put up at Castelfidardo had also been hard to account for, but this she did by repeating a rumour that General Lamorcière had, at a dinner given to his staff in Rome, drunk to the health of "Henri Cinq": Lamorcière, therefore, did not truly represent the Emperor. What Elizabeth might have admired in her hero was his agility in sitting on both sides of the fence.

During this rush of events, on October 8, the Brownings left Siena. On the 7th Elizabeth, sitting under her favourite fig tree in the garden of Villa Alberti, decided to commemorate it in pen-and-ink; perhaps with some inward premonition that to-morrow there must be a last good-bye to this place of quietude on the "windy hill."

One may suppose that the Brownings returned to Casa Guidi before they went south again to Rome; and that (if we place in 1860, as I think we should, a note to a Mrs. Matthews [1]) "a disastrous letter," perhaps containing grave news of Henrietta, made Browning hurry on the journey before November 23. "I hope," he wrote, "that the change of scene and respite from bad news for a day or two will enable her to recover strength in some degree." But the journey proved, in his own words, "a wretched business." Elizabeth was chafing to arrive that she might have fresh news from England. When in Rome they heard nothing, Browning telegraphed to George Barrett. George's reply was so serious that Browning prepared his wife for the worst: on November 23 a letter told of Henrietta's death. Elizabeth was prostrated with silent bitter grief. A little later she wrote to Fanny Haworth:

It is a great privilege to be able to talk and cry; but I cannot you know. I have suffered very much, and feel tired and beaten. Now, it's all being lived down; thrown behind or pushed before, as such things must be if we are to live: not forgetting, not feeling any tie slackened, loving unchangeably, and believing how mere a line this is to overstep between the living and the dead.

Perhaps some of the bitterness, a sense of personal loss extending back over the death of father and friends to a terrible summer in 1840, went into that poem called "My Heart and I"; masked though the feeling is by the fiction of a lost lover:

[1] Myers Collection.

> *Enough! we're tired, my heart and I.*
> *We sit beside the headstone thus,*
> *And wish that name were carved for us.*
> *The moss reprints more tenderly*
> *The hard types of the mason's knife,*
> *As heaven's sweet life renews earth's life*
> *With which we're tired, my heart and I.*

This time the Brownings lodged at 126, Via Felice (now Via Sestina) high up by the Pincian Gardens.[2] There Elizabeth, though in failing health and with a load of grief on her, made verses, political or in the popular vein of sentiment; and in one case turning a poem into literal Italian as a trial piece for Dall'Ongaro, that terse and witty patriotic poet, to translate. This poem, "A View across the Roman Campagna," composed in early 1861, recaptures the apocalyptic vision of earlier days. It is a direct attack upon the Papacy; an attack so outspoken that if Elizabeth had lived and Dall'Ongaro had put it into a language the Italian cardinals could read, surely no further sojourn in Rome would have been possible for this bold heretic, famous though she was.

Perhaps, at a risk of spoiling the effect of the whole strong work, some quotation may be given. The Church is imagined as a ship "heaving silently like a mighty ship in pain" while "over the dumb Campagna-sea"

> *Alone and silent as God must be,*
> *The Christ walks. Aye, but Peter's neck*
> *Is stiff to turn on the foundering deck.*

Peter, his nets "heavy with silver fish," "reckons his gains": not for him the perilous leap of faith upon heaving waters:

> *Peter, Peter! He does not speak;*
> *He is not rash as in old Galilee:*
> *Safer a ship, though it toss and leak,*
> *Than a reeling foot on a rolling sea!*
> *And he's got to be round in the girth, thinks he.*

Elizabeth was left much alone at this time. Browning, restless since last winter, unable to compose, had to seek a channel for his enormous energy beyond hard riding. Elizabeth could fill in a fallow time with books, but Browning was never able to

[2] A plaque commemorates the stay here, 1835–42, of Nikolai Gogol.

concentrate for long on the printed page. At one time he had amused himself with drawing, but now, inspired by his friend Story in the Palazzo Barberini close by, he threw himself to a degree beyond mere pastime into a study of sculpture, modelling in clay from the antique.

It was natural that Elizabeth should deplore this devotion to an art not his own; however much he might be discouraged by neglect, beyond the small circle of Pre-Raphaelites, of himself by the British public. Even if Robert had not already been hailed, honoured in America with public reading and study, Elizabeth would have known her husband to be a major poet. Neglect among the English extended to those in Rome, many of whom knew Browning only as the handsome amusing husband of a famous woman poet. His success in society was undoubted, but it was on his own obvious personal qualifications. "The women," Elizabeth wrote to his sister with an indulgent smile, "adore him everywhere far too much for decency."

A possible embarrassment was now occupying Elizabeth's mind as she sat so much alone. That autumn, stirred by an account in the New York *Independent* of a funeral oration by Henry Ward Beecher over the body of Annie Howard,[3] she had sent to that journal "De Profundis," written after Bro's death, the manuscript of which had probably been found again in that box of papers restored to her in London. This being published in December 1860, she feared might be taken for a lament over the loss of her sister. Explaining the situation to Isa Blagden she added:

it's not my way to grind up my green griefs to make bread of. But that poem exaggerates nothing—represents a condition from which the writer had already partly emerged, after the greatest suffering; the only time in which I have known what absolute despair is.

She made it clear that the cause of her misery dated back to before she met Browning, but could not mention Bro even to this intimate friend. It may be that, in the midst of new grief, Elizabeth's mind was painfully directed back to the tragic loss of her brother by a resemblance in her own child: Browning

---

[3] Daughter of Mrs. John T. Howard, who, with Mrs. Stowe, had visited Elizabeth in 1860.

tells us that at one period of boyhood Pen was strikingly like a drawing of Bro at the same age.

However deep sorrow might be, Elizabeth was still able to surmount it with courage: even in December she could write that life "has rolled into the ruts again and goes." She was seeing a few people, among them Val Prinsep "in the roses and lilies of youth." Prinsep, a man of magnificent physique and great strength, is now chiefly memorable, not as an artist, but as the original of Taffy in *Trilby*; he was also the grandson of that eccentric India merchant James Pattle, whose last return to England, in the spirit and partially out of spirits, has been so deliciously commemorated by Virginia Woolf.

Another Englishman met at this time brought Elizabeth news of Naples, where matters were not going too smoothly under the Italian Government. Elsewhere in Italy too there were obvious difficulties in this time of change; such as the position, especially from a financial point of view, of the Pope in Rome and the question of Venetia. "There is much talk of war in the spring," Elizabeth wrote Mrs. Martin, "and if Austria will not cede Venetia war must be." But there was no war again in Elizabeth's lifetime: Venice lay in fetters for another six years. On February 18 the first Italian parliament decreed Victor Emmanuel King of Italy. On March 31 Great Britain, the first power to do so, gave the new country official recognition.

In Rome feeling for the King was strong, but Napoleon's troops were there to protect the Holy See, and to remain for another five years. These troops were, however, on friendly terms with the people and not unsympathetic to patriots. When there was a great demonstration of twenty thousand Romans after Victor Emmanuel was decreed King of Italy, French soldiers, making sure that the Papal troops kept out of sight, marched about with them on two days. Then, Elizabeth tells us, a French officer turned to the crowds with a friendly smile and said: "*Gioventù Romana, basta così. Adesso bisogna andare a casa, poichè mi farebbe grandissimo dispiacere d'aprire ad alcuno la strada delle carceri.*" [4] "*Grazie, grazie, grazie,*" came from the people, always quick in intelligence, before they dispersed.

---

[4] "Young Romans, that's enough. You must go home now. I should hate to put any one of you on the road to prison."

Of this friendly attitude Penini, to his great satisfaction, obtained direct evidence. Falling in with French troops on the Pincio, he made friends with "ever so many captains" and marched back with them to barracks. "They hope," the boy excitedly told his mother, "that I *would not think* they were like the Papalini. No indeed. They hoped I knew the French were different quite; and that, though they protected the Holy Father, they certainly didn't mean to fight for him. What *they* wanted was V. E. King of Italy. *Napoleon veut l'Italie Libre.* I was to *understand that, and remember it.*" But Napoleon did not recognize the new state until June.

If Elizabeth was wrong in predicting war in Italy that year, she was right in regard to another land dear to her. America was on the brink of civil war. She herself held steadily to the view that the North must at all costs prevent secession, though her friend Story, an American, argued that it would be wiser to let the South go.

As a mild winter wore into spring, a spring unusually cold, Elizabeth was thinking with dread of a visit that summer to Robert's father and sister, whom he had not seen for three years now. Sadly she reflected that, because of her, that devoted family had not been together for longer than a total of three weeks in all during the last fourteen years. If Robert could have only been got to agree she would gladly have sent him and Penini without her. A bright ray, however, on the gloomy prospect of a difficult journey, one to her now even hazardous, was that in Paris, or near it, Arabel might come to her.

In April Joseph Severn, newly appointed British Consul in Rome, came to visit Elizabeth. She found him "among the persons the most interesting" to her. It was in his arms that John Keats had died:

I make him tell me the most minute details—some very painful. Keats revolted against death, on that deeply tragic ground (always so affecting to me as an artist) of his gift being undeveloped in him—of having a work to do with his right hand, which he must let fall. "In ten years," said he, "I should be a great 'poet'—and now, I have not even philosophy enough to die by. ."

In April too there came to Rome that inveterate and charming traveller Hans Christian Andersen; delighting all who met him and especially the children. At a children's party given by the Storys he read "The Ugly Duckling"; then Robert, dressed for the part, gave "The Pied Piper" and all present, men, women, children, lined up behind him. Through the great rooms of the Barberini Palace they marched and countermarched, with Story deputizing on his flute for the magic music that drew the children from Hamelin Town.

Andersen came to visit Elizabeth in emotional mood, kissing her hand, seeming indeed "in a general *verve* for embracing." She found him "very earnest, very simple, very childlike." Pen thought him "not really pretty," observing shrewdly: "He is rather like his own ugly duck, but his mind has *developed* into a swan." It is good to think that this bright being, half angel, half child, was one of the last to delight a suffering woman very near her end now. The poem she wrote upon him, "The North and the South," was to be her final poetic utterance.

But so far was the sanguine Robert, or perhaps Elizabeth herself, from realizing her condition that the Brownings were negotiating through Story for a six years' lease on an apartment in the Palazzo Barberini. One of her last preoccupations was how they should furnish this apartment.

In June they returned to Florence and there it soon became apparent that there was to be no more travelling for Elizabeth. "I am only fit," she wrote sadly to Sarianna on the 7th, "for a drag chain." That day she had heard of the sudden and untimely death of Cavour:

I can scarcely command voice or hand to name Cavour. *That great soul, which meditated and made Italy, has gone to the Diviner country. If tears or blood could have saved him to us, he should have had mine. I feel yet as if I could scarcely comprehend the greatness of the vacancy. A hundred Garibaldis for such a man.*

As Robert watched her shaking hand fly fast over the paper he knew she had written more than enough. The letter came to an abrupt end.

Even so, weak as she was, Browning had still no clue to her condition. Plans were made for a visit to Siena and for a return to Florence next spring; not to Casa Guidi, but to a villa outside the city gates. Perhaps this determination to abandon Casa Guidi was in itself a sign of some impending radical change: for years Elizabeth had clung to a home long felt to be inconvenient, too small, but where she had known much happiness. At Casa Guidi she had borne her child, and watched from its windows Italy in growth.

When she caught cold through sitting in a draught the usual remedies for congestion of the lungs failed to act: at one o'clock in the morning Robert went for Dr. Wilson.[5] Dr. Wilson reported that one lung was condensed and he suspected an abscess, but even he was not unduly alarmed: his patient had managed for so long to live on with damaged lungs. Elizabeth herself scoffed at his verdict, saying: "It is the old story—they don't know my case—I have been tapped and sounded so, and condemned so, repeatedly: this time it is said the right is the affected lung while the left is free—Dr. Chambers said just the contrary." It was not, she declared, as bad an attack as two years before.

At first Browning carried her during the day into their cool large drawing-room, where she sat in her chair and read the newspapers. Later a bed was put up for her in this room.

She began to doze heavily and seemed unaware that Robert was sitting up by her at night. Nourishment was pronounced essential, but she would take nothing but clear soup. Still Elizabeth refused to believe in the seriousness of her case. On the evening of Thursday, June 27, although her voice was almost completely gone, she was discussing their future plans. When Browning pointed out that, as she could not live in Florence either in full summer or in winter, it hardly seemed worth setting up another home there, Elizabeth said: "But I can't leave Florence. I like Florence." As they talked her mind wandered a little, but Browning thought this merely a result of the increased quantity of morphine the doctor had ordered.

When Isa Blagden came in on Friday evening full of an item of political news, Robert stopped the conversation for fear of exciting his wife, but Elizabeth waited until his back was turned and whispered a question. Her lively interest convinced Miss

[5] Dr. Grisanowsky was not in Florence at this time.

Blagden that she was really better. Wilson, when she came in to visit her former mistress, was of the same opinion. Even the doctor admitted some improvement.

That night, though Elizabeth's breathing was easier, she dozed constantly, only rousing a little and smiling if her husband spoke to her. At half past three on the 29th her condition made Browning uneasy. He sent for Dr. Wilson.

As he and the maid, Annunziata, attended her, sponging with hot water, feeding her with strong fowl-jelly from a spoon, Robert wondered if she was fully aware of their presence. He asked: "Do you know me?" She kissed him, speaking words of love, and said: "Our lives are held by God." As he gave her more jelly she put her arms round him, whispering: "God bless you" and kissing him repeatedly, Browning told his sister, with such vehemence

that when I laid her down she continued to kiss the air with her lips and several times raised her own hands and kissed them; I said "Are you comfortable?" "Beautiful." . . . *Then she motioned to have her hands sponged—some of the jelly annoying her—this was done, and she began to sleep again—the* last.

Browning raised her up. She died peacefully in his arms, her head against his shoulder.

The memory of those last tender words and her "God bless you" Browning was to cherish in profound gratitude. Never had she spoken to him in quite those tones before, laughing "with pleasure and *youth,* and I believe in some perfectly gracious way allowed by God suffered no pain whatever."

Elizabeth looked so tranquil, "perfectly beautiful" with a smile on her lips, that it was many hours before they could believe she was dead. Her aspect was that of a young girl.

On July 1 her body was laid in the Protestant Cemetery amid an extraordinary demonstration of grief. A crowd followed the funeral procession crying aloud in lament. "The Italians," her husband commented, "seem to have understood her by an instinct." As if to mark the passing of one so loved, who had ardently loved and served her adopted land, a great comet appeared unheralded that night, soon to be blazing over half the sky.

.   .   .

Robert Browning, that poet of married love, celebrated his devotion to Elizabeth Barrett in superb and characteristic verse, both directly and by implication; but there are no lines more pregnant with yearning love than those by the Florentine Dante which he transcribed in translation on a page of his lost wife's New Testament: "Thus I believe, thus I affirm, thus I am certain it is, that from this life I shall pass to another better, where that lady lives of whom my soul is enamoured."

Appendixes

APPENDIX 1. A BARRETT PLAY–BILL

THIS WRITTEN play-bill, in my possession, must be dated either 1824 or 1829. I am inclined to accept the latter date, as on the back of it are scribbled three words in Elizabeth's own writing, and these are in her more mature hand.

It will be noted that Rolla was played by Mr. E. Barrett. This would be either the father or Bro.

On Tuesday evening January twenty
at

Theatre Royal

Hope End

will be performed —

The Tragedy

of

Pizzarro

Ataliba .. Master C J Barrett.	Pizzarro .. Mr. Trant
Rolla .. Mr. E Barrett.	Darilla Master G Barrett
Alonzo ..	Valverde. Master S Barrett
	Las Casas. Mr H Trant

APPENDIX 2. AN EARLY POEM IN ITALIAN
BY ELIZABETH BARRETT

THIS APPEARS to be the best of Elizabeth's girlish exercises in Italian verse, and is perhaps worth putting on record if only for her affectionate but acute estimation of James Thomson in the last two lines of stanza 1: "Phœbus in giving thee his smile [literally 'laugh'] denied thee its full splendour."

A THOMSONI

O vate dolce e semplice
Poeta grato al core
Febo suo riso dandoti
Ti nega' il suo fulgore.

Tatto tua verga magica
   orbe   *vede* [1]
L'~~ochi~~ più bel si ~~vide~~
E il sol con fronte amabile
Più dolcemente ride

L'Inverno pur tua musica
Sente dal trono scuro
La State [L'estate] e lumi lucidi
Scopre con vel più puro.

L'alma natura guardati
Con ammiravol' amore
E il riso bel salutati
Suo figlio e il suo pittore.

E. B. Barrett

[1] The corrections in this line are in another hand, probably that of her Italian master.

APPENDIX 3. *SONNETS FROM THE PORTUGUESE*, XVI,
IN EARLY DRAFT, IN THE MORGAN LIBRARY, NEW YORK

SONNET XVI

And yet because thou art above me so,
Because thou art more strong, & like a king,
Thou canst prevail against my fears & fling
Thy purple round me till my heart shall grow
Too close against thy heart to henceforth know
Its separate trembling pulse—Oh, conquering
May prove as noble & complete a thing
In lifting upward as in beating low!
And as a soldier struck down by a sword,
Cries 'Here my strife ends' & sinks dead to earth;
Even so, beloved, I, at last, record. .
'My Doubt ends here—' If *thou* invite me forth,
I rise above abasement at the word!
Make thy love larger to enlarge my worth.

APPENDIX 4. AN ANECDOTE TOLD BY
G. G. GIANNINI

I HAVE TO THANK Signor G. G. Giannini, long an inhabitant of Florence, for the following anecdote translated from his own words:

She was a dwarfish figure with a body the size of a person of medium stature, but with legs hardly more than 30 centimetres in length.

One day she told me that she had happy recollections of a kind English lady, a poet. All she could remember of her identity was a Christian name, "Elisabetta."

As I was at that time taking a course in English and was interested in the principal English poets, I soon realized that she was talking of Mrs. Barrett Browning.

I asked her to describe the lady, but she could do nothing but repeat that she was so beautiful, with soft eyes and hair in long ringlets after the fashion of the time; and that she liked her very much.

One day I took her a portrait of Mrs. Browning, a print which I had taken out of a volume of poetry.

When I handed it to her the old woman gave a start and gazed at it in astonishment for a long time: she smiled, wept, and finished up by kissing it repeatedly.

"It is she, the kind lady: I fancy I see her now just as when I was sitting on a little stool at her feet and she was caressing me."

It was then that she was moved to give me her confidence, speaking of a youthful peccadillo.

Even she, so unkindly treated by Nature, had loved . . . and been loved in return.

"I was quite a good-looking girl," she told me, "when people saw me at the window. And it was at the window that I attracted the attention of a fair-haired Austrian officer. There was an Austrian garrison in Florence at that time, and we lived on the first floor of a house near the Pitti Palace. My father was groom to the Grand Duke. The fair officer began to court me, passing and repassing under my windows until I should appear.

I was foolish enough to encourage his attentions. At eighteen, even if Nature *had* been unkind to me, my heart beat just as with any girl of my age. It was very stupid of me—but I did want to enjoy just that one moment offered me. I flattered myself that I might be capable of winning the affection of young men."

But it couldn't last. One day she was coming out of the house with her mother when her admirer met her. His disillusionment was openly expressed in disdainful and insulting terms. It was like a blow from a bludgeon. She fainted and was carried into the house, to remain there many days in a high fever.

Her mother, being good at sewing and embroidery, numbered among her clients Elizabeth Browning. In talking with the poet the mother mentioned her daughter's plight and the pain this incident had caused her. Mrs. Browning asked the mother to bring her daughter; she would like to talk to her, to console her.

The memory of this first meeting was still vivid in the old woman's recollection. She remembered the young lady with fair [*sic*] curls deep in a big armchair, her shoulders enveloped in a wide silk shawl. She made the girl sit on a little stool at her feet and, stroking her hair, spoke many kind words, which touched her heart like a balm. After this first meeting Mrs. Browning often asked for her and many hours were passed in her company sewing. It was the girl's only joy, the only sunshine in her life, a great recompense for the cruel disillusionment of which she had been the victim.

It was a pity the old woman could not remember, so as to repeat them, the soothing phrases murmured by the English poet, phrases that succeeded in bringing back peace to her heart.

When several months later the Brownings' son had occasion to visit Florence, where he was born, I took him to old Girolama. He remembered her well, having often played with her as a child. He took an interest in her and often asked me to help her with money on his behalf.

G. G. Giannini

Florence

The old woman was named Girolama François, a name French in origin, but her father and mother were Florentines.—G.G.G.

APPENDIX 5. CHAPMAN & HALL

Why did Elizabeth in 1850 leave Moxon, "the most poetical publisher," who had been the first to publish her work at his own expense? We do not know.

We do know, however, that Browning after his marriage, recognizing perhaps that he could hardly now ask his father to continue to subsidize him, looked round for some firm who would take the risk of publication; in his case, unpopular as he still was, a real hazard. It was Chapman & Hall who, after an introduction by Browning's friend and admirer, John Forster, took that risk, publishing in 1848 an edition in two volumes containing "Paracelsus" and the contents of the eight numbers of *Bells and Pomegranates.* Whether Chapman & Hall stipulated that Browning's wife, the more popular of the two, should also become one of their authors, or whether Elizabeth merely followed her husband's lead out of loyalty or for convenience in having a common publisher, we cannot tell. There appears to have been no personal break with Moxon: the Brownings remained on good terms with him.

APPENDIX 6. A NOTE ON
ROBERT WIEDEMAN BARRETT BROWNING [1849–1912]

(For an excellent, concise account of Pen Browning's life see
"Robert Browning and His Son," by Gertrude Reese, *PMLA,*
Vol. LXI, September 1946.)

AFTER ELIZABETH'S DEATH Browning resolved to devote his life
to her child; but his ideas as to the bringing up of a boy differed
from hers. Her emphasis had been—rightly in Pen's case as it
turned out—on languages and the arts, but Browning's aim was
to make his boy, if not a scholar as enthusiastic as himself and
his father, at least a man of the conventional acquirements of
that day. Pen should go to Oxford and receive that hall-mark of
an English gentleman denied to himself.

It had been said that Browning, on his wife's death, immediately shore off Pen's curls and took away his girlish attire: altered in appearance, Pen was taken from sunny Italy, from the
Italians he loved, to live in a rather dreary part of London, at
Paddington, by the Regent's Park Canal. There he was put to
his books but, though an affectionate good-natured boy, he did
not work as hard as his brilliant, ambitious father desired: it
was perhaps unfortunate that Browning did defer to his wife's
wishes in one respect by not sending Pen to school. He therefore lacked the stimulus of competition. When the boy was old
enough for Oxford Browning tried to enter him at Balliol, a
college of high attainment, but Jowett, the Master, though
Browning's friend, could not bring himself to admit the lad. Pen
went to Christ Church, where he ran up the usual undergradu-
ate debts and spent a good deal of time in active sport and
playing billiards.

Pen, however, had been allowed to keep up his drawing and,
after leaving Oxford in 1871 with no academic distinction, expressed a wish to become an artist. Browning sent him to Ant-
werp to study and there, in the right atmosphere, he began to
work, making rapid progress in both painting and sculpture.
Browning exerted himself to obtain worldly success for his son,

quite simply in his great affection using all his now not inconsiderable influence. That Pen was an artist of some ability is certain, judging both from works reproduced in the Browning Catalogue of 1913 (including portraits in paint and stone of his father) and by awards and distinctions gained in both France and Belgium.

In 1887 he married a rich American, Fanny Coddington, but the marriage was an unhappy one. It is noticeable that, once free from economic dependence on his father, he went to live in Italy: how far the sharp severance from what was practically his native land had harmed the boy we cannot know. There, in Venice, he bought the Palazzo Rezzonico and took into his household Wilson and Ferdinando. After Ferdinando's death in 1893 Wilson remained with Pen, dying in 1902. For many years her mind was enfeebled.

In 1889 Browning went to live in Italy; but on December 12 he died. Sarianna joined her nephew, whose wife left him soon after. Sarianna died in 1903, remembered by those who saw her as an intelligent, vivacious old lady.

With his powerful father no longer alive, a father he loved and was anxious to please, Pen became the lazy man he was in later life. Painting was given up and a large part of his time was spent gossiping in the street with Italians. To lovers of Browning he was a profound disappointment, a "commonplace," a "very ordinary" man, but he honoured his parents and kept up their memory; though not unfortunately to the extent of having letters, documents, and mementoes secured in any one central place after his death. At the great Browning Sale in 1913 holographs, documents, pictures, furniture, all except a few pieces kept by the Moulton-Barrett family were scattered.

In money matters Pen inherited rather the heedlessness of his mother than his father's caution: when he wanted to buy Casa Guidi in their memory he could not afford it. In Florence, where he lived towards the end of his life, Pen befriended and spent much of his time with that love of his babyhood Edith Story, who, though she had made a brilliant marriage with the Marchese Peruzzi, fell upon evil times. It was she who attended him on his deathbed at Asolo in 1912.

MAIN BOOKS OF REFERENCE

Letters of Elizabeth Barrett Browning Addressed to Richard Hengist Horne, edited by S. R. Townshend Mayer. 2 vols. Richard Bentley, 1888.

The Letters of Elizabeth Barrett Browning, edited by Frederic G. Kenyon. 2 vols. 3rd edition, Smith, Elder, 1898.

"Twenty Unpublished Letters of Elizabeth Barrett to Hugh Stuart Boyd," by Bennet Weaver. *PMLA*, Vol. LXV, No. 4, June 1950.

Letters from Elizabeth Barrett to B. R. Haydon, edited by Martha Hale Shackford (Oxford University Press, 1939).

The Letters of Robert Browning and Elizabeth Barrett Barrett, 1845–1846. 2 vols. Smith, Elder, 1899.

Elizabeth Barrett Browning: Letters to her Sister, 1846–1859, edited by Leonard Huxley. John Murray, 1929.

From Robert & Elizabeth Browning, edited by William Rose Benét. John Murray, 1936.

Robert Browning and Alfred Domett, edited by Frederic G. Kenyon. Smith, Elder, 1906.

Letters of Robert Browning collected by Thomas J. Wise, edited by Thurman L. Hood. John Murray, 1933.

Robert Browning and Julia Wedgwood, edited by Richard Curle. John Murray, 1937.

Letters to Robert Browning and Other Correspondents, edited by Thomas J. Wise. 1916.

Dearest Isa, Robert Browning's Letters to Isabella Blagden, edited by Edward C. McAleer. University of Texas Press, 1951.

"New Letters from Mrs. Browning to Isa Blagden," by Edward C. McAleer. *PMLA*, Vol. LXVI, No. 5, September 1951.

· · ·

The Family of the Barrett, by Jeannette Marks. New York: The Macmillan Company; 1938.

Life and Letters of Robert Browning, by Mrs. Sutherland Orr. 2nd edition, Smith, Elder, 1891.

The Life of Robert Browning, by W. Hall Griffin and H. C. Minchin. Revised edition, Methuen, 1938.

The Brownings, Their Life and Art, by Lilian Whiting. Hodder & Stoughton, 1911.

"Robert Browning and His Son," by Gertrude Reese. *PMLA,* Vol. LXI, No. 3, September 1946.

Hitherto Unpublished Poems and Stories, edited by H. Buxton Forman. 2 vols. The Boston Bibliophile Society, 1914.

The Poet's Enchiridion, edited by H. Buxton Forman. The Boston Bibliophile Society, 1914.

The Battle of Marathon, a Poem, by E. B. Barrett. W. Lindsell, 1820.

An Essay on Mind, with Other Poems. James Duncan, 1824.

Prometheus Bound, translated from the Greek of Æschylus, by the Author of "An Essay on Mind," with Other Poems. A. J. Valpy, 1833.

The Seraphim, and Other Poems, by Elizabeth B. Barrett. Saunders & Otley, 1838.

A New Spirit of the Age, edited by R. H. Horne. 2 vols. Smith, Elder, 1844 (contributions by Elizabeth Barrett Barrett).

Poems, by Elizabeth Barrett Barrett. 2 vols. Edward Moxon, 1844.

Poems, by Elizabeth Barrett Browning. 2 vols. 2nd edition, Chapman & Hall, 1850 (includes retranslated *Prometheus Bound* and "Sonnets from the Portuguese").

Casa Guidi Windows, A Poem, by Elizabeth Barrett Browning. Chapman & Hall, 1851.

Two Poems, by Elizabeth Barrett Browning and Robert Browning. Chapman & Hall, 1854.

Aurora Leigh, by Elizabeth Barrett Browning. Chapman & Hall, 1857.

Poems Before Congress, by Elizabeth Barrett Browning. Chapman & Hall, 1860.

Last Poems, by Elizabeth Barrett Browning. Chapman & Hall, 1863.

The Greek Christian Poets and the English Poets, by Elizabeth Barrett Browning. Chapman & Hall, 1863.

Psyche Apocalyptè: A Lyrical Drama, Projected by Elizabeth Barrett Browning and R. H. Horne. Hazell, Watson & Viney, for private circulation, 1876.

Letters to William Allingham, edited by H. Allingham and E. Baumer Williams. Longmans, Green, 1911.

Red Letter Days, by Mrs. Andrew Crosse. Richard Bentley, 1892.

Anna Jameson, Letters and Friendships, edited by Mrs. Steuart Erskine. T. Fisher Unwin, 1915.

Memoirs of the Life of Anna Jameson, by Gerardine Macpherson. Longmans, Green, 1878.

The Life and Letters of Mary Russell Mitford, edited by A. G. L'Estrange, Vols. II, III. Richard Bentley, 1870.

The Friendships of Mary Russell Mitford, edited by A. G. L'Estrange, Vol. II. Hurst & Blackett, 1882.

Mary Russell Mitford, Correspondence, edited by Elizabeth Lee. Unwin, 1914.

Letters of Anne Thackeray Ritchie, edited by Hester Ritchie. John Murray, 1924.

D. G. Rossetti, His Family Letters. Ellis & Elvey, 1895

Pre-Raphaelitism Papers, 1854–1872, edited by William Rossetti. George Allen, 1899.

William Wetmore Story and His Friends, by Henry James. 2 vols. Edinburgh: Blackwood. Boston: Houghton, Mifflin; 1903.

"Correspondence of Harriet Beecher Stowe and Elizabeth Barrett Browning," by Hazel Harrod. *Studies in English,* University of Texas, Vol. XXVII, No. 1, June 1948.

Alfred, Lord Tennyson, a Memoir by his son. Macmillan, 1906.

What I Remember, by Thomas Adolphus Trollope, Vol. II. Richard Bentley, 1888.

Catalogues, the Browning Sales, Sotheby, 1913 and 1937, and various.

INDEX

A NOTE ON THE TYPE

THE TEXT of this book is set in Caledonia, *a Linotype face designed by W. A. Dwiggins. It belongs to the family of printing types called "modern face" by printers—a term used to mark the change in style of type-letters that occurred about 1800. Caledonia borders on the general design of Scotch Modern, but is more freely drawn than that letter.*

The book was composed, printed, and bound by The Plimpton Press, Norwood, Massachusetts. The typography and binding design are by W. A. Dwiggins.

WAD